PETERSON'S
ULTIMATE GMAT TOOL KIT

Mark Alan Stewart

WITHDRAWN FROM COLLECTION

PROPERTY OF PENN HIGHLANDS CC

THOMSON
★
PETERSON'S

Australia • Canada • Mexico • Singapore • Spain • United Kingdom • United States

THOMSON

PETERSON'S

About Thomson Peterson's

Thomson Peterson's (www.petersons.com) is a leading provider of education information and advice, with books and online resources focusing on education search, test preparation, and financial aid. Its Web site offers searchable databases and interactive tools for contacting educational institutions, online practice tests and instruction, and planning tools for securing financial aid. Thomson Peterson's serves 110 million education consumers annually.

For more information, contact Thomson Peterson's, 2000 Lenox Drive, Lawrenceville, NJ 08648; 800-338-3282; or find us on the World Wide Web at www.petersons.com/about.

© 2004 Thomson Peterson's, a part of The Thomson Corporation
Thomson Learning™ is a trademark used herein under license.

Editors: Mandie Rosenberg and Joe Ziegler; Production Editor: Alysha Bullock; Composition Manager: Gary Rozmierski; Manufacturing Manager: Ray Golaszewski; Cover and Interior Design: Allison Sullivan.

ALL RIGHTS RESERVED. No part of this work covered by the copyright herein may be reproduced or used in any form or by any means—graphic, electronic, or mechanical, including photocopying, recording, taping, Web distribution, or information storage and retrieval systems—without the prior written permission of the publisher.

For permission to use material from this text or product, submit a request online at www.thomsonrights.com

Any additional questions about permissions can be submitted by e-mail to thomsonrights@thomson.com

ISBN 0-7689-1486-8

Printed in the United States of America

10 9 8 7 6 5 4 3 2 1   06 05 04

First Edition

Petersons.com/publishing

Check out our Web site at www.petersons.com/publishing to see if there is any new information regarding the test and any revisions or corrections to the content of this book. We've made sure the information in this book is accurate and up-to-date; however, the test format or content may have changed since the time of publication.

Credits

"The American Renaissance," by James S. Turner, *Humanities*, Vol.13, No. 2 (March/April 1992). Published by The National Endowment for the Humanities.

"Arnold's Double-Sided Culture," by John P. Farrell, *Humanities*, Vol. 12, No. 3 (May/June 1991), pp. 26–30. Published by The National Endowment for the Humanities.

"The Artful Encounter," by Richard Wendorf, *Humanities*, Vol. 14, No. 4 (July/August 1993), pp. 9–12. Published by The National Endowment for the Humanities.

"The Debate Over Mozart's Music," by Neal Zaslaw, *Humanities*, Vol. 14, No. 5 (September/October 1993), pp. 26–27. Published by The National Endowment for the Humanities.

" 'I Am Christina Rossetti,' " by Antony H. Harrison, *Humanities*, Vol. 14, No. 4 (July/August 1993), pp. 33–37. Published by The National Endowment for the Humanities.

"Images of Dorothea Lange," by Therese Thau Heyman, *Humanities*, Vol. 14, No. 5 (September/October 1993), pp. 6, 8–10. Published by The National Endowment for the Humanities.

"Large Format Expands *Little Buddha*," by Bob Fisher, *American Cinematographer*, Vol. 75, No. 5 (May 1994), p. 41. Reprinted by permission of *American Cinematographer*.

Contents

ABOUT THIS TOOL KIT **1**
    Your Tools 1
    About This Book 2
    Oh, the Sidebars You'll See..................... 4

PART I: EVERYTHING YOU EVER WANTED TO KNOW ABOUT THE GMAT

Chapter 1: The GMAT—In a Nutshell 6

Chapter 2: The GMAT—Up Close 41

PART II: ANALYTICAL WRITING ASSESSMENT

Chapter 3: Analytical Writing Assessment 72
    Take It to the Next Level..................... 103

PART III: QUANTITATIVE ABILITY

Chapter 4: Problem Solving 136
    Take It to the Next Level..................... 152

Chapter 5: Data Sufficiency 164
    Take It to the Next Level..................... 177

Chapter 6: Math Review—Number Forms, Relationships, and Sets 190
    Take It to the Next Level..................... 214

Chapter 7: Math Review—Number Theory and Algebra 230
    Take It to the Next Level..................... 258

Chapter 8: Math Review—Geometry 279
    Take It to the Next Level..................... 303

PART IV: VERBAL ABILITY

Chapter 9: Critical Reasoning 332
    Take It to the Next Level..................... 357

Chapter 10: Sentence Correction 380
    Take It to the Next Level.................. 406
Chapter 11: Reading Comprehension 429
    Take It to the Next Level.................. 445

PART V: THREE PRACTICE TESTS

Practice Test 1 470
    Answers and Explanations 497
Practice Test 2 512
    Answers and Explanations 537
Practice Test 3 553
    Answers and Explanations 577

PART VI: APPENDIX

Determining Your Score 594

About This Tool Kit

Your Tools

Peterson's Ultimate GMAT Tool Kit provides the complete package you need to score your personal best on the GMAT and get into your top-choice MBA program. Unlike any book previously published, this tool kit contains many features that used to be available only to those who purchased expensive test-prep classes.

e-Tutoring

Use the CD to go online to register for one-to-one math help from a live expert when you need it. Tutoring is offered using an online white board shared by you and the tutor that allows you to communicate with one another in real time. However, if you prefer, you can submit your math question instead and receive an answer within 24 hours.

The free tutoring offered with this product is limited to 30 minutes, although you may purchase more time if you need it. A written response to a submitted questions counts as 20 minutes. The tutoring service is available for six months from the date you register online. The e-tutoring service offered to purchasers of this 2005 edition will expire on January 1, 2006.

This service is available 24 hours a day seven days a week for most of the year. During the summer it is available from 9 a.m. to 1 a.m. Eastern time. Due to low demand, the service is not available during several holiday periods including Thanksgiving, Christmas, and Easter, Labor Day, and Memorial Day.

Remember, to register for this service you will need the CD that accompanies this book. You will also need to refer to this book to provide the access code when prompted.

About This Tool Kit

Essay Scoring

The CD that accompanies this book allows you to go online to write 2 practice test essays online and receive a score for each of them that approximates your performance on the essays in the actual GMAT. In addition to a score, you will also receive constructive feedback on your essays, including tips to improve your score.

With this tool kit, you get scoring for 2 practice test essays—one analysis of an issue and one analysis of an argument. If you wish, for a fee, you may obtain scoring information and feedback for additional practice essays you write online. Please note: Your practice test essays will be scored by a computer, but for the actual GMAT test, the essays are scored by a combination of a computer program and a human scorer.

To register for this essay-scoring service you need the CD that accompanies this book. In addition, you will need to refer to this book to provide the access code when prompted. The scoring of 2 essays is offered free to purchasers of the 2005 edition and this offer will expire on December 31, 2005.

Computer-Adaptive Tests on CD

The actual GMAT is a computer-adaptive test (CAT)—the test questions you so depend on your performance on previous questions. On the CD-ROM that accompanies this book, you will receive 3 practice GMAT CATs that carefully reproduce the experience you can expect on test day. The additional three practice tests in the book can be used for further practice.

About This Book

Of course, another tool in your *Ultimate GMAT Tool Kit* is this book itself. It is structured so that you gain proven test-taking strategies to do your best on the exam, a thorough review of all content on the GMAT, and a complete understanding of how to attack the GMAT essays.

Part I: Everything You Ever Wanted to Know about the GMAT

Part I focuses on the "big picture." Here you'll learn about the overall structure of the GMAT and what the test sections cover. You'll also examine the directions for each type of question and see what typical test questions look like. Then, you'll learn strategies for GMAT preparation as well as general test-taking strategies.

About This Book

Parts II–IV: Study Guides for the GMAT

This book's GMAT study guide is unique in that it offers you the opportunity to study each part of the exam, and then you can *Take It to the Next Level*—using the section in each chapter that covers advanced topics and concepts you may encounter on the GMAT. Each section covers all four test sections and all general question types and both contain example questions. The unique ability to *Take It to the Next Level* feature will help you tailor your GMAT prep to your individual needs.

Should You Take it to the Next Level?

You should start with the general instruction if either of the following describes you:

- You're a GMAT "newbie" and you are just beginning your GMAT prep.
- The B-school you want to attend doesn't require especially high GMAT scores for admission.

You can go directly to *Take It to the Next Level* if you're a repeat GMAT test-taker whose scores were high the first time around but your GMAT goals are now even higher. Of course, regardless of your goals for the GMAT and for college admission, you can always work through both levels. In fact, that's what we recommend to anyone with enough study time before exam day.

Part V: Three Practice GMATs

In Part V, you'll find three full-length, practice GMATs. Each test covers all four test sections and includes a mix of easy, moderate, and difficult questions. To accurately measure your performance on the practice tests, be sure to adhere strictly to the time limits for each and every section.

You can take all three practice tests after completing your self-study (Parts II–IV). Or, you can take one practice test beforehand as a diagnostic tool. If your scores show that you rank above the 80th percentile on a test, you can skip over the basics to *Take It to the Next Level* for that test. Then, after you've completed your self-study, take the remaining two practice tests to measure your improvement.

PETERSON'S
getting you there

About This Tool Kit

Oh, the Sidebars You'll See

Throughout this book you'll encounter four different types of sidebars. (Flip through this book, and you'll see oodles of each one.) Here's a look at the types of sidebars you'll see:

Alert! Warns you about a common testing trick or ploy that might trip you up during the test if you're not careful.

Note Signals information that may not be a "need-to-know" fact, but that you might find rounds out your knowledge of the topic at hand.

Tip Signals a tip, strategy, or fine point related to the topic or example at hand.

X-Ref Signals a reference to a concept or other information located elsewhere in the book.

PART I

Everything You Ever Wanted to Know about the GMAT

The GMAT—In a Nutshell 6

The GMAT—Up Close 41

Chapter 1

The GMAT—In a Nutshell

Your GMAT prep begins with an overview of the test. In this chapter, you'll:

- Learn Key acronyms related to the GMAT.
- Look at the overall structure of the GMAT and what each of the four test sections cover.
- Familiarize yourself with the computerized aspects of the test.
- Examine the directions for each for each general question type.
- See what typical test questions look like.
- Find out how the GMAT is scored and evaluated.
- Find out how your scores are reported to the business schools.
- Learn strategies for GMAT preparation.
- Learn general GMAT test-taking strategies.

Key Acronyms

1. **GMAT** (*Graduate Management Admission Test*): This standardized test provides graduate business schools (as well as vocational counselors and prospective applicants) with predictors of academic performance in MBA programs. Approximately 850 graduate business schools worldwide *require* GMAT scores for admission. Another 450 graduate business schools use—but don't require—GMAT scores to access applicants' qualifications.

2. **GMAC** (*Graduate Management Admission Council*): This organization develops guidelines, policies, and procedures for the graduate business school admission process, and provides information about the admission process to the schools and to prospective applicants. The GMAC consists of representatives from more than 100 graduate business schools.

Chapter 1: The GMAT—In a Nutshell

3. **CAT** (*Computer-Adaptive Test*): Except for some locations outside of North America, the GMAT is now offered only by computer. CAT refers to the computerized version of the GMAT. Taking a computer-adaptive test means that each section of the test starts with a question of moderate difficulty. If you answer correctly, the computer will follow it with a more difficult question. If you answer it incorrectly, the following question will be easier.

The GMAT at a Glance

The GMAT contains three parts: an Analytical Writing Assessment section, a Quantitative Ability section, and a Verbal Ability section. The total testing time (excluding breaks) is 3 hours, 30 minutes. Here's the basic structure of the test:

ANALYTICAL WRITING ASSESSMENT (Sections 1 and 2)

- Analysis of an Issue (1 writing task, 30-minute time limit)
- Analysis of an Argument (1 writing task, 30-minute time limit)

Optional break (5-minute time limit)

QUANTITATIVE ABILITY (Section 3)

(37 multiple-choice questions, 75-minute time limit)

- Problem Solving (22–23 questions)
- Data Sufficiency (14–15 questions)

Optional break (5-minute time limit)

VERBAL ABILITY (Section 4)

(41 multiple-choice questions, 75-minute time limit)

- Critical Reasoning (14–15 questions)
- Sentence Correction (14–15 questions)
- Reading Comprehension (12–13 questions, divided among four sets)

Sequence of Exam Sections

Sections 1 and 2 (the two timed essay sections) always appear first (in either order), *before* the two timed multiple-choice sections. Section 3 is always Quantitative Ability, and section 4 is always Verbal Ability.

Sequence of Questions in Quantitative and Verbal

In each of the two multiple-choice sections, question types are interspersed. Here's a typical sequence for each section (on your GMAT, the sequence might be different):

Quantitative Ability (Typical Sequence of Questions)	
Questions 1–2	Problem Solving
Questions 3–7	Data Sufficiency
Questions 8–13	Problem Solving
Question 14	Data Sufficiency
Question 15	Problem Solving
Question 16	Data Sufficiency
Questions 17–21	Problem Solving
Questions 22–27	Data Sufficiency
Questions 28–34	Problem Solving
Question 35	Data Sufficiency
Questions 36–37	Problem Solving
Verbal Ability (Typical Sequence of Questions)	
Questions 1–3	Sentence Correction
Questions 4–5	Critical Reasoning
Questions 6–8	Reading Comprehension
Question 9	Sentence Correction
Questions 10–11	Critical Reasoning
Questions 12–14	Sentence Correction
Questions 15–17	Reading Comprehension
Questions 18–21	Critical Reasoning
Questions 22–24	Sentence Correction
Questions 25–26	Critical Reasoning
Question 27	Sentence Correction
Questions 28–30	Reading Comprehension
Questions 31–33	Critical Reasoning
Questions 34–35	Sentence Correction
Questions 36	Critical Reasoning
Questions 37–39	Reading Comprehension
Question 40	Critical Reasoning
Question 41	Sentence Correction

Chapter 1: The GMAT—In a Nutshell

Ground Rules

Here are some basic procedural rules for the GMAT (later in this chapter we'll cover test-taking procedures in greater detail):

- Once the timed test begins, you cannot stop the testing clock.
- If you finish any section before the time limit expires, you have the option of proceeding immediately to the next section.
- Once you exit a section, you can't return to it.
- Pencils and "scratch" paper are provided for all exam sections.
- You select a multiple-choice answer by clicking on an oval next to the choice. (All multiple-choice questions include five answer choices.)
- You compose both essays using the word processor built into the GMAT testing system. (Handwritten essays are not permitted.)

The Four Timed GMAT Sections

Here's a quick look at what each of the four timed test sections covers.

> **X-Ref**
>
> Later in this chapter, you'll see example questions in all of the formats described here.

Analysis of an Issue (1 Essay, 30 Minutes)

This 30-minute section tests your ability to present a position on an issue effectively and persuasively. Your task is to compose an essay in which you respond to a brief (1–2 sentence) opinion about an issue of general intellectual interest. You should consider various perspectives, and take a position on the issue and argue for that position. Your essay will be evaluated based on content, organization, writing style, and mechanics (grammar, syntax, word usage, etc.).

Analysis of an Argument (1 Essay, 30 Minutes)

This 30-minute section is designed to test your critical-reasoning and analytical-writing skills. Your task is to compose an essay in which you critique a paragraph-length argument based on the strength of the evidence presented in support of it and on the argument's logic (line of reasoning). You can also indicate what additional evidence would help you evaluate the argument and how the argument could be improved. Like your Issue-Analysis essay, your Argument-Analysis essay will be evaluated based on content, organization, writing style, and mechanics.

Quantitative Ability (37 Questions, 75 Minutes)

This 75-minute section consists of 37 multiple-choice questions designed to measure your basic mathematical skills; understanding of basic mathematical concepts; and ability to reason quantitatively, solve quantitative problems, and interpret graphical data. The Quantitative Ability section covers the following topics:

- Arithmetical operations
- Integers, factors, and multiples
- The number line and ordering
- Decimals, percentages, ratios, and proportion
- Exponents and square roots
- Descriptive statistics (mean, median, mode, range, standard deviation)
- Basic probability, permutations, and combinations
- Operations with variables
- Algebraic equations and inequalities
- Geometry, including coordinate geometry

Algebraic concepts on the GMAT are those normally covered in a first-year high school algebra course. The GMAT does not cover more advanced areas such as trigonometry and calculus.

Each Quantitative question appears in one of two formats (any of the topics listed above is fair game for either format):

PROBLEM SOLVING questions require you to solve a mathematical problem and then select the correct answer from among five answer choices. Some of these questions will be "story" problems—cast in a real-world setting.

DATA SUFFICIENCY problems each consist of a question followed by two statements labeled (1) and (2). Your task is to analyze each of the two statements to determine whether it provides sufficient data to answer the question and, if neither suffices alone, whether both statements together suffice. *Every Data Sufficiency question includes the same five answer choices.* As with certain Problem Solving questions, some of these questions will be so-called "story" problems—cast in a real-world setting.

Verbal Ability (41 Questions, 75 Minutes)

This 75-minute section consists of 41 multiple-choice questions. Each question will be one of the following three types (each type covers a distinct set of verbal and verbal-reasoning skills):

CRITICAL REASONING questions measure your ability to understand, criticize, and draw reasonable conclusions from arguments. Each argument consists of a brief one-paragraph passage.

SENTENCE CORRECTION questions measure your command of the English language and of the conventions of Standard Written English. Areas tested include grammar, diction, usage, and effective expression (but not punctuation). In each question, part (or all) of a sentence is underlined. Your task is to determine which is correct—the original underlined part or one of four alternatives.

READING COMPREHENSION questions measure your ability to read carefully and accurately, to determine the relationships among the various parts of the passage, and to draw reasonable inferences from the material in the passage. You'll encounter four sets of questions; all questions in a set pertain to the same passage. The passages are drawn from for a variety of subjects, including the humanities, the social sciences, the physical sciences, ethics, philosophy, and law.

Your GMAT Scores

You'll receive four scores for the GMAT:

1. A scaled *Quantitative* score on a 0–60 scale
2. A scaled *Verbal* score on a 0–60 scale
3. A *total* score, on a 200–800 scale, based on both your Quantitative and Verbal scores
4. An *AWA* score on a 0–6 scale, which averages (to the nearest one-half point) the final scores for each of your two GMAT essays

For each of these four scores you'll also receive a percentile rank (0–99%). A percentile rank of 60%, for example, indicates that you scored higher than 60% (and lower than 40%) of all other test-takers. Percentile ranks reflect your performance relative to the entire GMAT test-taking population during the most recent three-year period.

> In Part IV, you'll find tables that convert scaled scores to percentile ranks.

X-Ref

How the Quantitative and Verbal Sections Are Scored

The scoring system for the Quantitative and Verbal sections is a bit tricky. Your score for each of these two sections is based on three factors:

- The *number* of questions you answer correctly
- The *difficulty level* of the questions you answer correctly
- The *range* of question types and topics among the questions you answer correctly

So, even if you don't respond to all 37 Quantitative (or 41 Verbal) questions, you can still attain a high score for the section if a high percentage of your responses are correct—especially if you respond correctly to a wide variety of question types. The CAT system's scoring algorithms are well-guarded ETS secrets; however, knowing exactly how the system works wouldn't affect your exam preparation or test-taking strategy, anyway.

> Some questions on each of your two multiple-choice sections won't be scored. The test-makers include unscored, "pre-test" questions on the GMAT in order to assess their integrity, fairness, and difficulty. Some of these questions might show up as scored questions on the GMAT in the future. Pre-test questions are mixed in with scored questions, and you won't be able to tell them apart—so don't risk trying.

Note

How the GMAT Essays Are Scored

The evaluation and scoring system for GMAT essays is also a bit tricky. Initially, one person will read and evaluate your Issue-Analysis essay, while a different person reads and evaluates your Argument-Analysis essay. Each reader will award a single score on a scale of 0–6 in whole-point intervals (6 is highest).

Readers apply a *holistic* scoring approach, meaning that a reader will base his or her evaluation on the overall quality of your writing. In other words, instead of awarding separate sub-scores for content, organization, writing style, and mechanics, the reader will consider how effective your essay is *as a whole*—accounting for all of these factors.

> **Note**
>
> All GMAT readers are college or university faculty; most teach in the field of either English or Communications. Each reader evaluates your writing independently of other readers, and no reader is informed of other readers' scores.

Scoring Criteria for the GMAT Essays

All readers are trained by ETS in applying the same scoring criteria. Here are the essential requirements for a top-scoring ("6") Issue-Analysis essay (note that you can attain a top score of 6 even if your essay contains minor errors in grammar, word usage, spelling, and punctuation):

1. The essay develops a position on the issue through the use of incisive reasons and persuasive examples.
2. The essay's ideas are conveyed clearly and articulately.
3. The essay maintains proper focus on the issue and is well organized.
4. The essay demonstrates proficiency, fluency, and maturity in its use of sentence structure, vocabulary, and idiom.
5. The essay demonstrates an excellent command of the elements of Standard Written English, including grammar, word usage, spelling, and punctuation—but may contain minor flaws in these areas.

Here are the essential requirements for a top-scoring ("6") Argument-Analysis essay (notice that the last two requirements are the same as for a top-scoring Issue-Analysis essay):

1. The essay identifies the key features of the argument and analyzes each one in a thoughtful manner.
2. The essay supports each point of critique with insightful reasons and examples.
3. The essay develops its ideas in a clear, organized manner, with appropriate transitions to help connect ideas.
4. The essay demonstrates proficiency, fluency, and maturity in its use of sentence structure, vocabulary, and idiom.
5. The essay demonstrates an excellent command of the elements of Standard Written English, including grammar, word usage,

spelling, and punctuation—but may contain minor flaws in these areas.

The criteria for lower scores are the same as the ones above; the only difference is that the standard for quality decreases for successively lower scores.

> **Note:** The scoring criteria for all six score levels are published in the official GMAT *Bulletin* as well as directly at the official GMAT Web site.

Computerized Rating of Your Two Essays

While two human readers evaluate your GMAT essays (one reader per essay), a computer program called *E-Rater®* will evaluate your essays in terms of grammar, syntax (sentence structure), repetitiveness (overuse of the same phrases), sentence length, and spelling. Like human readers, E-Rater awards a score of 0–6 for each essay.

In many respects, E-Rater is similar to the grammar- and spell-checkers built into popular word-processing programs such as Word and WordPerfect. However, E-Rater is custom-designed for ETS to weigh certain criteria more heavily than others. For instance, very little weight is given to minor mechanical errors (e.g., in punctuation and spelling). Also, E-Rater overlooks so-called "gray" areas of grammar (e.g., use of the passive voice), and flags certain problems (e.g., repetitiveness) that off-the-shelf checkers might not. Of course, E-Rater is only useful to a point. It cannot evaluate your ideas or how persuasively you have presented and supported those ideas. That's what human readers are for.

> **Note:** According to the testing service, the human readers' and E-Rater's combined evaluation takes into account more than 50 structural and linguistic criteria altogether.

Computation of Your AWA Score

Here are the specific steps involved in calculating your AWA score:

1. As mentioned above, one reader will read and score your Issue-Analysis essay, and a different reader will read and score your Argument-Analysis essay. Each reader will award a single score on a scale of 0–6 in whole-point intervals (6 is highest).

2. E-Rater will also evaluate and award a score of 0–6 for each essay.

Chapter 1: The GMAT—In a Nutshell

3. For either essay, if the human reader's score differs from E-Rater's score by more than one point, a second human reader will read and score the essay (and E-Rater's score will be disregarded).

4. For each essay, your final score is the average of the scores awarded by the human reader and E-Rater (or by the second human reader).

5. You final AWA score is the average of your final scores for each essay; AWA scores are rounded up to the nearest half-point.

Here's an example showing how the AWA scoring system works:

4	Reader A's evaluation of the Issue-Analysis essay
2	E-Rater's evaluation of the Issue-Analysis essay
3	Reader B's evaluation of the Issue-Analysis essay
3.5	Final score for the Issue-Analysis essay
3	Reader C's evaluation of the Argument-Analysis essay
3	E-Rater's evaluation of the Argument-Analysis essay
3	Final score for the Argument-Analysis essay
3.5	*AWA score*

Notice in this example that a second human reader evaluated the Issue-Analysis essay, and that the average of the two final scores (3.25) has been rounded up (to 3.5).

Score Reporting

Once the GMAT readers have read and scored your two essays, ETS will mail you an official score report for all four sections. (Expect your score report within ten days after testing.) At the same time, ETS will transmit a score report to each B-school you've designated to receive your score report. (You can direct reports to as many as five schools without charge.)

At this time, score reports don't include the GMAT essays themselves, although ETS is working on it. Eventually, the CAT system will provide disclosure of each test-taker's complete exam (including the questions).

> **Note**
>
> GMAT absences and cancellations also appear on your official report, but will not adversely affect your chances of admission.

How B-Schools Evaluate GMAT Scores

Each business school develops and implements its own policies for evaluating GMAT scores. Some schools place equal weight on GMAT scores and GPA, others weigh GMAT scores more heavily, whereas others weigh GPA more heavily. ETS reports your three most recent GMAT scores to each business school receiving your scores and transcripts. Most schools simply *average* reported scores. (Quantitative, Verbal, Total, and AWA scores are each averaged separately for this purpose.)

A minority of schools have refined this approach by disregarding a score that is sufficiently lower than another score for the same ability—on the basis that the low score unfairly distorts the test-taker's ability in this area. Other schools disregard all but your highest score of each type in any event. (This approach is increasingly uncommon, since it discriminates in favor of test-takers who can afford to take the GMAT repeatedly.)

> **Note**
>
> Any B-school will gladly tell you which method it uses among the three mentioned above. But don't expect any school to tell you exactly how much weight it places on each exam section or on different admission criteria (such as GMAT scores, GPA, work experience, and personal statements).

How the Computer-Adaptive GMAT Works

A "computer-adaptive" feature of the GMAT CAT makes it an entirely different animal than convention paper-based tests. The following are five key features that set the CAT apart.

1. **During the two multiple-choice sections, the GMAT CAT will continually adapt to your ability level.**

    The "A" in CAT stands for "Adaptive," which means that during each of the two multiple-choice sections the testing system tailors its difficulty level to your level of ability. How? The initial few questions *of each type* are average in difficulty level. As you respond *correctly* to questions, the CAT system steps you up to more difficult questions. Conversely, as you respond *incorrectly* to questions, the CAT steps you down to easier ones. Thus, the CAT builds a customized test for you, drawing on its *very* large pool of multiple-choice questions.

Chapter 1: The GMAT—In a Nutshell

Alert!

Early in an exam section, the CAT can shift from the easiest level to a very challenging level (or vice versa) in as few as 3 or 4 successive questions. But later in the section, when your ability level is well established, the difficulty level will not vary as widely.

2. The GMAT CAT does not let you skip questions.

Given the adaptive nature of the test, this makes sense. The computer-adaptive algorithm cannot determine the appropriate difficulty level for the next question without a response (correct or incorrect) to each question presented in sequence.

3. The GMAT CAT does not let you return to any question already presented (and answered).

Why not? The computer-adaptive algorithm that determines the difficulty of subsequent questions depends on the correctness of prior responses. For example, suppose you answer question 5 incorrectly. The CAT responds by posing slightly easier questions. Were the CAT to let you return to question 5 and change your response to the correct one, the questions following question 5 would be easier than they should have been, given your amended response. In other words, the process by which the CAT builds your GMAT and determines your score would be undermined.

4. The GMAT CAT does not require you to answer all available questions.

The CAT gives you the *opportunity* to respond to a total of 37 Quantitative and 41 Verbal questions. But the CAT does *not* require you to finish either section. The CAT will tabulate a score regardless of the number of available questions you've answered, except if you fail to respond to at least one question during a section, in which case an "NS" (no score) will appear on your score report *for that section only*.

Note

During each of the two essay sections, if you fail to key in (type) at least one character using the CAT word processor, you'll automatically receive a score of 0 (on a scale of 0 to 6) for that section; this score will appear on your report.

5. During each section, the GMAT CAT automatically warns you when time is running out.

When 5 minutes remain during each timed section, the on-screen clock (in the upper left corner of the screen) will blink silently several times to warn you. This 5-minute warning will be your only reminder.

> **Alert!**
> Beepers and alarms aren't allowed in the testing room, although silent timing devices are permitted.

The GMAT CAT Interface

The three simulated screen shots on pages 19, 21, and 22 show the GMAT CAT interface for the AWA sections, the Quantitative Ability section, and the Verbal Ability section. Let's first examine the features of the interface that are common to all exam sections.

The CAT Title Bar

A dark title bar will appear across the top of the computer screen at all times during all test sections. (You cannot hide this bar.) The CAT title bar displays three items:

- **Left corner:** The time remaining for the current section (hours and minutes)
- **Middle:** The name of the test (GMAT) and current section number
- **Right corner:** The current question number and total number of questions in the current section

Chapter 1: The GMAT—In a Nutshell

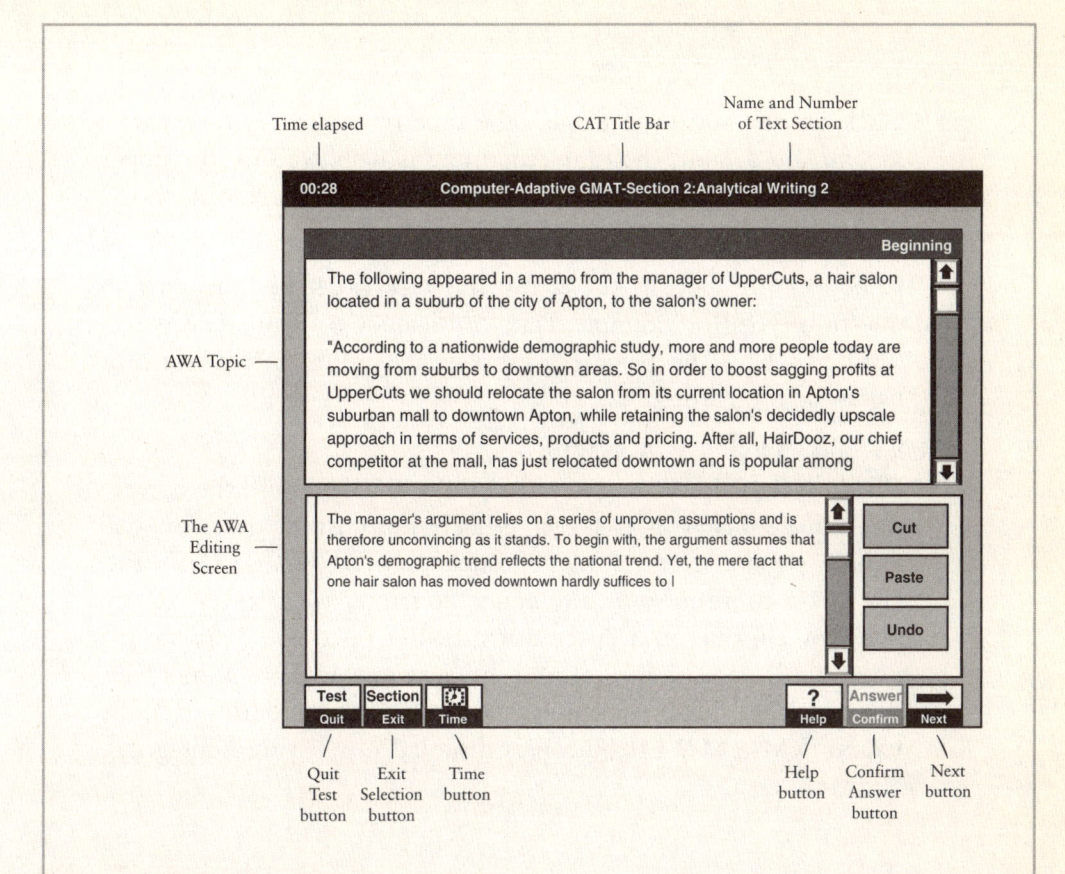

[Figure: CAT screen showing Computer-Adaptive GMAT-Section 2: Analytical Writing 2, with labels — Time elapsed (00:28), CAT Title Bar, Name and Number of Text Section, AWA Topic, The AWA Editing Screen, Quit Test button, Exit Selection button, Time button, Help button, Confirm Answer button, Next button. AWA Topic text: "The following appeared in a memo from the manager of UpperCuts, a hair salon located in a suburb of the city of Apton, to the salon's owner: 'According to a nationwide demographic study, more and more people today are moving from suburbs to downtown areas. So in order to boost sagging profits at UpperCuts we should relocate the salon from its current location in Apton's suburban mall to downtown Apton, while retaining the salon's decidedly upscale approach in terms of services, products and pricing. After all, HairDooz, our chief competitor at the mall, has just relocated downtown and is popular among". Editing screen text: "The manager's argument relies on a series of unproven assumptions and is therefore unconvincing as it stands. To begin with, the argument assumes that Apton's demographic trend reflects the national trend. Yet, the mere fact that one hair salon has moved downtown hardly suffices to |"]

The CAT Toolbar

A series of six buttons appear in a toolbar across the bottom of the computer screen at all times during all test sections. (You cannot hide the toolbar.) Here's a description of each button's function:

QUIT TEST

Click on this button to stop the test and cancel your scores for the *entire* test. (Partial score cancellation is not allowed in any event.) If you click here, a dialog box will appear on the screen, asking you to confirm this operation. Stay away from this button unless you're absolutely sure you wish your GMAT score for the day to vaporize and you're willing to throw away your GMAT registration fee.

EXIT SECTION

Click on this button if you finish the section before the allotted time expires and wish to proceed immediately to the next section. A dialog box will appear on the screen asking you to confirm this operation. Stay away from this button unless you've already answered every question in the current section and don't feel you need a breather before starting the next one!

TIME

Click on this button to display the time remaining to the nearest *second*. By default, the time remaining is displayed (in the upper left corner) in hours and minutes, but not to the nearest second.

HELP

Click on this button to access the directions for the current question type (for example, Data Sufficiency or Sentence Correction), as well as the general test directions and the instructions for using the toolbar items.

NEXT and CONFIRM ANSWER

Click on the NEXT button when you're finished with the current question. When you click on NEXT, the current question will remain on the screen until you click on CONFIRM ANSWER. Until you confirm, you can change your answer as often as you wish (by clicking on a different oval). But once you confirm, the question disappears forever and the next one appears in its place. Whenever the NEXT button is enabled (appearing dark gray), the CONFIRM ANSWER button is disabled (appearing light gray), and vice versa.

The AWA Screen

As illustrated in the screen shot on page 19, the AWA prompt appears at the top of your screen, and your essay response appears below it as you type your response. (The screen in the figure includes the first several lines of a response.) Notice that you have to scroll down to read the entire topic and question. You compose your essays using the CAT word processor. (Just ahead, you'll look closely at its features and limitations.)

The Quantitative and Verbal Screens

To respond to multiple-choice questions, click on one of the ovals to the left of the answer choices. You can't use the keyboard to select answers. Notice that the answer choices are *not* lettered; you'll click on blank ovals.

> In the sample questions throughout this book, the answer choices are lettered for easy reference to corresponding explanations.

X-Ref

Split screens. For some multiple-choice questions, the screen splits either horizontally or vertically.

Reading Comprehension: The screen splits vertically. The left side displays the passage; the right side displays the question and answer choices.

Quantitative questions that include figures: The screen splits horizontally. The figures appears at the top; the question and answer choices appear at the bottom.

Vertical Scrolling. For some multiple-choice questions, you'll have to scroll up and down (using the vertical scroll bar) to view all the material that pertains to the current question.

Reading Comprehension: Passages are too long for you to see on the screen in their entirety; you'll need to scroll.

Quantitative questions that include figures: Some figures—especially charts and graphs—won't fit on the screen in their entirety; you might need to scroll.

```
01:06          Computer-Adaptive GMAT-Section 3:Quantitative          21 of 37
```

Richard began driving from home on a trip averaging 30 miles per hour. How many miles per hour must Carla drive on average to catch up to him in exactly 3 hours if she leaves 30 minutes after Richard?

○ 35
○ 55
○ 39
○ 40
○ 60

| Test | Section | [⟳] | | ? | Answer | → |
| Quit | Exit | Time | | Help | Confirm | Next |

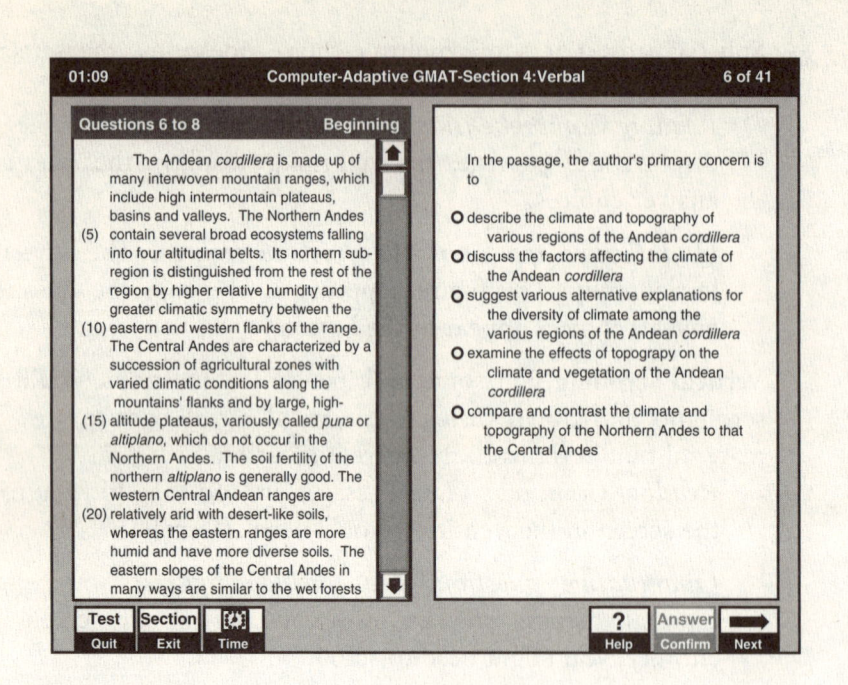

The CAT's Word Processor

During the two GMAT essay sections, you'll use the simple word processor built into the CAT system. While the word processor includes some features standard in programs like Word and WordPerfect, it also lacks many of these programs' features.

Keyboard Commands for Navigation and Editing

Here are the navigational and editing keys available in the CAT word processor:

- **Backspace** removes the character to the left of the cursor.
- **Delete** removes the character to the right of the cursor.
- **Home** moves the cursor to the beginning of the line.
- **End** moves the cursor to the end of the line.
- **Arrow Keys** move the cursor up, down, left, or right.
- **Enter** inserts a paragraph break (starts a new line).
- **Page Up** moves the cursor up one page (screen).
- **Page Down** moves the cursor down one page (screen).

Certain often-used features of standard word processing programs are not available in the CAT word processor. For example, no keyboard commands are available for:

- TAB—disabled (does not function)
- Beginning/end of paragraph (not available)
- Beginning/end of document (not available)
- No key combinations (using the CTRL, ALT, or SHIFT key) or other so-called "macros" are available for editing functions. (You'll use your mouse for cutting and pasting text.)

Mouse-Driven Navigation and Editing Functions

Just as with other word processors, to navigate the editing screen you can simply point the cursor to the position at which you wish to begin typing, then click. The CAT word processor also includes mouse-driven CUT, PASTE, and UNDO.

Selecting text you wish to cut. You select text the same way as with standard word processing programs: either (1) hold down your mouse button while sweeping the I-beam on the screen over the desired text, or (2) hold down the SHIFT key and use the navigation keys to select text.

The CUT Button. If you wish to delete text but want to save it to a temporary clipboard for pasting elsewhere, select that text (see above) then click on the CUT button. Cutting text is not the same as deleting it. When you delete text (using the DELETE key), you cannot paste it elsewhere in your document (but see UNDO below).

The PASTE button. If you wish to move text from one position to another, select and cut the text, then reposition your cursor where you want the text to go and click on the PASTE button.

The UNDO button. Click on this button to undo the most recent delete, cut, or paste that you performed.

Limitations of CUT and UNDO. The following mouse-driven features are not available:

- DRAG-AND-DROP cut-and-paste (not available)
- COPY (not available; to copy you need to cut, then paste, in the same spot)
- MULTIPLE UNDO (the CAT word processor stores *only your most recent* delete, cut, or paste, or keyboard entry.)

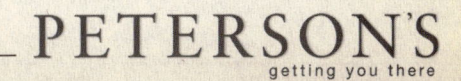

The vertical scroll bar. Once you key in ten lines or so, you'll have to scroll to view your entire response. A vertical scroll bar also appears to the right of the AWA prompt. Be sure to scroll all the way down to make sure you've read the entire prompt.

Spell-checking, grammar-checking, fonts, attributes, hyphenation. The CAT word processor does not include a spell-checker or grammar-checker, nor does it allow you to choose typeface or point size. Neither manual nor automatic hyphenation is available. Attributes such as bold, italics, and underlining are not available.

> **Note**
>
> As for words that you would otherwise italicize or underline (such as titles or non-English words), it's okay to leave them as is. The readers understand the limitations of the CAT word processor.

The GMAT CAT Test-Taking Experience

When you take a test as important as the GMAT, it's a good idea to minimize test anxiety by knowing exactly what to expect on exam day—aside from the timed test itself. Let's walk you through the various pre-test and post-test procedures and describe the physical testing environment.

When You Arrive at the Test Center

Here's what you can expect when you arrive at the test center:

- The supervisor will show you a roster, which includes the names of test-takers scheduled for that day, and will ask you to initial the roster next to your name, and indicate on the roster your arrival time.

- The supervisor will ask you to read a two-page list of testing procedures and rules. (I'll cover all these rules in the pages immediately ahead.)

- The supervisor will give you a "Nondisclosure Statement." You're to read the printed statement, then *write* the statement (in the space provided on the form) and sign it. In the statement, you agree to the testing policies and rules, and you agree not to reproduce or disclose any of the actual test questions. The supervisor will not permit you to enter the exam room until you've written and signed the statement.

Chapter 1: The GMAT—In a Nutshell

- You'll probably have to sit in a waiting room until the supervisor calls your name. A 5- to 10-minute wait beyond your scheduled testing time is not uncommon. (Taking the GMAT CAT is like going to the dentist—in more than one respect!)

- The supervisor will check your photo identification. (You won't be permitted to take the test unless you have one acceptable form of photo identification with you.)

- The test center will provide a secure locker (free of charge) for stowing your personal belongings during the test.

- To help ensure that nobody else takes any part of the exam in your place, the supervisor will take a photograph of you.

- The supervisor might give you some rudimentary tips about managing your time during the exam. Just ignore the supervisor's tips, because they might not be good advice for you!

- Before you enter the testing room, you must remove everything from your pockets except your photo I.D. and locker key.

- The supervisor will provide you with several pieces of scratch paper (stapled together), along with two pencils. These are the only items you'll have in hand as you enter the testing room.

Testing Procedures and Rules

- If you want to exit the testing room for any reason, you must raise your hand and wait for the supervisor to come in and escort you from the room. (You won't be able to pause the testing clock for any reason.)
- No guests are allowed in the waiting room during your test.
- No food or drink is allowed in the testing room.
- No hats are allowed.
- You must sign out whenever you exit the testing room.
- You must sign in whenever you re-enter the testing room (the supervisor will ask to see your photo I.D. each time).
- If you need more scratch paper during the exam, just raise your hand and ask for it. The supervisor will happily replace your bundle with a fresh one.
- The supervisor will replace your tired pencils with fresh, sharp ones upon your request anytime during the exam (just raise your hand).

What You Should Know about the CAT Testing Environment

- Individual testing stations are like library carrels; they're separated by half-walls.
- The height of your chair's seat will be adjustable and the chair will swivel. Chairs at most testing centers have arms.
- Computer monitors are generally of the 15-inch variety. You can adjust contrast. If you notice any flickering, ask the supervisor to move you to another station. (You won't be able to tell if you monitor has color capability, because the GMAT is strictly a black-and-white affair.)

> **Alert!**
> You can't change the size of the font on the screen, unless you specifically request before the exam begins that a special ZOOMTEXT function be made available to you.

- If your mouse has two buttons, you can use either button to click your way through the exam (both buttons serve the same function). Don't expect that nifty wheel between buttons for easy scrolling, because you're not going to get it. For all you gamers and laptop users, trackballs are available, but only if you request one before you begin the test.
- Testing rooms are not soundproof. During your test, you might hear talking and other noise from outside the room.
- Expect the supervisor to escort other test-takers in and out of the room during your test. Do your best to ignore this potential distraction.
- If the testing room is busy, expect to hear lots of mouse-clicking during your test. Because the room is otherwise fairly quiet, the incessant mouse-clicking can become annoying!
- Earplugs are available upon request.
- Expect anything in terms of room temperature, so dress in layers.
- You'll be under continual audio and video surveillance. To guard against cheating, and to record any irregularities or problems in the testing room as they occur, the room is continually audiotaped and videotaped. (Look for the cameras or two-way mirrors, then smile and wave!)

Chapter 1: The GMAT—In a Nutshell

Before You Begin the Test—The Computer Tutorial

Okay, the supervisor has just escorted you into the inner sanctum and to your station, and has wished you luck. (Some supervisors have been known to encourage test-takers to "have fun!") Before you begin the test, the CAT System will lead you through a tutorial which includes five sections (each section steps you through a series of "screens"):

1. How to use the mouse (6 screens)
2. How to select and change an answer (6 screens)
3. How to scroll the screen display up and down (6 screens)
4. How to use the toolbars (21 screens); here you'll learn how to:
   - Quit the test.
   - Exit the current section.
   - Access the directions.
   - Confirm your response and move to the next question.
5. How to use the AWA word processor features (14 screens)

> **Note:** If you want to see what some of the tutorial screens look like, ETS provides a variety of samples in its official GMAT *Bulletin*.

Here's what you need to know about the CAT tutorial:

- You won't be able to skip any section or any screen during the tutorial.

- As you progress, the system requires that you demonstrate competency in using the mouse, selecting and confirming answer choices, and accessing the directions. So you can't begin taking the actual test unless you've shown that you know how to use the system. (Don't worry: no test-taker has ever flunked the CAT system competency test.)

- At the end of each tutorial section (series of screens), you can repeat that section, at your option. But once you leave a section you can't return to it.

> **Alert!**
> Don't choose to repeat any tutorial section. Why not? If you do, you'll be forced to step through the entire sequence of screens in that section again (an aggravating time-waster, especially for the 21-screen section!)

- The AWA section of the tutorial allows you to practice using the word processor.
- If you carefully read all the information presented to you, expect to spend about 20 minutes on the tutorial.

> **Tip**
> On test day, you'll already know how the CAT system works. So step through the tutorial as quickly as you can, reading as little as possible. You can easily dispense with the tutorial in 5–10 minutes this way. Remember: The less time you spend with the tutorial, the less fatigued you'll be during the exam itself.

Post-Test GMAT CAT Procedures

Okay, it's been about 4 hours since you first entered the testing center, and you've just completed the second of two multiple-choice GMAT sections. You may think you've finished the CAT, but the CAT has not quite finished with you yet! There are a few more hoops to jump through before you're done.

1. **Respond to a brief questionnaire.** The CAT will impose on you a brief questionnaire (presented in a series of screens) about your test-taking experience (believe it or not, these questions are multiple-choice, just like the exam itself). The questionnaire might ask you, for example:

    - Whether your supervisor was knowledgeable and helpful
    - Whether the testing environment was comfortable
    - How long you waited after you arrived at the testing site to begin the test
    - Whether you were distracted by noise during your exam

2. **Cancel your test, at your option.** The most important question you'll answer while seated at your testing station is this next one. The CAT will ask you to choose whether to:

    - Cancel your scores (no scores are recorded; partial cancellation is not provided for) *or* see your scores immediately.

Chapter 1: The GMAT—In a Nutshell

Once you elect to see your scores, you can no longer cancel them—ever! So you should take a few minutes to think it over. The CAT gives you 5 minutes to choose. If you haven't decided within 5 minutes, the CAT will automatically show you your scores (and you forfeit your option to cancel).

Alert!

If you click on the CANCEL SCORES button, the CAT will then give you yet another 5 minutes to think over your decision. So you really have 10 minutes altogether to make up your mind.

3. **View and record your scores.** If you elect to see your scores, you should write them down on your scratch paper. When you leave the testing room, the supervisor will allow you to transcribe them onto another sheet of paper (one that you can take home with you), so that you don't have to memorize them.

4. **Direct your scores to the schools of your choice.** Once you've elected to see your scores, the CAT will ask you to select the schools you wish to receive your score report (the CAT provides a complete list of schools).

Tip

You can select as many as five schools at this time—without incurring an additional fee. This is your last chance for a freebie, so you should take full advantage of it. Be sure to compile your list of five schools before exam day.

Before You Leave the Testing Center

Upon exiting the testing room for the final time, the following will happen:

1. The supervisor will collect your pencils and scratch paper, and will count the number of sheets of paper to make sure you aren't trying to sneak out with any. (Then, if you're lucky, you'll be allowed to watch while the supervisor ceremoniously rips up your scratch paper and drops it in the trash basket!)

2. The supervisor will remind you to collect your belongings from your locker (if you used one), and turn in your locker key.

3. The supervisor will provide you with an ETS pamphlet that explains how to interpret your test scores. (You can take this home with you.)

> **Note:** The supervisor might also provide you with a postcard-sized invitation to "blow the whistle" on anybody you suspect of cheating on the exam (the invitation ends with the assurance: "Confidentiality guaranteed").

Top 10 Tips for GMAT Prep

Regardless of what books, software, or other GMAT-prep resources you're using, certain time-tested strategies for GMAT prep never go out of style. To attain your optimal GMAT score, and to maximize your chances of getting into your first-choice B-school, heed the following points of sage advice.

1. Don't Neglect Your Weaknesses

In gearing up for the GMAT, many test-takers make the mistake of focusing on their strengths while neglecting their weaknesses. They tell themselves: "I can't handle this tough stuff right now; so I'll either face it later or skip it altogether and hope to make some lucky guesses on the exam."

But, you can't hide any of your individual GMAT scores from B-school admissions officers. So, don't spin your GMAT-prep wheels by spending more time than you need on any one area of the GMAT, or by rehashing what you already know. Devote more time to improving on your weaknesses than basking in your strengths.

2. Don't Neglect the Two GMAT Essay Sections

GMAT "prep neglect" is especially commonplace when it comes to the two GMAT essay sections—a bit ironic, considering that it's impossible to guess, or "fake," your way through an essay. What's more, the B-schools are focusing more and more on the GMAT essays to help them make tough decisions among applicants—many of whom appear equally qualified otherwise. So, your AWA score might very well make the difference between acceptance and rejection, especially for a B-school where you're a borderline candidate.

> **Alert!** Fast, accurate typists have a clear advantage when it comes to the two GMAT essay sections—no doubt about it. So if you're a poor typist, work on improving your speed and skill before exam day.

Chapter 1: The GMAT—In a Nutshell

3. Practice under Exam Conditions

When it comes to GMAT prep, there's simply no substitute for "putting yourself to the test" by taking practice questions under simulated testing conditions. Here are some suggestions:

- Adhere to the time limits that each exam section imposes.
- If possible, use a word processor for composing your practice essays; use only the features available on the CAT word processor.
- If possible, take at least one computer-based practice test.
- Also, do not underestimate the role that endurance plays on the GMAT. Half the battle is just making it through the half-day ordeal with your wits intact. Condition yourself by taking at least one full-length practice test straight through, with only a few short breaks.

4. Take the Real GMAT Once—Just for Practice

If you have time and can afford it, you should register for and take the real GMAT once as a dress rehearsal—just to get comfortable with the testing environment. You'll rid yourself of a lot of anxiety and nervousness and, if you're like most test-takers, you'll be far more relaxed and focused the second time around. In fact, ETS statistics show that among repeaters, more than 90% improve their score the second time around. Those are great odds!

5. Keep Practice Scores in Perspective

If you're like most GMAT test-takers, you've set your sights on two or three particular colleges or universities as your top choices, and you have a good idea what GMAT scores you'll need for getting into those schools. So perhaps you've set a goal for your GMAT scores. That's understandable. But don't psyche yourself out by obsessing over your practice-test scores. Gloating over high scores can lead to complacency and overconfidence, while brooding over low scores can result in discouragement and self-doubt. Either way, you're sabotaging yourself. The bottom line: Try to concern yourself not with test scores themselves but rather with what you can constructively do between now and exam day to improve these scores.

6. Maintain the Right "GMATitude"

It's important to maintain a positive attitude about the GMAT. But, it's also important to keep your self-confidence from swelling to the point of complacency and overconfidence. Think you can just "wing it" on the

Part I: Everything You Ever Wanted to Know about the GMAT

GMAT and still crush the competition? Think again. Even if you were a curve-raiser in college, there are thousands of others like you who are taking the GMAT very seriously and who would be more than happy to bump you down the GMAT-scoring curve. Enough said?

7. Be Realistic in Your Expectations

You'd love perfect GMAT scores, wouldn't you? And in theory, your capable of attaining them. But in reality, you probably won't score as highly as you'd like to. Accept your limitations. With regular study and practice, you'll perform as well as you can reasonably expect to perform. Also be realistic about the benefits you expect from this or any other GMAT preparation book. There's only so much that you can do in a few weeks—or even several months—to boost your GMAT score.

8. Take Steps to Minimize GMAT Anxiety

Test anxiety, whether before or during a test, can only hinder your performance. Although it's a good idea to try to keep a lid on it, don't expect to eliminate it entirely. If you're starting to feel the heat, try the following anxiety-busting techniques.

- Practice testing under exam conditions is the best method of reducing test anxiety. As you become more comfortable in a simulated testing environment, your nerves will begin to settle down, and the real test will seem more like "just another day at the office."

- Join (or form) a GMAT study group. Openly discuss your insecurities about the GMAT, and you'll notice that they begin to dissipate.

- Before taking practice tests, try simple relaxation techniques such as stretching, quieting your thoughts, deep breathing, or whatever else works for you. Some people find a quick burst of vigorous exercise to be highly effective.

- You'll be anxious about the GMAT only if you're actually thinking about it. So during the weeks that you're gearing up for the test, keep yourself preoccupied with your everyday activities. Try not to discuss the GMAT with others except during planned study sessions or classes.

Chapter 1: The GMAT—In a Nutshell

9. Know When You've Peaked

Preparing for the GMAT is a bit like training for an athletic event. You need to familiarize yourself with the event, learn to be comfortable with it, and build up your skill and endurance. At some point—hopefully around exam day—your motivation, interest, and performance will peak. Sure, it takes *some* time and effort to get comfortable with the exam, to correct poor test-taking habits, to bone up on whatever math and grammar you might have forgotten, to develop an instinct for recognizing wrong-answer choices, and to find your optimal pace. But there's a point beyond which additional study and practice confer little or no additional benefit. Don't drag out the process by starting several months in advance or by postponing the GMAT to give yourself more time than you really need for preparation.

10. Take the GMAT Early to Allow Yourself the Option of Retaking It

Most graduate business schools admit new students for the fall term only. Although application deadlines vary widely among schools, if you take the GMAT no later than the November prior to matriculation, you'll meet almost any application deadline. Ideally, you should take the GMAT early enough so that you can take the exam a second time if necessary and still meet application deadlines. In any event, schedule the GMAT so that you're sure you will have adequate time to prepare beforehand.

Top 10 GMAT Test-Taking Tips

In Parts II–IV, you'll learn strategies and tips for specific test sections and question types. Right now, however, review some general strategies for the GMAT. Even if you've read about these strategies elsewhere, of if they seem like common sense to you, it's a good idea to reinforce them in your mind.

1. Know Your Optimal Pace, and Stay on It

Time is definitely a factor on every section of the GMAT. On the multiple-choice sections, expect to work at quicker pace than is comfortable for you. Similarly, the 30-minute time limit for each AWA response requires a lively writing pace, allowing little time for editing, revising, and fine-tuning.

During the multiple-choice sections, check your pace after every 10 questions or so (three times during a section), and adjust it accordingly so that you have time to at least consider every question in the section. During each essay section be sure to leave yourself enough time to cover all your main points and to wrap up your essay with a brief concluding paragraph. The best way to avoid the time squeeze is to practice under timed conditions, so that you get a sense for your optimal pace.

2. If You're Not Sure What the Correct Answer Is, Don't Dwell on It . . . Move on

This tip is closely related to the previous one. You might find yourself reluctant to leave a question until you're sure your answer is correct. The design of the CAT contributes to this mind set, because your reward for correct responses to difficult questions is greater than your reward for easier questions. But a stubborn attitude will only defeat you, because it reduces the number of questions you may attempt, which in turn can lower your score. Set aside your perfectionist tendencies and remember: You can miss quite a few questions and still score high. Develop a sense of your optimal pace—one that results in the greatest number of *correct* responses.

3. Take Your Time with the First Few Quantitative and Verbal Questions

The CAT uses your responses to the first few questions to move you either up or down the ladder of difficulty. Of course, you want to move up the ladder, not down. So take great care with the initial questions—perhaps moving at a somewhat slower pace. Otherwise, you'll have to answer several questions just to reverse the trend by proving to the CAT that you're smarter than it thinks you are.

4. Avoid Random Guesswork, If Possible

If you must guess, always try to eliminate obvious wrong-answer choices first, then go with your hunch. Eliminating even one choice improves your odds. If you're out of time on a section, there's no advantage to guessing randomly on the remaining questions. Why? You might luck out and guess correctly. However, incorrect responses move you down the ladder of difficulty, and correct responses to easier questions aren't worth as much as correct responses to more difficult questions. So on balance, there's no net advantage to guessing randomly.

5. Read Each Question in Its Entirety, and Read Every Answer Choice

You'll discover in the days ahead that the test-makers love to bait you with tempting wrong-answer choices. This applies to every type of multiple-choice question on the exam. So unless you're quickly running out of time, never confirm an answer until you've read all the choices! This blunder is one of the leading causes of incorrect responses on the GMAT.

6. Maintain an Active Mind Set

During the GMAT, it's remarkably easy to fall into a passive mode—one in which you let your eyes simply pass over the words while you hope that the correct response jumps out at you as you scan the answer choices. Fight this tendency by interacting with the test as you read it. Keep in mind that each question on the GMAT is designed to measure a specific ability or skill. So try to adopt an active, investigative approach to each question, in which you ask yourself:

- What skill is the question measuring?
- What is the most direct thought process to determine the correct response?
- How might a careless test-taker be tripped up on this type of question?

Answering these three questions is, in large part, what the rest of this book is all about.

7. Use Your Pencil and Scratch Paper

Using pencil and paper helps keep you in an active mode. Making brief notes and drawing diagrams and flow charts will help keep your thought process clear.

8. Move the Keyboard Aside for the Multiple-Choice Sections

You won't use the keyboard at all for these sections. So put your scratch paper right in front of you, and get the keyboard out of the way.

9. Know the Test Directions Inside and Out—Before You Take the Test

Just before the first question of each type (e.g., Data Sufficiency or Reading Comprehension) the CAT will display the directions for that question type. The clock will be running, so dismiss the directions as quickly as possible by clicking on the DISMISS DIRECTIONS button. time to read (This advice presupposes that you already know the directions—which of course you will!)

10. Use the 5-Minute Breaks, but Keep an Eye on the Time

Remember: The GMAT CAT clock is always running, even during the two scheduled 5-minute breaks. By all means, take advantage of these breaks to leave the room, perhaps grab a quick snack from your locker, and do some stretching or relaxing. But don't get too relaxed! Five minutes goes by very quickly, and the test will begin after that time has elapsed—with or without you!

Resources for GMAT Preparation

How much should you "invest" in your GMAT education—in terms of both time and money? The conventional wisdom is that since the GMAT is one of the most important tests you'll ever take, you should invest as much time and money in it as possible. However, the law of diminishing returns applies to GMAT preparation. This book, along with a few other thoughtfully selected resources, can provide virtually all of the potential benefits of a full-blown GMAT prep course.

GMAT Books

The number of available books for GMAT prep is overwhelming. Here are some suggestions to help you cut through the glut:

- Peruse a book carefully before committing to it. Yes, this means visiting your local brick-and-mortar bookstore.

- Look for a book that emphasizes skill development, not just practice questions.

- Rule out any book that emphasizes so-called "secrets" and "shortcuts," or makes the test out to be easier than it appears. Do you really think the GMAC and ETS would devise a test that can be "cracked" like a cheap safe? If so, think again.

Chapter 1: The GMAT—In a Nutshell

- Limit the number of comprehensive GMAT books you use to two or three altogether. Any more any you'll find yourself reading the same strategies and test-taking tips again.

- Identify your weakest skill area, and supplement this book with a workbook targeted at that area.

If you must shop for GMAT books at an online bookstore, ignore customer comments and ratings, especially if they are few in number. Laudatory comments are often submitted anonymously by the publishers themselves, while derogatory comments are often factually inaccurate, unfair, and inflammatory.

The bottom line: You don't need to spend more than $40 to $50, on three or four books altogether, to be fully prepared for the GMAT.

Online GMAT Resources

The Web is now littered with GMAT advice and practice questions—freely available for public consumption. To separate the wheat from the chaff, limit your GMAT web-surfing to the official GMAC site (www.mba.com) and the sites of test-prep publishers with a time-tested reputation for producing high-quality content, such as Peterson's (www.petersons.com).

GMAT-Prep Courses

Would it be worthwhile to enroll in a live GMAT-prep course? Well, here are the advantages:

1. The dynamics of a live classroom setting can help you learn difficult concepts by affording different perspectives. (But why not start your own study group? You're just as likely to gain useful insights from your peers as from a GMAT instructor.)

2. Having made a substantial financial investment, you'll probably be motivated to get your money's worth out of that investment. (But this is an expensive head game, isn't it? And if you can't afford the course, it doesn't matter anyway.)

3. You're less likely to procrastinate with a set class schedule. (But if you're disciplined enough this is no advantage.)

4. All the materials are provided, so you don't need to decide which books and/or software to buy. (But is this really a significant benefit?)

PETERSON'S
getting you there

5. You can commiserate and compare notes with your classmates. In fact, GMAT prep classes typical morph into de facto pre-MBA support groups. (But why not start your own GMAT study/support group?)

Here are some drawbacks and caveats to keep in mind if you're thinking about taking a GMAT prep-course:

1. They're expensive; you can easily spend $1,000. (If you're near a university, you might find a course sponsored by the university, perhaps through its extension program, for a fraction of the cost of a private course.)

2. Despite their claims, private test-prep companies pass along no "secrets" to you—nothing at all that you can't find for yourself in test-prep books.

3. The popular test-prep services require each of their GMAT instructors to have taken the real GMAT and attained a high score (typically above the 90th percentile). But this screen hardly ensures that your instructor will be an effective teacher.

4. During peak times of the year, you might have difficulty scheduling out-of-class time in the computer lab, at least during reasonable hours.

5. If you're not located in a major urban area or near a large college or university, the class location might be too remote for you.

If you decide to enroll in a GMAT prep-course, keep in mind the following points of advice:

1. Ask about the policy for repeating the course. Insist on an option to repeat the course at least once without charge at any time (not just within the next year).

2. Ask about merit-based or financial-based "scholarships" (fee reductions).

3. If you repeat the course, be sure to arrange for a different instructor; just as with GMAT books, each GMAT instructor has his or her own teaching style.

4. The most significant benefit of a GMAT course is the live classroom; so be sure to attend as many classes as you can.

5. Take full advantage of the chance to meet other students and set up out-of-class study sessions. As we've already noted, you can learn just as much from your peers as from an instructor.

Chapter 1: The GMAT—In a Nutshell

GMAT Availability and Registration

The computer-based GMAT is administered year-round at more than 500 locations, most of which are in North America. Testing centers are located at Prometric Testing Centers, Sylvan Learning Centers, certain colleges and universities, and ETS (Educational Testing Service) field offices. The official GMAT *Bulletin* contains a complete list of GMAT computer-based test centers; an updated list is available at the GMAC Web site (www.mba.com).

Registering for the GMAT

To take the computer-based GMAT, you must schedule an appointment by using any of the following four methods:

1. Make an appointment online, via the GMAC Web site (www.mba.com).

2. Call the test center of your choice directly. A current test center list is available at the GMAC Web site (www.mba.com).

3. Call a central registration number: 1-800-GMAT-NOW (1-800-462-8669).

4. Make an appointment by mail. (You'll need to complete and mail the Authorization Voucher Request Form in the official GMAT *Bulletin*; you should receive your Authorization Voucher about four weeks after you mail the request form, and you cannot schedule a test appointment until you've received your voucher.)

You might be able to sit for the GMAT within a few days after scheduling an appointment. However, keep in mind that popular test centers may experience backlogs of up to several weeks. Also, you might find it more difficult to schedule a weekend test date than a weekday test date. So be sure to plan ahead and schedule your GMAT early enough to meet your B-school application deadlines.

> **Note:** In certain areas outside of North America, the computer-based network is not yet available, and the GMAT is still administered as a paper-based exam. A complete list of international paper-based testing locations and test dates is available at the GMAC Web site (www.mba.com).

Obtaining Up-to-Date GMAT Information

For detailed information about GMAT registration procedures, consult the official GMAC Web site (www.mba.com), or refer to the printed GMAT *Bulletin*, published annually by the GMAC. This free bulletin is available directly from ETS and GMAC, as well as through career-planning offices at most four-year colleges and universities. You can also download the *Bulletin* from the GMAC Web site. The official GMAC Web site and *Bulletin* both provide detailed and current information about:

- Test center locations, telephone numbers, and hours of operation
- Registration procedures
- Accommodations for disabled test-takers
- Requirements for admission to the GMAT
- Registration and reporting fees, and refund policies
- Repeating the test
- The paper-based GMAT (availability, registration procedures, etc.)
- Official scoring criteria for the AWA essays
- How GMAT scores should be used by the institutions

The GMAT *Bulletin* is published only once a year, so for the most up-to-date official information you should check the GMAC Web site.

Contacting the Testing Service

To obtain the *Bulletin*, or for other information about the GMAT, you can contact ETS using any of the following methods:

Telephone:
1-609-771-7330 (general inquiries and publications)
1-800-462-8669 (CAT registration only)

E-mail:
gmat@ets.org

World Wide Web:
www.mba.com
www.ets.org (the ETS home page)

Mail:
GMAT
Educational Testing Service
P.O. Box 6103
Princeton, NJ 08541-6103

Chapter 2

The GMAT—Up Close

In Chapter 1, you learned that the GMAT consists of three parts and that test questions come in seven different formats. Here's a recap:

Test Section	Question Formats
Analytical Writing Assessment (Sections 1 and 2)	Analysis of an Issue Analysis of an Argument
Quantitative Ability (Section 3)	Problem Solving Data Sufficiency
Verbal Ability (Section 4)	Critical Reasoning Sentence Correction Reading Comprehension

In this chapter, you'll examine each format in detail. Specifically, you'll:

- Learn what abilities and content areas the format covers
- Examine the test directions
- Look at one or two example questions
- Review the format's key features

Note

For each multiple-choice format, you'll look at two questions—one a bit easier than average, the other a bit tougher than average—along with explanatory answers. You can use these sample questions to help determine if you should *Take It to the Next Level*.

Analytical Writing Assessment (AWA)

In Chapter 1, you learned that the GMAT Analytical Writing Assessment consists of two separate timed sections: (1) Analysis of an Issue and (2) Analysis of an Argument. These two sections have a lot in common. For each section:

- You compose an essay response using the test's built-in word processor.
- Your time limit is 30 minutes.
- Your essay topic, or "prompt," is drawn randomly from a large pool.
- Your essay will be evaluated based on four broad areas: (1) content, (2) organization, (3) writing style, and (4) mechanics (grammar, syntax, word usage, etc.).

Here, you'll take a closer look at each of the two AWA sections.

Analysis of an Issue (1 Writing Task, 30 Minutes)

During the Issue-Analysis section, your task is to compose an essay in which you respond to a brief (1–2 sentence) opinion about an issue of general intellectual interest. You should consider various perspectives, take a position on the issue, and argue that position.

What's Covered

The Issue-Analysis section is designed to test your ability to present a position on an issue effectively and persuasively. In scoring your Issue essay, readers will consider how effectively you do the following:

- Recognize and deal with the complexities and implications of the issue.
- Organize, develop, and express your ideas.
- Support your ideas (with reasons and examples).
- Control the elements of Standard Written English.

Test Directions

During the pre-test tutorial, as well as at the start of your timed Issue-Analysis section, the GMAT will present to you one screen providing directions and guidelines specific to the Issue-Analysis writing task. The screen will describe the task generally, and indicate the four general scoring criteria. Here's essentially what you'll see on this screen:

Chapter 2: The GMAT—Up Close

> This writing task is designed to test your ability to present a position on an issue effectively and persuasively. Your task is to analyze the issue presented, considering various perspectives, and to develop your own position on the issue. In scoring your Issue essay, readers will consider how effectively you:
>
> - Recognize and deal with the complexities and implications of the issue.
> - Organize, develop, and express your ideas.
> - Support your ideas (with reasons and examples).
> - Control the elements of Standard Written English.

The screen will also indicate rules and guidelines for the Issue writing task. Here's essentially what you'll see further down the screen:

> - Your time limit is 30 minutes.
> - Writing on any topic other than the one presented is unacceptable.
> - The topic will appear as a brief statement on an issue of general interest.
> - You are free to accept, reject, or qualify the statement.
> - You should support your perspective with reasons and/or examples from such sources as your experience, observation, reading, and academic studies.
> - You should take a few minutes to plan your response before you begin typing.
> - You should leave time to reread your response and make any revisions you think are needed.

Part I: Everything You Ever Wanted to Know about the GMAT

> **Note:** You can access the directions and guidelines at any time during the Issue-Analysis section by clicking on the HELP button.

What Issue-Analysis Questions Look Like

Each Issue-Analysis topic in the official pool consists of a statement of opinion, which appears in quotes, followed by a brief *directive* (statement of your task). Here's an example, which is similar to some of the topics in the official pool—although you won't see this one on your exam (the directive follows the quoted statement):

> "People often complain that the introduction of new labor-saving machines costs workers their jobs. However, most new technologies create more jobs than they destroy."

> Discuss the extent to which you agree or disagree with the foregoing statement. Support your perspective using reasons and/or examples from your experience, observation, reading, or academic studies.

Although each statement in the official GMAT pool is distinct, many of them cover similar thematic ground. Here are the different themes to look for (understandably, more topics involve business issues than any other type):

- Business—organizational structure/behavior, management
- Culture and social mores, attitudes, values
- Business productivity, efficiency, and teamwork
- Business—labor and employment issues
- Education—its overall role and objectives
- Government's role in ensuring the welfare of its citizens
- Technology and its impact on business and society
- Keys to individual success
- Business—its overall role and objectives in society
- Business ethics
- Personal qualities and values
- Government's role in regulating business, commerce, speech
- "Global village" issues
- Bureaucracy and "the system"

- Business—advertising and marketing
- Learning lessons from history
- Individual power and influence

> **Note**
> These categories are not mutually exclusive; in other words, many Issues could fall into more than one category.

Key Facts about GMAT Issue Analysis

Here are some key facts about the Issue-Analysis section (most of these are review):

- **The CAT will select your topic randomly from a large pool.** You won't be able to choose among topics.

- **All directives in the official pool are not identical.** Your directive might differ slightly from the one in the preceding example. For example, your directive might ask you: "In your opinion, how accurate is the foregoing statement?" Regardless of how the directive is framed, however, you essential task is always the same: adopt a position on the issue, then support it with sound reasons and relevant examples.

- **There is no "correct" answer.** What's important is how effectively you present and support your position, not what your position is.

- **The Issue-Analysis section is not intended to test your technical knowledge of any topic.** Of course, you'll need some familiarity with the topic at hand. But, don't worry if you're no expert on the subject. The test-makers are far more interested in your ability to assemble a well-organized, cohesive essay under time pressure than in your knowledge of any specific subject.

- **GMAT readers appreciate your time constraint and focus less on minutia than on the big picture.** In evaluating and scoring your essay, the readers will focus primarily on substance and organization. You writing "style" and your mechanics (grammar, syntax, word usage, etc.) are secondary factors, which will come into play only if problems in these areas interfere with the reader's understanding of the ideas you're intending to convey in your essay. You won't be penalized for errors in spelling and punctuation—unless these errors are frequent and egregious. (The CAT word processor does not include a grammar- or spell-checker.)

Analysis of an Argument (1 Writing Task, 30 Minutes)

During the Argument-Analysis section, your task is to compose an essay in which you critique a paragraph-length argument based on the strength of the evidence presented in support of it and on the argument's logic (line of reasoning). You can also indicate what additional evidence would help you evaluate the argument, and how the argument could be improved.

What's Covered

The Argument-Analysis section is designed to test your critical-reasoning and analytical-writing skills. In scoring your Argument essay, the reader will consider how effectively you:

- Identify and analyze the key elements of the argument.
- Organize, develop, and express your critique.
- Support your ideas (with reasons and examples).
- Control the elements of Standard Written English.

Test Directions

During the pre-test tutorial, as well as at the start of your timed Issue-Analysis section, the GMAT will present two screens of directions and guidelines specific to the Argument-Analysis writing task. The first screen will describe the task generally and indicate the four general scoring criteria. Here's essentially what you'll see on the first screen:

> This writing task is designed to test your critical-reasoning skills as well as your writing skills. Your task is to critique the stated argument in terms of its logical soundness and in terms of the strength of the evidence offered in support of the argument. In scoring your Argument essay, the reader will consider how effectively you:
>
> - Identify and analyze the key elements of the argument.
> - Organize, develop, and express your critique.
> - Support your ideas (with reasons and examples).
> - Control the elements of Standard Written English.

Chapter 2: The GMAT—Up Close

The screen will then indicate additional rules and guidelines. Here's essentially what you'll see farther down the screen:

- Your time limit is 30 minutes.
- You must critique the logical soundness of the argument presented.
- A critique of any other argument is unacceptable.
- You should take a few minutes to plan your response before you begin typing.
- You should develop your ideas fully and organize them in a coherent manner.
- You should leave time to reread your response and make any revisions you think are needed.

The second screen will indicate specific guidelines for critiquing the Argument. Here's essentially what you'll see on the second screen:

- You are not being asked to agree or disagree with any of the statements in the argument.
- You should analyze the argument's line of reasoning.
- You should consider questionable assumptions underlying the argument.
- You should consider the extent to which the evidence presented supports the argument's conclusion.
- You may discuss what additional evidence would help strengthen or refute the argument.
- You may discuss what additional information, if any, would help you to evaluate the argument's conclusion.

Note

You can access the two screens of directions and guidelines at any time during the Argument-Analysis section by clicking on the HELP button.

What Argument-Analysis Questions Look Like

The Argument on your exam will be drawn randomly from a large pool. Each Argument in the official pool consists of a paragraph-length passage, which presents the *argument* itself, followed by a *directive* (statement of your task). The directive is the same for every Argument in the official pool.

The Argument will appear as a quotation from a specified fictitious source. Here's an example similar to the ones in the official pool—although you won't see this one on your exam (the directive follows the Argument):

> The following recommendation appeared in a memo from the Hillsville City Council to the city's mayor:
>
> "The private firm Trashco provides refuse pickup and disposal as well as recycling services for the town of Plattsburg. Trashco's total fees for these services are about two thirds what Hillsville pays Ridco for the same services. In order to save enough money to construct a refuse transfer station within our city limits, Hillsville should discontinue using Ridco's services and use Trashco's services instead."
>
> Discuss how well reasoned you find this argument. In your discussion, be sure to analyze the line of reasoning and the use of evidence in the argument. For example, you may need to consider what questionable assumptions underlie the thinking and what alternative explanations or counterexamples might weaken the conclusion. You can also discuss what sort of evidence would strengthen or refute the argument, what changes in the argument would make it more logically sound, and what, if anything, would help you to better evaluate its conclusion.

Key Facts about GMAT Argument Analysis

Here are some key facts about the Argument-Analysis section (most are review):

- **The CAT will randomly select your Argument-Analysis prompt from a large pool.** As in the Issue-Analysis section, you won't be able to choose among topics.

- **All Arguments in the official pool contain the same directive.** Learn the directive that follows the quoted Argument before the exam, and you won't need to read it during the exam.

- **The Argument-Analysis task is much different than the Issue-Analysis task.** There's no "correct' answer to any Issue-Analysis question. But, when it comes to the Argument-Analysis task, it's a different story. The argument that you critique will contain *at least*

Chapter 2: The GMAT—Up Close

three major problems in the use of evidence, reasoning, and logic; to score high on your Argument-Analysis essay, you must identify and discuss each major problem.

- **You don't need technical knowledge or special training in logic to score high.** GMAT arguments are designed so that you can analyze them by applying general reasoning skills and common sense.

- **GMAT readers appreciate your time constraint and focus less on minutia than on the big picture.** Just as with the Issue-Analysis section, the readers will focus primarily on substance and organization. You writing "style" and your mechanics (grammar, syntax, word usage, etc.) are secondary factors, and you won't be penalized for errors in spelling and punctuation unless these errors are frequent and egregious.

The Quantitative Ability Section (37 Questions, 75 Minutes)

Before examining the two question formats—Problem Solving and Data Sufficiency—that the test-makers use for Quantitative Ability questions, let's first cover what's common to both formats.

Both types of questions—Problem Solving and Data Sufficiency—are designed to measure the following general skills:

- Your proficiency in arithmetical operations
- Your proficiency at solving algebraic equations
- Your ability to convert verbal information to mathematical terms
- Your ability to visualize geometric shapes and numerical relationships
- Your ability to devise intuitive and unconventional solutions to conventional mathematical problems

Here's a breakdown of the specific areas covered on the Quantitative section, along with their frequency of appearance:

Properties of Numbers and Arithmetical Operations
(13–17 Questions)

- Linear ordering (positive and negative numbers, absolute value)
- Properties of integers (factors, multiples, prime numbers)
- Arithmetical operations
- Laws of arithmetic

- Fractions, decimals, and percentages
- Ratio and proportion
- Exponents (powers) and roots
- Average (arithmetic mean), mode, and median
- Basic probability

Algebraic Equations and Inequalities (11–15 Questions)

- Simplifying linear and quadratic algebraic expressions
- Solving equations with one variable (unknown)
- Solving equations with two variables (unknowns)
- Solving factorable quadratic equations
- Inequalities

Geometry, Including Coordinate Geometry (5–8 Questions)

- Intersecting lines and angles
- Perpendicular and parallel lines
- Triangles
- Quadrilaterals (4-sided polygons)
- Circles
- Rectangular solids (three-dimensional figures)
- Cylinders
- Pyramids
- Coordinate geometry

Interpreting Statistical Charts, Graphs, and Tables (2–4 Questions)

- Pie charts
- Tables
- Bar graphs
- Line charts

Algebraic concepts on the GMAT are those normally covered in a first-year high school algebra course. The Quantitative Ability section does NOT cover these skills and math areas:

- Complex calculations involving large and/or unwieldy numbers
- Advanced algebra concepts

- Formal geometry proofs
- Trigonometry
- Calculus
- Statistics (except for simple probability, arithmetic mean, and median)

The following assumptions apply to all Quantitative questions:

- All numbers used are real numbers.
- All figures lie on a plane unless otherwise indicated.
- All lines shown as straight are straight. Lines that appear "jagged" can be assumed to be straight (lines can look somewhat jagged on the computer screen).

> **Note**
>
> Additional assumptions about figures (diagrams and graphics) are different for Problem Solving questions than for Data Sufficiency questions. (You'll look at these assumptions when you examine each of the two formats just ahead.)

Problem Solving (22–23 questions)

Problem Solving questions require you to work to a solution (a numerical value or other expression), and then find that solution among the five answer choices.

What's Covered
Any of the Quantitative areas listed on page 49 is fair game for a Problem Solving question.

Test Directions
The directions on the following page are essentially what you'll see during the pre-test tutorial and just prior to your first Problem Solving questions (you can access these directions at any time by clicking on the HELP button).

> **Directions:** Solve this problem and indicate the best of the answer choices given.
>
> **Numbers:** All numbers used are real numbers.
>
> **Figures:** A figure accompanying a Problem Solving question is intended to provide information useful in solving the problem. Figures are drawn as accurately as possible EXCEPT when it is stated in a specific problem that its figure is not drawn to scale. Straight lines may sometimes appear jagged. All figures lie on a plane unless otherwise indicated.
>
> To review these directions for subsequent questions of this type, click on HELP.

What Problem Solving Questions Look Like

Let's look at two Problem Solving questions that are similar to what you might see on the GMAT. (Answer choices are lettered A–E here. Remember, though, that on the actual GMAT, you'll select among choices by clicking on one of five blank ovals, not letters.) This first problem is easy to understand, and no formulas or tricky math is needed to solve it. Among GMAT test-takers, about 80% would answer this question correctly.

Village A's population, which is currently 6,800, is decreasing at a rate of 120 each year. Village B's population, which is currently 4,200, is decreasing at a rate of 80 each year. At these rates, in how many years will the population of the two villages be equal?

A. 9
B. 11
C. 13
D. 14
E. 16

The correct answer is C. One way to solve this problem is to subtract 120 from A's population while adding 80 to B's population—again and again until the two are equal—keeping track of the number of times you perform these simultaneous operations. (You'll find that number to be 13.) But there's a faster way to solve the problem that also helps you avoid computation errors. The difference between the two populations is currently 2,600 (6,800 − 4,200). Each year that gap closes by 200 (120 + 80). So you can simply divide 2,600 by 200 to determine the

Chapter 2: The GMAT—Up Close

number of years for the gap to close completely. That's easy math: 2,600 ÷ 200 = 13.

Now here's a more difficult Problem Solving question. To handle it, you need to understand rules involving exponents and their effect on the size and sign (positive or negative) of fractional numbers. Among GMAT test-takers, only about 50% would respond correctly to this question.

If $-27 = \left(\dfrac{1}{3}\right)^k$, what is the value of k?

A. -9
B. -3
C. $-\dfrac{1}{3}$
D. $\dfrac{1}{3}$
E. 3

The correct answer is B. This question is asking you to determine the power that must be raised to in order to obtain -27. First, look at the numbers in the question. Note that $-27 = (-3)^3$. That's a good clue that the answer to the question must involve the number -3. If the number we were raising to the power of k were -3, then the value of k would be 3. But, the number we're raising to the power is k is $-\dfrac{1}{3}$, which is the *reciprocal* of -3. (By definition, the product of a number and its reciprocal is 1.) So, you need to apply the rule that a negative exponent reciprocates its base. In other words, raising a base number to a negative power is the same as raising the base number's reciprocal to the power's absolute value. Therefore:

$$\left(-\dfrac{1}{3}\right)^{-3} = (-3)^3$$

As you can see, that value of k is -3.

> **Note**
> In the preceding questions, we've labeled the answer choices A through E. Remember that on the actual GMAT CAT screen, you'll select your choice by clicking on one of five *blank ovals* (instead of choosing among *lettered* answer choices).

Part I: Everything You Ever Wanted to Know about the GMAT

Key Facts about GMAT Problem Solving
Important features of the Problem Solving format to keep in mind (some of these points are review).

- **Numerical answer choices are listed in order—from smallest in value to greatest in value.** Notice in our first sample question that the numerical values in the answer choices got *larger* as you read down from A to E. That's the way it is with every Problem Solving question whose answer choices are all numbers.

> **Note**
>
> There is one exception to this pattern. If a question asks you which answer choice is greatest (or smallest) in value, the answer choices will not necessarily be listed in ascending order of value—for obvious reasons.

- **Some Problem Solving questions will include figures (geometry figures, graphs, and charts).** Most of the 5–8 geometry questions will be accompanied by some type of figure. Also, each Data Interpretation question will be accompanied by a chart or graph.

- **Figures are drawn accurately unless the problem indicates otherwise.** Accompanying figures are intended to provide information useful in solving the problems. They're intended to help you, not to mislead or trick you by their visual appearance. If a figure is not drawn to scale, you'll see this warning near the figure: "Note: Figure not drawn to scale."

> **Alert!**
>
> It's a whole different ball game when it comes to Data Sufficiency questions, in which figures are *not* necessarily drawn to scale.

Data Sufficiency (14–15 questions)
The Data Sufficiency format is unique to the GMAT; you won't find it on any other standardized test. Each Data Sufficiency consists of a question followed by two statements—labeled (1) and (2). Your task is to analyze each of the two statements to determine whether it provides sufficient data to answer the question and, if neither suffices alone, whether both statements together suffice.

What's Covered
Data Sufficiency problems cover the same mix of arithmetic, algebra, and geometry as Problem Solving questions. (Any of the Quantitative areas listed on page 49 is fair game for a Data Sufficiency question.)

Chapter 2: The GMAT—Up Close

Test Directions

The following directions are essentially what you'll see during the pre-test tutorial and just prior to your first Data Sufficiency question. (You can access these directions at any time by clicking on the HELP button.) Notice that some of the directions are new—in other words, they don't apply to Problem Solving questions.

> **Directions:** This Data Sufficiency problem consists of a question and two statements, labeled (1) and (2), in which certain data are given. You have to decide whether the data given in the statements are sufficient for answering the question. Using the data given in the statements plus your knowledge of mathematics and everyday facts (such as the number of days in July or the meaning of *counterclockwise*), you must indicate whether:
>
> Statement 1 ALONE is sufficient, but statement 2 alone is not sufficient to answer the question asked;
>
> Statement 2 ALONE is sufficient, but statement 1 alone is not sufficient to answer the question asked;
>
> BOTH statements (1) and (2) TOGETHER are sufficient to answer the question asked; but NEITHER statement ALONE is sufficient;
>
> EACH statement ALONE is sufficient to answer the question asked;
>
> Statements (1) and (2) TOGETHER are NOT sufficient to answer the question asked, and additional data specific to the problem are needed.
>
> **Numbers:** All numbers used are real numbers.
>
> **Figures:** A figure accompanying a data sufficiency problem will conform to the information given in the question, but will not necessarily conform to the additional information in statements (1 and 2).
>
> Lines shown as straight can be assumed to be straight and lines that appear jagged can also be assumed to be straight.
>
> You may assume that positions of points, angles, regions, etc., exist in the order shown and that angle measures are greater than zero.
>
> All figures lie in a plane unless otherwise indicated.
>
> **Note:** In Data Sufficiency problems that ask you for the value of a quantity the data given in the statements are sufficient only when it is possible to determine exactly one numerical value for the quantity.
>
> To review these directions for subsequent questions of this type, click on HELP.

What Data Sufficiency Questions Look Like

As already noted, each Data Sufficiency consists of a question followed by two statements labeled (1) and (2). Let's look at two examples, similar to what you'll encounter on the GMAT. (Answer choices are lettered A–E here. Remember, though, that on the actual GMAT, you'll select among choices by clicking on one of five blank ovals, not letters.) This first question is a bit easier than average. Of all GMAT test-takers, about 85% would respond correctly to it.

How many quarts of oil will a car burn during a 3,600 mile trip?

(1) The car burns half a quart of oil every 1,000 miles.

(2) At a price of $1.50 per quart, the car uses $2.70 worth of oil during the trip.

A. Statement 1 ALONE is sufficient, but statement 2 alone is not sufficient to answer the question asked.
B. Statement 2 ALONE is sufficient, but statement 1 alone is not sufficient to answer the question asked.
C. BOTH statements (1) and (2) TOGETHER are sufficient to answer the question asked; but NEITHER statement ALONE is sufficient.
D. EACH statement ALONE is sufficient to answer the question asked.
E. Statements (1) and (2) TOGETHER are NOT sufficient to answer the question asked, and additional data specific to the problem are needed.

The correct answer is D. To answer the question, you need to know the rate (the number of miles per quart) at which the car burns oil. Statement (1) provides the information you need. A half quart of oil is burned per 1,000 miles; therefore, the car will burn 3.6 that amount over 3,600 miles. Although you don't need to do the math, the answer to the question is $(3.6)(.5) = 1.8$. You've narrowed the answer choices to (A) and (D). But, can you see that statement (2) alone also provides the information you need to determine the rate? The amount of oil used = $2.70 ÷ $1.50. Again, although you don't need to do the math, the quotient (and the answer to the question) is *1.8*. Since either statement alone suffices to answer the question, the correct answer choice is (D).

This next Data Sufficiency question is a bit more difficult than average. Only about 55% of all GMAT test-takers would respond correctly to it.

Chapter 2: The GMAT—Up Close

What is the absolute value of the sum of two numbers?

(1) The product of the two numbers is 6.

(2) One number is 5 less than the other number.

- A. Statement 1 ALONE is sufficient, but statement 2 alone is not sufficient to answer the question asked.
- B. Statement 2 ALONE is sufficient, but statement 1 alone is not sufficient to answer the question asked.
- C. BOTH statements (1) and (2) TOGETHER are sufficient to answer the question asked; but NEITHER statement ALONE is sufficient.
- D. EACH statement ALONE is sufficient to answer the question asked.
- E. Statements (1) and (2) TOGETHER are NOT sufficient to answer the question asked, and additional data specific to the problem are needed.

The correct answer is C. Calling one number x and the other number y, statement (1) alone tells us only that $xy = 6$, but gives no information about their sum. This narrows the answer choice options to (B), (C), and (E). Statement (2) alone tells us that the relationship between the two numbers can be written as $y = x-5$, but gives no information about their sum. The correct answer choice must be either (C) or (E). By considering statements (1) and (2) together, you can substitute $x-5$ for y in the equation $xy = 6$:

$$x(x - 5) = 6$$
$$x^2 - 5x = 6$$
$$x^2 - 5x - 6 = 0$$

You can factor the quadratic expression into two binomial factors, then find the roots of the equation—that is, the possible values of x:

$$x - 6 = 0 \text{ or } x + 1 = 0$$
$$x = 6 \text{ or } -1$$

Hence, either $x = 6$ and $y = 1$, with sum 7, or $x = -1$ and $y = -6$, with sum -7. In either case, the absolute value of their sum is the same: 7. Since both statements together provide one and only one answer to the question, the correct answer choice is (C).

You can also analyze this problem less formally. Based on statement (1) alone, try to think of some possibilities for the values of the two numbers that satisfy statement (1). Just using integers, the following four pairs should occur to you: 1 and 6, 2 and 3, −1 and −6, or −2 and −3. Since there's more than one possibility, you can rule out answer choices (A) and (D). Statement (2) alone presents an infinite number of possibilities, doesn't it? So you can also rule out choice (B). Together, statements (1) and (2) seem to rule out all integer pairs except (1, 6) and (−1, −6). In either case, the absolute value of their sum is 7. But what about non-integers? Answering this question is where a bit of intuition or trial-and-error is required. You may try a few non-integer number pairs, to satisfy you that none work.

Key Facts about GMAT Data Sufficiency

Keep in mind the following important features of the Data Sufficiency format (some of these points are review):

- **The answer choices are the same for all Data Sufficiency questions.** One feature that makes Data Sufficiency questions unique among other types of GMAT questions is that the answer choices are exactly the same for all Data Sufficiency questions.

- **Data Sufficiency questions can vary widely in difficulty level.** Assuming you're familiar with their unique format, these questions are neither inherently easier nor more difficult than Problem Solving questions. The level of difficulty and complexity can vary widely (depending on the correctness of your responses to earlier questions).

- **A Data Sufficiency question that asks for a specific numerical value is answerable only if** *one and only one value* results. Some, but not all, Data Sufficiency questions will ask for a particular *numerical value*. For example:

    - What is the area of the circle?
    - What is the value of *x*?
    - What is the area of triangle *ABC*?
    - How much did Sam pay for his book?

> **Alert!** You must keep in mind that in any Data Sufficiency question, if the answer choices consist of numerical values only (no variables), then the question is answerable only if *one and only one value* results—not a range of numbers, not a positive or negative number, not an expression that includes a variable.

Chapter 2: The GMAT—Up Close

- **The two statements (1 and 2) will *not* conflict with each other.** Perhaps you're wondering which response you should choose—(D) or (E)—if you can answer the question with either statement alone, but get two conflicting answers. Don't worry; this won't happen. If you can answer the question using either statement alone, *the answer will be the same in both cases*. In other words, statements 1 and 2 will *never* conflict with one another. Why? The test-makers design Data Sufficiency questions to avoid the "D vs. E" conundrum.

- **Figures are not necessarily drawn to scale, unless noted otherwise.** Any figure accompanying a Data Sufficiency question will conform to the information in the question itself, but will not necessarily conform to either statement 1 or 2. So although the figures are not designed to mislead you, they are not necessarily drawn to scale.

> **Tip**
> In Data Sufficiency questions, just like in Problem Solving questions, rely on the information in the question and statements, not on a figure's appearance.

- **Calculating is not what Data Sufficiency is primarily about.** Expect to do far less number crunching and equation solving for Data Sufficiency questions than for Problem Solving questions. What's being tested here is your ability to recognize and understand *principles*, not to work step-by-step toward a solution. (That's what Problem Solving is about.)

The Verbal Ability Section (41 Questions, 75 Minutes)

The Verbal Ability section contains questions in three distinct formats:

- Critical Reasoning (14–15 questions)
- Sentence Correction (14–15 questions)
- Reading Comprehension (12–13 questions)

Regardless of the format, each and every question in the Verbal Ability section is five-choice multiple-choice. Otherwise, each of the three formats is quite distinct. In the pages ahead, you examine each one up close.

Critical Reasoning (14–15 questions)

Critical Reasoning questions are designed to measure your ability to understand, criticize, and draw reasonable conclusions from arguments.

What's Covered

GMAT Critical Reasoning questions cover various aspects of reasoning and evaluating arguments. Here are the three basic aspects on which *most* of the exam's 14–15 Critical Reasoning questions are based:

- Identifying assumptions underlying an argument
- Understanding the effect of additional evidence on an argument
- Drawing strong inferences from stated premises

Some GMAT Critical Reasoning questions will involve specific forms of reasoning or argument evaluation. Look for any of the following forms on your exam:

- Recognizing a hypothesis that provides a good explanation for a set of observations
- Recognizing an effective strategy, based on a set of premises and a stated objective
- Making valid deductions from stated premises, or recognizing an additional premise needed to validate a stated conclusion
- Recognizing similarities in reasoning between different arguments

Test Directions

There are no special instructions for GMAT Critical Reasoning. The following simple directions are essentially what you'll see during the pre-test tutorial and just prior to your first Critical Reasoning question (you can access these directions at any time by clicking on the HELP button):

> **Directions:** For this question, select the best of the answer choices given.

What Critical Reasoning Questions Look Like

Each Critical Reasoning question consists of a paragraph-length passage, followed by a question about the passage and five answer choices. Let's look at two Critical Reasoning questions that are similar to what you might see on the GMAT. (Answer choices are lettered A–E here.

Chapter 2: The GMAT—Up Close

Remember, though, that on the actual GMAT you'll select among choices by clicking on one of five blank ovals, not letters.)

This first question is a bit easier than average; among GMAT test-takers, about 80% would answer it correctly.

Ten years ago, Brand 1 was the most popular beer among consumers. Today, however, consumers spend twice the amount on Brand 2, another brand of beer, than on Brand 1, even though Brand 2 is nearly twice as expensive as Brand 1.

Which of the following, if true, would best explain the apparent discrepancy described above?

A. Consumers of beer as a group consider a beer's taste more important than its price.
B. Brand 2 beer has decreased in price over the last ten years.
C. Over the last ten years, wine has become a more popular beverage among consumers than beer.
D. Brand 2 beer is more readily available to consumers today than Brand 1 beer.
E. The minimum age at which a person can legally drink beer is lower today than ten years ago.

The correct answer is D. The best answer choice must explain why Brand 2 beer is more popular than Brand 1 beer despite its higher price. Only choice (D) provides an adequate explanation. If Brand 1 beer is not available, while Brand 2 is, then obviously a consumer will purchase Brand 2 and not Brand 1. Choice (A) might explain the discrepancy if consumers prefer the taste of Brand 2 beer over that of Brand 1 beer; however, we don't know whether this is the case. Choice (B) might explain an increase in sales of Brand 2 beer; however, it fails to explain why Brand 2 is more popular today than Brand 1. Choice (C) might explain declining beer consumption generally; however, the popularity of wine is irrelevant to the popularity of one brand of beer compared to another brand of beer. Choice (E) might explain an increase in beer sales generally, but it does not explain why consumers buy more Brand 2 beer than Brand 1 beer.

This next Critical Reasoning question is a bit more difficult than average. Only about 50% of all GMAT test-takers would respond correctly to it.

Company Spokesperson: Charges that our corporation has discriminated against women in its hiring and promotion practices are demonstrably untrue. In fact, statistics show that greater than sixty percent of our corporation's employees are women.

The answer to which of the following questions would be most relevant in evaluating the argument above?

A. What is the average tenure, or length of employment, among the company's women employees?
B. What percentage of the company's employees in higher-level management positions are women?
C. What percentage of employees in competing companies are women?
D. How has the percentage of women employees at the company changed over time?
E. Is the chief executive officer of the company a man or a woman?

The correct answer is B. What makes this question difficult is that some of the incorrect answer choices are somewhat relevant to the argument; but their relevance is neither as clear nor as direct as choice (B). Let's start with the correct answer. Although a large percentage of the company's employees are women, it is entirely possible that these women generally occupy low-level positions while male employees generally hold higher-level jobs. One possible explanation for such a discrepancy would be that, when deciding whom to promote, the company discriminates against women. Hence, the answer to the question in choice (B) is highly relevant to evaluating the spokesperson's denial that the company engages in this type of discrimination. The issue raised in choice (A) would be relevant to whether the company's employee-termination practices are discriminatory, especially if the average tenure for women turned out to be significantly briefer than for men. However, the issue of tenure is not directly relevant to the company's hiring or promotion practices. Nor is the issue raised in choice (C) directly relevant to the argument. For example, assume that the percentage of the company's employees that are women is typical among firms in its industry. So what? Perhaps all of the firms discriminate against women, or perhaps none do. As for choice (D), the company's practices in the past are not directly relevant to its current practices. Choice (E) focuses on only one high-level employee, hardly a sufficient statistical sampling to prove a pattern of discrimination. Also, even with a female CEO, a company could very well engage in hiring and promotion practices that are unfair to women.

Chapter 2: The GMAT—Up Close

Key Facts about GMAT Critical Reasoning
Keep in mind the following important features of Critical Reasoning questions:

- **Your knowledge of the topic at hand is not important in answering Critical Reasoning questions.** The test-makers design Critical Reasoning questions so that you can analyze and answer them without regard to what is factual (or not) in the real world. Also, whatever your personal opinions or viewpoints about the issue that an argument raises, they are irrelevant to analyzing the argument and answering the question.

- **Distinctions in quality between answer choices can be subtle.** GMAT Critical Reasoning is not a "black-and-white" affair in which one answer is perfect while each of the others is completely wrong. A typical Critical Reasoning question stem contains a word such as "best" or "most." That's because more than one answer choice usually has merit—it's just that the correct answer choice is the strongest among the bunch. (To master GMAT Critical Reasoning, you'll need to become comfortable with these shades of gray.)

- **Each piece of information in the paragraph is usually important in answering the question.** Occasionally, a Critical Reasoning paragraph will include superfluous information, which does not come into play at all in analyzing the argument and answering the question. But this is the exceptional case.

Sentence Correction (14–15 questions)

Sentence Correction questions are designed to measure your command of the English language and of the conventions of Standard Written English.

What's Covered
GMAT Sentence Correction covers two areas of English language proficiency:

1. *Correct expression*, measured by your ability to recognize errors in grammar, diction, and word usage

2. *Effective expression*, measured by your ability to improve sentences that are poorly worded or structured

GMAT Sentence Correction does NOT cover these other areas of English language proficiency:

1. *Punctuation* (except that comma placement can come into play if it affects the meaning of a sentence)
2. *Vocabulary* (you won't have to memorize long lists of obscure words just for GMAT Sentence Correction)
3. *Slang and colloquialisms* (informal expressions don't appear at all in Sentence Correction questions)

Test Directions

The following set of directions are essentially what you'll see during the pre-test tutorial and just prior to your first Sentence Correction question (you can access these directions at any time by clicking on the HELP button):

> **Directions:** This question presents a sentence, all or part of which is underlined. Beneath the sentence you will find five ways of phrasing the underlined part. The first of these repeats the original; the other four are different. If you think the original is best, choose the first answer; otherwise, choose one of the other answers.
>
> This question tests correctness and effectiveness of expression. In choosing your answer, follow the requirements of Standard Written English; that is, pay attention to grammar, choice of words, and sentence construction. Choose the answer that produces the most effective sentence; this answer should be clear and exact, without awkwardness, ambiguity, redundancy, or grammatical error.

What Sentence Correction Questions Look Like

In each Sentence Correction question, part of a sentence (or the whole sentence) will be underlined. The first answer choice will simply restate the underlined part "as is." The other four choices present alternatives to the original underlined phrase.

Let's look at two questions that are similar to what you might see on the GMAT. (Answer choices are lettered A–E here. Remember, though, that on the actual GMAT you'll select among choices by clicking on one of five blank ovals, not letters.) This first question is a bit easier than average; among GMAT test-takers, about 80% would answer this question correctly.

Chapter 2: The GMAT—Up Close

A thesaurus can be a useful tool for <u>writers, providing he knows how to use it</u> correctly.

- A. writers, providing he knows how to use it
- B. writers, providing he knows how to use such a book
- C. a writer, providing he knows how to use them
- D. writers, providing she knows how to use it
- E. writers, providing they know how to use it

The correct answer is E. A pronoun and the noun to which it refers (called the *antecedent*) should be consistent; both should be either singular or plural. In the original sentence, however, the singular pronoun *he* is inconsistent with its plural antecedent *writers*. Among the four alternatives, only choices (C) and (E) fix this problem. In choice (C), both are singular, while in choice (E) both are plural; either is acceptable. Choice (C), however, creates another pronoun-antecedent error. Notice that it replaces the singular pronoun *it* with the plural *them*. Since the intended antecedent is *thesaurus*, which is singular, the plural pronoun *them* is incorrect, and you can eliminate choice (C). Choice (E) is the best version of the underlined part; it fixes the problem with the original version without creating any new errors.

Here's a Sentence Correction question that's a bit more difficult than average. Of all GMAT test-takers, only about 55% would respond correctly to it.

Frank Lloyd Wright was a preeminent architect of the twentieth century, and <u>there have been many less talented people who, both in the past and today, have</u> imitated his style.

- A. there have been many less talented people who, both in the past and today, have
- B. a great number of less talented people of today, as well as in the past, have
- C. many less talented people, both in the past and today, have
- D. there are many less talented people, today as well as in the past, who
- E. many people less talented than Wright who, today as well as in the past, have

The correct answer is C. The original version contains no grammatical errors. However, the phrase *there have been many less talented people who* is wordy. Choice (C) provides a more concise and graceful version, without introducing any new errors. In choice (B), *a great number of* is wordy; also, the two phrases *of today* and *in the past* lack grammatical parallelism. Choice (D) provides a less wordy version than the original, but is still not as effective as choice (C). As for choice (E), it too is unnecessarily wordy; what's more, within the construction of choice (E), the word *who* creates an incomplete sentence and should be omitted.

Key Facts about GMAT Sentence Correction

Keep in mind the following important features of Sentence Correction questions (some of these points are review):

- **Any part of the sentence might be underlined.** The underlined part may appear at the beginning, middle, or end of the sentence. Also, in some cases, the entire sentence will be underlined. Expect all of these variations on your exam.

- **The first answer choice simply restates the underlined part "as is."** The other four choices present alternatives to the original underlined phrase.

- **The best answer choice isn't always perfect.** The best choice among the five will not contain any grammatical errors. However, it may make for a less-than-ideal sentence, at least in your opinion. But remember: You're looking for the best version of the five, not the perfect version.

- **More than one answer choice may be grammatically correct.** These questions cover not just grammar, but also effective expression. So don't select an answer choice just because it results in a grammatically correct sentence. Another answer choice may be clearer, more concise, or less awkward—and therefore better.

- **A single Sentence Correction item can cover a lot of ground.** Don't expect each Sentence Correction item to isolate and test you on one, and only one, rule of grammar or aspect of written expression. Typically, by the time you've read all five choices, you've seen a variety of grammatical errors and other problems—at least among the four incorrect choices.

- **Punctuation doesn't matter.** You won't find errors in punctuation in these sentences (except as part of larger errors involving sentence structure).

- **You won't need any knowledge of the topic at hand in order to handle a question.** You're at no disadvantage if you know little or nothing about the topic of any particular sentence. For instance, in handling the second question above, experts on Frank Lloyd Wright would not have any advantage over other test-takers, would they?

Chapter 2: The GMAT—Up Close

Reading Comprehension (12–13 questions)

GMAT Reading Comprehension questions are designed to measure your ability to read carefully and accurately, to determine the relationships among the various parts of the passage, and to draw reasonable inferences from the material in the passage. On the GMAT, you'll encounter four sets of Reading Comprehension questions; all questions in a set pertain to the same passage and are presented in sequence.

What's Covered
GMAT Reading Comprehension tests on the following reading skills (you can think of these skills as question types):

- Recognizing the main point or primary purpose of the passage
- Recalling information explicitly stated in the passage
- Making inferences from specific information stated in the passage
- Recognizing the purpose of specific passage information
- Applying and extrapolating from the ideas presented in the passage

Test Directions
The following set of directions are essentially what you'll see during the pre-test tutorial and just prior to your first group of Reading Comprehension questions (you can access these directions at any time by clicking on the HELP button):

> **Directions:** The questions in this group are based on the content of a passage. After reading the passage, choose the best answer to each question. Answer all questions on the basis of what is *stated* or *implied* in the passage.

What Reading Comprehension Sets Look Like
Each Reading Comprehension set consists of a reading passage along with a series of 3–4 questions about the passage. Here's a typical passage. Go ahead and read it now.

> Line Urodeles, a class of vertebrates that includes small, lizard-like creatures such as newts and salamanders, have an enviable ability to regenerate arms, legs, tails, heart muscle, jaws, spinal cords, and other organs that are injured or destroyed by
> (5) accidents or those who prey on them. Planaria, which are a

type of simple worm, have their own form of regenerative power. A single worm can be sliced and diced into hundreds of pieces, each piece giving rise to a completely new animal. However, while both urodeles and planaria have the capacity
(10) to regenerate, they use different means to accomplish this feat.

In effect, urodeles turn back the biological clock. First, the animal heals the wound at the site of the missing limb. Then, various specialized cells at the site, such as bone, skin, and blood cells, lose their identity and revert to cells as unspecial-
(15) ized as those in the embryonic limb bud. This process is called dedifferentiation, and the resulting blastema, a mass of unspecialized cells, proliferates rapidly to form a limb bud. Ultimately, when the new limb takes shape, the cells take on the specialized roles they had previously cast off.

(20) In contrast, planaria regenerate using cells called neoblasts. Scattered within the planarian body, these neoblasts remain in an unspecialized, stem-cell state, which enables them at need to differentiate into any cell type. Whenever planaria are cut, the neoblasts migrate to the site and form a blastema by them-
(25) selves. It is interesting to note that this mechanism is similar to that following reproductive fission in these animals, and that species incapable of this form of asexual reproduction have poorly developed regenerative capacities.

Now, look at two questions based on the preceding passage. (Answer choices are lettered A–E here. Remember, though, that on the actual GMAT you'll select among choices by clicking on one of five blank ovals, not letters.) This first question is a bit easier than average; among GMAT test-takers, about 80% would answer this question correctly.

The author's primary purpose in the passage is to

A. describe the roles of blastema in regenerating urodeles and planaria.
B. describe how urodeles use the process of dedifferentiation to regenerate.
C. contrast the mechanisms by which urodeles and planaria accomplish regeneration.
D. show how methods of cellular regeneration have evolved in different animal species.
E. explain the link between reproductive fission and regeneration in simple worms.

Chapter 2: The GMAT—Up Close

The correct answer is C. The last sentence of the first paragraph sets forth this central theme: that urodeles and planaria differ in the means they use to regenerate. The paragraphs that follow provide the details that reveal those differences. The second paragraph discusses how urodeles regenerate, while the third paragraph discusses how planaria regenerate. (Notice the phase "In contrast," which begins the third paragraph.) Each of the incorrect choices distorts the author's central focus in the passage.

Here's a question that's a bit more difficult than average. Of all GMAT test-takers, only about 50% would respond correctly to it.

In the final sentence of the passage (lines 25–28), the author implies that

- A. reproductive fission and regeneration in certain planaria differ solely in the quantity of new planaria produced.
- B. planaria that reproduce sexually use the process of dedifferentiation to regenerate entirely new animals.
- C. asexual reproduction is related to regeneration in planaria but not in urodeles.
- D. the genetic makeup of planaria created through regeneration would be the same as in those created through reproductive fission.
- E. those planaria that reproduce by splitting themselves in two are more likely to regenerate using the same mechanism.

The correct answer is E. The idea in the final sentence of this passage is difficult to grasp, making this question difficult to answer. The sentence says essentially that those species of planaria that do not engage in reproductive fission (i.e., splitting) are more likely to regenerate themselves in this way than those species of planaria that do. Choice (E) expresses the same essential idea conversely: species of planaria that reproduce asexually (by fission, or splitting) are the ones that are more likely to be able to regenerate in the same way.

Key Facts about GMAT Reading Comprehension

Keep in mind the following important features of GMAT Reading Comprehension (some of these points are review):

- **Passages appear on the left side of the computer screen, and questions appear (one at a time) on the right side.** You'll have to scroll vertically to read each entire passage, even the short ones (as in the simulated screen shot on page 21).

- **Reading Comprehension questions are designed to test a lot more than just your short-term memory and your knack for finding information quickly.** Although your ability to recall what you've read is part of what's being tested, all but the easiest questions also gauge your ability to assimilate, interpret, and apply the ideas presented.

- **Some questions require that you focus on an isolated sentence or two; others require that you assimilate information from various parts of the passage.** Understandably, questions that cover disparate parts of a passage tend to be tougher than ones that you can answer just by reading a particular sentence or two.

- **Questions about information appearing early in the passage** *tend* to come before other questions. However, this isn't a hard-and-fast rule; don't assume you can simply scroll down the passage to answer each question in turn.

- **Tougher questions include not only a "best" response but also a tempting second-best response.** Recognizing the difference in quality between the two most viable responses is the key to answering the questions correctly.

- **Reading Comprehension questions are not designed to test your vocabulary.** Sure, you'll find the occasional advanced, technical, or obscure word. But the test-makers don't intentionally load the passages with tough vocabulary. Also, if a reading passage introduces a technical term, don't worry—the passage will supply all you need to know about the term to respond to the questions.

- **Reading Comprehension passages are condensed from larger works in the humanities, social sciences, and physical sciences.** Specific sources include professional journals, dissertations, and periodicals of intellectual interest. The test-makers edit the source material in order to pack it with test-worthy material.

- **All reading passages are not created equal—that is, equally difficult.** Comparatively tough passages are typically written in a dryer, more "academic" style than easier ones. Syntax is more complex, and vocabulary more advanced. The passage's topic might deal with ideas and concepts that are more difficult to grasp, or it might be written, organized, or edited in a way that makes it more difficult to assimilate.

- **Prior knowledge of a passage's subject matter is not important. All questions are answerable based solely on information in the passage.** The exam includes passages from a variety of disciplines, so it is unlikely that any particular test-taker knows enough about two or more of the areas included on the test to hold a significant advantage over other test-takers.

PART II

Analytical Writing Assessment

Analytical Writing Assessment   72

PART II

Chapter 3

Analytical Writing Assessment

Welcome to Analytical Writing Assessment. At this point, you'll learn the basics about writing effective GMAT Issue-Analysis and Argument-Analysis essays—ones that will earn you a better-than-average Analytical Writing Assessment score of at least 4 on the 0–6 scale. Specifically, you will learn the following:

- A step-by-step approach to brainstorming, organizing, composing, and proofreading your essays, all comfortably within the 30-minute time limit for each writing task

- Success keys to scoring higher with your essays than most GMAT test-takers

- Useful tips for writing mechanics and for developing a writing style that's appropriate for the GMAT

Issue Analysis—Your 7-Step Game Plan

For a high-scoring Issue essay, you need to accomplish these four basic tasks:

1. Recognize and deal with the complexities and implications of the Issue.

2. Organize, develop, and express your ideas in a coherent and persuasive manner.

3. Support your ideas with sound reasons and relevant examples.

4. Demonstrate adequate control of the elements of Standard Written English (grammar, syntax, and usage).

The 30 minutes you're allowed to write your Issue essay isn't much time, so you will need to use the time wisely. This does *not* mean using every one of your 30 minutes to peck away at the keyboard like mad. You should spend some time up front thinking about what you should write and how you should organize your ideas. And you should save some time at the end to proofread and fine-tune your essay. Here's a 7-step game plan to help you budget your time so you can accomplish all four tasks listed above within your 30-minute time limit (suggested times are parenthesized):

1. Brainstorm and make notes (3 min.).
2. Review your notes, and decide on a viewpoint (1 min.).
3. Organize your ideas into a logical sequence (1 min.).
4. Compose a brief introductory paragraph (2 min.).
5. Compose the body of your response (16 min.).
6. Compose a brief concluding or summary paragraph (2 min.).
7. Proofread for significant mechanical problems (5 min.).

Notice that, by following the suggested times for each step, you'll spend about 5 minutes planning your essay, 20 minutes writing it, and 5 minutes proofreading it.

> **Note**
> These suggested time limits for each step are merely guidelines, not hard-and-fast rules. As you practice composing your own Issue essays under timed conditions, start with these guidelines; then, adjust to a pace that works best for you.

In the following pages, you'll walk through each step in turn, applying the following Issue statement, which is similar to some of the statements in the official pool

Issue Statement 1 (and directive)

"Schools should be responsible not only for teaching academic skills but also for teaching ethical and social values."

Discuss the extent to which you agree or disagree with the foregoing statement. Support your perspective using reasons and/or examples from your experience, observation, reading, or academic studies.

1. Brainstorm and Make Notes (3 min.)

Your first step in developing your Issue essay is to brainstorm for ideas that are relevant to the topic. Try to think of some reasons and examples supporting not just one side, but *both* sides, of the issue. As you conjure up ideas, don't commit to a position on the issue, and don't try to filter out what you think might be unconvincing reasons or weak examples. Just let all your ideas flow onto your scratch paper, in no particular order. (You can sort through them during steps 2 and 3.) Here's what a test-taker's notes for Issue statement 1 on page 73 might look like after a few minutes of brainstorming:

> Whose values?
>   Amish
>   suburbanites
>   yuppies
>   Southern Baptists
> pluralism
> schools need focus
> sex education
> classroom cooperation vs. competition
> teachers set examples—indirectly
> drugs & violence

Notice that the first several lines reflect one train of thought (If schools were to teach ethical values, whose values would they teach?) while the other notes reflect other random ideas. The notes are somewhat of a hodgepodge, but that's okay. The point of brainstorming is just to generates a bunch of ideas—the raw material for your Issue essay. Let your ideas flow freely, and you'll have plenty of fodder for that essay.

2. Review Your Notes, and Decide on a Viewpoint (1 min.)

Decide on the basic point of view (either "pro" or "con") you want to defend in your essay. In other words, decide whether you are going to basically agree or disagree with the statement. Your notes from step 1 should help you decide. Review the ideas you jotted down, and then ask yourself whether you can make a stronger case for or against the statement.

> **Alert!**
> Keep in mind: There is no "correct" viewpoint or position on any GMAT issue. So don't waste time debating over what viewpoint you should defend. Just go with the flow—choose whatever viewpoint seems easiest or most "natural" for you to defend.

Next, pick the three or four ideas from your notes that best support your viewpoint. These should be ideas that you think make sense, that support your viewpoint reasonably well, and that you know enough about to write at least a few sentences on. Put a checkmark next to these ideas, to signify that they are the ones you're certain you want to use in your essay. If there aren't enough ideas, take one or two of the ideas you like and elaborate on them. Think of related ideas, add details or examples, and use these to fill out your list.

It's perfectly acceptable to strongly agree or disagree with the Issue statement. But it's also okay to *qualify* the statement, which means that your agreement (or disagreement) with it is less than complete.

3. Organize Your Ideas into A Logical Sequence (1 min.)

Next, decide on a sequence for the ideas. The best sequence might be obvious. One idea may lead logically to another. Your ideas might involve historical examples, which lead chronologically from one to another. Or, your ideas might range from the personal level to the family or community level, then to the societal or global level. Any of these schemes suggests a certain natural sequence for your Issue essay.

If there's no obvious sequence, one effective approach is to decide which two ideas you like best—the two you consider most convincing or that you happen to know the most about and can develop most fully—and earmark these ideas to discuss *first* and *last* (in either order) in the body of your essay. Then sequence the remaining ideas in any order, but *between* your two best ideas. Why sequence your ideas this way? The most emphatic and memorable parts of any essay are its beginning and end. It makes sense that your best material should go there, where it will have the greatest possible impact on the reader.

X-Ref

The suggested sequence on page 76 is a basic one that works well in many cases. But there are a myriad of other effective ways to organize ideas for your Issue essay. At the Next Level, you'll explore some of these alternatives.

Part II: Analytical Writing Assessment

Once you've decided on a sequence for your ideas, number them accordingly in your notes. Here's an example of how a test-taker might turn the notes on statement 1 into a simple outline:

> 2. ✔ <u>Whose values?</u>
>   Amish
>   suburbanites
>   yuppies
>   Southern Baptists
> 1. ✔ pluralism
> 3. ✔ schools need focus
>   sex education
>   classroom cooperation vs. competition
>   teachers set examples-indirectly
>   drugs & violence
> 4. ✔ U.S. Schools lag

Notice that this test-taker has decided to essentially *disagree* with the statement—that is, to take the position that schools should teach academics only and not ethical values. The first three points in his notes all fit nicely into an argument for this viewpoint. He also thought of a fourth idea that he thought might make a good ending—that U.S. schools lag behind most other countries in academic standards, and so time must not be taken away from teaching academic subjects to teach ethics. So he made a note of that idea, and checked it off as well.

He decided to start with the idea that America is pluralistic. From this idea, it makes sense to ask, "Whose values would be taught in schools?" and use the examples listed. This leads nicely into the point about focusing on academics and, finally, the argument about how U.S. students lag behind others.

4. Compose a Brief Introductory Paragraph (2 min.)

Now that you've spent about five minutes planning your essay, its time to compose it. You'll begin with a brief introductory paragraph, in which you should accomplish the following:

1. Demonstrate that you understand the issue that the statement raises.

2. Let the reader know that you have a clear viewpoint on the issue.

3. Anticipate the ideas you intend to present in your essay's body paragraphs.

You can probably accomplish all three tasks in 2–3 sentences. In your introductory paragraph, don't go into detail about your reasoning, and don't provide specific examples. This is what the body paragraphs of the essay are for. Also, don't begin your introductory paragraph by repeating the statement verbatim. This amounts to wasted time, since the reader is already familiar with the topic. Instead, show the reader from the very first sentence that you're thinking for yourself.

Here's an introductory paragraph for statement 1—based on the test-taker's outline on page 76:

Introductory paragraph (Issue Statement 1)

Schools, especially in a pluralistic nation such as the United States, should limit what they teach to academic subjects—leaving it to parents and clergy to teach ethics. To do otherwise, as the statement suggests, is to invite trouble, as this essay will show.

5. Compose the Body of Your Essay (16 min.)

During step 4, your chief ambition is to get your main points—and supporting reasons and examples—from your brain and your scratch paper onto the computer screen! Here's what you need to keep in mind as you compose your body paragraphs:

- Be sure the first sentence of each paragraph begins a distinct train of thought and clearly conveys to the reader the essence of the paragraph.

- Arrange your paragraphs so that your essay flows logically and persuasively from one point to the next. Stick to your outline, but be flexible.

- Try to devote at least two, but no more than three or four, sentences to each main point in your outline.

- Don't worry if you don't have time to include every single point from your outline. The readers understand that time constraints prevent most test-takers from covering every point they want to make.

- Don't stray from the issue at hand, or from the points you seek to make. Be sure to stay well focused on both.

Now, here are the body paragraphs of a response to statement 1—based on the outline on page 76:

Four-paragraph body (Issue Statement 1)

If our schools are to teach values, the most important question to answer is: Whose values would they teach? After all, not all ethical values are the same. The Amish have a way of life that stresses simplicity and austerity; they shun modern conveniences and even such activities as dancing. By contrast, the typical young urban family—"yuppies," as they're often called—enjoys buying the latest electronic gadgets and going on expensive vacations. Either group might be offended by the values of the other.

True, Amish and yuppie children aren't likely to attend the same schools; but what about children from Jewish and fundamentalist Christian households? These two religious groups may live in the same town or neighborhood, and either one might very well be incensed if the other group's moral teachings were imposed on them.

The only way to avoid the inevitable conflicts that teaching ethics would bring to our schools is by allowing teachers to focus on what they're paid to do: teach academics. We send children to school to learn math, English, history, and science. How would we feel if our kids came home ignorant about geometry but indoctrinated with someone else's religious or ethical ideas? Justly annoyed, I think.

Moreover, consider that schoolchildren in the U.S. lag behind those in most other nations in academic achievement. In light of this fact, it would seem foolish for us to divert classroom time from teaching academics to teaching "morality."

Notice the following features of these body paragraphs, which show that the test-taker tried to stick to his outline, while at the same time remaining flexible as new ideas for content or organization occurred to him:

- Point 2 in the outline ("Whose values?") became the basis for *two* paragraphs (the second and third ones), not just one.

- After writing about the Amish and yuppies, the test-taker seemed to realize that the contrast between them, while illustrating the point, was a bit exaggerated. Rather than replacing the entire paragraph with a more realistic pairing, which would have meant substantial time wasted, the test-taker *added* the third paragraph to provide a more down-to-earth pairing.

- The suburbanites got left out of the essay altogether, possibly because they seemed unnecessary. (Or, perhaps the test-taker realized that he was running short on time.)

6. Compose a Brief Concluding or Summary Paragraph (2 min.)

Unless your essay has a clear ending, the reader might think you didn't finish in time. That's not the impression you want to make; so be sure to make time to wrap up your discussion. Convey the main thrust of your essay in a clear, concise, and assertive way. Two or three sentences should suffice. If an especially insightful concluding point occurs to you, the final sentence of your essay is a good place for it.

Here's a brief but effective concluding paragraph for the essay on Issue statement 1. Notice that it assures the reader that the test-taker has organized his time well and finished the writing task. Also, notice that this brief summary does not introduce any new reasons or examples; it's just a quick recapitulation.

Final paragraph (Issue Statement 1)

> Ironically, what is most ethical for our schools to do in the interest of educating our children is to avoid becoming entangled in ethical issues. Stick to academics, and let families and clergy teach morality in their own way and on their own time.

7. Proofread for Glaring Mechanical Problems (5 min.)

To score high on your Issue essay, you don't need to compose a flawless work of art. The readers won't reduce your score for the occasional awkward sentence and minor error in punctuation, spelling, grammar, or diction (word choice and usage). Don't get hung up on whether each sentence is something your English composition professor would be proud of. Instead, use whatever time remains to read your essay from start to finish and fix the most glaring mechanical problems. Here are some suggestions for what you should and, just as importantly, what you should *not*, try to accomplish during this final step:

- Find and rework awkward sentences, especially ones where the point you're trying to make is not clear.

- Find and correct accidentally omissions of words, garbled phrases, grammatical errors, and typographical errors. It doesn't take much time to fix these kinds of errors, and the time spent will go a long way toward making a positive impression on the reader.

- Correct spelling errors *only* when they might prevent the reader from understanding the point at hand.
- Don't spend *any* of your valuable time correcting punctuation or removing extra character spaces between words.
- Don't get drawn into drastic rewriting. Accept that your essay is what it is and that you don't have time to reshape it substantially.

From beginning to end (including the introductory, body, and concluding paragraphs), the preceding sample essay runs just over 300 words in length. It is neither lengthy nor a literary masterpiece. Nevertheless, it expresses a clear viewpoint, it's smartly organized, it employs relevant reasons and examples, and it's crisp and effective in style. In short, it contains all the elements of a high-scoring GMAT Issue essay.

Success Keys for Writing a GMAT Issue-Analysis Essay

Here's our very best advice for GMAT Issue Analysis, parsed out into bite-size pieces. Some of these tips reiterate suggestions made earlier in this lesson—suggestions that are well worth underscoring. Others are new here. Apply these points of advice to Part V's practice tests, and then review them again, just before exam day. You'll be glad you did!

Adopt a Viewpoint . . . Any Viewpoint

It's perfectly acceptable to strongly agree or disagree with an Issue statement. Don't worry that your position may appear somewhat "right-wing" or "left-wing," or even outside the mainstream altogether. Just be sure to provide sound reasons and relevant examples to justify your strong viewpoint. It's also perfectly okay to *qualify* the statement—in other words, to accept (or reject) it only in part or to a limited extent. Again, just be sure to justify your "middle-ground" position with sound reasoning and relevant examples.

At the Next Level, you'll explore the various ways you can "qualify" Issue statements, and you'll learn how to develop an essay that accounts for "pros" and "cons" of both sides of an issue.

Explain How Your Examples Support Your Viewpoint

Anyone can simply list a long string of examples and claim that they illustrate a point. But GMAT readers are looking for incisive analysis, not fast typing. For each example you cite, be sure to tell the reader how it supports the point you're trying to make. Otherwise, you argument will be unconvincing, and your score might suffer as a result.

Appeal to Reason, Not Emotion

Avoid inflammatory statements, and don't preach or proselytize. Approach the Issue writing task as an intellectual exercise in which you dispassionately argue for a certain viewpoint. Do not use it as a forum for sharing your personal belief system. It's perfectly appropriate to criticize particular behavior, policies, or viewpoints as operating against the best interest of a business or of a society. But refrain from either condemning or extolling based on personal moral grounds. Also avoid demagoguery (appeal to prejudice or emotion) and jingoism (excessive patriotism).

Spare the Reader Rote Facts and Technical Details

The Issue essay is not like a game of *Jeopardy!* or *Trivial Pursuit*. You will not score points simply by recounting statistics, compiling long lists, or conjuring up little-known facts. And, don't try to impress the reader with your technical knowledge of any particular subject. Resist the temptation to use the Issue essay as a forum to recapitulate your senior-year thesis. This is not the place to convince the reader of your firm grasp of the finest points of foreign policy, macroeconomic theory, or market analysis. That's what your GPA and undergraduate transcripts are for.

Avoid Obvious and Hackneyed Examples

Many GMAT test-takers will rely heavily on today's headlines and on history's most illustrious and notorious figures. If you can, avoid relying on these all-too-obvious examples. Try to dig a bit deeper, showing the reader a broader, more literate perspective.

> **Tip**
> Most GMAT readers reside in the United States. If you reside elsewhere, cite examples from your own region of the world. You're more likely to pique the reader's interest, which can only operate in your favor.

Don't Dwell on One Point; But Don't Try to Cover Everything, Either

Avoid harping on one point you believe to be the most convincing one, or on one example that you know a lot about or you feel best illustrates your point. Instead, try to cover as many points in your outline as you have time for, devoting no more than one paragraph to each one.

At the same time, if you try to cover everything you can think of about the issue at hand, you're likely to become frustrated, and you might even panic as the testing clock ticks away your 30 minutes. The readers understand your time constraints. So don't worry if you're forced to leave the secondary and more tangential points on your scratch paper. Stick to your outline, ration your time, and you'll be fine.

Keep It Simple; the Reader Will Reward You for It

Don't make the Issue writing task more onerous than it needs to be for you to attain a solid score. Keep your sentences clear and simple. Use a straightforward structure for your essay. Avoid using "fancy" words just to impress the reader. Don't waste time ruminating over how you can come across as ultra-brilliant, mega-insightful, or super-eloquent. Finally, don't waste brain-power or keystrokes trying to be clever, creative, or humorous. Be forewarned: Dazzling the reader with your amazing wit and wisdom is *not* the way to score points.

Look Organized and in Control of the Task

Use every tool at your disposal to show the reader that you can write well under pressure. Use logical paragraph breaks—one after your introduction, one between each of your main points, and one before your concluding paragraph. Be sure to present your main points in a logical, easy-to-follow sequence. (If you don't get it right the first time, you can use the word processor's cut-and-paste features to rearrange your ideas.) Your essay's "bookends"—the introductory and concluding paragraph—are especially key to looking organized and in control. First of all, make sure they're there! Then, make sure they're consistent with each other, and that they reveal your viewpoint and recap your reasons for your viewpoint.

Chapter 3: Analytical Writing Assessment

It's Quality, Not Quantity, That Counts

The only limitation on your essay's length is the practical one that the 30-minute time limit imposes. But, do the readers prefer brief or longer Issue essays? Well, it all depends on the essay's quality. A lengthy essay that's articulate and that includes many insightful ideas that are well supported by examples will score higher than a briefer essay that lacks substance. On the other hand, an essay that's concise and to the point can be more effective than a long-winded, rambling one.

Don't worry about the word length of your essay. GMAT readers don't count words. As long as you incorporate into your essay all the suggested elements you learned about in this lesson, you don't need to worry about length. Just keep in mind that it's quality, not quantity, that counts.

Don't Lose Sight of Your Primary Objectives

The official scoring criteria for the Issue essay boil down to four broad objectives. Never lose sight of them during the 30-minute Issue section. After brainstorming and making notes, but before you start typing, ask yourself:

1. Do I have a clear viewpoint on the issue?
2. Do I support my viewpoint with sound reasons and relevant examples?
3. Do I have in mind a clear, logical structure for presenting my ideas?

Once you can confidently answer "Yes" to each question, start composing your essay. Then, once you're finished your draft, ask yourself the same three questions again, as well as this fourth one:

4. Have I demonstrated good grammar, diction (word choice and usage), and syntax (sentence structure)?

Once you can answer "Yes" to all four questions, rest assured that you've produced a solid, high-scoring Issue essay.

Argument Analysis—Your 7-Step Game Plan

For a high-scoring Argument essay, you need to accomplish these four basic tasks:

1. Identify and analyze the Argument's key elements.
2. Organize, develop, and express your critique in a coherent and logically convincing manner.
3. Support your ideas with sound reasons and supporting examples.
4. Demonstrate adequate control of the elements of Standard Written English (grammar, syntax, and usage).

Just as for the Issue Analysis, you should spend some time up front thinking about what you will write and how you will organize your ideas. Again, save some time at the end to proofread and fine-tune your essay. Here's a 7-step game plan to help you budget your time so you can accomplish all four tasks listed above within your 30-minute time limit (suggested times are parenthesized):

1. Read the Argument, and identify its conclusions (1 min.).
2. Examine the Argument's evidence to determine how strongly it supports the Argument's conclusion(s). (3 min.).
3. Organize and prioritize your points of critique (1 min.).
4. Compose a brief introduction (2 min.).
5. Compose the body of your response (16 min.).
6. Compose a concluding paragraph (2 min.).
7. Proofread for significant mechanical problems (5 min.).

Notice that, by following the suggested time limits for each step, you'll spend about 5 minutes planning your essay, 20 minutes writing it, and 5 minutes proofreading it.

> **Note**
> These time limits for each step are merely guidelines, not hard-and-fast rules. As you practice composing your own Argument essays under timed conditions, start with these guidelines, then adjust to a pace that works best for you.

Chapter 3: Analytical Writing Assessment

In the following pages, you'll walk through each step in turn, applying the following Argument statement, which is similar to some of the statements in the official pool:

Argument 1 (and directive)

> The following appeared in a memo from the manager of UpperCuts hair salon:
>
> "According to a nationwide demographic study, more and more people today are moving from suburbs to downtown areas. In order to boost sagging profits at UpperCuts, we should take advantage of this trend by relocating the salon from its current location in Apton's suburban mall to downtown Apton, while retaining the salon's decidedly upscale ambiance. Besides, Hair-Dooz, our chief competitor at the mall, has just relocated downtown and is thriving at its new location, and the most prosperous hair salon in nearby Brainard is located in that city's downtown area. By emulating the locations of these two successful salons, UpperCuts is certain to attract more customers."
>
> Discuss how well reasoned you find this argument. In your discussion be sure to analyze the line of reasoning and the use of evidence in the argument. For example, you may need to consider what questionable assumptions underlie the thinking and what alternative explanations or counterexamples might weaken the conclusion. You can also discuss what sort of evidence would strengthen or refute the argument, what changes in the argument would make it more logically sound, and what, if anything, would help you better evaluate its conclusion.

1. Read The Argument, and Identify Its Conclusion(s) (1 Min.)

Every GMAT Argument consists of the following basic elements:

1. *Evidence* (stated premises that the Argument does not dispute)
2. *Assumptions* (unstated premises needed to justify a conclusion)
3. *Conclusions* (inferences drawn from evidence and assumptions)

As you read an Argument for the first time, identify its *final* conclusion as well as its *intermediate* conclusion (if any). Why is this first step so important? Unless you are clear about the Argument's conclusions, it's impossible to evaluate the author's reasoning or the strength of the evidence offered in support of them. And that's what the Argument writing task is all about!

You'll probably find the *final* conclusion in the Argument's first or last sentence. The Argument might refer to it as a "claim," a "recommendation," or a "prediction." An intermediate conclusion, upon which the final conclusion depends, might appear anywhere in the Argument. Not every Argument contains an intermediate conclusion.

Did you identify and distinguish between the intermediate and final conclusions in the Argument involving UpperCuts? Here they are:

Intermediate conclusion:

"By emulating the locations of these two successful salons, UpperCuts is certain to attract more customers."

Final conclusion:

"In order to boost sagging profits at UpperCuts, we should . . . relocat[e] the salon from its current location in Apton's suburban mall to downtown Apton, while retaining the salon's decidedly upscale ambiance."

Notice that the Argument's final conclusion relies on its intermediate conclusions. Here's the essential line of reasoning:

UC will gain customers if it moves downtown. *(Intermediate conclusion)*

Therefore, UC will boost its profits *simply* by moving downtown. *(Final conclusion)*

Always jot down an Argument's intermediate conclusion (if any) and its final conclusion—in shorthand like we've provided above. You'll need to refer to them time and again as you develop your points of critique and compose your essay.

2. Identify and Examine the Argument's Evidence to Determine How Strongly It Supports the Argument's Conclusion(s) (3 Min.)

Most Arguments contain at least two or three items of information, or evidence, that are used in support of its conclusion(s). Identify them, label them, and jot them down in shorthand on your scratch paper. Argument 1 contains three distinct items of evidence:

Chapter 3: Analytical Writing Assessment

Evidence (item 1):

"According to a nationwide demographic study, more and more people today are moving from suburbs to downtown areas."

Evidence (item 2):

"Hair-Dooz, our chief competitor at the mall, has just relocated downtown and is thriving at its new location."

Evidence (item 3):

". . . the most prosperous hair salon in nearby Brainard is located in that city's downtown area."

Next, analyze each item as to how much support it lends to the Argument's intermediate and final conclusions. For the most part, what you should look for are any unsubstantiated or unreasonable *assumptions* upon which the Argument's conclusions depend. For example, an Argument might rely on one of these assumptions, yet fail to provide evidence to support it.

- An event that occurs after another was caused by the other (a false-cause problem).

- Two things that are similar in one way are similar in other ways (a false-analogy problem).

- A statistical sample of a group is representative of the group as a whole.

Also check for problems with the Argument's *internal logic* (for example, self-contradictions or circular reasoning). These types of problems don't occur commonly in GMAT Arguments; but you should be on the lookout for them, anyway.

Just as for your Issue essay, don't filter your ideas during this crucial brainstorming step! Let them all flow onto your scratch paper. (You'll sort them out in step 3.)

> **X-Ref**
>
> Without exception, each Argument in the official pool contains at least three or four discrete assumptions or other problems—that's how the test-makers design them. When you *Take It to the Next Level*, you'll examine in detail the most common flaws in GMAT Arguments.

Below is an example of what a test-taker's notes for Argument 1 might look like after a few minutes of brainstorming:

> inter. concl.—UC will gain customers downtown
> final concl.—UC will improve profits downtown
>
> - demog. study—is Apton typical?   no trend
>   reverse trend
>
> - success of HD—is location key?   marketing
>   key stylist
>
> - success of B salon—downtown location key?
>   —is Apton like Brainard?
>   (demog.)
>
> - other problems
>   —relocation expenses offset revenues
>   —UC must establish new clientele
>   —competition from HD
>   (suff. demand for both salons?)
>   —demand for "upscale" salon downtown?

3. Organize and Prioritize Your Points of Critique (1 Min.)

Using your notes from step 2 as a guide, arrange your ideas into paragraphs (probably three or four, depending on the number of problems built into the Argument). Take a minute to consider whether any of the flaws you identified overlap and whether any can be separated into two distinct problems. In many cases, the best sequence in which to organize your points of critique is the same order in which reasoning problems arise in the Argument.

Just as you would for your Issue essay, try to use your notes as an outline, numbering points according to their logical sequence. The next page shows an example of what the test-taker's notes for Argument 1 look like after organizing them (arrows indicate where he intend to discuss a point; "[FC]" refers to final conclusion):

> *inter. concl.* UC will gain customers downtown
> *final concl.* UC will improve profits downtown
> ① • demog. study is Apton typical? — no trend / reverse trend
> ② • success of HD is location key? — marketing / key stylist
> ③ • success of B salon downtown location key?
>   is Apton like Brainard? (demog.)
> • other problems
> [FC] ④ relocation expenses offset revenues
>   UC must establish new clientele
>   competition from HD
>   (suff. demand for both salons?)
>   demand for upscale salon downtown?

4. Compose a Brief Introductory Paragraph (2 Min.)

Now that you've spent about five minutes planning your essay, its time to compose it. Don't waste time repeating the quoted Argument; the reader, whom you can assume is already well familiar with the Argument, is interested in your critique—not in your transcription skills. Here's what you should try to accomplish in your initial paragraph:

1. *Identify* the Argument's final conclusion.

2. *Describe* briefly the Argument's line of reasoning and evidence in support of its conclusion.

3. *Allude* generally to the problems with the Argument's line of reasoning and use of evidence.

You can probably accomplish all three task in 2–3 sentences. Here's a concise introductory paragraph of a response to Argument 1:

> Citing a general demographic trend and certain evidence about two other hair salons, the manager of UpperCuts (UC) concludes here that UC should relocate from suburban to downtown Apton in order to attract more customers and, in turn, improve its profitability.

However, the manager's argument relies on a series of unproven assumptions and is therefore unconvincing as it stands.

Your introductory paragraph is the least important component of your essay. So, you might consider waiting until you've completed your critique of the Argument before composing your introduction. If you're running out of time for your introduction, begin your essay with a sentence like one of the following two, then delve right into your first point of critique—without a paragraph break:

> This argument suffers from numerous flaws which, considered together, render untenable the conclusion that UpperCuts should relocate to downtown Apton. One such flaw involves . . .

> I find the argument for moving UpperCuts salon downtown specious at best, because it relies on a series of unproven and doubtful assumptions. One such assumption is that . . .

5. Compose the Body of Your Response (16 Min.)

As in the Issue essay, your chief aim during this step is to peck madly at your keyboard in order to get your ideas onto the screen! Here's what you need to keep in mind as you compose your body paragraphs:

- Try to devote a separate paragraph to each major point of your critique—but be flexible. Sometimes it makes more sense to discuss related points in the same paragraph.

- Be sure the first sentence of each paragraph conveys to the reader the essence of the problem you're dealing with in that paragraph.

- For each of the Argument's assumptions, try to provide at least one example or counterexample (a hypothetical scenario) that, if true, would undermine the assumption.

- Try to devote no more than three or four sentences to any one point in your outline. Otherwise, you risk running out of time without discussing all of the Argument's major problems.

- Arrange your paragraphs so that your essay flows logically from one point of critique to the next.

- Don't worry if you don't have time to discuss each and every point of critique or example that you noted during step 2. The readers understand your time constraint.

Chapter 3: Analytical Writing Assessment

> **Tip**
> Try to stick to your outline, but be flexible. Start with whichever points of critique strike you as the most important, are clearest in your mind, and are easiest to articulate. (You can always rearrange your points later, during step 6, using the word processor's cut-and-paste feature.)

Here's the body of a test-taker's response to Argument 1. As you read these four paragraphs, notice that each paragraph addresses a distinct, critical assumption—a certain condition that must be true to justify one of the Argument's conclusions. Also notice that each paragraph describes at least one scenario that, if true, would serve to undermine an assumption.

One such assumption is that Apton reflects the cited demographic trend. The mere fact that one hair salon has moved downtown hardly suffices to show that the national trend applies to Apton specifically. For all we know, in Apton there is no such trend, or perhaps the trend is in the opposite direction, in which event the manager's recommendation would amount to especially poor advice.

Even assuming that downtown Apton is attracting more residents, relocating downtown might not result in more customers for UC, especially if downtown residents are not interested in UC's upscale style and prices. Besides, Hair-Dooz might draw potential customers away from UC, just as it might have at the mall. Without ruling out these and other reasons why UC might not benefit from the trend, the manager can't convince me that UC would attract more customers by moving downtown.

Even if there was a high demand for UC's service in downtown Apton, an increase in the number of patrons would not necessarily improve UC's profitability. UC's expenses might be higher downtown, in which case it might be no more, or perhaps even less, profitable downtown than at the mall.

As for the Brainard salon, its success might be due to particular factors that don't apply to UC. For example, perhaps the Brainard salon thrives only because it is long-established in downtown Brainard. Or perhaps hair salons generally fare better in downtown Brainard than downtown Apton, due to demographic differences between the two areas. In short, the manager simply cannot justify his proposal on the basis of the Brainard salon's success.

6. Compose a Concluding Paragraph (2 Min.)

Unless your essay has a clear ending, the reader might think you didn't finish on time; so be sure to make time for a final paragraph that clearly "wraps up" your essay. Your final paragraph is *not* the place to introduce any new points of critique. Instead, *recapitulate* the Argument's problems—e.g., a series of unproven assumptions—in two or three sentences. Here's a final paragraph in response to Argument 1:

> In sum, the argument relies on what might amount to two poor analogies between UC and two other salons, as well as a sweeping generalization about demographic trends, which may or may not apply to Apton. Thus, even though the manager has provided some scant evidence to support the recommendation, on balance I find the argument unconvincing at best.

Notice that this paragraph does not introduce any new points of critique. It's just a brief recap of the argument's major problems, along with a reiteration of why the Argument is weak.

> **Tip**
> Another tack for your concluding paragraph is to recap in terms of how the argument could be strengthened and/or how additional information might be needed to evaluate it. Although these two elements are optional, incorporating one or both into your essay can boost your score.

From beginning to end (including the introductory, body, and concluding paragraphs), the preceding sample essay runs just under 400 words in length—brief enough to plan and write in 30 minutes. It's well organized; it articulates the Argument's major problems; it supports each point of critique with relevant examples; and it's crisp, clear, and convincing. In short, it contains all the elements of a high-scoring GMAT Argument essay.

7. Review for Coherence and Proofread for Significant Mechanical Problems (5 Min.)

Be sure to reserve time to check the flow of your essay, paying particular attention to the first sentence of each paragraph. Check to see if you should rearrange paragraphs so that they appear in a more logical sequence. Also, proofread for glaring mechanical problems. Your Argument essay, like your Issue essay, need not be flawless in order to earn a high score. The readers won't mark you down for the occasional awkward sentence and minor error in punctuation, spelling, grammar, or diction (word choice and usage). Use whatever time remains to fix the most glaring mechanical problems. Correct spelling and punctuation errors only when they're likely to interfere with the reader's understanding of the point at hand.

Chapter 3: Analytical Writing Assessment

Success Keys for Writing a GMAT Argument-Analysis Essay

In the following pages, we've distilled our very best advice for GMAT Argument-Analysis down to bite-sized nuggets that you can easily digest. Many of them reiterate suggestions we've already made—suggestions that are well worth underscoring. Others are new here. Apply these points of advice to Part III's practice tests, and then review them again just before exam day. You'll be glad you did!

Ferreting Out the Flaws Is Half the Battle

Built into each and every GMAT Argument are at least three or four distinct reasoning problems. That's how the test-makers design them. To earn a high score, first and foremost, your essay must identify these problems. After brainstorming and making notes, if you haven't isolated at least three major flaws, then you can be sure that you've missed at least one. Read the Argument again—*very* carefully. (Even a few overlooked words can be key.)

Ration your time to be sure the reader knows you've recognized each and every problem listed in your notes. Don't worry if 30 minutes isn't enough time for you to discuss each problem in detail. When it comes to analyzing GMAT Arguments, remember that breadth is better than depth.

> **Alert!** GMAT Arguments are not all created equal. Some are flawed in more ways than others. The greater the number of distinct flaws, the more forgiving the reader will be. So if an Argument contains as many as five or six distinct problems, and you overlook one or two of them, you can still attain a high score—perhaps even a top score of 6 assuming your essay is outstanding in all other respects.

Viewpoints and Opinions Don't Matter—At All

In sharp contrast to the Issue essay, your Argument essay is not the place to present viewpoints or opinions about an issue that the Argument might touch up on. Your analysis must focus strictly on the Argument's logical features and on how strongly its evidence supports its conclusions.

For instance, consider an Argument for electing a certain political candidate because she has a record of being tough on crime. In an Issue essay involving the problem of violent crime, it would be perfectly appropriate to present various viewpoints on this social issue—weighing alternative approaches to the problem in general. But these viewpoints are irrelevant to the Argument writing task.

Don't Leave Any Point of Critique Without Support

Don't neglect to support each point of your critique with at least one example or counterexample that helps the reader understand the particular flaw you're pointing out. Keep your examples and counterexamples hypothetical ("What if . . . ," "Suppose that . . . ," or It's possible that . . ." or "Perhaps . . .") You don't need to go into great detail; one or two for each point of critique will suffice. Unless you provide some support for each point of critique, your score might suffer.

But what if you think you won't have enough time to provide supporting detail for each and every point of critique in your notes? Don't despair. Look for two or three points that are related to the same item of evidence (for example, points that all involve the same statistical survey). Then, plan to touch briefly on each one *in the same paragraph*. Grouping them together this way will make sense to the reader, who might not notice what's missing as much as the fact that you're very organized!

Don't Look for the "Fatal Flaw"; Instead, Treat Every Problem as a Contributing Cause of Death

Avoid dwelling on one particular flaw that you think is the most serious one—or on one realistic example or counterexample that you think, if true, would spell certain death for the entire Argument. Otherwise, you risk running out of time to identify all the problems you've listed in your notes.

Also, don't try to rank any flaw as "more serious" or "less serious" than another. True, one particular flaw might be more damaging to an Argument than others. But by identifying it as "the most serious problem with the Argument," you're committing yourself to defend this claim, by weighing that problem against all the others. Do you really have time for this kind of analysis? No! Nor do the GMAT readers expect or want this from you. In short, you're best off applying equal treatment to each of the Argument's problems.

There's No Need to Impress with Technical Terminology

Scholars in the academic fields of Critical Reasoning and Logic rely on all sorts of formal terminology (much of which comes from the Latin language), for the kinds of reasoning flaws that you'll find in GMAT Arguments. For example, *post hoc* reasoning refers to faulty "After this, therefore because of this" reasoning. But you won't score any points with GMAT readers by tossing around such terminology in your Argument essay. Besides, if you refer a technical term, you'll then need to define it for the reader, which will only consume your precious time. So don't bother!

Go with the Logical Flow

Try to organize your points of critique to reflect the Argument's line of reasoning—from its evidence and assumptions to its intermediate conclusion (if any), then to its final conclusion. Fortunately, most GMAT Arguments are already organized this way—so that your points of critique can simply follow the quoted Argument from beginning to end.

But don't assume that this sequence will be the most logical one. Regardless of the sequence of ideas in the quoted Argument, try to group together all your points of critique that involve the same item of evidence (for example, a statistical survey or study). Also, it makes logical sense to address problems involving the Argument's intermediate conclusion before those involving its final conclusion.

Look Organized and in Control

As with the Issue essay, use every means at your disposal to show that reader that, even under significant time pressure, you know how to organize your ideas and convey them in writing. Use logical paragraph breaks, present your points of critique in a logical sequence, and try to save time for brief introductory and concluding paragraphs.

Don't Lose Sight of Your Primary Objectives

The official scoring criteria for the Argument essay boil down to four broad objectives. Never lose sight of them during your 30-minute Argument section. After brainstorming and making notes, but before you start typing, ask yourself:

1. Have I clearly identified each of the Argument's major problems?
2. Can I support each point of my critique with at least one relevant example or counter-example?
3. Do I have in mind a clear, logical structure for presenting my points of critique?

Once you can confidently answer "Yes" to each question, start composing your essay. Then, once you're finished your draft, ask yourself the same three questions, as well as this fourth one:

4. Have I demonstrated good grammar, diction (word choice and usage), and syntax (sentence structure)?

Once you can answer "Yes" to all four questions, rest assured that you've produced a solid, high-scoring Argument essay.

Writing Style and Mechanics

The testing service instructs GMAT readers to place less weight on writing style and mechanics than on content and organization. But, this doesn't mean that the first two factors won't influence the reader or affect your Analytical Writing Assessment score. Indeed, they might! If the way you write interferes with the reader's understanding of your ideas, then be prepared for a disappointing score. And, in any event, poor writing will predispose the reader to award a lower score, regardless of your ideas or how you organize them. To ensure yourself a high Analytical Writing Assessment score, strive for writing that is:

- Appropriate in tone and "voice" for graduate-level, academic writing

- Varied in sentence length and structure (to add interest and variety as well as to demonstrate maturity and sophistication in writing style)

- Clear and concise (easy to follow and direct rather than wordy or verbose)

- Correct in grammar, mechanics, and usage (conforming to the requirements of Standard Written English)

- Persuasive in style (using rhetorical devices effectively)

All of this is easier said than done, of course. Don't worry if you're not a natural when it comes to writing effective prose. You can improve your writing for your exam, even if your time is short. Start by reading the suggestions and guidelines in the following pages. But, keep in mind: improvement in writing comes mainly with practice. So you'll also need to apply what you learn here to the practice tests in Part III of this book.

> This section covers all writing aspects listed above except grammar and persuasiveness (the last item). The rules of grammar you reviewed in the Sentence Correction lessons of this book are the same ones you should keep in mind as you compose and proofread your essays. And, if you advance to the Next Level that's where you'll pick up ideas for developing a persuasive writing style.

X-Ref

Overall Tone and Voice

In general, you should try to maintain a somewhat formal tone throughout both your essays. An essay that comes across as conversational is probably a bit too informal for the GMAT. Here's a brief list of additional guidelines:

Chapter 3: Analytical Writing Assessment

1. The overall tone should be critical, but not inflammatory or emotional. Don't try to overstate your position by using extreme or harsh language. Don't attempt to elicit a visceral or emotional response from the reader. Appeal instead to the reader's intellect.

2. When it comes to your main points, a very direct, even forceful voice is perfectly acceptable. But don't overdo it; when it comes to the details, use a more dispassionate approach.

3. Don't try to make your point with "cutesy" or humorous remarks. Avoid puns, double-meanings, plays on words, and other forms of humor. Not that GMAT readers don't have a sense of humor; it's just that they leave it at the door when they go to work for ETS. (That sentence exhibits just the sort of "humor" you should avoid in your essays.)

4. Sarcasm is entirely inappropriate for your GMAT essays. Besides, the reader might not realize that you're being sarcastic, in which case your remark will only serve to confuse the reader.

Sentence Length and Variety

To ensure a high Analytical Writing Assessment score, strive for sentences that are varied in length and structured in a manner that helps convey their intended meaning, rather than obscuring or distorting it. Here are some specific warnings and suggestions:

- Sentences that vary in length make for a more interesting and persuasive essay. For rhetorical emphasis, try using an abrupt short sentence for a crucial point, either before or after longer sentences that elucidate that point. For additional variety, use a semicolon to transform two sentences involving the same train of thought into one; and use the word "and" to connect your two independent clauses (just as in this sentence).

- Sentences that use the same essential structure can help convey your line of reasoning to the reader. Try using the same structure for a list of reasons or examples.

- Sentences that essentially repeat (verbatim) throughout your essay suggest an immature, unsophisticated writing style. Try to avoid using so-called "template" sentences over and over—especially for the first (or last) sentence of each body paragraph.

> **Alert!**
>
> To speed up the writing process, some GMAT test-takers copy and paste certain phrases and sentences, then "tweak" them to avoid the template look. There's nothing wrong *per se* with this strategy. But you'll probably find that it takes more time than it's worth. You're better off composing each sentence from scratch.

Clear and Concise Writing

You're more likely to score high on your GMAT essays with writing that is clear and concise. Frequent occurrences of awkward, wordy, or redundant phrases can lower your Analytical Writing Assessment score by a notch—especially if these problems interfere with the reader's understanding of your essay. And, although punctuation is the least important aspect of your GMAT essays, the habitual overuse, underuse, or misuse of commas can also contribute to lowering your score.

Wordy and awkward phrases

With enough words, anyone can make the point; but it requires skill and effort to make your point with concise phrases. As you proofread your essay, if a sentence seems clumsy or too long, check for a wordy, awkward phrase that you can replace with a clearer, more concise one. Here are two examples (replace italicize phrases with the ones in parentheses):

Discipline is crucial to *the attainment of one's* objectives. (attain)

To indicate the fact that they are in opposition to a bill, legislators sometimes engage in filibusters. (To show their)

Look for the opportunity to change prepositional phrases into one-word modifiers:

The employee *with ambition* . . .

The *ambitious* employee . . .

You can often rework clauses with relative pronouns (*that*, *who*, *which*, etc.), omitting the pronoun:

The system, *which is* most efficient and accurate . . .

The most efficient and accurate system . . .

In your Argument essay, you can replace wordy phrases that signal a premise with a single word:

Wordier: the reason for, for the reason that, due to the fact that, in light of the fact that, on the grounds that

More concise: because, since, considering that

Redundant words and phrases

As you proofread your essays, check for words and phrases that express the same essential idea twice.

> *Both* unemployment levels *as well as* interest rates can affect stock prices. (Replace *as well as* with *and*, or omit *both*.)

> *The reason* science is being blamed for threats to the natural environment *is because* scientists fail to see that technology is only as useful, or as harmful, as those who decide how to use it. (Replace *because* with *that*, or omit *the reason* and *is*.)

Using too few (or too many) commas

Although punctuation is the least important aspect of your GMAT essays, too few or too many commas might interfere with the reader's understanding of a sentence. Too few commas might confuse the reader, while too many can unduly interrupt the sentence's flow. Here's the guideline: Use the minimum number of commas needed to ensure that the reader will understand your point.

Your Facility with the English Language

To ensure yourself top scores on your essays, strive to convince the readers that you possess a strong command of the English language—in other words, that you can use the language correctly, clearly, and persuasively in writing. To show the reader the requisite linguistic prowess, try to:

- Demonstrate a solid vocabulary.
- Use proper idioms (especially prepositional phrases).
- Use proper diction (word usage and choice).

Demonstrating a solid vocabulary

By all means, show the reader that you possess the vocabulary of a broadly educated individual, and that you know how to use it. But keep the following caveats in mind:

- Don't overuse SAT-style words just to make an impression. Doing so will only serve to warn the reader that you're trying to mask poor content with window dressing.

- Avoid obscure or archaic words that few readers are likely to know. The readers will not take time while reading essays to consult their unabridged dictionaries.

- Avoid technical terminology that only specialists and scholars in a specific field understand. GMAT readers are typically English-language generalists from the academic fields of English and Communications, not economic-policy analysts.

- Use Latin and other non-English terms *very* sparingly. After all, one of the primary skills being tested through the GMAT essays is your facility with the *English* language. However, the occasional use of Latin terms and acronyms—for example, *per se*, *de facto*, *ad hoc*, and especially *i.e.*, and *e.g.*,—are perfectly acceptable. Non-English words used commonly in academic writing—such as *vis-à-vis*, *caveat*, and *laissez faire*—are acceptable as well. Again, just don't overdo it.

> **Note**
>
> The rules for Standard Written English require that Latin and other non-English terms be italicized (or underlined). However, the GMAT word processor does not allow you to incorporate these attributes or special diacritical marks (as in *vis-à-vis*). So leave words such as these as is, but be sure they are terms that most educated people are familiar with.

- Avoid colloquialisms (slang and vernacular). Otherwise, instead of hitting a home run with your essay, your essay will turn out lousy, and you'll be out of luck and need to snake your way into a bottom-barrel B-school. (Did you catch the *five* colloquialisms in the preceding sentence?)

Your diction and use of idioms

In evaluating your essays, GMAT readers also take into account your *diction* and use of *idioms*—again, especially when problems in these areas interfere with the readers' understanding of your essays. Here you'll learn tips for avoiding, or at least minimizing, diction and idiom errors in your essays.

Diction (word choice and usage)

Diction refers to word choice as well as to the manner in which a word is used. For instance, you might confuse one word with another because the two words look or sound similar. Or you may choose a word that doesn't accurately convey your idea. Here's an example of each type of diction error:

One type of diction error:

The best way to *impede* employees to improve their productivity is to allow them to determine for themselves the most efficient way of performing their individual job tasks.

(The word *impede* means "to hinder or hamper"; in the context of this sentence *impede* should be replaced with a word such as *impel*, which means "propel or drive." The test-taker might have confused these two words.)

Another type of diction error:

Unless the department can supply a comparative cost-benefit analysis for the two alternative courses of action, I would remain *diffident* about following the department's recommendation.

(The word *diffident* means "reluctant, unwilling, or shy." A more appropriate word here would be *ambivalent*, which means "undecided or indecisive." Or perhaps the test-taker meant to use the word *indifferent* (thereby committing the first type of diction error).

What appear to be diction errors might in many instances be mere clerical (typing) errors. Accordingly, problems with your word choice and usage will adversely affect your scores only if they are obvious and occur frequently.

Idiom

An *idiom* is a distinctive (*idio*syncratic) phrase that is considered proper or improper based upon whether it has become acceptable over time—through repeated and common use. Here are two sentences, each of which contain an idiomatic prepositional phrase as well as another idiom.

Example (from a typical Issue essay):

The speaker's contention *flies in the face of* the empirical evidence and, *in any event*, runs contrary to common sense.

Example (from a typical Argument essay):

For all we know, last year was the only year in which the company earned a profit, in which case the vice president's advice might *turn out* especially poor in retrospect.

Tips for avoiding diction and idiom errors

Idioms don't rely on any particular rules of grammar; hence, they are learned over time by experience. As you might suspect, the English language contains more idiomatic expressions than you can shake a thesaurus at. Moreover, the number of possible diction errors isn't even limited to the number of entries in a comprehensive unabridged English dictionary. Although it is impossible in these pages to provide an adequate diction or idiom review, here are some guidelines to keep you on the straight and narrow when it comes to these aspects of your writing.

- If you're the least bit unsure about the meaning of a word you intend to use in your essay, don't use it. Why risk committing a diction blunder just to impress the reader with an erudite vocabulary? (And if you're not sure what "erudite" means, either find out or don't use it in your essays!)

- If a phrase sounds wrong to your ear, change it until it sounds correct to you.

- The fewer words you use, the less likely you'll commit an error in diction or idiom. So when in doubt, go with a relatively brief phrase that you still think conveys your point.

- If English is your second language, take heart: In evaluating and scoring your essays, GMAT readers take into account diction or idiom problems only to the extent that those problems interfere with a reader's understanding of your sentence's intended meaning. So as long as your writing is understandable to your EFL (English-as-first-language) friends, you don't need to worry.

> **Tip**
> If you have ample time before your exam, and you think your diction and use of idioms could stand considerable improvement, check for errors in your practice essays by consulting a reputable guide to English usage—or a trusted professor, colleague, or acquaintance who has a firm grasp of the conventions of Standard Written English.

Take It to the Next Level

Welcome to the Next Level of Analytical Writing Assessment. At this level, you'll learn advanced skills and techniques that will help you attain not only a solid Analytical Writing Assessment score, but no less than a top score of 6.

What's New at the Next Level

For the Issue-Analysis writing task, at the Next Level you'll learn to:

- Recognize and deal with the kinds of complexities inherent in GMAT Issues but that many test-takers overlook.
- Acknowledge and respond effectively to ostensible weaknesses of your viewpoint on an Issue.
- Acknowledge and respond effectively to the merits of viewpoints that are contrary to yours.

For the Argument-Analysis writing task, at the Next Level you'll learn to:

- Recognize each of the typical types of flaws you'll find in GMAT Arguments.
- Compose a concise and effective one-paragraph analysis of each type of flaw.
- Incorporate optional elements into your essay.

Here at the Next Level, you'll also learn to develop an especially mature and persuasive writing style—one that will leave a distinctively positive impression on any GMAT reader.

Issue Analysis—"Qualifying" Your Viewpoint

Most GMAT test-takers will essentially accept (agree with) or reject (disagree with) the Issue statement that the test presents to them. And that's okay. As long as you provide sound reasons and relevant examples in support of your position, you'll earn a solid score on your essay. But you're more likely to receive a top score of 6 if you demonstrate additional insight into the issue at hand.

One way to accomplish this is to think of ways that you can *qualify* the statement—or your viewpoint on it. What this means is that you agree (or disagree) with the statement only in part or to a certain extent. In other words, you neither completely agree nor completely disagree with the statement. Here are two Issue statements, which are typical of the ones in the official pool, each followed by a viewpoint that expresses how the test-taker might qualify it:

Issue Statement 1:

"To truly succeed in life, a person must assert his or her individuality rather than conforming to the expectations of others."

Viewpoint: Asserting individuality is important only to an extent. The key is to strike the optimal balance between individuality and conformity—a balance that varies depending on the particular activity or goal involved.

Issue Statement 2:

"The greatest responsibility of a leader—whether in politics, business, or the military—is to serve the interests of his or her followers."

Viewpoint: The statement's accuracy depends on the category. Legitimate political leadership must, by definition, serve the citizenry, but the same can't be said for either business or military leadership.

You might be wondering: By qualifying the statement, wouldn't I appear wishy-washy or indecisive? To the contrary! By "hedging your position" on the Issue, you'll impress the reader as thoughtful and insightful! Just be sure to persuade the reader (with sound reasons and relevant examples) that your qualified agreement (or disagreement) is justifiable.

On your exam, look especially for any of the following types of qualifiable Issue statements:

- A statement whose accuracy depends on various factors
- A statement that might be generally true (or untrue) but that fails to account for significant exceptional cases
- A statement that is unclear or vague in some way (in other words, the statement's accuracy depends on the meaning of key terms or how you interpret the statement as a whole)

- A statement that raises two distinct but related issues (one might be a threshold issue, which the statement ignores but that should be addressed before analyzing the main issue)

- A statement that has merit but overlooks legitimate competing interests or contributing factors—e.g., Issue Statement 1 above

- A statement that lists, or otherwise embraces, two or more distinct categories—e.g., Issue Statement 2 above (different categories often lend differing degrees of support to the statement)

> **Tip:** If you have time before exam day, select one or two dozen Issue statements from the official pool. Try to qualify each one using the preceding list to help you brainstorm ideas. Jot down your viewpoint in one or two sentences that could serve as an introduction to an essay.

Issue Analysis—Debating a Statement's "Pros" and "Cons"

Earlier in the chapter, we suggested that you take a few minutes up front to brainstorm and jot down ideas, listing points both for and against the statement as you think of them. As an advanced test-taker, you should think more consciously about "pros" and "cons" during this step. Think of this process as a *debate*, in which you formulate points and supporting examples to bolster one side of the issue. Then respond with *counterpoints* and *counterexamples*. (You can even go a step further, to *rebut* a counterpoint or counterexample.)

To organize the points of your debate, try creating two columns, one for points that support the statement (the "pro" column) and the other for opposing points (the "con" column). To help you see how this might work, here's what a test-taker's notes might look like after a few minutes of brainstorming "pros" and "cons" of Issue Statement 3.

Issue Statement 3:

"The best way to ensure protection and preservation of our natural environment is through government regulatory measures. We cannot rely on the voluntary efforts of individuals and private businesses to achieve these objectives."

PRO	CON
• self-interest rules ind. & bus. 　• e.g. auto emissions 　• but nations too • environ problems too widespread for ind. & bus. 　• but nations must cooperate	• lawmakers pander 　• but accountable to voters • enforcement problems 　• e.g. bus. relocate • bureaucratic problems 　• e.g. delays 　• e.g. compromises 　• e.g. admin. expense 　• but must put up with problems to save environ.

Notice that the test-taker supports each main point (indicated by a bullet) with one or more examples ("e.g.") and/or a counterpoint ("but").

> Don't worry if you don't quite understand what each of the preceding notes means. You'll find out what the test-taker had in mind as you a read complete essay based on these notes later in this chapter.

Issue Analysis—Developing Rhetorical Arguments

The word "rhetoric" refers to the art of persuasive argumentation. A rhetorically effective Issue essay does more than just itemize the best reasons and examples in support of one viewpoint on the issue. It also:

- Acknowledges possible problems with the writer's viewpoint, then defends that viewpoint by responding to those problems head-on
- Acknowledges at least one other position or viewpoint, then challenges that viewpoint directly

Hopefully, as you take notes on your Issue statement, ideas for responding to (or "countering") other viewpoints, and to possible problems with your own viewpoint will occur to you naturally. But if you do get stuck for ideas, draw upon the five tried-and-true techniques discussed in the following pages to get your rhetorical ideas flowing.

To illustrate each technique, we'll use examples based upon the following two Issue statements, the first of which you've already encountered in this lesson:

Issue Statement 3:

"The best way to ensure protection and preservation of our natural environment is through government regulatory measures. We cannot rely on the voluntary efforts of individuals and private businesses to achieve these objectives."

Issue Statement 4:

"Large businesses should focus on teamwork as the primary means of achieving success."

Turn it Around (Look for the "Silver Lining")

Argue that an apparent weakness (or strength) is actually not, or perhaps even just the opposite, if you view it from a different perspective. The notes/outline for Issue Statement 3 provide a good example. The writer might first cite evidence that lends *apparent* support to the opposing position.

Admittedly, businesses often attempt to avoid compliance by concealing their activities, or calculate the cost of polluting, in terms of punishment, then budget in advance for anticipated penalties and openly violate the law.

Then the writer might indicate how this point *actually* undermines that position.

. . . However, this behavior only serves to underscore the need for government intervention, because, left unfettered, this type of behavior would only exacerbate environmental problems.

Trivialize it ("Explain it Away")

Argue that an apparent weakness of your position (or strength of a different position) is trivial, minor, or insignificant. Issue Statement 4 provides a good opportunity to use this technique. The writer might first cite two examples that lend *apparent* support to those who might disagree with the statement:

Detractors might cite the heavy manufacturing and natural-resource industries, where the value of tangible assets—raw materials and capital equipment—are often the most significant determinant of business success.

Then the writer might *explain away* these examples.

. . . However, such industries are diminishing in significance as we move from an industrial society to an information age.

Appeal to Broader Considerations

Argue that any minor problems with your position seem trivial in light of the broad, and serious, implications that the Issue raises. The notes/outline for Issue Statement 3 provide a good example. The writer might first acknowledge a certain problem with her position.

Delays typically associated with bureaucratic regulation can thwart the purpose of the regulations, because environmental problems can quickly become grave indeed.

Then the writer might point out the broad societal consideration that puts this minor drawback in its proper perspective.

. . . But such delays seem trivial when we consider that many environmental problems carry not only a real threat to public health but also a potential threat to the very survival of the human species.

The "Lesser of Two Evils" Method

Argue that an opposing position is not stronger, but perhaps even weaker, in a certain respect. The notes/outline for Issue Statement 1 provides a good example. The writer might first acknowledge a certain weakness in his position.

Delays typically associated with bureaucratic regulation can thwart the purpose of the regulations, because environmental problems can quickly become grave indeed.

Then, the writer would point out an even greater weakness in the opposing position.

. . . However, given that unjustifiable reliance on volunteerism is the only alternative, government regulation seems necessary.

The "Greater of Two Virtues" Method

Argue that a certain merit of the opposing position is overshadowed by one or more virtues of your position. Issue Statement 4 provides a good opportunity to employ this rhetorical device. The writer might first admit that the opposing position is not without merit.

> No reasonable observer of the corporate business world could disagree that the leadership and vision of a company's key executives is of great importance to the organization's success.

The writer would then assert that the contrary position has even greater merit.

> . . . Yet chief executives of our most successful corporations would no doubt admit that without the cooperative efforts of their subordinates, their personal vision would never become reality.

Issue Analysis—How to Put It All Together

Here again are the notes on Issue Statement 3. The test-taker has now numbered his notes to indicate how he plans to organize his essay.

PRO	CON
① • self-interest rules ind. & bus. 　　• e.g. auto emissions 　　• but nations too ④ • environ problems too widespread for ind. & bus. 　　• but nations must cooperate	② • lawmakers pander 　　• but accountable to voters • enforcement problems 　　• e.g. bus. relocate ③ • bureaucratic problems 　　• e.g. delays 　　• e.g. compromises 　　• e.g. admin. expense 　　• but must put up with problems to save environ.

Notice that the test-taker has decided to begin and end the body of the essay with "pro" points, possibly because he weighed the evidence—the pros and cons—and thinks the "pro" points are the strongest arguments. He probably intends to agree, at least *on balance*, with the statement. Also notice that he plans to discuss two distinct "cons" both in the same paragraph (2), possibly because he doesn't have enough to say about them to justify devoting an entire paragraph to either one alone.

Now here's a full length essay on Issue Statement 3, which pulls together the techniques you have learned about up to this point in the lesson. It runs about 430 words in length—a bit longer than average, but still realistic given a 30-minute time limit. Certain words and phrases that you might use in almost any Issue essay are underlined—just to help you see how the ideas flow naturally and persuasively from one to the next. (The test's built-in word processor does *not* provide for underlining.) Notice the following features of the essay, which together boost the essay to the highest score level:

- The essay expresses overall but *qualified* agreement with the statement, a thoughtful viewpoint that shows the writer recognizes the issue's complexity.

- The body of the essay begins and ends with "pro" arguments for rhetorical impact. The "con" arguments are positioned between them.

- For each of the "con" arguments (third and fourth paragraphs), the writer immediately responds with persuasive counterpoints.

Notice also that the writer tried to follow his outline, while at the same time remaining flexible as new ideas for content or organization occurred to him. (Notice, for instance, that he repositioned certain points from the outline.) Also notice that the writer didn't incorporate every single point from his outline, perhaps because he simply didn't have time in 30 minutes to cover every point.

Essay (Issue Statement 3)

In asserting that government regulation is the "best" way to ensure environmental protection, the speaker fails to acknowledge certain problems inherent with government regulation. Nevertheless, I agree with the statement to the extent that exclusive reliance on individual or business volunteerism would be naive and imprudent, especially considering the stakes involved.

Experience tells us that individuals and private corporations tend to act in their own short-term economic and political interest, not on behalf of the environment or the public at large. For example, current technology makes possible the complete elimination of polluting emissions from automobiles. Nevertheless, neither automobile manufacturers nor consumers are willing or able to voluntarily make the short-term sacrifices necessary to accomplish this goal. Only the government holds the regulatory and enforcement power to impose the necessary standards and to ensure that we achieve these goals.

Admittedly, government penalties do not guarantee compliance with environmental regulations. Businesses often attempt to avoid compliance by concealing their activities, lobbying legislators to modify regulations, or moving operations to jurisdictions that allow their environmentally harmful activities. Others calculate the cost of polluting, in terms of punishment, then budget in advance for anticipated penalties and openly violate the law. However, this behavior only serves to underscore the need for government intervention, because left unfettered this type of behavior would only exacerbate environmental problems.

One must admit as well that government regulation, environmental or otherwise, is fraught with bureaucratic and enforcement problems. Regulatory systems inherently call for legislative committees, investigations, and enforcement agencies, all of which add to the tax burden on the citizens whom these regulations are designed to protect. Also, delays typically associated with bureaucratic regulation can thwart the purpose of the regulations, because environmental problems can quickly become grave indeed. However, given that unjustifiable reliance on volunteerism is the only alternative, government regulation seems necessary. Moreover, such delays seem trivial when we consider that many environmental problems carry not only a real threat to public health but also a potential threat to the very survival of the human species.

Finally, environmental issues inherently involve public health and are far too pandemic in nature for individuals or even businesses to solve on their own. Many of the most egregious environmental violations traverse state and sometimes national borders. Individuals and businesses have neither the power nor the resources to address these widespread hazards.

In the final analysis, only the authority and scope of power that a government possesses can ensure the attainment of agreed-upon environmental goals. Since individuals are unable and businesses are by nature unwilling to assume this responsibility, government must do so.

Issue Analysis—Rhetorical Effectiveness and Your Essay's Structure

How you arrange your ideas into paragraphs can make a big difference in your essay's persuasiveness. Chapter 2 introduced the basic strategy of starting the body of your essay with your best argument and finishing it with your second-best argument, sandwiching your other arguments between these two. And, you just saw in the preceding essay how you can adapt this strategy to a two-column list of "pros" and "cons"—sandwiching the "cons" in between the "pros."

As an advanced test-taker, you should consider alternative structures as well. Although the ways in which you can organize an Issue essay are limitless, five basic structures cover most situations.

> **Note:** In the following templates, the term "counterpoint" refers to a reason or example supporting a contrary position, and "rebuttal" refers to a response (reason or example) to a counterpoint (and in further support of the other position).

Try this first structure if your agreement or disagreement with the statement is *nearly unqualified*.

1st Paragraph: Main reason for your position → counterpoint → rebuttal

2nd Paragraph: Second reason for your position → counterpoint → rebuttal

3rd Paragraph: Third reason for your position → counterpoint → rebuttal

You can use the same structure to discuss two or more examples (or distinct areas) that lend support to your position:

1st Paragraph: One example (or area) that supports your position → counterpoint → rebuttal

2nd Paragraph: Another example (or area) that supports your position → counterpoint → rebuttal

3rd Paragraph: Another example (or area) that supports your position → counterpoint → rebuttal

Try this next structure to acknowledge *one* strong argument *against* your position, but where you have more reasons or examples *in support of* your position.

1st Paragraph: One reason (and/or example) in support of your position

2nd Paragraph: Another reason (and/or example) in support of your position

3rd Paragraph: Another reason (and/or example) in support of your position

Final Paragraph: Chief counter-argument → rebuttal

Try this next structure to acknowledge *one or more* strong arguments *against* your position, but where you have better reasons and/or examples in support of your position.

1st Paragraph: Chief counter-argument

Next Paragraph: Another counter-argument

Next Paragraph: One reason and/or example in support of your position

Next Paragraph: Another reason and/or example in support of your position

If the arguments for and against the statement's position are equally strong (e.g., if it all depends on the area under consideration), try the following structure for a balanced essay:

1st Paragraph (or 1st and 2nd Paragraphs): Area(s) or examples supporting one position

2nd Paragraph (or 3rd and 4th Paragraphs): Area(s) or examples supporting a contrary position

Finally, try the following structure to address two or more reasons in support of an opposing position, each one in turn:

1st Paragraph (or 1st and 2nd Paragraphs): Counter-argument → rebuttal

2nd Paragraph (or 3rd and 4th Paragraphs): Counter-argument → rebuttal

Next Paragraph: Counter-argument → rebuttal

> **Alert!** You need not adhere strictly to one of these structures in order to write an effective Issue essay. Try to be flexible. The particular ideas you've jotted down might come together best in some other, idiosyncratic format. In short, let your ideas drive your essay's structure, not vice versa.

Argument Analysis—Common Reasoning Flaws and How to Handle Them

In this section, you'll turn your attention from the Issue-Analysis writing task to the Argument-Analysis task. The test-maker intentionally incorporates into each Argument numerous reasoning flaws that render the Argument vulnerable to criticism. In a typical Argument, you can find three or four distinct areas for critique. The following are the most common types of problems with GMAT Arguments (memorize this list to help you brainstorm and ferret out flaws in any GMAT Argument):

- Confusing cause-and-effect with mere correlation or time sequence
- Drawing a weak analogy between two things
- Relying on a potentially unrepresentative statistical sample
- Relying on a potentially unreliable survey or poll
- Assuming that a certain condition is necessary and/or sufficient for a certain outcome
- Assuming that characteristics of a group apply to each group member (or vice-versa)
- Assuming that all things remain unchanged over time
- Assuming that two courses of action are mutually exclusive
- Relying on undefined, vague, or ambiguous terms

In the following pages, you'll learn more about each type of flaw, and you'll learn how to address each one in your Argument-Analysis essay.

> **Alert!** The sample Arguments you'll read in this section are each designed to focus on one particular reasoning flaw. Keep in mind: Most Arguments in the official pool are a bit longer and more involved.

Chapter 3: Analytical Writing Assessment

Confusing Cause-and-Effect with Mere Correlation or Time Sequence

Many GMAT Arguments rely on the claim that certain events cause other certain events. A cause-and-effect claim might be based on:

1. A significant *correlation* between the occurrence of two phenomena (both phenomena generally occur together)

2. A *temporal relationship* between the two (one event occurred after another)

A significant correlation or a temporal relationship between two phenomena is one indication of a cause-and-effect relationship between them. However, neither in itself suffices to prove such a relationship. Unless the Argument also considers and eliminates all other plausible causes of the presumed "result" (by the way, it won't), the Argument is vulnerable to criticism. To show the reader you understand this sort of false-cause problem, you need to accomplish all three of the following tasks:

1. *Identify* the false-cause problem (e.g., as one of the Argument's crucial assumptions).

2. *Elucidate* by providing at least one or two examples of other possible causes.

3. *Explain* how the false-cause problem undermines the Argument.

Here's an Argument that confuses causation with mere *temporal sequence*, followed by a succinct and effective critique.

Argument:

The following appeared in the editorial section of a newspaper:

> "Two years ago State X enacted a law prohibiting environmental emissions of certain nitrocarbon byproducts, on the basis that these byproducts have been shown to cause Urkin's disease in humans. Last year fewer State X residents reported symptoms of Urkin's disease than in any prior year. Since the law is clearly effective in preventing the disease, in the interest of public health this state should adopt a similar law."

Response:

> The editorial infers that State X's new law is responsible for the apparent decline in the incidence of Urkin's disease (UD) symptoms. However, the editorial's author ignores other possible causes of the decline—for example, a new UD cure or new treatment for

UD symptoms. Without eliminating alternative explanations such as these, the author cannot justify either the inference or the additional assertion that a similar law would be similarly effective in the author's state.

Drawing a Weak Analogy Between Two Things

A GMAT Argument might draw a conclusion about one thing (perhaps a city, school, or company) on the basis of an observation about a similar thing. However, in doing so, the Argument assumes that because the two things are similar in certain respects, they are similar in all respects, at least as far as the Argument is concerned. Unless the Argument provides sufficient evidence to substantiate this assumption (by the way, it won't), the Argument is vulnerable to criticism. The Argument cannot rely on these claims to support its recommendation.

To show the reader you understand the weak-analogy problem, you need to accomplish all three of the following tasks:

1. *Identify* the analogy (e.g., as one of the Argument's crucial assumptions).

2. *Elucidate* by providing at least one or two significant ways in which the two things might differ.

3. *Explain* how those differences, which render the analogy weak, undermine the Argument's conclusion.

Here's an Argument that contains a questionable analogy, followed by an effective 3-sentence analysis.

Argument:

The following was part of a speech made by the principal of Valley High School:

"Every year Dunston High School wins the school district's student Math SuperBowl competition. The average salary of teachers at Dunston is greater than at any other school in the district. Hence in order for Valley High students to improve their scores on the state's standardized achievement exams, Valley should begin awarding bonuses to Valley teachers whenever Valley defeats Dunston in the Math SuperBowl."

Response:

The principal's recommendation relies on what might be a poor analogy between Dunston and Valley. Valley teachers might be less responsive than Dunston teachers when it comes to monetary incentives, or Valley students might be less gifted than Dunston students when it comes to math. In short, what might have helped Dunston perform well at the Math SuperBowl would not necessarily help Valley perform better either at the SuperBowl or on the state exams.

> **X-Ref**
>
> Some GMAT Arguments actually rest on *more than one* weak analogy. Earlier in the chapter, you saw a simulated example—Argument 1 (page 85) relied on two distinct analogies. The second and fourth body paragraphs of the Argument's response (page 91) addressed each one, respectively.

Relying on a Potentially Unrepresentative Statistical Sample

A GMAT Argument might cite statistical evidence from a study, survey, or poll involving a "sample" group, then draw a conclusion about a larger group or population which the sample supposedly represents. But in order for a statistical sample to accurately reflect a larger population, the sample must meet two requirements:

1. The sample must be *significant in size* (number) as a portion of the overall population.

2. The sample must be *representative* of the overall population in terms of relevant characteristics.

Arguments that cite statistics from studies, surveys, and polls often fail to establish either of these two requirements. Of course this failure is by design of the test-maker, who is inviting you to call into question the reliability of the evidence. To show the reader you understand this statistical problem, you need to accomplish all three of the following tasks:

1. *Identify* the problem (e.g., as one of the Argument's crucial assumptions).

2. *Elucidate* by providing at least one or two respects in which key characteristics of a sample group might differ from those of the larger population.

3. *Explain* how those differences would undermine the Argument's conclusion.

Here's an Argument that relies on *two* potentially unrepresentative sample groups: (1) new graduates from a certain state's undergraduate programs and (2) new graduates from the state's graduate-level programs. The response that follows it provides a brief but effective critique.

Argument:

The following was part of an article appearing in a national magazine:

> "Our nation's new college graduates will have better success obtaining jobs if they do not pursue advanced degrees after graduation. After all, more than ninety percent of State X's undergraduate students are employed full-time within one year after they graduate, while less than half of State X's graduate-level students find employment within one year after receiving their graduate degrees."

Response:

The argument fails to consider that State X's new graduates might not be representative of the nation's as a whole, especially if the former group constitutes only a small percentage of the latter group. If it turns out, for example, that State X's undergraduate students are less motivated than the nation's average college student to pursue graduate-level study, then the argument's recommendation for all undergraduate students would be unwarranted.

Relying on Tainted Results from a Survey or Poll

As you just learned, a GMAT Argument might draw some conclusion involving a group based on statistical data about an *insufficient* or *unrepresentative* sample. However, this is not the only potential problem with statistical data. The *process* of collecting the data (i.e., the methodology) might be flawed in a way that calls into question the *quality* of the data, rendering the data "tainted" and therefore unreliable for the purpose of drawing any conclusions. In order for survey or poll results to be reliable in quality:

- The survey or poll responses must be *credible* (truthful and accurate). If respondents have reason to provide incomplete or false responses, the results are tainted (and therefore unreliable).

- The method of collecting the data must be *unbiased*. If responses are not mandatory, or if the survey's form predisposes subjects to respond in certain ways, then the results are tainted (and therefore unreliable).

- To show the reader that you recognize and understand this statistical problem, you need to accomplish all three of the following tasks:

1. *Identify* the problem (e.g., as one of the Argument's crucial assumptions).

2. *Elucidate* by providing at least one or two reasons, based on the Argument's information, why the statistical data might be tainted (and therefore unreliable).

3. *Explain* how the potentially tainted data might undermine the Argument's conclusion.

The following Argument relies on a survey that poses a potential *bias* as well as a *credibility* problem. The response contains all three elements required to address each problem, in a single paragraph.

Argument:

The following appeared in a memo from the director of human resources at Webco:

"Among Webco employees participating in our department's most recent survey, about half indicated that they are happy with our current four-day work week. These survey results show that the most effective way to improve overall productivity at Webco is to allow each employee to choose for himself or herself either a four-day or five-day work week."

Response:

The survey methodology might be problematic in two respects. First, we are not informed whether the survey required that respondents choose their work week preference between alternatives. If it did, then the results might distort the preferences of the respondents, who might very well prefer a work schedule choice not provided for in the survey. Secondly, we are not informed whether survey responses were anonymous, or even confidential. If they were not, then respondents might have provided responses that they believed their superiors would approve of, regardless of whether the responses were truthful. In either event, the survey results would be unreliable for the purpose of drawing any conclusions about Webco employee preferences, let alone about how to improve overall productivity at Webco.

Assuming That a Certain Condition is Necessary and/or Sufficient for a Certain Outcome

A GMAT Argument might recommend a certain course of action, based on one or both of the following claims:

1. The course of action is *necessary* to achieve a desired result.

2. The course of action is *sufficient* to achieve the desired result.

With respect to claim 1, the Argument must provide evidence that no other means of achieving the same result are available (by the way, it won't). With respect to claim 2, the Argument must provide strong evidence that the proposed course of action by itself would be sufficient to bring about the desired result (by the way, it won't). Lacking this sort of evidence, the Argument cannot rely on these claims to support its recommendation.

To show the reader you understand necessary-condition and sufficient-condition problems, you need to accomplish all three of the following tasks:

1. *Identify* the problem (e.g., as one of the Argument's crucial assumptions).

2. *Elucidate* by providing at least one or two examples. For a necessary-condition problem, suggest other possible means of achieving the stated objective. For a sufficient-condition problem, suggest other conditions that might also be necessary for the outcome.

3. *Explain* how the problem undermines the Argument's conclusion.

Here's an Argument that assumes that a certain condition is *necessary* for a certain outcome. The response provides a brief but incisive analysis of the problem.

Argument:

The following appeared in a memo from a vice president at Toyco, which operates a large chain of toy stores:

> "Last year was the first year in which Playtime Stores, our main competitor, sold more toys than Toyco. Playtime's compensation for its retail sales force is based entirely on their sales. If Toyco is to recapture its leadership position in the toy-sales market, we must reestablish our former policy of requiring all our retail associates to meet strict sales quotas in order to retain their jobs."

Chapter 3: Analytical Writing Assessment

Response:
> The argument assumes that the proposed compensation policy is the only way that Toyco can once again sell more toys than Playtime. However, the vice president fails to consider and rule out possible alternative means of achieving this end—for example, opening new stores or adding new types of toys to the ones its stores already carry. Until the president does so, I will remain unconvinced that the proposed policy is a necessary means for Toyco to recapture market leadership.

> **X-Ref**
>
> Earlier in the chapter, Argument 1 (about UpperCuts hair salon) relied on a *sufficient*-condition assumption. Read again the third body paragraph of the response to that Argument (page 91), which addresses the problem.

Assuming That Characteristics of a Group Apply to Each Group Member (or vice-versa)

A GMAT Argument might point out some fact about a general group—such as students, employees, or cities—to support a claim about one particular member of that group. Or conversely, the Argument might point out some fact about a particular group member to support a claim about the entire group. In either scenario, unless the Argument supplies clear evidence that the member is
representative of the group as a whole (by the way, it won't), the Argument is vulnerable to criticism.

To show the reader you understand a group-member problem, you need to accomplish all three of the following tasks:

1. *Identify* the problem (e.g., as one of the Argument's crucial assumptions).

2. *Elucidate* by providing at least one or two significant ways in which the member might differ from the general group.

3. *Explain* how those key differences, which serve to refute the assumption, would undermine the Argument's conclusion.

Here's an Argument that assumes that characteristics of a group member apply to the group as a whole. Following the Argument is a response that shows how to handle the problem in one very succinct paragraph.

Argument:

The following is part of an article appearing in the entertainment section of a local newspaper:

> "At the local Viewer Choice video store, the number of available movies in VHS-tape format remains about the same as three years ago, even though the number of available movies on digital video disk, or DVD, has increased tenfold over the past three years. People who predict the impending obsolescence of the VHS format are mistaken, since demand for VHS movie rentals today clearly remains just as strong as ever."

Response:

> This argument assumes that Viewer Choice (VC) is typical of all video stores as a group. However, this isn't necessarily the case; VC might carry far more VHS tapes, as a percentage of its total inventory, than the average store. If so, then the argument has failed to discredit the prediction for the industry as a whole.

Assuming That All Things Remain Unchanged Over Time

A GMAT Argument might rely on evidence collected in the *past* in order to formulate some conclusion or recommendation concerning the *present* or the *future*. Similarly, an Argument might rely on evidence about *present* conditions to make a prediction or recommendation for the *future*. But unless the Argument provides clear evidence that key circumstances have remained, or will remain, unchanged over the relevant time period (by the way, it won't), the Argument is vulnerable to criticism.

To address this problem, you should accomplish each of the following three tasks:

1. *Identify* the problem (i.e., the poor assumption that all key circumstances remain fixed over time).
2. *Elucidate* by providing examples of conditions that might change from one time frame to the other.
3. *Evaluate* the argument in light of the problem.

Here's an Argument that provides evidence about the past to draw a conclusion about the present as well as the future, followed by a 3-sentence paragraph that addresses the problem.

Chapter 3: Analytical Writing Assessment

Argument:

The following appeared in a political campaign advertisement:

> "Residents of this state should vote to elect Kravitz as state governor in the upcoming election. During Kravitz's final term as a state senator, she was a member of special legislative committee that explored ways the state can reduce its escalating rate of violent crime. Elect Kravitz for governor, and our cities' streets will be safer than ever."

Response:

Assuming that at one time Kravitz was genuinely committed to fighting violent crime, the ad unfairly infers a similar commitment on Kravitz's part today and in the future while Kravitz serves as governor. Kravitz might hold entirely different views today, especially if her participation as a member of the committee occurred some time ago. Lacking better evidence that as governor Kravitz would continue to make crime fighting a high priority, the ad cannot persuade me to vote for Kravitz based on her committee membership.

Assuming That Two Courses of Action are Mutually Exclusive

An Argument might recommend one course of action over another in order to achieve the stated objective, without considering that it is possible to pursue both courses (that is, they are not mutually exclusive alternatives), thereby increasing the likelihood of achieving the objective. Here's a good example, along with a response that handles the flaw.

Argument:

Rivertown's historic Hill district used to be one of the city's main tourist attractions. Recently, however, the district's quaint older shops and restaurants have had difficulty attracting patrons. In order to reverse the decline in tourism to the district, Rivertown's City Council intends to approve construction a new shopping center called Hill Hub on one of the district's few remaining vacant parcels. However, the city's interests in attracting revenue from tourism would be better served were it to focus instead on restoring Hill district's older buildings and waging a publicity campaign touting the historically authentic character of the district.

Response:

> The argument seems to assume that the city must either approve the Hill Hub project or engage in the restoration and publicity efforts that the argument suggests, but that the city cannot do both. However, the argument provides absolutely no evidence that the city must choose between the two courses of action. Lacking any such evidence, it is entirely possible that implementing both plans would attract more dollars from tourists to the district than implementing either one alone.

Relying on Undefined, Vague, or Ambiguous Terms

An Argument might contain a statement (or word or phrase) that carries more than one possible meaning or is simply too vague to reasonably rely upon when it comes to drawing conclusions. Look for references to "some," "many," and "several" in lieu of providing precise percentages or numbers. Also look for references to a particular class, category, or group, without a clear explanation of what it includes or excludes. Here's an example, followed by an effective response:

Argument:

> A reliable recent study attests to the value of physical activity in increasing attention span among young children. Accordingly, in order to improve the overall learning levels among elementary-school children in our state, the state's board of education should mandate a daily exercise regimen for students at all our state's elementary schools.

Response:

> The Argument neglects to indicate what types of "physical activity" the study observed. For all I know, those activities amounted to play, as opposed to the recommended exercise "regimen," which might be more like work for children. Nor does the Argument indicate the age range of the "young children" observed in the study. Perhaps the children were pre-schoolers, whose attention spans might respond differently than school-age children to certain types of physical activity. In short, before I can determine the extent to which the study supports the recommendation, I need specific definitions of these important terms.

Chapter 3: Analytical Writing Assessment

Argument-Analysis—Adding Optional Elements to Your Essay

The directive for every GMAT Argument indicates that you *may* include either or both of the following in your essay:

- Suggestions as to how the Argument can be strengthened
- Additional information needed to evaluate the Argument

These two elements are *optional*, and you can score high on your Argument essay without them. Thus, do not take the time to add either of these two elements to your essay unless you're sure you've adequately addressed all of the Argument's major problems. Otherwise, you risk running out of time to accomplish that essential task.

But keep in mind: You're more likely to attain a top score of 6 if you add these additional elements, *all else being equal*. So, as you brainstorm your Argument essay, by all means, jot down your ideas about how the Argument can be strengthened and/or what additional information is needed to evaluate the Argument. Then, after you've finished your critique of the Argument and proofread your critique, check the clock. If you still have at least a few minutes, go ahead and add one or both elements.

You have two realistic choices as to where to include them in your essay:

1. List the suggestions (and/or additional information needed) in your *final*, concluding paragraph.
2. Incorporate the suggestions (and/or additional information needed) into your *body paragraphs*.

Here's how you might incorporate both elements into a final paragraph of an essay on Argument 1 about UpperCuts hair salon (we've underlined words and phrases that you could use in the final paragraph of nearly any Argument essay):

Optional elements added to an essay's final, concluding paragraph:

<u>In sum, the argument is a dubious one that relies on a series of unproven assumptions</u>—about Apton's and Brainard's demographics, the reasons for the success of the two other salons, and UC's future expenses. <u>To strengthen the argument, the manager should provide better evidence</u> of a demographic shift in Apton toward the downtown area, <u>and clear evidence that</u> those demographics portend success there for an upscale hair salon. <u>Even with this additional evidence, in order to properly evaluate the argument I would need to know why</u> Hair-Dooz relocated, what factors have contributed to the Brainard salon's success, what factors other than location might have contrib-

uted to UC's sagging profits at the mall, and what additional, offsetting expenses UC might incur at the new location.

Now here's how you might incorporate the same two elements into the body of an essay on the same Argument. (The optional elements are in italics—just to help you locate them.) Again, we've underlined words and phrases that you could use in nearly any Argument essay:

Optional elements incorporated into an essay's body paragraphs:

To begin with, the argument assumes that Apton's demographic trend reflects the national trend. Yet, the mere fact that one hair salon has moved downtown hardly suffices to infer any such trend in Apton; Hair-Dooz might owe its success at its new location to factors unrelated to Apton's demographics. In fact, for all we know, the trend in Apton might be in the opposite direction. *Thus, I would need to know whether more people are in fact moving to downtown Apton before I could either accept or reject the manager's proposal.*

Even if Apton's demographics do reflect the national trend, it is unfair to assume that UC will attract more customers simply by relocating downtown. It is entirely possible that the types of people who prefer living in downtown areas tend not to patronize upscale salons. It is also possible that Hair-Dooz will continue to impede upon UC's business, just as it might have at the mall. *Before I can accept that UC would attract more customers downtown, the manager would need to supply clear proof of a sufficient demand downtown for UC's service.*

Nor can the manager justify the recommended course of action on the basis of the Brainard salon's success. Perhaps hair salons generally fare better in downtown Brainard than downtown Apton, due to demographic differences between the two areas. Or perhaps the salon thrives only because it is long-established in downtown Brainard—an advantage that UC clearly would not have in its new location. *Accordingly, in order to determine whether the success of the Brainard salon portends success for UC in downtown Apton, I would need to know why the Brainard salon is successful in the first place.*

Finally, even assuming that the proposed relocation would attract more customers, an increase in the number of patrons would not necessarily result in improved profits. After all, profit is a function of expenses as well as revenue. Thus an increase in UC's expenses—due perhaps to higher rents downtown than at the mall—might very well offset increasing revenues, thereby frustrating UC's efforts to improve its profitability. *Before I could agree with the proposal, I would need to examine a comparative cost-benefit analysis for the two locations.*

Chapter 3: Analytical Writing Assessment

Writing Style and Mechanics

As you know by now, although GMAT readers place less weight on writing style and mechanics than on content and organization, the way you write *can* affect your Analytical Writing Assessment score, especially if you've written an otherwise borderline essay that has the reader "on the fence" between two scores. (It happens frequently!)

Earlier in the chapter, you learned some basic tips for style and mechanics. The Next Level moves on to more advanced techniques. Here, you'll learn the following:

- A variety of rhetorical devices that, if used appropriately and prudently, add persuasiveness to essays (especially your Issue essay)

- How to connect your ideas together with words and phrases that will help the reader follow your reasoning as you proceed from one point to the next

- The parlance of Critical Reasoning, and how to use it properly (in your Argument essay)

- How to refer to yourself, to the statement or Argument, and to the author of the statement or Argument

Alert!

As we've mentioned before, however, refinement and maturity in writing style come mainly with practice. So you should also apply what you learn here to the practice tests in Part V of this book.

Developing a Persuasive Writing Style

Earlier in this lesson, you learned how to develop persuasive *ideas* (especially for your Issue essay) and to structure and sequence your paragraphs in ways that enhance their persuasiveness. To further ensure a high Analytical Writing Assessment score, you should try to use particular words and phrases that can be especially effective rhetorically, but you should avoid words and phrases that amount to so-called "empty rhetoric." You can also use *irony*, and even *punctuation*, for rhetorical emphasis.

Rhetorical words and phrases—by functional category

Here's a reference list of rhetorical words and phrases, categorized by function. Some list items you encountered as underlined words and phrases in the examples throughout previous chapters, while others are new.

Take It to the Next Level

Use phrases such as these to subordinate an idea:

> although it might appear that, at first glance it would seem/appear that, admittedly

Use phrases such as these to argue for a position, thesis, or viewpoint:

> promotes, facilitates, provides a strong impetus, serves to, directly, furthers, accomplishes, achieves, demonstrates, suggests, indicates

Use phrases such as these to argue for a solution or direction based on public policy or some other normative basis:

> ultimate goal/objective/purpose, overriding, primary concern, subordinate, subsumed

Use phrases such as these to refute, rebut, or counter a proposition, theory, or viewpoint:

> however, closer scrutiny reveals, upon closer inspection/examination, a more thorough analysis, in reality, actually, when viewed more closely, when viewed from another perspective, further observation shows

Use phrases such as these to point out problems with a proposition, theory, or viewpoint:

> however, nevertheless, yet, still, despite, of course, serious drawbacks, problematic, countervailing factors

Use phrases such as these to argue against a position or viewpoint:

> works against, undermines, thwarts, defeats, runs contrary to, fails to achieve/promote/accomplish, is inconsistent with, impedes

Use phrases such as these to argue that the merits of one position outweigh those of another

> on balance, on the whole, all things considered, in the final analysis

X-Ref

To improve your power of persuasion, again, there's no substitute for practice. So you should try to incorporate these words and phrases into your essays as you take the practice tests in Part V of this book.

Avoid empty rhetoric

Many test-takers try to mask weak ideas by relying on strong rhetoric. Be careful in using words and phrases such as these for emphasis:

> clearly, absolutely, definitely, without a doubt, nobody could dispute that, extremely, positively, emphatically, unquestionably, certainly, undeniably, without reservation

It's okay to use these phrases. But keep in mind: By themselves, they add absolutely no substance to your ideas. So be sure that you have convincing reasons and/or examples to back up your rhetoric!

Using irony as a rhetorical device

In your Issue essay, look for the opportunity to use words in their ironic sense or as misnomers for rhetorical emphasis—in other words, to help make your point. Read the Issue statement closely for key words. Here's one example of each:

Example (irony):

> The speaker fails to consider the long-term cultural impact of the kinds of technological "advancements" I've just described.

Example (misnomer):

> The "knowledge" to which the statement refers is, in actuality, only subjective perception.

Be sure to use quotation marks for the ironic term or misnomer, whether or not you're quoting the Issue statement.

Using punctuation for rhetorical emphasis

You can also use punctuation for rhetorical emphasis. Here are some suggestions (try them out during the practice tests in Part III):

- Use em-dashes (two hyphens, or one hyphen preceded and followed by a space) in the middle of a sentence—instead of commas or parentheses—to set off particularly important parenthetical material (just like in this sentence). You can also use an em-dash before a concluding phrase instead of a comma—to help set off and emphasize what follows (just like in this sentence). But don't overuse the dash—or it will lose its punch (as in this paragraph).

- Use exclamation points for emphasis *very* sparingly. As in this paragraph, one per essay is plenty!

- Sentences that pose questions can be a useful rhetorical device. Like short, abrupt sentences, rhetorical questions can help persuade the reader—or at least help to make your point. They can be quite effective, especially in Issue essays. They also add interest and variety. Yet how many test-takers think to incorporate them into their essays? Not many. (By the way, we just posed a rhetorical question.) Just be sure to provide an answer to your question. And don't overdo it; one rhetorical question per essay is plenty.

- Avoid using UPPERCASE letters, *asterisks* or similar devices to flag words you would emphasize in rhetorical *speech*. To get your point across, rely instead on your choice of words and phrases as well as your sentence construction.

> **Note**
> As noted in Part I, the testing system's word processor does not permit the use of attributes such as bold, underlining, and italics—so those devices are not available for emphasis in any event.

Connecting Your Ideas Together

Your essays will not earn top scores unless your ideas flow naturally from one to the next, allowing the reader to easily follow your train of thought. To connect your ideas, develop your own arsenal of transition devices—words and phrases that serve as bridges between ideas—helping to convey your line of reasoning to the reader.

Each transition device should help the reader make certain connections or assumptions about the two areas that you are connecting. For example, some devices lead your reader forward and imply the building of an idea or thought, while others prompt the reader to compare ideas or draw conclusions from the preceding thoughts.

Here's a reference list that includes many of those devices—by functional category.

To signal addition:

and, again, and then, besides, equally important, finally, further, furthermore, nor, too, next, lastly, what's more

To connect ideas together:

furthermore, additionally, in addition, also, [first, second, . . .], moreover, most important/significantly, consequently, simultaneously, concurrently, next, finally

To signal comparison or contrast:

but, although, conversely, in contrast, on the other hand, whereas, but, except, by comparison, where, compared to, weighed against, vis-à-vis, while, meanwhile

To signal proof:

> because, for, since, for the same reason, obviously, evidently, furthermore, moreover, besides, indeed, in fact, in addition, in any case, that is

To signal exception:

> yet, still, however, nevertheless, in spite of, despite, of course, occasionally, sometimes, in rare instances, infrequently

To signal sequence (chronological, logical, or rhetorical):

> [first, second(ly), third(ly), . . .], next, then, now, at this point, then, after, in turn, subsequently, finally, consequently, previously, beforehand, simultaneously, concurrently

To signal examples:

> for example, for instance, perhaps, consider, take the case of, to demonstrate, to illustrate, as an illustration, one possible scenario, in this case, in another case, on this occasion, in this situation

To signal your reasoning from premise to conclusion:

> therefore, thus, hence, accordingly, as a result, it follows that, hence, therefore, accordingly, thus, as a result, in turn

Use these phrases for your concluding or summary paragraph:

> in sum, in the final analysis, in brief, summing up, in conclusion, to conclude, to recapitulate, in essence, in a nutshell

Tip: For insights and ideas about how use these transition words and phrases in your GMAT essays, read again the sample essays earlier in this chapter. Look particularly at the underlined words and phrases; they provide the glue to connect together the pieces of those essays.

Using the Language of Critical Reasoning

In your essays, you don't need to resort to the technical terminology of formal logic. However, you will need to use less technical words, such as "argument," "assumption," "conclusion," and possibly "premise" and "inference"—especially in your Argument essay. Be sure you understand what these words mean and that your use of them is idiomatic. Here are definitions for these terms and usage guidelines.

> **Argument:** The process of reasoning from premises to conclusion
>
> To describe a flawed argument, use adjectives such as *weak*, *poor*, *unsound*, *poorly reasoned*, *dubious*, *poorly supported*, and *problematic*.

To describe a good argument use adjectives such as *strong*, *convincing*, *well reasoned*, and *well supported*.

You don't "prove an argument"; rather, you "prove an argument (to be) true." (However, the word "prove" implies deduction and should be used sparingly, if at all, in your Argument essay.)

Premise: A proposition helping to support an argument's conclusion

Use the words *premise* and *evidence* interchangeably to refer to stated information that is not in dispute.

Assumption: Something taken for granted to be true in the argument. (Strictly speaking, assumptions are unstated, assumed premises.)

To describe an assumption, use adjectives such as *unsupported*, *unsubstantiated*, and *unproven*.

To describe a particularly bad assumption, use adjectives such as *unlikely*, *poor*, *questionable*, *doubtful*, *dubious*, and *improbable*.

To strengthen an argument, you *substantiate* an assumption or *prove* (or *show* or *demonstrate*) that the assumption is true. (However, be careful in using the word *prove*; it is a strong word that implies deduction.)

Strictly speaking, an assumption is neither "true" nor "false," neither "correct" nor "incorrect." Also, you don't "prove an assumption."

Conclusion: A proposition derived by deduction or inference from the premises of an argument.

To describe a poor conclusion, use adjectives such as *indefensible*, *unjustified*, *unsupported*, *improbable*, and *weak*.

To describe a good conclusion, use adjectives such as *well-supported*, *proper*, *probable*, *well-justified*, and *strong*.

Although you can "prove a conclusion" or "provide proof for a conclusion," again the word "proof" implies deduction. You're better off "supporting a conclusion" or "showing that the conclusion is probable."

Inference: The process of deriving from assumed premises (assumptions) either a strict conclusion or a conclusion that is to some degree probable.

You can describe an inference as *poor*, *unjustified*, *improbable*, or *unlikely*.

You can also describe an inference as *strong*, *justified*, *probable*, or *likely*.

Chapter 3: Analytical Writing Assessment

You can "infer that . . .", but the phrase "infer a conclusion" is awkward.

Deduction: The process of reasoning in which the conclusion follows necessarily from the premises. (Deduction is a specific kind of inference.)

> **Alert!**
>
> GMAT Arguments do not involve deduction; all inferences and conclusions involve probabilities, not certainties. So there's no reason to use any form of the word "deduction" in your Argument essay.

References to Yourself and to the Statement or Argument

In your essay, occasionally you'll need to refer to the Issue statement (or Argument) as well to its hypothetical source, whether a person or entity. You might also wish to refer to yourself from time to time. Here are some guidelines for handling these references.

Self-references

Self-references—singular as well as plural—are perfectly acceptable, though optional. Just be consistent.

"I disagree with . . ."

"In my view, . . ."

"Without additional evidence, we cannot assume that . . ."

References to the statement or Argument

In your Issue essay, refer to the statement as "this statement" or an alternative such as "this claim" or "this assertion." In your Argument essay, try using "argument" to refer to the passage's line of reasoning as a whole, or "recommendation" or "claim" to refer to specific conclusions.

References to the source of the statement or Argument

Be sure your references to a statement or Argument's source are appropriate. In your Issue essay, you can simply refer to the statement's source as the "speaker," for example. In your Argument essay, the first time you refer to the source, be specific and correct—e.g., "this editorial," "the ad," "the vice president," or "ACME Shoes." If no specific source is provided, try using "author" or "argument."

Part II: Analytical Writing Assessment

Pronoun references to an Argument's proponent

In your Argument essay, it's okay to save keystrokes by using an occasional pronoun. Just be sure that your pronouns are appropriate and consistent (male, female, or neither):

"The speaker argues . . . *Her* line of reasoning is . . . but *she* overlooks. . . ."

"The manager cites . . . in support of *his* argument . . . *He* then recommends . . ."

"To strengthen *its* conclusion, the city council must . . . *It* must also . . ."

Also, be sure that your pronoun references are clear. If a pronoun is separated from its antecedent (the noun that it describes) by one or more sentences, don't use a pronoun.

> **Note**
> Readers will disregard whether you use masculine, feminine, or gender-neutral terms in your essays. In other words, don't worry about your political correctness (or incorrectness) when it comes to gender. If you wish to use gender-neutral pronouns, that's fine. However, avoid alternating male and female examples and expressions; you might confuse the reader.

Shorthand references to an Argument's source and evidence

It's perfectly acceptable to save keystrokes with shorthand names or acronyms in place of multiple-word proper nouns. If you use an acronym, be sure to identify it the first time you use it. For example:

In this Argument, the marketing director for Specialty Manufacturing (SM) recommends that SM discontinue its line of.

Quoting the statement or Argument

Occasionally, it may be appropriate to quote key words or phrases from the Issue statement or Argument. For example, you may wish to point out to the reader a key phrase that is ambiguous or vague (e.g., "certain respondents"), or a term that is overly inclusive or exclusive (e.g., "only" or "all"). Just keep the number of quoted words and phrases to a minimum. Also, there's never any justification for quoting entire sentences.

PART III

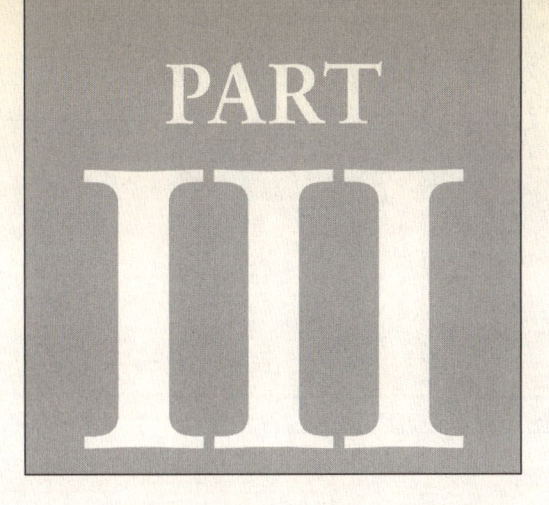

Quantitative Ability

Problem Solving *136*

Data Sufficiency *164*

Math Review—Number Forms, Relationships, and Sets *190*

Math Review—Number Theory and Algebra *230*

Math Review—Geometry *279*

Chapter 4

Problem Solving

Welcome to GMAT Problem Solving. In this chapter, you'll:

- Learn a step-by-step approach to handling any Problem Solving question
- Learn success keys for tackling Problem Solving questions

To handle GMAT Problem Solving questions, you'll need to be well versed in the fundamental rules of arithmetic, algebra, and geometry. Your knowledge of these basics is, to a large extent, what's being tested. (That's what the math reviews in Chapters 5–7 are all about.)

But, the test-makers are just as interested, if not more interested, in gauging your mental agility, flexibility, creativity, and efficiency when it comes to solving quantitative problems. More specifically, they design Problem Solving questions to help determine the following:

- Can you manipulate numbers with a certain end result already in mind?
- Can you see the dynamic relationships between numbers as you apply operations to them?
- Can you visualize geometric shapes and relationships between shapes?
- Can you devise unconventional solutions to conventional quantitative problems?
- Can you solve problems efficiently, by recognizing the easiest, quickest, or most reliable route to a solution?

This chapter will help give you the skills you need to answer "yes" to these questions. What follows might strike you as merely a series of tips, shortcuts, or secrets for GMAT Problem Solving. However, the skills you'll learn here are intrinsic to the test—and along with your knowledge of substantive rules of math—they're precisely what Problem Solving questions are designed to measure.

Problem Solving—Your 5-Step Game Plan

The first task in this chapter is to learn the five basic steps for handling any GMAT Problem Solving question. You'll apply these steps to three sample questions.

Sample Questions

Question 1 is a word problem involving *changes in percent*. (Word problems account for about half of the Quantitative questions.)

1. If Susan drinks 10% of the juice from a 16-ounce bottle immediately before lunch and 20% of the remaining amount with lunch, approximately how many ounces of juice are left to drink after lunch?

    A. 4.8
    B. 5.5
    C. 11.2
    D. 11.5
    E. 13.0

This next Problem Solving question involves the concept of *arithmetic mean* (simple average).

2. The average of 6 numbers is 19. When one of those numbers is removed, the average of the remaining 5 numbers is 21. What number was taken away?

    A. 2
    B. 8
    C. 9
    D. 11
    E. 20

Part III: Quantitative Ability

Here's a somewhat more difficult Problem Solving question. This one involves the concept of *proportion*.

3. If p pencils cost $2q$ dollars, how many pencils can you buy for c cents? [Note: 1 dollar = 100 cents]

   A. $\dfrac{pc}{2q}$

   B. $\dfrac{pc}{200q}$

   C. $\dfrac{50pc}{q}$

   D. $\dfrac{2pc}{c}$

   E. $200pcq$

> **Note:** Notice that instead of performing a numerical computation, your task in question 3 is to *express a computational process* in terms of letters. Expressions such as these are known as *literal expressions*, and they can be perplexing! On the GMAT, you'll probably find two or three of them among the 25–26 Problem Solving questions.

The 5-Step Plan

Here's the 5-step approach that will help you to handle any Problem Solving question. Just a few pages ahead, we'll apply this approach our three sample Problem Solving questions.

Step 1: Size up the question. Read the question and then pause for a moment to ask yourself:

- What specific subject area is being covered?
- What rules and formulas are likely to come into play?
- How complex is this question? (How many steps are involved in solving it? Does it require setting up equations, or does it require merely a few quick calculations?)
- Do I have a clue, off the top of my head, how I would begin solving this problem?

Determine how much time you're willing to spend on the problem, if any. Recognizing a "toughie" when you see it may save you valuable time; if you don't have a clue, take a guess and move on.

Chapter 4: Problem Solving

> **Note**
>
> Remember: The computerized GMAT testing system determines the difficulty level of your questions based on your responses to prior questions. So if you respond incorrectly to toughies, you'll see fewer of them later in your Quantitative section.

Step 2: Size up the answer choices. Before you attempt to solve the problem at hand, examine the answer choices. They can provide helpful clues about how to proceed in solving the problem and about what sort of solution you should be aiming for. Pay particular attention to the following:

- *Form:* Are the answer choices expressed as percentages, fractions, or decimals? Ounces or pounds? Minutes or hours? If the answer choices are expressed as equations, are all variables together on one side of the equation? As you work through the problem, rewrite numbers and expressions to the same form as the answer choices.

- *Value:* Are the answer choices extremely small valued numbers? Numbers between 1 and 10? Greater numbers? Negative or positive numbers? Do the answer choices vary widely in value, or their values clustered closely around an average? If all answer choices are tightly clustered in value, you can probably disregard decimal points and extraneous zeros in performing calculations. At the same time, however, you should be more careful about rounding off your figures where answer choices do not vary widely. Wide variation in value suggests that you can easily eliminate answer choices that don't correspond to the general value of number suggested by the question.

- *Other distinctive properties and characteristics:* Are the answer choices integers? Do they all include a variable? Do one or more include radicals (roots)? Exponents? Is there a particular term, expression, or number that they have in common?

Step 3: Look for a shortcut to the answer. Before plunging headlong into a problem, ask yourself if there's a quick, intuitive way to get to the correct answer. If the solution is a numerical value, perhaps only one answer choice is in the right ballpark. Also, some questions can be solved *intuitively*, without resort to equations and calculations. (You'll see how when we apply this step to our sample questions.)

Step 4: Set up the problem and solve it. If your intuition fails you, grab your pencil, roll up your sleeves, and do whatever computations, algebra, or other procedures are needed to solve the problem at hand. Simple problems may require just a few quick calculations, while complex algebra and geometry questions may require setting up and solving a series of equations.

Part III: Quantitative Ability

Step 5: Verify your response before moving on. After solving the problem, if your solution does *not* appear among the answer choices, go back and check your work. (You obviously made at least one mistake.) If your solution *does* appear among the choices, don't celebrate quite yet. Although there's a good chance your answer is correct, it's possible your answer is wrong, and that the test-maker anticipated your error by including a "sucker bait" answer choice—just for you and other test-takers who made the same mistake. (We'll look at some "sucker-bait" answer choices a few pages ahead.) So check the question to verify that your response corresponds to what the question calls for—in terms of value, expression, units of measure, and so forth. If it does, and you're confident that your work was careful and accurate, don't spend any more time checking your work. Confirm your response and move on to the next question.

Apply the 5-Step Plan

It's time to go back to the three sample questions you looked at a few pages back. Let's walk through them—one at a time–using the 5-step game plan you just learned.

Question 1

Question 1 is a relatively easy question. Approximately 80% of test-takers respond correctly to questions like it. Here's the question again:

1. If Susan drinks 10% of the juice from a 16-ounce bottle immediately before lunch and 20% of the remaining amount with lunch, approximately how many ounces of juice are left to drink after lunch?

    A. 4.8
    B. 5.5
    C. 11.2
    D. 11.5
    E. 13.0

Step 1: This problem involves the concept of *percent*—more specifically, *percentage decrease*. The question is asking you to perform two computations—in sequence. (The result of the first computation is used to perform the second one.) Percent questions tend to be relatively simple. All that is involved here is a two-step computation.

Chapter 4: Problem Solving

Step 2: The five answer choices in this question provide two useful clues:

1. Notice that they range in value from 4.8 to 13.0. That's a broad spectrum, isn't it? But what general value should we be looking for in a correct answer to this question? Without crunching any numbers, it's clear that most of the juice will still remain in the bottle, even after lunch. So you're looking for a value much closer to 13 than to 4. Eliminate (A) and (B).

2. Notice that each answer choice is carried to exactly one decimal place, and that the question asks for an *approximate* value. These two features are clues that you can probably round off your calculations to the nearest "tenth" as you go.

Step 3: You already eliminated (A) and (B) in step 1. But if you're on your toes, you can eliminate all but the correct answer without resort to precise calculations. Look at the question from a broader perspective. If you subtract 10% from a number, then 20% from the result, that adds up to *a bit less* than a 30% decrease from the original number. Thirty percent of 16 ounces is 4.8 ounces. So the solution must be a number that is a bit greater than 11.2 (16 − 4.8). Answer choice (D), 11.5, is the only choice that fits the bill!

> **Alert!** Many GMAT Problem Solving questions are designed to reward you for recognizing easier, more intuitive ways of narrowing down the choices to the correct answer. Don't skip over step 3. It's well worth your time to look for a shortcut to the correct answer choice.

Step 4: If your intuition fails you, go ahead and crunch the numbers. First, determine 10% of 16, then subtract that number from 16:

$$16 \times .1 = 1.6$$
$$16 - 1.6 = 14.4$$

Susan now has 14.4 ounces of juice. Now perform the second step. Determine 20% of 14.4, then subtract that number from 14.4:

$$14.4 \times .2 = 2.88$$

Round off 2.88 to the nearest tenth: 2.9

$$14.4 - 2.9 = 11.5$$

Step 5: The decimal number 11.5 is indeed among the answer choices. Before moving on, however, ask yourself whether your solution makes sense—in this case, whether the value of our number (11.5) "fits" what the question asks for. If you performed step 2, you should already realize that

Part III: Quantitative Ability

11.5 is in the right ballpark. If you're confident that your calculations were careful and accurate, confirm your response (D), and move on to the next question.

Question 2
Question 2 is average in difficulty. Approximately 60% of test-takers respond correctly to questions like it. Here's the question again:

2. The average of 6 numbers is 19. When one of those numbers is removed, the average of the remaining 5 numbers is 21. What number was taken away?

   A. 2
   B. 8
   C. 9
   D. 11
   E. 20

Step 1: This problem involves the concept of *arithmetic mean* (simple average). To handle this question, you need to be familiar with the formula for calculating the average of a series of numbers. But notice that the question does not ask for the average, but rather for one of the numbers in the series. This curveball makes the question a bit tougher than most arithmetic mean problems.

Step 2: Take a quick look at the answer choices for clues. Notice that the middle three are clustered closely together in value. So take a closer look at the two aberrations: (A) and (E). Choice (A) would be the correct answer to the question: "What is the difference between 19 and 21?" But this question is asking something entirely different, so you can probably rule out (A) as a sucker bait answer choice. Choice (E) might also be a sucker bait choice, since 20 is simply 19 + 21 divided by 2. If this solution strikes you as too simple, you've got good instincts! The correct answer is probably either (B), (C), or (D). If you're pressed for time, guess one of these, and move on to the next question. Otherwise, go to step 3.

> **Alert!**
> In complex questions, don't look for easy solutions. Problems involving algebraic formulas generally aren't solved simply by adding (or subtracting) a few numbers. Your instinct should tell you to reject easy answers to these kind of problems.

Chapter 4: Problem Solving

Step 3: If you're on your "intuitive toes," you might recognize a shortcut to the answer here. You can solve this problem quickly by simply comparing the two *sums*. Before the sixth number is taken away, the sum of the numbers is 114 (6 × 19). After removing the sixth number, the sum of the remaining numbers is 105 (5 × 21). The difference between the two sums is 9, which must be the value of the number removed.

Step 4: Lacking a burst of intuition (step 3), you can solve this problem in a conventional (and slower) manner. The formula for arithmetic mean (simple average) can be expressed this way:

$$AM = \frac{\text{sum of terms in the set}}{\text{number of terms in the set}}$$

In the question, you started with six terms. Let *a* through *f* equal those six terms:

$$19 = \frac{a + b + c + d + e + f}{6}$$
$$114 = a + b + c + d + e + f$$
$$f = 114 - (a + b + c + d + e)$$

Letting f = the number removed, here's the arithmetic-mean formula, applied to the remaining five numbers:

$$21 = \frac{a + b + c + d + e}{5}$$
$$105 = a + b + c + d + e$$

Substitute 105 for $(a + b + c + d + e)$ in the first equation:

$$f = 114 - 105$$
$$f = 9$$

The correct answer is C.

Step 5: If you have time, check to make sure you got the formula right, and check your calculations. Also make sure you didn't inadvertently switch the numbers 19 and 21 in your equations. (It's remarkably easy to commit this careless error under time pressure!) If you're satisfied that your analysis is accurate, confirm your answer and move on to the next question.

Part III: Quantitative Ability

> **Alert!**
> Take heed: On the GMAT, careless errors—such as switching two numbers in a problem—is far and away the leading cause of incorrect responses.

Question 3

Question 3 is moderately difficult. Approximately 50% of test-takers respond correctly to questions like it. Here's the question again:

3. If p pencils cost $2q$ dollars, how many pencils can you buy for c cents? [Note: 1 dollar = 100 cents]

   A. $\dfrac{pc}{2q}$

   B. $\dfrac{pc}{200q}$

   C. $\dfrac{50pc}{q}$

   D. $\dfrac{2pq}{c}$

   E. $200pcq$

Step 1: The first step is to recognize that this question involves a *literal expression*. Although it probably won't be too time-consuming, it may be a bit confusing. You should also recognize that the key to this question is the concept of *proportion*. It might be appropriate to set up an equation to solve for c. Along the way, expect to convert dollars into cents.

Step 2: The five answer choices provide a couple of useful clues:

- Notice that each answer choice includes all three letters (p, q, and c). So the solution you're shooting for must also include all three letters.

- Notice that every answer choice but (E) is a fraction. So anticipate building a fraction to solve the problem algebraically.

Step 3: Is there any way to answer this question besides setting up an algebraic equation? You bet! In fact, there are two ways. One is to use easy numbers for the three variables—for example, $p = 2$, $q = 1$, and $c = 100$. These simple numbers make the question easy to work with: "If 2 pencils cost 2 dollars, how many pencils can you buy for 100 cents?" Obviously, the answer to this question is 1. Therefore, plug in the numbers into each answer choice to see which choice provides an expression that equals 1.

Only choice (B) fits the bill: $\frac{(2)(100)}{(200)(1)} = 1$. Another way to shortcut the algebra is to apply some intuition to this question. If you strip away the pencils, *p*'s, *q*'s and *c*'s, in a very general sense the question is asking:

"If you can by an item for a dollar, how many can you buy for one *cent*?"

Since one cent (a penny) is $\frac{1}{100}$ of a dollar, you can buy $\frac{1}{100}$ of one item for a cent. So you're probably looking for a fractional answer with a large number in the denominator—something on the order of 100 (as opposed to a number such as 2, 3, or 6). Answer choice (B) is the only choice that appears to be in the correct ballpark. (B) is indeed the correct answer.

Step 4: You can also answer the question in a conventional manner using algebra. (This is easier said than done.) Here's how to approach it:

1. Express 2*q* dollars as 200*q* cents (1 dollar = 100 cents).

2. Let *x* equal the number of pencils you can buy for *c* cents.

3. Think about the problem "verbally," then set up an equation and solve for *x*:

"*p* pencils is to 200*q* cents as *x* pencils is to *c* cents"

"The ratio of *p* to 200*q* is the same as the ratio of *x* to *c*" (in other words, the two ratios are proportionate)

$$\frac{p}{200q} = \frac{x}{c}$$

$$\frac{pc}{200q} = x$$

> **Note**
>
> Don't worry if you didn't fully understand the way we set up and solved this problem. You'll learn more about how to handle GMAT proportion questions in this book's math review.

Step 5: Our solution, $\frac{pc}{200q}$, is indeed among the answer choices. If you arrived at this solution using the conventional algebraic approach (step 4), you can verify your solution by substituting simple numbers for the three variables (as we did in step 3). Or, if you arrived at your solution by plugging in numbers, you can check your work by plugging in a different set of numbers or by thinking about the problem conceptually (as in step 3). Once you're confident you've chosen the correct expression among

Part III: Quantitative Ability

the five choices, confirm your choice, and then move on to the next question. The correct answer is indeed B.

Success Keys for GMAT Problem Solving

Here are some basic tips you should follow for any type of Problem Solving question. Apply these "keys" to Part V's practice tests, and then review them again just before exam day.

Narrow Down Answer Choices Up Front by Sizing Up the Question

If the question asks for a number value, you can probably narrow down the answer choices by estimating the value and type of number you're looking for. Use your common sense and real-world experience to formulate a "ballpark" estimate for word problems.

Question 1

You can narrow down answer choices by looking at the problem from a "common sense" viewpoint. The five answer choices in this question provide some useful clues. Notice that they range in value from 4.8 to 13.0. That's a wide spectrum, isn't it? But what general value should you be looking for in a correct answer to this question? Without crunching any numbers, it's clear that most of the juice will still remain in the bottle, even after lunch. So you're looking for a value much closer to 13 than to 4. So you can safely eliminate (A) and (B).

Common Sense Can Sometimes Reveal the Right Answer

In many questions, you can eliminate all but the correct answer without resorting to precise calculations.

Question 1

Look at the question from a broader perspective. If you subtract 10% from a number, then 20% from the result, that adds up to *a bit less* than a 30% decrease from the original number. Thirty percent of 16 ounces is 4.8 ounces. So the solution must be a number that is a bit greater than 11.2 (16 − 4.8). Choice (D), 11.5, is the only choice that fits the bill!

Question 3

In Question 3, notice that c is a much greater number than either p or q. Only a fraction with c in the numerator and a large number in the denominator (or vice versa) is likely to yield a quotient you're looking for. With this in mind, choice (B) jumps off the paper at you as the likely choice!

Scan the Answer Choices for Clues to Solving the Problem

Scan the answer choices to see what all or most of them have in common—such as radical signs, exponents, factorable expressions, or fractions. Then try to formulate a solution that looks like the answer choices.

Question 3

Notice that each answer choice includes all three letters (p, q, and c). So the solution you're aiming for must also include all three letters. Also, notice that every answer but choice (E) is a *fraction*. So, anticipate building a fraction to solve the problem.

Don't Be Reeled in by Too-Obvious, Sucker-Bait Answer Choices

The test-makers will intentionally tempt or "bait" you with wrong-answer choices that result from making common errors in calculation and in setting up and solving equations. Don't assume that your response is correct just because your solution appears among the five answer choices! Rely instead on your sense for whether you understood what the question called for and performed the calculations and other steps carefully and accurately.

Question 1

In this question, each of the four incorrect choices is sucker bait:

A.	4.8	You performed the wrong calculation: 30% of 16 ounces = 4.8 ounces
B.	5.5	This is the number of ounces Susan drank. (The question asks for the amount remaining.)
C.	11.2	You performed the wrong calculation: 30% of 16 ounces = 4.8 ounces 16 − 4.8 = 11.2
D.	11.5	This is the correct answer.
E.	13.0	You confused percentages with raw numbers, erroneously converting 30% (10% + 20%) into 3.0: 16 − 3.0 = 13.0

Question 2
This question contains two sucker bait answer choices:

| A. | 2 | This would be the correct answer to the question: "What is the difference between 19 and 21?" But this question is asking something entirely different. |
| E. | 20 | 20 is simply 19 + 21 divided by 2. If this solution strikes you as too simple, you've got good instincts! |

Don't do More Work Than Needed to Get to the Answer

If the question asks for an approximation, that's a huge clue that precise calculations aren't necessary.

Question 1
Notice that each answer choice is carried to exactly one decimal place, and that the question asks for an approximate value. These two features are clues that you can probably round off your calculations to the nearest tenth as you go.

Look for Shortcuts to Conventional Ways of Solving Problems

The adage "There's more than one way to skin a cat" applies to many GMAT Problem Solving questions.

Question 2
You can solve this problem quickly by simply comparing the two *sums*. Before the sixth number is removed, the sum of the numbers is 114 (6×19). After removing the sixth number, the sum of the remaining numbers is 105 (5×21). The difference between the two sums is 9, which must be the value of the number.

Know When to Plug in Numbers for Variables

If the answer choices contain variables (like x and y), the question might be a good candidate for the "plug-in" strategy. Pick simple numbers (so the math is easy) and substitute them for the variables. You'll definitely need your pencil for this strategy.

Chapter 4: Problem Solving

Question 3

This question was a perfect candidate for the plug-in strategy. Instead of trying to figure out how to set up and solve an algebraic equation, in step 3 we used easy numbers for the three variables, then plugged those numbers into each answer choice to see which choice worked.

Know When to Work Backward from Numerical Answer Choices

If a Problem Solving question asks for a number value, and if you draw a blank as far as how to set up and solve the problem, don't panic. You might be able work backward by testing each answer choice. This might take a bit of time, but if you test the answer choices in random order, the statistical odds are that you'll only need to test three choices to find the correct one.

Question 2

You already learned that comparing the two sums is the quickest shortcut to the answer. But if this strategy didn't occur to you, working backward from the answer choices would be the next quickest method. After the sixth number is removed, the sum of the five remaining numbers is $21 \times 5 = 105$. So, to test an answer choice, add this sum to the number provided in the choice, dividing the new sum by 6. If the result is 19, you've found the correct choice. Here's how to do the math for choice (C), which is the correct answer choice:

$$\frac{105 + 9}{6} = \frac{114}{6} = 19$$

> **Tip**
>
> Problem Solving questions always list numerical answer choices in ascending order of value. So, if you use the strategy of working backward, start with the median value: choice (C). If (C) turns out too great, you know the correct answer must be either (A) or (B). Conversely, if (C) turns out too small valued, then either (D) or (E) must be correct. Of course, you might also be able to eliminate an answer choice right away by sizing up the questions (a previous strategy). Doing so would make your job even quicker!

Always Check Your Work

Always check your work. Here are three suggestions for doing so:

1. Do a reality check. Ask yourself whether your solution makes sense based upon what the question asks. (This check is especially appropriate for word problems.)

2. For questions where you solve algebraic equations, plug your solution into the equation(s) to make sure it works.

3. Confirm your calculations (except for the simplest no-brainers) with your calculator. It's amazingly easy to accidentally push the wrong button.

> **Alert!**
> Checking your calculations is especially crucial for questions asking for an approximation. Why? If your solution doesn't precisely match one of the five answer choices, you might conclude that you should just pick the choice that's closest to your solution—a big mistake if you miscalculated!

Question 1
A reality check on this question will tell you that answer choice (C), 11.5, seems about right, but that most of the other choices don't.

Read the Question One Last Time before Moving on

Among GMAT test-takers, simple carelessness in reading a Problem Solving question is by far the most likely cause of an incorrect answer. So even if your solution is among the choices, and you're confident your calculations are accurate, don't move on quite yet. Read the question again. Make sure you answered the precise question asked. For example, does the question ask for:

- Arithmetic mean or median?
- A circumference or an area?
- A sum or a difference?
- A perimeter or a length of one side only?
- An aggregate rate or a single rate?
- Total time or average time?

Also check to make sure you:

- Used the same numbers provided in the question
- Didn't inadvertently switch any numbers or other expressions
- Didn't use raw numbers where percentages were provided, or vice-versa

Question 1
The question asked for the amount of juice remaining, not the amount Susan drank. Also, a careless test-taker might subtract 10 ounces instead of 10%.

Question 2
A careless test-taker might inadvertently switch the numbers 19 and 21.

Question 3
The question asks for an answer in cents, not dollars.

Take It to the Next Level

Welcome to the Next Level of GMAT Problem Solving. At this point, you'll:

- Apply the success keys you learned earlier to more challenging Problem Solving questions
- Learn additional success keys that apply to certain types of Problem Solving questions, and apply these keys to example questions

What's New at the Next Level

Here at the Next Level, you'll explore some of the strategies you learned earlier in this chapter—applying them to GMAT-style questions that are a bit more challenging. You'll also learn some additional strategies that apply to certain types of Problem Solving questions.

Scan the Answer Choices for Clues to Solving the Problem

Scan the answer choices to see what all or most of them have in common—such as radical signs, exponents, factorable expressions, or fractions. Then, try to formulate a solution that looks like the answer choices.

If $a \neq 0$ or 1, then $\dfrac{\frac{1}{a}}{2 - \frac{2}{a}} =$

A. $\dfrac{1}{2a - 2}$

B. $\dfrac{2}{a - 2}$

C. $\dfrac{1}{a - 2}$

D. $\dfrac{1}{a}$

E. $\dfrac{2}{2a - 1}$

The correct answer is A. Notice what all the answer choices have in common: Each one is a fraction in which the denominator contains the variable a. And, there are no fractions in either the numerator or the denominator. That's a clue that your job is to manipulate the expression given in the question so that the result includes these features. First, place the denominator's two terms over the common denominator a. Then, divide a from the denominators of both the numerator fraction and the denominator fraction (this is a shortcut to multiplying the numerator fraction by the reciprocal of the denominator fraction):

$$\dfrac{\frac{1}{a}}{2 - \frac{2}{a}} = \dfrac{\frac{1}{a}}{\frac{2a - 2}{a}} = \dfrac{1}{2a - 2}$$

Use Common-Sense "Guesstimates" to Narrow the Field—But Know the Limits of This Strategy

If the question asks for a numerical value, you can probably narrow down the answer choices by estimating the value and type of number you're looking for. Use your common sense and real-world experience to formulate a "ballpark" estimate for word problems. But keep in mind: Don't expect to eliminate all answer choices but the correct one by common sense alone.

A spinner containing seven equal regions numbered 1 through 7 is spun two times in a row. What is the probability that the first spin yields an odd number and the second spin yields an even number?

A. $\dfrac{2}{7}$

B. $\dfrac{12}{49}$

C. $\dfrac{5}{14}$

D. $\dfrac{1}{2}$

E. $\dfrac{4}{7}$

The correct answer is B. This problem involves the concept of probability. Common sense about basic probability should tell you that, with odds of *close to* 50% of spinning the desired type of number on each of the two spins, the odds of spinning such a number twice in a row should be less than 50%. So, you can eliminate choices (D) and (E). Your odds of answering the question correctly are now 1 in 3. But notice that the remaining choices—(A), (B), and (C)—are closely grouped in value. Also notice that, in each of these remaining choices, the denominator contains the sort of number you could end up with when you apply a mathematical operation to the numbers given in the question.

Conclusion: You've probably reached the limits of applying common sense, and you'll need to solve the problem mathematically to find the correct choice. Here's how to do it. There are four odd numbers (1, 3, 5, and 7) and three even numbers (2, 4, and 6) on the spinner. So, the chances of yielding an odd number with the first spin are 4 in 7, or $\dfrac{4}{7}$. The chances of yielding an even number with the second spin are 3 in 7, or $\dfrac{3}{7}$. To determine the probability of both events occurring, combine the two individual probabilities by multiplication:

$$\dfrac{4}{7} \times \dfrac{3}{7} = \dfrac{12}{49}$$

Chapter 4: Problem Solving

> **Alert!**
>
> Notice the sucker-bait answer choice in this question: Answer choice (D) provides the simple average of the two individual probabilities: $\frac{4}{7}$ and $\frac{3}{7}$. Aside from the fact that $\frac{1}{2}$, or 50%, is too high a probability from a common-sense viewpoint, should strike you as too easy a solution to what appears to be a complex problem.

Know When to Plug in Numbers for Variables

If the answer choices contain variables (like *x* and *y*), the question might be a good candidate for the "plug-in" strategy. Pick simple numbers (so the math is easy), and substitute them for the variables. You'll definitely need your pencil for this strategy.

If a train travels *r* + 2 miles in *h* hours, which of the following represents the number of miles the train travels in 1 hour and 30 minutes?

A. $\dfrac{3r + 6}{2h}$

B. $\dfrac{3r}{h + 2}$

C. $\dfrac{r + 2}{h + 3}$

D. $\dfrac{r}{h + 6}$

E. $\dfrac{3}{2}(r + 2)$

The correct answer is A. This is an algebraic word problem involving rate of motion (speed). You can solve this problem either conventionally or by using the plug-in strategy.

The conventional way: Notice that all of the answer choices contain fractions. This is a clue that you should try to create a fraction as you solve the problem. Here's how to do it. Given that the train travels *r* + 2 miles in *h* hours, you can express its rate in miles per hour as $\dfrac{r+2}{h}$. In $\dfrac{3}{2}$ hours, the train would travel $\dfrac{3}{2}$ this distance:

$$\left(\dfrac{3}{2}\right)\left(\dfrac{r+2}{h}\right) = \dfrac{3r+6}{2h}$$

Take It to the Next Level

The plug-in strategy: Let $r = 8$ and $h = 1$. Given these values, the train travels 10 miles ($8 + 2$) in 1 hour. Obviously, in $1\frac{1}{2}$ hours the train will travel 15 miles. Start plugging these r and h values into the answer choices. You won't need to go any further than choice (A):

$$\frac{3r + 6}{2h} = \frac{3(8) + 6}{2(1)} = \frac{30}{2}, \text{ or } 15$$

> **Tip**
>
> Even if you had no clue how to handle this question, you could at least eliminate choice (E) out of hand. It omits h! Common sense should tell you that the correct answer must include both r and h.

Know When to Work Backward from Numerical Answer Choices

If a Problem Solving question asks for a number value, and if you draw a blank as far as how to set up and solve the problem, don't panic. You might be able to work backward by testing the answer choices, each one in turn.

> A ball is dropped 192 inches above level ground, and after the third bounce, it rises to a height of 24 inches. If the height to which the ball rises after each bounce is always the same fraction of the height reached on its previous bounce, what is this fraction?
>
> A. $\frac{1}{8}$
>
> B. $\frac{1}{4}$
>
> C. $\frac{1}{3}$
>
> D. $\frac{1}{2}$
>
> E. $\frac{2}{3}$
>
> **The correct answer is D.** The fastest route to a solution is to plug in an answer. Try choice (C), and see what happens. If the ball bounces up $\frac{1}{3}$ as high as it started, then after the first bounce it will rise up $\frac{1}{3}$ as high as 192

inches, or 64 inches. After a second bounce, it will rise $\frac{1}{3}$ as high, or about 21 inches. But, the problem states that the ball rises to 24 inches after the *third* bounce. Obviously, if the ball rises less than that after two bounces, it'll be way too low after three. So, choice (C) cannot be the correct answer.

We can see that the ball must be bouncing higher than one third of the way; so the correct answer must be a greater fraction, either choice (D) or choice (E). You've already narrowed your odds to 50%. Try plugging in choice (D), and you'll see that it works: $\frac{1}{2}$ of 192 is 96; $\frac{1}{2}$ of 96 is 48; and $\frac{1}{2}$ of 48 is 24.

Although it would be possible to develop a formula to answer the question, doing so would be senseless, considering how quickly and easily you can work backward from the answer choices.

Know When Not to Work Backward from Numerical Answer Choices

Working backward from numerical answer choices works well when the numbers are easy, and when few calculations are required, as in the preceding question. In other cases, applying algebra might be a better way.

> How many pounds of nuts selling for 70 cents per pound must be mixed with 30 pounds of nuts selling at 90 cents per pound to make a mixture that sells for 85 cents per pound?
>
> A. 10
> B. 12
> C. 15
> D. 20
> E. 24

The correct answer is A. Is the easiest route to the solution to test the answer choices? Let's see. First of all, calculate the total cost of 30 pounds of nuts at 90 cents per pound: 30 × .90 = $27. Now, start with choice (C). 15 pounds of nuts at 70 cents per pound costs $9.50. The total cost of this mixture is $36.50, and the total weight is 45 pounds. Now you'll need to perform long division. The average weight of the mixture turns out to be between 81 and 82 cents—too small valued for the 85 cent average given in the question. At least you can eliminate choice (C).

You should realize by now that testing the answer choices might not be the most efficient way to tackle this question. Besides, there are ample

Part III: Quantitative Ability

opportunities for calculation errors. Instead, try solving this problem algebraically—by writing and solving a system of equations. Here's how to do it. The cost (in cents) of the nuts selling for 70 cents per pound can be expressed as $70x$, letting x equal the number that you're asked to determine. You then add this cost to the cost of the more expensive nuts ($30 \times 90 = 2,700$) to obtain the total cost of the mixture, which you can express as $85(x + 30)$. You can state this algebraically and solve for x as follows:

$$70x + 2,700 = 85(x + 30)$$
$$70x + 2,700 = 85x + 2,550$$
$$150 = 15x$$
$$10 = x$$

10 pounds of 70-cent-per-pound nuts must be added in order to make a mixture that sells for 85 cents per pound.

Avoid Heavy Lifting; Look for the Easiest Route to the Answer

If the question asks for an approximation, then you know that precise calculations won't be necessary, and you can safely "round off" the numbers as you go. But, even in other questions, you can sometimes eliminate all but the correct answer without resort to precise calculations.

What is the difference between the sum of all positive even integers less than 102 and the sum of all positive odd integers less than 102?

A. 0
B. 1
C. 50
D. 51
E. 101

The correct answer is D. To see the pattern, compare the initial terms of each sequence:

even integers: {2,4,6, . . . 100}
odd integers: {1,3,5, . . . , 99,101}

Notice that, for each successive term, the odd integer is one less than the corresponding even integer. There are a total of 50 corresponding integers, so the difference between the sums of all these corresponding integers is 50. But the odd-integer sequence includes one additional integer: 101. So the difference is ($-50 + 101$), or 51.

Chapter 4: Problem Solving

If a Geometry Problem Provides a Figure, Mine it for Clues

Most geometry problems are accompanied by figures. They're there for a reason! The pieces of information a figure provides can lead you, step-by-step, to the answer.

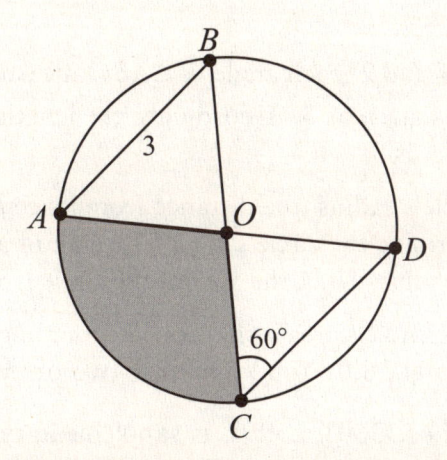

If O is the center of the circle in the figure above, what is the area of the shaded region, expressed in square units?

A. $\dfrac{3}{2}\pi$

B. 2π

C. $\dfrac{5}{2}\pi$

D. $\dfrac{8}{3}\pi$

E. 3π

The correct answer is E. This question asks for the area of a portion of the circle defined by a central angle. To answer the question, you'll need to determine the area of the entire circle as well as what percent (portion) of that area is shaded. This multi-step question is as complex as any you might encounter on the GMAT. But there's no need to panic; just start with what you know, then move step-by-step toward the answer. Mine the figure for a piece of information that might provide a starting point. $\triangle OCD$ is your first "stepping stone." Here are the steps to the answer:

You know that $\overline{OC}$ and $\overline{OD}$ are congruent (equal in length) because each one is the circle's radius. In any triangle, angles opposite congruent sides are also congruent (the same size, or degree measure). Thus, ∠ODC must measure 60°—just like ∠OCD.

For any triangle, the sum of the measures of all three interior angles is 180°. Thus, ∠COD measures 60°, just like the other two angles.

Vertical angles created by two intersecting lines are congruent. Thus, ∠AOB also measures 60°.

By the same reasoning as in steps 1 and 2, each angle of △ABO measures 60°. Notice that the length of $\overline{AB}$ is given as 3. Accordingly, the length of each and every side of both triangles is 3.

Since this length (3) is also the circle's radius (the distance from its center to its circumference), you can determine the circle's area. The area of any circle is πr^2, where r is the circle's radius. Thus, the area of the circle is 9π.

Now determine what portion of the circle's area is shaded. The four angles formed at the circle's center (O) total 360°. You know that two of these angles account for 120°, or $\frac{1}{3}$ of those 360°. ∠AOC is supplementary to ∠DOC; that is, the two angles combine to form a straight line, and so their measures total 180°. Therefore, ∠AOC measures 120°.

120° is $\frac{1}{3}$ of 360°. Thus, the shaded portion accounts for $\frac{1}{3}$ the circle's area, or 3π.

> **Tip**
>
> If you look at the 60° angle in the figure, you might recognize right away that both triangles are equilateral and, extended out to their arcs, form two "pie slices," each one $\frac{1}{6}$ the size of the whole "pie" (the circle). What's left are two big slices, each of which is twice the size of a small slice. So the shaded area must account for $\frac{1}{3}$ the circle's area. With this intuition, the problem is reduced to the simple mechanics of calculating the circle's area, then dividing it by 3.

If A Geometry Problem Doesn't Provide A Figure, Sketch One

A geometry problem that does not provide a diagram might cry out for one. That's your cue to take pencil to scratch paper and draw one yourself.

> A rancher uses 64 feet of fencing to create a rectangular horse corral. If the ratio of the corral's length to width is 3:1, which of the following most closely approximates the minimum length of additional fencing needed to divide the rectangular corral into three triangular corrals, one of which is exactly twice the area of the other two?
>
> A. 24 feet
> B. 29 feet
> C. 36 feet
> D. 41 feet
> E. 48 feet

The correct answer is B. Your first step is to determine the dimensions of the rectangular corral. Given a 3:1 length-to-width ratio, you can solve for the width (w) of the field using the perimeter formula:

$$2(3w) + 2(w) = 64$$
$$8w = 64$$
$$w = 8$$

Accordingly, the length of the rectangular corral is 24 feet. Next, determine how the rancher must configure the additional fencing to meet the stated criteria. This calls for a bit of sketching to help you visualize the dimensions. Only two possible configurations create three triangular corrals with the desired ratios:

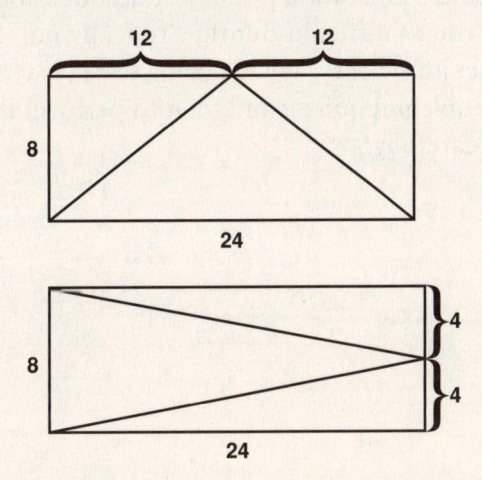

The top figure requires less fencing. You can determine this fact by calculating each length (using the Pythagorean theorem). Or you can also use logic and visualization. Here's how. As a rectangle becomes flatter ("less square"), the shorter length approaches zero (0), at which point the minimum amount of fencing needed in the top configuration would decrease, approaching the length of the longer side. However, in the bottom design, the amount of fencing needed would increase, approaching twice the length of the longer side.

Your final step is to calculate the amount of fencing required by the top design, applying the Theorem (let x = either length of cross-fencing):

$$8^2 + 12^2 = x^2$$
$$64 + 144 = x^2$$
$$208 = x^2$$
$$x = \sqrt{208} \approx 14.4$$

Thus, a minimum of approximately 28.8 feet of fencing is needed. Answer choice (B) approximates this solution.

> **Tip**
>
> Since the question asks for an approximation, it's a safe bet that estimating $\sqrt{208}$ to the nearest integer will suffice. If you learned your "times table," you know that $14 \times 14 = 196$, and $15 \times 15 = 225$. So $\sqrt{200}$ must be between 14 and 15. That's close enough to zero in on choice (B), which provides twice that estimate.

To Handle "Defined Operation" Questions, Just Plug in the Numbers

At least one of your 25–26 Problem Solving questions will probably be an example of what's called a "defined operation." These questions look weird and therefore might strike you as difficult. But they're really not. In fact, the math turns out to be ridiculously easy. What's being tested is your ability to understand what the problem requires, and then to perform the simple arithmetical calculations, carefully!

Let $\langle{}^b_a{}^{\ }_d{}^c\rangle$ be defined for all numbers a, b, c, and d by $\langle{}^b_a{}^{\ }_d{}^c\rangle$ = $ac - bd$. If $x = \langle{}^4_5{}^{\ }_1{}^2\rangle$, what is the value of $\langle{}^{10}_x{}^{\ }_1{}^2\rangle$?

A. 1
B. 2
C. 18
D. 38
E. 178

The correct answer is B. In defining the diamond-shaped figure as "$ac - bd$," the test-makers are saying that whenever you see four numbers in a diamond like this, you should plug them into the mathematical expression shown in the order given. The question itself then requires you to perform this simple task twice.

First, let's figure out the value of x. If x is the diamond labeled as x, then $a = 5$, $b = 4$, $c = 2$, and $d = 1$. Now, we plug those numbers into the equation given, and do the simple math:

$x = (5 \times 2) - (4 \times 1)$

$x = 10 - 4$

$x = 6$

Now, we tackle the second step. Having figured out the value of x, we can plug it into our second diamond, where $a = 6$, $b = 10$, $c = 2$, and $d = 1$. Again, plug in the numbers and do the math:

$(6 \times 2) - (10 \times 1) = 12 - 10 = 2$

As you can see, the math is very easy; the trick is understanding what the test-makers are doing, which is "defining" a new math operation, and then carefully plugging in the numbers and working out the solution. With a little practice, you'll never get a "defined operation" question wrong.

Chapter 5

Data Sufficiency

Welcome to GMAT Data Sufficiency. At this point, you'll learn the following:

- A step-by-step approach to handling any Data Sufficiency question
- Success keys for tackling Data Sufficiency questions

Data Sufficiency—Your 5-Step Game Plan

The first task in this chapter is to learn the five basic steps for handling a GMAT Data Sufficiency question. You'll apply these steps to the following four sample questions. At the risk of giving away the answers up front, the correct answer is different for each question. Take a minute or two to attempt each one. (We'll analyze all four questions a few pages ahead.)

> **Note**
>
> We've labeled the answer choices here A through E. Remember, however, that on the actual GMAT CAT screen, you'll select your choice by clicking on one of five *blank ovals* (instead of *lettered* answer choices). But the answer choices themselves will always be exactly the same (and in the same order) as A through E here.

Chapter 5: Data Sufficiency

Sample Questions

1. If a jewelry merchant bought a particular ring for $10,000 and sold the ring to Judith, how much did Judith pay for the ring?

   (1) The merchant's profit from the sale was 50%.

   (2) The amount that the merchant paid for the ring was two-thirds the amount that Judith paid for the ring.

   A. Statement (1) ALONE is sufficient, but statement (2) alone is NOT sufficient to answer the question asked.
   B. Statement (2) ALONE is sufficient, but statement (1) alone is NOT sufficient to answer the question asked.
   C. BOTH statements (1) and (2) TOGETHER are sufficient to answer the question asked, but NEITHER statement ALONE is sufficient.
   D. Each statement ALONE is sufficient to answer the question asked.
   E. Statements (1) and (2) TOGETHER are NOT sufficient to answer the question asked, and additional data specific to the problem are needed.

2. The symbol □ represents the third digit in the 5-digit number 62,□79. What number does □ represent?

   (1) 62,□79 is a multiple of 3.

   (2) The sum of the digits of 62,□79 is divisible by 4.

   A. Statement (1) ALONE is sufficient, but statement (2) alone is NOT sufficient to answer the question asked.
   B. Statement (2) ALONE is sufficient, but statement (1) alone is NOT sufficient to answer the question asked.
   C. BOTH statements (1) and (2) TOGETHER are sufficient to answer the question asked, but NEITHER statement ALONE is sufficient.
   D. Each statement ALONE is sufficient to answer the question asked.
   E. Statements (1) and (2) TOGETHER are NOT sufficient to answer the question asked, and additional data specific to the problem are needed.

3. If $xy \neq 0$, is $x > y$?

   (1) $|x| > |y|$

   (2) $x = 2y$

   A. Statement (1) ALONE is sufficient, but statement (2) alone is NOT sufficient to answer the question asked.
   B. Statement (2) ALONE is sufficient, but statement (1) alone is NOT sufficient to answer the question asked.
   C. BOTH statements (1) and (2) TOGETHER are sufficient to answer the question asked, but NEITHER statement ALONE is sufficient.
   D. Each statement ALONE is sufficient to answer the question asked.
   E. Statements (1) and (2) TOGETHER are NOT sufficient to answer the question asked, and additional data specific to the problem are needed.

4.

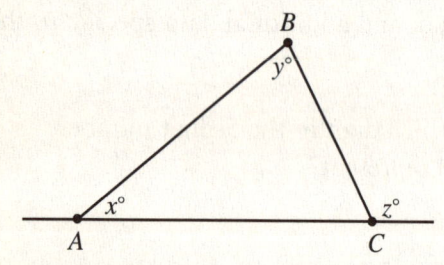

In the figure above, is $\overline{AB}$ equal in length to $\overline{AC}$?

   (1) $x + y = z$

   (2) $y = 180 - z$

   A. Statement (1) ALONE is sufficient, but statement (2) alone is NOT sufficient to answer the question asked.
   B. Statement (2) ALONE is sufficient, but statement (1) alone is NOT sufficient to answer the question asked.
   C. BOTH statements (1) and (2) TOGETHER are sufficient to answer the question asked, but NEITHER statement ALONE is sufficient.
   D. Each statement ALONE is sufficient to answer the question asked.
   E. Statements (1) and (2) TOGETHER are NOT sufficient to answer the question asked, and additional data specific to the problem are needed.

Note: Some Data Sufficiency questions will include diagrams (geometry figures, graphs, and charts), but most won't.

The 5-Step Plan

Here's the 5-step approach that will help you to handle any Data Sufficiency question. Just a few pages ahead, we'll apply this approach to four sample Data Sufficiency questions.

Step 1: Size up the question first. As with Problem Solving questions, assess what specific mathematical area is being tested (e.g., what mathematical rules and formulas come into play). By determining what you're up against, you're well on your way to dealing with the question. Data Sufficiency questions, just like Problem Solving questions, vary widely in difficulty level. Try to get a feel for your limitations in handling complex questions. Determine how much time you're willing to spend on the question, if any.

Step 2: Size up the two statements and look for a shortcut to the correct answer. Before you plunge into a full-blown analysis of statement (1), read both statements and ask yourself:

- Do the statements provide essentially the same information? If so, the answer is probably either choice (D) or choice (E).
- Does either statement establish a solvable system of equations (for example, two equations in two variables)?
- Does a statement seem to merely repeat (paraphrase) all or some of the information in the question? (If so, you can't answer the question with that statement alone.)

Asking yourself questions such as these may in some cases enable you to determine the correct answer choice without doing any more work. Otherwise, proceed to step 3.

Step 3. Consider statement (1) alone. If the information provided in statement (1) suffices to answer the question, eliminate choices (B), (C), and (E) as viable answer choices. On the other hand, if statement (1) is insufficient alone, eliminate choices (A) and (D) as viable answer choices.

Tip: If you're pressed for time, after step 3, take your best guess and move on. Your odds of selecting the correct answer choice are pretty good at this point.

Step 4. Consider statement (2) alone. If the information provided in statement (2) suffices to answer the question, eliminate choices (A), (C), and (E) as viable answer choices. On the other hand, If statement (2) is insufficient alone, eliminate choices (B) and (D) as viable answer choices.

Step 5. If neither statement alone suffices to answer the question, consider both statements together. Now if you can answer the question, the correct answer choice is (C). If you still don't have enough information, the correct answer choice is (E).

Apply the 5-Step Plan

It's time to go back to the three sample questions you looked at a few pages back. Let's walk through them—one at a time—using the 5-step game plan you just learned.

> **Note**
>
> By now you're probably familiar with the five answer choices, so we won't bother including them with the questions from now on.

Question 1

Question 1 is a relatively easy question. Approximately 85% of test-takers respond correctly to questions like it. Here's the question again:

1. If a jewelry merchant bought a particular ring for $10,000 and sold the ring to Judith, how much did Judith pay for the ring?

    (1) The merchant's profit from the sale was 50%.

    (2) The amount that the merchant paid for the ring was two-thirds of the amount that Judith paid for the ring.

Step 1: The focus of this question is the concept of *percent increase*—in the context of a word problem involving *profit*. This type of question is usually fairly easy, so you can expect to determine the correct response within a minute—without resorting to an educated guess. It should be worth investing your time on this one.

Step 2: Notice that the two statements (1 and 2) provide the same information—only in different ways! This is a huge clue that the correct answer choice is either (D) or (E). You'll still have to consider one of the two statements alone, but that should suffice.

Step 3: Consider the premise, along with statement (1) *alone*. (Disregard statement (2) for now.) Given that the merchant paid $10,000 for the ring, if the merchant earned a 50% profit from the sale to Judith, determining Judith's ring price is a simple matter of adding 50% of $10,000 to $10,000:

$$\$10,000 + .5(\$10,000) = \text{Judith's ring price}$$

At this point, it's clear that you can determine Judith's ring price by simple multiplication and addition. Don't waste time actually computing Judith's ring price. You know that statement (1) alone suffices to answer the question and that's all you need to know! Eliminate choices (B), (C), and (E) from consideration. The correct choice must be either (A) or (D).

Step 4: If you're not convinced that both statements say essentially the same thing, go ahead and consider the premise along with statement (2) *alone*. (Disregard statement (1) for now.) If the merchant's cost was $\frac{2}{3}$ the amount Judith paid, then Judith paid $\frac{3}{2}$ of the merchant's cost. Determining Judith's ring price is a simple matter of multiplying $10,000 by $\frac{3}{2}$:

$$\$10,000 \times \frac{3}{2} = \text{Judith's ring price}$$

At this point, it's clear that you can determine Judith's ring price by simple multiplication. As in step 3, don't waste time actually computing that price. You know that statement (2) alone suffices to answer the question and that's all you need to know!

Step 5: This step is unnecessary here. There's no need to consider both statements together. You know that either statement (1) or (2) alone suffices to answer the question, so you can eliminate choices (C) and (E). The correct answer must be D.

Question 2

Question 2 is average in difficulty level. Approximately 65% of test-takers respond correctly to questions like it. Here's the question again:

2. The symbol □ represents the third digit in the 5-digit number 62,□79. What number does □ represent?

   (1) 62,□79 is a multiple of 3.

   (2) The sum of the digits of 62,□79 is divisible by 4.

Part III: Quantitative Ability

Step 1: This question is testing on *factors* and *divisibility*. The peculiar use of a "placeholder" is a typical GMAT technique for testing your understanding of integers and digits. Questions such as these are usually straightforward once you know the basic rules as well as a few shortcuts for divisibility.

Step 2: Both statements appear to add different information to the question. So there's no obvious shortcut here. (Go on to step 3.)

Step 3: Consider statement (1) alone. If the sum of the digits of a number is divisible by 3, the number is also divisible by 3. Excluding the digit represented by □, the sum of the digits in the number 62, □79 is 24. Accordingly, if the number is a multiple of (divisible by) 3, the missing digit must be 0, 3, 6, or 9. Since there's more than one possible value for □, statement (1) alone is insufficient to answer the question. Eliminate answer choices (A) and (D).

Step 4: Consider statement (2) alone. The number that □ represents can be 0, 4, or 8. Thus, statement (2) alone is insufficient to answer the question. Eliminate answer choice (B).

Step 5: Consider statements (1) and (2) together. The two statements together establish that the missing digit is 0, because 0 is the only common number in between the two lists of possible values for □. Thus, statements (1) and (2) together are sufficient to answer the question, and the correct answer choice is (C).

Question 3

Question 3 is moderately difficult. Approximately 45% of test-takers respond correctly to questions like it. Here's the question again:

3. If $xy \neq 0$, is $x > y$?

   (1) $|x| > |y|$

   (2) $x = 2y$

Step 1: This is a typical *absolute value* question. Whenever you see inequalities and variables but no numbers, that's a clue that you'll need to consider different types of numbers—such as negative numbers, positive numbers, fractions, and perhaps the numbers 0 and 1—to determine the correct answer choice. Getting to the answer might entail performing some simple calculations, and perhaps a bit of trial and error (plugging in possible values).

Step 2: Both statements appear to add different information to the question. So there's no obvious shortcut here. But a good reasoned guess at this point would be that the correct answer choice is (E). Why? Because the question doesn't restrict the value of either x or y (except that neither can equal 0). So if you're pressed for time, guess choice (E) and move on to the next question. Otherwise, go on to step 3.

Step 3: You must consider both positive and negative values for x and y. Given $|x| > |y|$, an x-value of either 4 or -4 and a y-value of 2, for example, satisfies the inequality but results in two different answers to the question. Thus, statement (1) alone is insufficient to answer the question. Eliminate answer choices (A) and (D).

Step 4: Similarly, given $x = 2y$, if you use negative values for both x and y (for example, $x = -4$ and $y = -2$), the answer to the question is *no*; but if you use positive values (for example, $x = 4$ and $y = 2$), the answer to the question is *yes*. Thus, statement (2) alone is insufficient. Eliminate answer choice (B).

Step 5: Statements (1) and (2) together are still insufficient. For example, if $x = -4$ and $y = -2$, both statements (1) and (2) are satisfied, $x < y$, and the answer to the question is *no*. However, if $x = 4$ and $y = 2$, statements (1) and (2) are both satisfied, but $x > y$, and the answer to the question is *yes*. Eliminate answer choice (C). The correct answer must be E.

Question 4

Question 4 is a relatively difficult question. Approximately 30% of test-takers respond correctly to questions like it. Here's the question again:

4.

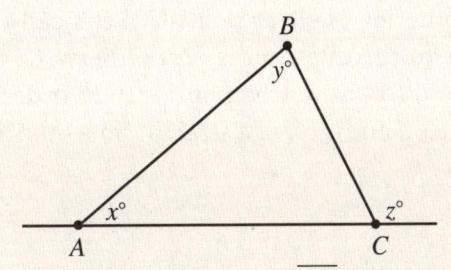

In the figure above, is $\overline{AB}$ equal in length to $\overline{AC}$?

(1) $x + y = z$
(2) $y = 180 - z$

Step 1: This question is a *geometry* problem involving the *isosceles triangle*. (You'll see anywhere from five to eight geometry questions on your GMAT CAT.) This question involves three distinct rules of geometry. Two of these rules (A and C below) apply specifically to triangles:

Rule A: If two angles of a triangle are congruent, then the two sides opposite those angles are congruent.

Part III: Quantitative Ability

Rule B: If angles formed from the same vertex form a straight line, their degree measures total 180 (and they are known as "supplementary" angles).

Rule C: In any triangle, the sum of the degree measures of the three interior angles is 180.

If you're unfamiliar with any of the three rules in step 1, you won't get very far with this question! So if you're pressed for time, and if you're particularly weak in this area of geometry, consider taking a guess and moving on.

Step 2: Intuition alone probably won't get you very far on this question. If you're really on your toes, you'll notice that statement (1) merely restates Rule C (see step 1) in a different form. Also, because statement (2) includes a number, this statement is probably more likely than statement (1) to suffice in answering the question. (This amounts to little more than a guess, however.) So let's move on to step 3.

> **Alert!** Don't shortcut the analysis by simply measuring the lengths of $\overline{AB}$ and $\overline{AC}$ with your eye. Take heed: Data Sufficiency figures are not necessarily drawn to scale. So analyze these problems using your knowledge of mathematics, not your eye!

Step 3: Consider statement (1) alone. Given Rule A (see step 1) to answer the question, you need to know whether angle y is congruent to the triangle's unidentified angle—the interior angle at point C. Let's call this angle a. If $a = y$, then the answer to the question is *yes*. Otherwise, the answer is *no*. In either case, we need to know whether $a = y$ in order to answer the question. Together, angles a and z form a straight line—the line passing through points A and C:

$$a + z = 180$$
$$a = 180 - z$$

The sum of x, y, and a is 180 (Rule C). You can substitute $(180 - z)$ for a in this equation, and manipulate the result so that it is identical to the equation in statement (1):

$x + y + a = 180$	Rule C (sum of angle measures is 180°)
$x + y + (180 - z) = 180$	substituting $(180 - z)$ for a
$x + y - z = 0$	subtract 180 from each side
$x + y = z$	add z to each side

Statement (1) essentially restates a rule that is true for any triangle, so it is insufficient alone to answer the question. Eliminate answer choices (A) and (D) as viable choices.

> **Tip:** You could have shortcut this entire analysis had you already been aware of the rule that an exterior angle of a triangle is always congruent to the sum of the two remote interior angles.

Step 4: Now consider statement (2) disregarding statement (1) for now. The expression $(180 - z)$ equals our third unidentified angle, which we called a in step 3. Given that $(180 - z)$ also equals y, the two angles a and y are congruent (equal in degree measure). The two sides opposite a and y must also be congruent (see Rule A). Thus, statement (2) alone suffices to answer the question.

Step 5: Because statement (1) alone is insufficient to answer the question, while statement (2) alone is sufficient, the correct answer choice is (B). There's no need to consider the two statements together. Based on statement (2), the answer to the question itself is *yes*, but you don't need to go this far. Had neither (1) nor (2) alone been sufficient to answer the question, you would have then considered both statements together to determine whether the correct answer choice is (C) or (E).

Success Keys for GMAT Data Sufficiency

Here are some basic tips you should follow for Data Sufficiency questions. Apply these keys to Part III's practice tests, and then review them again just before exam day.

Memorize the Answer Choices

Don't just learn the directions—memorize the answer choices. (Remember: they are always the same.) This way you'll save time because you won't need to refer to them for every question.

Be Sure to Consider Each Statement Alone

After analyzing statement (1), you'll be surprised how difficult it can be to purge the information in Statement (1) from your mind and start with a clean slate in considering Statement (2). Be alert at all times to this potential problem.

Don't Do More Work Than Necessary

Keep in mind that the Data Sufficiency format does not require you to answer the question. So once you've convinced yourself that a statement (1 or 2) suffices to answer the question, stop right there! You'd only be wasting your precious time by figuring out the answer itself.

Question 1

Once you recognized that each statement provides the missing piece to compute Judith's ring cost, you know the correct answer is D. There's no need to do the math.

Look for a Quicker, More Intuitive Route to the Correct Answer

The GMAT is testing, among other skills, your ability to find ingenious, unconventional, and intuitive solutions to conventional problems. Always look for a shortcut to performing calculations. You'll save time, and you'll avoid common computational errors.

Question 2

As you tackle more questions like question 3, you'll learn to recognize when an answer depends on which values are used, and you won't have to bother plugging in "test" numbers.

Don't Perform Endless Calculations

You shouldn't have to do involved calculations to get to the answer in a Data Sufficiency question. A few simple calculations may be required; but if you're doing a lot of number crunching, you've probably missed the mathematical principal the question is asking about.

Question 3

Had we not used an organized approach to the problem, we would have had no choice but to start plugging in digit after digit (0 through 9). The more number crunching, the greater the chance for error.

Never Rely Solely on a Diagram (Figure)

Although a figure will conform to the information in the question, it won't necessarily conform to either statement (1) or (2). So don't use a Data Sufficiency figure to estimate or measure values, shapes, lengths, or other sizes. For example, don't rely on a figure's appearance to determine whether:

- One line segment is longer than another.
- One angle is larger (greater in degree measure) than another.

- Two lines are parallel or perpendicular.
- Two triangles are the same shape or size.
- One segment of a pie chart is larger than another segment.
- Rely instead on the numbers and textual information provided in the question and statements.

Question 4
In the figure, it appears that $\overline{AB}$ is equal in length to $\overline{AC}$. If you had relied on the figure, your response to the question would have been wrong!

Consider All the Possibilities When It Comes to Unknowns

When analyzing a Data Sufficiency question involving unknowns (variables such as x and y), unless the question explicitly restricts their value, consider positive *and* negative values, as well as fractions and the numbers zero (0) and 1. If the answer to the question depends on what kind of value you plug in, then the correct answer must be E.

Question 3
We needed to consider negative as well as positive numbers; otherwise, we would have gotten the question wrong.

Look for Two Statements That Say Essentially the Same Thing

Check to see if the two statements provide essentially the same information—just in a slightly different form. If they're the same, you know the correct answer choice must be either D or E.

Question 1
Notice that the two statements provided the same information—just in different forms

Check each statement to see if it provides numbers needed to answer the question

Use this approach for any Data Sufficiency problem involving formulas and calculations, where the question asks for a number. In a problem involving rate of motion (speed), for instance, if the question asks for a speed but does not provide the time (or does not provide the distance), rule out a statement that doesn't supply the missing piece of the formula.

Question 3
In analyzing this question, we recognized early that neither statement alone supplies the numbers we need.

Don't Try to Do All the Work in Your Head
As with Problem Solving questions, don't try to do too much work in your head. Avoid careless errors by using your pencil and scratch paper for all but the simplest mathematical steps. (Remember: Scratch paper and pencils will be provided at the testing center.)

Question 3
How far would you get with Question 3 without doing some pencil work—at a minimum, scratching out the two statements in different forms? Not very far!

If You're Running out of Time, Make a Reasoned Guess by Eliminating Answer Choices
Keep in mind that if statement (1) alone is insufficient to answer the question, you can eliminate choices (A) and (D). On the other hand, once you've determined that one of the statements alone is sufficient, you can eliminate choices (C) and (E). At this point, your odds of guessing correctly are 1 in 3, which is a lot better than 1 in 5 for a compete random guess. So if you're having trouble analyzing one statement, but are confident that the other statement is sufficient alone, make a guess and move on to the next question.

Questions 1–4
In any of the four example questions, we could have stopped part way through our analysis and taken a reasoned guess. Remember: If you can get as far as ruling out one answer choice, you can rule out two. At that point, your odds look pretty good!

Take It to the Next Level

Welcome to the Next Level of GMAT Data Sufficiency, along with GMAT Data Analysis. At this point, you'll:

- Apply the success keys you learned earlier in the chapter to more challenging Data Sufficiency questions
- Learn additional success keys that apply to certain types of Data Sufficiency questions, and apply these keys to example questions
- Learn a step-by-step approach to handling any Data Analysis question
- Learn success keys for tackling Data Analysis questions

What's New at the Next Level

Here at the Next Level, you'll further explore some of the strategies listed above—applying them to GMAT-style questions that are a bit more challenging. You'll also learn some additional strategies that apply to certain types of Data Sufficiency questions.

Next, you'll take a look at a special type of GMAT Quantitative problem, which the test-makers call *Data Analysis*. These questions involve reading, interpreting, and analyzing data presented in graphical form—graphs, charts, and tables—and often come in pairs. (Data Analysis questions can appear in either format—Problem Solving or Data Sufficiency.)

Data Sufficiency Strategies

In this section, you'll learn strategies for handling Data Sufficiency problems and see examples of each strategy.

Plug in "Easy" Numbers—But Don't Forget Negatives, Fractions, Zero, and One

If a Data Sufficiency question involves variables, you can easily confuse yourself by thinking about the problem purely abstractly. You should also experiment with different numerical values. Take pencil to paper and scratch out some scenarios. This technique will help you see what's behind the problem at hand. Just be sure to try all the different "types" of numbers that the problem allows (greater numbers, lesser numbers, positive and negative numbers, non-integers, as well as 0 and 1). If the answer to the question depends on what kind of values you plug in, then the correct answer choice must be (E).

If a, b, c, and d are all positive integers, is $\frac{a}{b}$ greater than $\frac{c}{d}$?

(1) $a > c$

(2) $b > d$

The correct answer is E. Neither statement alone allows you to compare the values of the two fractions. To see this, try plugging in some simple numbers. For example, let $a = 4$ and $c = 2$, in accordance with statement (1). Since you can choose any values for b and d, the possible values of either fraction are infinite in number, and so you can see that statement (1) alone is insufficient to answer the question. By the same reasoning, statement (2) alone is also insufficient.

Now, consider the two statements together. Again, let $a = 4$ and $c = 2$, in accordance with statement (1). Now, start plugging in some values for b and d that meet the condition in statement (2), which is that $b > d$. Can you answer *yes* to the question? Easily; for example, $b = 1$ and $d = -1$. Can you answer *no* to the question? Easily; here's just one possible way: $b = 4$ and $d = 1$. Stop here! You've found two different answers to the question and so you know the correct answer must be E.

Look for Two Statements That Say Essentially the Same Thing

In most Data Sufficiency questions, one numbered statement will obviously provide different information than the other statement. But, this isn't always the case. One skill that the test-makers will test is your ability to recognize two statements that provide essentially the same information—just in a slightly different form. If they're the same, you know the correct answer choice must be either (D) or (E).

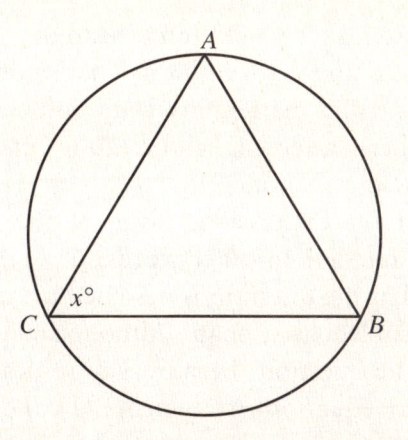

Is the triangle in the figure above equilateral?

(1) Minor arc AB has a degree measure of 120°.

(2) $x = 60$

The correct answer is E. The two statements tell us the same thing—that angle C measures 60°, as it would if the triangle were equilateral. But without further information, we can't tell that angles A and B are also 60° angles. It's possible, for instance, that angle A measures 59° while angle B measures 61°—in which case the triangle is *not* equilateral. Since we can't know for sure, the answer must be choice (E).

Alert! The triangle inscribed in the circle certainly *looks* equilateral (which means that all three sides are equal in length). But, the apparent dimensions of the triangle in the diagram are irrelevant to answering the question. Only the facts given in the question and in the two numbered statements are important.

Focus on Quantitative Concepts, Not on Number Crunching

Data Sufficiency focuses more on mathematical concepts than on working toward a quantitative solution (which is what Problem Solving questions are primarily about). So, be sure to size up the problem at hand. Ask yourself: "What rule, principle, formula, is the question covering?" Once you've figured this out, you should be able to you handle the problem without breaking a sweat.

What is the value of $p^2 - q^2$?

(1) $p + q = -4$

(2) $p - q = 4$

The correct answer is C. Many test-takers would jump headlong into trying various values for p and q in trial-and-error fashion. That's not the way to approach this problem—or for that matter, any Data Sufficiency problem. Before you evaluate either statement alone, look at the expressions given in the problem. Did you notice that $p^2 - q^2$ is the difference of two squares, and that the expressions given in the two statements provide its two binomial factors? In other words: $p^2 - q^2 = (p + q)(p - q)$. This is the concept that the question is designed to cover. Once you see this, handling the problem is a snap. Although neither statement alone suffices to answer the question (because you're dealing with a quadratic rather than a linear equation), statements (1) and (2) together provide the two binomials, allowing you to answer the question. (To calculate the answer, you would simply multiply: $-4 \times 4 = -16$.)

Don't do More Work Than Necessary

Keep in mind that the Data Sufficiency format does not require you to answer the question. So once you've convinced yourself that a statement (1 or 2) suffices to answer the question, stop right there! You'd only be wasting your precious time by figuring out the answer itself.

What is the average weight of the 5 members of a football team?

(1) The average weight of the three heaviest team members is 340 pounds.

(2) The two lightest team members weigh 275 and 290 pounds, respectively.

The correct answer is C. To calculate the average of a group of numbers, you must have two pieces of information: The total of the numbers and the number of numbers. In this case, the only missing piece of information is the total weight of the team members. (You already know the number of numbers involved: 5.) Neither statement (1) nor (2) alone gives you the players' total weight. But if you combine statements (1) and (2), you can determine it. You'd multiply 340 by 3 (to get the combined weight of the heaviest team members) and add 275 and 290 (the weights of the two lightest members). *But there's no need to actually perform these steps.* All that matters is that you can tell that it would be theoretically possible to make these calculations and so determine the average. This is enough to get the correct answer, choice (C).

Don't Assume Any Information Not Stated in the Problem

One of the skills the test-makers are measuring is your ability to distinguish facts provided in a Data Sufficiency problem from unsupported assumptions made out of carelessness or inattention. There's a natural tendency to "invent" facts that aren't really there so that you can answer the question. No test-taker is immune to this tendency. You might be surprised how many "smart" GMAT test-takers slip up in this way, robbing themselves of precious Quantitative score points.

> What percentage of the female students in a certain history class are majoring in economics?
>
> (1) 50 percent of the students in the class are male and 50 percent are female.
>
> (2) 50 percent of all students in the class are majoring in economics.

The correct answer is E. Many test-takers would carelessly *assume* that the percent of students majoring in economics is the same for the class's male students as for it's female students. If this were the case, then you could easily answer the question. (The answer would be 50.) But the problem provides no information to support this assumption! Thus, the correct answer must be choice (E).

Beware of Statements That Are Irrelevant or That Provide Facts Already Supplied in the Question

Ask yourself what kind of information each statement provides. A statement is more likely to be *sufficient* to answer the question if:

- It provides specific numerical values not given in the premise.
- It adds something new to the premise.
- It provides information that strikes you as relevant to the question.

On the other hand, a statement is more likely to be *insufficient* to answer the question if:

- It does not provide any specific numerical values that the premise leaves unknown.
- It seems redundant—simply paraphrasing the premise (or some part of it).
- The information strikes you as irrelevant to the premise or question.

A certain granola recipe calls for a simple mixture of raisins costing $3.50 per pound with oats. At a cost of $2.00 per pound for the granola mixture, how many pounds of oats must be added to 10 pounds of raisins?

(1) The granola mixture is packaged in one-pound bags.

(2) Oats cost $1.00 per pound.

The correct answer is A. The question itself provides two of the three facts you need to answer it: the cost per pound of raisins and the cost per pound of the mixture. Statement (1) alone provides no useful information for answering the question. So, without even looking at statement (1), you've eliminated answer choices (A), (C), and (D)! Statement (2) provides the third needed fact: the cost per pound of oats.

Although you don't need to do the math, here's how you would answer the question with the additional information provided by statement (2). Think of the quantities as costs per pound and multiply the cost by the weight. The total mixture will consist of 10 pounds of raisins at $3.50 per pound, or ($3.50)(10), plus "x" pound of oats at $1.00 per pound, or ($1.00)(x). The mixture costs $2.00 per pound, and it will be (10 + x) pounds:

$$(3.50)(10) + (1.00)(x) = (2.00)(10 + x)$$
$$35 + x = 20 + 2x$$
$$15 = x$$

15 pound of oats are needed.

Don't Assume That Any Diagrams Provided Are Accurate

Although a diagram will conform to the information in the question, it won't necessarily conform to either statement (1) or (2). So don't use a Data Sufficiency figure to estimate or measure values, shapes, lengths, or other sizes. For example, don't rely on a figure's appearance to determine:

- Whether one line segment is longer than another
- Whether one angle is larger (greater in degree measure) than another
- Whether two lines are parallel or perpendicular
- Whether two triangles are the same shape or size
- Whether one segment of a pie chart is larger than another segment
- Rely instead on the numbers and the textual information provided in the question and in the two statements.

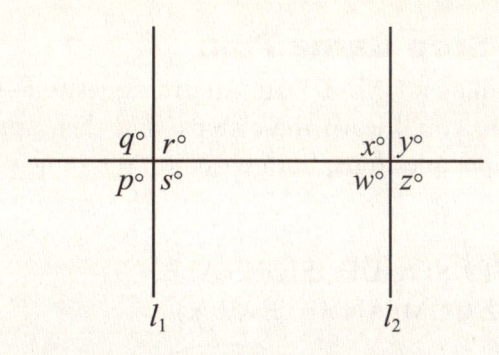

In the figure above, is l_1 parallel to l_2?

(1) $q + y = s + w$

(2) $p + x = 180$

The correct answer is B. If you were to rely on the appearance of the figure, you'd see that the two lines look parallel. But, remember: When it comes to GMAT Data Sufficiency, never measure with your eye! Rely instead on the numbers and other information in the problem. Here's how to analyze this problem. Vertical angles (formed by intersecting lines) are always congruent. Thus, $q = s$ and $y = w$. Accordingly, $q + y$ must equal $s + w$ in any event, and statement (1) alone does not suffice to answer the question. Given statement (2) alone, since p and x are supplementary, p must equal y as well as w (because $y + x = 180$ and $w + x = 180$). Thus, corresponding angles are congruent and the two lines are parallel.

Data Analysis Strategies

Data Analysis questions are designed to gauge your ability to read and analyze data presented in statistical charts, graphs, and tables—and to calculate figures such as percentages, ratios, fractions, and averages based on the numbers you glean from graphical data. Data Analysis questions can appear in either of the two basic formats: Problem Solving and Data Sufficiency.

Expect to find 2–4 Data Analysis questions (typically in sets of two questions) interspersed with other Quantitative questions. Each question in a set pertains to the same graphical data. Each question (and each set) involves either *one or two* distinct graphical displays. Four types appear most frequently:

1. Pie charts
2. Tables
3. Bar graphs
4. Line graphs

Part III: Quantitative Ability

Data Analysis—Your 5-Step Game Plan

There are 5 basic steps for handling a GMAT Data Analysis question—or set of questions. In this section, you'll learn these steps, and then apply them to the following two sample questions, both based on the same two *pie charts*.

1. INCOME AND EXPENSES–DIVISIONS A, B, C,
   AND D OF XYZ COMPANY (YEAR X)

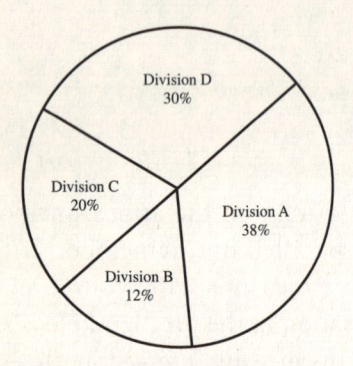

   INCOME
   (Total Income = $1,560,000)

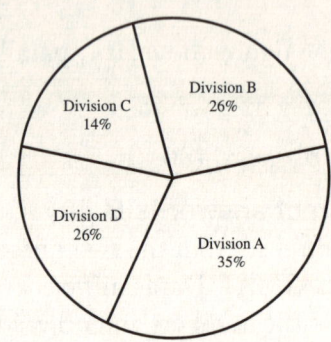

   Division D 30%
   Division C 20%
   Division A 38%
   Division B 12%

   EXPENSES
   (Total Expenses = $495,000)

   Division C 14%
   Division B 26%
   Division D 26%
   Division A 35%

   During year X, by approximately what amount did Division C's income exceed Division B's expenses?

   A. $125,000
   B. $127,000
   C. $140,000
   D. $180,000
   E. $312,000

2. With respect to the division whose income exceeded its expenses by the greatest percent among the four divisions, by approximately what amount did the division's income exceed its own expenses?

   A. $69,000
   B. $90,000
   C. $150,000
   D. $185,000
   E. $230,000

Chapter 5: Data Sufficiency

Before learning and applying the 5 steps, note the following key features of Data Analysis question sets:

- The questions tend to be long and wordy. Get used to it; that's the way the test-makers design them. You'll probably find that you have more trouble interpreting the questions than the figures.

- Bar graphs and line charts are drawn to scale. (You'll see a bar graph and a line chart during this chapter's Mini-Test.) Pie charts will are not necessarily drawn to scale (you'll see a note letting you know that it's not). Visual scale is irrelevant when it comes to analyzing tables.

- Important assumptions will be provided. Any additional information that you might need to know to interpret the figures will be indicated above and below the figures. (Be sure to read this information.)

- Nearly all questions ask for an approximation. You'll see some form of the word *approximate* in nearly all Data Analysis questions. This is because the test-makers are trying to gauge your ability to interpret graphical date, not your ability to crunch numbers to the "nth" decimal place.

- Many of the numbers used are *almost* round. This feature relates to the previous one. The GMAT rewards test-takers who recognize that rounding off numbers (to an appropriate extent) will suffice to get to the right answer. So they pack Data Analysis figures with numbers that are close to "easy" ones. (The numbers in our pie chart set serve as good examples. For example, $1,560,000 is close to $1,500,000 million and $495,000 is close to $500,000.)

- Figures are not drawn to deceive you or to test your eyesight. In bar graphs and line charts, you won't be asked to split hairs to determine values. These figures are designed with a comfortable margin for error in visual acuity. Just don't round up or down too far.

The 5-Step Plan

Here's the 5-step approach that will help you to handle any set of Data Analysis questions. Just a few pages ahead, we'll apply this approach to this 2-question set on page 187.

Step 1: Look at the "big picture" first. Before plunging into the question(s), read all the information above and below the figure(s). Look particularly for:

- Totals (dollar figures or other numbers)
- Whether the numbers are in thousand or millions

Part III: Quantitative Ability

- How two or more figures are labeled
- Whether graphical data is expressed in numbers or percentages

Step 2: Read the entire Data Analysis question very carefully. As you do, divide the question into parts, each of which involves a distinct step in getting to the answer. Pay particular attention to whether the question asks for:

- An approximation
- A percentage or a raw number
- A comparison
- An increase or a decrease

In breaking the question down into tasks, look for a shortcut to save yourself work. (Many Data Analysis questions can be answered either the quick way or the slow way.)

Step 3: Perform the steps needed to get to the answer. Look for a shortcut to the answer. Round numbers up or down (but not too far) as you go.

Step 4: Check choices (A) through (E) for your answer. If the question asks for a number, find the choice closest to your answer. Look for other answer choices are "too close for comfort." If you see any, or if your solution is nowhere near any of the choices, go to Step 5.

Step 5: Check your calculations, and make sure the value and form (number, percentage, total, etc.) of your solution conforms with what the question asks. Check your rounding technique. Did you round off in the wrong direction? Did you round off too far?

Apply the 5-Step Plan

It's time to go back to the sample question set you looked at a few pages back. Let's walk through both questions, using the 5-step game plan you just learned.

Step 1: Size up the two charts, and read the information above and below them. Notice that we're only dealing with one company during one year here. Notice also that dollar totals are provided, but that the pie segments are expressed only as percentages. That's a clue that your main task in this set will be to calculate dollar amounts for various pie segments. Now read the first question.

Question 1

Question 1 is a moderately difficult question. Approximately 50% of test-takers respond correctly to questions like it. Here's the question again:

Chapter 5: Data Sufficiency

1. During year X, by approximately what amount did Division C's income exceed Division B's expenses?

   A. $125,000
   B. $127,000
   C. $140,000
   D. $180,000
   E. $312,000

You already performed step 1, so move ahead to step 2.

Step 2: This question involves three tasks: (1) calculate Division C's income, (2) calculate Division B's expenses, and (3) compute their difference. There's no shortcut to these three tasks, so go on to step 3.

Step 3: Division B's expenses accounted for 26% of XYZ's total expenses, given as $495,000. Rounding off these figures to 25% and $500,000, Division B's expenses totaled approximately $125,000. Income from Division C sales was 20% of total XYZ income, given as $1,560,000. Rounding this total down to $1,500,000, income from Division C sales was approximately $300,000. Income from Division C sales exceeded Division B's expenses by approximately $175,000.

Step 4: The only answer choice close to this solution is (D). If you have extra time, go to step 5.

Step 5: Make sure you started with the right numbers. Did you compare C's income with B's expense (and not some other combination)? If you're satisfied that the numbers you used were the right ones and that your calculations are okay, move on to the next question.

Question 2

Question 2 is a difficult question. Approximately 30% of test-takers respond correctly to questions like it. Here's the question again:

2. With respect to the division whose income exceeded its own expenses by the greatest percent among the four divisions, by approximately what amount did the division's income exceed its own expenses?

   A. $69,000
   B. $90,000
   C. $150,000
   D. $185,000
   E. $230,000

Part III: Quantitative Ability

Step 2: This is a complex question. First, you need to compare profitability—in dollar amount—among the four divisions. You can rule out Division B, since its expenses exceeded its income. That leaves Divisions A, C, and D.

Step 3: For Divisions A, C, and D, compare percent of income and percent of expenses:

> Division A: 38% of total income and 35% of total expenses (37% difference)

> Division C: 20% of total income and 14% of total expenses (6% difference)

> Division D: 30% of total income and 26% of total expenses (4% difference)

Division C's income was a bit more than $300,000 (20% of $1,500,000). Division C's expenses were approximately $75,000 (15% of $500,000). Division C's income exceeded it's expenses by approximately $225,000.

Step 4: Answer choice (E), $230,000, is the only one close to our approximation.

Step 5: If you have time, rethink Step 3. Make sure you're convinced that Division C's percentage profit was greater than either A's or D's. Also, ask yourself if $230,000 in the right ballpark. If you're confident in your analysis, move on to the next question.

Success Keys for GMAT Data Analysis

Here are some basic tips you should follow for any type of Data Analysis question. Apply these keys to Part III's practice tests, and then review them again just before exam day.

Scroll Vertically to See the Entire Display

Some vertical scrolling may be necessary to view the entire display, especially the information above and below the chart, graph, or table. Don't forget to scroll up and down as you analyze each question.

Don't Confuse Percentages with Raw Numbers

Most data analysis questions involve raw data as well as *proportion*—in terms of either percent, fraction, or ratio (usually percent). Always ask yourself: "Is the solution to this problem a *raw* number or a *proportional* number?" You can be sure that the testing service will "bait" you with appealing incorrect answer choices!

Be Sure to Go to the Appropriate Chart (Or Part of A Chart) for Your Numbers

This point of advice may seem obvious; nevertheless, reading the wrong data is probably the leading cause of incorrect responses to data analysis questions! To ensure that you don't commit this careless error, point your finger to the proper line, column, or bar on the screen; put your finger right on it, and don't move it until you're sure you've got the correct data.

To Save Time, Round Off Numbers—But Don't Distort Values

Most Data Analysis questions ask for approximate values. So, to save time, it's okay to round off numbers; rounding off to the nearest appropriate unit or half-unit usually suffices to get to the correct answer. But don't get too rough in your approximations. Also, be sure to round off numerators and denominators of fractions in the same direction (either both up or both down), unless you're confident that a rougher approximation will suffice. Otherwise, you'll distort the value of the number.

Handle Lengthy, Confusing Questions One Part at a Time

Data Analysis questions can be wordy and confusing. Don't panic. Keep in mind that lengthy questions almost always call for two discreet tasks. For the first task, read only the first part of the question. When you're done, go back to the question and read the next part.

Don't Split Hairs in Reading Line Charts and Bar Graphs

These are the two types of figures that are drawn to scale. If a certain point on a chart appears to be about 40% of the way from one hash mark to the next, don't hesitate to round up to the halfway point. (The number 5 is usually easier to work with than 4 or 6.)

Formulate a Clear Idea as to the Overall Size of the Number the Question is Calling for

The test-makers pack Data Analysis questions with "sucker bait" answer choices for test-makers who make common computational errors. The best way to keep yourself from falling into their trap is to ask yourself what sort of ballpark number you're looking for in a correct answer. You might ask yourself:

- Is it a double digit number?
- Is it a percentage that is obviously greater than 50 percent?
- Is it a great raw number in the thousands?

By keeping the big picture in mind, you'll catch the fact that you made an error in calculation.

Chapter 6

Math Review—Number Forms, Relationships, and Sets

In this chapter, first you'll focus on various forms of numbers and relationships between numbers. Specifically, you'll learn how to:

- Combine fractions using the four basic operations
- Combine decimal numbers by multiplication and division
- Compare numbers in percentage terms
- Compare percent changes with number changes
- Rewrite percents, fractions, and decimal numbers written in one form as another
- Determine ratios between quantities and determine quantities from ratios
- Set up equivalent ratios (proportions)

Next, you'll explore the following topics, all of which involve sets (defined groups) of numbers or other objects:

- Simple average and median (two ways that a set of numbers can be described as a whole)
- Arithmetic series (the pattern from one number to the next in a linear sequence of numbers)
- Permutations (the possibilities for arranging a set of objects)
- Combinations (the possibilities for selecting groups of objects from a set)
- Probability (the statistical chances of a certain event, permutation, or combination occurring)

Chapter 6: Math Review—Number Forms, Relationships, and Sets

Alert!

Although this is the most basic of all the math-review chapters in this book, don't think for a minute that you should skip it. The skills covered here are basic building blocks for other types of questions—the ones you'll encounter in the chapters to follow.

Percent, Fraction, and Decimal Equivalences

Any real number can be expressed as a fraction, a percent, or a decimal number. For instance, $\frac{2}{10}$, 20%, and .2 are all different forms of the same quantity, or value. GMAT math questions often require you to rewrite one form as another as part of solving the problem at hand. You should know how to write any equivalence quickly and confidently.

To rewrite a percent-as-a-decimal, move the decimal point two places to the *left* (and drop the percent sign). To rewrite a decimal-as-a-percent, move the decimal point two places to the *right* (and add the percent sign).

$9.5\% = .095$

$.004 = .4\%$

To rewrite a percent-as-a-fraction, *divide* by 100 (and drop the percent sign). To rewrite a fraction-as-a-percent, *multiply* by 100 (and add the percent sign). Percents greater than 100 are equivalent to numbers greater than 1.

$$810\% = \frac{810}{100} = \frac{81}{10} = 8\frac{1}{10}$$

$$\frac{3}{8} = \frac{300}{8}\% = \frac{75}{2}\% = 37\frac{1}{2}\%$$

Alert!

Percents greater than 100 or less than 1 (such as 457% and .067%) can be confusing, because it's a bit harder to grasp the magnitude of these numbers. To guard against errors when writing, keep in mind the general magnitude of the number you're dealing with. For example, think of .09% as just less than .1%, which is one-tenth of a percent, or a thousandth (a pretty small valued number). Think of $\frac{.4}{5}$ as just less than $\frac{.5}{5}$, which is obviously $\frac{1}{10}$, or 10%. Think of 668% as more than 6 times a complete 100%, or between 6 and 7.

Part III: Quantitative Ability

To rewrite a fraction as a decimal, simply divide the numerator by the denominator, using long division. A fraction-to-decimal equivalence might result in a precise value, an approximation with a repeating pattern, or an approximation with no repeating pattern:

$\frac{5}{8} = .625$	The equivalent decimal number is precise after three decimal places.
$\frac{5}{9} \approx .555$	The equivalent decimal number can only be approximated (the digit 5 repeats indefinitely).
$\frac{5}{7} \approx .714$	The equivalent decimal number can only be approximated (there is no repeating pattern by carrying the calculation to additional decimal places).

Certain fraction-decimal-percent equivalents show up on the GMAT more often than others. The numbers in the following tables are the test-makers' favorites because they reward test-takers who recognize quick ways to deal with numbers. Memorize these conversions so that they're second nature to you on exam day.

Percent	Decimal	Fraction	Percent	Decimal	Fraction
50%	.5	$\frac{1}{2}$	$16\frac{2}{3}\%$	$.16\frac{2}{3}$	$\frac{1}{6}$
25%	.25	$\frac{1}{4}$	$83\frac{1}{3}\%$	$.83\frac{1}{3}$	$\frac{5}{6}$
75%	.75	$\frac{3}{4}$	20%	.2	$\frac{1}{5}$
10%	.1	$\frac{1}{10}$	40%	.4	$\frac{2}{5}$
30%	.3	$\frac{3}{10}$	60%	.6	$\frac{3}{5}$
70%	.7	$\frac{7}{10}$	80%	.8	$\frac{4}{5}$
90%	.9	$\frac{9}{10}$	$12\frac{1}{2}\%$	.125	$\frac{1}{8}$
$33\frac{1}{3}\%$	$.33\frac{1}{3}$	$\frac{1}{3}$	$37\frac{1}{2}\%$	.375	$\frac{3}{8}$
$66\frac{2}{3}\%$	$.66\frac{2}{3}$	$\frac{2}{3}$	$62\frac{1}{2}\%$	.625	$\frac{5}{8}$
			$87\frac{1}{2}\%$	.875	$\frac{7}{8}$

Simplifiying and Combining Fractions

A GMAT question might ask you to combine fractions using one or more of the four basic operations (addition, subtraction, multiplication, and division). The rules for combining fractions by addition and subtraction are very different than the ones for multiplication and division.

Addition and Subtraction and the LCD

To combine fractions by addition or subtraction, the fractions *must* have a common denominator. If they already do, simply add (or subtract) numerators. If they don't, you'll need to find one. You can always multiply all of the denominators together to find a common denominator, but it might be a big number that's clumsy to work with. So instead, try to find the *least (or lowest) common denominator* (LCD) by working your way up in multiples of the largest of the denominators given. For denominators of 6, 3 and 5, for instance, try out successive multiples of 6 (10, 12, 18, 24 . . .), and you'll hit the LCD when you get to 30.

$$\frac{5}{3} - \frac{5}{6} + \frac{5}{2} =$$

A. $\frac{15}{11}$

B. $\frac{5}{2}$

C. $\frac{15}{6}$

D. $\frac{10}{3}$

E. $\frac{15}{3}$

The correct answer is D. To find the LCD, try out successive multiples of 6 until you come across one that is also a multiple of both 3 and 2. The LCD is 6. Multiply each numerator by the same number by which you would multiply the fraction's denominator to give you the LCD of 6. Place the three products over this common denominator. Then, combine the numbers in the numerator. (Pay close attention to the subtraction sign!) Finally, simplify to lowest terms:

$$\frac{5}{3} - \frac{5}{6} + \frac{5}{2} = \frac{5(\overset{2}{\cancel{10}}) - 5(\overset{1}{\cancel{5}}) + 5(\overset{3}{\cancel{15}})}{\underset{6}{\cancel{30}}}$$

$$= \frac{\overset{10}{\cancel{50}} - \overset{5}{\cancel{25}} + \overset{15}{\cancel{75}}}{\underset{6}{\cancel{30}}}$$

$$= \frac{100}{30}, \text{ or } \frac{10}{3}$$

Multiplication and Division

To multiply fractions, multiply the numerators and multiply the denominators. The denominators need not be the same. To divide one fraction by another, multiply by the reciprocal of the divisor (the number after the division sign).

Multiplication:	Division:
$\frac{1}{2} \times \frac{5}{3} \times \frac{1}{7} = \frac{(1)(\cancel{5})(1)}{(2)(3)(7)} = \frac{\cancel{5}}{42}$	$\frac{\frac{2}{5}}{\frac{3}{4}} = \frac{2}{\cancel{5}} \times \frac{4}{3} = \frac{(2)(4)}{(5)(3)} = \frac{8}{15}$

To simplify the multiplication or division, cancel factors common to a numerator and a denominator before combining fractions. It's okay to cancel across fractions. Take, for instance the operation $\frac{3}{4} \times \frac{4}{9} \times \frac{3}{2}$. Looking just at the first two fractions, you can factor out 4 and 3, so the operation simplifies to $\frac{1}{1} \times \frac{1}{3} \times \frac{3}{2}$. Now, looking just at the second and third fractions, you can factor out 3 and the operation becomes even simpler: $\frac{1}{1} \times \frac{1}{1} \times \frac{1}{2} = \frac{1}{2}$.

Apply the same rules in the same way to variables (letters) as to numbers.

$$\frac{2}{a} \times \frac{b}{4} \times \frac{a}{5} \times \frac{8}{c} = ?$$

A. $\dfrac{ab}{4c}$

B. $\dfrac{10b}{9c}$

C. $\dfrac{8}{5}$

D. $\dfrac{16b}{5ac}$

E. $\dfrac{4b}{5c}$

The correct answer is E. Since you're dealing only with multiplication, look for factors and variables (letters) in any numerator that are the same as those in any denominator. Canceling common factors leaves

$$\frac{2}{1} \times \frac{b}{1} \times \frac{1}{5} \times \frac{2}{c}.$$

Multiply numerators and combine denominators and you get $\dfrac{4b}{5c}$.

Mixed Numbers and Multiple Operations

A *mixed number* consists of a whole number along with a simple fraction—for example, the number $4\frac{2}{3}$. Before combining fractions, you might need to rewrite a mixed number as a fraction. To do so, follow these three steps:

1. Multiply the denominator of the fraction by the whole number.
2. Add the product to the numerator of the fraction.
3. Place the sum over the denominator of the fraction.

For example, here's how to rewrite the mixed number $4\frac{2}{3}$ into a fraction:

$$4\frac{2}{3} = \frac{(3)(4) + 2}{3} = \frac{14}{3}$$

To perform multiple operations, always perform multiplication and division before you perform addition and subtraction.

Part III: Quantitative Ability

$$\frac{4\frac{1}{2}}{1\frac{1}{8}} - 3\frac{2}{3} = ?$$

A. $\frac{1}{3}$

B. $\frac{3}{8}$

C. $\frac{11}{6}$

D. $\frac{17}{6}$

E. $\frac{11}{2}$

The correct answer is (A). First, rewrite all mixed numbers as fractions. Then, eliminate the complex fraction by multiplying the numerator fraction by the reciprocal of the denominator fraction (cancel across fractions before multiplying):

$$\frac{\frac{9}{2}}{\frac{9}{8}} - \frac{11}{3} = \left(\frac{9}{2}\right)\left(\frac{8}{9}\right) - \frac{11}{3} = \left(\frac{1}{1}\right)\left(\frac{4}{1}\right) - \frac{11}{3} = \frac{4}{1} - \frac{11}{3}$$

Then, express each fraction using the common denominator 3, then subtract:

$$\frac{4}{1} - \frac{11}{3} = \frac{12-11}{3} = \frac{1}{3}$$

Place Value and Operations with Decimals

Place value refers to the specific value of a digit in a decimal. For example, in the decimal 682.793:

The digit 6 is in the "hundreds" place.

The digit 8 is in the "tens" place.

The digit 2 is in the "ones" place.

The digit 7 is in the "tenths" place.

The digit 9 is in the "hundredths" place.

The digit 3 is in the "thousandths" place.

So, you can express 682.793 as follows:

$$600 + 80 + 2 + \frac{7}{10} + \frac{9}{100} + \frac{3}{1,000}.$$

To approximate, or round off, a decimal, round any digit less than 5 down to 0, and round any digit greater than 5 up to 0 (adding one digit to the place value to the left).

The value of 682.793, to the nearest hundredth, is 682.79.

The value of 682.793, to the nearest tenth, is 682.8.

The value of 682.793, to the nearest whole number, is 683.

The value of 682.793, to the nearest ten, is 680.

The value of 682.793, to the nearest hundred, is 700.

Multiplying decimals. The number of decimal places (digits to the right of the decimal point) in a product should be the same as the total number of decimal places in the numbers you multiply. So to multiply decimals quickly:

1. Multiply, but ignore the decimal points.
2. Count the total number of decimal places among the numbers you multiplied.
3. Include that number of decimal places in your product.

Here are two simple examples:

(23.6)(.07)	3 decimal places altogether
(236)(7) = 1652	Decimals temporarily ignored
(23.6)(.07) = 1.652	Decimal point inserted
(.01)(.02)(.03)	6 decimal places altogether
(1)(2)(3) = 6	Decimals temporarily ignored
(.01)(.02)(.03) = .000006	Decimal point inserted

Dividing decimal numbers. When you divide (or compute a fraction), you can move the decimal point in both numbers by the same number of places either to the left or right without altering the quotient (value of the fraction). Here are three related examples:

$$11.4 \div .3 = \frac{11.4}{.3} = \frac{114}{3} = 38$$

$$1.14 \div 3 = \frac{1.14}{3} = \frac{14}{300} = .38$$

$$114 \div .003 = \frac{114}{.003} = \frac{11,400}{3} = 3,800$$

> **Tip:** Eliminate decimal points from fractions, as well as from percents, to help you see more clearly the magnitude of the quantity you're dealing with.

GMAT questions involving place value and decimals usually require a bit more from you than just identifying a place value or moving around a decimal point. Typically, they require you to combine decimals with fractions or percents.

Which of the following is nearest in value to $\frac{1}{3} \times .3 \times \frac{1}{30} \times .03$?

A. $\frac{99}{1,000,000}$

B. $\frac{33}{100,000}$

C. $\frac{99}{100,000}$

D. $\frac{33}{10,000}$

E. $\frac{99}{10,000}$

The correct answer is (A). There are several ways to convert and combine the four numbers provided in the question. One method is to combine the two fractions: $\frac{1}{3} \times \frac{1}{30} = \frac{1}{90}$. Then, combine the two decimals: $.3 \times .03 = .009$. Finally, combine the two products: $.011 \times .009 \approx$

Chapter 6: Math Review—Number Forms, Relationships, and Sets

.000099. Each answer choice expresses a fraction, so you need to rewrite .000099 as a fraction by carefully counting place values. The final digit is in the "millionth" place. Choice (A) provides the fractional equivalent of this number.

Simple Problems Involving Percent

On the GMAT, a simple problem involving percent might ask you to perform any one of these four tasks:

1. Find a percent of a percent.
2. Find a percent of a number.
3. Find a number when a percent is given.
4. Find what percent one number is of another.

The following examples show you how to handle these four tasks (task 4 is a bit trickier than the others):

1. Finding a percent of a percent	*What is 2% of 2%?* Rewrite 20% as .20, then multiply: $.02 \times .02 = .004$, or .4%
2. Finding a percent of a number	*What is 35% of 65?* Rewrite 35% as .35, then multiply: $.35 \times 65 = 22.75$
3. Finding a number when a percent is given	*7 is 14% of what number?* Translate the question into an algebraic equation, writing the percent as either a fraction or decimal: $7 = 14\%$ of x $7 = .14x$ $x = \dfrac{7}{.14} = \dfrac{1}{.02} = \dfrac{100}{2} = 50$

Part III: Quantitative Ability

4. Finding what percent one number is of another	90 *is what % of 1,500?* Set up an equation to solve for the percent: $$\frac{90}{1,500} = \frac{x}{100}$$ $$1,500x = 9,000$$ $$15x = 90$$ $$x = \frac{90}{15}, \text{ or } 6$$

Percent Increase and Decrease

> **X-Ref**
> In example 4, you set up a proportion. (90 is to 1,500 as x is to 100.) You'll need to set up a proportion for other types of GMAT questions as well, including questions about ratios, which you'll look at a bit later in this chapter.

The concept of percent change is one of the test-makers' favorites. Here's the key to answering questions involving this concept: Percent change always relates to the value *before* the change. Here are two simple illustrations:

10 increased by what percent is 12?	1. The amount of the increase is 2. 2. Compare the change (2) to the original number (10). 3. The change in percent is , or 20.
12 decreased by what percent is 10?	1. The amount of the decrease is 2. 2. Compare the change (2) to the original number (12). 3. The change is $\frac{1}{6}$, or $16\frac{2}{3}$, or approximately 16.6%. (Did you remember from the equivalents table on page 192 that?)

Chapter 6: Math Review—Number Forms, Relationships, and Sets

Notice that the percent increase from 10 to 12 (20%) is not the same as the percent decrease from 12 to 10 ($16\frac{2}{3}$%). That's because the original number (before the change) is different in the two questions.

A typical GMAT percent-change problem will involve a story—about a type of quantity such as tax, profit or discount, or weight—in which you need to calculate successive changes in percent. For example:

- An increase, then a decrease (or vice versa)
- Multiple increases or decreases

Whatever the variation, just take the problem one step at a time and you'll have no trouble handling it.

> A stereo system original priced at $500 is discounted by 10%, then by another 10%. If a 20% tax is added to the purchase price, how much would a customer buying the system at its lowest price pay for it, including tax, to the nearest dollar?
>
> A. $413
> B. $480
> C. $486
> D. $500
> E. $512

The correct answer is C. After the first 10% discount, the price was $450 ($500 minus 10% of $500). After the second discount, which is calculated based on the $450 price, the price of the stereo is $405 ($450 minus 10% of $450). A 20% tax on $405 is $81. Thus, the customer has paid $405 + $81 = $486.

Part III: Quantitative Ability

A percent-change problem might also involve an accompanying chart or graph, which provides the numbers needed for the calculation.

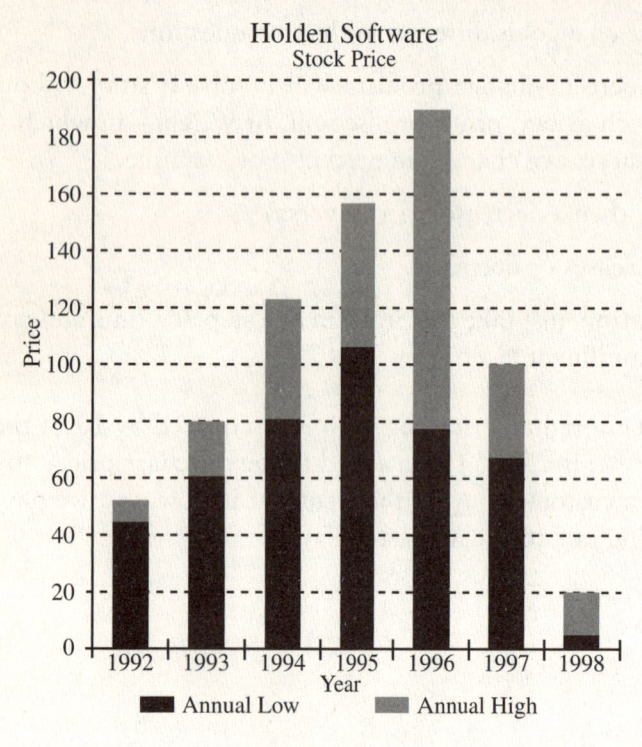

Holden Software Stock Price

[Bar chart showing Annual Low (black) and Annual High (gray) prices for years 1992–1998]

Based on the graph above, the average low price of Holden Software stock for the two-year period 1993–1994 was approximately what percent lower than its average high price for the two-year period 1996–1997?

- A. 25
- B. 37
- C. 45
- D. 52
- E. 75

The correct answer is C. Average *low* prices (represented by black bars) for 1993 and 1994 were $60 and $80, respectively—which yield an average of $70 for the two-year period. Average *high* prices (represented by gray bars) for 1996 and 1997 were approximately $190 and $100, respectively—which yield an average of $145. The percent decrease from $145 to $70 is just less than 50%. The only possible answer choice is (C).

Chapter 6: Math Review—Number Forms, Relationships, and Sets

> **Tip**
>
> If a question based on a bar graph, line graph, or pie chart asks for an approximation, the test-makers are telling you that it's okay to round off numbers you glean from the chart or graph. For example, in the preceding question, a rough estimate of $145 for the high 1996 average was close enough to determine the correct answer choice.

Ratios and Proportion

A *ratio* expresses proportion or comparative size—the size of one quantity *relative to* the size of another. As with fractions, you can simplify ratios to simplest form by dividing common factors. For example, given a class of 28 students—12 freshmen and 16 sophomores:

- The ratio of freshmen to sophomores is 12:16, or 3:4.
- The ratio of freshmen to the total number of students is 12:28, or 3:7.
- The ratio of sophomores to the total number of students is 16:28, or 4:7.

Finding a Ratio

A GMAT question might ask you to determine a ratio based on given quantities. This is the easiest type of GMAT ratio question.

> A class of 56 students contains only freshmen and sophomores. If 21 of the students are sophomores, what is the ratio between the number of freshmen and the number of sophomores in the class?
>
> A. 3:5
> B. 5:7
> C. 5:3
> D. 7:4
> E. 2:1

The correct answer is C. Since 21 of 56 students are sophomores, 35 must be freshman. The ratio of freshmen to sophomores is 35:21. To simplify the ratio to simplest term, divide both numbers by 7, giving you a ratio of 5:3.

Determining Quantities from a Ratio (Part-to-Whole Analysis)

You can think of any ratio as parts adding up to a whole. For example, in the ratio 5:6, 5 parts + 6 parts = 11 parts (the whole). If the actual total quantity were 22, you'd multiply each element by 2: 10 parts + 12 parts = 22 parts (the whole). Notice that the ratios are the same: 5:6 is the same ratio as 10:22.

You might be able to solve a GMAT ratio question using this part-to-whole approach.

> A class of students contains only freshmen and sophomores. If 18 of the students are sophomores, and if the ratio between the number of freshmen and the number of sophomores in the class is 5:3, how many students altogether are in the class?
> A. 30
> B. 36
> C. 40
> D. 48
> E. 56

The correct answer is D. Using a part-to-whole analysis, look first at the ratio and the sum of its parts: 5 (freshman) + 3 (sophomores) = 8 (total students). These aren't the actual quantities, but they're proportionate to those quantities. Given 18 sophomores altogether, sophomores account for 3 parts—each part containing 6 students. Accordingly, the total number of students must be $6 \times 8 = 48$.

Determining Quantities from a Ratio (Setting Up a Proportion)

Since you can express any ratio as a fraction, you can set two equivalent, or proportionate, ratios equal to each other, as fractions. So the ratio 16:28 is proportionate to the ratio 4:7 because $\frac{16}{28} = \frac{4}{7}$. If one of the four terms is missing from the equation (the proportion), you can solve for the missing term using algebra. So if the ratio 3:4 is proportionate to 4:x, you can solve for x in the equation $\frac{3}{4} = \frac{4}{x}$. Using the *cross-product* method, equate product of numerator and denominator across the equation:

$$(3)(x) = (4)(4)$$
$$3x = 16$$
$$x = \frac{16}{3}, \text{ or } 5\frac{1}{3}$$

Or, since the numbers are simple, shortcut the algebra by asking yourself what number you multiply the first numerator (3) by for a result that equals the other numerator (4):

$$3 \times \frac{4}{3} = 4 \text{ (a no-brainer calculation)}.$$

So you maintain proportion (equal ratios) by also multiplying the first denominator (4) by $\frac{4}{3}$:

$$4 \times \frac{4}{3} = \frac{16}{3} \text{ (another no-brainer calculation)}$$

Even if the quantities in a question strike you as decidedly "unround," it's a good bet that doing the math will be easier than you might first think.

If 3 miles is equivalent to 4.83 kilometers, then 11.27 kilometers are equivalent to how many miles?

A. 1.76
B. 5.9
C. 7.0
D. 8.4
E. 16.1

The correct answer is (C). The question essentially asks, "3 is to 4.83 as *what* is to 11.27?" Set up a proportion, then solve for x by the cross-product method:

$$\frac{3}{4.83} = \frac{x}{11.27}$$
$$(4.83)(x) = (3)(11.27)$$
$$x = \frac{(3)(11.27)}{4.83}$$
$$x = \frac{33.81}{4.83}, \text{ or } 7$$

Notice that, despite all the intimidating decimal numbers, the solution turns out to be a tidy number: 7. That's typical of the GMAT.

Arithmetic Mean (Simple Average), Median, Mode, and Range

Arithmetic mean (simple average), median, mode, and range are four different ways to describe a set of terms quantitatively. Here's the definition of each one:

arithmetic mean (average): In a set of n measurements, the sum of the measurements divided by n

median: The middle measurement after the measurements are ordered by size (or the average of the two middle measurements if the number of measurements is odd)

mode: The measurement that appears most frequently in a set

range: The difference between the greatest measurement and the least measurement

For example, given a set of six measurements, $\{8,-4,8,3,2,7\}$:

mean = 4	$(8 - 4 + 8 + 3 + 2 + 7) \div 6 = 24 \div 6 = 4$
median = 5	The average of 3 and 7—the two middle measurements in the set ordered in this way: $\{-4,2,3,7,8,8\}$
mode = 8	8 appears twice (more frequently than any other measurement)
range = 12	The difference between 8 and -4

For the same set of values, the mean (simple average) and the median can be, but are not necessarily, the same. For example: The set $\{3,4,5,6,7\}$ has both a mean and median of 5. However, the set $\{-2,0,5,8,9\}$ has a mean of 4 but a median of 5.

The GMAT covers arithmetic *mean* far more frequently than median, mode, or range, so let's focus on problems involving mean. First of all, in finding a simple average, be sure the numbers being added are all of the same form or in terms of the same units.

Chapter 6: Math Review—Number Forms, Relationships, and Sets

What is the average of $\frac{1}{5}$, 25%, and .09?

- A. .18
- B. 20%
- C. $\frac{1}{4}$
- D. .32
- E. $\frac{1}{3}$

The correct answer is A. Since the answer choices are not all expressed in the same form, first rewrite numbers as whichever form you think would be easiest to work with when you add the numbers together. In this case, the easiest form to work with is probably the decimal form. So, rewrite the first two numbers as decimals, and then find the sum of the three numbers: .20 + .25 + .09 = .54. Finally, divide by 3 to find the average: .54 ÷ 3 = .18.

To find a missing number when the average of all the numbers in a set is given, plug into the arithmetic-mean formula all the numbers you know—which include the average, the sum of the other numbers, and the number of terms. Then, use algebra to find the missing number. Or, you can try out each answer choice, in turn, as the missing number until you find one that results in the average given.

The average of five numbers is 26. Four of the numbers are –12, 90, –26, and 10. What is the fifth number?

- A. 16
- B. 42
- C. 44
- D. 68
- E. 84

The correct answer is D. To solve the problem algebraically, let x = the missing number. Set up the arithmetic-mean formula, then solve for x:

$$26 = \frac{(90 + 10 - 12 - 26) + x}{5}$$

$$26 = \frac{62 + x}{5}$$

$$130 = 62 + x$$

$$68 = x$$

Or, you can try out each answer choice in turn. Start with the middle value, 44 (choice (C)). The sum of 44 and the other four numbers is 106. Dividing this sum by 5 gives you 21.2—a number less than the average of 26 that you're aiming for. So you know the fifth number is greater than 44—and that leaves choices (D) and (E). Try out the number 68 (choice (D)), and you'll obtain the average of 26.

> **Tip**
>
> Remember: numerical answer choices are listed in ascending order of value. So, when working backward from numerical answer choices, start with choice (C), which is the median value. If (C) is either too great or too less, you've narrowed down the options to two: (A) and (B) or (D) and (E).

If the numbers are easy to work with, you might be able to determine a missing term, given the simple average of a set of numbers, without resorting to algebra. Simply apply a dose of logic.

If the average of six consecutive multiples of 4 is 22, what is the greatest of these integers?

A. 22
B. 24
C. 26
D. 28
E. 32

The correct answer is E. You can answer this question with common sense—no algebra required. Consecutive multiples of 4 are 4, 8, 12, 16,. . . . Given that the average of six such numbers is 22, the two middle terms (the third and fourth terms) must be 20 and 24. (Their average is 22.) Accordingly, the fifth term is 28, and the sixth and greatest term is 32.

Chapter 6: Math Review—Number Forms, Relationships, and Sets

Arithmetic Series

In an *arithmetic series* of numbers, there is a constant (unchanging) difference between successive numbers in the series. In other words, all numbers in an arithmetic series are evenly spaced. All of the following are examples of an arithmetic series:

- Successive integers
- Successive even integers
- Successive odd integers
- Successive multiples of the same number
- Successive integers ending in the same digit

On the GMAT, questions involving an arithmetic series might ask for the average or the sum of a series. When the numbers to be averaged form an arithmetic (evenly spaced) series, the average is simply the median (the middle number or the average of the two middle numbers if the number of terms is even). In other words, the mean and median of the set of numbers are the same. Faced with calculating the average of a long series of evenly-spaced integers, you can shortcut the addition.

What is the average of the first 20 positive integers?

A. $7\frac{1}{2}$
B. 10
C. $10\frac{1}{2}$
D. 15
E. 20

The correct answer is C. Since the terms are evenly spaced, the average is halfway between the 10th and 11th terms—which happen to be the integers 10 and 11. So, the average is $10\frac{1}{2}$. (This number is also the median.) If you take the average of the first term (1) and the last term (20), you get the same result:

$$\frac{1+20}{2} = \frac{21}{2}, \text{ or } 10\frac{1}{2}$$

Finding the sum (rather than the average) of an arithmetic (evenly spaced) series of numbers requires only one additional step: multiplying the average (which is also the median) by the number of terms in the series. The trickiest aspect of this type of question is determining the number of terms in the series.

What is the sum of all odd integers between 10 and 40?

- A. 250
- B. 325
- C. 375
- D. 400
- E. 450

The correct answer is C. The average of the described numbers is 25—halfway between 10 and 40 (in other words, half the sum of 10 and 40). The number of terms in the series is 15. (The first term is 11, and the last term is 39.) The sum of the described series of integers = $25 \times 15 = 375$.

> **Alert!** When calculating the average or sum of a series of evenly-spaced numbers, be careful when counting the number of terms in the series. For instance, the number of positive *odd* integers less than 50 is 25, but the number of positive *even* integers less than 50 is only 24.

Permutations

A *permutation* is an arrangement of objects in which the order (sequence) is important. Each arrangement of the letters A, B, C, and D, for example, is a different permutation of the four letters. There are two different ways to determine the number of permutations for a group of objects.

1. List all the permutations, using a methodical process to make sure you don't overlook any. For the letters A, B, C, and D, start with A in the first position, then list all possibilities for the second position, along with all possibilities for the third and fourth positions (you'll discover six permutations):

A B C D	A C B D	A D B C
A B D C	A C D B	A D C B

Placing B in the first position would also result in 6 permutations. The same applies to either C or D in the first position. So the total number of permutations is $6 \times 4 = 24$.

2. Use the following formula (let n = the number of objects, and limit the number of terms to the counting numbers, or positive integers):

Number of permutations = $n(n - 1)(n - 2)(n - 3) \ldots$

The number of permutations can be expressed as $n!$ ("n factorial"). Using the factorial formula is much easier than compiling a list of permutations. For example, try applying the formula to the letters A, B, C, and D:

$4! = 4(4 - 1)(4 - 2)(4 - 3) = 4 \times 3 \times 2 \times 1 = 24$

Five tokens—one red, one blue, one green, and two white—are arranged in a row, one next to another. If the two white tokens are next to each other, how many arrangements according to color are possible?

A. 12
B. 16
C. 20
D. 24
E. 30

The correct answer is (D). The two white tokens might be in positions 1 and 2, 2 and 3, 3 and 4, or 4 and 5. For each of these four possibilities, there are 6 possible color arrangements (3!) for the other three tokens (which all differ in color). Thus, the total number of possible arrangements is 4×6, or 24.

> **Tip**
>
> You can shortcut common factorial calculations by memorizing them:
>
> $3! = 6$, $4! = 24$, and $5! = 120$.

Combinations

A *combination* is a group of certain objects selected from a larger set. The order of objects in the group is not important. You can determine the total number of possible combinations by listing the possible groups in a methodical manner. For instance, to determine the number of possible three-letter groups among the letters A, B, C, D, and E, work methodically, starting with A as a group member paired with B, then C, then D, then E. Be sure not to repeat combinations (repetitions are indicated in parentheses here).

A, B, C	(A, C, B)	(A, D, B)	(A, E, B)
A, B, D	A, C, D	(A, D, C)	(A, E, C)
A, B, E	A, C, E	A, D, E	(A, E, D)

> **Alert!** Notice that each parenthesized combination backtracks to an earlier letter. So, to be sure you don't repeat any combination, make sure you don't backtrack to an earlier object.

Perform the same task assuming B is in the group, then assuming C is in the group (all combinations not listed here repeat what's already listed).

B, C, D	C, D, E
B, C, E	
B, D, E	

The total number of combinations is 10.

How many two-digit numbers can be formed from the digits 1 through 9, if no digit appears twice in a number?

A. 36
B. 72
C. 81
D. 144
E. 162

The correct answer is B. Each digit can be paired with any of the other 8 digits. To avoid double counting, account for the possible pairs as follows: 1 and 2–9 (8 pairs), 2 and 3–9 (7 pairs), 3 and 4–9 (6 pairs), and so forth. The total number of distinct pairs is $8 + 7 + 6 + 5 + 4 + 3 + 2 + 1 = 36$. Since the digits in each pair can appear in either order, the total number of possible two-digit numbers is 2×36, or 72.

> **X-Ref** You can approach combination problems as *probability* problems as well. Why? You can think of the "probability" of any single combination as "one divided by" the total number of combinations (a fraction between zero and 1). Use whichever method is quickest for the question at hand. The topic of probability is next.

Probablility

Probability refers to the statistical chances, of an event occurring (or not occurring). By definition, probability ranges from 0 to 1. (Probability is never negative, and it's never greater than 1.) Here's the basic formula for determining probability:

$$\text{Probability} = \frac{\text{number of ways the event can occur}}{\text{total number of possible occurrences}}$$

If you randomly select one candy from a jar containing two cherry candies, two licorice candies, and one peppermint candy, what is the probability of selecting a cherry candy?

A. $\frac{1}{6}$

B. $\frac{1}{5}$

C. $\frac{1}{3}$

D. $\frac{2}{5}$

E. $\frac{3}{5}$

The correct answer is D. There are two ways among five possible occurrences that a cherry candy will be selected. Thus, the probability of selecting a cherry candy is $\frac{2}{5}$.

> **Tip**
>
> To calculate the probability of an event NOT occurring, just *subtract* the probability of the event occurring *from 1*. So, referring to the preceding question, the probability of NOT selecting a cherry candy is $\frac{3}{5}$. (Subtract $\frac{2}{5}$ from 1.)

Take It to the Next Level

This Next Level focuses first on the following specific applications of fractions, percents, decimals, ratios, and proportion (with special emphasis on how the test-makers incorporate algebraic features into GMAT questions covering these concepts):

- Altering fractions and ratios
- Ratios involving more than two quantities
- Proportion problems with variables

Next, you'll explore how the test-makers design tougher-than-average GMAT questions involving the following topics (all of which we've covered in this chatper except the second and third topics listed here):

- Arithmetic mean (simple average) and median (two ways that a set of numbers can be measured as a whole)
- Standard deviation (a quantitative expression of the dispersion of a set of measurements)
- Geometric series (the pattern from one number to the next in an exponential sequence of numbers)
- Permutations (the possibilities for arranging a set of objects)
- Combinations (the possibilities for selecting groups of objects from a set)
- Probability (the statistical chances of a certain event, permutation, or combination occurring)

Altering Fractions and Ratios

An average test-taker might assume that *adding* the same *positive* quantity to a fraction's numerator (p) and to its denominator (q) leaves the fraction's value $\left(\frac{p}{q}\right)$ unchanged. But this is true *if and only if* the original numerator and denominator were equal to each other. Otherwise, the fraction's value will change. Remember the following three rules, which apply to any positive numbers x, p, and q (the first one is the no-brainer you just read):

If $p = q$, then $\dfrac{p}{q} = \dfrac{p+x}{q+x}$. (The fraction's value remains unchanged and is always 1.)

If $p > q$, then $\dfrac{p}{q} > \dfrac{p+x}{q+x}$. (The fraction's value will *decrease*.)

If $p < q$, then $\dfrac{p}{q} < \dfrac{p+x}{q+x}$. (The fraction's value will *increase*.)

A GMAT question might ask you to alter a ratio by adding or subtracting from one (or both) terms in the ratio. The rules for altering ratios are the same as for altered fractions. In either case, set up a proportion and solve algebraically for the unknown term.

> A drawer contains exactly half as many white shirts as blue shirts. If four more shirts of each color are added to the drawer, the ratio of blue to white shirts would be 8:5. How many blue shirts does the drawer contain?
>
> A. 14
> B. 12
> C. 11
> D. 10
> E. 9

The correct answer is B. Represent the original ratio of white to blue shirts by the fraction $\dfrac{x}{2x}$, where x is the number of white shirts, then add 4 to both the numerator and denominator. Set this fraction equal to $\dfrac{5}{8}$ (the ratio after adding shirts). Cross-multiply to solve for x:

$$\dfrac{x+4}{2x-4} = \dfrac{5}{8}$$
$$8x + 32 = 10x + 20$$
$$12 = 2x$$
$$x = 6$$

The original denominator is $2x$, or 12.

> **Tip**
>
> When you add (or subtract) the same number from both the numerator and denominator of a fraction—or from each term in a ratio—you alter the fraction or ratio—unless the original ratio was 1:1 (in which case the ratio goes unchanged).

Ratios Involving More than Two Quantities

You approach ratio problems involving three or more quantities the same way as those involving only two quantities. The only difference is that there are more "parts" that make up the "whole."

Three lottery winners—X, Y, and Z—are sharing a lottery jackpot. X's share is $\frac{1}{5}$ of Y's share and $\frac{1}{7}$ of Z's share. If the total jackpot is $195,000, what is the dollar amount of Z's share?

A. $15,000
B. $35,000
C. $75,000
D. $105,000
E. $115,000

The correct answer is D. At first glance, this problem doesn't appear to involve ratios. (Where's the colon?) But it does. The ratio of X's share to Y's share is 1:5, and the ratio of X's share to Z's share is 1:7. So you can set up the following triple ratio:

$X:Y:Z = 1:5:7$

X's winnings account for 1 of 13 equal parts (1 + 5 + 7) of the total jackpot. $\frac{1}{13}$ of $195,000 is $15,000. Accordingly, Y's share is 5 times that amount, or $75,000, and Z's share is 7 times that amount, or $105,000.

> In handling word problems involving ratios, think of a whole as the sum of its fractional parts, as in the method used to solve the preceding problem: $\frac{1}{13}$ (X's share) + $\frac{5}{13}$ (Y's share) + $\frac{7}{13}$ (Z's share) = 1 (the whole jackpot).

Proportion Problems with Variables

A GMAT proportion question might use *letters* instead of numbers—to focus on the process rather than the result. You can solve these problems algebraically or by using the plug-in strategy.

> A candy store sells candy only in half-pound boxes. At *c* cents per box, which of the following is the cost of *a* ounces of candy? [1 pound = 16 ounces]
>
> A. $\dfrac{c}{a}$
>
> B. $\dfrac{a}{16c}$
>
> C. ac
>
> D. $\dfrac{ac}{8}$
>
> E. $\dfrac{8c}{a}$

The correct answer is D. This question is asking: "*c* cents is to one box as *how many cents* are to *a* ounces?" Set up a proportion, letting *x* equal the cost of *a* ounces. Because the question asks for the cost of *ounces*, convert 1 box to 8 ounces (a half pound). Use the cross-product method to solve quickly:

$$\frac{c}{8} = \frac{x}{a}$$

$$8x = ca$$

$$x = \frac{ca}{8}$$

You can also use the plug-in strategy for this question—either instead of algebra or, better yet, to check the answer you chose using algebra. Pick easy numbers to work with, such as 100 for *c* and 8 for *a*. At 100 cents per 8-ounce box, 8 ounces of candy costs 100 cents. Plug in your numbers for *a* and *c* into each answer choice. Only choice (D) gives you the number 100 you're looking for.

Simple Average and Median

For any set of terms, the *arithmetic mean* (*AM*), also called the *simple average*, is the sum of the terms ($a + b + c + \ldots$) divided by the number of terms (n) in the set.

$$AM = \frac{(a + b + c + \ldots)}{n}$$

On the GMAT, easier questions involving simple average might ask you to add numbers together and divide a sum. A tougher question might ask you to perform one or both of these tasks (both of which involve algebra):

- Find the value of a number that changes an average from one number to another express simple average in terms of variables instead of just numbers

- When an additional number is added to a set, and the average of the numbers in the set changes as a result, you can determine the value of the number that's added by applying the arithmetic-mean formula twice.

The average of three numbers is -4. If a fourth number is added, the arithmetic mean of all four numbers is -1. What is the fourth number?

A. -10
B. 2
C. 8
D. 10
E. 16

The correct answer is C. To solve the problem algebraically, first determine the sum of the three original numbers by the arithmetic-mean formula:

$$-4 = \frac{a + b + c}{3}$$

Then, apply the formula again accounting for the additional (fourth) number. The new average is -1, the sum of the other three numbers is -12, and the number of terms is 4. Solve for the missing number (x):

$$-1 = \frac{-12 + x}{4}$$
$$-4 = -12 + x$$
$$8 = x$$

Chapter 6: Math Review—Number Forms, Relationships, and Sets

You approach arithmetic-mean problems that involve *variables* instead of (or in addition to) numbers in the same way as those involving only numbers. Just plug-in the information you're given to the arithmetic-mean formula, and then solve the problem algebraically.

If A is the average of P, Q, and another number, which of the following represents the missing number?

A. $3A - P - Q$
B. $A + P + Q$
C. $3A - P + Q$
D. $A - P + Q$
E. $3A - P + Q$

The correct answer is A. Let x = the missing number. Solve for x by the arithmetic-mean formula:

$$A = \frac{P + Q + x}{3}$$

$$3A = P + Q + x$$

$$3A - P - Q = x$$

Alert! Should you try using the plug-in strategy to solve this problem, testing each answer choice by substituting simple numbers for P, Q, and A? No; it's too complex. So you'll need to be flexible. Try using shortcuts wherever you can, but recognize their limitations.

Standard Deviation

Standard deviation is a measure of dispersion among members of a set. Computing standard deviation involves these steps:

1. Compute the arithmetic mean (simple average) of all terms in the set.

2. Compute the difference between the mean and each term.

3. Square each difference you computed in step (2).

4. Compute the mean of the squares you computed in step (3).

5. Compute the non-negative square root of the mean you computed in step (4).

For example, here's how you'd determine the standard deviation of Distribution A: {−1, 2, 3, 4}:

1. Arithmetic mean $= \dfrac{-1 + 2 + 3 + 4}{4} = \dfrac{8}{4} = 2$.

2. The difference between the mean (2) and each term: $2 - (-1) = 3$; $2 - 2 = 0$; $3 - 2 = 1$; $4 - 2 = 2$.

3. The square of each difference: $\{3^2, 0^2, 1^2, 2^2\} = \{9, 0, 1, 4\}$

4. The mean of the squares: $\dfrac{9 + 0 + 1 + 4}{4} = \dfrac{14}{4} = \dfrac{7}{2}$

5. The standard deviation of Distribution A $= \sqrt{\dfrac{7}{2}}$

A GMAT question might ask you to calculate standard deviation (as in the preceding example). Or, a question might ask you to *compare* standard deviations. You might be able to make the comparison without precise calculations—by remembering to the follow this general rule: *The greater the data are spread away from the mean, the greater the standard deviation.* For example, consider these two distributions:

Distribution A: {1, 2.5, 4, 5.5, 7}

Distribution B: {1, 3, 4, 5, 7}

In both sets, the mean and median is 4, and the range is 6. But the standard deviation of A is greater than that of B, because 2.5 and 5.5 are further away than 3 and 5 from the mean.

Which of the following distributions has the greatest standard deviation?

A. {−1, 1, 3}
B. {1, 2, 5}
C. {0, 4, 5}
D. {−3, −1, 2}
E. {2, 3, 6}

The correct answer is C. Notice that in each of the choices (A), (B), and (E), the distribution's range is 4, but that in choice (C) and choice (D), the range is 5. So, the correct answer is probably either (C) or (D). Focusing on these two choices, notice that the middle term in choice (C), 4, is skewed further away from the mean than the middle term in choice (D). That's a good indication that (C) provides the distribution having the greatest standard deviation.

Chapter 6: Math Review—Number Forms, Relationships, and Sets

Geometric Series

In a *geometric series* of numbers, each term is a constant multiple of the preceding one; in other words, the ratio between any term and the next one is constant. The multiple (or ratio) might be obvious by examining the series—for example:

In the geometric series 2, 4, 8, 16, . . . , you can easily determine that the constant multiple is 2 (and the ratio of each term to the next is 1:2).

In the geometric series 1, −3, 9, −27, . . . , you can easily determine that the constant multiple is −3 (and the ratio of each term to the next is 1:−3).

Once you know the multiple (or ratio), you can answer any question asking for an unknown term—or for either the sum or the average of certain terms.

In a geometric series, each term is a constant multiple of the preceding one. If the third and fourth numbers in the series are 8 and −16, respectively, what is the first term in the series?

A. −32
B. 4
C. 2
D. 4
E. 64

The correct answer is C. The constant multiple is −2. But since you need to work backward from the third term (8), apply the *reciprocal* of that multiple twice. The second term is $(8)\left(-\frac{1}{2}\right) = -4$. The first term is $(-4)\left(-\frac{1}{2}\right) = 2$.

In a geometric series, each term is a constant multiple of the preceding one. What is the sum of the first four numbers in a geometric series whose second number is 4 and whose third number is 6?

A. 16
B. 19
C. $22\frac{1}{2}$
D. $21\frac{2}{3}$
E. 20

The correct answer is D. The constant multiple is $\frac{3}{2}$. In other words, the ratio of each term to the next is 3:2. Since the second term is 4, the first term is $4 \times \frac{2}{3} = \frac{8}{3}$. Since the third term is 6, the fourth term is $6 \times \frac{3}{2} = \frac{18}{2}$, or 9. The sum of the four terms $= \frac{8}{3} + 4 + 6 + 9 = 21\frac{2}{3}$.

> **Alert!** You can't calculate the average of terms in a geometric series simply by averaging the first and last term in the series. That's because the progression is geometric, not arithmetic. Instead, you need to add up the terms, then divide by the number of terms.

You can also solve geometric series problems by applying a special formula. But you'll need to memorize it because the test won't provide it. In the following formula, r = the constant multiple (or the ratio between each term and the preceding one), a = the first term in the series, n = the position number for any particular term in the series, and T = the particular term itself:

$$ar^{(n-1)} = T$$

You can solve for any of the formula's variables, as long as you know the values for the other three. Following are two examples:

If $a = 3$ and $r = 2$, then the third term $= (3)(2)^2 = 12$, and the sixth term $= (3)(2)^5 = (3)(32) = 96$.

If the sixth term is $-\frac{1}{16}$ and the constant ratio is $\frac{1}{2}$, then the first term $(a) = -2$:

$$a\left(\frac{1}{2}\right)^5 = -\frac{1}{16}$$

$$a\left(\frac{1}{32}\right) = -\frac{1}{16}$$

$$a\left(-\frac{1}{16}\right)(32) = -2$$

The algebra is simple enough—but you need to know the formula, of course.

In a geometric series, each term is a constant multiple of the preceding one. If the first three terms in a geometric series are -2, x, and -8, which of the following could be the sixth term in the series?

A. $-4{,}096$
B. $-1{,}024$
C. 512
D. $1{,}024$
E. $2{,}048$

The correct answer is E. Since all pairs of successive terms must have the same ratio, $\frac{-2}{x} = \frac{x}{-8}$. By the cross-product method, $x^2 = 16$, and hence $x = \pm 4$. Applying the formula you just learned, for $+4$, the sixth term would be $(-2)(4)^5 = -2{,}048$, while for -4 it would be $2{,}048$.

Permutations

A *permutation* is an arrangement of objects in which the order (sequence) is important. Each arrangement of the letters A, B, C, and D, for example, is a different permutation of the four letters. There are two different ways to determine the number of permutations for a group of distinct objects.

1. List all the permutations, using a methodical process to make sure you don't overlook any.

2. Use the following formula (let n = the number of objects) and limit the number of terms to the counting numbers, or positive integers:

$$\text{Number of permutations} = n(n-1)(n-2)(n-3)\ldots$$

For example, the number of arrangements (permutations) of the four letters A, B, C, and D is $4! = 4 \times 3 \times 2 \times 1 = 24$.

To handle a tougher permutation question, you might need to calculate multiple permutations, then add them together—applying a dose of logic along the way.

Five children—two boys and three girls—are standing in a single-file line. If the first in line is a girl, how many different arrangements of the five children are possible?

A. 16
B. 20
C. 36
D. 45
E. 72

The correct answer is E. Label the five children B1, B2, G1, G2, and G3. If G1 is first in line, with the other four children in any order, the number of permutations is 4!, or 24. The same applies to either G2 or G3 in the first position. So the total number of permutations is $4! + 4! + 4! = 72$.

Combinations

A *combination* is a group of certain objects selected from a larger set. The order of objects in the group is not important. You can determine the total number of possible combinations by listing the possible groups in a methodical manner. On the GMAT, a simple combination question will involve the selection of one or more objects from *one* larger set. A more complex combination question might require you to determine the number of combinations involving *two or more* sets of objects.

Chapter 6: Math Review—Number Forms, Relationships, and Sets

From a group of three violinists and four pianists, a judge must select two violinists and two pianists to perform at a music recital. How many different combinations of musicians might perform at the recital?

A. 9
B. 12
C. 18
D. 24
E. 30

The correct answer is C. The judge must select two of three violinists, for a total of three possible combinations. The judge must select two of four pianists, for a total of six possible combinations. For each pair of violinists, there are six possible pairs of pianists. Thus, the total number of four-musician combinations is $6 \times 3 = 18$.

A combination question might also incorporate a permutation feature, making it even more challenging.

From a group of three singers and three comedians, a show organizer must select two singers and two comedians to appear one after another in a show. How many different ways can the organizer arrange performers for the show?

A. 72
B. 90
C. 136
D. 180
E. 216

The correct answer is E. The organizer must select two of three singers, for a total of 3 possible combinations. Similarly, the judge must select two of three comedians, for a total of 3 possible combinations. For each pair of singers, there are 3 possible pairs of comedians. Thus, the total number of four-performer combinations is 3×3, or 9. The four performers can appear in any order in the show. So, for each four-performer combination, there are 24 permutations (4!, or $4 \times 3 \times 2 \times 1$). The total number of possible arrangements, then, is 24×9, or 216.

Probability

Here's the basic formula for determining the probability of an event occurring:

$$\text{Probability} = \frac{\text{number of ways the event can occur}}{\text{total number of possible occurrences}}$$

For example, a standard deck of 52 playing cards contains 12 face cards. The probability of selecting a face card from a standard deck is $\frac{12}{52}$, or $\frac{3}{13}$. On the GMAT, a tougher probability question will involve this basic formula, but will also add a complication of some kind. It might require you to determine any of the following:

- Certain missing facts needed for a given probability
- Probabilities involving two (or more) *independent* events
- Probabilities involving an event that is *dependent* on another event

Alert!

Think twice before you try to "intuit" the answer for these three types of probability questions. Probabilities involving complex scenarios such as these are often greater or less than you might expect.

Missing Facts Needed for a Given Probability

In this question type, instead of calculating probability, you determine what missing number is needed for a given probability. Don't panic; just plug what you know into the basic formula, and solve for the missing number.

A piggy-bank contains a certain number of coins, of which 53 are dimes and 19 are nickels. The remainder of the coins in the bank are quarters. If the probability of selecting a quarter from this bank is $\frac{1}{4}$, how many quarters does the bank contain?

A. 30
B. 27
C. 24
D. 21
E. 16

The correct answer is C. On its face, this question looks complicated, but it's really not. Just plug what you know into the probability formula. Let x = the number of quarters in the bank (this is the numerator of the formula's fraction), and let $x + 72$ = the total number of coins (the fraction's denominator). Then solve for x (use the cross-product method to clear fractions):

$$\frac{1}{4} = \frac{x}{x + 72}$$
$$x + 72 = 4x$$
$$72 = 3x$$
$$24 = x$$

Probability Involving Two (or More) Independent Events

Two events are independent if neither event affects the probability that the other will occur. (You'll look at dependent events a few pages ahead.) On the GMAT, look for either of these scenarios involving independent events:

- The random selection of one object from *each of two or more groups*
- The random selection of one object from a group, then *replacing* it and selecting again (as in a "second round" or "another turn" of a game)

In either scenario, the simplest calculation involves finding the probability of two events both occurring. All you need to do is multiply together their individual probabilities:

(probability of event 1 occurring) × (probability of event 2 occurring) = (probability of both events occurring)

For example, assume that you randomly select one letter from each of two sets: {A,B} and {C,D,E}. The probability of selecting A and C = $\frac{1}{2} \times \frac{1}{3}$, or $\frac{1}{6}$.

Tip: To calculate the probability that two events will *not both* occur, *subtract from 1* the probability of both events occurring. To determine the probability that *three* events will all occur, just multiply the third event's probability by the other two.

If one student is chosen randomly out of a group of seven students, then one student is again chosen randomly from the same group of seven, what is the probability that two different students will be chosen?

A. $\dfrac{36}{49}$

B. $\dfrac{6}{7}$

C. $\dfrac{19}{21}$

D. $\dfrac{13}{14}$

E. $\dfrac{48}{49}$

The correct answer is E. You must first calculate the chances of picking *the same student twice* by multiplying together the two individual probabilities for the student: $\dfrac{1}{7} \times \dfrac{1}{7} = \dfrac{1}{49}$. The probability of picking the same student twice, added to the probability of not picking the same student twice, equals 1. So to answer the question, subtract $\dfrac{1}{49}$ from 1.

> **Alert!**
>
> In one selection, the probability of *not* selecting a certain student from the group of seven is $\dfrac{6}{7}$ (the probability of selecting the student, subtracted from 1). But does this mean that the probability of not selecting the same student twice $= \dfrac{6}{7} \times \dfrac{6}{7} = \dfrac{36}{49}$? No! Make sure you understand the difference.

Probability Involving a Dependent Event

Two distinct events might be related in that one event affects the probability of the other one occurring — for example, randomly selecting one object from a group, then selecting a second object from the same group *without replacing the first selection*. Removing one object from the group *increases the odds* of selecting any particular object from those that remain.

You handle this type of problem as you would any other probability problem: Calculate individual probabilities, then combine them.

Chapter 6: Math Review—Number Forms, Relationships, and Sets

In a random selection of two people from a group of five—A, B, C, D, and E—what is the probability of selecting A and B?

A. $\dfrac{2}{5}$

B. $\dfrac{1}{5}$

C. $\dfrac{1}{10}$

D. $\dfrac{1}{15}$

E. $\dfrac{1}{20}$

The correct answer is C. You need to consider each of the two selections separately. In the first selection, the probability of selecting either A or B is $\dfrac{2}{5}$. But the probability of selecting the second of the two is $\dfrac{1}{4}$—because after the first selection only four people remain from whom to select. Since the question asks for the probability of selecting both A and B (as opposed to either one), multiply the two individual probabilities: $\dfrac{2}{5} \times \dfrac{1}{4} = \dfrac{2}{20} = \dfrac{1}{10}$.

You can also approach a question such as this one as a *combination* problem. For this question, here are all the possibilities:

A and either B, C, D, or E (4 combinations)

B and either C, D, or E (3 combinations)

C and either D or E (2 combinations)

D and E (1 combination)

There are 10 possible combinations, so the probability of selecting A and B is 1 in 10.

Alert!

Strategies such as plugging-in test numbers, working backwards, and even sizing up the answer choices don't work for most probability questions (including the preceding one).

Take It to the Next Level

Chapter 7

Math Review—Number Theory and Algebra

In this chapter, first you'll broaden your arithmetical horizons by dealing with numbers in more abstract, theoretical settings. You'll examine the following topics:

- The concept of absolute value
- Number signs and integers—and what happens to them when you apply the four basic operations
- Factors, multiples, divisibility, prime numbers, and the "prime factorization" method
- The rules for combining exponential numbers (base numbers and "powers") using the four basic operations
- The rules for combining radicals using the four basic operations
- The rules for simplifying terms containing radical signs

Then, you'll review the following basic algebra skills:

- Solving a linear equation in one variable
- Solving a system of two equations in two variables—by substitution and by addition-subtraction
- Recognizing unsolvable linear equations when you see them
- Handling algebraic inequalities

Basic Properties of Numbers

You'll begin this chapter by reviewing the basics about integers, number signs (positive and negative), and prime numbers. First, make sure you're up to speed on the following definitions, which you'll need to know for this chapter as well as for the test:

Chapter 7: Math Review—Number Theory and Algebra

- **Absolute value (of a real number):** The number's distance from zero (the origin) on the real-number line. The absolute value of x is indicated as $|x|$. (The absolute value of a negative number can be less than, equal to, or greater than a positive number.)

- **Integer:** Any non-fraction number on the number line: $\{\ldots -3, -2, -1, 0, 1, 2, 3, \ldots\}$. Except for the number zero (0), every integer is either positive or negative. Every integer is either even or odd.

- **Factor (of an integer n):** Any integer that you can multiply by another integer for a product of n.

- **Prime number:** Any positive integer that has exactly two positive factors: 1 and the number itself. In other words, a prime number is not divisible by (a multiple of) any positive integer other than itself and 1.

Alert!

The factors of any integer n include 1 as well as n itself. Zero (0) and 1 are not prime numbers; 2 is the first prime number.

Number Signs and the Four Basic Operations

The four basic operations are addition, subtraction, multiplication, and division. Be sure you know the sign of a number that results from combining numbers using these operations. Here's a table that includes all the possibilities (a "?" indicates that the sign depends on which number has the greater absolute value):

Addition	Subtraction	Multiplication	Division
(+) + (+) = +	(+) − (−) = (+)	(+) × (+) = +	(+) ÷ (+) = +
(−) + (−) = −	(−) − (+) = (−)	(+) × (−) = −	(+) ÷ (−) = −
(+) + (−) = ?	(+) − (+) = ?	(−) × (+) = −	(−) ÷ (+) = −
(−) + (+) = ?	(−) − (−) = ?	(−) × (−) = +	(−) ÷ (−) = +

GMAT problems involving combining numbers by addition or subtraction usually incorporate the concept of absolute value, as well as the rule for subtracting negative numbers.

Part III: Quantitative Ability

$|-1 - 2| - |5 - 6| - |-3 + 4| = ?$

A. -5
B. -3
C. 1
D. 3
E. 5

The correct answer is C. First, determine each of the three absolute values:

$|-1 - 2| = |-3| = 3$

$|5 - 6| = |-1| = 1$

$|-3 + 4| = |1| = 1$

Then combine the three results: $3 - 1 - 1 = 1$.

Because multiplication (or division) involving two negative terms always results in a positive number:

- Multiplication or division involving any *even* number of negative terms gives you a positive number.
- Multiplication or division involving any *odd* number of negative terms gives you a negative number.

A number N is the product of seven negative numbers, and the number M is the product of six negative numbers and one positive number. Which of the following holds true for all possible values of M and N?

I. $M \times N < 0$
II. $M - N < 0$
III. $N + M < 0$

A. I only
B. II only
C. I and II only
D. II and III only
E. I, II, and III

The correct answer is C. The product of seven negative numbers is always a negative number. (M is a negative number.) The product of six negative numbers is always a positive number, and the product of two positive numbers is always a positive number. (N is a positive number.) Thus, the product of M and N must be a negative number; (I) is always true. Subtracting a positive number N from a negative number M always results in a negative number less than M; (II) is always true. However, whether (III) is true depends on the values of M and N. If $|N| > |M|$, then $N + M > 0$, but if $|N| < |M|$, then $N + M < 0$.

Integers and the Four Basic Operations

When you combine integers using a basic operation, whether the result is an odd integer, an even integer, or a non-integer depends on the numbers you combined. Here's a table that summarizes all the possibilities:

Addition and Subtraction
integer ± integer = integer
even integer ± even integer = even integer
even integer ± odd integer = odd integer
odd integer ± odd integer = even integer
Multiplication and Division
integer × integer = integer
integer ÷ non-zero integer = integer, but only if the numerator is divisible by the denominator (if the result is a quotient with no remainder)
odd integer × odd integer = odd integer
even integer × non-zero integer = even integer
even integer ÷ 2 = integer
odd integer ÷ 2 = non-integer

GMAT questions that test you on the preceding rules sometimes look like algebra problems, but they're really not. Just apply the appropriate rule or, if you're not sure of the rule, plug in simple numbers to zero-in on the correct answer.

If P is an odd integer, and if Q is an even integer, which of the following expressions CANNOT represent an even integer?

A. $3P - Q$
B. $3P \times Q$
C. $2Q \times P$
D. $3Q - 2P$
E. $32P - 2Q$

The correct answer is A. Since 3 and P are both odd integers, their product ($3P$) must also be an odd integer. Subtracting an even integer (Q) from an odd integer results in an odd integer in all cases.

Factors, Multiples, and Divisibility

Figuring out whether one number (f) is a factor of another (n) is no big deal. Just divide n by f. If the quotient is an integer, then f is a factor of n (and n is divisible by f). If the quotient is not an integer, then f is not a factor of n, and you'll end up with a *remainder* after dividing. For example, 2 is a factor of 8 because $8 \div 2 = 4$, which is an integer. On the other hand, 3 is not a factor of 8 because $8 \div 3 = \frac{8}{3}$, or $2\frac{2}{3}$, which is a non-integer. (The remainder is 2.)

Remember these basic rules about factors, which are based on the definition of the term "factor":

1. Any integer is a factor of itself.
2. 1 and −1 are factors of all integers.
3. The integer zero has an infinite number of factors, but is not a factor of any integer.
4. A positive integer's greatest factor (other than itself) will never be greater than one half the value of the integer.

On the "flip side" of factors are multiples. If f is a factor of n, then n is a multiple of f. For example, 8 is a multiple of 2 for the same reason that 2 is a factor of 8—because $8 \div 2 = 4$, which is an integer.

As you can see, factors, multiples, and divisibility are simply different aspects of the same concept. So, a GMAT question about factoring is also about multiples and divisibility.

Chapter 7: Math Review—Number Theory and Algebra

If $n > 6$, and if n is a multiple of 6, which of the following is always a factor of n?

A. $n - 6$
B. $n + 6$
C. $\dfrac{n}{3}$
D. $\dfrac{n}{2} + 3$
E. $\dfrac{n}{2} + 6$

The correct answer is C. Since 3 is a factor of 6, 3 is also a factor of any positive-number multiple of 6. Thus, if you divide any multiple of 6 by 3, the quotient will be an integer. In other words, 3 will be a factor of that number (n). As for the incorrect choices, $n - 6$ (choice A) is a factor of n only if $n = 12$. $n + 6$ (choice (B)) can never be a factor of n because $n + 6$ is greater than n. With choice (D), you always end up with a remainder of 3. You can eliminate choices (D) and (E) because the greatest factor of any positive number (other than the number itself) is half the number, which in this case is $\dfrac{n}{2}$.

> **Tip**
>
> Although the plug-in strategy works for the preceding question, you should try out more than one sample value for n. If $n = 12$, choices (A), (C), and (E) all are viable. But try out the number 18, and choice (C) is the only factor of n. (To be on the safe side, you should try out at least one additional sample value as well, such as 24.)

Prime Numbers and Prime Factorization

A *prime number* is a positive integer that is divisible by (a multiple of) only two positive integers: itself and 1. Just for the record, here are all the prime numbers less than 50:

2 3 5 7

11 13 17 19

23 29

31 37

41 43 47

Determining all the factors of great integers can be tricky; it's easy to overlook some factors. To find all factors of a great number, use a method called

235

Part III: Quantitative Ability

prime factorization. Divide the number by each prime number in turn, starting with 2 and working up from there (2,3,5,7,11 ...), then try to find factors for the quotients as well, using the same method. Test prime numbers up to the point where your quotient is no greater than the greatest factor you've already found. For example, here's how you apply prime factorization to the number 110 (prime-number quotients are shown in italics):

$110 \div 2 = 55$, and $55 = 5 \times 11$

$110 \div 3 =$ non-integer

$110 \div 5 = 22$, and $22 = 2 \times 11$

$110 \div 7 =$ non-integer

$110 \div 11$ (already covered)

The prime factor quotients are 2, 5, and 11, and their product is 110. (That's no coincidence.) *The product of all prime-number quotients will equal your original number.* A number's prime factorization refers to all its prime factors multiplied together.

> **Note**
>
> To find all other *positive* factors of a number, combine any two or more prime factors by multiplication.

Which of the following is a prime factorization of 144?

A. $2^4 \times 3^2$
B. 4×3^3
C. $2^3 \times 12$
D. $2^2 \times 3 \times 5$
E. $2 \times 3^2 \times 4$

The correct answer is A. Divide 144 by its least possible prime factor, which is 2. Continue to divide the result by 2, and you ultimately obtain a prime-number quotient: $144 \div 2 = 72 \div 2 = 36 \div 2 = 18 \div 2 = 9 \div 3 = 3$.

Exponents (Powers)

An *exponent*, or *power*, refers to the number of times a number (referred to as the *base number*) is multiplied by itself, plus 1. In the number 2^3, the base number is 2 and the exponent is 3. To calculate the value of 2^3, you multiply 2 by itself twice: $2^3 = 2 \times 2 \times 2 = 8$.

Chapter 7: Math Review—Number Theory and Algebra

On the GMAT, questions involving exponents usually require you to combine two or more terms that contain exponents. To do so, you need to know some basic rules. Can you combine base numbers—using addition, subtraction, multiplication, or division—*before* applying exponents to the numbers? The answer depends on which operation you're performing.

Combining Exponents by Addition or Subtraction

When you add or subtract terms, you cannot combine base numbers or exponents. It's as simple as that.

$a^x + b^x \neq (a + b)^x$

$a^x - b^x \neq (a - b)^x$

If you don't believe it, try plugging in a few easy numbers. Notice that you get a different result depending on which you do first: combine base numbers or apply each exponent to its base number:

$(3 + 4)^2 = 7^2 = 49$

$3^2 + 4^2 = 9 + 16 = 25$

If $x = -2$, then $x^5 - x^2 - x = ?$

A. -70
B. -58
C. -34
D. 4
E. 26

The correct answer is C. You cannot combine exponents here, even though the base number is the same in all three terms. Instead, you need to apply each exponent, in turn, to the base number, then subtract:

$x^5 - x^2 - x = (-2)^5 - (-2)^2 - (-2) = -32 - 4 + 2 = -34$

Combining Exponents by Multiplication or Division

It's a whole different story for multiplication and division. First, remember these two simple rules:

1. You can combine base numbers first, but only if the exponents are the same:

$a^x \times b^x = (ab)^x$

2. You can combine exponents first, but only if the base numbers are the same. When multiplying these terms, add the exponents. When dividing them, subtract the denominator exponent from the numerator exponent:

$$a^x \times a^y = a^{(x+y)}$$

$$\frac{a^x}{a^y} = a^{(x-y)}$$

When the same base number (or term) appears in both the numerator and denominator of a fraction, you can factor out, or cancel, the number of powers common to both.

Which of the following is a simplified version of $\frac{x^2 y^3}{x^3 y^2}$?

A. $\frac{y}{x}$

B. $\frac{x}{y}$

C. $\frac{1}{xy}$

D. 1

E. $x^5 y^5$

The correct answer is A. The simplest approach to this problem is to factor out, x^2 and y^2 from numerator and denominator. This leaves you with x^1 in the denominator and y^1 in the numerator.

> **Tip:** "Canceling" a base number's powers in a fraction's numerator and denominator is actually a shortcut to applying the rule $\frac{a^x}{a^y} = a^{(x-y)}$ along with another rule, $a^{-x} = \frac{1}{a^x}$, that you'll review immediately ahead.

Additional Rules for Exponents

To cover all your bases, also keep in mind these three additional rules for exponents:

1. When raising an exponential number to a power, multiply exponents:

$$(a^x)^y = a^{xy}$$

Chapter 7: Math Review—Number Theory and Algebra

2. Any number other than zero (0) raised to the power of 0 (zero) equals 1:

   $a^0 = 1 \;[a \neq 0]$

3. Raising a base number to a negative exponent is equivalent to 1 divided by the base number raised to the exponent's absolute value:

   $a^{-x} = \dfrac{1}{a^x}$

The preceding three rules are all fair game for the GMAT. In fact, a GMAT question might require you to apply more than one of these rules.

$(2^3)^2 \times 4^{-3} =$

A. $\dfrac{1}{8}$

B. $\dfrac{1}{2}$

C. $\dfrac{2}{3}$

D. 1

E. 16

The correct answer is D. $(2^3)^2 \times 4^{-3} = 2^{(2)(3)} \times \dfrac{1}{4^3} = \dfrac{2^6}{4^3} = \dfrac{2^6}{2^6} = 1$

Exponents You Should Know

For the GMAT, memorize the exponential values in the following table. You'll be glad you did, since these are the ones you're most likely to see on the exam.

	Power and Corresponding Value						
Base	2	3	4	5	6	7	8
2	4	8	16	32	64	128	256
3	9	27	81	243			
4	16	64	256				
5	25	125	625				
6	36	216					

Roots and Radicals

On the flip side of exponents and powers are roots and radicals. The *square root* of a number n is a number that you "square" (multiply by itself, or raise to the power of 2), to obtain n.

$2 = \sqrt{4}$ (the square root of 4) because 2×2 (or 2^2) = 4

The *cube root* of a number n is a number that you raise to the power of 3 (multiply by itself twice) to obtain n. You determine greater roots (for example, the "fourth root") in the same way. Except for square roots, the radical sign will indicate the root to be taken.

$2 = \sqrt[3]{8}$ (the cube root of 8) because $2 \times 2 \times 2$ (or 2^3) = 8

$2 = \sqrt[4]{16}$ (the fourth root of 16) because $2 \times 2 \times 2 \times 2$ (or 2^4) = 16

For the GMAT, you should know the rules for simplifying and for combining radical expressions.

Simplifying Radicals

On the GMAT, always look for the possibility of simplifying radicals by moving what's under the radical sign to the outside of the sign. Check inside your square-root radicals for perfect squares: factors that are squares of nice tidy numbers or other terms. The same advice applies to perfect cubes, and so on.

$\sqrt{4a^2} = 2a$	4 and a^2 are both perfect squares; remove them from under the radical sign, and find each one's square root.
$\sqrt{8a^3} = \sqrt{(4)(2)a^3}$ $= 2a\sqrt{2a}$	8 and a^3 are both perfect cubes, which contain perfect-square factors; remove the perfect squares from under the radical sign, and find each one's square root.

You can simplify radical expressions containing fractions in the same way. Just be sure that what's in the denominator under the radical sign stays in the denominator when you remove it from under the radical sign.

$$\sqrt{\frac{20x}{x^3}} = \sqrt{\frac{(4)(5)}{x^2}} = \frac{2\sqrt{5}}{x}$$

$$\sqrt[3]{\frac{3}{8}} = \sqrt[3]{\frac{3}{2^3}} = \frac{1}{2}\sqrt[3]{3}$$

Chapter 7: Math Review—Number Theory and Algebra

Tip: Whenever you see a non-prime number under a square-root radical sign, factor it to see if it contains perfect-square factors you can move outside the radical sign. The same applies to cube roots and other, greater roots. More than likely, this step is needed to solve the problem at hand.

$$\sqrt{\frac{28a^6b^4}{36a^4b^6}} =$$

A. $\dfrac{a}{b}\sqrt{\dfrac{a}{2b}}$

B. $\dfrac{a}{2b}\sqrt{\dfrac{a}{b}}$

C. $\dfrac{a}{3b}\sqrt{7}$

D. $\dfrac{a^2}{3b^2}\sqrt{2}$

E. $\dfrac{2a}{3b}$

The correct answer is C. Divide a^4 and b^4 from the numerator and denominator of the fraction. Also, factor out 4 from 28 and 36. Then, remove perfect squares from under the radical sign:

$$\sqrt{\frac{28a^6b^4}{36a^4b^6}} = \sqrt{\frac{7a^2}{9b^2}} = \frac{a\sqrt{7}}{3b}, \text{ or } \frac{a}{3b}\sqrt{7}$$

Tip: In GMAT questions involving radical terms, you might want to remove a radical term from a fraction's denominator to match the correct answer. To accomplish this, multiply both numerator and denominator by the radical value. (This process is called "rationalizing the denominator.") Here's an example of how to do it:

$$\frac{3}{\sqrt{15}} = \frac{3\sqrt{15}}{\sqrt{15}\sqrt{15}} = \frac{3\sqrt{15}}{15} = \frac{3\sqrt{15}}{15}, \text{ or } \frac{1}{5}\sqrt{15}$$

Combining Radical Terms

The rules for combining terms that include radicals are quite similar to those for exponents. Keep the following two rules in mind; one applies to addition and subtraction, while the other applies to multiplication and division.

Addition and subtraction: If a term under a radical is being added to or subtracted from a term under a different radical, you cannot combine the two terms under the same radical.

$$\sqrt{x} + \sqrt{y} \neq \sqrt{x+y}$$
$$\sqrt{x} - \sqrt{y} \neq \sqrt{x-y}$$
$$\sqrt{x} + \sqrt{x} = 2\sqrt{x}, \text{ not } \sqrt{2x}$$

On the GMAT, if you're asked to combine radical terms by adding or subtracting, chances are you'll also need to simplify radical expressions along the way.

$$\sqrt{24} - \sqrt{16} - \sqrt{6} =$$

A. $\sqrt{6} - 4$
B. $4 - 2\sqrt{2}$
C. 2
D. $\sqrt{6}$
E. $2\sqrt{2}$

The correct answer is A. Although the numbers under the three radicals combine to equal 2, you cannot combine terms this way. Instead, simplify the first two terms, then combine the first and third terms:

$$\sqrt{24} - \sqrt{16} - \sqrt{6} = 2\sqrt{6} - 4 - \sqrt{6} = \sqrt{6} - 4.$$

Multiplication and Division: Terms under different radicals can be combined under a common radical if one term is multiplied or divided by the other, but only if the radical is the same.

$$\sqrt{x}\sqrt{x} = (\sqrt{x})^2, \text{ or } x$$
$$\sqrt{x}\sqrt{y} = \sqrt{xy}$$
$$\frac{\sqrt{x}}{\sqrt{y}} = \sqrt{\frac{x}{y}}$$
$$\sqrt[3]{x}\sqrt{x} = ?$$

(you cannot easily combine $\sqrt[3]{x}\sqrt{x} = x^{\frac{1}{3}}x^{\frac{1}{2}} = x^{\frac{1}{3}+\frac{1}{2}} = x^{\frac{5}{6}}$)

$(2\sqrt{2a})^2 =$

A. $4a$
B. $4a^2$
C. $8a$
D. $8a^2$
E. $6a$

The correct answer is C. Square each of the two terms, 2 and $\sqrt{2a}$, separately. Then combine their squares by multiplication: $(2\sqrt{2a})^2 = 2^2 \times (\sqrt{2a})^2 = 4 \times 2a = 8a$.

Roots You Should Know

For the GMAT, memorize the roots in the following table. If you encounter one of these radical terms on the exam, chances are you'll need to know its equivalent integer to answer the question.

In the table on the following page, notice that positive numbers have two square roots, one positive and one negative. Also notice that positive numbers have only one cube root, which is a *positive* number; while negative numbers have only one cube root, which is a *negative* number.

X-Ref

You'll explore further the relationship between roots and number signs if you advance to the Next Level.

Square roots of "perfect square" integers	Cube roots of "perfect cube" integers (positive and negative)
$\sqrt{121} = \pm 11$	$\sqrt[3]{(-)8} = (-)2$
$\sqrt{144} = \pm 12$	$\sqrt[3]{(-)27} = (-)3$
$\sqrt{169} = \pm 13$	$\sqrt[3]{(-)64} = (-)4$
$\sqrt{196} = \pm 14$	$\sqrt[3]{(-)125} = (-)5$
$\sqrt{225} = \pm 15$	$\sqrt[3]{(-)216} = (-)6$
$\sqrt{625} = \pm 25$	$\sqrt[3]{(-)343} = (-)7$
	$\sqrt[3]{(-)512} = (-)8$
	$\sqrt[3]{(-)729} = (-)9$
	$\sqrt[3]{(-)1000} = (-)10$

Linear Equations in One Variable

Algebraic expressions are usually used to form equations, which set two expressions equal to each other. Most equations you'll see on the GMAT are *linear* equations, in which the variables don't come with exponents. To solve any linear equation containing one variable, your goal is always the same: Isolate the unknown (variable) on one side of the equation. To accomplish this, you may need to perform one or more of the following operations on both sides, depending on the equation:

1. Add or subtract the same term from both sides
2. Multiply or divide by the same term on both sides
3. Clear fractions by cross-multiplication
4. Clear radicals by raising both sides to the same power (exponent)

Performing any of these operations on *both* sides does not change the equality; it merely restates the equation in a different form.

Chapter 7: Math Review—Number Theory and Algebra

Alert!

The operation you perform on one side of an equation must also be perform on the other side; otherwise, the two sides won't be equal!

Let's take a look at each of these four operations to see when and how to use each one.

1. Add or subtract the same term from both sides of the equation.

To solve for x, you may need to either add or subtract a term from both sides of an equation—or do both.

If $2x - 6 = x - 9$, then $x =$

A. -9
B. -6
C. -3
D. 2
E. 6

The correct answer is C. First, put both x-terms on the left side of the equation by subtracting x from both sides; then combine x-terms:

$$2x - 6 - x = x - 9 - x$$
$$x - 6 = -9$$

Next, isolate x by adding 6 to both sides:

$$x - 6 + 6 = -9 + 6$$
$$x = -3$$

2. Multiply or divide both sides of the equation by the same non-zero term.

To solve for x, you may need to either multiply or divide a term from both sides of an equation. Or, you may need to multiply and divide.

If $12 = \dfrac{11}{x} - \dfrac{3}{x}$, then $x =$

A. $\dfrac{3}{11}$

B. $\dfrac{1}{2}$

C. $\dfrac{2}{3}$

D. $\dfrac{11}{12}$

E. $\dfrac{11}{3}$

The correct answer is C. First, combine the x-terms:

$$12 = \dfrac{11 - 3}{x}$$

Next, clear the fraction by multiplying both sides by x:

$12x = -3$

$12x = 8$

Finally, isolate x by dividing both sides by 12:

$$x = \dfrac{8}{12}, \text{ or } \dfrac{2}{3}$$

3. If each side of the equation is a fraction, your best bet is to cross-multiply.

Where the original equation equates two fractions, use cross-multiplication to eliminate the fractions. Multiply the numerator from one side of the equation by the denominator from the other side. Set the product equal to the product of the other numerator and denominator. (In effect, cross-multiplication is a shortcut method of multiplying both sides of the equation by both denominators.)

If, $\dfrac{7a}{8} = \dfrac{a+1}{3}$, then $a =$

A. $\dfrac{8}{13}$

B. $\dfrac{7}{8}$

C. 2

D. $\dfrac{7}{3}$

E. 15

The correct answer is A. First, cross-multiply as we've described:

$(3)(7a) = (8)(a + 1)$

Next, combine terms (distribute 8 to both a and 1):

$21a = 8a + 8$

Next, isolate a-terms on one side by subtracting $8a$ from both sides; then combine the a-terms:

$21a - 8a = 8a + 8 - 8a$

$13a = 8$

Finally, isolate a by dividing both sides by its coefficient 13:

$\dfrac{13a}{13} = \dfrac{8}{13}$

$a = \dfrac{8}{13}$

Part III: Quantitative Ability

4. Square both sides of the equation to eliminate radical signs. Where the variable is under a square-root radical sign, remove the radical sign by squaring both sides of the equation. (Use a similar technique for cube roots and other roots.)

   If $3\sqrt{2x} = 2$, then $x =$

   A. $\frac{1}{18}$

   B. $\frac{2}{9}$

   C. $\frac{1}{3}$

   D. $\frac{5}{4}$

   E. 3

The correct answer is B. First, clear the radical sign by squaring all terms:

$$(3^2)(\sqrt{2x})^2 = 2^2$$
$$(9)(2x) = 4$$
$$18x = 4$$

Next, isolate x by dividing both sides by 18:

$$x = \frac{4}{18}, \text{ or } \frac{2}{9}$$

Linear Equations in Two Variables

What we've covered up to this point is pretty basic stuff. If you haven't quite caught on, you should probably stop here and consult a basic algebra workbook for more practice. On the other hand, if you're with us so far, let's forge ahead and add another variable. Here's a simple example:

$$x + 3 = y + 1$$

Quick... what's the value of x? It depends on the value of y, doesn't it? Similarly, the value of y depends on the value of x. Without more information about either x or y, you're stuck; well, not completely. You can express x in terms of y, and you can express y in terms of x:

$$x = y - 2$$
$$y = x + 2$$

Let's look at one more:

$$4x - 9 = \frac{3}{2}y$$

Solve for x in terms of y:

$$4x = \frac{3}{2}y + 9$$
$$x = \frac{3}{8}y + \frac{9}{4}$$

Solve for y in terms of x:

$$\frac{4x - 9}{\frac{3}{2}} = y$$
$$\frac{2}{3}(4x - 9) = y$$
$$\frac{8}{3}x - 6 = y$$

To determine numerical values of x and y, you need a system of two linear equations with the same two variables. Given this system, there are two different methods for finding the values of the two variables:

1. The *substitution* method
2. The *addition-subtraction* method

Next, we'll apply each method to determine the values of two variables in a two-equation system.

Part III: Quantitative Ability

> You can't solve one equation if it contains two unknowns (variables). You either need to know the value of one of the variables, or you need a second equation.

The Substitution Method

To solve a system of two equations using the substitution method, follow these steps (we'll use x and y here):

1. In *either* equation, isolate one variable (x) on one side.
2. Substitute the expression that equals x in place of x in the other equation.
3. Solve that equation for y.
4. Now that you know the value of y, plug it into *either* equation to find the value of x.

If $\frac{2}{5}p + q = 3q - 10$, and if $q = 10 - p$, then $\frac{p}{q} =$

A. $\frac{5}{7}$

B. $\frac{3}{2}$

C. $\frac{5}{3}$

D. $\frac{25}{6}$

E. $\frac{36}{6}$

The correct answer is A. Don't let the fact that the question asks for $\frac{p}{q}$ (rather than simply p or q) throw you. Because you're given two linear equations with two unknowns, you know that you can first solve for p and q, then divide p by q. First thing's first: Combine the q-terms in the first equation:

$$\frac{2}{5}p = 2q - 10$$

Next, substitute $(10 - p)$ for q (from the second equation) in the first equation:

$$\frac{2}{5}p = 2(10 - p) - 10$$

$$\frac{2}{5}p = 20 - 2p - 10$$

$$\frac{2}{5}p = 10 - 2p$$

Move the p-terms to the same side, then isolate p:

$$\frac{2}{5}p + 2p = 10$$

$$\frac{12}{5}p = 10$$

$$p = \left(\frac{5}{12}\right)(10)$$

$$p = \frac{25}{6}$$

Substitute $\frac{25}{6}$ for p in either equation to find q (we'll use the second equation):

$$q = 10 - \frac{25}{6}$$

$$q = \frac{60}{6} - \frac{25}{6}$$

$$q = \frac{35}{6}$$

The question asks for $\frac{p}{q}$, so do the division:

$$\frac{p}{q} = \frac{\frac{25}{6}}{\frac{35}{6}} = \frac{25}{35}, \text{ or } \frac{5}{7}$$

The Addition-Subtraction Method

Another way to solve for two unknowns in a system of two equations is with the
addition-subtraction method. Here are the steps:

1. Make the coefficient of *either* variable the same in both equations (you can disregard the sign) by multiplying every term in one of the equations.

2. Make sure the equations list the same variables in the same order.

3. Place one equation above the other.

4. Add the two equations (work down to a sum for each term), or subtract one equation from the other, to eliminate one variable.

5. You can repeat steps 1–3 to solve for the other variable.

If $3x + 4y = -8$, and if $x - 2y = \frac{1}{2}$, then $x =$

A. -12

B. $-\frac{7}{5}$

C. $\frac{1}{3}$

D. $\frac{14}{5}$

E. 9

The correct answer is B. To solve for x, you want to eliminate y. You can multiply each term in the second equation by 2, then add the equations:

$$3x + 4y = -8$$
$$2x - 4y = 1$$
$$\overline{5x + 0y = -7}$$

$$x = -\frac{7}{5}$$

Since the question asked only for the value of x, stop here. If the question had asked for both x and y (or for y only), you could have multiplied both sides of the second equation by 3, then subtracted the second equation from the first:

$$3x + 4y = -8$$

$$3x - 6y = \frac{3}{2}$$

$$0x + 10y = -9\frac{1}{2}$$

$$10y = -\frac{19}{2}$$

$$y = -\frac{19}{20}$$

Which Method Should You Use?

> **Note:** If a question requires you to find values of both unknowns, you can combine the two methods. For example, after using addition-subtraction to solve for x in the last question, you can then substitute, the value of x, into either equation to find y.

Which method, substitution or addition-subtraction, you should use depends on what the equations look like to begin with. To see what we mean, look again at this system:

$$\frac{2}{5}p + q = 3q - 10$$

$$q = 10 - p$$

Notice that the second equation is already set up nicely for the substitution method. This system is an ideal candidate for the substitution method. You could use addition-subtraction instead; however, you'd just have to rearrange the terms in both the equations first:

$$\frac{2}{5}p - 2q = -10$$

$$p + q = 10$$

Now, look again at the following system:

$$3x + 4y = -8$$
$$x - 2y = \frac{1}{2}$$

Notice that the *x*-term and *y*-term already line up nicely here. Also, notice that it's easy to match the coefficients of either *x* or *y*: multiply both sides of the second equation by either 3 or 2. This system is an ideal candidate for addition-subtraction. To appreciate this point, try using substitution instead. You'll discover that it takes far more number crunching.

> **Tip**
> To solve a system of two linear equation in two variables, use addition-subtraction if you can quickly and easily eliminate one of the variables. Otherwise, use substitution.

Linear Equations that Cannot be Solved

Never assume that one linear equation with one variable is solvable. If you can reduce the equation to $0 = 0$, then you can't solve it. In other words, the value of the variable could be any real number. The test-makers generally use the Data Sufficiency format to cover this concept.

If $3x - 3 - 4x = x - 7 - 2x + 4$, then what is the value of *x* ?

(1) $x > -1$

(2) $x < 1$

The correct answer is E. All terms on both sides subtract out:

$$3x - 3 - 4x = x - 7 - 2x + 4$$
$$-x - 3 = -x - 3$$
$$0 = 0$$

Thus, even considering both statements together, *x* could equal any real number between -1 and 1 (not just the integer 0).

In some cases, what appears to be a system of two equations in two variables might actually be the same equation expressed in two different ways. In other words, what you're really dealing with are two equivalent equations, which you cannot solve. The test-makers generally use the Data Sufficiency format to cover this concept.

Does $a = b$?

(1) $a + b = 30$

(2) $2b = 60 - 2a$

The correct answer is E. An unwary test-taker might assume that the values of both *a* and *b* can be determined with both equations together, because they appear at first glance to provide a system of two linear equations with two unknowns. Not so! You can easily manipulate the second equation so that it is identical to the first:

$2b = 60 - 2a$
$2b = 2(30 - a)$
$b = 30 - a$
$a + b = 30$

As you can see, the equation $2b = 60 - 2a$ is identical to the equation $a + b = 30$. Thus, *a* and *b* could each be any real number. You can't solve one equation in two unknowns, so the correct answer must be (E).

> **Tip**
> Whenever you encounter a Data Sufficiency question that calls for solving one or more linear equations, stop in your tracks before taking pencil to paper. Size up the equation to see whether it's one of the two unsolvable kinds you learned about here. If so, then unless you're given more information, the correct answer will be (E).

Solving Algebraic Inequalities

You can solve algebraic inequalities in the same manner as equations. Isolate the variable on one side of the equation, factoring and eliminating terms wherever possible. However, one important rule distinguishes inequalities from equations: Whenever you multiply or divide both sides of an inequality by a negative number, you must reverse the inequality symbol. Simply put: If $a > b$, then $-a < -b$.

$12 - 4x < 8$	original inequality
$-4x < -4$	12 subtracted from each side; inequality unchanged
$x > 1$	both sides divided by -4; inequality reversed

Part III: Quantitative Ability

Here are some general rules for dealing with algebraic inequalities. Study them until they're second nature to you, because you'll put them to good use on the GMAT.

1. Adding or subtracting unequal quantities to (or from) equal quantities:

   If $a > b$, then $c + a > c + b$

   If $a > b$, then $c - a < c - b$

2. Adding unequal quantities to unequal quantities:

   If $a > b$, and if $c > d$, then $a + c > b + d$

3. Comparing three unequal quantities:

   If $a > b$, and if $b > c$, then $a > c$

4. Combining the same *positive* quantity with unequal quantities by multiplication or division:

   If $a > b$, and if $x > 0$, then $xa > xb$

   If $a > b$, and if $x > 0$, then $\frac{a}{x} > \frac{b}{x}$

   If $a > b$, and if $x > 0$, then $\frac{x}{a} < \frac{x}{b}$

5. Combining the same *negative* quantity with unequal quantities by multiplication or division:

   If $a > b$, and if $x < 0$, then $xa < xb$

   If $a > b$, and if $x < 0$, then $\frac{a}{x} < \frac{b}{x}$

   If $a > b$, and if $x < 0$, then $\frac{x}{a} > \frac{x}{b}$

If $a > b$, and if $c > d$, then which of the following must be true?

- A. $a - b > c - d$
- B. $a - c > b - d$
- C. $c + d < a - b$
- D. $b + d < a + c$
- E. $a - c < b + d$

The correct answer is D. Inequality questions can be a bit confusing, can't they? In this problem, you need to remember that if unequal quantities (*c* and *d*) are added to unequal quantities of the same order (*a* and *b*), the result is an inequality in the same order. This rule is essentially what answer choice (D) says.

> **Alert!**
>
> When handling inequality problems, you might think that by simply plugging in some sample numbers, you can zero-in on the correct answer. Be careful! The wrong-answers might look right, depending on the values you use for the different variables.

Take It to the Next Level

This Next Level focuses on the following advanced topics involving number theory and algebra:

- The impact of exponents and radicals on the magnitude and sign of numbers
- Factoring quadratic expressions
- Finding the roots of quadratic equations by factoring
- Finding the roots of quadratic equations by applying the quadratic formula
- Factoring non-linear equations in two variables
- Algebraic expressions and problem-solving involving certain types of word problems

Exponents and the Real Number Line

Raising base numbers to powers can have surprising effects on the magnitude and/or sign—negative vs. positive—of the base number. You need to consider four separate regions of the real-number line:

1. Values greater than 1 (to the right of 1 on the number line)
2. Values less than −1 (to the left of −1 on the number line)
3. Fractional values between 0 and 1
4. Fractional values between −1 and 0

The next table indicates the impact of positive-integer exponent (x) on base number (n) for each region.

Chapter 7: Math Review—Number Theory and Algebra

$n > 1$	n raised to any power: $n^x > 1$ (the greater the exponent, the greater the value of n^x)
$n < -1$	n raised to even power: $n^x > 1$ (the greater the exponent, the greater the value of n^x)
	n raised to odd power: $n^x < 1$ (the greater the exponent, the lesser the value of n^x)
$0 < n < 1$	n raised to any power: $0 < n^x < n < 1$ (the greater the exponent, the lesser the value of n^x)
$-1 < n < 0$	n raised to even power: $0 < n^x < 1$ (the greater the exponent, the lesser the value of n^x, approaching 0 on the number line)
	n raised to odd power: $-1 < n^x < 0$ (the greater the exponent, the greater the value of n^x, approaching 0 on the number line)

The preceding set of rules are simple enough to understand. But when you apply them to a GMAT question, it can be surprisingly easy to confuse yourself, especially if the question is designed to create confusion.

If $-1 < x < 0$, which of the following must be true?

I. $x < x^2$
II. $x^2 < x^3$
III. $x < x^3$

A. I only
B. II only
C. I and II only
D. I and III only
E. I, II, and III

The correct answer is D. The key to analyzing each equation is that raising x to successively greater powers moves the value of x closer to zero (0) on the number line.

(I) must be true. Since x is given as a negative number; x^2 must be positive and thus greater than x.

(II) cannot be true. Since x is given as a negative number; x^2 must be positive, while x^3 must be negative. Thus, x^2 is greater than x^3.

(III) must be true. Both x^3 and x are negative fractions between 0 and -1, but x^3 is closer to zero (0) on the number line—that is, greater than x.

Roots and the Real Number Line

As with exponents, the root of a number can bear a surprising relationship to the mgnitude and/or sign (negative vs. positive) of the number (another of the test-makers' favorite areas). Here are four rules you should remember:

1. If $n > 1$, then $1 < \sqrt[3]{n} < \sqrt{n} < n$ (the greater the root, the lesser the value). However, if n lies between 0 and 1, then
   $$n < \sqrt{n} < \sqrt[3]{n} < 1$$
   (the greater the root, the greater the value).

$n = 64$	$n = \dfrac{1}{64}$
$1 < \sqrt[3]{64} < \sqrt{64} < 64$	$\dfrac{1}{64} < \sqrt{\dfrac{1}{64}} < \sqrt[3]{\dfrac{1}{64}} < 1$
$1 < 4 < 8 < 64$	$\dfrac{1}{64} < \dfrac{1}{8} < \dfrac{1}{4} < 1$

2. Every negative number has exactly one cube root, and that root is a negative number. The same holds true for all other odd-numbered roots of negative numbers.

$\sqrt[3]{-27} = -3$	$\sqrt[5]{-32} = -2$
$(-3)(-3)(-3) = -27$	$(-2)(-2)(-2)(-2)(-2) = -32$

3. Every positive number has two square roots: a negative number and a positive number (with the same absolute value). The same holds true for all other even-numbered roots of positive numbers.
   $$\sqrt{16} = \pm 4$$
   $$\sqrt[4]{81} = \pm 3$$

4. Every positive number has only one *cube* root, and that root is always a positive number. The same holds true for all other odd-numbered roots of positive numbers.

Note: The square root (or other even-number root) of any negative number is an imaginary number, not a real number. That's why the preceding rules don't cover these roots.

Which of the following inequalities, if true, is sufficient alone to show that $\sqrt[3]{x} < \sqrt[5]{x}$?

A. $-1 < x < 0$
B. $0 < x < 1$
C. $|x| < -1$
D. $|x| > 1$
E. $x < -1$

The correct answer is E. If $x < -1$, then applying a greater root yields a *lesser negative* value—further to the left on the real number line.

Factorable Quadratic Expressions in One Variable

A *quadratic expression* includes a "squared" variable, such as x^2. An equation is quadratic if you can express it in this general form:

$$ax^2 + bx + c = 0,$$

where:

x is the variable

a, b, and c are constants (numbers)

$a \neq 0$

b can equal 0

c can equal 0

Here are four examples (notice that the b-term and c-term are not essential; in other words, either b or c, or both, can equal zero):

Quadratic Equation	Same Equation, but in the form: $ax^2 + bx + c = 0$
$2w^2 - 16$	$2w^2 - 16 = 0$ (no b-term)
$x^2 = 3x$	$x^2 - 3x = 0$ (no c-term)
$3y = 4 - y^2$	$y^2 + 3y - 4 = 0$
$7z = 2z^2 - 15$	$2z^2 - 7z - 15 = 0$

Part III: Quantitative Ability

Every quadratic equation has exactly two solutions, called *roots*. (But the two roots might be the same.) On the GMAT, you can often find the two roots by *factoring*. To solve any factorable quadratic equation, follow these three steps:

1. Put the equation into the standard form: $ax^2 + bx + c = 0$.

2. Factor the terms on the left side of the equation into two linear expressions (with no exponents).

3. Set each linear expression (root) equal to zero and solve for the variable in each one.

Factoring Simple Quadratic Expressions

Some quadratic expressions are easier to factor than others. If either of the two constants b or c is zero, factoring requires no sweat. In fact, in some cases, no factoring is needed at all:

A quadratic with no c term	A quadratic with no b term
$2x^2 = x$	$2x^2 - 4 = 0$
$2x^2 - x = 0$	$2(x^2 - 2) = 0$
$x(2x -) = 0$	$x^2 - 2 = 0$
$x = 0, 2x - 1 = 0$	$x^2 = 2$
$x = 0, \frac{1}{2}$	$x = \sqrt{2}, -\sqrt{2}$

Alert!

When dealing with a quadratic equation, your first step is usually to put it into the general form $ax^2 + bx + c = 0$. But keep in mind: The only essential term is ax^2.

Factoring Quadratic Trinomials

A trinomial is simply an algebraic expression that contains three terms. If a quadratic expression contains all three terms of the standard form $ax^2 + bx + c$, then factoring becomes a bit trickier. You need to apply the **FOIL** method, in which you add together these terms:

(F) the product of the first terms of the two binomials

(O) the product of the outer terms of the two binomials

(I) the product of the inner terms of the two binomials

(L) the product of the last (second) terms of the two binomials

Note the following relationships:

(F) is the first term (ax^2) of the quadratic expression

(O + I) is the second term (bx) of the quadratic expression

(L) is the third term (c) of the quadratic expression

You'll find that the two factors will be two binomials. The GMAT might ask you to recognize one or both of these binomial factors.

Which of the following is a factor of $x^2 - x - 6$?

A. $(x + 6)$
B. $(x - 3)$
C. $(x + 1)$
D. $(x - 2)$
E. $(x + 3)$

The correct answer is B. Notice that x^2 has no coefficient. This makes the process of factoring into two binomials easier. Set up two binomial shells: $(x \quad)(x \quad)$. The product of the two missing second terms (the "L" term under the FOIL method) is -6. The possible integral pairs that result in this product are $(1,-6)$, $(-1,6)$, $(2,-3,)$, and $(-2,3)$. Notice that the second term in the trinomial is $-x$. This means that the sum of the two integers whose product is -6 must be -1. The pair $(2,-3)$ fits the bill. Thus, the trinomial is equivalent to the product of the two binomials $(x + 2)$ and $(x - 3)$.

To check your work, multiply the two binomials using the FOIL method:

$$(x + 2)(x - 3) = x^2 - 3x + 2x - 6$$
$$= x^2 - x + 6$$

Note: If the preceding question had asked you to determine the roots of the equation $x^2 - x - 6 = 0$, you'd simply set each of the binomial factors equal to 0 (zero), then solve for x in each one. The solution set (the two possible values of x) includes the roots -2 and 3.

How many different values of x does the solution set for the equation $4x^2 = 4x - 1$ contain?

- A. None
- B. One
- C. Two
- D. Four
- E. Infinitely many

The correct answer is B. First, express the equation in standard form: $4x^2 - 4x + 1 = 0$. Notice that the c-term is 1. The only two integral pairs that result in this product are $(1,1)$ and $(-1-1)$. Since the b-term $(-4x)$ is negative, the integral pair whose product is 1 must be $(-1-1)$. Set up a binomial shell:

$(? - 1)(? - 1)$

Notice that the a-term contains the coefficient 4. The possible integral pairs that result in this product are $(1,4)$, $(2,2)$, $(-1,-4)$, and $(-2,-2)$. A bit of trial-and-error reveals that only the pair $(2,2)$ works. Thus, in factored form, the equation becomes $(2x - 1)(2x - 1) = 0$. To check your work, multiply the two binomials using the FOIL method:

$$(2x - 1)(2x - 1) = 4x^2 - 2x - 2x + 1$$
$$= 4x^2 - 4x + 1$$

Since the two binomial factors are the same, the two roots of the equation are the same. In other words, x has only one possible value. (Although you don't need to find the value of x in order to answer the question, solve for x in the equation $2x - 1 = 0$; $x = \frac{1}{2}$.)

Chapter 7: Math Review—Number Theory and Algebra

Stealth Quadratic Equations

Some equations that appear linear (variables include no exponents) may actually be quadratic. Following, you will see the two GMAT situations you need to be on the lookout for.

1. The same variable inside a radical also appears outside:

$$\sqrt{x} = 5x$$
$$(\sqrt{x})^2 = (5x)^2$$
$$x = 25x^2$$
$$25x^2 - x = 0$$

2. The same variable that appears in the denominator of a fraction also appears elsewhere in the equation:

$$\frac{2}{x} = 3 - x$$
$$2 = x(3 - x)$$
$$2 = 3x - x^2$$
$$x^2 - 3x + 2 = 0$$

In both scenarios, you're dealing with a quadratic (non-linear) equation in one variable. So, in either equation, there are two roots. (Both equations are factorable, so go ahead and find their roots.) The test-makers often use the Data Sufficiency format to cover this concept.

What is the value of x?

(1) $6x = \sqrt{3x}$

(2) $x > 0$

The correct answer is C. An unwary test-taker might assume that the equation in statement (1) is linear—because x is not squared. Not so! Clear the radical by squaring both sides of the equation, then isolate the x-terms on one side of the equation and you'll see that the equation is quite quadratic indeed:

$$36x^2 = 3x$$
$$36x^2 - 3x = 0$$

To ferret out the two roots, factor out $3x$, then solve for each root:

$$3x(12x - 1) = 0$$
$$3x = 0;\ 12x - 1 = 0$$
$$x = 0, \frac{1}{12}$$

Since there is more than one possible value for x, statement (1) alone is insufficient to answer the question. Statement (2) alone is obviously insufficient. But the two together eliminate the root value 0, leaving $\frac{1}{12}$ as the only possible value of x.

The Quadratic Formula

For some quadratic equations, although rational roots exist, they're difficult to find. For example, $12x^2 + x - 6 = 0$ can be solved by factoring, but the factors are not easy to see:

$$12x^2 + x - 6 = (3x - 2)(4x + 3)$$

Faced with a quadratic equation that's difficult to factor, you can always use the quadratic formula, which states that, for any equation of the form $ax^2 + bx + c = 0$:

$$x = \frac{-b \pm \sqrt{b^2 - 4ac}}{2a}$$

In the equation $12x^2 + x - 6 = 0$, for example, $a = 12$, $b = 1$, and $c = -6$. Plugging these value into the quadratic formula, you'll find that the two roots are $\frac{2}{3}$ and $-\frac{3}{4}$.

> **Note**
>
> Some quadratic equations have no rational roots (solutions). Referring to the quadratic formula, if $\sqrt{b^2 - 4ac}$ turns out to be a negative number, then its square root will be *imaginary*, and hence so will the roots of the quadratic equation at hand. But, the GMAT doesn't test you on imaginary numbers. In other words, you'll find only real-number (rational) roots of any GMAT quadratic equation.

Chapter 7: Math Review—Number Theory and Algebra

Non-Linear Equations in Two Variables

In the world of math, solving non-linear equations in two or more variables can be *very* complicated, even for bona-fide mathematicians. But on the GMAT, all you need to remember are these three general forms:

Sum of two variables, squared: $(x + y)^2 = x^2 + 2xy + y^2$

Difference of two variables, squared: $(x - y)^2 = x^2 - 2xy + y^2$

Difference of two squares: $x^2 - y^2 = (x + y)(x - y)$

You can verify these equations using the FOIL method:

$(x + y)^2$	$(x - y)^2$	$(x + y)(x - y)$
$= (x + y)(x + y)$	$= (x - y)(x - y)$	$= x^2 + xy - xy - y^2$
$= x^2 + xy + xy + y^2$	$= x^2 - xy - xy + y^2$	$= x^2 - y^2$
$= x^2 + 2xy + y^2$	$= x^2 - 2xy + y^2$	

For the GMAT, memorize the three equations listed here. When you see one form on the exam, it's a sure bet that your task is to rewrite it as the other form.

If $x^2 - y^2 = 100$, and if $x + y = 2$, then $x - y =$

A. -2
B. 10
C. 20
D. 50
E. 200

The correct answer is D. If you're on the lookout for the difference of two squares, you can handle this question with no sweat. Use the third equation you just learned, substituting 2 for $(x + y)$, then solving for $(x - y)$:

$x^2 - y^2 = (x + y)(x - y)$
$100 = (x + y)(x - y)$
$100 = (2)(x - y)$
$50 = (x - y)$

Part III: Quantitative Ability

> **Tip**
>
> What about working backward from the answer choices to solve this problem? Go ahead and try it. You don't get very far, do you? There are two lessons here: (1) You usually can't solve quadratics using a shortcut, and (2) always look for one of the three common quadratic forms; if you see it, rewrite it as its equivalent form to answer the question as quickly and easily as possible.

Weighted Average Problems

You solve *weighted average* problems using the arithmetic mean (simple average) formula, except you give the set's terms different weights. For example, if a final exam score of 90 receives *twice* the weight of each of two mid-term exam scores 75 and 85, think of the final-exam score as *two* scores of 90—and the total number of scores as 4 rather than 3:

$$WA = \frac{75 + 85 + (2)(90)}{4} = \frac{340}{4} = 85$$

Similarly, when some numbers among terms might appear more often than others, you must give them the appropriate "weight" before computing an average.

> During an 8-hour trip, Brigitte drove 3 hours at 55 miles per hour and 5 hours at 65 miles per hour. What was her average rate, in miles per hour, for the entire trip?
>
> A. 58.5
> B. 60
> C. 61.25
> D. 62.5
> E. 66.25

The correct answer is C. Determine the total miles driven: $(3)(55) + (5)(65) = 490$. To determine the average over the entire trip, divide this total by 8, which is the number of total hours: $490 \div 8 = 61.25$.

A tougher weighted-average problem might provide the weighted average and ask for one of the terms, or require conversions from one unit of measurement to another—or both.

Chapter 7: Math Review—Number Theory and Algebra

A certain olive orchard produces 315 gallons of oil annually, on average, during four consecutive years. How many gallons of oil must the orchard produce annually, on average, during the next six years, if oil production for the entire 10-year period is to meet a goal of 378 gallons per year?

A. 240
B. 285
C. 396
D. 420
E. 468

The correct answer is D. In the weighted-average formula, 315 annual gallons receives a weight of 4, while the average annual number of gallons for the next six years (x) receives a weight of 6:

$$378 = \frac{1{,}260 + 6x}{10}$$

$$3{,}780 = 1{,}260 + 6x$$

$$3{,}780 - 1{,}260 = 6x$$

$$420 = x$$

This solution (420) is the average number of gallons needed per year, on average, during next 6 years.

> **Tip:** To guard against calculation errors, check your answer by sizing up the question. Generally, how great a number are you looking for? Notice that the stated goal is a bit greater than the annual average production over the first four years. So you're looking for an answer that is greater than the goal — a number somewhat greater than 378 gallons per year. You can eliminate choice (A) and (B) out of hand. The number 420 fits the bill.

Currency (Coin and Bill) Problems

Currency problems are similar to weighted-average problems in that each item (bill or coin) is weighted according to its monetary value. Unlike weighted average problems, however, the "average" value of all the bills or coins is not at issue. In solving currency problems, remember the following:

- You must formulate algebraic expressions involving both *number* of items (bills or coins) and *value* of items.

- You should convert the value of all moneys to a common currency unit before formulating an equation. If converting to cents, for example, you must multiply the number of nickels by 5, dimes by 10, and so forth.

Jim has $2.05 in dimes and quarters. If he has four fewer dimes than quarters, how much money does he have in dimes?

   A. 20 cents
   B. 30 cents
   C. 40 cents
   D. 50 cents
   E. 60 cents

The correct answer is B. Letting x equal the number of dimes, $x + 4$ represents the number of quarters. The total value of the dimes (in cents) is $10x$, and the total value of the quarters (in cents) is $25(x + 4)$ or $25x + 100$. Given that Jim has $2.05, the following equation emerges:

$$10x + 25x + 100 = 205$$
$$35x = 105$$
$$x = 3$$

Jim has three dimes, so he has 30 cents in dimes.

You could also solve this problem without formal algebra, by plugging in each answer choice in turn. Let's try this strategy for choices (A) and (B):

   A. 20 cents is 2 dimes, so Jim has 6 quarters. 20 cents plus $1.50 adds up to $1.70. Wrong answer!
   B. 30 cents is 3 dimes, so Jim has 7 quarters. 30 cents plus $1.75 adds up to $2.05. Correct answer!

> **Tip**
>
> You can also solve most GMAT currency problems by working backward from the answer choices.

Chapter 7: Math Review—Number Theory and Algebra

Mixture Problems

In GMAT mixture problems, you combine substances with different characteristics, resulting in a particular mixture or proportion, usually expressed as percentages. Substances are measured and mixed by either volume or weight — rather than by number (quantity).

How many quarts of pure alcohol must you add to 15 quarts of a solution that is 40% alcohol to strengthen it to a solution that is 50% alcohol?

A. 4.0
B. 3.5
C. 3.25
D. 3.0
E. 2.5

The correct answer is D. You can solve this problem by working backward from the answer choices—trying out each one in turn. Or, you can solve the problem algebraically. The original amount of alcohol is 40% of 15. Letting x equal the number of quarts of alcohol that you must add to achieve a 50% alcohol solution, $.4(15) + x$ equals the amount of alcohol in the solution after adding more alcohol. You can express this amount as 50% of $(15 + x)$. Thus, you can express the mixture algebraically as follows:

$$(.4)(15) + x = (.5)(15 + x)$$
$$6 + x = 7.5 + .5x$$
$$.5x = 1.5$$
$$x = 3$$

You must add 3 quarts of alcohol to obtain a 50% alcohol solution.

Investment Problems

GMAT investment problems involve interest earned (at a certain percentage rate) on money over a certain time period (usually a year). To calculate interest earned, multiply the original amount of money by the interest rate:

amount of money × interest rate = amount of interest on money

For example, if you deposit $1,000 in a savings account that earns 5% interest annually, the total amount in the account after one year will be $1,000 + .05($1,000) = $1,000 + $50 = $1,050.

GMAT investment questions usually involve more than simply calculating interest earned on a given principal amount at a given rate. They usually call for you to set up and solve an algebraic equation. When handling these problems, it's best to eliminate percent signs.

> Dr. Kramer plans to invest $20,000 in an account paying 6% interest annually. How much more must she invest at the same time at 3% so that her total annual income during the first year is 4% of her entire investment?
>
> A. $32,000
> B. $36,000
> C. $40,000
> D. $47,000
> E. $49,000

The correct answer is C. Letting x equal the amount invested at 3%, you can express Dr. Kramer's total investment as $20,000 + x$. The interest on $20,000 plus the interest on the additional investment equals the total interest from both investments. You can state this algebraically as follows:

$$.06(20,000) + .03x = .04(20,000 + x)$$

Multiply all terms by 100 to eliminate decimals, then solve for x:

$$6(20,000) + 3x = 4(20,000 + x)$$
$$120,000 + 3x = 80,000 + 4x$$
$$40,000 = x$$

She must invest $40,000 at 3% for her total annual income to be 4% of her total investment ($60,000).

> **Alert!**
>
> In solving GMAT investment problems, by all means size up the question to make sure your calculated answer is in the right ballpark. But don't rely on your intuition to derive a *precise* solution. Interest problems can be misleading. For instance, you might have guessed that Dr. Kramer would need to invest more than *twice* as much at 3% than at 6% to lower the overall interest rate to 4%. Not true!

Problems Involving Rate of Production or Work

A *rate* is a fraction that expresses a quantity per unit of time. For example, the rate at which a machine produces a certain product is expressed this way:

$$\text{rate of production} = \frac{\text{number of units produced}}{\text{time}}$$

A simple GMAT rate question might simply provide two of the three terms, and then ask you for the value of the third term. To complicate matters, the question might also require you to convert a number from one unit of measurement to another.

A printer can print pages at a rate of 15 pages per minute, how many pages can it print in $2\frac{1}{2}$ hours?

A. 1,375
B. 1,500
C. 1,750
D. 2,250
E. 2,500

The correct answer is D. Apply the following formula:

$$\text{rate} = \frac{\text{no. of pages}}{\text{time}}$$

The rate is given as 15 minutes, so convert the time ($2\frac{1}{2}$ hours) to 150 minutes. Determine the number of pages by applying the formula to these numbers:

$$15 = \frac{\text{no. of pages}}{150}$$

$$(15)(150) = \text{no. of pages}$$
$$2{,}250 = \text{no. of pages}$$

A more challenging type of rate-of-production (work) problem involves two or more workers (people or machines) working together to accomplish a task or job. In these scenarios, there's an inverse relationship between the number of workers and the time that it takes to complete the job; in other words, the more workers, the quicker the job gets done.

A GMAT work problem might specify the rates at which certain workers work alone and ask you to determine the rate at which they work together, or vice versa. Here's the basic formula for solving a work problem:

$$\frac{A}{x} + \frac{A}{y} = 1$$

In this formula:

- x and y represent the time needed for each of two workers, x and y, to complete the job alone.
- A represents the time it takes for both x and y to complete the job working in the *aggregate* (together).

So each fraction represents the portion of the job completed by a worker. The sum of the two fractions must be 1 if the job is completed.

> **Note**
>
> In the real world, teamwork often creates a synergy whereby the team is more efficient than the individuals working alone. But on the GMAT, you can assume that no additional efficiency is gained by two or more workers working together.

One printing press can print a daily newspaper in 12 hours, while another press can print it in 18 hours. How long will the job take if both presses work simultaneously?

- **A.** 7 hours, 12 minutes
- **B.** 9 hours, 30 minutes
- **C.** 10 hours, 45 minutes
- **D.** 15 hours
- **E.** 30 hours

The correct answer is A. Just plug the two numbers 12 and 18 into our work formula, then solve for A:

$$\frac{A}{12} + \frac{A}{18} = 1$$

$$\frac{3A}{36} + \frac{2A}{36} = 1$$

$$\frac{5A}{36} = 1$$

$$5A = 36$$

$$A = \frac{36}{5}, \text{ or } 7\frac{1}{5}.$$

Both presses working simultaneously can do the job in $7\frac{1}{5}$ hours—or 7 hours, 12 minutes.

> **Tip:** Had you needed to guess the answer, you could have easily ruled out choices (D) and (E), which both nonsensically suggest that the aggregate time it takes both presses together to produce the newspaper is *longer* than the time it takes either press alone. Remember: In work problems, use your common sense to narrow down answer choices!

Problems Involving Rate of Travel (Speed)

GMAT rate problems often involve rate of travel (speed). You can express a rate of travel this way:

$$\text{rate of travel} = \frac{\text{distance}}{\text{time}}$$

An easier speed problem will involve a *single* distance, rate, and time. A tougher speed problem might involve different rates, such as:

- Two different times over the same distance
- Two different distances covered in the same time

In either type, apply the basic rate-of-travel formula to each of the two events. Then solve for the missing information by algebraic substitution. Use essentially the same approach for any of the following scenarios:

- One object making two separate "legs" of a trip — either in the same direction or as a round trip

Part III: Quantitative Ability

- Two objects moving in the same direction
- Two objects moving in opposite directions

Janice left her home at 11 a.m., traveling along Route 1 at 30 mph. At 1 p.m., her brother Richard left home and started after her on the same road at 45 mph. At what time did Richard catch up to Janice?

A. 2:45 p.m.
B. 3:00 p.m.
C. 3:30 p.m.
D. 4:15 p.m.
E. 5:00 p.m.

The correct answer is E. Notice that the distance Janice covered is equal to that of Richard—that is, distance is constant. Letting x equal Janice's time, you can express Richard's time as $x - 2$. Substitute these values for time and the values for rate given in the problem into the speed formula for Richard and Janice:

Formula: rate $\times$ time = distance

Janice: $(30)(x) = 30x$

Richard: $(45)(x - 2) = 45x - 90$

Because the distance is constant, you can equate Janice's distance to Richard's, then solve for x:

$30x = 45x - 90$

$15x = 90$

$x = 6$

Janice had traveled six hours when Richard caught up with her. Because Janice left at 11:00 a.m., Richard caught up with her at 5:00 p.m.

How far in kilometers can Scott drive into the country if he drives out at 40 kilometers per hour (kph), returns over the same road at 30 kph, and spends eight hours away from home, including a one-hour stop for lunch?

A. 105
B. 120
C. 145
D. 180
E. 210

The correct answer is B. Scott's actual driving time is 7 hours, which you must divide into two parts: his time spent driving into the country and his time spent returning. Letting the first part equal x, the return time is what remains of the seven hours, or $7 - x$. Substitute these expressions into the motion formula for each of the two parts of Scott's journey:

Formula: rate $\times$ time = distance

Going: $(40)(x) = 40x$

Returning: $(30)(7 - x) = 210 - 30x$

Because the journey is round trip, the distance going equals the distance returning. Simply equate the two algebraic expressions, then solve for x:

$40x = 210 - 30x$

$70x = 210$

$x = 3$

Scott traveled 40 mph for 3 hours, so he traveled 120 miles.

Tip: Regardless of which type of speed problem you're dealing with, you should always start with the same task: set up *two* distinct equations patterned after the simple rate-of-travel formula ($r \times t = d$).

Problems Involving Overlapping Sets

Overlapping set problems involve distinct sets that share some number of members. GMAT overlapping set problems come in one of two varieties:

- Single overlap (easier)
- Double overlap (tougher)

Each of the 24 people auditioning for a community-theater production is either an actor, a musician, or both. If 10 of the people auditioning are actors and 19 of the people auditioning are musicians, how many of the people auditioning are musicians but not actors?

A. 10
B. 14
C. 19
D. 21
E. 24

Part III: Quantitative Ability

The correct answer is B. You can approach this relatively simple problem without formal algebra: The number of actors plus the number of musicians equals 29 (10 + 19 = 29). However, only 24 people are auditioning. Thus, 5 of the 24 are actor-musicians, so 14 of the 19 musicians must not be actors.

You can also solve this problem algebraically. The question describes three mutually exclusive sets: (1) actors who are not musicians, (2) musicians who are not actors, and (3) actors who are also musicians. The total number of people among these three sets is 24. You can represent this scenario with the following algebraic equation (n = number of actors/musicians), solving for $19 - n$ to answer the question:

$$(10 - n) + n + (19 - n) = 24$$
$$29 - n = 24$$
$$n = 5$$
$$19 - 5 = 14$$

Adrian owns 60 neckties, each of which is either 100% silk or 100% polyester. Forty percent of each type of tie is striped, and 25 of the ties are silk. How many of the ties are polyester but not striped?

A. 18
B. 21
C. 24
D. 35
E. 40

The correct answer is B. This double-overlap problem involves four distinct sets: striped silk ties, striped polyester ties, non-striped silk ties, and non-striped polyester ties. Set up a table representing the four sets, filling in the information given in the problem, as shown in the next figure:

	silk	polyester	
striped			40%
non-striped		?	60%
	25	35	

Given that 25 ties are silk (see the left column), 35 ties must be polyester (see the right column). Also, given that 40% of the ties are striped (see the top row), 60% must be non-striped (see the bottom row). Thus, 60% of 35 ties, or 21 ties, are polyester and "non-striped."

Chapter 8

Math Review—Geometry

In this chapter, you'll review the fundamentals involving plane geometry, starting with the following:

- Relationships among angles formed by intersecting lines
- Characteristics of any triangle
- Characteristics of special right triangles
- The Pythagorean theorem
- Characteristics of squares, rectangles, and parallelograms
- Characteristics of circles

Then, you'll review the basics of coordinate geometry:

- The characteristics of the *xy*-plane
- Defining and plotting points and lines on the plane
- Applying the midpoint and distance formulas to problems involving line segments

Lines and Angles

Lines and line segments are the basic building blocks for most GMAT geometry problems. A GMAT geometry question might involve nothing more than intersecting lines and the angles they form. To handle the question, just remember four basic rules about angles formed by intersecting lines:

1. Vertical angles (angles across the vertex from each other and formed by the same two lines) are equal in degree measure, or *congruent* (≅). In other words, they're the same size.

2. If adjacent angles combine to form a straight line, their degree measures total 180. In fact, a straight line is actually a 180° angle.

3. If two lines are perpendicular (⊥) to each other, they intersect, forming right (90°) angles.

4. The sum of the measures of all angles where two or more lines intersect at the same point is 360° (regardless of how many angles are involved).

> **Note:** The symbol (≅) symbolizes that two geometric features are *congruent*, which means that they are identical (the same size, length, degree measure, etc.). The equation $AB \cong CD$ means that line segment AB is congruent (equal in length) to line segment CD. The two equations $\angle A \cong \angle B$ and $m\angle A = m\angle B$ are two different ways of symbolizing the same relationship: that the angle whose vertex is at point A is congruent (equal in degree measure, or size) to the angle whose vertex is at point B. (The letter m symbolizes degree measure.)

Angles Formed by Intersecting Lines

When two or more lines intersect at the same point, they form a "wheel-spoke" pattern with a "hub." On the GMAT, "wheel-spoke" questions require you to apply one or more of the preceding four rules.

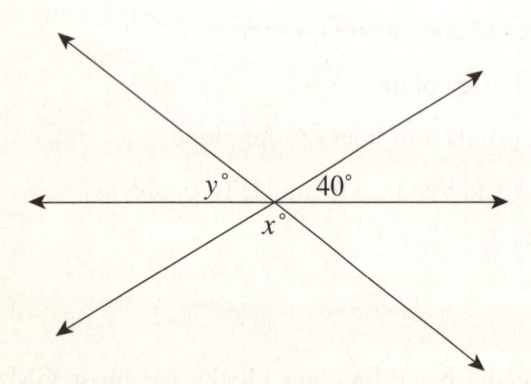

The figure above shows three intersecting lines. What is the value of $x + y$?

A. 50
B. 80
C. 130
D. 140
E. 150

The correct answer is D. The angle vertical to the one indicated as 40° must also measure 40°. That 40° angle, together with the angles whose measures are $x°$ and $y°$, combine to form a straight (180°) line. In other words, $40 + x + y = 180$. Thus, $x + y = 140$.

A slightly tougher "wheel-spoke" question might focus on overlapping angles and require you to apply rule 1 (about vertical angles) to determine the amount of the overlap. Look at this next "wheel-spoke" figure:

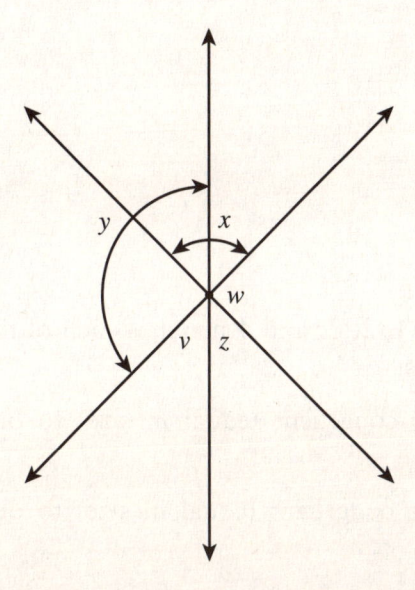

A GMAT question about the preceding figure might test your ability to recognize one of the following relationships:

$x + y - z = 180$	$x + y$ exceeds 180 by the amount of the overlap, which equals z, the angle vertical to the overlapping angle.
$x + y + v + w = 360$	The sum of the measures of all angles, excluding z, is 360°; z is excluded because it is already accounted for by the overlap of x and y.
$y - w = z$	w equals its vertical angle, so $y - w$ equals the portion of y vertical to angle z.

Parallel Lines and Transversals

GMAT problems involving parallel lines also involve at least one transversal, which is a line that intersects each of two (or more) lines. Look at this next figure, in which $l_1 \parallel l_2$ and $l_3 \parallel l_4$:

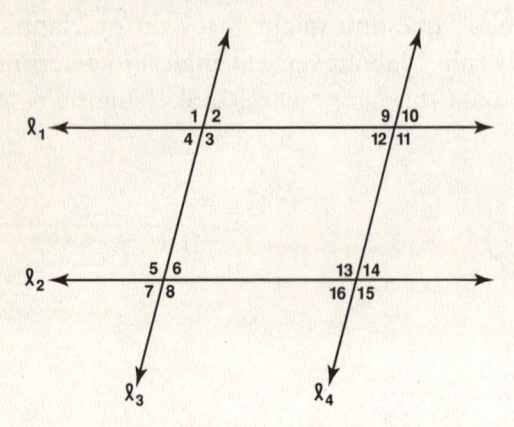

The upper-left "cluster" of angles 1, 2, 3, and 4 matches each of the three other clusters. In other words:

All the odd-numbered angles are congruent (equal in size) to one another.

All the even-numbered angles are congruent (equal in size) to one another.

If you know the size of just one angle, you can determine the size of all 16 angles!

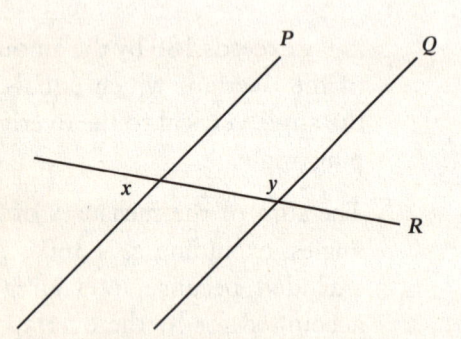

In the figure above, lines P and Q are parallel to each other. If m∠x = 75°, what is the measure of ∠y?

- A. 75°
- B. 85°
- C. 95°
- D. 105°
- E. 115°

The correct answer is D. The angle "cluster" where lines *P* and *R* intersect corresponds to the cluster where lines *Q* and *R* intersect. Thus, ∠*x* and ∠*y* are supplementary (their measures add up to 180°). Given that ∠*x* measures 75°, ∠*y* must measure 105°.

Triangles

The *triangle* (a three-sided polygon) is the test-makers' favorite geometric figure. You'll need to understand triangles not only to solve "pure" triangle problems but also to solve certain problems involving four-sided figures, three-dimensional figures, and even circles. After a brief review of the properties of any triangle, you'll focus on right triangles (which include one right, or 90°, angle).

Properties of All Triangles

Here are four properties that all triangles share:

1. *Length of the sides.* Each side is shorter than the sum of the lengths of the other two sides. (Otherwise, the triangle would collapse into a line.)

2. *Angle measures.* The measures of the three angles total 180°.

3. *Angles and opposite sides.* Comparative angle sizes correspond to the comparative lengths of the sides opposite those angles. For example, a triangle's largest angle is opposite its longest side. (The sides opposite two congruent angles are also congruent.)

Alert! Don't take this rule too far! The ratio among angle sizes need not be identical to the ratio among lengths of sides! For example, if a certain triangle has angle measures of 30°, 60°, and 90°, the ratio of the angles is 1:2:3. But this does not mean that the ratio of the opposite sides is also 1:2:3? No, it doesn't, as you'll soon learn.

4. *Area.* The area of any triangle is equal to one-half the product of its base and its height (or "altitude"): Area = $\frac{1}{2}$ × base × height. You can use any side as the base to calculate area.

> **Alert!** Do not equate altitude (height) with any particular side. Instead, imagine the base on flat ground, and drop a plumb line straight down from the top peak of the triangle to define height or altitude. The only type of triangle in which the altitude equals the length of one side is the *right* triangle.

Right Triangles and the Pythagorean Theorem

In a right triangle, one angle measures 90° (and, of course, each of the other two angles measures less than 90°). The *Pythagorean theorem* expresses the relationship among the sides of any right triangle. In the following expression of the Theorem, a and b are the two *legs* (the two shortest sides) that form the right angle, and c is the *hypotenuse*—the longest side, opposite the right angle:

$$a^2 + b^2 = c^2$$

For any right triangle, if you know the length of two sides, you can determine the length of the third side by applying the Theorem. For example:

If the two shortest sides (the legs) of a right triangle are 2 and 3 units long, then the length of the triangle's third side (the hypotenuse) is $\sqrt{13}$ units:

$$2^2 + 3^2 = (\sqrt{13})^2;\ 13 = c^2;\ c = \sqrt{13}$$

If a right triangle's longest side (hypotenuse) is 10 units long and another side (one of the legs) is 5 units long, then the third side is $5\sqrt{3}$ units long:

$$a^2 + 5^2 = 10^2;\ a^2 = 75;\ a = \sqrt{75} = \sqrt{(25)(3)} = 5\sqrt{3}$$

Pythagorean Triplets

A Pythagorean triplet is a specific ratio among the sides of a triangle that satisfies the Pythagorean theorem. In each of the following triplets, the first two numbers represent the comparative lengths of the two legs, whereas the third—and greatest—number represents the comparative length of the hypotenuse (on the GMAT, the first four appear far more frequently than the last two):

$1:1:\sqrt{2}$	$1^2 + 1^2 = (\sqrt{2})^2$
$1:\sqrt{3}:2$	$1^2 + (\sqrt{3})^2 = 2^2$
3:4:5	$3^2 + 4^2 = 5^2$
5:12:13	$5^2 + 12^2 = 13^2$
8:15:17	$8^2 + 15^2 = 17^2$
7:24:25	$7^2 + 24^2 = 25^2$

Each triplet above is expressed as a *ratio* because it represents a proportion among the triangle's sides. All right triangles with sides having the same proportion, or ratio, have the same shape. For example, a right triangle with sides of 5, 12, and 13 is smaller but exactly the same shape (proportion) as a triangle with sides of 15, 36, and 39.

Two boats leave the same dock at the same time, one traveling due east at 10 miles per hour and the other due north at 24 miles per hour. How many miles apart are the boats after three hours?

A. 68
B. 72
C. 88
D. 98
E. 110

The correct answer is D. The distance between the two boats after three hours forms the hypotenuse of a triangle in which the legs are the two boats' respective paths. The ratio of one leg to the other is 10:24, or 5:12. So you know you're dealing with a 5:12:13 triangle. The slower boat traveled 30 miles (10 mph × 3 hours). Thirty corresponds to the number 5 in the 5:12:13 ratio, so the multiple is 6 (5 × 6 = 30). 5:12:13 = 30:72:98.

> **Tip**
>
> To save valuable time on GMAT right-triangle problems, learn to recognize given numbers (lengths of triangle sides) as multiples of Pythagorean triplets.

Pythagorean Angle Triplets

In two (and only two) of the unique triangles identified in the preceding section as Pythagorean side triplets, all degree measures are *integers*:

1. The corresponding angles opposite the sides of a $1:1\sqrt{2}$ triangle are 45°, 45°, and 90°.

2. The corresponding angles opposite the sides of a $1:\sqrt{3}:2$ triangle are 30°, 60°, and 90°.

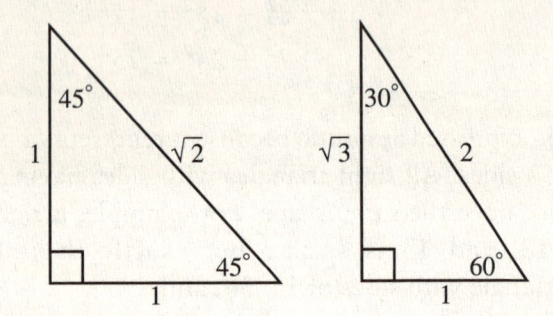

If you know that the triangle is a right triangle (one angle measures 90°) and that one of the other angles is 45°, then given the length of any side, you can determine the unknown lengths. For example:

- If one leg is 5 units long, then the other leg must also be 5 units long, while the hypotenuse must be $5\sqrt{2}$ units long.

- If the hypotenuse (the longest side) is 10 units long, then each leg must be $5\sqrt{2}$ units long. Divide hypotenuse by $\sqrt{2}$:

$$\frac{10}{\sqrt{2}} = \frac{10\sqrt{2}}{2} = 5\sqrt{2}$$

Similarly, if you know that the triangle is a right triangle (one angle measures 90°) and that one of the other angles is either 30° or 60°, then given the length of any side you can determine the unknown lengths. For example:

- If the shortest leg (opposite the 30° angle) is 3 units long, then the other leg (opposite the 60° angle) must be $3\sqrt{3}$ units long, and the hypotenuse must be 6 units long (3×2).

- If the longer leg (opposite the 60° angle) is 4 units long, then the shorter leg (opposite the 30° angle) must be $\frac{4\sqrt{3}}{3}$ units long (divide by $\sqrt{3}$: $\dfrac{4}{\sqrt{3}} = \dfrac{4\sqrt{3}}{3}$), while the hypotenuse must be $\dfrac{8\sqrt{3}}{3}$ (twice as long as the shorter leg).

- If the hypotenuse is 10 units long, then the shorter leg (opposite the 30° angle) must be 5 units long, while the longer leg (opposite the 60° angle) must be $5\sqrt{3}$ units long (the length of the shorter leg multiplied by $\sqrt{3}$).

In the figure below, $\overline{AC}$ is 8 units long, $m\angle ABD = 45°$, and $m\angle DAC = 60°$. How many units long is $\overline{BD}$?

A. $\dfrac{7}{3}$

B. $2\sqrt{2}$

C. $\dfrac{5}{2}$

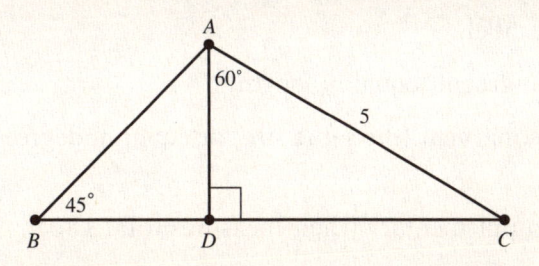

D. $\dfrac{3\sqrt{3}}{2}$

E. $\dfrac{7}{2}$

The correct answer is C. To find the length of $\overline{BD}$, you first need to find $\overline{AD}$. Notice that $\triangle ADC$ is a 30°-60°-90° triangle. The ratio among its sides is 1:$\sqrt{3}$:2. Given that $\overline{AC}$ is 5 units long, $\overline{AD}$ must be $\dfrac{5}{2}$ units long. (The ratio 1:2 is equivalent to the ratio $\dfrac{5}{2}$:5. Next, notice that $\triangle ABD$ is a 45°-45°-90° triangle. The ratio among its sides is 1:1:$\sqrt{2}$. You know that $\overline{AD}$ is $\dfrac{5}{2}$ units long. Thus, $\overline{BD}$ must also be $\dfrac{5}{2}$ units long.

> **X-Ref**
>
> A 45°-45°-90° triangle is special type of *isosceles* triangle—a triangle with two congruent sides. If you advance, you'll look more closely at this type of triangle, as well as at another special type: the *equilateral* triangle (a triangle whose three sides are all congruent).

Rectangles, Squares, and Parallelograms

Rectangles, squares, and parallelograms are types of *quadrilaterals*—four-sided geometric figures. Here are the characteristics that apply to all rectangles, squares, and parallelograms:

- The sum of the measures of all four interior angles is 360°.
- Opposite sides are parallel.
- Opposite sides are congruent (equal in length).
- Opposite angles are congruent (the same size, or equal in degree measure).
- Adjacent angles are supplementary (their measures total 180°).

A rectangle is a special type of parallelogram in which all four angles are right angles (90°). A square is a special type of rectangle in which all four sides are congruent (equal in length). For the GMAT, you should know how to determine the perimeter and area of each of these three types of quadrilaterals. Referring to the next three figures, here are the formulas (l = length and w = width):

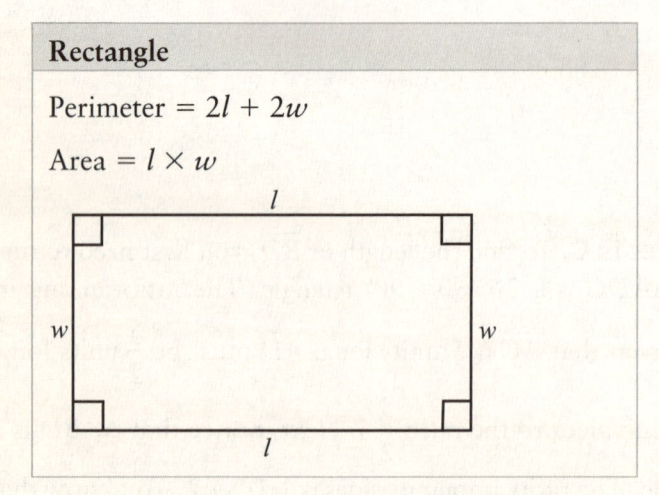

Rectangle

Perimeter = $2l + 2w$

Area = $l \times w$

Square

Perimeter = 4s [s = side]

Area = s^2

Area = $\left(\dfrac{1}{2}\right)(\text{diagonal})^2$

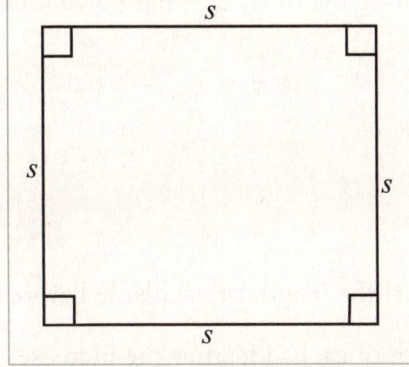

Parallelogram

Perimeter = 2l + 2w

Area = base (b) × altitude (a)

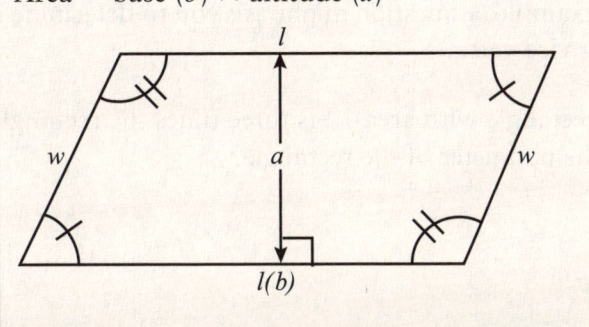

GMAT questions involving squares come in many varieties. For example, you might need to determine area, given the length of any side or either diagonal, or perimeter. Or, you might need to do just the opposite—find a length or perimeter given the area. For example:

The area of a square with a perimeter of 8 is 4.
($s = 8 \div 4 = 2$; $s^2 = 4$)

The perimeter of a square with an area of 8 is $8\sqrt{2}$.
($s = \sqrt{8} = 2\sqrt{2}$; $4s = 4 \times 2\sqrt{2}$)

The area of a square with a diagonal of 6 is 18.

$$A = \left(\frac{1}{2}\right)6^2 = \left(\frac{1}{2}\right)(36) = 6$$

Or, you might need to determine a change in area resulting from a change in perimeter (or vice versa).

> If a square's sides are each increased by 50%, by what percent does the square's area increase?
>
> A. 75%
> B. 100%
> C. 125%
> D. 150%
> E. 200%

The correct answer is C. Letting s = the length of each side before the increase, area = s^2. Let $\frac{3}{2}s$ = the length of each side after the increase, the new area = $\left(\frac{3}{2}s\right)^2 = \frac{9}{4}s^2$. The increase from s^2 to $\frac{9}{4}s^2$ to is $\frac{5}{4}$, or 125%.

GMAT questions involving non-square rectangles also come in many possible flavors. For example, a question might ask you to determine area based on perimeter, or vice versa.

> The length of a rectangle with area 12 is three times the rectangle's width. What is the perimeter of the rectangle?
>
> A. 10
> B. 12
> C. 14
> D. 16
> E. 20

The correct answer is D. The ratio of length to width is 3:1. The ratio 6:2 is equivalent, and $6 \times 2 = 12$ (the area). Thus, the perimeter = $(2)(6) + (2)(2) = 16$.

Or, a question might require you to determine a combined perimeter or area of adjoining rectangles.

Chapter 8: Math Review—Geometry

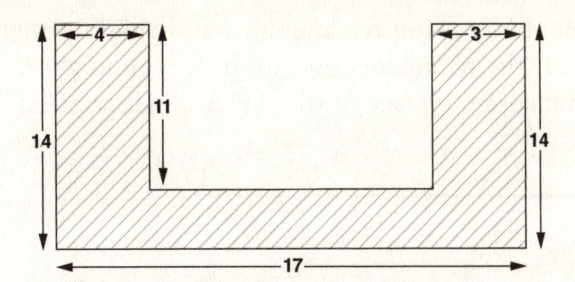

In the figure above, all intersecting line segments are perpendicular. What is the area of the shaded region, in square units?

A. 84
B. 118
C. 128
D. 139
E. 238

The correct answer is C. The figure provides the perimeters you need to calculate the area. One way to find the area of the shaded region is to consider it as what remains when a rectangular shape is cut out of a larger rectangle. The area of the entire figure without the "cut-out" is $14 \times 17 = 238$. The "cut-out" rectangle has a length of 11, and its width is equal to $17 - 4 - 3 = 10$. Thus, the area of the cut-out is $11 \times 10 = 110$. Accordingly, the area of the shaded region is 238 110 = 128.

Another way to solve the problem is to partition the shaded region into three smaller rectangles, as shown in the next figure, and sum up the area of each.

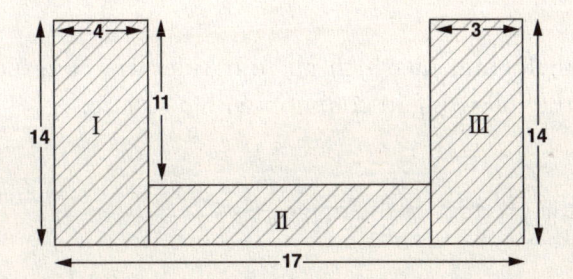

A GMAT question about a non-rectangular parallelogram might focus on angle measures. These questions are easy to answer. In any parallelogram, opposite angles are congruent, and adjacent angles are supplementary. (Their measures total 180°.) So, if one of a parallelogram's angles measures 65°, then the opposite angle must also measure 65°, while the two other angles each measure 115°.

A more difficult question about a non-rectangular parallelogram might focus on area. To determine the parallelogram's altitude, you might need to apply the Pythagorean theorem (or one of the side or angle triplets).

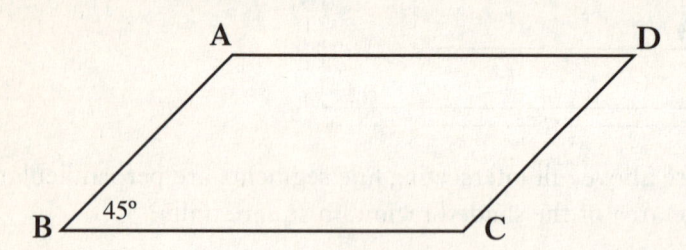

In the figure above, $\overline{AB} \parallel \overline{CD}$ and $\overline{AD} \parallel \overline{BC}$. If $\overline{BC}$ is 4 units long and $\overline{CD}$ is 2 units long, what is the area of quadrilateral $ABCD$?

A. 4
B. $4\sqrt{2}$
C. 6
D. 8
E. $6\sqrt{2}$

The correct answer is B. Since $ABCD$ is a parallelogram, its area = base (4) × altitude. To determine altitude (a), draw a vertical line segment connecting point A to $\overline{BC}$, which creates a 45°-45°-90° triangle. The ratio of the triangle's hypotenuse to each leg is $\sqrt{2}:1$. The hypotenuse $\overline{AB} = 2$. Thus, the altitude (a) of $ABCD$ is $\frac{2}{\sqrt{2}}$, or $\sqrt{2}$. Accordingly, the area of $ABCD = 4 \times \sqrt{2}$, or $4\sqrt{2}$.

> **Tip**
>
> A non-rectangular parallelogram in which all four sides are congruent (called a *rhombus*) has the following in common with a square:
>
> - Perimeter = 4s
> - Area = one-half the product of the diagonals

Circles

For the GMAT, you'll need to know the following basic terminology involving circles:

Circumference: The distance around the circle (its "perimeter").

Radius: The distance from a circle's center to any point on the circle's circumference.

Diameter: The greatest distance from one point to another on the circle's circumference (twice the length of the radius).

Chord: A line segment connecting two points on the circle's circumference (a circle's longest possible chord is its diameter, passing through the circle's center).

You'll also need to apply the two basic formulas involving circles (r = radius, d = diameter):

- Circumference = $2\pi r$, or πd
- Area = πr^2

> **Note:** The value of π is approximately 3.14, or $\frac{22}{7}$. For the GMAT, you won't need to work with a value for π any more precise. In fact, in most circle problems, the solution is expressed in terms of π rather than numerically.

With the two formulas, all you need is one value—area, circumference, diameter, or radius—and you can determine all the others. For example:

Given a circle with a diameter of 6:
radius = 3
circumference = $(2)(3)\pi = 6\pi$
area = $\pi(3)^2 = 9\pi$

If a circle's circumference is 10π centimeters long, what is the area of the circle, in square centimeters?

A. 12.5
B. 5π
C. 22.5
D. 25π
E. 10π

The correct answer is D. First, determine the circle's radius. Applying the circumference formula $C = 2\pi r$, solve for r:

$10\pi = 2\pi r$
$5 = r$

Then, apply the area formula, with 5 as the value of r:

$A = \pi(5)^2 = 25\pi$

Part III: Quantitative Ability

> A GMAT circle problem might involve other types of geometric figures as well—such as triangles, squares and non-square rectangles, and tangent lines. If you advance, you'll learn how to handle these hybrid problems.
>
> X-Ref

Coordinate Signs and the Four Quadrants

GMAT *coordinate geometry* questions involve the rectangular *coordinate plane* (or *xy*-plane) defined by two axes—a horizontal *x-axis* and a vertical *y-axis*. You can define any point on the coordinate plane by using two coordinates: an *x-coordinate* and a *y-coordinate*. A point's *x*-coordinate is its horizontal position on the plane, and its *y*-coordinate is its vertical position on the plane. You denote the coordinates of a point with (x,y), where x is the point's *x*-coordinate and y is the point's *y*-coordinate.

The center of the coordinate plane—the intersection of the x and y axes—is called the *origin*. The coordinates of the origin are $(0,0)$. Any point along the *x*-axis has a *y*-coordinate of 0 $(x,0)$, and any point along the *y*-axis has an *x*-coordinate of 0 $(0,y)$. The coordinate signs (positive or negative) of points lying in the four quadrants I-IV in this next figure are as follows:

Quadrant I $(+,+)$

Quadrant II $(-,+)$

Quadrant III $(-,-)$

Quadrant IV $(+,-)$

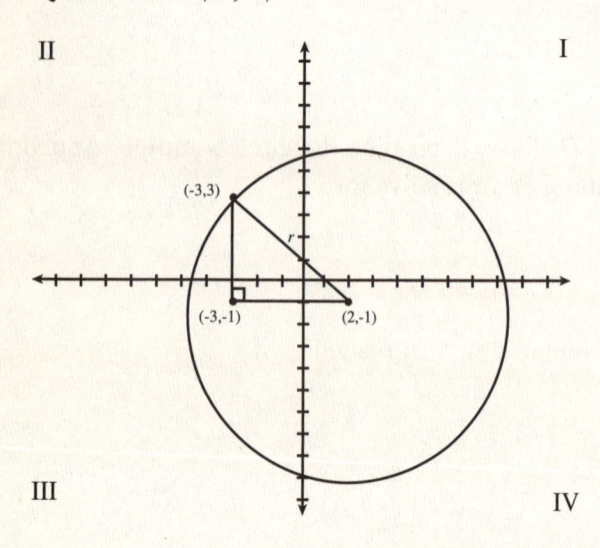

> **Note:** Notice that we've plotted three different points on this plane. Each point has its own unique coordinates. Before you read on, make sure you understand why each point is identified (by two coordinates) as it is.

Defining a Line on the Coordinate Plane

You can define any line on the coordinate plane by the equation:

$y = mx + b$

In this equation:

- The variable m is the slope of the line.
- The variable b is the line's y-intercept (where the line crosses the y-axis).
- The variables x and y are the coordinates of any point on the line. Any (x,y) pair defining a point. on the line can substitute for the variables x and y.

Determining a line's *slope* is often crucial to solving GMAT coordinate geometry problems. Think of the slope of a line as a fraction in which the numerator indicates the vertical change from one point to another on the line (moving left to right) corresponding to a given horizontal change, which the fraction's denominator indicates. The common term used for this fraction is "rise-over-run."

You can determine the slope of a line from any two pairs of (x,y) coordinates. In general, if (x_1,y_1) and (x_2,y_2) lie on the same line, calculate the line's slope as follows (notice that you can subtract either pair from the other):

$$\text{slope } (m) = \frac{y_2 - y_1}{x_2 - x_1} \text{ or } \frac{y_1 - y_2}{x_1 - x_2}$$

> **Alert!** In applying the preceding formula, be sure to subtract corresponding values! For example, a careless test-taker calculating the slope might subtract y_1 from y_2 but subtract x_2 from x_1. Also, be sure to calculate "rise-over-run," and *not* "run-over-rise"—another careless, but common, error.

Part III: Quantitative Ability

For example, here are two ways to calculate the slope of the line defined by the two points $P(2,1)$ and $Q(-3,4)$:

$$\text{slope } (m) = \frac{4-1}{-3-2} = \frac{3}{-5}$$

$$\text{slope } (m) = \frac{1-4}{2-(-3)} = \frac{-3}{5}$$

A GMAT question might ask you to identify the slope of a line defined by a given equation, in which case you simply put the equation in the standard form $y = mx + b$, then identify the m-term. Or, it might ask you to determine the equation of a line, or just the line's slope (m) or y-intercept (b), given the coordinates of two points on the line.

> On the xy-plane, at what point along the vertical axis (the y-axis) does the line passing through points $(5, -2)$ and $(3,4)$ intersect that axis?
>
> A. -8
> B. $-\frac{5}{2}$
> C. 3
> D. 7
> E. 13

The correct answer is E. The question asks for the line's y-intercept (the value of b in the general equation $y = mx + b$). First, determine the line's slope:

$$\text{slope } m = y2 - y1x2 - x1 = 4 - -23 - 5 = 6$$
$$-2 = -3$$

In the general equation ($y = mx + b$), $m = -3$. To find the value of b, substitute either (x,y) value pair for x and y, then solve for b. Substituting the (x,y) pair $(3,4)$:

$$y = -3x + b$$
$$4 = -3(3) + b$$
$$4 = -9 + b$$
$$13 = b$$

To determine the point at which two non-parallel lines intersect on the coordinate plane, first determine the equation for each line. Then, solve for x and y by either substitution or addition-subtraction.

Chapter 8: Math Review—Geometry

In the standard xy-coordinate plane, the xy-pairs (0,2) and (2,0) define a line, and the xy-pairs (−2,−1) and (2,1) define another line. At which of the following points do the two lines intersect?

A. $\left(\dfrac{4}{3}, \dfrac{2}{3}\right)$

B. $\left(\dfrac{3}{2}, \dfrac{4}{3}\right)$

C. $\left(-\dfrac{1}{2}, \dfrac{3}{2}\right)$

D. $\left(\dfrac{3}{4}, -\dfrac{2}{3}\right)$

E. $\left(-\dfrac{3}{4}, -\dfrac{2}{3}\right)$

The correct answer is A. For each line, formulate its equation by determining slope (m), then y-intercept (b). For the pairs (0,2) and (2,0):

$$y = \left(\dfrac{0-2}{2-0}\right)x + b \text{ (slope} = -1)$$

$$0 = -2 + b$$

$$2 = b$$

The equation for the line is $y = -x + 2$. For the pairs (−2, −1) and (2,1):

$$y = \left(\dfrac{1-(-1)}{2-(-2)}\right)x + b \left(\text{slope} = \dfrac{1}{2}\right)$$

$$1 = \dfrac{1}{2}(2) + b$$

$$0 = b$$

The equation for the line is $y = \frac{1}{2}x$. To find the point of intersection, solve for x and y by substitution. For example:

$$\frac{1}{2}x = -x + 2$$

$$\frac{3}{2}x = 2$$

$$x = \frac{4}{3}$$

$$y = \frac{2}{3}$$

The point of intersection is defined by the coordinate pair $\left(\frac{4}{3}, \frac{2}{3}\right)$.

Graphing a Line on the Coordinate Plane

You can graph a line on the coordinate plane if you know the coordinates of any two points on the line. Just plot the two points, and then draw a line connecting them. You can also graph a line from one point on the line, if you know either the line's slope or its *y*-intercept.

A GMAT question might ask you to recognize the value of a line's slope (*m*) based on a graph of the line. If the graph identifies the precise coordinates of two points, you can determine the line's precise slope (and the entire equation of the line). Even without any precise coordinates, you can still estimate the line's slope based on its appearance.

Lines that slope *upward* from left to right:

- A line sloping *upward* from left to right has a positive slope (*m*).
- A line with a slope of 1 slopes upward from left to right at a 45° angle in relation to the *x*-axis.
- A line with a fractional slope between 0 and 1 slopes upward from left to right but at less than a 45° angle in relation to the *x*-axis.
- A line with a slope greater than 1 slopes upward from left to right at more than a 45° angle in relation to the *x*-axis.

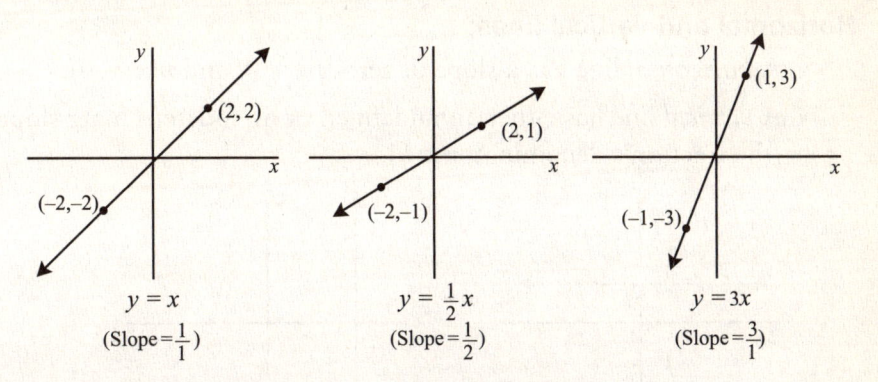

$y = x$	$y = \frac{1}{2}x$	$y = 3x$
(Slope $= \frac{1}{1}$)	(Slope $= \frac{1}{2}$)	(Slope $= \frac{3}{1}$)

Lines that slope *downward* from left to right:

- A line sloping *downward* from left to right has a negative slope (m).

- A line with a slope of -1 slopes downward from left to right at a 45° angle in relation to the x-axis.

- A line with a fractional slope between 0 and -1 slopes downward from left to right but at less than a 45° angle in relation to the x-axis.

- A line with a slope less than -1 (for example, -2) slopes downward from left to right at more than a 45° angle in relation to the x-axis.

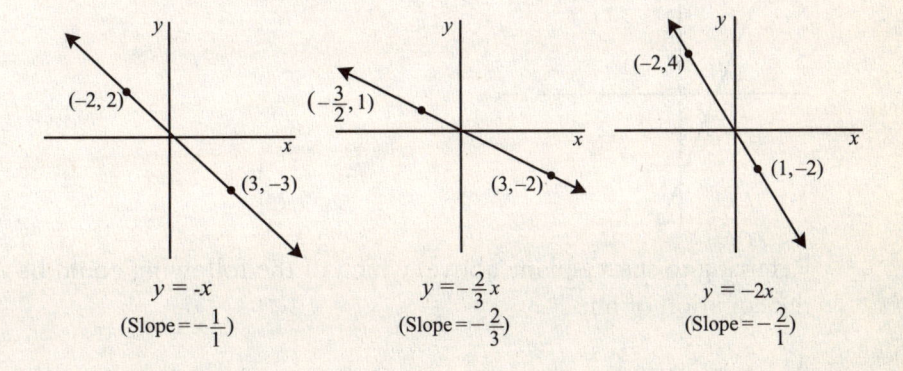 $y = -x$	$y = -\frac{2}{3}x$	$y = -2x$
(Slope $= -\frac{1}{1}$)	(Slope $= -\frac{2}{3}$)	(Slope $= -\frac{2}{1}$)

Horizontal and vertical lines:
- A *horizontal* line has a slope of zero ($m = 0$, and $mx = 0$).
- A *vertical* line has either an undefined or an indeterminate slope (the fraction's denominator is 0).

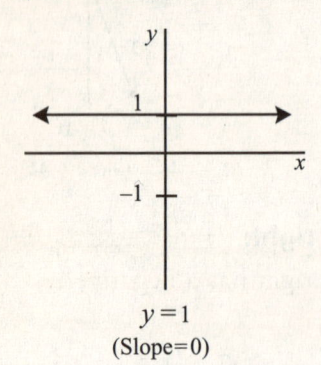

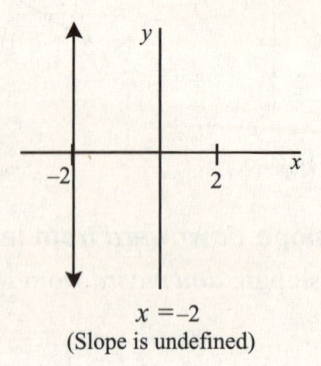

$y = 1$
(Slope=0)

$x = -2$
(Slope is undefined)

> **Tip**
> Parallel lines have the same slope (the same *m*-term in the general equation). The slope of a line perpendicular to another is the negative reciprocal of the other line's slope. (The product of the two slopes is 1. For example, a line with slope $\frac{3}{2}$ is perpendicular to a line with slope $-\frac{2}{3}$.

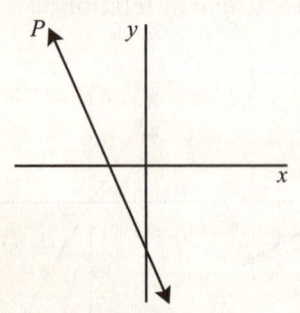

Referring to the *xy*-plane above, which of the following could be the equation of line *P* ?

A. $y = \frac{2}{5}x - \frac{5}{2}$

B. $y = -\frac{5}{2}x + \frac{5}{2}$

C. $y = \frac{5}{2}x - \frac{5}{2}$

D. $y = \frac{2}{5}x + \frac{2}{5}$

E. $y = -\frac{5}{2}x - \frac{5}{2}$

The correct answer is E. Notice that line P slopes downward from left to right at an angle greater than 45°. Thus, the line's slope (m in the equation $y = mx + b$) < -1. Also notice that line P crosses the y-axis at a negative y-value (that is, below the x-axis). That is, the lines y-intercept (b in the equation $y = mx + b$) is negative. Only choice (E) provides an equation that meets both conditions.

The Midpoint and Distance Formulas

To be ready for GMAT coordinate geometry, you'll need to know these two formulas. To find the coordinates of the midpoint of a line segment, simply average the two endpoints' x-values and y-values:

$$x_M = \frac{x_1 + x_2}{2} \text{ and } y_M = \frac{y_1 + y_2}{2}$$

For example, the midpoint between $(-3,1)$ and $(2,4) = \left(\frac{-3+2}{2}, \frac{1+4}{2}\right)$, or $\left(-\frac{1}{2}, \frac{5}{2}\right)$.

A GMAT question might simply ask you to find the midpoint between two given points. Or, it might provide the midpoint and one endpoint, and then ask you to determine the other point.

In the standard xy-coordinate plane, the point $M(-1,3)$ is the midpoint of line segment whose endpoints $A(2,-4)$ and B. What are the xy-coordinates of point B?

A. $(-1,-2)$
B. $(-3,8)$
C. $(8,-4)$
D. $(5,12)$
E. $(-4,10)$

The correct answer is E. Apply the midpoint formula to find the x-coordinate of point B:

$$-1 = \frac{x+2}{2}$$
$$-2 = x + 2$$
$$-4 = x$$

Apply the midpoint formula to find the *y*-coordinate of point *B*:

$$3 = \frac{y-4}{2}$$
$$6 = y - 4$$
$$10 = y$$

To find the *distance* between two points that have the same *x*-coordinate (or *y*-coordinate), simply compute the difference between the two *y*-values (or *x*-values). Otherwise, the line segment is neither vertical nor horizontal, and you'll need to apply the *distance formula*, which is actually the Pythagorean theorem in thin disguise (it measures the length of a right triangle's hypotenuse):

$$d = \sqrt{(x_1 - x_2)^2 + (y_1 - y_2)^2}$$

For example, the distance between $(-3,1)$ and $(2,4) =$.

$$\sqrt{(-3-2)^2 + (1-4)^2} = \sqrt{25 + 9} = \sqrt{34}.$$

A GMAT question might ask for the distance between two defined points (as in the example above). Or, it might provide the distance, and then ask for the value of a missing coordinate—in which case you solve for the missing *x*-value or *y*-value in the formula.

> **Alert!**
>
> In the distance formula, it doesn't matter which of the two points (x_1, y_1) signifies, or which point (x_2, y_2) signifies. But whichever pair you choose as (x_1, y_1), be sure not to inadvertently switch x_1 with x_2, or y_1 with y_2.

Take It to the Next Level

Here at the Next Level, you'll review the following advanced topics involving plane and coordinate geometry:

- Properties of isosceles and equilateral triangles
- Properties of trapezoids
- Properties of polygons (including those with more than four sides)
- Relationships between arcs and other features of circles
- Relationships between circles and tangent lines
- Relationships created by combining a circle with another geometry figure (such as a triangle or another circle)
- Properties of cubes, other rectangular solids, and cylinders
- Plotting and defining 2-dimensional figures (triangles, rectangles, and circles) on the *xy*-plane

Isosceles Triangles

An *isosceles* triangle has the following special properties:

1. Two of the sides are congruent (equal in length).
2. The two angles opposite the two congruent sides are congruent (equal in size, or degree measure).

If you know any two angle measures of a triangle, you can determine whether the triangle is isosceles.

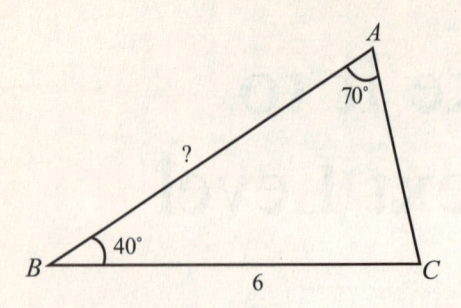

In the figure above, $\overline{BC}$ is 6 units long, $m\angle A = 70°$, and $m\angle B = 40°$. How many units long is $\overline{AB}$?

A. 5
B. 6
D. 7
C. 8
E. 9

The correct answer is B. Since $m\angle A$ and $m\angle B$ add up to 110°, $m\angle C = 70°$ (70 + 110 = 180), and you know the triangle is isosceles. What's more, since $m\angle A = m\angle C$, $\overline{AB} \cong \overline{BC}$. Given that $\overline{BC}$ is 6 units long, $\overline{AB}$ must also be 6 units long.

In any isosceles triangle, lines bisecting the triangle's three angles each bisect its opposite side. The line bisecting the angle connecting the two congruent angles divides the triangle into two congruent right triangles. So, if you know the lengths of all three sides of an isosceles triangle, you can determine the area of the triangle by applying the Pythagorean theorem.

Two sides of a triangle are each 8 units long, and the third side is 6 units long. What is the area of the triangle, expressed in square units?

A. 14
B. $12\sqrt{3}$
C. 18
D. 22
E. $3\sqrt{55}$

The correct answer is E. Bisect the angle connecting the two congruent sides (and in $\triangle ABC$ on the following page). The bisecting line is the triangle's height (h), and the triangle's base, which is 6 units long.

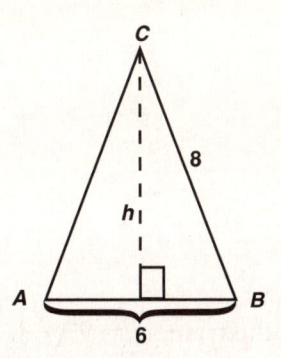

You can determine the triangle's height (h) by applying the Pythagorean theorem:

$$3^2 + h^2 = 8^2$$
$$h^2 = 64 - 9$$
$$h^2 = 55$$
$$h = \sqrt{55}$$

A triangle's area is half the product of its base and height. Thus, the area of $\triangle ABC = \frac{1}{2}(6)\sqrt{55} = 3\sqrt{55}$

Equilateral Triangles

An equilateral triangle has the following three properties:

1. All three sides are congruent (equal in length)
2. The measure of each angle is 60°.
3. Area $= \dfrac{s^2 \sqrt{3}}{4}$ (s = any side)

Any line bisecting one of the 60° angles divides an equilateral triangle into two right triangles with angle measures of 30°, 60°, and 90°; in other words, into two $1:\sqrt{3}:2$ triangles, as shown in the right-hand triangle in the next figure. (Remember that Pythagorean angle triplet?)

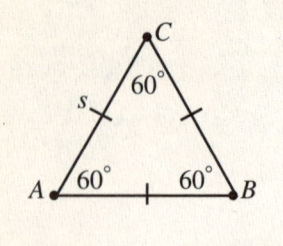

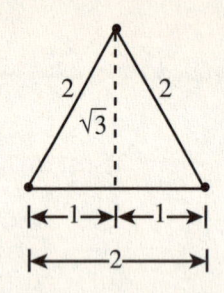

In the left-hand triangle, if $s = 6$, the area of the triangle $= 9\sqrt{3}$. To confirm this formula, bisect the triangle into two 30°-60°-90° ($1:\sqrt{3}:2$) triangles (as in the right-hand triangle in the preceding figure). The area of this equilateral triangle is $\frac{1}{2}(2)\sqrt{3}$, or $\sqrt{3}$. The area of each smaller right triangle is $\frac{\sqrt{3}}{2}$.

> On the GMAT, equilateral triangles often appear in problems involving *circles*, as you'll see later in this chapter.

Trapezoids

A trapezoid is a special type of quadrilateral. The next figure shows a trapezoid. All trapezoids share these properties:

1. Only one pair of opposite sides are parallel ($\overline{BC} \parallel \overline{AD}$).

2. The sum of the measures of all four angles is 360°.

3. Perimeter $= AB + BC + CD + AD$

4. Area $= \dfrac{BC + AD}{2} \times$ altitude (that is, one-half the sum of the two parallel sides multiplied by the altitude).

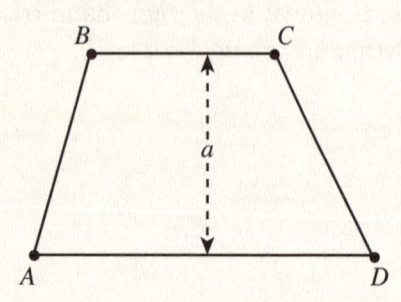

On the GMAT, a trapezoid problem might require you to determine either the altitude, the area, or both.

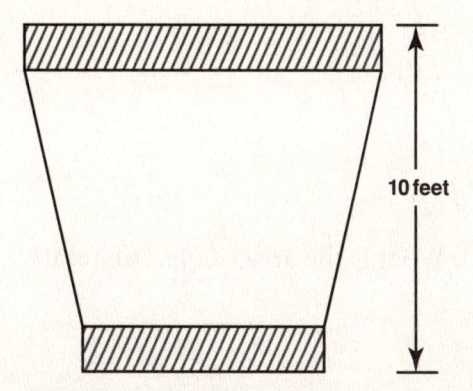

10 feet

To cover the floor of an entry hall, a 1' × 12' strip of carpet is cut into two pieces, shown as the shaded strips in the figure above, and each piece is connected to a third carpet piece as shown. If the 1' strips run parallel to each other, what is the total area of the carpeted floor, in square feet?

A. 46
B. 48
C. 52.5
D. 56
E. 60

The correct answer is E. The altitude of the trapezoidal piece is 8. The sum of the two parallel sides of this piece is 12' (the length of the 1'×12' strip before it was cut). You can apply the trapezoid formula to determine the area of this piece:

$$A = 8 \times \frac{12}{2} = 48$$

The total area of the two shaded strips is 12 square feet, so the total area of the floor is 60 square feet.

A GMAT trapezoid problem might require you to find the trapezoid's altitude by the Pythagorean theorem.

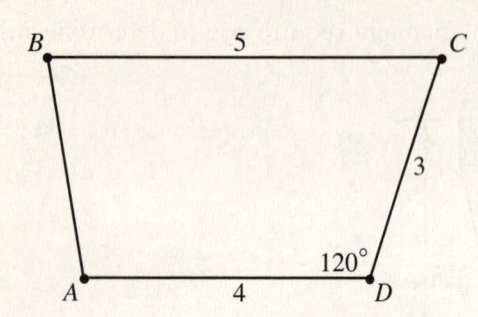

In the figure above, $\overline{BC} \parallel \overline{AD}$. What is the area of quadrilateral ABCD?

A. $5\sqrt{2}$

B. $\dfrac{9\sqrt{3}}{2}$

C. $\dfrac{27\sqrt{3}}{4}$

D. $\dfrac{27}{2}$

E. 16

The correct answer is C. The figure shows a trapezoid. To find its area, first determine its altitude by creating a right triangle:

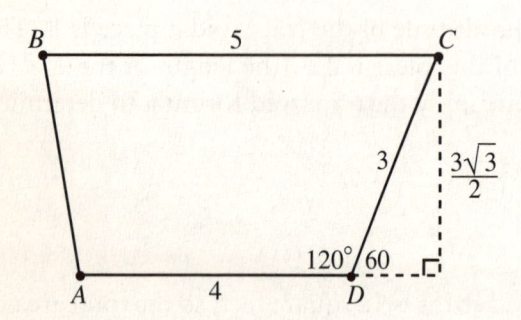

This right triangle conforms to the 30°-60°-90° Pythagorean angle triplet. Thus, the ratio of the three sides is $1:\sqrt{3}:2$. The hypotenuse is given as 3, so the trapezoid's altitude is $\dfrac{3\sqrt{3}}{2}$. Now you can calculate the area of the trapezoid:

$$\left(\dfrac{1}{2}\right)(4+5)\left(\dfrac{3\sqrt{3}}{2}\right) = \left(\dfrac{9}{2}\right)\left(\dfrac{3\sqrt{3}}{2}\right) = \dfrac{27\sqrt{3}}{4}$$

Polygons

Polygons include all plane figures formed only by straight lines. Up to this point, we've focused on only two types of polygons: three-sided ones (triangles) and four-sided ones (quadrilaterals). Now take a quick look at the key characteristics of all polygons.

> **Note**
>
> A polygon in which all sides are congruent and all angles are congruent is called a *regular* polygon. But for the GMAT, you don't need to know the terminology—just the principle.

You can use the following formula to determine the sum of the measures of all interior angles of *any* polygon whose angles each measure less than 180° (n = number of sides):

$(n - 2)(180°)$ = sum of interior angles

For *regular* polygons, the average angle measure is also the measure of every angle. But for any polygon (except for those with an angle exceeding 180°), you can find the average angle measure by dividing the sum of the measures of the angles by the number of sides. One way to shortcut the math is to memorize the angle sums and averages for polygons with 3 − 8 sides:

3 sides: $(3 - 2)(180°) = 180° \div 3 = 60°$

4 sides: $(4 - 2)(180°) = 360° \div 4 = 90°$

5 sides: $(5 - 2)(180°) = 540° \div 5 = 108°$

6 sides: $(6 - 2)(180°) = 720° \div 6 = 120°$

7 sides: $(7 - 2)(180°) = 900° \div 7 \approx 129°$

8 sides: $(8 - 2)(180°) = 1080° \div 8 = 135°$

A GMAT question might simply ask for the measure of any interior angle of a certain regular polygon; to answer it, just apply the preceding formula. If the polygon is not regular, you can add up known angle measures to find unknown angle measures.

If exactly two of the angles of the polygon shown below are congruent, what is the LEAST possible sum of the degree measures of two of the polygon's interior angles?

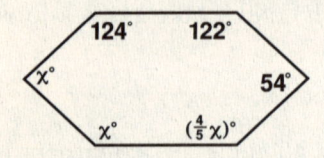

A. 162°
B. 174°
C. 176°
D. 204°
E. 216°

The correct answer is B. The figure shows a hexagon. The sum of the measures of six angles is 720°. Subtracting the measures of the three known angles from 720° leaves 420°, which is the sum of the measures of the three unknown angles. Set up an equation, then solve for x:

$$x + x + \frac{4}{5}x = 420$$

$$\frac{14}{5}x = 420$$

$$x = (420)\frac{5}{14} = (30)(5) = 150$$

Of the three unknown angles, two are either 150° each. The other is 120°. The polygon's two least possible angles measure 54° and 120°. Their sum is 174°.

Another, more difficult, type of problem requires you to determine the area of a polygon, which might be either regular or irregular. To do so, you need to partition the polygon into an assemblage of smaller geometric figures.

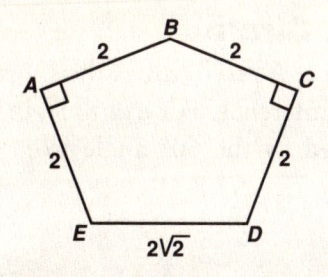

What is the area of polygon *ABCDE* shown above?

A. $4 + 2\sqrt{3}$
B. $3 + 3\sqrt{2}$
C. $6\sqrt{3}$
D. $2 + 6\sqrt{2}$
E. $8\sqrt{2}$

The correct answer is A. Divide the polygon into three triangles as shown below. The area of each of the two outer triangles $= \frac{1}{2}bh = \frac{1}{2}(2)(2) = 2$. (Their combined area is 4.) Since the two outer triangles are both $1:1:\sqrt{2}$ right triangles, $\overline{BE} \cong \overline{BD}$, and both line segments are $2\sqrt{2}$ units long. Accordingly, the central triangle is equilateral. Calculate its area:

$$\frac{s^2\sqrt{3}}{4} = \frac{(2\sqrt{2})^2\sqrt{3}}{4} = \frac{8\sqrt{3}}{4} = 2\sqrt{3}$$

Thus, the area of the polygon is $4 + 2\sqrt{3}$.

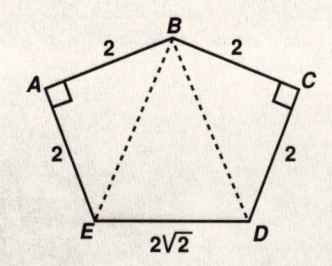

Advanced Circle Problems

GMAT circle problems sometimes involve other geometric figures as well, so they're inherently tougher than average. The most common such "hybrids" involve triangles, squares, and other circles. In the next sections, you'll learn all you need to know to handle any hybrid problem.

Arcs and Degree Measures of a Circle

An *arc* is a segment of a circle's circumference. A *minor arc* is the shortest arc connecting two points on a circle's circumference. For example, in the next figure, minor arc *AB* is the one formed by the 60° angle from the circle's center (*O*).

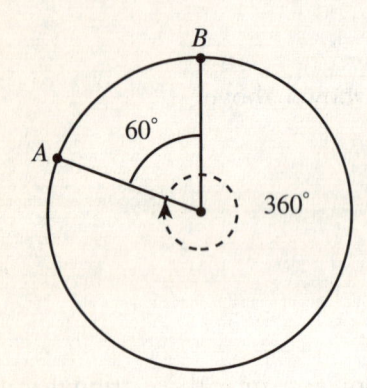

A circle, by definition, contains a total of 360°. The length of an arc relative to the circle's circumference is directly proportionate to the arc's degree measure as a fraction of the circle's total degree measure of 360°.

For example, in the preceding figure, minor arc *AB* accounts for $\frac{60}{360}$, or $\frac{1}{6}$, of the circle's circumference.

> **Note**
> An arc of a circle can be defined either as a length (a portion of the circle's circumference) or as a degree measure.

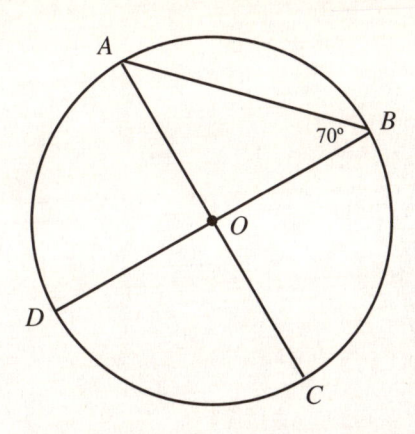

Circle O, as shown in the figure above, has diameters of $\overline{DB}$ and $\overline{AC}$ and has a circumference of 9. What is the length of minor arc BC?

A. 4

B. $\dfrac{11}{3}$

C. $\dfrac{7}{2}$

D. $\dfrac{13}{4}$

E. 3

The correct answer is C. Since $\overline{AO}$ and $\overline{OB}$ are both radii, we have isosceles $\triangle AOB$ thus making m$\angle BAC$ = 70°. From this we can find m$\angle AOB$ = 40°. $\triangle BOC$ is supplementary to $\angle AOB$, therefore m$\angle BOC$ = 140°. (Remember: Angles from a circle's center are proportionate to the arcs they create.) Since m$\angle BOC$ accounts for $\dfrac{140}{360}$ or $\dfrac{7}{18}$ of the circle's circumference, we have the length of minor arc $BC = \left(\dfrac{7}{18}\right)(9)\dfrac{7}{2}$.

Circles and Inscribed Polygons

A polygon is *inscribed* in a circle if each vertex of the polygon lies on the circle's circumference. The next figure shows an inscribed square. The square is partitioned into four congruent triangles, each with one vertex at the circle's center (O).

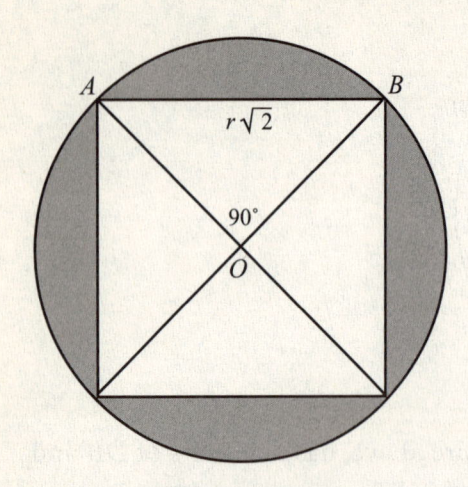

Look at any one of the four congruent triangles—for example, $\triangle ABO$. Notice that $\triangle ABO$ is a *right* triangle with the 90° angle at the circle's center. The length of each of the triangle's two legs ($\overline{AO}$ and $\overline{BO}$) equals the circle's radius (r). Accordingly, $\triangle ABO$ is a right isosceles triangle, m$\angle OAB$ = m$\angle OBA$ = 45°, and $AB = r\sqrt{2}$. (The ratio of the triangle's sides is $1:1:\sqrt{2}$.) Since $\overline{AB}$ is also the side of the square, the area of a square inscribed in a circle is $(r\sqrt{2})^2$, or $2r^2$. (The area of $\triangle ABO$ is $\frac{r^2}{2}$ or one fourth the area of the square.)

You can also determine relationships between the inscribed square and the circle:

- The ratio of the inscribed square's area to the circle's area is $2:\pi$.
- The *difference* between the two areas—the total shaded area—is $\pi r^2 - 2r^2$.
- The area of each crescent-shaped shaded area is $\frac{1}{4}(\pi r^2 - 2r^2)$.

The next figure shows a circle with an inscribed regular hexagon. (In a regular polygon, all side are congruent.) The hexagon is partitioned into six congruent triangles, each with one vertex at the circle's center (O).

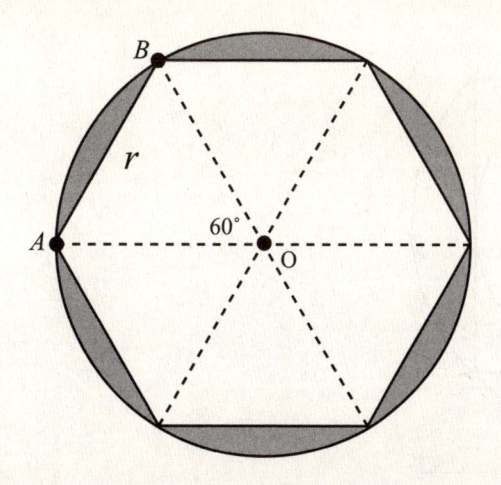

Look at any one of the six congruent triangles—for example, $\triangle ABO$. Since all six triangles are congruent, $m\angle AOB = 60°$, (one sixth of 360°). You can see that the length of $\overline{AO}$ and $\overline{BO}$ each equals the circle's radius (r). Accordingly, $m\angle OAB = m\angle OBA = 60°$, $\triangle ABO$ is an equilateral triangle, and $\overline{AB} = r$.

Applying the area formula for equilateral triangles: Area of $\triangle ABO = \frac{r^2\sqrt{3}}{4}$. The area of the hexagon is 6 times the area of $\triangle ABO$, or $\frac{3r^2\sqrt{3}}{2}$. You can also determine relationships between the inscribed hexagon and the circle. For example, the *difference* between the two areas—the total shaded area—is $\pi r^2 - \frac{3r^2\sqrt{3}}{2}$.

Part III: Quantitative Ability

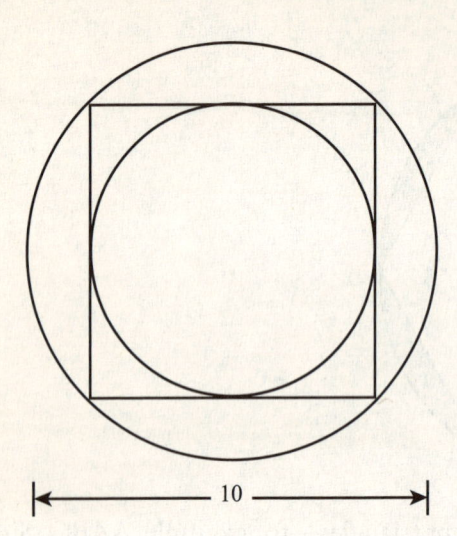

[Figure: A large circle containing a square, which contains a smaller circle tangent to the square at four points. The diameter of the large circle is labeled 10.]

The figure above shows a square that is tangent to one circle at four points, and inscribed in another. If the diameter of the large circle is 10, what is the diameter of the smaller circle?

A. $\dfrac{5\sqrt{3}}{2}$

B. 5

C. 2π

D. $5\sqrt{2}$

E. 7.5

The correct answer is D. The square's diagonal is equal in length to the large circle's diameter, which is 10. This diagonal is the hypotenuse of a triangle whose legs are two sides of the square. The triangle is right isosceles, with sides in the ratio $1:1:\sqrt{2}$. The length of each side of the square $= \dfrac{10}{\sqrt{2}}$, or $5\sqrt{2}$. This length is also the diameter of the small circle.

Tangents and Inscribed Circles

A circle is *tangent* to a line (or line segment) if they intersect at one and only one point (called the *point of tangency*). Here's the key rule to remember about tangents: A line that is tangent to a circle is *always* perpendicular to the line passing through the circle's center and the point of tangency.

The next figure shows a circle with center O inscribed by a square. Point P is one of four points of tangency. By definition, $\overline{OP} \perp \overline{AB}$.

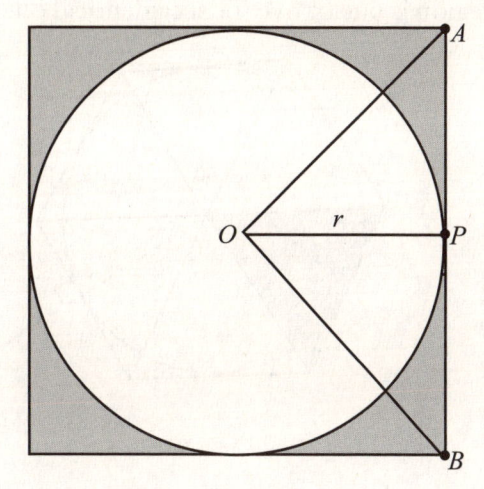

Also, notice the following relationships between the circle in the preceding figure and the inscribing square (r = radius):

- Each side of the square is 2r in length.

- The square's area is $(2r)^2$, or $4r^2$.

- The ratio of the square's area to that of the inscribed circle is $\frac{4}{\pi}$:1.

- The *difference* between the two areas—the total shaded area—is $4r^2 - \pi r^2$.

- The area of each separate (smaller) shaded area is $\frac{1}{4}(4r^2 - \pi r^2)$.

For *any* regular polygon (including squares) that inscribes a circle:

- The point of tangency between each line segment and the circle *bisects* the segment.

- Connecting each vertex to the circle's center creates an array of congruent angles, arcs, and triangles.

Part III: Quantitative Ability

For example, the left-hand figure below shows a regular pentagon, and the right-hand figure shows a regular hexagon. Each polygon inscribes a circle. In each figure, the shaded region is one of five (or six) identical ones.

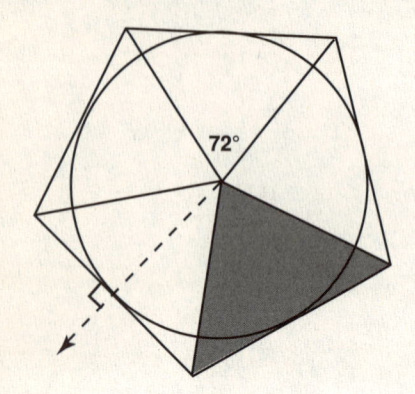

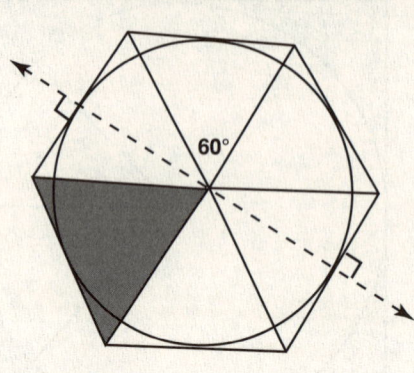

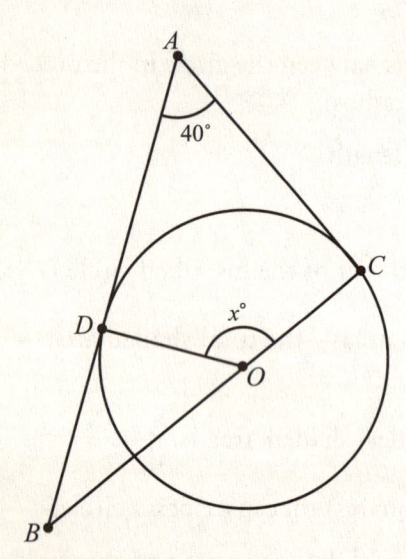

In the figure above, a circle with center O is tangent to $\overline{AB}$ at point D and tangent to $\overline{AC}$ at point C. If $m\angle A = 40°$, then $x =$

A. 140
B. 145
C. 150
D. 155
E. 160

The correct answer is A. Since $\overline{AC}$ is tangent to the circle, $\overline{AC} \perp \overline{BC}$. Accordingly, $\triangle ABC$ is a right triangle, and m$\angle B = 50°$. Similarly, $\overline{AB} \perp \overline{DO}$, $\triangle DBO$ is a right triangle, and $\angle DOB = 40°$. $\angle DOC$ (the angle in question) is supplementary to $\angle DOB$. Thus, m$\angle DOC = 140°$ ($x = 140$).

Comparing Circles

On the GMAT, questions asking you to compare circles come in two varieties. You will be required to do one of the following:

- Calculate the *difference* between radii, circumferences, or areas.
- Determine *ratios* involving the two circles and their radii, circumference, and areas.

To calculate a *difference* between the radii, circumferences, or areas, just calculate each area or circumference, then subtract. And if the question asks you for a difference between proportionate *segments* of the two circles, first find the difference between the circular areas, then calculate the fractional portion. No sweat.

To handle questions involving ratios, you need to understand that the relationship between a circle's radius or circumference and its area is *exponential*, not linear (because $A = \pi r^2$). For example, if one circle's radius is *twice* that of another, the ratio of the circles' areas is 1:4 $[\pi r^2 : \pi(2r)^2]$. If the larger circle's radius is *three* times that of the smaller circle, the ratio is 1:9 $[\pi r^2 : \pi(3r)^2]$. A 1:4 ratio between radii results in a 1:16 area ratio (and so forth).

> **Tip**
> The same proportions apply if you compare circumferences and areas. If the circumference ratio is 2:1, then the area ratio is 4:1. If the circumference ratio is 4:1, then the area ratio is 16:1.

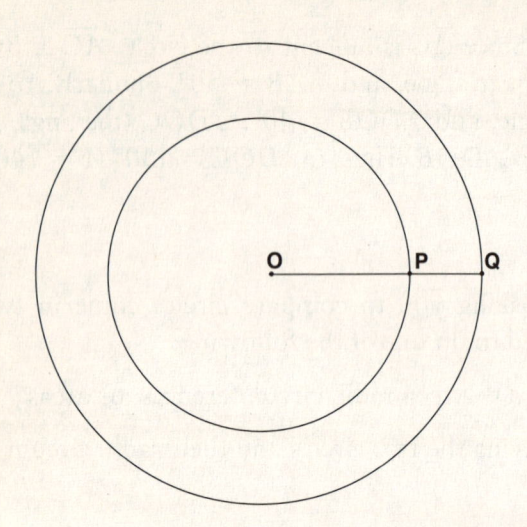

In the figure above, point O lies at the center of both circles. If the length of $\overline{OP}$ is 6 and the length of $\overline{PQ}$ is 2, what is the ratio of the area of the smaller circle to the area of the larger circle?

A. $\dfrac{3}{8}$

B. $\dfrac{7}{16}$

C. $\dfrac{1}{2}$

D. $\dfrac{9}{16}$

E. $\dfrac{5}{8}$

The correct answer is D. The ratio of the small circle's radius to that of the large circle is 6:8, or 3:4. Since Area = πr^2, the area ratio is $\pi(3)^2 : \pi(4)^2$, or 9:16.

Cubes and Other Rectangular Solids

GMAT questions about *rectangular solids* always involve one or both of two basic formulas (l = length, w = width, h = height):

Volume = lwh

Surface Area = $2lw + 2wh + 2lh = 2(lw + wh + lh)$

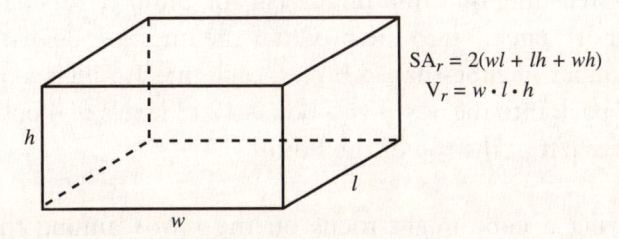

$SA_r = 2(wl + lh + wh)$
$V_r = w \cdot l \cdot h$

For *cubes*, the volume and surface-area formulas are even simpler than for other rectangular solids (let s = any edge):

Volume = s^3, or $s = \sqrt[3]{\text{Volume}}$

Surface Area = $6s^2$

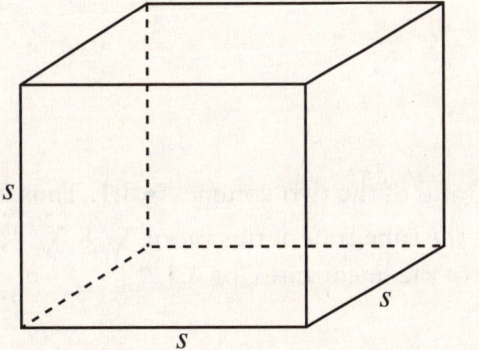

$SA_c = 6s^2$
$V_c = s^3$

A GMAT question might require you to apply any one of the formulas. Plug what you know into the formula, then solve for whatever characteristic the question asks for. Or, a question might require you to deal with the formulas for both surface area and volume.

A closed rectangular box with a square base is 5 inches in height. If the volume of the box is 45 square inches, what is the box's surface area in square inches?

A. 45
B. 66
C. 78
D. 81
E. 90

The correct answer is C. First, determine the dimensions of the square base. The box's height is given as 5. Accordingly, the box's volume (45) = $5lw$, and $lw = 9$. Since the base is square, the base is 3 inches long on each side. Now you can calculate the total surface area: $2lw + 2wh + 2lw = (2)(9) + (2)(15) + (2)(15) = 78$.

> **Tip**
>
> A variation on the preceding question might ask the number of smaller boxes you could fit, or "pack," into the box that the question describes. For instance, the number of cube-shaped boxes, each one 1.5 inches on a side, that you could pack into the 3 × 3 × 5 box is 12 (3 levels of 4 cubes, with a half-inch space left at the top of the box).

A test question involving a cube might focus on the *ratios* among the cube's linear, square, and cubic measurements.

> If the volume of one cube is 8 times greater than that of another, what is the ratio of the area of one square face of the larger cube to that of the smaller cube?
>
> A. 16:1
> B. 12:1
> C. 8:1
> D. 4:1
> E. 2:1

The correct answer is D. The ratio of the two volumes is 8:1. Thus, the linear ratio of the cubes' edges is the cube root of this ratio: $\sqrt[3]{8}:\sqrt[3]{1}$, or 2:1. The area ratio is the square of the linear ratio, or 4:1.

Cylinders

The only kind of cylinder the GMAT covers is a "right" circular cylinder (a tube sliced at 90° angles). The *surface area* of a right cylinder is the sum of the areas of:

1. The circular base
2. The circular top
3. The rectangular surface around the cylinder's vertical face (visualize a rectangular label wrapped around a soup can)

The area of the vertical face is the product of the circular base's circumference (i.e., the rectangle's width) and the cylinder's height. Thus, given a radius r and height h of a cylinder:

Surface Area $(SA) = 2\pi r^2 + (2\pi r)(h)$

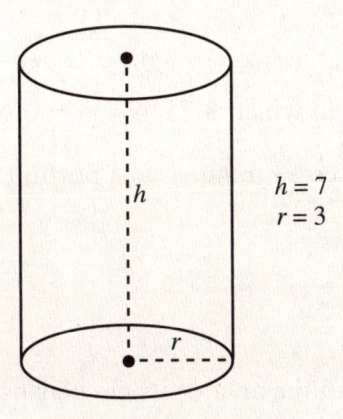

$h = 7$
$r = 3$

Given a cylinder's radius and height, you can determine its *volume* by multiplying the area of its circular base by its height:

Volume $= > \pi r^2 h$

On the GMAT, a cylinder problem might require little more than a straightforward application of formula for either surface area or volume. As with rectangular-solid questions, just plug what you know into the formula, then solve for what the question asks. For example:

Given a radius of 3 and a height of 7, a right cylinder's volume $= \pi(3)^2(7) = 63\pi$.

A tougher cylinder problem might require you to apply other math concepts. It also might call for you to convert one unit of measure into another.

One hose dispenses water at the rate of one gallon per minute, and a second hose dispenses water at the rate of $1\frac{1}{2}$ gallons per minute. At the same time, the two hoses begin filling a cylindrical tank whose diameter is 14 inches and whose height is 10 inches. Which of the following most closely approximates the water level, measured in inches up from the tank's circular base, after $1\frac{1}{2}$ minutes? [231 cubic inches = 1 gallon]

A. 3.5
B. 4.2
C. 4.8
D. 5.6
E. 6.7

The correct answer is D. After $1\frac{1}{2}$ minutes, the two hoses have dispensed a total of 3.75 gallons. Set up a proportion in which 3.75 as a portion of the tank's volume equals the water level after $1\frac{1}{2}$ minutes as a portion of the tank's height:

$$\frac{3.75}{V} = \frac{x}{10}$$

The volume of the cylindrical pail is equal to the area of its circular base multiplied by its height:

$$V = \pi r^2 h \approx \left(\frac{22}{7}\right)((49)(10)) \approx 1{,}540 \text{ cubic inches}$$

The *gallon* capacity of the pail = 1,540 ÷ 231, or about 6.7. Plug this value into the proportion, then solve for x:

$$\frac{3.75}{6.7} = \frac{x}{10}$$
$$6.7x = 37.5$$
$$x = 5.6$$

Coordinate Geometry

To handle GMAT questions involving the standard *xy*-coordinate plane, you'll need to be able to perform the following basic tasks covered earlier in this chapter:

- Plotting points on the coordinate plane
- Determining the slope of a line (or line segment) on the plane
- Interpreting and formulating the equation of a line
- Finding the midpoint of a line segment
- Finding the distance between two points

Notice that all these tasks involve points and lines (line segments) only. In this section, you'll explore coordinate-geometry problems involving two-dimensional geometric figures—especially triangles and circles.

Triangles and the Coordinate Plane

On the GMAT, a question might ask you to find the perimeter or area of a triangle defined by three particular points. As you know, either calculation requires that you know certain information about the lengths of the triangle's sides. Apply the distance formula (or the standard form of the Pythagorean theorem) to solve these problems.

On the *xy*-plane, what is the perimeter of a triangle with vertices at points $A(-1,-3)$, $B(3,2)$, and $C(3,-3)$?

A. 12
B. $10 + 2\sqrt{3}$
C. $7 + 5\sqrt{2}$
D. 15
E. $9 + \sqrt{41}$

The correct answer is E. The figure below shows the triangle on the coordinate plane:

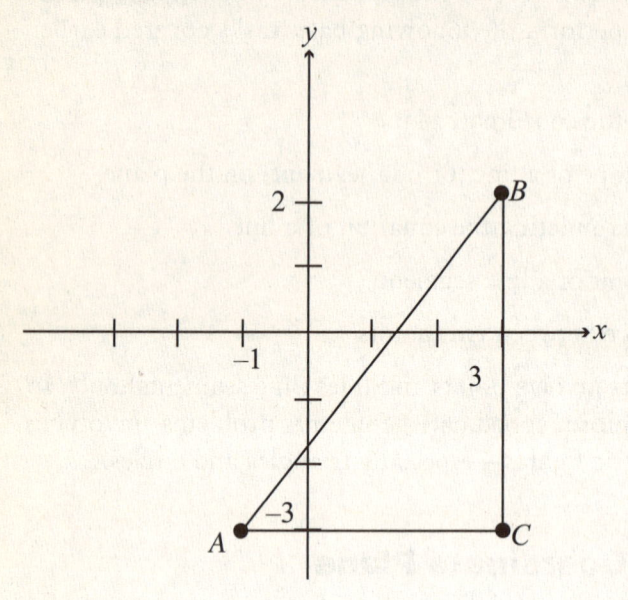

$AC = 4$ and $BC = 5$. Calculate AB (the triangle's hypotenuse) by the distance formula or, since the triangle is right, by the standard form of the Pythagorean theorem: $(AB)^2 = 4^2 + 5^2$; $(AB)^2 = 41$; $AB = \sqrt{41}$. The triangle's perimeter $= 4 + 5 + \sqrt{41} = 9 + \sqrt{41}$.

> **Note**
>
> Since the triangle is right, had the preceding question asked for the triangle's area instead of perimeter, all you'd need to know are the lengths of the two legs ($\overline{AC}$ and $\overline{BC}$). The area is $\left(\dfrac{1}{2}\right)(4)(5) = 10$.

To complicate these questions, the test-makers might provide vertices that do not connect to form a right triangle. (Answering this type of question requires the extra step of finding the triangle's altitude.) Or, they might provide only two points, then require that you construct a triangle to meet certain conditions.

Chapter 8: Math Review—Geometry

On the xy-plane, the xy-coordinate pairs $(-6,2)$ and $(-14, -4)$ define one line, and the xy-coordinate pairs $(-12,1)$ and $(-3, -11)$ define another line. What is the unit length of the longest side of a triangle formed by the y-axis and these two lines?

A. 15
B. 17.5
C. 19
D. 21.5
E. 23

The correct answer is D. For each line, formulate its equation by determining slope (m), then y-intercept (b):

For the pairs $(-6,2)$ and $(-14, -4)$	For the pairs $(-12,1)$ and $(-3,-11)$
$y = \frac{6}{8}x + b$ (slope $= \frac{3}{4}$)	$y = \frac{12}{9}x + b$ (slope $= -\frac{4}{3}$)
$2 = \frac{3}{4}(-6) + b$	$1 = -\frac{4}{3}(-12) + b$
$2 = -4\frac{1}{2} + b$	$1 = \frac{48}{3} + b$
$2 + 4\frac{1}{2} = b$	$1 - 16 = b$
$6\frac{1}{2} = b$	$-15 = b$

The two y-intercepts are $6\frac{1}{2}$ and -15. Thus the length of the triangle's side along the y-axis is 21.5. But is this the longest side? Yes. Notice that the slopes of the other two lines (l_1 and l_2) are negative reciprocals of each other: $\left(\frac{3}{4}\right)\left(-\frac{4}{3}\right) = -1$. This means that they're perpendicular, forming the two legs of a right triangle in which the y-axis is the hypotenuse (the longest side).

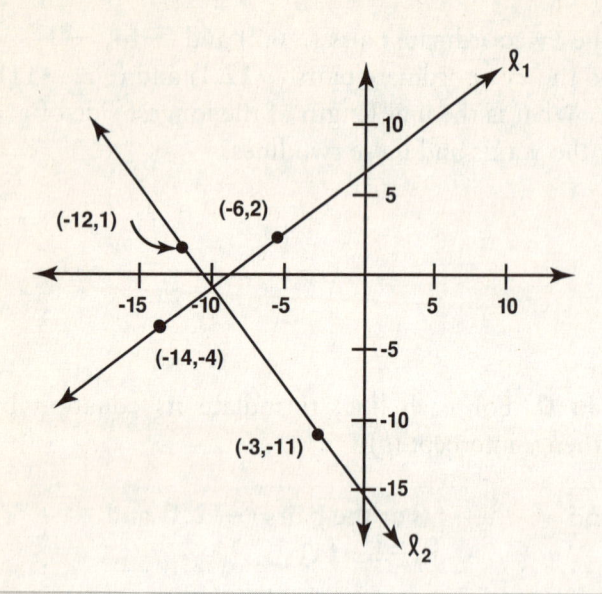

> If the preceding question had instead asked for the point at which the two lines intersect, to answer the question you would formulate the equations for both lines, then solve for *x* and *y* with this system of two equations in two variables.

Circles and the Coordinate Plane

A GMAT question might ask you to find the circumference or area of a circle defined by a center and one point along its circumference. As you know, either calculation requires that you know the circle's radius. Apply the distance formula (or the standard form of the Pythagorean theorem) to find the radius and to answer the question.

On the xy-plane, a circle has center $(2,-1)$, and the point $(-3,3)$ lies along the circle's circumference. What is the square-unit area of the circle?

A. 36π
B. $\dfrac{81\pi}{2}$
C. 41π
D. 48π
E. 57π

Chapter 8: Math Review—Geometry

The correct answer is A. The circle's radius is the distance between its center $(2,-1)$ and any point along its circumference, including $(-3,3)$. Hence, you can find r by applying the distance formula:

$$\sqrt{(-3-2)^2 + (-3-(-1))^2} = \sqrt{25+16} = \sqrt{41}.$$

The area of the circle $= \pi(\sqrt{41})^2 = 41\pi$.

Alert!

In any geometry problem involving right triangles, look out for the Pythagorean triplet "fake-out," in which you'll see the correct ratio—but between the wrong two sides. For instance, in the preceding problem, the lengths of the two legs of a triangle whose hypotenuse is the circle's radius are 4 and 5. But the triangle does *not* conform to the 3:4:5 Pythagorean side triplet! Instead, the ratio is $4:5:\sqrt{41}$.

PART IV

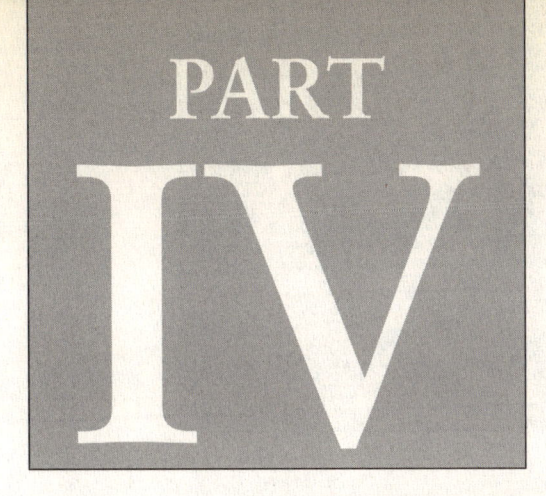

Verbal Ability

Critical Reasoning *332*

Sentence Correction *380*

Reading Comprehension *429*

PART IV

Chapter 9

Critical Reasoning

Welcome to GMAT Critical Reasoning. In this chapter, you'll:
- Briefly review the basic terminology you need to know for GMAT Critical Reasoning.
- Learn a step-by-step approach to handling any Critical Reasoning question.
- Learn how to recognize and handle each of the three basic, and most common, types of Critical Reasoning questions.
- Learn success keys for tackling Critical Reasoning questions.

Need-to-Know Terminology

For GMAT Critical Reasoning, you won't need to know the technical terminology of formal logic, except for a few basic terms. Here are the ones you should know before you proceed any further.

ARGUMENT: The process of reasoning—from premises to conclusion.

PREMISE: A proposition helping to support the argument's conclusion; premises form the basis on which reasoning proceeds; premises are often signaled with words and phrases such as *since*, *because*, and *given that*.

ASSUMPTION: Something taken for granted to be true in the argument; strictly speaking, assumptions are actually unstated, assumed premises.

CONCLUSION: A proposition derived by inference from the premises of an argument. Conclusions are typically signaled by words and phrases such as *hence*, *as a result*, *consequently*, *therefore*, and *it follows that*.

INFERENCE: The process of deriving, from assumed premises, either the strict logical conclusion or a conclusion that is to some degree probable.

Chapter 9: Critical Reasoning

> **Note**
>
> Don't get hung up on precise dictionary definitions. The GMAT won't ask you to define terms or try to trick you based on semantics; that's not what the GMAT is about. But, the test-makers *will* use these terms in phrasing Critical Reasoning questions—so you should have at least a layperson's understanding of what they mean.

Critical Reasoning—Your 6-Step Game Plan

The first task in this chapter is to learn the six basic steps for handling a GMAT Critical Reasoning question. You'll apply these steps to the following sample question:

> Among customers of breakfast restaurants, more order fresh fruit for breakfast than any other menu item. However, a recent health-research report indicates that eating eggs does not pose as significant a health risk as previously thought. In response to this report, operators of breakfast restaurants should increase the number of eggs but decrease the amount of fresh fruit they order from their suppliers.
>
> Which of the following, if true, would be the best reason to reject the recommendation made in the argument above?
>
> **A.** Eating eggs still poses a substantial health risk, especially for males over age fifty.
> **B.** Most fresh fruits are available only seasonally, whereas eggs are available any time of the year.
> **C.** Alternatives to breakfast egg dishes, such as pancakes and cereals, are growing in popularity at breakfast restaurants.
> **D.** Many customers of breakfast restaurants who order eggs also order fresh fruit.
> **E.** Compared to fresh fruits, pre-prepared fruit juices are growing in popularity among people who dine at breakfast restaurants.

Step 1: Read the question "stem" (the actual question or prompt that follows the passage). Reading the question stem first will tell you what you should think about as you read the passage. Be sure you understand the specific task that the question is asking you to perform.

Step 2: Read the passage and identify its key elements. Identify the argument's conclusion (if any) and its premises. If the passage contains a conclusion (most Critical Reasoning passages do), try to follow the argument's line of reasoning from premise(s) to conclusion. To help yourself along, try reading the passage again, starting with the conclusion. (Critical Reasoning passages are brief, so a second reading won't take much time.)

Step 3: Try to formulate your own answer to the question.

Step 4: Read the five answer choices, looking for one that provides something similar to one of the "best" answers you've formulated. But, don't assume that your home-grown "best" answer will look exactly the way you imagined it. Just look for a choice that conveys the same general idea. Also, keep an open mind to a possible "best" answer that hasn't yet occurred to you.

Step 5: If you're still not sure what the best answer choice is, eliminate whichever ones you can. Eliminate choices that make no sense to you, that don't seem directly relevant to the argument, or that accomplish just the opposite of what the question asks for.

Step 6: Compare the quality of the remaining (viable) answer choices. Try to determine which is qualitatively better than the others. Don't try to make ultra-fine semantic distinctions, parse words, or second-guess the test-makers. The qualitative difference between the best and any runner-up choice will be clear enough—if your thinking is straight enough.

Now let's walk through the sample question about breakfast restaurants, using this 6-step approach.

Step 1: This question stem tells you quite a bit about the passage as well as what to look for in a viable answer choice. The stem essentially asks you to recognize how the argument can be weakened. Since it refers to the "argument above," you know that the passage will contain at least one premise (information that you should assume is factual) as well as a conclusion, which, in this case, will be in the form of a "recommendation."

Step 2: The passage's last sentence expresses the argument's conclusion, while the first two sentences indicate the premises on which the conclusion is based. So, what's the line of reasoning here; in other words, what's the logical connection between the premises and the recommendation? Apparently, the passage's author thinks that breakfast-restaurant customers now know that its okay to eat eggs, so a significant number will begin ordering eggs *instead of* (as a substitute for) fresh fruit; based on this reasoning, it would make sense for restaurants to get ready for the shift in demand toward eggs and away from fresh fruits—by adjusting their supplies accordingly. If you find this line of reasoning a bit questionable — in other words, if you think it's full of holes—you're on the right track! Proceed to Step 3.

Chapter 9: Critical Reasoning

Step 3: The question essentially asks how you'd weaken the argument. So now's the time to critique it—to shoot some big holes in it. Ask yourself what else is needed to justify the recommendation, based solely on the premises. Doesn't the logical leap from premises to conclusion rely on certain assumptions about a significant number of breakfast-restaurant patrons? Here are three such assumptions (have any of these occurred to you?):

- Customers are actually aware of the report (otherwise, why anticipate increased demand for eggs?).
- Customers would prefer eggs over fresh fruit, even if they knew about the report (otherwise, why anticipate a shift in demand from fresh fruit to eggs?).
- Customers consider eggs a suitable substitute for fresh fruit (otherwise, why decrease the supply of fresh fruit?).

Any one of these assumptions would form a good basis for a "best" answer to the question. To draft that best answer, all you'd need to do is *refute* any one of those assumptions—in other words, point out that any of the following is true:

- Customers are *not* aware of the report.
- Customers would *not* prefer eggs over fresh fruit (even if they knew about the report).
- Customers do *not* consider eggs a suitable substitute for fresh fruit.

Step 4: Notice that the statement in choice (D) (*Many customers of breakfast restaurants who order eggs also order fresh fruit*) is not quite the same as saying that eggs are not a substitute for fresh fruit (the last of our home-grown answers from Step 3). Yet, the essence of the critique is essentially the same: It's unfair to assume, without any supporting evidence, that a significant number of customers are going to switch from fruit to eggs. Notice that (D) uses the word "many," leaving open the possibility that for *some* customers, these two choices might be mutually exclusive. So does that mean that there's probably a better answer choice? No; it's a pretty safe bet that (D) is the best choice. But go ahead and consider the other choices, anyway, just in case. Tentatively earmark (D) as your selection, then continue to Step 5.

Step 5: Consider each of the other four answer choices in turn:

Choice (A) also tends to weaken the argument. (If eating eggs is risky, this fact would tend to discourage, rather than encourage, people from eating them.) But if (A) is to significantly weaken the argument, we need to assume that a significant percentage of breakfast-restaurant customers are males over the age of fifty. Since (A) depends heavily on this additional assumption, it is not as effective as (D) in weakening the argument. Earmark it as a "runner-up."

Choice (B) is difficult to assess without more information, isn't it? The fact that fresh fruits are seasonal might have a bearing on whether owners should decrease their fruit supplies at a particular time. (For example, you could argue that, when fresh fruit is plentiful, lowering the supply might be safer than when it is not.) But what does that have to do with increasing egg supply? Absolutely nothing. As you can see, it's a real stretch to defend (B) as directly relevant to the argument at all, let alone as a statement that would clearly weaken the argument. Eliminate it!

Choice (C) provides a reason why restaurant owners might want to decrease their supply of eggs. So (C) does tend to weaken the argument. But (C) helps refute only half of what the argument recommends. What about the recommendation to decrease fresh fruit supplies? Whether alternatives to eggs are gaining in popularity has no clear relationship on the demand for fresh fruit. So earmark (C) as another "runner-up."

Choice (E) provides a reason why restaurant owners might want to decrease their supply of fresh fruit—which is part of what the argument recommends. So (E) actually tends to support, or strengthen, the argument—just the opposite of what you're looking for in the best choice. Eliminate (E)!

Step 6: Reflect again on the three most viable choices—the ones that tend to weaken the argument. Notice that choices (A) and (C), the two runners-up, both pale in comparison to (D) in terms of how seriously they weaken the argument. You can confidently confirm your selection: (D).

> **Tip**
>
> In the preceding question, the difference between (D), the best choice, and the two runner-up choices, (A) and (C), is just the degree of qualitative difference that's typical of the GMAT. On the actual exam, you won't need to make judgment calls that are any closer than the ones made here.

Chapter 9: Critical Reasoning

Assumption Questions

In an assumption question, the passage will contain a series of premises and a conclusion. However, in order for the argument's conclusion to be probable, at least one additional premise must be *assumed*. In other words, the argument will rely on at least one *assumption*. Your task is to identify which of the five answer choices indicates an assumption. Think of the structure of the argument this way:

Argument: stated premise(s) + assumption → inference (conclusion)

You know you're dealing with an assumption question when the question stem looks something like one of the following (a question stem might refer to specific passage information as well):

"The argument in the passage depends on which of the following assumptions?"

"Which of the following is an assumption that enables the conclusion above to be properly drawn?"

"The conclusion drawn in the first sentence logically depends on which of the following assumptions?"

How to Identify an Argument's Assumptions

To identify an argument's assumptions, always ask yourself this question:

"In addition to the stated premises, what *must* be assumed as factual to justify the argument's logical leap from premises to conclusion—for the conclusion to be probable?"

Try asking and answering this question for Arguments 1 and 2 below. For each argument, try to think of at least one or two assumptions, then jot them down on paper. (On the GMAT, premises and conclusions are not labeled as they are here.)

Argument 1:

Premise: More new Jupiter Motors automobiles were sold this year than any other brand.

Premise: Jupiter Motors automobiles have the lowest sticker prices, which are the manufacturers' suggested retail prices, of any new automobiles on the market.

Conclusion: Consumers rank low purchase price as the most important factor when purchasing new automobiles.

Argument 2:

Premise: Three years ago a business tax credit for research and development was enacted into law for the purpose of stimulating these business activities.

Premise: Overall business profits have risen steadily since the enactment of this law.

Conclusion: The tax credit has failed to achieve its objective of stimulating research and development.

Now read the following assumptions. Think about each assumption until you understand the necessary link it provides in the argument's chain of reasoning—from premises to conclusion. Without the assumption the argument falls apart, doesn't it?

Assumption (Argument 1): Comparative sticker prices coincide with comparative prices consumers actually pay for new automobiles.

Assumption (Argument 2): New investment in research and development does not generally enhance business profits within a brief (three-year) period.

Did you identify these necessary assumptions, or did you instead jot down various propositions that merely lend additional support to the argument, such as the ones below? Any of these propositions, if factual, *might* lend support to the argument, rendering its conclusion more probable. Yet the argument would not fall apart without them, would it?

Additional supporting evidence (Argument 1):

- The supply of new automobiles other than Jupiter Motors automobiles is sufficient to meet demand for them.

- Jupiter Motors salespeople are no more adept at salesmanship than salespeople who sell other automobiles.

- Warranties, service contracts, and other purchase incentives besides sticker price are no more attractive for Jupiter Motors automobiles than those of other brands.

- Jupiter Motors automobiles provide no advantage over other brands with respect to features other than price—such as safety, functionality, and appearance.

Additional supporting evidence (Argument 2):

- The tax credit is small compared to the costs of new research and development.

- The general economic climate for business has remained at least as healthy as it was three years ago.

- Taxes on businesses have otherwise remained at current levels or declined during the same time period.

- Major corporate research initiatives begun prior to the enactment of the law began to enhance profits during the last three years.

Be sure you understand the qualitative difference between *necessary* assumptions and merely *helpful* additional evidence. Why? *In any GMAT assumption question, the best answer choice will provide a necessary assumption.*

> **X-Ref**
>
> GMAT Assumption questions have a lot in common with the GMAT Argument-Analysis section, where your primary task is to identify the argument's assumptions. The key difference is that you write your own response rather than pick one among five choices.

A Typical Assumption Question

Now that you know how to identify and distinguish between necessary assumptions and other supporting evidence, attempt the following GMAT-style assumption question. (This one is a bit easier than average.) As you tackle the question, follow these steps:

1. Identify the argument's conclusion and premises.

2. Try to identify at least one *necessary* assumption and jot it down—before reading the answer choices.

3. Scan the answer choices for that assumption—or one similar to it.

4. Earmark other choices you think provide supporting evidence.

5. For each remaining answer choice, ask yourself why it is not a viable choice.

Then read the analysis of the question and of each answer choice.

For several consecutive years, poultry prices at each of three statewide grocery-store chains have exceeded the national average by about fifty percent. Also, the per-pound difference in poultry prices among the three stores never amounted to more than a few pennies, while among grocery stores in other states, the prices varied by nearly a dollar over the same period. The three chains must have conspired to not compete among themselves and to fix their poultry prices at mutually agreed-upon levels.

The claim that the three grocery-store chains conspired to fix poultry prices rests on which of the following assumptions for the time period referred to above?

- A. No other grocery store charged higher prices for poultry other than the three chains.
- B. Average poultry prices in the state where the three chains operate exceeded the national average.
- C. The price that grocery stores paid for poultry did not vary significantly from state to state.
- D. Consumers in the state where the three chains operate generally prefer poultry over other meats, even if poultry is more expensive than other meats.
- E. Other grocery stores operating in the same state as the three chains also sell poultry to consumers.

The correct answer is C. The argument relies on the assumption that all other possible factors in the price grocery stores charge for poultry were essentially the same in the state where the three chains operate as in other states. One such factor is wholesale price (the price grocery stores pay suppliers for poultry). A higher wholesale price generally leads to higher prices for consumers. Answer choice (C) expressly eliminates this factor. Admittedly, an "ideal" answer choice would provide a more sweeping statement—that all factors possibly affecting poultry price were the same from state to state. Nevertheless, (C) is the only answer choice that serves to affirm the assumption; thus (C) is the best choice.

Choice (A) admittedly provides *some support* for the argument. Higher poultry prices at another store would weaken the argument that the three chains conspired to fix prices; thus given the inverse—that no other store charges higher poultry prices—the argument's conclusion becomes more probable. However, (A) is not a necessary assumption. Even if a certain grocery store charged higher prices for poultry during the period, this fact would probably not be statistically significant in light of the much lower national average—especially if that store were located in another state and therefore did not compete with the three chains.

Choice (B) actually serves to *weaken* the argument. Given (B), the greater the number of other grocery stores in the same state the more likely that these other stores also charged high prices for poultry. This fact would in turn help refute the claim that the three chains were motivated by any concern other than to compete effectively against other stores in the state.

Choice (D) is *not relevant* to the argument, which is concerned with poultry prices charged by the three chains compared to poultry prices in other states, *not* compared to prices of other meats.

Choice (E) actually *weakens* the argument. The more competitors, the less likely these three chains together hold a statewide poultry monopoly. (Monopolists are more likely to charge whatever price they wish for their products.)

Tips for Tackling Assumption Questions

1. Formulate your own "best" answer as your read the passage—by filling in the missing logical link between the argument's premises and its conclusion. If you know what to look for among the five answer choices, you'll be more likely to find it, and less likely to fall prey to the test-maker's wrong-answer ploys.

2. Don't spend too much time brainstorming; if the missing link (a necessary assumption) doesn't occur to you within 10 or 15 seconds, go ahead and read the answer choices.

3. If a necessary assumption occured to you as you read the passage, scan the answer choices quickly for it (or a statement similar to it). If you spot it, immediately select it (click on the button to the left of it) as your tentaive choice.

4. If more than one answer choice seems viable to you, for each choice ask yourself whether the proposition provides a link in the argument's chain of reasoning. If it doesn't, eliminate that answer choice even if it lends support to the argument.

5. Look out for the following types of wrong answers (in addition to those that provide supporting but unessential additional evidence):

    - Additional information that serves to *weaken* the argument
    - Superfluous information, which is not directly relevant to the argument

Additional-Evidence Questions—Weakening the Argument

In this type of question, the passage will look just like a passage for an assumption question; the passage will contain a series of premises, along with a conclusion whose probability depends on one or more assumptions. Here's the basic structure again:

Argument: stated premise(s) + assumption(s) → inference (conclusion)

In a weakening-evidence question, however, your task is to identify which of the five answer choices *most seriously weakens* the argument. You know you're dealing with an weakening-evidence question when the question stem looks similar to one of the following (a question stem might refer to specific passage information as well):

"Which of the following, if true, would most weaken the argument above?"

"The argument in the passage would be most seriously weakened if it were true that"

"Which of the following, if true, is most damaging to the conclusion above?"

"Which of the following statements, if true, provides the best evidence that the reasoning in the argument above is flawed?"

"Each of the following, if true, raises a consideration against the conclusion above, EXCEPT:"

(Your task here is to identify the only answer choice that does NOT weaken the argument.)

How to Weaken an Argument

To understand how an argument by inference can be weakened, consider Argument 1 on page 337. Here it is again:

Argument 1

Premise: More new Jupiter Motors automobiles were sold this year than any other brand.

Premise: Jupiter Motors automobiles have the lowest sticker prices, which are the manufacturers' suggested retail prices, of any new automobiles on the market.

Conclusion: Consumers rank low purchase price as the most important factor when purchasing new automobiles.

There are many ways to weaken an argument like the one above. One way is to essentially point out as a matter of fact that the conclusion is false, or that a stated premise needed for the conclusion to be probable is false. However, in a GMAT weakening-evidence question, you're unlikely to find either method among the five choices—because both are bit too obvious. Instead, the test-makers prefer the following two methods:

1. Directly refute a necessary assumption—in other words, provide evidence that the assumption is false as a matter of fact.

    New automobiles with comparatively high sticker prices are often sold to consumers for less than automobiles with lower sticker prices.

Chapter 9: Critical Reasoning

2. Refute other possible supporting evidence—evidence that does not pertain directly to a necessary assumption but that, if true, would nevertheless increase the conclusion's probability.

   Example A: Production at the plants of Jupiter Motors' main competitor has been hampered by numerous labor strikes during the last three years.

   Example B: Warranties and other non-price purchase incentives vary widely among retailers of new automobiles.

Here's what you need to know about these two methods when analyzing a GMAT weakening-evidence question:

- A method-1 answer choice is always better than a method-2 choice, because the former is a *direct* attack on a *necessary* assumption.

- If no method 1 proposition appears among the answer choices, then the best choice will be the best among the method-2 propositions listed. (*Example A* above would be a better choice than *Example B*. Why? *Example B* leaves open the possibility that non-price incentives at Jupiter retailers are *less* attractive than at other retailers, which would actually *strengthen* the Argument.)

> **Tip**
>
> In weakening-evidence questions, don't expect any answer choice to directly refute or contradict the Argument's conclusion or one of its premises. Although either method is a great way to annihilate an Argument, the choice would be too easy to spot as the best one.

A Typical Weakening-Evidence Question

Now that you know how to weaken an Argument, and distinguish between propositions that merely weaken and those that completely undermine the Argument, take another look at the GMAT-style question you encountered near the beginning of this chapter. (This question is average in difficulty level.) This time around, as you tackle the question, do the following:

1. Identify the argument's conclusion and premises.

2. Try to identify at least one *necessary* assumption and jot it down—before reading the answer choices.

3. Scan the answer choices for a proposition that directly refutes, or contradicts, that assumption.

Part IV: Verbal Ability

4. Earmark other choices you think serve to weaken the Argument—then rank them in quality (degree of damage to the conclusion).

5. For each remaining answer choice, ask yourself why it is not a viable choice.

Then read the analysis of the question and of each answer choice.

Worldwide retail sales of home entertainment systems, which include a television and an audio system, increased twenty-five percent this year over last year. At the same time, worldwide retail sales of new automobiles declined by about the same percent. These statistics show that consumers can no longer afford to purchase both types of products during the same year.

Which of the following, if true, would cast most serious doubt on the conclusion drawn above?

A. Fewer advertisements for new cars appeared on television during the most recent year than during the previous year.
B. Consumers are spending more money on home entertainment systems than on new cars.
C. People who own home entertainment systems do not drive their automobiles as often as other people.
D. Prices of home entertainment systems and new cars were higher during the most recent year than during the previous year.
E. The reliability of automobiles this year improved significantly over last year.

The correct answer is E. The argument relies on the assumption that all other possible factors influencing consumers' buying decisions respecting the two products remained unchanged from last year to this year. An ideal "best" answer would directly refute or provide strong evidence against this assumption.

Choice (E) accomplishes this better than any other choice—by providing an alternative explanation for the fact that consumers are buying fewer new cars *and* more entertainment centers. Specifically, if a car is more reliable, then it is less likely to be replaced by a new one. By the same token, if people keep their cars longer and do not need to spend much money to repair them, then people can better afford to purchase other consumer items such as entertainment centers.

Choice (A) might explain why sales of new cars have declined. However, (A) does not explain increased sales of home entertainment centers.

Choice (B) reinforces the argument's premise, thereby *strengthening* the argument.

Choice (C) is irrelevant to the argument. (C) provides a reason why people with home entertainment systems might replace their cars less often. However, even if this were the case, it would have no bearing on whether these people can afford both items.

Choice (D) does not explain why consumers have chosen one type of product over another.

Tips for Tackling Weakening-Evidence Questions

1. As you read the passage try to identify at least one *necessary* assumption. There are two general types of assumptions that are especially common in weakening-evidence arguments:

    - The assumption that *all other factors are equal*—if the argument

    - The assumption that *all other relevant conditions remain unchanged over time*, if the argument seeks to explain or predict change from one point in time (or period of time) to another

2. Scan the answer choices for a proposition that directly refutes an assumption. If you spot one, immediately select it (click on the button to the left of it) as your tentative choice.

3. In all likelihood, more than one answer choice will serve to weaken the argument. Always select a choice that directly addresses, and attacks, a necessary assumption over any other choice that weakens the argument.

4. Before confirming your selection, ask yourself whether your choice serves to destroy a logical link needed for a convincing argument; if it doesn't, look for a better answer choice.

5. If no answer choice refutes a necessary assumption (it could happen), you'll need to weigh the comparative quality of all answer choices that serve to weaken the argument.

6. Look out for the following types of wrong answers:

    - A statement that affirms a necessary assumption—in other words, that accomplishes just the opposite of what the question asks for.

- A statement that serves to strengthen (rather than weaken) the argument in some other way.

- A statement that could either strengthen or weaken the argument, depending on additional unknown facts.

- A statement that contains superfluous information, which is not directly relevant to the argument.

> **Alert!** When handling a weakening-evidence question, what if no answer choice hits directly on what you're sure is a key assumption behind the argument? Don't assume that your powers of reasoning have failed you. Perhaps the argument depends on other assumptions as well. Or perhaps the particular question wasn't designed to test you on recognizing assumptions.

Additional-Evidence Questions—Supporting the Argument

For a supporting-evidence question, your task is to identify which of five propositions provides *the most support* for the argument—just the opposite as for a weakening-evidence question. You know you're dealing with a supporting-evidence question when the question stem looks similar to one of the following (a question stem might refer to specific passage information as well):

"Which of the following, if true, most strongly supports the author's argument?"

"Which of the following statements, if true, would most strengthen the argument above?"

"Which of the following, if true, provides the best indication that the conclusion in the argument above was logically well supported?"

"Which of the following best completes the passage below?"

How to Strengthen an Argument

To understand how an argument by inference can be supported or strengthened, consider Argument 2 on page 338. Here it is again:

Argument 2:
Premise: Three years ago a business tax credit for research and development was enacted into law for the purpose of stimulating these business activities.

Premise: Overall business profits have risen steadily since the enactment of this law.

Conclusion: The tax credit has failed to achieve its objective of stimulating research and development.

There are *two* methods of strengthening an argument like this one (the first is more effective):

1. Provide a necessary assumption (assert it is factual) or provide strong evidence that it is factual.

    Example: Investing in research and development does not generally enhance profitability until several years after the investment.

2. Provide evidence that adds weight or credibility to the argument, but that does not affirm a necessary assumption.

    Example A: Costs of certain raw materials used in many areas of research and development have increased since the law was enacted.

    Example B: Many large corporations curtailed significant research and development shortly before the law was enacted.

Here's what you need to know about these two methods for analyzing a GMAT supporting-evidence question:

- A proposition that affirms a necessary assumption (method 1) provides better support for an argument than one that does not.

- If no method-1 proposition appears among the answer choices, then the best choice will be the strongest method-2 proposition listed. (*Example A* above would be a better choice than *Example B*. Why? The degree of support *Example B* lends to the argument depends entirely on our assumption that new research and development cannot enhance profits within three years; *Example A* lends support to the argument irrespective of this assumption.)

> **Tip:** The best way to strengthen an argument is to affirm an assumption; the best way to weaken it is to refute an assumption. If you're beginning to think that assumptions are what GMAT Critical Reasoning is mainly about, you're absolutely correct!

A Typical Supporting-Evidence Question

Now that you know how to strengthen an argument and distinguish among propositions of varying degrees of support, attempt the following GMAT-style supporting-evidence question. (This one is average in difficulty.) As you tackle the question:

- Identify the argument's conclusion and premises.

- Try to identify at least one *necessary* assumption and jot it down—before reading the answer choices.

- Scan the answer choices for a proposition that essentially provides that assumption.

- Earmark other choices you think serve to strengthen the argument—then rank them in quality (degree of support).

- For each remaining answer choice, ask yourself why it is not a viable choice.

Then read the analysis of the question and of each answer choice.

> In an experiment involving addicted cigarette smokers, each subject was unknowingly administered either the new drug Nico-Gone or a placebo. One year later, less than a third of the subjects who were administered Nico-Gone had resumed smoking, compared with about two thirds of the subjects who were administered a placebo. These reports confirm that Nico-Gone is effective in curing addiction to cigarette smoking.
>
> Which of the following, if true, most strongly supports the conclusion above?
>
> A. One year after the experiment, the percentage of the experiment's subjects who were cigarette smokers was less than the percentage of the general population who were smokers.
> B. Other reliable studies indicate that cigarette smokers often falsely inform others that they are not smokers.
> C. During the year following the experiment, cigarettes were readily available to all of the subjects.
> D. One year after the experiment, the total number of subjects who were cigarette smokers was less than the number who were smokers one year prior to the experiment.
> E. During the year following the experiment, some of the subjects received other treatment to help them avoid cigarette smoking.

Chapter 9: Critical Reasoning

The correct answer is C. The argument relies on the major unstated assumption that no factor other than the experiment at issue was responsible for the reported result one year after the experiment. (C) provides evidence that lends credence to this assumption. If cigarettes were unavailable to some of the subjects during the year, this fact would be the primary explanation for any decrease in the number of smokers among the subjects.

Choice (A) does lend *some* measure of support to the argument. However, (A) fails to provide the specific difference between the two percentages; a small percentage would not be statistically significant, especially if the number of subjects participating in the experiment was small. Thus, (A) is qualitatively not as strong as (C).

Choice (B) actually *weakens* the argument, by providing evidence that the results as reported by the subjects themselves might have been unreliable.

Choice (D) fails to provide sufficient information to support the argument. Specifically, (D) fails to distinguish between the subjects receiving Nico-Gone and those receiving the placebo. (D) also fails to account for the possibility that the number of subjects who smoked might have changed significantly during the year immediately preceding the experiment.

Choice (E) actually *weakens* the argument by providing evidence that some factor other than Nico-Gone might have been responsible for the reported results.

Tips for Tackling Supporting-Evidence Questions

1. As you read the passage, try to identify a *necessary* assumption. There are two general types of assumptions that are especially common in supporting-evidence questions:

   - The assumption that *all other factors are equal*—if the argument seeks to explain certain differences between two phenomena

   - The assumption that *all other relevant conditions remain unchanged over time*—if the argument seeks to explain or predict some sort of change from one point in time (or period of time) to another

2. Scan the answer choices for a proposition that provides that assumption. If you spot it, immediately select it (click on the button to the left of it) as your tentative choice.

3. In all likelihood, more than one answer choice will serve to strengthen the argument. Always select a choice that directly affirms a necessary assumption over any other choice.

4. If no answer choice affirms a necessary assumption, you'll need to weigh the comparative quality of all answer choices that serve to strengthen the argument.

5. Look out for the following types of wrong answers:

    - A statement that weakens rather than strengthens the argument
    - A statement that could either strengthen or weaken the argument, depending on additional unknown facts
    - A statement that contains superfluous information, which is not directly relevant to the argument

Inference Questions

For a GMAT inference question, the passage will simply provide a series of premises—information that you are to accept as factual. Your task is to identify among the five answer choices the statement that provides the most reliable, or probable, conclusion from the passage information. Expect to encounter at least one or two questions of this type on the GMAT.

You know you're dealing with an inference question when the question stem looks similar to one of the following:

"Which of the following statements draws the most reliable conclusion from the information above?"

"Which of the following conclusions about . . . is best supported by the passage?"

"Which of the following can most properly be inferred from the information in the passage above?"

Notice that each of these question stems contains the word "most" or "best." These are important words. For an inference question, even the best answer choice will *not necessarily* follow from the premises; yet it will be *more probable* than any other answer choice.

Chapter 9: Critical Reasoning

> **X-Ref**
>
> Arguments in which conclusions are necessarily either true or false involve *deductive* reasoning. GMAT necessary-inference questions are distinct, which you'll discover if you advance to the Next Level.

How to Identify a Strong Inference

How do you recognize a probable, or reliable, inference among five answer choices and distinguish it from less reliable ones? The best way to answer this question is by example. Consider the following two GMAT-style passages. After reading each one, ask yourself: "Given this information, what else is probably true?" Try to think of at least one answer—then jot it down as if you were drafting your own best answer choice for a GMAT inference question. (Expect an easier time with passage 1 than 2.)

Passage 1
Many sociologists argue that science-fiction television programs play a crucial role in fostering the belief that intelligent aliens have visited Earth. However, in countries where relatively few people have access to television, belief that intelligent aliens have visited Earth is at least as prevalent as in other countries.

Passage 2
To subsidize the profits of domestic farms that grow a certain crop, country X imposes a tariff on exports of the crop. As a result, foreign food-product manufacturers that must use the crop in their products find it more difficult to compete with country X businesses that must use the same crop in their products.

Next, for each passage read the following conclusions (inferences). Think about each one until you understand that the one listed as a possible best answer choice *makes sense*; in other words, that it is *reasonably inferable* from the passage and *probable to some degree*. Then compare it to the ones listed as typical wrong-answer choices. Notice that each of these unreliable inferences depends on additional, unsubstantiated assumptions, and is therefore far less probable.

Conclusions (inferences) from Passage 1
Reliable inference (potential "best" answer choice):

> Science-fiction television programs are not the only factor in determining whether a person believes intelligent aliens have visited Earth.

Unreliable inferences (typical wrong-answer choices):
- Science-fiction television programs do not affect whether people believe that intelligent aliens have visited Earth.
- People who do not watch television are more likely to believe that intelligent aliens have visited Earth than people who do.
- Science-fiction television programming is not realistic enough to persuade people that intelligent aliens have visited Earth.

Conclusions (inferences) from Passage 2
Reliable inference (potential "best" answer choice):

> Importing the crop from country X is less costly for foreign businesses than if these businesses obtain the crop from another source.

Unreliable inferences (typical wrong-answer choices):
- The farms of country X are the only sources of the crop.
- Other countries that produce the crop also impose export tariffs on the crop.
- The total demand for the crop produced in country X declined as a result of the export tariff.

Compare the reliable inferences to the unreliable ones listed above. Notice that the unreliable ones either depend on additional assumptions that find no support in the passage and/or go too far—beyond the reliable inference to one that amounts to a sweeping, all-encompassing conclusion.

A Typical Inference Question

Now that you know how to identify and distinguish between reliable and unreliable inferences, attempt the following GMAT-style inference question, which is average in difficulty. As you tackle the question, follow these steps:

1. Try to answer the question "What else is probably true" after reading the passage, but before reading the answer choices. If you think of an answer, jot it down.

2. Scan the answer choices for your answer, or one similar to it.

3. If there's no answer choice similar to the one you thought of, analyze each one in turn to determine how strongly the passage supports it.
4. For each statement you eliminated, be sure you can think of an additional assumption needed for the statement to make sense as a conclusion.

Then, read the analysis of the question and of each answer choice.

During each of the last five years, both the demand for beverage containers and the quantity of beverage containers recycled to produce new beverage containers have increased steadily. At the same time, the number of freshly cut trees used to produce beverage containers has declined each year.

If the statements above are all true, they provide most support for which of the following conclusions about the last five years?

A. The number of new beverage containers not made of recycled materials has decreased.
B. More beverage containers have been recycled for producing new beverage containers than have not been recycled for this purpose.
C. Recycled beverage containers have been used only for making new beverage containers.
D. The number of beverage containers made of tree materials has decreased.
E. The number of used beverage containers not being recycled has decreased.

The correct answer is A. The fact that the number of recycled beverage cotainers has been increasing while the number of new trees used to make beverage containers has been declining lends considerable support to (A). Moreover, (A) allows for the possibilty that some beverage containers are made of recycled materials other than tree materials. Admittedly, demand for beverage containers in general has increased recently, reducing the likelihood that (A) is true. On balance, however, (A) is more strongly supported than any of the other answer choices.

Choice (B) is not inferable from the statements, which provide information about *changes* in numbers from one year to the next, not *total* numbers. The passage provides no information which would permit a comparison between the total numbers of recycled beverage containers and non-recycled beverage containers.

Choice (C) is not inferable. The passage provides no information permitting the sweeping inference that the increasing demand for beverage containers has been so great as to necessitate the use of *all* recycled beverage containers to meet this increased demand.

Choice (D) is not inferable. Although the decrease in the number of freshly cut trees each year tends to show that (D) might be true, the increase in demand for beverage containers and in the number of recycled beverage containers tend to show just the opposite. In any event, (D) also requires more information (additional assumptions) about the *percentage* of beverage containers, both new and recycled, made of tree products.

Choice (E) is not inferable. Just because the number of beverage containers being recycled has increased each year, it is unfair to conclude that the number of beverage containers *not* being recycled has been decreasing. In fact, given the increased demand for beverage containers in general, it is just as likely that consumers are recycling more beverage containers *and* discarding more beverage containers.

Tips for Tackling Inference Questions

1. All statements in the passage are premises; thus, you should assume they are all factual (even if in real life they seem somewhat dubious).

2. Remember: Your task is not to recognize what *must* be true, but rather to recognize what's *most likely* to be true among the five conclusions listed.

3. Formulating a possible "best" answer might help you zero in on the best answer choice. But don't expect this technique to work as reliably for inference questions as for the other question types covered in this chapter.

4. If an answer choice makes sense as a conclusion only if additional facts are assumed, you can safely eliminate it.

5. If an answer choice draws a sweeping conclusion—an all-encompassing generalization—you can probably eliminate it as the best answer choice. When in doubt, choose a narrower conclusion over a broader one.

Chapter 9: Critical Reasoning

Success Keys for GMAT Critical Reasoning

Here are some basic tips you should follow for any type of Critical Reasoning question—the types you encountered so far in this chapter, as well as those you'll examine if you advance to the Next level. Apply these "keys" to Part V's practice tests, and then review them again just before exam day.

Always Read the Question Stem First

The question "stem" refers to the question (or prompt) itself, NOT to the passage or the answer choices. Read the stem *before* reading the passage. It will contain useful clues about what to look for and think about as you read the passage. (Reading answer choices before reading the passage is wasted time, because you'll invariably need to read them again.)

Assume That All Premises Are Factual

As you read the passage, assume that all premises—statements asserted as factual—are indeed factual. Critical Reasoning questions are not designed to test your real-world knowledge of passage topics. Although the premises often resemble real-world facts, whether they are factual is beside the point.

Identify the Conclusion to Clear Up Your Confusion

Most passages will contain a conclusion. The conclusion might appear at the beginning, in the middle, or at the end of the passage. If a passage confuses you, look for the conclusion, then try to follow the argument's line of reasoning *from* premises *to* conclusion.

Read Every Answer Choice before Confirming Your Selection

Remember: the test directions ask you to select the *best* among the five choices, and the qualitative difference between the best and second-best choices can be subtle. Unless you carefully consider all five answer choices, you might select the second-best one without even reading the best one.

Critical Reasoning Takes Time; So Pace Yourself Accordingly

For most test-takers, Critical Reasoning questions require more thought than Sentence Correction and Reading Comprehension questions (the other types of Verbal Ability questions). Moreover, for all but the easiest Critical Reasoning questions, you'll probably need to read the passage *and* answer choices twice before deciding on an answer. So, plan to devote a bit more time to Critical Reasoning questions (at least two minutes per question, on average) than to other Verbal Ability questions.

Don't Second Guess Your Instincts

When in doubt, go with your initial hunch about whether an answer choice is viable or not. It's remarkably easy to over-analyze any Critical Reasoning question to the point that you second-guess your own judgment. Although you should carefully consider all five answer choices, don't disregard your instincts.

Take It to the Next Level

Welcome to the Next Level GMAT Critical Reasoning. At this point, you'll:

- Learn how to recognize and handle four additional, and more unusual, types of Critical Reasoning questions
- Learn general strategies for tackling these question types

What's New at the Next Level

Here in this Next Level chapter, you'll look at four additional question types, each of which involves a quirkier, more specific form of reasoning or argument evaluation. Expect at least three of these types on your exam; but don't expect more than one question of any type.

- *Hypothesis* questions. For these questions, your task is to recognize a hypothesis that provides a reasonable explanation for a set of observations.

- *Strategy* questions. For these questions, your task is to recognize an effective course of action based on a set of premises and a stated objective.

- *Necessary-inference* questions. For these questions, your task is to distinguish, based on a set of premises, valid deductions from invalid ones, or to recognize an additional premise needed to validate a stated conclusion.

- *Parallel-argument* questions. For these questions, your task is to recognize similarities in reasoning (that might be flawed) between different arguments.

Strategy Questions

In a GMAT strategy question, the passage sets up a scenario where a decision-maker must develop a plan, or *strategy*, for solving a "real-life" problem such as:

- An undesirable economic or sociological trend
- A decline in a certain business's revenue or profitability
- An increasingly serious public-health threat
- Declining performance levels among workers or students

Typically, the problem at hand is an undesirable trend or development that the decision-maker hopes to either halt or reverse. The question stem will indicate the decision-maker's objective. Your task is to identify, among the five answer choices, the strategy or course of action that would be most *effective*, *efficient*, or *appropriate* in achieving the stated objective. Expect to encounter no more than one question of this type on the GMAT.

You know you're dealing with a strategy question when the question stem looks similar to one of the following:

"Which of the following strategies would be most likely to reverse the decline in . . . ?"

"To prevent the continued loss of . . . , it would be best for [decision-maker] to"

"Among the following proposals, which one, if implemented, is likely to be most effective in discouraging . . . ?"

Notice that each of these question stems contains the word "most" or "best." These are important words. For a strategy question, even the best answer choice will *not necessarily* achieve the decision-maker's objective; yet, it will be *more likely* to achieve that objective than any other answer choice.

How to Identify the Best Strategy

How do you recognize the "best" strategy among five choices and distinguish it from less effective, efficient, or appropriate ones? To answer this question for yourself, consider the following GMAT-style passage:

At Xenon Company, overall worker productivity, which depends primarily on the amount of time workers spend at their workstations, has been declining recently. Meanwhile, instead of either bringing lunch from home or eating lunch in the company's cafeteria, an increasing number of Xenon workers have been dining out for lunch, which usually takes more time than eating lunch at the Xenon premises.

Given the passage information, ask yourself: *How would I reverse the decline in worker productivity at Xenon?* Well, based on the passage, you know that eating out tends to reduce productivity because it takes more time away from actual work than does eating on the premises. So, to increase productivity, it would make sense to implement a plan that encourages workers to stay on the premises for lunch or, conversely, that discourages them from going out for lunch. Notice that the general strategy here is to encourage workers not just to eat in the cafeteria, and not just to bring lunch from home, but, more generally, to remain on Xenon premises for lunch. This is an important distinction, as you're about to see!

Alert! When analyzing a GMAT strategy passage, try to think in terms of general strategy rather than specific actions. Why? In all likelihood, any one of a limitless number of specific actions might help in achieving the stated goal; so the chances of your conjuring up the one listed as the best answer choice are rather slim.

Now read the following list of possible actions (i.e., answer choices). Think about each one until you understand why the one listed as the best course of action is more likely to discourage Xenon workers from leaving Xenon's premises for lunch than any of the others.

Alternative Courses of Action

Effective action (potential "best" answer choice):

Impose stricter limits on the amount of time Xenon's workers are allowed for lunch breaks.

Actions that would have no clear, direct effect (typical wrong-answer choices):

- Allow Xenon workers greater flexibility in determining when they start and end their workdays.

- Establish free after-work nutrition and cooking classes for Xenon workers.

Actions that could either help or harm, depending on other facts (typical wrong-answer choices):

- Replace the vendor that currently provides Xenon's cafeteria food service with a different one.

- Begin charging workers a fee for parking in Xenon's employee parking lot.

Actions that would help but are too narrow (typical wrong-answer choices):

- Provide a greater variety of menu choices at the company cafeteria.
- Install a kitchenette on the premises for workers to prepare their own lunches.

Notice the three categories of typical wrong-answer choices. Actions that are unlikely to have any direct impact on worker productivity are the easiest to recognize as incorrect answers. Actions that might be effective, depending on other circumstances, are a bit tougher to recognize as incorrect. Finally, actions that clearly help to achieve the objective, but not to as great an extent as the best choice, are the ones that lure most test-takers away from the correct choice.

A Typical Strategy Question

Now that you know how to identify and distinguish between effective and less effective strategies, attempt the following GMAT-style strategy question, which is more difficult than average due to the kinds of wrong-answer choices that follow it. In tackling the question, follow these steps:

1. Before reading the answer choices, try to answer the question, "What general strategy would help achieve the objective?" If you think of a strategy, jot it down.

2. Scan the answer choices for a specific course of action that would implement that strategy effectively.

3. For each other answer choice, ask yourself why it's less effective than the one you selected. (Keep in mind the wrong-answer categories you just learned about.)

Chapter 9: Critical Reasoning

Then, read the analysis of the question and of each answer choice.

> Company Q, a manufacturer of consumer products, offers a manufacturer's rebate through retailers that sell its products. Retailers offer their own rebate as well on company Q products, and company Q reimburses the retailer for a portion of each such rebate. Both company Q and its retailers are currently losing money on overall sales of company Q products as a result of the rebate scheme.
>
> Which of the following plans, if implemented, is most likely to be effective in reversing the losses that company Q and its retailers are currently experiencing from overall sales of company Q products?
>
> A. Restrict both types of rebates to purchases of products priced only below a certain amount.
> B. Restrict both types of rebates to purchases of certain higher-priced products only.
> C. Develop a new advertising campaign designed to boost retail sales of company Q's newest products.
> D. Reduce the amount of the rebate that retailers offer on purchases of company Q products.
> E. Discontinue reimbursement to retailers for any portion of rebates on company Q products that retailers pay to consumers.

The correct answer is D. Notice that the objective is twofold: (1) decrease company X's losses *and* (2) decrease the retailers' losses. The most effective strategy would help achieve not just one but *both* objectives. The manufacturer and retailer currently share the cost of rebates that the retailer pays to consumers. Both can reduce their overall costs, thereby reducing losses, by lowering the amount of the retail rebate—as (D) provides—and continuing to share the rebate costs. Hence, the course of action that (D) suggests is likely to be effective in achieving both stated objectives.

Choice (A) suggests a plan that wouldn't necessarily reduce losses for either company Q or its retailers. In fact, the plan is just as likely to increase those losses. How? If company Q and its retailers discontinue rebate offers on certain items, then sales of those items are more likely to decline. Since the passage states that it is the rebate items that are responsible for current losses, sales of non-rebate items are less likely to generate losses, and might even generate profits. A decline in sales of profitable items would only add to the overall losses for company X and its retailers.

Choice (B) is incorrect for essentially the same reason as (A). Restricting the rebate to purchases of only certain items might actually *increase* losses, especially if consumers buy fewer profit-generating (non-rebate) items as a result of the new rebate restrictions.

Choice (C) suggests a plan that is just as likely, if not more likely, to *increase* losses as decrease them. Why? First, the ad campaign will no doubt add to costs. Second, if the ads are effective, there's no reason to believe that consumers enticed by the ads would not take advantage of the rebate offers; the more money paid as rebates, the greater the losses for company Q and its retailers.

Choice (E) suggests a plan that would obviously help reduce company Q's losses, since it would no longer need to reimburse its retailers. By the same token, however, the plan would *increase* losses for retailers, who would now pay the entire rebate. Since the stated objective is to reduce losses not just for company Q but also for its retailers, plan (E) is too narrow to be the "best" plan.

> **Tip**
>
> In handling basic inference questions like the ones you encountered earlier in the chapter, we suggested that, when in doubt, you should choose a narrow conclusion over a broader one. This advice also applies to strategy questions—but with a twist. For instance, in answering the previous question, (E) suggests a course of action whose effect would be too narrow, which is exactly why (E) is not the best answer!

Tips for Tackling Strategy Questions

1. All statements in the passage are premises; so you should assume they are all factual. Also, accept the scenario at face value, even though it oversimplifies real life.

2. Before you read the answer choices, try to formulate an effective *general* strategy rather than a *specific* course of action. (Otherwise, you might be frustrated by not finding your proposal listed as an answer choice.) Then scan the answer choices for a course of action that carries out the strategy.

3. Remember: Your job is to determine which plan is *most likely* to achieve the objective, not which one *will* do so. You won't find any bullet-proof plan—one that would work no matter what happens—among the answer choices. So don't waste time looking for one. Improve your odds of picking the best answer choice by at least eliminating the most unlikely ones. Look for choices that "get it backwards" (that suggest plans that are sure to hurt the cause) or that strike you as nonsense (that aren't directly relevant to the objective).

4. Watch out for proposals that could either help of hinder, depending on other circumstances. If there's a possible "fip side" to a proposed course of action, eliminate it.

Hypothesis Questions

In a GMAT hypothesis question, the passage provides two pieces of evidence (factual information) that seem inconsistent or in conflict with each other (paradoxical). The passage might involve a "real-world" scenario like one of these:

- An apparent discrepancy between results of different experiments or statistical studies
- Two seemingly contrary economic, business, or sociological trends
- Conflicting conclusions drawn by two different individuals based on the same set of facts
- A surprising difference between two things that are ostensibly similar in other ways

Your task is to recognize a logical explanation (hypothesis) for the apparent discrepancy, conflict, or difference. You know you're dealing with a hypothesis question when the question stem looks similar to one of the following:

"Which of the following best explains the apparent discrepancy between the . . . ?"

"Which of the following, if true, would provide the best explanation for the seemingly contradictory results of the two studies described above?"

"Each of the following, if true, could help account for the simultaneous increase in . . . and . . . EXCEPT:"

> **Note**
>
> Although the test-makers use the term hypothesis in describing this question type, you're unlikely to see this actual term in a question stem. Instead, look for a word such as "explanation."

How to Recognize an Effective Hypothesis

In tackling this question type, the best way to recognize an effective hypothesis is to first formulate a broader explanation for the apparent discrepancy or conflict. Let's do just that, by analyzing three brief passages.

Passage 1
While on Diet X, most dieters reduce their daily calorie intake from previous levels. However, people who try Diet X generally gain rather than lose weight over the course of the diet.

What might explain the apparent discrepancy between reduced caloric intake and weight gain? One good general explanation is that calorie intake is only one of many factors that determine a person's body weight. (One or two such factors might come to your mind.)

Passage 2
A study comparing the benefits of different popular diets observed that dieters tend to lose more weight while in Diet Y than while on Diet X. However, Diet X calls for a lower daily-calorie intake than Diet Y.

What might explain the surprising comparative results of the two diets? One general explanation is that Diet X and Diet Y might differ in certain other respects—one of which might account for the counter-intuitive results. (One or two such respects might come to your mind.)

Passage 3
One independent study on the benefits of dieting observed that people on Diet X lost more weight, on average, than people on Diet Y. However, another such study observed just the opposite—that people on Diet X tended to lose less weight than people on Diet Y.

What might explain the apparent conflict between the results of the two studies? One general explanation is that studies often vary in methodology, and that different methodologies can yield different results. (One or two possible differences in methodology might come to your mind.)

Now examine different hypotheses involving each passage. Notice that each hypothesis provides a specific scenario rather than a general explanation, and that the effective hypotheses support the general explanations we just formulated. Also notice that each poor hypothesis falls into one of these categories (try to determine which category each one belongs to):

- It relies heavily on certain assumed facts.
- It helps explain only one aspect of the discrepancy or conflict.
- It's not directly relevant to the discrepancy or conflict.
- It actually makes the discrepancy or conflict *more* inexplicable.

Hypotheses Based on Passage 1

Effective hypothesis (possible "best" answer choice):
  Diet X makes a person too tired to engage in the kinds of exercise that help a person lose weight.

Poor hypotheses (typical wrong-answer choices):
  - Most people who try Diet X find it to be bland and lacking in variety.
  - Most people who try Diet X have already tried other diets but failed to lose weight as a result of those diets.

Hypotheses Based on Passage 2

Effective hypothesis (possible "best" answer choice):
  Dieters find Diet X more restrictive than Diet Y and therefore more difficult to stay on.

Poor hypotheses (typical wrong-answer choices):
  - Other diets are far more effective than either Diet X or Diet Y.
  - More people on Diet Y than on Diet X are first-time dieters.
  - Diet X is more effective than Diet Y in satisfying a dieter's appetite.

Hypotheses Based on Passage 3

Effective hypothesis (possible "best" answer choice):
  One of the studies observed only first-time dieters, while the other study observed only dieters who had previously lost weight on other diets.

Poor hypotheses (typical wrong-answer choices):
  - Among dieters as a group, Diet X is currently more popular than Diet Y.

- Neither study continued to observe the dieters' weight after discontinuing the diet.
- Although lower in calories than Diet Y, Diet X is more effective in satisfying a dieter's appetite.

> **Alert!**
> In a typical hypothesis passage, the number of scenarios that would help explain the facts is virtually limitless. So if you happen to conjure up a few good scenarios, keep an open mind. The answer choices may or may not list one of them. That's why we suggest that, when you try to explain the facts for yourself, think in general terms.

A Typical Hypothesis Question

In each of the three passages you just analyzed, the discrepancy or conflict was relatively easy to identify and explain. Now that you've seen some easier passages, try tackling a more difficult GMAT-style hypothesis question. (What makes this question tricky is that it actually involves *two* paradoxes.) As you grapple with it, follow these steps:

1. Before reading the answer choices, try to formulate a general explanation for both paradoxes. Jot down your idea.

2. Scan the answer choices for a scenario that supports your explanation.

3. For each other answer choice, ask yourself why it fails to adequately explain the paradox. (Keep in mind the wrong-answer categories you just learned about.)

Then, read the analysis of the question and of each answer choice.

> Kiki birds breed more effectively in some temperatures than in others. During the period from 1991 to 1995, the kiki bird population in a certain region increased, despite a moratorium, or official ban, on the hunting of the kiki bird's chief predator. During the period from 1996 to 2000, the kiki bird population in the same region declined, despite ideal breeding temperatures during that period.
>
> Which of the following, if true, best explains why the kiki bird population increased during the period from 1991 to 1995, then declined during the period from 1996 to 2000?
>
> - A. During the period from 1991 to 1995, temperatures in the region were ideally suited for kiki bird breeding.
> - B. The moratorium on the hunting of the kiki bird's chief predator was rigorously enforced only after 1995.
> - C. Ideal breeding temperatures for the kiki bird's chief predator differ from those for the kiki bird.
> - D. The kiki bird is only one of many animal species that is potential prey for the bird's chief predator.
> - E. During the period from 1996 to 2000, the population of the kiki bird's chief predator increased throughout the region.

The correct answer is B. The passage presents a double-paradox: How could the bird's population increase in the face of an ostensible threat to its survival, then decrease when breeding conditions were ideal? A comprehensive explanation would need to account for both the increase and subsequent decrease in population. One explanation is that some other condition likely to have an impact on the kiki bird population changed from one time period to the other. (B) provides such a condition—a specific scenerio that supports this explanation. Without enforcement of the moratorium, a greater number of the kiki bird's predators might be killed, which would tend to stabilize and perhaps even result in an increase in the kiki bird population. Conversely, enforcing the moratorium would tend to increase the predator's population, thereby possibly decreasing the bird's population.

Choice (A) explains why the kiki bird population increased from 1991 to 1995, but not why the kiki bird population declined from 1996 and 2000.

Choice (C) actually makes the paradox more inexplicable by providing an additional reason why the kiki bird population should have *increased* during the period from 1996 to 2000.

Choice(D) is completely irrelevant to the paradox—it serves neither to explain nor reinforce it.

Choice (E) explains why the kiki bird population decreased from 1996 to 2000, but not why the kiki bird population decreased from 1991 to 1995.

Tips for Tackling Hypothesis Questions

1. All statements in the passage are premises; so you should assume they are all factual.

2. Before you read the answer choices, try to formulate a *general* explanation for the discrepancy or conflict, rather than a *specific* scenario. (Otherwise, you might be frustrated by not finding your scenario listed as an answer choice.) Then scan the answer choices for a scenario that supports your explanation.

3. Remember: Your job is to zero in on an answer choice that *helps* explain the facts—that provides *one possible* explanation. No one hypothesis is going to cover all the bases; so don't waste time looking for it.

Watch out for the following types of wrong-answer choices:

- The incomplete or partial explanation (you're looking for a choice that helps explain all the facts)

- The choice that "gets it backward"—that makes the discrepancy or paradox even more inexplicable

- The choice that assumes too much—that helps explain only if certain additional facts are assumed

- The irrelevant scenario (it's on the topic, but doesn't relate to the discrepancy or conflict)

Necessary-Inference Questions

In this type of GMAT question, an argument's conclusion will be *necessarily* inferable (or not inferable) from its premises—in other words, necessarily true (or false). Expect to encounter at least one necessary-inference question on the GMAT.

GMAT necessary-inference questions come in two varieties. In one type, the passage provides a series of premises, and your task is to determine which of the five answer choices must be true (or false) based on the premises. You know you're dealing with this type when the question stem looks similar to one of the following:

Chapter 9: Critical Reasoning

"If the statements above are true, which of the following statements can logically be derived from them?"

"Which of the following must be true on the basis of the statements above?"

"Which of the following can be correctly inferred from the statements above?"

"If the statements above are true, any of the following statements might also be true EXCEPT:"

In the second type of necessary-inference question, the passage provides one or more premises along with a conclusion, and your task is to determine what additional premise is required for the conclusion to be necessarily inferable (true). You know you're dealing with this type when the question stem looks similar to one of the following:

"The passage's conclusion is true only if which of the following statements is also true?"

"The conclusion of the argument above cannot be true unless which of the following is true?"

"Any of the following, if introduced into the argument as an additional premise, makes the argument above logically correct EXCEPT:"

Notice the absence of words such as *best*, *most*, and *least* in both groups of questions above. That's because, for this type of question, evaluating the argument does not involve a conclusion's probability but rather its certainty—whether it is true or false, valid or invalid, correct or incorrect, inferable or not inferable—based on the premises. So the mode of reasoning for necessary-inference questions is entirely different than for the question types we've covered up to this point. If you're ready to shift to this other mode, read on.

> **Note**
>
> Necessary-inference questions involve deductive reasoning, which is actually a specific kind of inference. You'll see this term used often in the following pages. A logician might define deduction as the process of drawing specific inferences from general laws or propositions. Since the definition is a bit technical, the test-makers avoid using any form of the term in Critical Reasoning questions.

Forms and Fallacies of Deductive Reasoning

To master GMAT necessary-inference questions, you need to recognize certain basic argument forms and fallacies. (A "fallacy" is simply an argument by deduction whose conclusion is incorrect—or whose *inference is invalid*.) The following series of forms are the ones you're most likely to encounter on the GMAT. The best way to identify a form is to first use symbols in premises and conclusions, then analyze an example that matches the form.

Based on the following premise, there is only one valid inference. Notice that the valid inference switches A with B, and negates both.

Argument 1

Premise: If A, then B.

Valid inference: If not B, then not A.

Invalid inference: If B, then A.

Invalid inference: If not A, then not B.

Example (Argument 1)

Premise: If I strike the window with a hammer, the window will break.

Valid inference: If the window is not broken, then I have not struck it with a hammer.

Invalid inference: If the window is broken, I have struck it with a hammer.

Invalid inference: If I do not strike the window with a hammer, the window will not break.

(*Both invalid inferences overlook that the window might be broken for any number of reasons besides my having struck it with a hammer.*)

The following argument form and accompanying fallacies are logically identical to the ones above.

Argument 2

Premise: All A are B.

Valid inference: All non-B's are non-A's. (No non-B is an A.)

Invalid inference: All B are A.

Invalid inference: No non-A's are B's.

Example (Argument 2)

Premise: All red gremlins are spotted.

Valid inference: No gremlin that is not spotted is red.

Invalid inference: All spotted gremlins are red.

Invalid inference: No gremlins that are not red are spotted.

(Both invalid inferences overlook that a spotted gremlin might be a color other than red.)

This next form involves two premises and a third symbol, (C), allowing inferences (and inviting fallacies) in addition to the ones covered in arguments 1 and 2 above.

Argument 3

Premise: If A, then B.

Premise: If B, then C.

Valid inference: If A, then C.

Valid inference: If not C, then not A.

Invalid inference: If not A, then not C.

Invalid inference: If C, then A.

Example (Argument 3)

Premise: If I strike the window with a hammer, the window will break.

Premise: If the window is broken, the cold outside air will blow into the house.

Valid inference: If I strike the window with a hammer, then the cold outside air will blow into the house.

Valid inference: If the cold outside air has not blown into the house, then I have not struck the window with a hammer.

Invalid inference: If I do not strike the window with a hammer, the window will not break.

Invalid inference: If cold outside air has blown into the house, I have struck the window with a hammer.

The following argument is logically identical to argument 3 above.

Argument 4

Premise: All A are B.

Premise: All B are C.

Valid inference: All A are C.

Valid inference: No non-C is an A.

Invalid inference: No non-A is a C.

Invalid inference: All C are A.

Example (Argument 4)

Premise: All red gremlins are spotted.

Premise: All spotted gremlins are female.

(*Assumption:* A gremlin must be either male or female, but not both.)

Valid inference: All red gremlins are female.

Valid inference: No male gremlin is red.

Invalid inference: No gremlin that is not red is female.

Invalid inference: All female gremlins are red.

In arguments 1–4, each statement is essentially an all-or-none assertion (signaled by words such as "all" and "no"). In this next series of arguments, the word "some" is introduced into a premise. For each form, try conjuring up your own example (perhaps involving red, spotted, and female gremlins).

Argument 5

Premise: Some A are B.

Valid inference: Some B are A.

Invalid inference: Some A are not B.

Invalid inference: Some B are not A.

(In formal logic the word "some" means at least one and possibly as many as all; thus the premise allows for the possibility that all A are B, and that all B are A.)

Argument 6

Premise: Some A are B.

Premise: Some B are C.

Valid inference: Some B are A.

Valid inference: Some C are B.

Invalid inference: Some A are C.

Invalid inference: Some C are A.

(If a B is an A, it is not necessarily a C as well; in other words, the set of B's that are also A's does not necessarily overlap the set B's that are also C's.)

Argument 7

Premise: Some A are B.

Premise: All B are C.

Valid inference: Some B are A.

Valid inference: Some A are C.

Valid inference: Some C are A.

Invalid inference: All C are B.

Invalid inference: All C are A.

The following two arguments involve "either-or" forms:

Argument 8

Premise: Either A or B, but not both.

Valid inference: If A, then not B.

Valid inference: If B, then not A.

Valid inference: If not B, then A.

Valid inference: If not A, then B.

Argument 9

Premise: Either A or B, but not both.

Premise: Either B or C, but not both.

Valid inference: If B, then not C (and not A).

Valid inference: If A, then C (but not B).

Valid inference: If C, then A (but not B).

Part IV: Verbal Ability

A Typical Necessary-Inference Question

Now that you know how to recognize various forms of deductive reasoning and distinguish between valid and invalid inferences, attempt the following GMAT-style question, which is a bit more difficult than average for this question type. As you tackle the question, follow these steps:

1. Try to reduce the passage to simple statements using symbols (letters). Jot down the premise and conclusion using those symbols.

2. Before reading the answer choices, try to determine the missing premise for yourself.

3. Scan the answer choices for your answer.

4. For each answer choice you eliminated, try to determine what valid conclusion (if any) would be inferable by adding the premise provided in the answer choice.

Then, read the analysis of the question and of each answer choice.

> **X-Ref**
>
> Notice that this question provides the conclusion, then asks about the necessary premise that's missing; it's an example of one of the two basic types of necessary-inference questions.

In the country of Xania, periods of political instability are always accompanied by a volatile Xania stock market and by volatility of Xania's currency compared to currencies of other countries. At the present time, Xania's currency is experiencing volatility. Hence, the Xania stock market must also be experiencing volatility.

Which of the following allows the conclusion above to be properly drawn?

A. Whenever Xania is politically stable, the Xania currency is stable as well.
B. Whenever the Xania currency is stable, Xania is politically stable as well.
C. Whenever the Xania stock market is unstable, Xania is politically unstable as well.
D. Whenever the Xania stock market is unstable, the Xania currency is unstable as well.
E. Whenever the Xania stock market is stable, the Xania currency is stable as well.

The correct answer is A. The argument boils down to the following:

Premise 1: If there is political instability, then the stock market is volatile (unstable).

Premise 2: If there is political instability, then the currency is volatile (unstable).

Premise 3: The currency is volatile (unstable).

Conclusion: The stock market is volatile (unstable).

To reveal the argument's structure, let's reduce it to symbols:

Premise 1: If A, then B.

Premise 2: If A, then C.

Premise 3: C.

Conclusion: B.

The conclusion above requires the following additional premise:

Premise 4: If the currency is volatile (unstable), then there is political instability.

Premise 4: If C, then A.

Only answer choice (A) provides this essential premise. Note that premise number 4 above is essentially the same proposition as answer choice (A). In other words, the following two propositions are logically identical:

Premise 4: If C, then A.

Answer choice (A): If not A, then not C.

Choice (B) merely reiterates premise number 2. In other words, the following two statements are essentially the same:

If X, then Y.

If not Y, then not X.

Choice (C) commits the following fallacy:

Premise: If X, then Y.

Conclusion: If Y, then X.

Choice (D) would lead to the conclusion that if the stock market is volatile (unstable), then the currency is volatile (unstable). In other words, (D) commits the same fallacy as (C):

Premise: If X, then Y.

Conclusion: If Y, then X.

Choice (E) merely reiterates the argument's conclusion. In other words, the following two statements are essentially the same:

If X, then Y.

If not Y, then not X.

Tips for Tackling Necessary-Inference Questions

1. If the question asks for a missing premise, identify the premise(s) and conclusion in the passage.

2. If you're having trouble following the logic, reduce each part of the passage to simple statements using letters as symbols. Write down the form of the argument on paper.

3. Pre-phrase the answer to the question by determining the additional premise needed for the conclusion to be valid (or the conclusion that necessarily follows from the stated premises).

4. Express your answer using symbols.

5. If you're having trouble making sense of a particular statement in the passage, try to rephrase it so its logical meaning is clearer. Eliminating double-negatives can be particularly helpful.

   Confusing: Only gremlins that are spotted are red.

   Clear: All red gremlins are spotted.

   Confusing: If a gremlin is not spotted, then it cannot be red.

   Confusing: A gremlin is spotted only if it is red.

   Clear: If a gremlin is red, then it must be spotted.

6. Look out for the following types of wrong answers:

   - A statement that results in one of the logical fallacies identified in this chapter.

   - A statement that merely reiterates a stated premise (or stated conclusion), expressing it in a slightly different way.

Parallel-Argument Questions

In this type of question, the passage and the five answer choices each provide an argument (one or more premises and a conclusion). Your task is to determine which of the five choices provides the argument most similar *in its pattern of reasoning* to the pattern in the passage. Don't expect to encounter more than one question of this type on the GMAT.

Chapter 9: Critical Reasoning

You know you're dealing with a parallel-argument question when the question stem looks similar to one of the following (notice that the first two are essentially the same, but the third one suggests a slightly different task):

"Which of the following is most like the argument above in its logical structure?"

"Which of the following illustrates a pattern of reasoning most similar to the pattern of reasoning in the argument above?"

"The flawed reasoning in the argument above is most similar to the reasoning in which of the following arguments?"

> **Tip**
> Parallel-argument questions almost always involve deductive reasoning. To handle these questions, you apply the forms and fallacies you just learned to the unique parallel-argument format.

A Typical Parallel-Argument Question

Attempt the following GMAT-style parallel-argument question, which is average in difficulty. As you tackle the question, follow these steps:

1. Try to reduce the passage to simple statements using symbols (letters). Jot down the premise and conclusion using these symbols.
2. Perform the same task (step 1) for each answer choice.
3. Compare the pattern of reasoning in each answer choice to the pattern in the original passage.

Then, read the analysis of the question and of each answer choice.

Very few software engineers have left MicroFirm Corporation to seek employment elsewhere. Thus, unless CompTech Corporation increases the salaries of its software engineers to the same level as those of MicroFirm, these CompTech employees are likely to leave CompTech for another employer.

The flawed reasoning in the argument above is most similar to the reasoning in which of the following arguments?

A. Robert does not gamble, and he has never been penniless. Therefore, if Gina refrains from gambling she will also avoid being penniless.
B. If Dan throws a baseball directly at the window, the window pane will surely break. The window pane is not broken, so Dan has not thrown a baseball directly at it.
C. If a piano sits in a humid room the piano will need tuning within a week. This piano needs tuning. Therefore, it must have sat in a humid room for at least a week.
D. Diligent practice results in perfection. Hence, one must practice diligently in order to achieve perfection.
E. More expensive cars are stolen than inexpensive cars. Accordingly, owners of expensive cars should carry auto theft insurance, whereas owners of inexpensive cars should not.

The correct answer is D. The original argument's line of reasoning is essentially as follows:

Premise: The well-paid engineers at MicroFirm do not quit their jobs.

Conclusion: If CompTech engineers are not well-paid, they will quit their jobs.

To reveal the argument's logical structure, let's express it using letters as symbols:

Premise: All A's are B's.

Conclusion: If not A, then not B.

The reasoning is fallacious (flawed), because it fails to account for other possible reasons why MicroFirm engineers have not left their jobs. (Some B's might not be A's.)

Choice (D) is the only answer choice the demonstrates the same essential pattern of flawed reasoning. To recognize the similarity we can rephrase the argument's sentence structure to match the essence of the original argument:

Premise: All people who practice diligently (A) achieve perfection (B).

Conclusion: If one does not practice diligently (not A) one cannot achieve perfection (not B).

Choice (A) reasons essentially as follows: One certain A is B. Therefore, if A then B. This reasoning is flawed, but in a different respect than the reasoning in the original argument.

Choice (B) reasons essentially as follows: If A, then B. Not B. Therefore, not A. This reasoning is sound (not flawed).

Choice (C) reasons essentially as follows: If A, then B. Therefore, if B, then A. This reasoning is flawed, but in a different respect than the reasoning in the original argument.

Choice (E) does not involve deductive reasoning and can't easily be expressed in symbols. Without additional evidence, it's impossible to determine the strength of the argument.

Tips for Tackling Parallel-Argument Questions

1. Before reading the answer choices, reduce the original passage to its basic structure.

2. Express the argument in general terms—perhaps using letters as symbols—that incorporate the argument's logic but not its subject matter.

3. Don't equate logical structure with sequence. The passage might provide the conclusion first, while the best answer choice provides its conclusion last (or vice-versa). In other words, try to identify parallel *logic*—not parallel *sequence*.

4. Don't equate logical structure with subject matter. Be suspicious of any answer choice involving a topic that is similar to that of the passage. Although that answer choice *might* be the best one, more than likely it is not.

Chapter 10

Sentence Correction

Welcome to GMAT Sentence Correction. At this point, you'll:

- Learn a step-by-step approach to handling any Sentence Correction question
- Learn to recognize and fix basic grammatical errors and problems with sentence structure and verbosity
- Learn success keys for tackling GMAT Sentence Correction

Sentence Correction—Your 4-Step Game Plan

The first task in this chapter is to learn the four basic steps for handling a GMAT Sentence Correction question. You'll apply these steps to the following sample question:

<u>Despite sophisticated computer models for assessing risk, such a model is nevertheless</u> limited in their ability to define what risk is.

- A. Despite sophisticated computer models for assessing risk, such a model is nevertheless
- B. Sophisticated computer models, which assess risk, are nevertheless
- C. Despite their sophistication, computer models for assessing risk are
- D. Assessment of risk can be achieved with sophisticated computer models, but these models are
- E. Assessing risk with sophisticated computer models is limited because such models are

Chapter 10: Sentence Correction

Step 1: Read the original sentence carefully. As you do so, ask yourself:

- Does it sound odd or wrong to my ear?
- Do any errors in grammar jump out at me?
- Is the sentence confusing, and would I have to read it again to try and figure out what it means?

If your answer to any of these questions is "yes," you can confidently eliminate choice (A), the original underlined part, even if you're not sure why it's wrong.

Step 2: Plug your remaining choices, one at a time, into the original sentence, and read the entire *revised* sentence. As you do so, ask yourself the same three questions as in Step 1, and eliminate any choice for which your answer to any of those questions is "yes."

Step 3: If you still haven't narrowed the choices down to a clear winner, compare the remaining candidates. Resolve close judgment calls in favor of:

- A briefer, more concise version
- A version that more accurately conveys the intended meaning of the sentence
- A less awkward version

Step 4: Verify your selection before confirming your response. Check your selection one more time by plugging it into the sentence. If it sounds right, confirm your response, and move on.

Now let's walk through the sample question about computer models, using this 4-step approach.

Step 1: Upon a first reading, doesn't "such a model" sound a bit awkward? That's a good clue that (A) is not the correct response. In fact, the original sentence contains two flaws. One is a grammatical error: the plural pronoun *their* is used to refer to the singular noun *model*. Either both should be plural or both should be singular, but they must match! The word *their* in not part of the underlined phrase, so look for an answer choice that uses *models* instead of *model*. (In grammatical terminology, the original sentence contains an error in "pronoun-antecedent agreement.") The other flaw is one of ineffective expression: the first clause (before the comma) is structured differently than the second clause, and the result is an awkward and confusing sentence. So you should look for an answer choice that renders the sentence clearer and perhaps a bit more concise—one that helps the sentence sound a bit sweeter and "flow" more smoothly.

Part IV: Verbal Ability

Step 2: Substitute each answer choice in turn for the underlined part. Choice (B) does not contain any grammatical errors. But doesn't the phrase *which assess risk* appear to describe computer models in general rather than models for assessing risk? Surely, this isn't the intended meaning of the sentence. (B) is a perfect example of an answer choice that is wrong because it either distorts, confuses, or obscures the intended meaning of the sentence. Eliminate (B). Choice (C) takes care of both problems with the original sentence. The plural noun *models* matches the plural pronoun *their*, and both clauses are now constructed in a similar way, making for a clearer and briefer sentence. (C) is probably the correct answer, but read the remaining choices anyway. Choice (D) sounds pretty good when you read it as part of the sentence, doesn't it? No grammatical errors jump out at you. So is it a toss-up between (C) and (D)? Well, go on to (E) for now, then come back to the (C)-versus-(D) debate. Choice (E) incorrectly uses the phrase *is limited* to describe *assessing risk*. It is the computer models' ability, *not* assessing risk, that is limited. Eliminate (E).

> **Alert!**
> Don't select an answer choice as the correct one just because it fixes every flaw in the original sentence. If (A) is flawed, you can be certain that one or two of the answer choices will fix the flaw, *but* create a new flaw!

Step 3: Go back to (C) and (D). Is one less awkward than the other? More concise? Closer in meaning to the original version? Perhaps you noticed that the first clause in (D) (*assessment of risk can be achieved*) sounds a bit awkward. So you've got a good reason to choose (C) over (D).

Step 4: Check (C) one more time by plugging it into the sentence: *Despite their sophistication, computer models for assessing risk are limited in their ability to define what risk is.* Sounds great! Confirm your response, and move on to the next question.

Grammatical Errors Involving Parts of Speech

In the remainder of this chapter, you'll examine basic kinds of grammatical errors and problems with sentence structure and written expression. These are the ones that, for most test-takers, are easiest to recognize and most straightforward to fix. In addition to learning how to fix these problems, you'll see how the GMAT might test you on each one.

We'll start with grammatical errors involving *parts of speech*—which include adjectives, adverbs, pronouns, and verbs. Here are the kinds of errors we'll cover in the pages ahead:

- Error in choice between adjective and adverb
- Error in choice of adjective for comparisons
- Error in choice of personal pronoun
- Error in pronoun-antecedent agreement
- Error in subject-verb agreement

Tip: By the way, immersing yourself in the rules of English grammar and the guidelines for effective written expression (as you're about to do) will help you not only for Sentence Correction questions but also for the two Analytical Writing Assessment (AWA) sections of the GMAT. So pay close attention; your efforts here will be doubly rewarded on exam day!

Error in Choice Between Adjective and Adverb

Adjectives describe nouns, while *adverbs* describe verbs, adjectives, and other adverbs. Adverbs generally end with *-ly*, while adjectives don't. Look for adjectives incorrectly used as adverbs (and vice versa).

incorrect: The movie ended *sudden*.

correct: The movie ended *suddenly*.

(The adverb *suddenly* describes the verb *ended*.)

Although adverbs generally end with *-ly*, some adverbs don't. Also, if you're dealing with two adverbs in a row, sometimes the *-ly* is dropped from the second adverb. There are no hard-and-fast rules here. Trust your ear as to what sounds correct.

incorrect: Risk-takers drive fastly, play hardly, and arrive lately for their appointments.

correct: Risk-takers drive *fast*, play *hard*, and arrive *late* for their appointments.

incorrect: The Canadian skater jumps *particularly highly*.

correct: The Canadian skater jumps *particularly high*.

Part IV: Verbal Ability

Also keep in mind that adjectives, not adverbs, should be used to describe verbs involving the senses (sight, taste, smell, hearing, touch).

incorrect: Dinner tasted *deliciously*.

incorrect: Dinner tasted *awful* delicious.

correct: Dinner tasted *awfully* delicious.

(The adjective *delicious* is used to describe the verb *tasted*, while the adverb *awfully* is used to describe *delicious*.)

Now look at how the test-makers might try to slip one of these errors past you in a GMAT sentence. In the question below, the original sentence is flawed, so (A) is correct. Your choice is between (C) and (D).

> **Note:** To help you focus on the specific grammatical error at hand, we'll simplify the Sentence Correction format by listing just *three* answer choices, and by limiting the kinds of errors to one or two. Actual GMAT questions include five answer choices, of course.

A recent report from the Department of Energy suggests that over the next two decades demand for crude oil will <u>increase at an alarming fast rate, and greatly exceeds</u> most economists' previous forecasts.

- A. increase at an alarming fast rate, and greatly exceeds
- B. ***
- C. increase at an alarmingly fast rate, greatly exceeding
- D. be at an increasingly alarming rate and will greatly exceed
- E. ***

The correct answer is C. The original sentence incorrectly uses the adjective *alarming* instead of the adverb *alarmingly* to describe the adjective *fast*. The original sentence also contains an additional, and more conspicuous, flaw. The phrase *and greatly exceeds* improperly suggests that the rate is increasing alarmingly at the present time. However, the sentence as a whole makes clear that this is a future event. (C) corrects both of these problems. Although (D) also corrects both problems, it creates a new flaw. The use of the word *be* to refer to *demand* is an awkward and inappropriate expression of the idea which the sentence attempts to convey. *Be* suggests one point in time, but the sentence intends to describe the changing demand over a period of time.

Chapter 10: Sentence Correction

> **Alert!**
>
> Because this sort of error is generally easy to spot in a sentence, the GMAT test-makers will probably try to sneak it past you by including another (and possibly more conspicuous) flaw as well, in the hope that you'll carelessly overlook the incorrect adjective or adverb. Beat them at their own game by looking carefully at adjectives and adverbs, *especially when they appear in pairs* (as in the sample question above)!

Error in Choice of Adjective for Comparisons

As you read a GMAT sentence, pay close attention to any adjective ending in *-er*, *-ier*, *-est*, and *-iest*. Adjectives ending in *-er* and *-ier* should be used to compare *two* things, while adjectives ending in *-est* and *-iest* should be used when dealing with three or more things.

Comparative form (two things)	Superlative form (three or more things)
brighter	brightest
greater	greatest
fewer	fewest
lesser	least
more	most
better	best

incorrect: Frank is less intelligent than the other four students.

correct: Frank is the *least* intelligent among the *five* students.

correct: Frank is *less* intelligent than *any* of the other four students (The word *any* is singular, so the comparative form is proper.)

Another way of making a comparison is to precede the adjective with a word such as *more*, *less*, *most*, or *least*. But if both methods are used together, the sentence is incorrect.

incorrect: Francis is *more healthier* than Greg.

correct: Francis is *healthier* than Greg.

Part IV: Verbal Ability

Now, look at a GMAT-style sentence involving the kinds of issues we just covered. The original version (A) is faulty, so your choice is between the two alternative versions listed here.

<u>The more busier the trading floor at the stock exchange, the less opportunities</u> large institutional investors have to influence the direction of price by initiating large leveraged transactions.

- A. The more busier the trading floor at the stock exchange, the less opportunities
- B. ***
- C. ***
- D. The busier trading floor at the stock exchange results in less opportunities
- E. The busier the trading floor at the stock exchange, the fewer opportunities

The correct answer is E. In the original sentence, the phrase *more busier* incorrectly uses both comparative methods. (E) corrects this flaw by using *busier*. The original sentence includes another flaw as well. The phrase *less opportunities* is incorrect; the word *fewer* should be used instead of *less* in referring to numbers of things—as opposed to the amount of one thing. (E) corrects this flaw. However, (D) does not.

Error in Choice of Personal Pronoun

Personal pronouns are words such as *they*, *me*, *his*, and *itself*—words that refer to specific people, places, and things. Pronouns take different forms, called "cases," depending on how they are used in a sentence. Just for the record, you'll find all the various cases in the following table.

	Subjective Case	Possessive Case	Objective Case	Objective Case —Reflexive
first-person singular	I	my, mine	me	myself
first-person plural	we	our, ours	us	ourselves
second-person singular	you	your, yours	you	yourself
second-person plural	you	your, yours	you	yourselves

Chapter 10: Sentence Correction

	Subjective Case	Possessive Case	Objective Case	Objective Case —Reflexive
third-person singular	he, she, it	his, her, hers, its	him, her, it	himself, herself, itself
third-person plural	they	their, theirs	them	themselves

You can generally trust your ear when it comes to detecting personal-pronoun errors. In some cases, however, your ear can betray you, so make sure you are "tuned in" to the following uses of pronouns.

incorrect: Either him or Trevor *would be* the best spokesman for our group.

incorrect: The best spokesperson for our group *would be* either him or Trevor.

correct: Either Trevor or *he would be* the best spokesperson for our group.

correct: The best spokesperson for our group *would be* either *he* or Trevor.

(Any form of the verb *to be* is followed by a subject pronoun, such as *he*.)

incorrect: One can't help admiring *them* cooperating with one another.

correct: One can't help admiring *their cooperating* with one another.

(The *possessive* form is used when the pronoun is part of a "noun clause," such as *their cooperating*.)

incorrect: In striving to understand others, we also learn more about *us*.

correct: In striving to understand others, *we* also learn more about *ourselves*. (A *reflexive* pronoun is used to refer to the sentence's subject.)

> **Alert!** What appears to be a reflexive pronoun may not even be a real word! Here's a list of "non-words," any of which might masquerade as a reflexive pronoun in a GMAT sentence: *ourself*, *our own selves*, *theirselves*, *theirself*, *themself*, *their own self*, and *their own selves*.

387

PETERSON'S
getting you there

Part IV: Verbal Ability

Now, look at a GMAT-style sentence involving the issue of pronoun case. The original version (A) is faulty, so your choice is between the two alternative versions listed here.

> Those of the legislators opposing the swampland protection bill have only theirselves to blame for the plight of the endangered black thrush bird.

   A. of the legislators opposing the swampland protection bill have only theirselves
   B. ***
   C. Those legislators, who opposed the swampland protection bill, have only themselves to blame
   D. Those legislators who opposed the swampland protection bill have only themselves to blame
   E. ***

The correct answer is D. The original sentence suffers from two flaws. First, *theirselves* is a non-word and should be replaced with the reflexive pronoun *themselves*. Second, the phrase *those of the legislators opposing*, while not grammatically incorrect, is awkward and confusing. (D) provides a briefer and clearer alternative phrase and corrects the pronoun error. (C) also corrects the pronoun error, but creates a new problem by setting off a portion of the sentence with commas. In doing so, (C) infers that all of "those legislators" are opposed the bill, thereby distorting the intended meaning of the original sentence.

> **Note**
>
> In GMAT sentences, you'll find very few (if any) first-person or second-person personal pronouns. Why do the test-makers shun pronouns such as *we*, *you*, and *our*? Because GMAT sentences are academic in nature, not conversational or informal. (But you probably already noticed that, didn't you?)

Error in Pronoun-Antecedent Agreement

An *antecedent* is simply the noun to which a pronoun refers. In GMAT sentences, make sure that pronouns agree in *number* (singular or plural) with their antecedents.

   singular: Studying other artists actually helps a young *painter* develop *his* or *her* own style.

   plural: Studying other artists actually helps young *painters* develop *their* own style.

But what's the rule for pronouns that refer to nouns describing a group of people or things (called *collective nouns*)? The same rule applies here as for subject-verb agreement: the pronoun can either be singular or plural, depending on whether the collective noun is used in a singular or plural sense.

>**correct:** The legislature hesitates to punish *its* own members for ethics violations. (*Legislature* used in the singular sense.)
>
>**correct:** The planning *committee* recessed, but Jack continued to work without *them*.(*Committee* used in the plural sense.)

Singular pronouns are generally used in referring to antecedents such as *each*, *either*, *neither*, and *one*.

>**correct:** *Neither* of the two countries imposes an income tax on *its* citizens.
>
>**correct:** *One* cannot be too kind to *oneself*.

When it comes to antecedents such as *anyone*, *anybody*, *everybody*, *everyone*, or *a person*, the rules of English grammar get a bit fuzzy. For instance, any grammarian would agree that the first sentence below is correct, but whether the second one is correct is hotly debated among grammarians.

>**correct:** If *anyone* offends you, please don't confront *him* or *her*.
>
>**proper?** If *anyone* offends you, please don't confront *them*.

Because the rule of grammar here is unsettled, rest assured that you will not encounter these words as pronoun antecedents on the GMAT.

Now, look at a GMAT-style sentence involving pronoun-antecedent agreement. The original version (A) is faulty, so your choice is between the two alternative versions.

Many powerful leaders throughout history, such as President Nixon during the Watergate debacle, had become victimized by his own paranoia.

- A. Many powerful leaders throughout history, such as President Nixon during the Watergate debacle, had become victimized by his own paranoia.
- B. Many powerful leaders throughout history, such as President Nixon during the Watergate debacle, have become victims of their own paranoia.
- C. Throughout history, many a powerful leader, such as President Nixon during the Watergate debacle, have by his or her own paranoia become a victim.
- D. ***
- E. ***

The correct answer is B. The original sentence intends to make the point that *many leaders* (plural) *have* (plural verb) become victimized by *their* (plural pronoun) own paranoia. However, by using the singular *had* and *his*, the final clause seems to refer to *Nixon* instead of to *leaders*. (B) correctly uses the plurals *have* and *their*. In (C), the plural subject *leaders* has been transformed into a singular subject (*many a powerful leader*). This form is grammatically acceptable. However, the subject's verb, as well as any pronouns that refer to the subject, should now be singular as well. Although the singular *his or her* is correct, the plural verb *have* is incorrect. So (C) contains a subject-verb agreement error. (C) also improperly separates the words *have* and *become*. The phrase *have become* is an example of an "infinitive" verb form. Have you ever heard the phrase "split infinitive"? (C) provides a good example of one; and it's grammatically incorrect.

Error in Subject-Verb Agreement

A verb should always "agree" in number—either singular or plural—with its subject. A singular subject takes a singular verb, while a plural subject takes a plural verb.

    correct (singular): The *parade was* spectacular.

    correct (singular): Both *parades were* spectacular.

    correct (plural): The parade *and* the pageant *were* spectacular.

Chapter 10: Sentence Correction

Don't be fooled by any words or phrases that might separate the verb from its subject. In each sentence below, the singular verb *was* agrees with its subject, the singular noun *parade*.

correct: The *parade* of cars *was* spectacular.

correct: The *parade* of cars and horses *was* spectacular.

An intervening clause set off by commas can serve an especially effective "smokescreen" for a subject-verb agreement error. Pay careful attention to what comes immediately before and after the intervening clause. Reading the sentence without the clause often reveal a subject-verb agreement error.

incorrect: John, as well as his sister, *were* absent from school yesterday.

correct: *John*, as well as his sister, *was* absent from school yesterday.

Here's a GMAT-style sentence that raises a subject-verb agreement issue. The original version (A) is faulty, so your choice is between the two alternative versions listed here.

Grade school instruction in ethical and social values, particularly the <u>values of respect and of tolerance, are</u> required for any democracy to thrive.

A. values of respect and of tolerance, are
B. value of respect, together with tolerance, is
C. values of respect and tolerance, is
D. ***
E. ***

The correct answer is (C). In the original sentence, the subject of the plural verb *are* is the singular noun *instruction*. The correct answer choice must correct this subject-verb agreement problem. Also, the second *of* in the underlined phrase should be deleted because its use results in an awkward and nonsensical clause, which seems to suggest that *of tolerance* is a value. Both (B) and (C) correct the problem by changing *are* to *is* and by dropping the second *of*. However, (B) creates two new problems. First, using the word *value* instead of *values* distorts the meaning of the underlined phrase. Respect and tolerance are not referred to in (B) as values. However, the original sentence, considered as a whole, clearly intends to refer to respect and tolerance as examples of ethical and social *values*. Secondly, the phrase *together with tolerance* (set off by commas), adds an unnecessary clause and results in a sentence that is wordy and awkward. (C) is clearer and more concise.

> **Tip**
>
> Keep a keen eye out for GMAT sentences that separate verbs from their subjects. In every one of these sentences, it's a sure bet that the test-makers are testing you on subject-verb agreement.

Problems Involving a Sentence's Structural Elements

Now, let's move ahead to another broad area covered in GMAT Sentence Correction: *sentence structure*. Here are the specific kinds of structural problems we'll cover in this section:

- Sentence fragments (incomplete sentences)
- Two main clauses connected improperly
- Faulty parallelism involving lists, or "strings"
- Faulty parallelism involving correlatives

Sentence Fragments (Incomplete Sentences)

It was probably your fifth- or sixth-grade teacher who first informed you that a sentence must include both a subject and a predicate. Well, your teacher was right, and the GMAT is here to remind you. Grammarians call incomplete sentences "sentence fragments."

fragment: Expensive private colleges, generally out of financial reach for most families with college-aged children.

fragment: Without question, responsibility for building and maintaining safe bridges.

On the GMAT, you probably won't have any trouble recognizing a sentence fragment. However, an especially long fragment might escape your detection if you're not paying close attention.

Chapter 10: Sentence Correction

Now, look at a GMAT-style example of a sentence fragment. The original version (A) is faulty, so your choice is between the two alternative versions listed here.

One cannot deny that, even after the initial flurry of the feminist movement subsided, Congresswoman Bella Abzug, undeniably her female constituency's truest voice, <u>as well as its most public advocate</u>.

A. as well as its most public advocate
B. who was her constituency's most public advocate
C. ***
D. was also its most public advocate
E. ***

The correct answer is D. If you use (D), the sentence can be distilled down to this: *One cannot deny that Bella Abzug was its [the feminist movement's] most public advocate.* Adding the verb *was* is the key to transforming the original fragment into a complete sentence. Neither (A) nor (C) provides the verb needed for a complete sentence.

> **Tip**
>
> If you're not sure whether it's a complete sentence, ask yourself two questions: (1) What's the subject? and (2) Where's the verb that establishes a predicate?

Two Main Clauses Connected Improperly

A *main clause* is any clause that can stand alone as a complete sentence. There's nothing wrong with combining two main clauses into one sentence—as long as the clauses are properly connected. On the GMAT, look for any of these three flaws:

- No punctuation between main clauses
- A comma between main clauses, but no connecting word (such as *and*, *or*, *but*, *yet*, *for*, *so*).
- A confusing or inappropriate connecting word

incorrect:
   Dan ran out of luck Mike continued to win.

   Dan ran out of luck, Mike continued to win.

   Dan ran out of luck, or Mike continued to win.

correct:
>Dan ran out of luck, *but* Mike continued to win.
>
>Dan ran out of luck, *while* Mike continued to win.
>
>Dan ran out of luck, *yet* Mike continued to win.

Here's a GMAT-style sentence that focuses on the comma-splice issue. The original version (A) is faulty, so your choice is between the two alternative versions listed here.

>The Aleutian Islands of Alaska include many islands near the mainland, <u>the majority of them are</u> uninhabited by humans.
>
>A. the majority of them are
>B. ***
>C. so the majority of them are
>D. ***
>E. yet the majority of them are

The correct answer is E. Notice that (E) includes a connecting word (*yet*) that gives the sentence a reasonable meaning by underscoring the contrast between the mainland (which is populated) and the unpopulated nearby islands. Although (C) adds a connecting word (*so*), this word is inappropriate—inferring that the islands are unpopulated *because* they are near the mainland. The resulting sentence is nonsensical, so (C) can't be the best answer choice. (By the way, notice the appropriate use of *so* as a connector in the preceding sentence!)

Faulty Parallelism Involving a List or "String"

Sentence elements that are grammatically equal should be constructed similarly; otherwise the result will be what is referred to as *faulty parallelism*. For instance, whenever you see a list, or "string," of items in a sentence, look for inconsistent or mixed use of:

- Prepositions (such as *in*, *with*, or *on*)
- Gerunds (verbs with an *-ing* added to the end)
- Infinitives (plural verb preceded by *to*)
- Articles (such as *a* and *the*)

faulty: Flight 82 travels first to Boise, then to Denver, then Salt Lake City. (*To* precedes only the first two of the three cities in this list.)

parallel: Flight 82 travels first to Boise, then Denver, then Salt Lake City.

parallel: Flight 82 travels first to Boise, then to Denver, then to Salt Lake City.

faulty: Being understaffed, lack of funding, and being outpaced by competitors soon resulted in the fledgling company's going out of business. (Only two of the three listed items begin with the gerund *being*.)

parallel: Understaffed, underfunded, and outpaced by competitors, the fledgling company soon went out of business.

parallel: As a result of understaffing, insufficient funding, and outpacing on the part of its competitors, the fledgling company soon went out of business.

faulty: Among *the* mountains, *the* sea and desert, we humans have yet to fully explore only the sea.

parallel: Among *the* mountains, sea and desert, we humans have yet to fully explore only the sea.

parallel: Among *the* mountains, *the* sea and *the* desert, we humans have yet to fully explore only the sea.

Now, look at a GMAT-style sentence involving lists and faulty parallelism. The original version (A) is faulty, so your choice is between the two alternative versions listed here.

Long before the abolition of slavery, many freed indentured servants were able to acquire property, to interact with people of other races, and maintain their freedom.

- A. to interact with people of other races and
- B. interact with people of other races, and maintain
- C. ***
- D. to interact with people of other races, as well as maintaining
- E. ***

The correct answer is B. Notice the string of three items in this sentence. In the original version, the second item repeats the preposition *to*, but the third item does not. (B) corrects this faulty parallelism. (D) improperly mixes the use of a prepositional phrase (beginning with *to*) with a construction that uses a gerund (*maintaining*) instead.

Part IV: Verbal Ability

> **Alert!**
>
> Just because all items in a string are parallel, don't assume that the string is problem-free! Repeating the same preposition, article, or other modifier before each item in a string can sometimes result in an awkward and unnecessarily wordy sentence. In other instances, repeating the modifier may be necessary to achieve clarity.
>
> **awkward:** Some pachyderms can go for days at a time without water or without food or without sleep.
>
> **better:** Some pachyderms can go for days at a time without water, food, or sleep.
>
> **unclear:** Going for broke and broke usually carry identical consequences.
>
> **clear:** Going for broke and going broke usually carry identical consequences.

Faulty Parallelism Involving Correlatives

You just saw how items in a list can suffer from faulty parallelism. Now look at how this grammatical error shows up in what are called *correlatives*. Here are the most commonly used correlatives:

- either . . . or . . .
- neither . . . nor . . .
- both . . . and . . .
- not only . . . but also . . .

Whenever you spot a correlative in a sentence, make sure that the element immediately following the first correlative term is parallel in construction to the element following the second term.

faulty: Those wishing to participate should *either* contact us by telephone *or* should send e-mail to us.

parallel (but repetitive): Those wishing to participate *either should* contact us by telephone *or should* send e-mail to us.

parallel: Those wishing to participate should *either* contact us by telephone *or* send e-mail to us.

Now, look at how faulty parallelism in a correlative might appear in a GMAT sentence. The original version (A) is faulty, so your choice is between the two alternative versions listed here.

Species diversity in the Amazon basin results not <u>from climate stability, as once believed, but</u> climate disturbances.

A. from climate stability, as once believed, but
B. only from climate stability, as once believed, but instead from
C. ✳✳✳
D. ✳✳✳
E. from climate stability, as once believed, but rather from

The correct answer is (E). As it stands, the original sentence might carry one of two very different meanings: (1) stability and disturbances *both* contribute to species diversity, or (2) disturbances, *but not* stability, contribute to species diversity. The reason for the ambiguity is the use of an improper correlative as well as faulty parallelism (*from* appears only in the first correlative term). The correct answer choice must make the sentence's meaning clear, probably by using one of two correlatives: *not only . . . but also* or *not . . . but rather*. Also, the two correlative terms must be parallel. (E) corrects the faulty parallelism (*from* appears in each correlative term) and clears up the sentence's meaning. Although (B) corrects the parallelism problem, it uses the nonsensical (and improper) correlative *not only . . . but instead*.

Redundancy, Wordiness, Awkwardness, and Omissions

In addition to covering grammar and sentence structure, GMAT Sentence Correction also tests you on your skill at recognizing and fixing the following types of problems involving written expression:

- Redundancy (repeating the same idea)
- Wordiness (using more words than needed to make the point)
- Awkwardness (using clumsy, confusing, or overly complicated wording)
- Omissions (omitting words that are needed for clarity or sentence sense)

The problems of wordiness and awkwardness will show up in the majority of the 14–15 Sentence Correction questions on the GMAT. So always be on the lookout for them in both the original sentences or in one or more of the answer choices.

Redundant Words and Phrases

Look for words and phrases that express the same idea twice. This syndrome is known as "redundancy." In many cases, correcting the problem is as simple as omitting one of the redundant phrases.

redundant: *The reason that* we stopped for the night was *because* we were sleepy.

redundant: *Because* we were sleepy, we *therefore* stopped for the night.

better: We stopped for the night because we were sleepy.

redundant: The *underlying* motive *behind* his seemingly generous offer was old-fashioned greed.

better: The motive behind his seemingly generous offer was old-fashioned greed.

better: The underlying motive for his seemingly generous offer was old-fashioned greed.

redundant: One of the fossils is twenty thousand years old *in age*.

better: One of the fossils is twenty thousand years old.

redundant: The German Oktoberfest takes place *each October of every year*.

better: The German Oktoberfest takes place *every October*.

redundant: *At the same time* that lightning struck, we *simultaneously* lost our electric power.

better: At the same time that lightning struck, we lost our electric power.

redundant: *Both* unemployment *as well as* interest rates can affect stock prices.

better: Both unemployment levels and interest rates can affect stock prices.

better: Unemployment levels as well as interest rates can affect stock prices.

redundant: Not only does dinner smell good, but it *also* tastes good *too*.

better: Not only does dinner smell good, but it tastes good too.

Now look at a GMAT-style sentence that raises the issue of redundancy. The original version (A) is faulty, so your choice is between the two alternative versions listed here.

<u>Due to a negligible difference in Phase III results as between patients using the drug and those using a placebo, the Food and Drug Administration refused to approve it on this basis.</u>

- **A.** Due to a negligible difference in Phase III results between patients using the drug and those using a placebo, the Food and Drug Administration refused to approve the drug on this basis.
- **B.** The Food and Drug Administration refused to approve the drug based upon a negligible difference in Phase III results as between patients using it and those using a placebo.
- **C.** Due to a negligible difference in Phase III results as between patients using the drug and those using a placebo, the Food and Drug Administration refused to approve the drug.
- **D.** ***
- **E.** ***

The correct answer is C. There are three distinct problems with the original version. First, *due to* and *on this basis* serve the same function—to express that the FDA's refusal was based on the Phase III results. (The redundancy is easy to miss since one phrase begins the sentence while the other phrase ends it.) Secondly, the intended antecedent of *it* is *the drug*, but the intervening noun *placebo* obscures the reference. Thirdly, the sentence is ambiguous. Did the FDA refuse to approve the drug, or did it approve the drug on some basis other than the one mentioned in the sentence? The sentence is ambiguous as to which meaning is intended. (C) corrects all three problems, simply by omitting *on this basis* and by replacing *it* with *the drug*. (B) corrects the first two problems by omitting *due to* and reconstructing the sentence. But (B) fails to clarify the meaning of the sentence.

Alert!

On the GMAT, be on the lookout for sentences having the following "themes" and keywords. Redundancies are most likely to spring up in these kinds of sentences:

- Words establishing cause-and-effect (because, since, if, then, therefore)
- References to time (age, years, hours, days)
- Words used in conjunctions (both, as well, too, also)

Superfluous (Unnecessary) Words

You just took a look at one variety of unnecessary verbiage: redundancy. Now look at some other kinds of sentences in which certain words can simply be omitted without affecting the meaning or effectiveness of the original sentence. Remember: Briefer is better!

Each sentence in the first group below contains an *ellipsis*: a word or phrase that can be omitted because it is clearly implied. (In the incorrect version, the ellipsis is italicized.)

superfluous: The warmer the weather *is*, the more crowded the beach *is*.

concise: The warmer the weather, the more crowded the beach.

superfluous: He looks exactly like Francis *looks*.

concise: He looks exactly like Francis.

superfluous: That shirt is the ugliest *shirt that* I have ever seen.

concise: That shirt is the ugliest I have ever seen.

Each sentence in the next group includes a superfluous preposition. (In the incorrect version, the preposition is italicized.)

superfluous: The other children couldn't help *from* laughing at the girl with mismatched shoes.

concise: The other children couldn't help laughing at the girl with mismatched shoes.

superfluous: One prominent futurist predicts a nuclear holocaust by the year *of* 2020.

concise: One prominent futurist predicts a nuclear holocaust by the year 2020.

superfluous: They made the discovery *in* around December of last year.

concise: They made the discovery around December of last year.

superfluous: The waiter brought half *of* a loaf of bread to the table.

concise: The waiter brought half a loaf of bread to the table.

Chapter 10: Sentence Correction

Superfluous words can also appear in a series of parallel clauses. Both versions of the next sentence use proper parallelism, but briefer is better—as long as the meaning of the sentence is clear.

> **superfluous:** My three goals in life are to be healthy, *to be* wealthy, and *to be* wise.

> **concise:** My three goals in life are to be healthy, wealthy, and wise.

Here's a GMAT-style sentence that contains superfluous words. The original version (A) is faulty, so your choice is between the two alternative versions listed here.

> Only through a comprehensive, federally funded vaccination program can a new epidemic of tuberculosis be curbed, just like the spread of both cholera <u>as well as the spread of typhoid was curbed</u>.
>
> A. as well as the spread of typhoid was curbed
> B. ✱✱✱
> C. ✱✱✱
> D. and typhoid
> E. as well as typhoid was curbed

The correct answer is D. The original sentence suffers from no fewer than three distinct verbiage problems. First, the correlative *both . . . as well as* is redundant (and improper). Since *both* is not underlined, *as well as* should be replaced with *and*. Secondly, because the preposition *like* sets up an ellipsis, *were curbed* is implied and can be omitted. Thirdly, the second occurrence of *the spread of* can be omitted since it is implied through the use of parallel construction. (D) pares down the underlined phrase to its most concise form. (E) fails to correct the redundant correlative *both . . . as well as*. (E) also fails to omit the unnecessary *was curbed*.

Wordy and Awkward Phrases

Just because a sentence is grammatically acceptable, you shouldn't assume that there is no room for improvement. You've already seen that unnecessary words can sometimes be omitted, thereby improving a GMAT sentence. Now, look at some phrases that can be *replaced* with clearer, more concise ones.

> **wordy:** Failure can *some of the time* serve as a prelude to success.

> **concise:** Failure can *sometimes* serve as a prelude to success.

wordy: *As a result of Greg's being* a compulsive overeater, *it is not likely that he will* live past the age of fifty.

concise: *Because Greg is* a compulsive overeater, *he is unlikely* to live past the age of fifty.

wordy: Before the mother eats, she feeds *each and every one* of her offspring.

concise: Before the mother eats, she feeds *each* of her offspring.

wordy: There are fewer buffalo on the plains today than *there ever were* before.

concise: There are fewer buffalo on the plains today than *ever* before.

wordy: Discipline is crucial to *the attainment of* one's objectives.

concise: Discipline is crucial to *attaining* one's objectives.

wordy: Her husband was waiting for her on the platform *at the time of the train's arrival*.

concise: Her husband was waiting for her on the platform *when the train arrived*.

awkward: Calcification *is when* (or *is where*) calcium deposits form around a bone.

concise: Calcification *occurs when* calcium deposits form around a bone.

awkward: *There are* eight cats in the house, *of which* only two have been fed.

concise: Of the eight cats in the house, only two have been fed.

awkward: The wind poses a serious threat to the old tree, and *so does* the snow.

awkward: The wind and snow both pose a serious threat to the old tree.

Now, take a look at a wordy *and* awkward GMAT-style sentence. The original version (A) is faulty, so your choice is between the two alternative versions listed here.

To avoid confusion between oral medications, <u>different pills' coatings should have different colors, and pills should be different in shape and size</u>.

- A. different pills' coatings should have different colors, and pills should be different in shape and size
- B. pills should differ in color as well as in shape and size
- C. ✱✱✱
- D. pills should be able to be distinguished by their color, shape, and size
- E. ✱✱✱

The correct answer is B. There are several problems with the original sentence. The first is that *different pills' coatings* is very awkward. Secondly, the word *coatings* is probably superfluous here; *color* suffices to make the point. Thirdly, *have different colors* is awkward (*differ in color* would be better). Fourthly, the phrase *be different* is ambiguous (different from what?). Finally, a parallel series including color, shape, and size would be more concise and less awkward than the construction used in the sentence. (B) corrects all these problems. In (D), the phrase *be able to be distinguished* is wordy and very awkward; the phrase *be distinguishable* would be better.

> **Note**
>
> The wordy and awkward phrases that the GMAT can throw at you are limited in variety only by the collective imagination of the test-makers. The phrases we've provided here are just a small sampling.

Omitting a Necessary Word

On the flip side of redundancy and wordiness is the error of *omission*. Excluding a necessary word can obscure or confuse the meaning of the sentence. Check especially for the omission of key "little" words—prepositions, pronouns, conjunctives, and especially the word *that*.

omission: The newscaster announced the voting results were incorrect. (What did the newscaster announce: the results or the fact that the results were incorrect?)

clearer: The newscaster announced *that* the voting results were incorrect.

Part IV: Verbal Ability

Look out especially for an omission that results in an illogical comparison, as in the following sentences. It can easily slip past you if you're not paying close attention.

illogical: The color of the blouse is different from the skirt.

logical: The color of the blouse is different from *that* of the skirt.

illogical: China's population is greater than any country in the world. (This sentence draws an illogical comparison between a population and a country and illogically suggests that China is not a country.)

logical: China's population is greater than *that of* any *other* country in the world.

> **Alert!**
>
> As you've just seen, one little word can make all the difference! Your mind can easily trick you by filling in a key word that is not actually there. The moral here is: Read every GMAT sentence slowly and carefully!

Success Keys for GMAT Sentence Correction

Here's a checklist of tips for handling GMAT Sentence Correction questions. Some of these tips reiterate suggestions made earlier—suggestions that are worth underscoring. Others are new here. Apply these points of advice to Part V's practice tests, and then review them again, just before exam day.

Read the Answer Choices Very Carefully; One Little Word Can Make all the Difference

The difference between answer choices can be subtle: perhaps one extra little word, or perhaps a word replaced by a different one. It's easy to overlook these differences if you rush through a question. Take your time, and read carefully.

For Each Choice, Review the *Entire* Sentence—Not Just the Underlined Part

GMAT Sentence Correction questions are not nearly as time-consuming as other Verbal questions. So take your time; plug each version into the sentence, then read the entire sentence. Sure, you'll see the occasional answer choice that's grammatically incorrect apart from the rest of the sentence. But such cases are the exception, not the rule.

Don't Choose an Answer Just Because It Fixes Every Flaw in the Original Version

If the original version is flawed, it's a sure bet that one or two of the other answer choices will fix the flaw *but* create a new flaw!

Trust Your Ear

If an answer choice doesn't sound right as you read it in the context of the sentence, eliminate it. There's no need to analyze it any further.

Don't be Thrown by a Nonsensical Answer Choice

If an answer choice seems confusing or unclear, don't assume that you are at fault for not understanding the sentence. Some answer choices will simply not make much sense. Don't waste your time analyzing the answer choice to determine why it is wrong. Eliminate it!

Eliminate Answer Choices that Change the Meaning of the Original Sentence

If an answer choice alters, distorts, or confuses the meaning of the original sentence, it cannot be the best choice, even if it is grammatically correct.

Resolve Close Judgment Calls in Favor of Briefer Answer Choices

If it comes down to a coin flip between two answer choices, keep your penny in your pocket and select the briefer (more concisely worded) choice. But don't assume that shorter choices are automatically better than longer ones. Apply this technique only when your decision comes down to that coin flip.

Never Assume the Original Sentence is Wrong

This is probably the most common Sentence Correction mistake among GMAT test-takers. There's a tendency to assume there is a better choice than the original version. But keep in mind that in about one out of five Sentence Correction questions, the original sentence will be better than any of the four alternatives.

Take It to the Next Level

Welcome to the Next Level GMAT Sentence Correction. Here, you'll:

- Learn to recognize and fix challenging grammatical problems involving parts of speech
- Learn to distinguish between verb tenses
- Learn to recognize and correct improper mixing and shifting of tense, voice, and mood
- Learn to recognize and handle challenging problems involving sentence structure

What's New at the Next Level

Here at the Next Level, you'll learn to:

- Recognize and fix challenging grammatical problems involving parts of speech
- Distinguish between verb tenses
- Recognize and correct improper mixing and shifting of tense, voice, and mood
- Recognize and handle challenging problems involving sentence structure

> **Note:** To help you focus on the specific grammatical errors or other flaws at hand, we'll simplify the Sentence Correction format by listing just *three* answer choices, and by limiting the kinds of flaws to one or two. Actual GMAT questions include five answer choices, of course.

Chapter 10: Sentence Correction

Errors Involving Parts of Speech

Earlier in the chapter covered grammatical errors involving parts of speech that are most basic and that the GMAT covers most frequently. Here at the Next Level, you'll focus on the trickiest, most testworthy rules of grammar involving pronoun choice and subject-verb agreement:

- Error in choice of *relative* pronoun
- Errors in agreement between a *pronoun* or *compound* subject and verb

Error in Choice of Relative Pronoun

The English language includes only a handful of *relative* pronouns: *which*, *who*, *that*, *whose*, *whichever*, *whoever*, and *whomever*. Don't worry about what the term "relative pronoun" means. Instead, just remember the following rules about when to use each one:

1. Use *which* to refer to things.

2. Use either *who* or *that* to refer to people.

    incorrect: Amanda, *which* was the third performer, was the best of the group.

    correct: Amanda, *who* was the third performer, was the best of the group.

    correct: The first employee *that* fails to meet his or her sales quota will be fired.

    correct: The first employee *who* fails to meet his or her sales quota will be fired.

3. Whether you should use *which* or *that* depends on what the sentence is supposed to mean.

    one meaning: The third page, *which* had been earmarked, contained several typographical errors.

    different meaning: The third page *that* had been earmarked contained several typographical errors.

    (The first sentence merely describes the third page as earmarked. The second sentence also suggests that the page containing the errors was the third earmarked page.)

4. Whether you should use *who* (*whoever*) or *whom* (*whomever*) depends on the grammatical function of the person (or people) being referred to. Confused? Don't worry; just take a look at the

sample sentences here, and you shouldn't have any trouble deciding between *who* and *whom* on the GMAT.

incorrect: It was the chairman *whom* initiated the bill.

correct: It was the chairman *who* initiated the bill.

incorrect: First aid will be available to *whomever* requires it.

correct: First aid will be available to *whoever* requires it.

incorrect: The team members from East High, *who* the judges were highly impressed with, won the debate.

correct: The team members from East High, with *whom* the judges were highly impressed, won the debate.

On the GMAT, to make sure that *who (whoever)* and *whom (whomever)* are being used correctly, try substituting a regular pronoun, then rearrange the clause (if necessary) to form a simple sentence. If a subject-case pronoun works, then *who (whoever)* is the right choice. On the other hand, if an object-case pronoun works, then *whom (whomever)* is the right choice. Here's how it works with the foregoing sentences:

It was the chairman *whom* initiated the bill.

He initiated the bill.

(*He* is a subject-case pronoun, so *whom* should be replaced with *who*.)

First aid will be available to *whomever* requires it.

She requires it.

(*She* is a subject-case pronoun, so *whomever* should be replaced with *whoever*.)

The team members from East High, *who* the judges were highly impressed with, won the debate.

The judges were impressed with *them*.

(*Them* is an object-case pronoun, so *who* should be replaced by *whom*.)

Chapter 10: Sentence Correction

Now, look at a GMAT-style sentence that focuses on a relative-pronoun issue. The original version (A) is faulty, so your choice is between the two alternative versions listed here.

The Civil War's <u>bloodiest battle was initiated on behalf of those, the indentured black slaves, for who life was most precious</u>.

- A. bloodiest battle was initiated on behalf of those, the indentured black slaves, for who life was most precious
- B. indentured black slaves, for whom life was most precious bloodiest battle, initiated the war's bloodiest battle
- C. ***
- D. ***
- E. bloodiest battle was initiated on behalf of the indentured black slaves, for whom life was most precious

The correct answer is E. The original sentence suffers from two flaws. First, the relative pronoun *who* should be replaced with *whom*. (Replace the last clause with: *Life was most precious for them*. The pronoun *them* is an object-case pronoun, so the correct choice is *whom*.) Secondly, the word *those*, probably intended to refer to the slaves, should be deleted because it is unnecessary and because it confuses the meaning of the sentence. The comma following *those* should also be omitted. (E) corrects both flaws. (B) also corrects both flaws, but it radically alters the sentence's meaning, improperly suggesting that the slaves initiated the bloodiest battle (rather than properly communicating that it was on the slaves behalf that the battle was fought).

Error in Subject-Verb Agreement (Pronoun and Compound Subjects)

Determining whether a sentence's subject is singular or plural isn't always as simple as you might think. You can easily determine whether a personal pronoun such as *he*, *they*, and *its* is singular or plural. But other pronouns are not so easily identified as either singular or plural. Here are two lists, along with sample sentences, to help you keep these pronouns straight in your mind.

Singular pronouns:
anyone, anything, anybody
each
either, neither
every, everyone, everything, everybody
nobody, no one, nothing
what, whatever
who, whom, whoever, whomever

correct: *Every* possible cause *has* been investigated.

correct: *Each* one of the children here *speaks* fluent French.

correct: *Neither* of the pens *has* any ink remaining in *it*.

correct: *Whatever* he's doing is very effective.

correct: *Everything* she touches *turns* to gold.

Even when they refer to a "compound" subject joined by *and*, the pronouns listed above remain *singular*

correct: *Each adult and child* here *speaks* fluent French.

correct: *Every* possible *cause and suspect was* investigated.

Plural pronouns:
- both
- few
- many
- several
- some
- others

correct: *Few* would *argue* with that line of reasoning.

correct: *Many claim* to have encountered alien beings.

correct: *Some thrive* on commotion, while *others need* quiet.

It's especially easy to overlook a subject-verb agreement problem in a sentence involving a compound subject (multiple subjects joined by connectors such as the word *and* or the word *or*). If joined by *and*, a compound subject is usually plural (and takes a plural verb). But if joined by *or*, *either . . . or*, or *neither . . . nor*, compound subjects are usually singular.

plural: The chorus *and* the introduction *need* improvement.

singular: *Either* the chorus *or* the introduction *needs* improvement.

singular: *Neither* the chorus *nor* the introduction *needs* improvement.

But what if one subject is singular and another is plural? Which form should the verb take? Here's the rule: Look to see which subject is *nearer* to the verb; the verb should agree with that subject.

plural: Either the rhythm or the *lyrics need* improvement.

singular: Either the lyrics or the *rhythm needs* improvement.

In some cases, you can't tell whether a subject is singular or plural without looking at how it's used in the sentence. This is true of so-called *collective* nouns and nouns of *quantity*. These might call for either a singular verb or a plural verb, depending on whether the noun is used in a singular or plural sense.

> **correct:** Four years *is* too long to wait. (*four years* used in singular sense)
>
> **correct:** Four years can *pass* by quickly. (*four years* used in plural sense)
>
> **correct:** The majority *favors* the Republican candidate. (*majority* used in singular sense)
>
> **correct:** The majority of the voters here *favor* the Republican candidate. (*majority* used in plural sense)

Here's a GMAT-style sentence that contains a compound subject. The original version (A) is faulty, so your choice is between the two alternative versions listed here.

> Neither his financial patron or Copernicus himself were expecting the societal backlash resulting from him denouncing the Earth-centered Ptolemaic model of the universe.
>
> A. or Copernicus himself were expecting the societal backlash resulting from him
> B. ***
> C. nor Copernicus himself was expecting the societal backlash resulting from his
> D. nor Copernicus were expecting the societal backlash resulting from him
> E. ***

The correct answer is C. The original sentence actually contains three grammatical errors! First, *neither* should be paired with *nor* instead of *or*. Secondly, the singular verb *was* should be used instead of the plural *were* because *neither . . . nor* calls for a singular subject and because both parts of the subject (*patron* and *Copernicus*) are singular. Thirdly, the phrase *him denouncing* (which grammarians call a "noun clause") is improper; *denouncing* is a gerund (a verb turned into a noun by adding *-ing*), and gerunds always take possessive pronouns (*his*, in this case). (C) corrects all three errors without creating any new ones. (D) corrects the first error, but not the other two. Also, notice that (D) deletes *himself* from the original sentence. In doing so, (D) obscures the intended meaning of the sentence, which makes it clear, through the use of *himself*, that the word "his" (appearing twice in the sentence) refers to Copernicus rather than to someone else. So (D) creates a new error!

Problems Involving Tense, Voice, and Mood

You've arrived at what some grammarians would consider the inner sanction of Standard Written English: tense, voice, and mood. These three concepts are among the trickiest covered GMAT Sentence Correction. In this section, you'll focus on the following types of problems involving these three concepts (notice the similarities):

- Error in verb tense and shifting or mixing of tenses in a confusing manner
- Awkward use of either the active or passive voice; needlessly mixing the two voices
- Improper use of the subjunctive mood; needless mixing of the subjunctive mood and one of the tenses

Error in Verb Tense and Improper Tense Shifting and Mixing

Tense refers to how a verb's form indicates the *time frame* (past, present, or future) of the sentence's action. You won't need to know the names of the tenses for the GMAT, of course. But here they are anyway (all six of them), in case you're interested. Notice that we've used the singular form of the confusing verb *to have* in order to illustrate how verb form differs among different tenses. All of these sentences are correct.

simple present: He *has* enough money to buy a new car.

simple past: He *had* enough money after he was paid to by a new car.

simple future: He *will have* enough money after he is paid to buy a new car.

present perfect: He *has had* enough food but *has* continued to eat anyway.

past perfect: He *had had* enough food but *had* kept eating anyway.

future perfect: He *will have had* enough food once he *has* finished eating the dessert.

Chapter 10: Sentence Correction

With many verbs, the same form is used for all tenses, except that *-ed* is added for the past tenses—as in *walk*, *walked*. However, other verbs use distinctive forms for different tenses—as in *see, saw, seen*. Use your ear to determine whether the form sounds correct.

incorrect: The pilot seen the mountain but was flying too low to avoid a collision.

correct: The pilot *saw* the mountain but was flying too low to avoid a collision.

An incorrect sentence might needlessly *mix* tenses or *shift* tense from one time frame to another in a confusing manner.

incorrect: If it rains tomorrow, we cancel our plans.

correct: If it rains tomorrow, we *will cancel* our plans.

incorrect: When Bill arrived, Sal still did not begin to unload the truck.

correct: When Bill arrived, Sal still *had not begun* to unload the truck.

Our warning about mixing and shifting tenses also applies to the sentences like these:

incorrect: *To go* to war is *to have traveled* to hell.

correct: *To go* to war is *to go* to hell.

correct: *To have gone* to war is *to have traveled* to hell.

incorrect: *Seeing* the obstacle *would have allowed* him to alter his course.

correct: *Having seen* the obstacle *would have allowed* him to alter his course.

correct: *Seeing* the obstacle *would allow* him to alter his course.

> **Note:** By the way, verbs preceded by *to* (for example, *to go*) are called *infinitives*, and verbs turned into nouns by tacking an *-ing* the end (for example, *seeing*) are called *gerunds*. Of course, you don't need to know that for the GMAT.

Now look at how a tense-shift problem might appear in a GMAT-style sentence. The original version (A) is faulty, so your choice is between the two alternative versions listed here.

> Companies that <u>fail in their making cost-of-living adjustments of salaries of workers could not</u> attract or retain competent employees.

A. fail in their making cost-of-living adjustments of salaries of workers could not
B. ***
C. ***
D. will fail to adjust worker salaries to reflect cost-of-living changes can neither
E. fail to make cost-of-living adjustments in their workers' salaries cannot

The correct answer is E. The original sentence mixes present tense (*fail*) with past tense (*could not attract*). Also, the phrases *fail in their making* and *of salaries of workers* are awkward and unnecessarily wordy. (E) renders the sentence consistent in tense by replacing *could* with *can*. (E) is also more concise than the original sentence. (D) improperly mixes future tense (*will fail*) with present tense *can . . . retain*. (D) also uses *neither* to form the improper correlative pair *neither . . . or*. (The proper correlative pair is *neither . . . nor*.)

Inappropriate Use of the Passive Voice

In a sentence expressed in the *active voice*, the subject "acts upon" an object. Conversely, in a sentence expressed in the passive voice, the subject "is acted upon" by an object. The passive voice can sound a bit awkward, so the active voice is generally preferred.

> **passive (awkward):** The book was read by the student.
>
> **active (better):** The student read the book.
>
> **passive (awkward):** Repetitive tasks are performed tirelessly by computers.
>
> **active (better):** Computers perform repetitive tasks tirelessly.

Mixing the active and passive voices results in an even more awkward sentence.

> **mixed (awkward):** Although the house was built by Gary, Kevin built the garage.

Chapter 10: Sentence Correction

> **passive (less awkward):** Although the house was built by Gary, the garage was built by Kevin.
>
> **active (best):** Although Gary built the house, Kevin built the garage.

Although the active voice is usually less awkward than the passive voice, sometimes the passive voice is appropriate for emphasis or impact.

> **active (less effective):** Yesterday a car hit me.
>
> **passive (more effective):** Yesterday I was hit by a car.
>
> **passive (more effective):** Sunrise over the Tetons *is surpassed* in beauty only *by* the sun itself.
>
> **active (less effective):** Only the sun itself *surpasses* the Tetons in beauty.

> **Alert!**
>
> Keep in mind that the passive voice is *not* grammatically wrong. So don't eliminate an answer choice merely because it uses the passive voice. Check for grammatical errors among all five choices. If the one that uses the passive voice is the only one without a grammatical error, then it's the best choice.

Here's a GMAT-style sentence that focuses on the use of the passive voice. The original version (A) is faulty, so your choice is between the two alternative versions listed here.

> <u>It is actually a chemical in the brain that creates the sensation of eating enough, a chemical that is</u> depleted by consuming simple sugars.
>
> A. It is actually a chemical in the brain that creates the sensation of eating enough, a chemical that is
> B. ***
> C. The sensation of having eaten enough is actually created by a chemical in the brain that is
> D. A chemical actually creates the sensation in the brain of having eaten enough, and this chemical is
> E. ***

The correct answer is C. The original sentence isn't terrible, but it includes two flaws. First, the awkward *eating enough* should be replaced; *having eaten enough* is the proper idiom here. Both (C) and (D) correct this flaw. Second, notice that *a chemical* appears twice in the sentence. A more effective sentence would avoid repetition. Only (C) avoids repeating this phrase by reconstructing the first clause. In doing so, (C) admittedly uses the passive voice. Nevertheless, (C) is more concise and less awkward

415

overall than the original sentence. One more point about (D): It also creates a new problem. It separates *the sensation* from *of having eaten enough*, thereby creating an awkward and confusing clause. The phrase *in the brain* should be moved to either an earlier or later position in the sentence.

Error in Using the Subjunctive Mood

The *subjunctive mood* should be used to express a *wish* or a *contrary-to-fact* condition. These sentences should include words such as *if, had, were* and *should*.

incorrect: I wish it *was* earlier.

correct: I wish it *were* earlier.

incorrect: Suppose he speeds up suddenly.

correct: Suppose he *were* to speed up suddenly.

incorrect: If the college lowers its tuition, I would probably enroll.

correct: *Should* the college lower its tuition, I *would* probably enroll.

correct: *If* the college *were* to lower its tuition, I *would* probably enroll.

incorrect: *Had* he driven slower, he will recognize the landmarks from now on.

correct: *Had* he driven slower, he *would* recognize the landmarks from now on.

correct: *If* he *had* driven slower, he *would* recognize the landmarks from now on.

Tip

The subjunctive mood can be tricky because it uses its own idiomatic verb forms and because you can't always trust your ear when it comes to catching an error. Just remember: If the sentence uses a regular verb tense (past, present, future, etc.) to express a wish or contrary-to-fact condition, then it is grammatically incorrect, even if the subjunctive verb form is also used. Look, for example, at the *incorrect* sample sentences from above.

- I wish it *was* earlier. (*It was earlier* uses past tense.)
- Suppose he speeds up suddenly. (*He speeds up quickly* uses present tense.)
- If the college lowers its tuition, I would probably enroll. (The first clause uses present tense, while the second clause uses subjunctive form.)
- *Had* he driven slower, he will recognize the landmarks from now on. (The first clause uses subjunctive form, while the second clause uses future tense.)

The subjunctive mood is also used in clauses of recommendation, request, suggestion, or demand. These clauses should include the word *that*:

incorrect: Ann suggested we should go to the Chinese restaurant.

correct: Ann *suggested that* we go to the Chinese restaurant.

incorrect: I insist you be quiet.

correct: I *insist that* you be quiet.

incorrect: The supervisor preferred all workers wear uniforms from now on.

correct: The supervisor *preferred that* all workers wear uniforms from now on.

Now, look at a GMAT-style sentence designed to test you on the use of the subjunctive mood. The original version (A) is faulty, so your choice is between the two alternative versions listed here.

> The Environmental Protection Agency would be overburdened by its detection and enforcement duties <u>if it fully implemented all of its own regulations completely</u>.

- **A.** if it fully implemented all of its own regulations completely
- **B.** if it was to implement all of its own regulations completely
- **C.** were it to fully implement all of its own regulations
- **D.** ***
- **E.** ***

The correct answer is C. The original sentence poses two problems. First, the sentence clearly intends to express a hypothetical or contrary-to-fact situation; yet the underlined phrase does not use the subjunctive *were*. Secondly, *fully* and *completely* are redundant; one of them should be deleted. (C) corrects both problems without creating a new one. (B) corrects the redundancy problem by deleting *fully*. However, it incorrectly uses *was* instead of the subjunctive *were*.

Sentence Structure and Sense

Sentence structure refers to how a sentence's parts fit together as a whole. You know a sentence is poorly structured when its ideas are confusing, vague, ambiguous, or nonsensical—or even when its structure places undue emphasis (or de-emphasis) on certain ideas.

Problems involving sentence structure can be challenging to fix because there are no hard-and-fast rules of grammar to tell you what the best solution is. And since there are many acceptable ways to make any statement, the distinction between a highly effective structure and a less effective one can be subtle.

Here are the specific types of structural problems you'll examine in this section:

- Improper placement of modifiers
- Confusing pronoun references
- Dangling modifier errors
- Rhetorical imbalance between sentence parts
- Improper splitting of a grammatical unit
- Too many subordinate clauses in a row

Chapter 10: Sentence Correction

Improper Placement of Modifiers

A *modifier* is a word or phrase that describes, restricts, or qualifies another word or phrase. Modifying phrases are typically set off with commas, and many such phrases begin with a relative pronoun (*which*, *who*, *that*, *whose*, and *whom*). Modifiers should generally be placed as close as possible to the word(s) they modify. Positioning a modifier in the wrong place can result in a confusing or even nonsensical sentence.

> **misplaced:** His death shocked the entire family, which occurred quite suddenly.
>
> **better:** His death, which occurred quite suddenly, shocked the entire family.
>
> **misplaced:** *Nearly dead*, the police finally found the victim.
>
> **better:** The police finally found *the victim, who was nearly dead*.
>
> **unclear:** Bill punched Carl while wearing a mouth protector.
>
> **clear:** While wearing a mouth protector, Bill punched Carl.

Modifiers such as *almost*, *nearly*, *hardly*, *just* and *only* should immediately precede the word(s) they modify, even if the sentence sounds correct with the parts separated. For example:

> **misplaced:** Their one-year old child *almost* weighs *forty pounds*.
>
> **better:** Their one-year old child weighs *almost forty pounds*.

Note the position of *only* in the following sentences:

> **clear:** *Only the assistant* was able to detect obvious errors.
>
> **unclear:** The assistant was *only* able to detect obvious errors.
>
> **unclear:** The assistant was able to *only* detect *obvious errors*.
>
> **clear:** The assistant was able to detect *only obvious errors*.

Part IV: Verbal Ability

Now, look at a GMAT-style sentence that misplaces a modifier. The original version (A) is faulty, so your choice is between the two alternative versions listed here.

<u>Exercising contributes frequently to not only a sense of well being but also to longevity.</u>

- A. Exercising contributes frequently to not only a sense of well being but also to longevity.
- B. ***
- C. Exercising frequently contributes not only to a sense of well being but to longevity.
- D. ***
- E. Frequent exercise contributes not only to a sense of well being but also to longevity.

The correct answer is E. In the original sentence, *frequently* is probably intended to describe (or modify) *exercising* (frequent exercise). But separating these words makes it appear as though *frequently* describes *contributing*, which makes no sense in the overall context of the sentence. The original sentence also contains a "parallelism" error. The phrase after *not only* should parallel the phrase after *but also*, so that the two phrases can be interchanged and still make sense grammatically. But in the original sentence, the two phrases are not parallel. (E) corrects both problems. In (E), it is clear that what is "frequent" is *exercise* (rather than *contributing*). Also, the phrases following each part of the *not only . . . but also* pair are now parallel. (Notice that each phrase begins with *to*.) (C) fails to clear up the confusion as to whether *frequently* describes *exercising* or *contributes*. Also, (C) improperly uses *not only . . . but* instead of the proper idiom *not only . . . but also*.

> **Alert!**
>
> The general rule about placing modifiers near the words they modify applies *most* of the time. In some cases, however, trying to place a modifier near the words it modifies actually confuses the meaning of the sentence, as with the modifier *without his glasses* in the sentences below.
>
> **unclear:** Nathan can read the newspaper and *shave without his glasses*. (It is unclear whether *without his glasses* refers only to *shave* or to both *shave* and *read the newspaper*.)
>
> **unclear:** *Without his glasses*, Nathan can read the newspaper and can shave. (This sentence implies that these are the only two tasks Nathan can perform without his glasses.)
>
> **clear:** *Even without his glasses*, Nathan can read the newspaper and shave. It is important not to apply the modifier rule mechanically. Instead, check to see whether the sentence as a whole makes sense.

Confusing Pronoun Reference

A pronoun (e.g., *she*, *him*, *their*, *its*) is a "shorthand" way of referring to an identifiable noun—person(s), place(s) or thing(s). Nouns to which pronouns refer are called *antecedents*. Make sure every pronoun in a sentence has a clear antecedent!

unclear: Minutes before Kevin's meeting with Paul, *his* wife called with the bad news. (Whose wife called—Kevin's or Paul's?)

clear: *Kevin's* wife called with the bad news minutes before *his* meeting with Paul.

clear: Minutes before Kevin's meeting with Paul, *Kevin's* wife called with the bad news.

Pronoun reference errors are usually corrected in one of two ways:

1. By placing the noun and pronoun as near as possible to each other without other nouns coming between them (second sentence above)
2. By replacing the pronoun with its antecedent (third sentence above)

Also, look for the vague use of *it*, *you*, *that* or *one*—without clear reference to a particular antecedent.

vague: When one dives in without looking ahead, *you* never know what will happen. (Does *you* refer to the diver or to the broader *one*?)

clear: *One* never knows what will happen when *one* dives in without looking ahead.

clear: When *you* dive in without looking ahead, *you* never know what will happen.

vague: When the planets are out of alignment, *it* can be disastrous. (*It* does not refer to any noun.)

clear: Disaster can occur when the planets are out of alignment.

Part IV: Verbal Ability

The following GMAT-style sentence contains more than one confusing pronoun reference. The original version (A) is faulty, so your choice is between the two alternative versions listed here.

E-mail accounts administered by <u>an employer belong to them, and they can be seized and used</u> as evidence against the employee.

- A. an employer belongs to them, and they can be seized and used
- B. employers belong to them, who can seize and use it
- C. an employer belong to the employer, who can seize and use the accounts
- D. ✱✱✱
- E. ✱✱✱

The correct answer is C. There are two pronoun problems in the original sentence. First, *them* is used vaguely, without clear reference to *employers*, which seems to be the intended antecedent. Adding to this confusion is that the pronoun *them* is plural, yet its intended antecedent *employer* is singular. In addition, the antecedent of *they* is unclear because it is separated from its intended antecedent, *accounts*, by two other nouns (*them* and *employer*). (C) corrects the first problem by replacing the pronoun *them* with its (singular) antecedent *employer*. (C) also corrects the second problem by using *who*, which clearly refers to *employer*, since the two words appear immediately next to each other. (B) is riddled with problems! First, (B) does not correct the vague use of *them* (although the use of the plural *employers* is an improvement). Second, (B) leaves it unclear as to which noun *who* refers; presumably, *who* refers to *them*, yet the antecedent of *them* is uncertain. Thirdly, although the pronoun *it* is intended to refer to *accounts*, the reference is unclear because the pronoun and antecedent are separated by other nouns. Finally, the pronoun *it* is singular, yet its antecedent *accounts* is plural (they should both be either singular or plural).

> **Tip**
> When you see a pronoun in a GMAT sentence, ask yourself: "To what noun does this pronoun refer?" If the answer is the least bit unclear, you can rule out that version of the sentence as the best choice.

Chapter 10: Sentence Correction

Dangling Modifier Errors

A *dangling modifier* is a modifier that doesn't refer to any particular word(s) in the sentence. The best way to correct a dangling-modifier problem is to reconstruct the sentence.

> **dangling:** *Set by an arsonist*, firefighters were unable to save the burning building. (This sentence makes no reference to whatever was set by an arsonist.)
>
> **better:** Firefighters were unable to save the burning building from *the fire set by an arsonist*.

Despite the rule against dangling modifiers, certain dangling modifiers are acceptable because they're idiomatic.

> **acceptable:** *Judging* from the number of violent crimes committed every year, our nation is doomed. (Although the sentence makes no reference to whomever is judging, it is acceptable anyway.)
>
> **acceptable:** *Considering* that star's great distance from the earth, its brightness is amazing. (Although this sentence makes no reference to whomever is considering, it is acceptable anyway.)

> **Tip:** If you encounter a dangling modifier in a GMAT sentence that you've heard many times from well-educated people, then it's probably one of those idiomatic exceptions to the prohibition against dangling modifiers.

Now, look at a GMAT-style sentence that contains a dangling modifier. The original version (A) is faulty, so your choice is between the two alternative versions listed here.

<u>By imposing artificial restrictions in price on oil suppliers, these suppliers will be forced</u> to lower production costs.

- A. By imposing artificial restrictions in price on oil suppliers, these suppliers will be forced
- B. Imposing artificial price restrictions on oil suppliers will force these suppliers
- C. By imposing on oil suppliers artificial price restrictions, these suppliers will be forced
- D. ***
- E. ***

The correct answer is B. The original sentence includes a dangling modifier. The sentence makes no reference to whomever (or whatever) is imposing the price restrictions. (B) corrects the problem by reconstructing the sentence. (B) also improves on the original sentence by replacing *restrictions in price* with the more concise *price restrictions*. (C) does not correct the dangling modifier problem. Also, the grammatical construction of the first clause in (C) is awkward and confusing.

Rhetorical Imbalance Between Sentence Parts

An effective sentence gets its point across by placing appropriate emphasis on its different parts. If you're dealing with two equally important ideas, they should be separated as two distinct "main clauses," and they should be similar in length (to suggest equal importance).

unbalanced: Julie and Sandy were the first two volunteers for the fund-raising drive, *and* they are twins.

balanced: Julie and Sandy, *who* are twins, were the first two volunteers for the fund-raising drive.

commingled (confusing): Julie and Sandy, *who* are twins, are volunteers.

separated (balanced): Julie and Sandy are twins, *and* they are volunteers.

On the other hand, if you're dealing with only one main idea, be sure that it receives greater emphasis (as a main clause) than the other ideas in the sentence.

equal emphasis (confusing): Jose and Victor were identical twins, *and* they had completely different ambitions.

emphasis on second clause (better): *Although* Jose and Victor were identical twins, they had completely different ambitions.

Chapter 10: Sentence Correction

Here's a GMAT-style example of a rhetorically-challenged sentence. The original version (A) is faulty, so your choice is between the two alternative versions listed here.

<u>Treating bodily disorders by non-invasive methods is generally painless, and these methods</u> are less likely than those of conventional Western medicine to result in permanent healing.

A. Treating bodily disorders by non-invasive methods is generally painless, and these methods
B. Treating bodily disorders by non-invasive methods is generally painless, but they
C. ***
D. ***
E. Although treating bodily disorders by non-invasive methods is generally painless, these methods

The correct answer is E. Notice that the original sentence contains two main clauses, connected by *and*. Two problems should have occurred to you as you read the sentence: (1) the connector *and* is inappropriate to contrast differing methods of treatment (it fails to get the point across), and (2) the second clause expresses the more important point but does not receive greater emphasis than the first clause. (E) corrects both problems by transforming the first clause into a subordinate one and by eliminating the connecting word *and*. What about choice (B)? Replacing *and* with *but* is not as effective in shifting the emphasis to the second clause as the method used in (B). Moreover, by replacing *these methods* with *they*, (B) creates a pronoun-reference problem, making it unclear whether *they* refers to *disorders* or to *methods*.

Improper Splitting of a Grammatical Unit

Splitting clauses or phrases (by inserting another clause between them) often results in an awkward and confusing sentence.

split: The value of the dollar *is not*, relative to other currencies, *rising* universally.

better: The value of the dollar *is not rising* universally relative to other currencies.

split: The government's goal this year *is to provide* for its poorest residents *an economic safety net*.

split: *The government's goal* is to provide an economic safety net *this year* for its poorest residents.

better: The government's goal this year is to provide an economic safety net for its poorest residents.

In GMAT sentences, look closely for *split infinitives*. An infinitive is the plural form of an action verb, preceded by the word "to." If *to* is separated from its corresponding verb, then you're dealing with a "split infinitive" and the sentence is grammatically incorrect!

improper (split): The executive was compelled *to*, by greed and ambition, *work* more and more hours each day.

correct: The executive was compelled by greed and ambition, *to work* more and more hours each day.

improper (split): Meteorologists have been known *to* inaccurately *predict* snowstorms.

correct: Meteorologists have been known *to predict* snowstorms inaccurately.

Now, look at a GMAT-style sentence with a split personality. The original version (A) is faulty, so your choice is between the two alternative versions listed here.

<u>Typographer Lucian Bernhard was influenced, perhaps more so than any of his contemporaries, by Toulouse-Lautrec's emphasis on large, unharmonious lettering.</u>

- A. Typographer Lucian Bernhard was influenced, perhaps more so than any of his contemporaries, by Toulouse-Lautrec's emphasis on large, unharmonious lettering.
- B. Perhaps more so than any of his contemporaries, typographer Lucian Bernhard was influenced by Toulouse-Lautrec's emphasis on large, unharmonious lettering.
- C. ***
- D. ***
- E. Typographer Lucian Bernhard was influenced by Toulouse-Lautrec's emphasis on large, unharmonious lettering perhaps more so than any of his contemporaries.

The correct answer is B. The original sentence awkwardly splits the main clause with an intervening subordinate one (set off by commas). Both (B) and (E) keep the main clause intact. However, (E) creates a pronoun reference problem: It's unclear as to whom the pronoun *his* refers—Bernhard or Toulouse-Lautrec.

Chapter 10: Sentence Correction

> **Tip:** Whenever you see a clause set off by commas in the middle of the sentence, check the words immediately before and after the clause. If keeping those words together would sound better to your ear or would more effectively convey the sentence's main point, then the sentence (answer choice) is wrong, and you can safely eliminate it!

Too Many Subordinate Clauses in a Row

A *subordinate clause* is one that does not stand on its own as a complete sentence. Stringing together two or more subordinate clauses can result in an awkward and confusing sentence.

awkward: Barbara's academic major is history, *which* is a very popular course of study among liberal arts students, *who* are also contributing to the popularity of political science as a major.

better: Barbara's academic major is history, which along with political science, is a very popular course of study among liberal arts students.

Now, look at a GMAT-style sentence that suffers from this sort of error. The original version (A) is faulty, so your choice is between the two alternative versions listed here.

<u>By relying unduly on anecdotal evidence, which often conflicts with more reliable data, including data from direct observation and measurement, a scientist risks losing credibility among his or her peers.</u>

- A. By relying unduly on anecdotal evidence, which often conflicts with more reliable data, including data from direct observation and measurement, a scientist risks losing credibility among his or her peers.
- B. ***
- C. ***
- D. A scientist, by relying unduly on anecdotal evidence, which often conflicts with more reliable data, including data from direct observation and measurement, risks losing credibility among his or her peers.
- E. A scientist risks losing credibility among his or her peers by relying unduly on anecdotal evidence, which often conflicts with more reliable data, including data from direct observation and measurement.

The correct answer is E. The original sentence contains four clauses (separated by commas). The first three are all subordinate clauses! The result is that you are left in suspense as to who unduly relies on anecdotal evidence (first clause) until you reach the last (and main) clause. The solution is to rearrange the sentence to join the first and last clause, thereby minimizing the string of subordinate clauses and eliminating confusion. Choice (E) provides this solution. Choice (D) solves the problem only partially by moving only a section of the main clause (the scientist) to the beginning of the sentence. In fact, by doing so, (D) probably creates more confusion. Do you agree?

> *Subordination* of a dependent clause to a main clause can be achieved through the use of:
> - Words modifying relative pronouns: *which, who, that*
> - Words establishing time relationship: *before, after, as, since*
> - Words establishing a causal relationship: *because, since*
> - Words of admission or concession: *although, though, despite*
> - Words indicating place: *where, wherever*
> - Words of condition: *if, unless*

Chapter 11

Reading Comprehension

Welcome to GMAT Reading Comprehension. Here, you'll learn:

- The importance of reading GMAT passages "interactively"
- A step-by-step approach to handling Reading Comprehension questions
- Techniques for reading more effectively and efficiently
- Success keys for GMAT Reading Comprehension

X-Ref

The interactive reading techniques you'll learn here will help you handle any of the question types the test might deal you. Once you've mastered these techniques, move ahead to the Next Level to take a closer look at the test-maker's favorite question types and wrong-answer ploys.

*"Inter*active" Reading: The Key to Reading Comprehension

If you're like most GMAT test-takers, you'll experience at least one of the following problems as you tackle Reading Comprehension:

- Your concentration is poor—perhaps due to your lack of familiarity with or interest in the topic, or perhaps due to general test anxiety.
- Your reading pace is slow—so you have trouble finishing the Verbal section in time.
- To answer each question, you find yourself searching the passage again and again to find the information you need.
- You have trouble narrowing down the answer choices to one that's clearly the best.

Believe it or not, all of these problems are due to the same bad habit: *passive reading*, by which you simply read the passage from start to finish, giving equal time and attention to every sentence without thought as to what particular information might be key in answering the questions. You might call this approach the "osmosis strategy," since you're hoping to absorb what you need to know by simply allowing your eyes to glaze over the words.

What's the likely result of this osmosis strategy? You might remember some scattered facts and ideas, which will help you respond correctly to some easier questions. But the passive mind set won't take you very far when it comes to most of the questions, which measure your ability to *understand* the ideas in the passage rather than to simply *recall* information. Understanding a passage well enough to answer all the questions requires a highly *active* frame of mind—one in which you constantly *interact* with the text as you read, asking yourself questions such as these:

- What's the passage's main idea (or "thesis") and the author's overall concern or purpose?
- What does each part of the passage relate to the main idea and author's overall purpose?
- What's the author's line of reasoning, or so-called "train of thought"?

Interactive reading is the key to handling GMAT Reading Comprehension, and that's what this chapter is primarily about!

> **Alert!**
>
> Don't except to just walk into the GMAT testing room and apply the techniques you'll learn about here without practicing them first. You'll need to try them out first, during your GMAT practice testing, until you become comfortable with them.

Chapter 11: Reading Comprehension

Reading Comprehension—Your 7-Step Game Plan

The first task in this chapter is to learn the seven basic steps for handling a GMAT Reading Comprehension passage and question set. You'll apply these steps to the following sample passage and three questions:

> **Note**
>
> Passage lines are always numbered as shown here because questions occasionally refer to portions of the passage by line number.

Passage 1

Line   The encounter that a portrait records is most tangibly the sitting itself, which may be brief or extended, collegial or confrontational. Renowned photographer Cartier-Bresson has expressed his passion for portrait photography by characteriz-
(5)   ing it as "a duel without rules, a delicate rape." Such metaphors contrast quite sharply with Richard Avedon's conception of a sitting. While Cartier-Bresson reveals himself as an interloper and opportunist, Avedon confesses—perhaps uncomfortably—to a role as diagnostician and (by implication)
(10)   psychic healer: not as someone who necessarily transforms his subjects, but as someone who reveals their essential nature. Both photographers, however, agree that the fundamental dynamic in this process lies squarely in the hands of the artist.
    A quite-different paradigm has its roots not in confronta-
(15)   tion or consultation but in active collaboration between the artist and sitter. This very different kind of relationship was formulated most vividly by William Hazlitt in his essay entitled "On Sitting for One's Picture" (1823). To Hazlitt, the "bond of connection" between painter and sitter is most like the
(20)   relationship between two lovers. Hazlitt fleshes out his thesis by recalling the career of Sir Joshua Reynolds. According to Hazlitt, Reynold's sitters were meant to enjoy an atmosphere that was both comfortable for them and conducive to the enterprise of the portrait painter, who was simultaneously their
(25)   host and their contractual employee.

1. The author of the passage quotes Cartier-Bresson (line 5) in order to
   A. refute Avedon's conception of a portrait sitting.
   B. provide one perspective of the portraiture encounter.
   C. support the claim that portrait sittings are, more often than not, confrontational encounters.
   D. show that a portraiture encounter can be either brief or extended.
   E. distinguish a sitting for a photographic portrait from a sitting for a painted portrait

2. Which of the following characterizations of the portraiture experience as viewed by Avedon is most readily inferable from the passage?
   A. A collaboration
   B. A mutual accommodation
   C. A confrontation
   D. An uncomfortable encounter
   E. A consultation

3. Which of the following best expresses the passage's main idea?
   A. The success of a portrait depends largely on the relationship between artist and subject.
   B. Portraits, more than most other art forms, provide insight into the artist's social relationships.
   C. The social aspect of portraiture sitting plays an important part in the sitting's outcome.
   D. Photographers and painters differ in their views regarding their role in portrait photography.
   E. The paintings of Reynolds provide a record of his success in achieving a social bond with his subjects.

Step 1: Read the first question (including the answer choices), *before* you begin reading the passage. Try to anticipate what the passage is about and what sort of information you should be on the lookout for in order to answer the first question.

Step 2: Begin reading the passage, actively thinking about a possible thesis (main idea) and how the author attempts to support that thesis. Also, begin your reading with an eye for information useful in answering the first question.

Step 3: When you think you've learned enough to take a stab at the first question, go ahead and choose a *tentative* answer. You probably won't have to read very far to at least take a reasoned guess at the first question. But don't confirm your selection yet!

Step 4: Read the remainder of the passage, formulating an outline as you go. As you read, try to (1) separate main ideas from supporting ideas and examples; (2) determine the basic structure of the passage (e.g., chronology of events, classification of ideas or things, comparison between two or more ideas, events, or things); and (3) determine the author's opinion or position on the subject. Make notes on your scratch paper as needed to see the flow of the passage and to keep the passage's details straight in your mind.

Step 5: Sum up the passage; formulate a brief thesis (main idea) statement. Take a few seconds to review your outline. Then, in your own words, express the author's main point—in one sentence. Jot it down on your scratch paper. Your thesis statement should reflect the author's opinion or position (e.g., critical, supportive, neutral) toward the ideas presented in the passage.

Step 6: Confirm your selection for the first question. Eliminate any answer choice that is inconsistent with your thesis statement, that doesn't respond to the question, or that doesn't make sense to you.

Step 7: Move on to the remaining question(s), considering *all* of the answer choices for each question.

> **X-Ref**
>
> If you advance to the Next Level, you'll learn some tips to help you tackle different question types and to zero in on the best answer choices.

Now let's walk through Passage 1 (involving portraiture) and the sample questions about it, using this 7-step approach.

Step 1: The first question tells you a lot about what you might expect in the passage. In all likelihood, the passage will be primarily about the portraiture experience. The author will probably provide different viewpoints and insights on this experience from the perspective of particular artists.

Step 2: The first four sentences (lines 1–11) reinforce your initial prediction about the passage's content. Based on these initial lines, it appears that the author will indeed be comparing and contrasting different views of the portraiture experience. At this point you don't know whether the passage will involve the views of any artists other than Cartier-Bresson

Part IV: Verbal Ability

and Richard Avedon, nor do you know whether the author has any opinion on the subject. But you should be on the lookout for answers to these unknowns during Step 4.

Step 3: Consider question 1 based on what you've read so far. The author points out in lines 4–9 that Cartier-Bresson's conception is quite different from that of Avedon. Choices (A), (B), and (C) all appear to be viable choices, at least based on lines 4–9. But whether the author's purpose here is to *refute* Avedon's view (choice (A)), *support* Cartier-Bresson's view (choice (C)), or simply *provide* one of at least two perspectives without taking sides (choice (B)) remains to be seen. You'll have to read on to find out. In any event, you can probably eliminate (D) and (E), since neither one seems relevant to the Cartier-Bresson quotation. Don't confirm a selection yet; go on to Step 4.

Step 4: Your goal in Step 4 is to formulate an informal outline of the passage as you read from start to finish. You might want to jot down some key words and phrases to help you see how the ideas flow and to keep the four individuals discussed in the passage straight in your mind. Here's a good outline of the passage:

Paragraph 1

Contrast:

— CB: confrontation (rape)

— Avedon: diagnosis (consultation)

— BUT agree artist is key

Paragraph 2

3rd view: Hazlitt (writer)

— collaboration (like lovers)

— e.g. Reynolds

Tip

Make outlines and summaries as brief as possible. Don't write complete sentences; rather, just jot down key words.

Step 5: Now let's sum up the passage based on the outline you formulated in Step 4. It's a good idea to jot it down. Notice that the "thesis" is neutral; the author does not side with any viewpoint presented in the passage.

> *Thesis: Portraiture is a social experience, but artists disagree about their role in it.*

Step 6: Having read the entire passage, return to the question. Nowhere in the passage does the author attempt to either refute or support any of the viewpoints presented. So you can eliminate (A) and (C). Accordingly, (B) provides the best answer to the question. Notice also that (B) is consistent with our thesis statement. Regardless of the particular question, you can eliminate any answer choice that is inconsistent with your thesis statement.

Step 7: Move ahead to questions 2 and 3. In the following analysis, notice the qualitative difference (from best to worst) among the answer choices.

> **X-Ref**
>
> Also, note how we've labeled (in italics) what's wrong with some of the wrong-answer choices; you'll learn more about these and other wrong-answer ploys if you advance to the Next Level.

Question 2: The correct answer is E. In the first sentence of the second paragraph, the author distinguishes a "quite-different paradigm" (that is, the case of Reynolds) from the conceptions of Cartier-Bresson and Avedon in that the Reynolds paradigm "has its roots not in confrontation or consultation but in active collaboration between artist and sitter." The third sentence of the passage makes clear that Cartier-Bresson conceives the encounter as "confrontational"; thus, you can *reasonably infer* that the author characterizes an Avedon sitting as a "consultation."

Choice (B) is also a good response but nevertheless not as good as (E). Although the term "mutual accommodation," which does not appear in the passage, is not altogether inconsistent with Avedon's view, the term suggests a relationship in which both artist and painter allow for the other's needs or desires. Such a description is closer to Hazlitt's analogy of two lovers than to Avedon's view of the artist as diagnostician and psychic healer.

Choice (A) also has merit, yet it is not as good a response as either (B) or (E). Admittedly, the idea of "a collaboration" is not in strong opposition to the idea of "a consultation." However, the author explicitly ascribes this characterization to the Reynolds paradigm, not to Avedon's view. Thus, (A) *confuses the passage's information*.

Choices (C) and (D) are qualitatively the worst choices among the five. (C) *confuses the passage's information*. The quotation in the first paragraph makes it clear that Cartier-Bresson (not Avedon) conceives the encounter as "confrontational." (D) also *confuses the passage's information*. According to the passage, Avedon confesses "uncomfortably" to his role as diagnostician and psychic healer. It does not necessarily follow, however, that Avedon finds his encounters with his sitters to be uncomfortable.

Question 3: The correct answer is (C). Although this passage doesn't seem to convey a strong central idea or thesis, the author seems to be most concerned with emphasizing that a portrait sitting is a social encounter, not just an artistic exercise, and that artists consider their relationship with their sitters to be somehow significant. For this reason, (C) is a good statement of the author's main point.

Choice (A) also has merit. In fact, but for (C), (A) would be the best choice because it embraces the passage as a whole and properly focuses on the author's primary concern with exploring the relationship between artist and sitter. However, the passage does not discuss how or whether this relationship results in a "successful" portrait; thus, (A) *distorts the passage's information*.

Choice (D) has merit in that the author does claim that the Reynolds paradigm (described in the second paragraph) is "quite different" from the two paradigms that the first paragraph discusses. The latter does indeed involve a painter (Reynolds) whereas the other two paradigms involve photographers (Cartier-Bresson and Avedon). However, the author does not generalize from this fact that a portrait artist's approach or view depends on whether the artist is a painter or a photographer. Thus, (D) is a bit *off focus* and calls for an *unwarranted generalization*.

Choices (B) and (E) are qualitatively the worst among the five choices. (B) *distorts* the information in the passage and departs from the topic at hand. Although the passage does support the notion that a portrait might reveal something about the relationship between artist and sitter, the author neither states nor implies that a portrait reveals anything about the artist's other relationships. Moreover, nowhere in the passage does the author compare portraiture with other art forms.

Choice (E) is *too narrow* and refers to information *not mentioned* in the passage. The passage is not just about Reynolds, but about the portraiture encounter in general. Also, the author does not comment on Reynold's "success" or about how his relationship with his sitters might have contributed to his success.

Chapter 11: Reading Comprehension

Techniques for Interactive Reading

During Step 4 of the 7-step approach you just learned, you read the passage and formulated an outline that revealed its basic structure and how its ideas flowed from one to the next. In this section, we'll focus more closely on this step, which lies at the heart of GMAT Reading Comprehension.

Think of any GMAT reading passage as a structure of ideas. Each passage is designed to convey a number of ideas that are connected to one another in some way. If you understand these ideas *and* the connections between them, then you truly understand the passage as a whole. Focusing on structure helps you in several ways:

- It makes it easy to see the "big picture"—what the passage is about as a whole.
- It tells you the purpose of the supporting details—even when you don't know what those details are.
- The logical structure organizes all the information in the passage, making it easy to locate any detail to which a particular question might refer.
- The structure explains how the author's main points are related to one another.

It's no coincidence that the preceding list covers just about all you'll need to know to answer any of the questions the test might deal you!

Focus on the Passage's Logical Structure

Although GMAT passages don't invariably have clear-cut, logical structures, a structure of some kind is almost always present. Here's a list of the most common types of logical structures found in GMAT passages. Either alone or in combination, these structures underlie most of the passages you'll encounter on the exam.

- A theory or idea illustrated by two (or more) detailed examples or illustrations or supported by two (or more) arguments (the passage might also critique the theory based on the examples or arguments)
- Two (or more) alternative theories, each of which seek to explain a certain phenomenon (the passage might also argue for one theory over another)
- Pro and con arguments presented for both sides of a single issue

- A comparison and/or contrast between two (or more) events, ideas, phenomena, or people
- A cause-and-effect sequence showing how one event led to another (presented either in chronological order or via "flashback," with later events described *before* earlier ones)
- Two or three basic types, categories, or classes of a phenomenon identified and distinguished, beginning with main classes, and then possibly branching out to subclasses (this structure is most common in passages involving the natural sciences)

> **Tip**
>
> Each of the structures listed here scream out for paragraph breaks—to turn from one theory, reason, example, or class to another, or to separate pros from cons or similarities from differences. But don't assume a passage's structure will reveal itself so neatly. In fact, a passage with a complex structure might contain only one paragraph! The moral: Use paragraph breaks as structural clues, but don't rely on them as crutches.

Now let's look at a couple of examples. Here's the passage about portraiture that you read earlier in this chapter. This time, key portions are underlined to help you see its structure. Notice how nicely it fits into the comparison-contrast structural pattern.

Passage 1 (comparison and contrast)

Line   The encounter that a portrait records is most tangibly the
        sitting itself, which may be brief or extended, collegial or
        confrontational. Renowned photographer Cartier-Bresson has
        expressed his passion for portrait photography by characteriz-
(5)   ing it as "a duel without rules, a delicate rape." Such meta-
        phors contrast quite sharply with Richard Avedon's conception
        of a sitting. While Cartier-Bresson reveals himself as an
        interloper and opportunist, Avedon confesses—perhaps
        uncomfortably—to a role as diagnostician and (by implication)
(10)   psychic healer: not as someone who necessarily transforms his
        subjects, but as someone who reveals their essential nature.
        Both photographers, however, agree that the fundamental
        dynamic in this process lies squarely in the hands of the artist.
            A quite-different paradigm has its roots not in confronta-
(15)   tion or consultation but in active collaboration between the
        artist and sitter. This very different kind of relationship was
        formulated most vividly by William Hazlitt in his essay entitled
        "On Sitting for One's Picture" (1823). To Hazlitt, the "bond
        of connection" between painter and sitter is most like the

(20) relationship between two lovers. Hazlitt fleshes out his thesis by recalling the career of Sir Joshua Reynolds. <u>According to Hazlitt, Reynold's sitters</u> were meant to enjoy an atmosphere that was both comfortable for them and conducive to the enterprise of the portrait painter, who was simultaneously their
(25) host and their contractual employee.

Here's a new passage. This one has a typical cause-and-effect structure. Again, some key phrases are underlined to help reveal the structure.

Passage 2 (cause-and-effect sequence)

Line Scientists in the post-1917 Soviet Union occupied an ambiguous position—while the government encouraged and generally supported scientific research, it simultaneously thwarted the scientific community's ideal: freedom from geographic and
(5) political boundaries. A strong nationalistic <u>emphasis on science led at times to</u> the dismissal of all non-Russian scientific work as irrelevant to Soviet science. A 1973 article in *Literatunaya Gazeta*, a Soviet publication, insisted: "World science is based upon national schools, so the weakening of
(10) one or another national school inevitably leads to stagnation in the development of world science." According to the Soviet regime, socialist science was to be consistent with, and in fact grow out of, the Marxism-Leninism political ideology. <u>Toward this end</u>, some scientific theories or fields, such as relativity
(15) and genetics, were abolished. Where scientific work conflicted with political criteria, the work was often disrupted. <u>During the Stalinist purges</u> of the 1930s, many Soviet scientists simply disappeared. <u>In the 1970s</u>, Soviet scientists who were part of the refusenik movement lost their jobs and were barred from
(20) access to scientific resources. Nazi Germany during the 1930s and, more recently, Argentina imposed strikingly similar, though briefer, constraints on scientific research.

Although the structure of passage 2 is not quite as obvious as that of passage 1, the structure is nevertheless there, lying just beneath the details. Notice that the passage's opening describes the *cause* (Russia's insular political ideology), while the rest of the passage lists the *effects* (non-Russian work was deemed irrelevant, certain theories and fields were abolished, scientific work was disrupted, and scientists disappeared). The final two sentences (beginning with "in the 1970s") is a postscript that simply notes two similar cause-and-effect relationships in modern history.

Look for Structural Clues, or "Triggers"

"Triggers" are key words and phrases that provide clues to the structure and organization of the passage and the direction in which the discussion is flowing. The lists below contain many common trigger words and phrases. Be on the lookout for trigger words as you read the passage. They'll help you see the structure of the passage and follow the author's train of thought.

These words precede an item in a list (e.g., examples, classes, reasons, or characteristics):

- first, second, etc.
- in addition, also, another

These words signal that the author is contrasting two phenomena:

- alternatively, by contrast, however, on the other hand, rather than, while, yet

These words signal a logical conclusion based upon preceding material:

- consequently, in conclusion, then, thus, therefore, as a result, accordingly

These words signal that the author is comparing (identifying similarities between) two phenomena:

- similarly, in the same way, analogous, parallel, likewise, just as, also, as

These words signal evidence (factual information) used to support the author's argument:

- because, since, in light of

These words signal an example of a phenomenon:

- for instance, e.g., such as, . . . is an illustration of

> **Note**
>
> Obviously, it's not possible to circle or underline key words, or to otherwise annotate passages on the CAT computer screen as you could on the old paper-based GMAT. To help make up for this fact, the GMAT test-makers shortened the length of Reading passages by about half when they switched to computerized testing (under the theory that a briefer passage is easier to assimilate without annotating it).

The Art of Note-Taking and Outlining

As you're reading, make shorthand notes to summarize paragraphs or to indicate the flow of the passage's discussion. Notes can also help you locate details more quickly and recap the passage more effectively. Keep your notes as brief as possible—two or three words are enough in most cases to indicate a particular idea or component of the passage. For complicated or high-density passages, an outline is a good way to organize information and to keep particular details straight in your mind. The following situations are ideal for outlining:

1. If the passage categorizes or classifies various things, use an outline to help you keep track of which belong in each category.

2. If the passage mentions numerous individual names (e.g., of authors, artists, political figures, etc.), use notes to link them according to influence, agreement or disagreement, and so forth.

3. If the passage describes a sequence of events, use a time-line outline to keep track of the major features of each event in the sequence.

4. In chronological passages, mark historical benchmarks and divisions—centuries, years, decades, or historical periods—that help form the structure of the author's discussion.

5. Use arrows to physically connect words that signify ideas that link together; for example:

    - To clarify cause and effect in the natural sciences or in the context of historical events
    - To indicate who was influenced by whom in literature, music, psychology, etc.
    - To connect names (philosophers, scientists, authors, etc.) with dates, events, other names, theories, or schools of thought, works, etc.
    - To indicate the chronological order in which historical events occurred

To Preview . . . or Not to Preview

Many GMAT prep books recommend that, before reading a passage straight through from beginning to end, you *preview* the passage by reading the first (and perhaps the last) sentence of each paragraph. This technique supposedly provides clues about the scope of the passage, the author's thesis or major conclusions, and the structure and flow of the discussion. Although these techniques make sense *in theory*, there are several reasons why *in practice* they are rarely helpful on the GMAT:

- Once immersed in the passage itself, you'll quickly forget most if not all of what you learned from previewing.
- These techniques call for you to read the same material twice. Does that sound efficient to you?
- Previewing takes time—time that you might not be able to afford under timed testing conditions.
- Previewing involves rapid vertical scrolling, which adds to eye strain.
- While reading the beginning and end of each paragraph may be helpful for some passages, for others this technique will be of little or no help—and there's no way to know whether you're wasting your time until you've already wasted it.

> **Tip**
> The only situation in which you should preview is if you're running out of time. Some questions, especially the ones that refer to particular line numbers, you can answer quickly by reading just one paragraph—or perhaps just a few sentences. And a quick scan of the first and last few sentences of the passage *might* provide clues about the passage's main idea or primary purpose—so you can at least take educated guesses at some questions.

Success Keys for Reading Comprehension

We've covered a lot of ground in this chapter. To help you assimilate it all, here's a checklist of the salient, and sage, points of advice for improving your reading efficiency and comprehension as you read GMAT passages. Apply them to Part V's practice tests, and then review them again, just before exam day.

Take Notes and (for some passages) Make Outlines

As you're reading, make shorthand notes to summarize paragraphs or to indicate the flow of the passage's discussion. Keep your notes brief—just enough key words to remind you of the particular idea. For complicated or high-density passages, an outline is a good way to organize information and to keep particular details straight in your mind.

Pause Occasionally to Sum Up ad Anticipate

After you read each logical "block" (perhaps after each paragraph), pause a moment to evaluate the paragraph as a whole. Try to recapitulate or summarize the paragraph as two or three basic ideas. After each paragraph, answer the following questions for yourself:

- How would I sum up the discussion to this point?
- At what point is the discussion now?
- What basic points is the author trying to get across in this paragraph? Do these ideas continue a line of thought, or do they begin a new one?
- Where is the discussion likely to go from here?

Pay Attention to the Overall Structure of the Passage

Different types of reading passages are organized in various ways. The passage might be organized as a chronology of events, a critique of a theory, a comparison of two or more things, or a classification system. Understanding how the passage is organized—in other words, recognizing its structure—will help you articulate the passage's main idea and primary purpose, to understand the author's purpose in mentioning various details, and to distinguish between main points and minor details—all of which in turn will help you answer the questions.

Look for Structural Clues, or "Triggers"

Be on the lookout for trigger words as you read the passage. They'll help you see the passage's structure and following the author's train of thought.

Don't Get Bogged Down in Details

GMAT reading passages are packed with details: lists, statistics and other numbers, dates, titles, and so forth. If you try to absorb all of the details as you read, you'll not only lose sight of the main points but also lose reading speed. Don't get bogged down in the details; gloss over them. On your scratch paper, note where particular examples, lists, and other details are located. Then, if a particular question involving those details is included, you can quickly and easily locate them and read them more carefully.

Sum Up the Passage After You Read It

After reading the entire passage, take a few seconds to recap it. What was the author's main point and what were the major supporting points? Remind yourself about the flow of the discussion without thinking about all the details. Chances are you'll be able to answer at least one or two of the questions based just on your recap.

Don't Bother Previewing, Unless You're Short on Time

So-called "previewing" (skimming a passage or reading just the first and last few sentences of the passage) *might* allow you to make educated guesses and to answer certain detail questions. But use this strategy only if you're running out of time on the testing clock.

Try to Minimize Vertical Scrolling

You'll need to scroll to read the entire passage. But scrolling in order to re-read the passage uses up valuable time, as well as creating eye strain and fatigue. The best way to minimize rereading (and scrolling) is to take good notes.

Take It to the Next Level

Welcome to the Next Level of GMAT Reading Comprehension. Here, you'll:

- Learn how to recognize and handle the four basic, and most common, types of Reading Comprehension questions
- Learn how to recognize and handle the less common types of Reading Comprehension questions

What's New at the Next Level

Here at the Next Level, you'll focus on answering the questions rather than on reading and understanding the passages. First, you'll learn how to recognize and handle the four most common question types:

- Simple recall
- Recap
- Restatement
- Inference

To round out the chapter, you'll learn how to identify and deal with three other types of reading questions that occasionally appear on the GMAT (although far less frequently than the preceding ones):

- Application
- Logical continuation
- Method

For each of the seven question types, you'll learn how the test-makers design wrong-answer choices—and how to recognize them when you see them.

Part IV: Verbal Ability

> **Note:** Since you're at the Next Level, don't expect to encounter easy reading or "gimmee" questions in this chapter.

Sample Reading Passages

Most of the sample questions you'll analyze in this chapter are based on the following two passages. Go ahead and read both passages now. Also, earmark this page, since you'll refer back to it throughout the chapter.

Passage 1

Line   The arrival of a non-indigenous plant or animal species in a new location may be either intentional or unintentional. Rates of species movement driven by human transformations of natural environments as well as by human mobility—through
(5)   commerce, tourism, and travel—dwarf natural rates by comparison. While geographic distributions of species naturally expand or contract over historical time intervals (tens to hundreds of years), species' ranges rarely expand thousands of miles or across physical barriers such as oceans or mountains.
(10)   A number of factors confound quantitative evaluation of the relative importance of various entry pathways. Time lags often occur between establishment of non-indigenous species and their detection, and tracing the pathway for a long-established species is difficult. Experts estimate that non-
(15)   indigenous weeds are usually detected only after having been in the country for thirty years or having spread to at least ten thousand acres. In addition, federal port inspection, although a major source of information on non-indigenous species pathways, especially for agricultural pests, provides data only
(20)   when such species enter via scrutinized routes. Finally, some comparisons between pathways defy quantitative analysis—for example, which is more "important": the entry pathway of one very harmful species or one by which many but less harmful species enter the country?

Passage 2

Line   Scientists have long claimed that, in order to flourish and progress, their discipline requires freedom from ideological and geographic boundaries, including the freedom to share new scientific knowledge with scientists throughout the world. In

(5) the twentieth century, however, increasingly close links between science and national life undermined these ideals. Although the connection facilitated large and expensive projects, such as the particle-accelerator program, that would have been difficult to fund through private sources, it also
(10) channeled the direction of scientific research increasingly toward national security (military defense).

For example, scientists in the post-1917 Soviet Union found themselves in an ambiguous position. While the government encouraged and generally supported scientific
(15) research, it simultaneously imposed significant restrictions on science and scientists. A strong nationalistic emphasis on science led at times to the dismissal of all non-Russian scientific work as irrelevant to Soviet science. A 1973 article in *Literatunaya Gazeta*, a Soviet publication, insisted: "World
(20) science is based upon national schools, so the weakening of one or another national school inevitably leads to stagnation in the development of world science." According to the Soviet regime, socialist science was to be consistent with, and in fact grow out of, the Marxism-Leninist political ideology. Toward
(25) this end, some scientific theories or fields, such as relativity and genetics, were abolished. Where scientific work conflicted with political criteria, the work was often disrupted. During the Stalinist purges of the 1930s, many Soviet scientists simply disappeared. In the 1970s, Soviet scientists who were part of
(30) the refusenik movement lost their jobs and were barred from access to scientific resources. Nazi Germany during the 1930's and, more recently, Argentina, imposed strikingly similar, though briefer, constraints on scientific research.

Simple Recall Questions

For these questions, your job is to identify which answer choice provides information that appears in the passage and that the question asks about. The question stem might look something like one of these:

"Which of the following does the author mention as an example of . . . ?"

"According to the passage, . . . is caused by . . . ?"

This is the most common question type, and it's the easiest type because all that's required to handle it is to either remember or find the appropriate information in the passage.

Here's a good example, based on passage 1 (page 446):

> According to the passage, the rate at which plant or animal species move naturally across land
>
> A. might depend on the prevalence of animals that feed on the species.
> B. is hindered by federal port inspectors.
> C. is often slower than the rate at which they move across water.
> D. is slower than human-assisted rates.
> E. varies according to the size of the species.

The correct answer is D. Only the first paragraph talks about the rate of species movement, so it's there you'll find the answer to this question. In lines 3–6, the author states that rates of species movement driven by human transformations and mobility "dwarf natural rates by comparison." In other words, natural rates are slower than human-assisted rates, just as (D) provides.

Choice (A) might be true in the "real world," but the passage mentions nothing about predators, let alone about their affect on movement rates. So you can easily eliminate it.

Choice (B) confuses the passage's details. It refers to information in the second paragraph, which discusses problems in determining entry pathways. This paragraph has nothing to do with the rate of species movement. Also, did you notice that (B) is a bit nonsensical? How could port inspectors, who are located where ocean meets land, affect the rate at which a species moves *naturally* across land?

Choice (C) involves relevant information from the passage, but distorts that information. The last sentence in the first paragraph indicates that oceans and mountains are barriers that typically prevent species movement. But (C) implies that mountains pose a greater barrier than oceans. Nowhere in the passage does the author seek to compare rates across land with rates across water.

Choice (E) is completely unsupported by the passage, which never mentions the size of a species in any context.

Chapter 11: Reading Comprehension

> **Tip**
>
> In handling a Simple Recall question, don't expect the correct answer choice to quote the passage verbatim. That's generally not how the test-makers write them. Instead, they prefer to paraphrase what's in the passage. In the preceding question, for instance, the precise phrase "human-assisted movement" doesn't appear in the passage, does it? But that's no reason to eliminate (D), which turns out to be the correct answer choice.

Notice the types of wrong-answer ploys built into the preceding question:

- Bringing in *irrelevant details* from elsewhere in the passage
- *Distorting* what the passage says
- Bringing in *outside information* (not found anywhere in the passage)
- Providing a *nonsensical* response to the question at hand

These are the wrong-answer ploys you should always look for in a Simple Recall question.

To complicate a Simple Recall question, the test-makers might turn the question around by asking you to identify an exception to what the passage provides (with a word such as "except" or "least" in upper-case letters).

"The author mentions all of the following as examples of . . . EXCEPT:"
"According to the passage, . . . could be caused by any of the following EXCEPT:"

To handle this variation, eliminate all choices that the passage covers and that are relevant to the question, and you'll be left with one choice—the correct one. The following question, based on passage 1 (page 446)—is a typical example. Although this question is about as tough a Simple Recall question as you'll find on the GMAT, you'll probably agree that it's pretty easy. Here it is again, along with an explanatory answer:

Whether the entry pathway for a particular non-indigenous species can be determined is LEAST likely to depend upon which of the following?

A. Whether the species is considered to be a pest
B. Whether the species gains entry through a scrutinized route
C. The rate at which the species expands geographically
D. How long the species has been established
E. The size of the average member of the species

The correct answer is E. Nowhere in the passage does the author state or imply that the physical size of a species' members affects whether the entry pathway for the species can be determined.

You can easily eliminate choices (B), (C), and (D). All three are mentioned explicitly in the second paragraph as factors affecting how precisely the entry pathway(s) of a species can be determined.

Choice (A) is a bit trickier, and it's the runner-up choice. Unlike the other incorrect choices, (A) is not *explicitly* supported by the passage. However, the author mentions in the final paragraph that federal port inspection is "a major source of information on non-indigenous species pathways, especially for agricultural pests." Accordingly, whether a species is an agricultural pest might have some bearing upon whether or not its entry is detected (by port inspectors). Hence choice (A) is not as good as choice (E), which finds no support in the passage whatsoever.

> **Alert!** In a tougher Simple Recall question, one wrong-answer choice will be more tempting than the others because the passage will *implicitly* support it. Don't be fooled; you *will* find a better choice among the five.

Recap Questions

For these questions, your job is to recognize either the main idea, or thesis, of the passage (or a particular paragraph) *as a whole*, or the author's primary purpose or concern in the passage (or in a particular paragraph) *as a whole*. In other words, you job is to *recap* what the passage or paragraph is about. The question stem will look like one of these:

"Which of the following best expresses the main idea of the passage?"

"Among the following characterization, the passage is best viewed as"

"Which of the following would be the most appropriate title of the passage?"

"The author's primary purpose in the passage [or "*in the third paragraph*"] is to"

"The passage [or "*in the first paragraph*"] is primary concerned with"

To handle this question type, you'll need to recognize the passage's (or paragraph's) overall scope and main emphasis. Most of the wrong-answer choices will fall into these categories:

- Too broad (embracing ideas outside the scope of the passage or paragraph)

- Too narrow (focusing on only a certain portion or aspect of the discussion)
- Distorted (an inaccurate reflection of the passage's ideas or the author's perspective on the topic)

To complicate a Recap question, the test-makers might include a runner-up answer choice that's just a bit off the mark. Here's a moderately difficult Recap question that illustrates this tactic, along with an explanatory answer:

The author's primary purpose in the passage is to

A. examine the events leading up to the suppression of the Soviet refusenik movement of the 1970s.
B. define and dispel the notion of a national science as promulgated by the post-revolution Soviet regime.
C. describe specific attempts by the modern Soviet regime to suppress scientific freedom.
D. examine the major twentieth-century challenges to the normative assumption that science requires freedom and that it is inherently international.
E. point out the similarities and distinctions between scientific freedom and scientific internationalism in the context of the Soviet Union.

The correct answer is C. Notice that, with the exception of the very last sentence, the passage is entirely concerned with describing Soviet attempts to suppress scientific freedom. In the order mentioned, the attempts include thwarting science's ideals, emphasizing a national science, controlling scientific literature, and threatening and punishing renegade scientists. Choice (C) aptly expresses this overall concern.

Choice (D) is the runner-up. Admittedly, the passage does mention, in the final sentence, two other twentieth-century attempts to suppress scientific freedom. Had the passage continued by describing these two other attempts, (D) would probably have been the best answer choice. But since it doesn't, (D) is a bit *too broad*.

Choice (A) *distorts* the author's primary purpose. The author does not actually discuss any specific events that might have caused the suppression of the refusenik movement; rather, this historical phenomenon is mentioned simply as another example of the Soviet regime's long-term pattern of suppression.

Choice (B) *distorts* the author's perspective on the topic. Although the author does define the concept of national science, nowhere does the author attempt to dispel or disprove the concept.

Choice (E) *distorts* the author's message and is *too narrow*. Although the author does imply that scientific freedom and scientific internationalism are related, the author makes no attempt to examine their differences. What's more, the author's broader concern is quite different than to examine the relationship between these two types of scientific freedoms.

Now here's a Recap question that focuses on just one paragraph, the second one. An easier question would provide wrong-answer choices that refer to information in the *first* paragraph. But this question is a bit tougher; it doesn't allow you such an easy way to rule out wrong choices.

The second paragraph (lines 10–24) as a whole is concerned with

- **A.** identifying the problems in assessing the relative significance of various entry pathways for non-indigenous species.
- **B.** describing the events usually leading to the detection of a non-indigenous species.
- **C.** discussing the role that time lags and geographic expansion of non-indigenous species play in species detection.
- **D.** pointing out the inadequacy of the federal port inspection system in detecting the entry of non-indigenous species.
- **E.** explaining why it is difficult to trace the entry pathways for long-established non-indigenous species

The correct answer is A. In the first sentence of the second paragraph, the author claims that "[a] number of factors confound quantitative evaluation of the relative importance of various entry pathways." In the remainder of the paragraph, the author identifies three such problems: (1) the difficulty of early detection, (2) the inadequacy of port inspection, and (3) the inherent subjectivity in determining the "importance" of a pathway. Choice (A) provides a good "recap" of what the second paragraph accomplishes.

Choice (B) is *too narrow*. Although the author does mention that a species is usually not detected until it spreads to at least ten-thousand acres, the author mentions this single "event" leading to detection as part of the broader point that the unlikelihood of early detection contributes to the problem of quantifying the relative importance of entry pathways.

Choice (C) is a *distortion*. Although the author mentions these factors, they are not "discussed" in any detail, as (C) suggests. Also, the primary concern of the second paragraph is not with identifying the factors affecting species detection, but rather with identifying the problems in quantifying the relative importance of various entry pathways.

Choice (D) is *too narrow*. The author is concerned with identifying other problems as well as in determining the relative importance of various entry pathways.

Choice (E) is a *distortion*. Although the author asserts that it is difficult to trace an entry pathway once a species is well established, the author does not explain why this is so.

> **Tip**
>
> The best answer to a Recap question must embrace the whole passage (or paragraph) better than any other choice—while not extending beyond the passage's scope or concerns. Look for at least one answer choice that is too narrow, and at least one other that is too broad.

Restatement Questions

In handling a Restatement question, your job is to understand a specific idea the author is trying to convey in the passage. These questions are different than Simple Recall questions in that you won't find the answer explicitly in the text. And it's this feature that makes them more difficult. A Restatement question stem might look something like one of the following:

"Which of the following statements about . . . is most strongly supported by the passage's information?"

"With which of the following statements about . . . would the author most likely agree?"

"Which of the following best characterizes . . . as viewed by . . . ?"

Here's a good example of a moderately difficult Restatement question, based on passage 1 (page 446). Notice that the wrong-answer choices are designed to confuse you by combining details from the passage that relate to the question but that don't add up. Here's the question again, along with an explanatory answer:

Which of the following statements about species movement is best supported by the passage?

  A. Species movement is affected more by habitat modifications than by human mobility.
  B. Human-driven factors affect the rate at which species move more than they affect the long-term amount of such movements.
  C. Natural expansions in the geographic distribution of species account for less species movement than natural contractions do.
  D. Natural environments created by commerce, tourism, and travel contribute significantly to species movement.
  E. Movement of a species within a continent depends largely upon the geographic extent of human mobility within the continent.

The correct answer is E. This choice restates the author's point in the first paragraph that rates of species, movement driven by human transformation of the natural environment and by human mobility, dwarf natural rates by comparison (lines 3–6).

Choice (A) is the most tempting wrong-answer choice. Based on the passage, habitat modifications and human mobility can both affect species movement, as (A) implies. And the passage does make a comparison involving human-driven species movement. So (A) looks appealing. However, the comparison made in the passage is between natural species movement and human-driven movement, not between human modification of habitats and human mobility. So (A) *confuses the details* of the passage.

Choice (B) is easier to eliminate because it is completely *unsupported* by the passage, which makes no attempt to compare rate (interpreted either as frequency or speed) of species movement to total amounts of movement (distance).

Choice (C) is also easier to eliminate than (A). It is completely *unsupported* by the passage. The author makes no attempt to compare natural expansions to natural contractions.

Chapter 11: Reading Comprehension

Choice (D) is the easiest one to eliminate. You don't even need to read the passage to recognize that (D) is a *nonsensical* statement. Human mobility (commerce, tourism, and travel) do not create "natural" environments. It is human mobility itself, not the "natural environment" created by it, that contributes significantly to species movement.

> **Tip**
>
> In Reading Comprehension questions, many answer choices simply won't make sense, as with the nonsensical choice (D) in the preceding question. Don't be fooled into second-guessing yourself just because you don't understand what the answer choice means.

Here's a good example of how the test-makers might further boost the difficulty level of a Restatement question. As you read this question, which is based on passage 2 (page 446), notice that most of the wrong answer choices appear to respond to the question because they describe an "ambiguous position." What's more, most of the answer choices contain information that the passage supports. The use of these two wrong-answer ploys makes this question tougher than average.

> Which of the following best characterizes the "ambiguous position" (line 13) in which Soviet scientists were placed during the decades that followed the Bolshevik Revolution?
>
> **A.** The Soviet government demanded that their research result in scientific progress, although funding was insufficient to accomplish this goal.
> **B.** They were exhorted to strive toward scientific advancements, while at the same time the freedoms necessary to make such advancements were restricted.
> **C.** While they were required to direct research entirely toward military defense, most advancements in this field were being made by non-Soviet scientists with whom the Soviet scientists were prohibited contact.
> **D.** They were encouraged to collaborate with Soviet colleagues but were prohibited from any discourse with scientists from other countries.
> **E.** The Soviet government failed to identify those areas of research that it deemed most worthwhile, but punished those scientists with whose work it was not satisfied.

The correct answer is B. According to the passage, the ambiguous position of Soviet scientists was that the Soviet government encouraged and generally supported scientific research, while at the same time imposed significant restrictions upon its scientists (lines 13–16). Choice (B) restates this idea.

Choice (C) is the easiest one to eliminate. (C) is wholly *unsupported* by the passage, which neither states nor suggests either assertion made in (C), which in any case does not describe an ambiguous situation.

Choice (A) is *unsupported* by the passage. The author neither states nor suggests that the Soviets lacked sufficient funding. Although if true, (B) would indicate an ambiguous position for scientists, although that ambiguity is not the kind referred to in the passage.

Choice (E) is also *unsupported*. Although some Soviet scientists were indeed punished by the government, the author neither states nor implies that the government failed to identify those areas of research that it deemed most worthwhile. If true, (E) would indicate an ambiguous position for scientists; but as with choice (A), the ambiguity described in (E) is not the sort referred to in the passage.

Choice (D) is the most tempting wrong-answer choice. It's a better choice than either (A) or (E) because the passage supports it, at least implicitly. What's more, (D), if true, would present an ambiguous position for Soviet scientists. However, as with choices (A) and (E), the ambiguity that (D) describes doesn't reflect the nature of the ambiguity referred to in the passage.

> Don't panic when you come across a lengthy question or lengthy answer choices, as in the preceding question. Although more reading usually makes for a tougher question, don't assume you're up against as difficult a question as the preceding one. Otherwise, you might give up too soon on what turns out to be an easier question!

Alert!

Inference Questions

Inference questions test your ability to recognize what the author implies, or infers, but does not state explicitly—in other words, you are tested on your ability to "read between the lines." To make the inference, you'll need to see a logical connection between two bits of information in the passage (usually in two consecutive sentences) and draw a reasonable conclusion from them.

Chapter 11: Reading Comprehension

X-Ref — Inference questions resemble Critical Reading questions in that to answer them, you need to distinguish a reasonable, well-supported conclusion from unreasonable, poorly supported ones. But don't expect them to look exactly the same or require the same level of inferential reasoning as Critical Reading questions.

Look for two basic types of Inference questions on the GMAT. One type focuses just on the passage's ideas. Your job is to infer a specific idea from what's stated. The question stem will probably contain some form of the word "infer," as in these two examples:

"It can be inferred from the passage that the reason for . . . is that . . ."

"The discussion about . . . most reasonably infers which of the following?"

A second type of Inference question asks you to infer the *author's purpose* in mentioning a specific idea. Look for a question stem like one of these:

"The author mentions . . . (lines X-X) most probably in order to"

"The example discussed in lines X-X is probably intended to illustrate"

In designing either type of Inference question, the test-makers will often include a runner-up answer choice in which the inference is a bit more *speculative* than the inference in the best choice. Both of the following questions, based on passage 2 (page 446) incorporate this wrong-answer ploy.

Which of the following is most reasonably inferable from the passage's first paragraph (lines 1–11)?

- A. Expensive research projects such as the particle-accelerator program apply technology that can also be applied toward projects relating to national security.
- B. Scientific knowledge had become so closely linked with national security that it could no longer be communicated to scientific colleagues without restriction.
- C. Without free access to new scientific knowledge, scientists in different countries are less able to communicate with one another.
- D. Governments should de-emphasize scientific projects related to military defense and emphasize instead research that can be shared freely within the international scientific community.
- E. Government funding of scientific research undermines the ideal of scientific freedom to a greater extent than private funding.

Take It to the Next Level

The correct answer is B. The first two sentences establish that the link between science and national life undermined scientists' freedom to communicate with other scientists. The next sentence points to the channeling of scientific research toward protecting national security as a manifestation of that link. Notice the almost unavoidable inference here—that national security concerns were part of the "national life" that took precedence over scientific freedoms.

Choice (E) is the runner up. An argument can be made from the information in the first paragraph that government-funded research is more likely than privately-funded research to relate to matters affecting the national security (i.e., military defense). However, this inference is hardly as unavoidable as the one that (B) provides, is it? To compete with (B), the inference would need additional supporting evidence.

Choice (A) is unsupported. The author implies no connection between the particle-accelerator program and national security.

Choice (C) is nonsensical. Ready access to new scientific knowledge would require ready communication among scientists—not the other way around.

Choice (D) is unsupported. The author neither states nor suggests which areas of scientific research should be emphasized.

> The author quotes an article from *Literatunaya Gazeta* (lines 19–22) most probably in order to
>
> A. illustrate the general sentiment among members of the international scientific community during the time period.
> B. support the point that only those notions about science that conformed to the Marxist-Leninist ideal were sanctioned by the Soviet government.
> C. show the disparity of views within the Soviet intellectual community regarding the proper role of science.
> D. underscore the Soviet emphasis on the notion of a national science.
> E. support the author's assertion that the Marxist-Leninist impact on Soviet scientific freedom continued through the decade of the 1970s.

The correct answer is D. This part of the passage is concerned exclusively with pointing out evidence of the Soviet emphasis on a national science; given the content of the excerpt from *Literatunaya Gazeta*, you can *reasonably infer* that the author is quoting this article as one such piece of evidence.

Choice (A) is easy to rule out because it *distorts* the nature of the quoted article and runs *contrary* to the passage. The article illustrates the official Soviet position and possibly the sentiment among some members of the Soviet intellectual or scientific community. However, the article does not necessarily reflect the views of scientists from other countries.

Choice (C) is not likely to be the author's purpose in quoting the article, because the author does not discuss disagreement and debate among Soviet intellectuals.

Choice (E) is a bit tempting because it might in fact be true and because it is indeed supported by the information in the passage. But the author gives no indication as to when the article was written or published; thus, the article itself lends no support to (E).

Choice (B) is the runner-up choice that helps make this question tougher than it would be otherwise. The quoted article does indeed reflect the Marxist-Leninist ideal (at least as interpreted and promulgated by the government) and may in fact have been published only because it was sanctioned (approved) by the Soviet government. However, since this conclusion would require *speculation*, and since the quoted excerpt makes no mention of government approval or disapproval of certain scientific notions, it is not likely that (B) expresses the author's purpose in quoting the article.

> **Tip**
>
> When handling Inference questions, you need to know the difference between a reasonable inference, which no rational person could dispute based on the passage's information, and mere speculation, which requires additional information to hold water.

Method Questions

Method questions ask you to recognize *how* the author goes about making his points—rather than focusing on the points themselves. Some Method questions ask for the author's overall approach in the passage, while others ask about how a specific point is made or about the structure of a particular paragraph. In Method questions, the answer choices are usually stated very generally, and it's up to you to connect the general wording of the choices with what's going on in the passage.

A Method question can appear in many different forms. Here are just a few examples of what the question stem might look like:

"Which of the following best describes the approach of the passage?"

"In the last paragraph (lines X-X), the author proceeds by"

Part IV: Verbal Ability

"How does the second paragraph function in relation to the first paragraph?"

"Which of the following most accurately describes the organization of the second paragraph (lines X-X)?"

"Which of the following techniques is used in the second paragraph (lines X-X)?"

When you see a Method question, first let the question guide you to the appropriate area of the passage. Your notes or outline might suffice to determine how the author proceeds in making her points there. If not, reread that section carefully. Focus on what the author is doing; don't get bogged down in details. Again, Method questions concern how the author makes points, not what those points are.

Here's the last paragraph of a passage about Francis Bacon, a sixteenth-century philosopher of science. (As a whole, the passage explores the link between his thinking and the modern-day scientific establishment.) Read the paragraph, then answer the Method question based on it.

> Line No one questions the immense benefits already conferred by science's efficient methodology. However, since individual scientists must now choose between improving standards of living and obtaining financial support for their research, there
> (5) is cause for concern. In light of current circumstances, we must ask certain questions about science that Francis Bacon, from a sixteenth-century perspective, could not possibly have put to himself.

Which of the following most accurately describes the technique that the author employs in the last paragraph of the passage?

- A. An assertion is made and is backed up by evidence.
- B. A viewpoint is expressed and an opposing viewpoint is stated and countered.
- C. An admission is offered and is followed by a warning and recommendation.
- D. Contradictory claims are presented and then reconciled.
- E. A problem is outlined and a solution is proposed and defended.

The correct answer is C. The notion that no one questions the benefits of science does qualify as an admission in the context of the paragraph; that is, the author admits that science has given mankind enormous benefits. The author then goes on to voice his concern regarding the current state of the scientific enterprise. Note how the contrast signal word "however" flags us that some kind of change must come after the author admits that science has conferred immense benefits. Indeed, what comes next is, as (C) puts it, a warning: there is cause for concern. A recommendation appears in the final sentence, highlighted by the words "we must ask certain questions. . . ." Every element in (C) is present and accounted for, so (C) aptly describes the technique used in the paragraph.

Choice (A) indicates that the paragraph begins with an assertion, and we can surely accept that: the assertion that no one questions the benefits of science. Is this then backed up by evidence? No. The contrast signal word "however" tells us that some kind of change is coming, but does not provide evidence for the statement in the first sentence. And indeed, the paragraph does go in a different direction.

Choice (B) doesn't reflect what's going on in the paragraph. (B) claims that the final paragraph begins with a viewpoint, which it does. But does an opposing viewpoint follow—that is, an argument against the benefits of science? No; instead, concern is expressed about the way science is now conducted.

Choice (D) is incorrect because there are no contradictory claims here. The author admits that science has given humankind enormous benefits, but then goes on to voice his concern regarding the current state of the scientific enterprise. These things aren't contradictory, and nothing in the paragraph reconciles them, so (D) can't be the best choice.

As for (E), it's fair to say that a problem is outlined. (The problem is that securing financial support for scientific work might get in the way of scientists improving standards of living.) But does the author propose a solution? No. He recommends that serious questions be asked about the problem, but offers no solution of his own. Besides, the passage ends before any kind of defense of his recommendation is offered.

Part IV: Verbal Ability

Application Questions

These questions, which require you to apply the author's ideas to new situations, usually involve relatively broad inferences. You might be asked to interpret how the author's ideas apply to, or are affected by, other situations. To do this requires you to make logical connections between the author's stated ideas and other ideas not explicitly discussed in the passage. Or, you might be asked to assess the author's attitude (agreement or disagreement) toward some new situation.

Application questions often add or refer to new information, so there's no predictable question stem to look for. But, the stem might look something like one of these three:

"If it were determined that _____, what effect would this fact have on the author's assessment of _____ as presented in the passage?"

"Which of the following new discoveries, if it were to occur, would most strongly support the author's theory about _____ ?"

"Which of the following is most analogous to the situation of _____ described in the passage?"

In dealing with Application questions:

- Be on the lookout for wrong-answer choices that require you to make an inference not supported by the passage.

- Eliminate answer choices that contradict the author's main idea or position.

- Eliminate answer choices that distort the passage's ideas.

Here's another brief excerpt from a passage about Francis Bacon (the sixteenth-century philosopher of science), along with an Application question based on the excerpt.

Line   Francis Bacon contributed to the scientific enterprise a prophetic understanding of how science would one day be put to use in the service of technology and how this symbiotic relationship between the two would radically impact both man
(5)   and his surroundings. As inseparable as they are today, it is hard to imagine science and technology as inhabiting separate domains.

As discussed in the passage, the relationship between science and technology is best illustrated by which of the following scenarios?

- A. A biologist writes an article documenting a new strain of influenza that is subsequently published and taught in medical schools around the world
- B. A breakthrough in the field of psychology enables psychoanalysts to diagnose patients with greater accuracy
- C. An engineering firm hires a public relations agency to advertise the benefits of a labor-saving mechanical device
- D. A physics discovery leads to the development of a machine that helps researchers view previously uncharted areas of the ocean floor
- E. The development of a new software application that helps research scientists isolate genes that are responsible for certain diseases

The correct answer is D. If you're not sure what "symbiotic" means, you can figure it out by its context. We're told that science is used to help develop and contribute to technology, and that technology also contributes to science. So we need to find the choice that illustrates the same sort of link. (D) fits the bill: A scientific discovery in one area (physics) leads to the invention of a technology (a machine) that helps scientists in another field (oceanography) make new discoveries. The interplay between science and technology in this example is a good application of the author's description of "symbiotic relationship."

Nether (A) nor (B) account for technology; they involve only science. Since there's nothing in either choice about the interplay between science and technology, neither is as good a choice as (D).

As for (C), if there's a symbiotic relationship at work at all in (C), it's between technology (a new mechanical device) and marketing. There's nothing about science here, so this choice doesn't illustrate the interplay between science and technology.

Choice (E) is the runner-up choice. It illustrates how science (genetic research) can benefit from technology (a computer application). But it does not illustrate the reverse relationship—how technology can also benefit from science. So (E) does not illustrate as completely as (D) the symbiotic relationship the author describes.

Logical Continuation Questions

In this question type, the test-maker gauges your ability to determine the flow of the discussion and anticipate where it will go beyond the end of the passage—were the passage to continue. A Logical Continuation question stem might look something like one of the following:

"Which of the following would be the most logical continuation of the passage?"

"The author would probably continue the discussion by"

To answer a question of this type, it helps to have a general outline of the passage so that you know how it flows and therefore how it would continue to flow. However, just the final few sentences probably provide enough information for you to eliminate some of the wrong-answer choices—and possibly even zero-in on the best choice.

In dealing with Logical Continuation questions:

- Focus on the operative word (probably the first word) in each answer choice. This can help you narrow down the choices.

- Be on the lookout for wrong-answer choices that rehash what's already been covered in the passage. Although the discussion is unlikely to reverse course, don't automatically rule out this possibility.

Here's the final paragraph of a passage about the geography of a South American mountain range. Based only on this paragraph, you can narrow down the choices—and probably even hone-in on the best one!

Line   At the regional or macroscale level, vegetation patterns in the Northern and Central Andes tend to reflect climatic zones determined by latitude and altitude. At the local or mesoscale, however, this correspondence becomes less precise, as local
(5)   variations in soil type, slope, drainage, climate, and human intervention come into play.

Chapter 11: Reading Comprehension

Among the following, the passage would most logically continue by

A. describing the climate and topography of the portions of the Andean cordillera other than the Northern and Central regions.
B. discussing how high- and low-pressure systems affect the climate of the Amazon.
C. exploring how proximity to the equator affects vegetation in the Andean cordillera.
D. identifying problems in determining the relation between soil type and vegetation in the Andean cordillera.
E. examining the effects of vegetation patterns on the topography of the Andean cordillera.

The correct answer is C. In the final paragraph, the author asserts that altitude as well as latitude (proximity to the equator) determine climatic zones as reflected by vegetation patterns. Accordingly, a more detailed discussion about why different forms of vegetation appear at different latitudes is a logical continuation.

Choice (D) is the runner-up choice; it's consistent with the content of the final paragraph, and the author does suggest a relationship between soil type and vegetation (presumably, soil type determines what forms of vegetation will thrive). However, the paragraph neither indicates nor suggests any potential problems in determining such a relationship.

Choices (A) and (B) both ignore the direction of the final paragraph.

Choice (E) appears at first glance to be a viable answer because it includes the same subject matter (i.e., vegetation) as the final paragraph. However, (E) is a bit nonsensical—it is unlikely that vegetation would have much effect upon topography; even if it did, nothing in the final paragraph indicates that this is the direction in which the discussion is likely to turn.

Alert!

In handling a Logical Continuation question, the passage's final few sentences are sure to help you narrow down the answer choices. But, by all means, don't ignore the rest of the passage! Check your notes or outline for the flow of ideas from the passage's beginning to its end. The best answer choice should go with the overall flow.

The Test-Makers' Top 10 Wrong-Answer Ploys

If you read the analysis of each sample question in this chapter carefully, you learned a lot about how the test-makers design wrong-answer choices. Now here's a review of the types they resort to most often:

1. **The response distorts the information in the passage.** It might understate, overstate, or twist the passage's information or the author's point in presenting that information.

2. **The response uses information from the passage, but does not answer the question.** The information cited from the passage isn't useful to respond to the question at hand.

3. **The response relies on speculation or an unsupported inference.** It calls for some measure of speculation in that the statement is not readily inferable from the information given.

4. **The response is contrary to what the passage says.** It contradicts the passage's information or runs contrary to what the passage infers.

5. **The response gets something in the passage backwards.** It reverses the logic of an idea in the passage, confuses cause with effect, or otherwise turns information in the passage around.

6. **The response confuses one opinion or position with another.** It incorrectly represents the viewpoint of one person (or group) as that of another.

7. **The response is too narrow or specific.** It focuses on particular information in the passage that is too specific or narrowly focused in terms of the question posed.

8. **The response is too broad (general).** It embraces information or ideas that are too general or widely focused in terms of the question posed.

9. **The response relies on information that the passage does not mention.** It brings in information not found anywhere in the passage.

10. **The response is utter nonsense.** It makes almost no logical sense in the context of the question; it's essentially gibberish.

Success Keys for Answering Reading Comprehension Questions

Here's a checklist of tips for answering Reading Comprehension questions. Some of these tips reiterate suggestions made earlier in this chapter—suggestions that are worth underscoring—while others are new here. Apply these points of advice to Part V's practice tests, and then review them again, just before exam day.

Don't Second-Guess the Test-Maker

The directions for the GMAT Reading Comprehension sets instruct you to choose the "best" among the five answer choices. Isn't this awfully subjective? True, there is an element of subjective judgment involved in reading comprehension. However, these questions are reviewed, tested, and revised several times before they appear as scored questions on an actual GMAT. If you think there are two or more viable "best" choices, *you* (not the test-maker) have either misread or misinterpreted the passage, the question, or the answer choices.

Read Each and Every Answer Choice in its Entirety

As you know, you're looking for the "best" answer choice. Often, more than one choice will be viable. Don't hastily select or eliminate answer choices without reading them all. *GMAT test-takers miss more questions for this reason than for any other!*

> **X-Ref**
> If you read the beginning of this chapter, you already know that you should never confirm your selection for any question until you've read the entire passage—even if the first few questions seem clearly to involve the initial portion of the passage. It's always possible that information relevant to these questions will appear at the end of the passage.

Don't Over-Analyze Questions or Second-Guess Yourself

If you believe you understood the passage fairly well, but a particular answer choice seems confusing or a bit nonsensical, do not assume that it's your fault. Many wrong-answer choices simply don't make much sense. If an answer choice strikes you this way, don't examine it further; eliminate it. Similarly, if you've read and considered all five choices, and one strikes you as the best one, *more often than not, your initial hunch will be correct.*

Don't Overlook the Obvious
Reading Comprehension questions vary in difficulty level, and this means that many of the questions are rather easy. If a particular choice seems obviously correct or incorrect, don't assume that you are missing something. You might simply have come across a relatively easy question.

Eliminate Answer Choices that Run Contrary to the Main Idea
Regardless of the type of question you are dealing with, keep in mind the overall thesis, main idea, or point that the author is making in the passage as a whole. Any answer choice to any question that runs contrary to or is inconsistent with that thesis can be eliminated. You may be surprised how many questions can be answered correctly using only this guideline.

Be Alert to the Test-Makers' Favorite Wrong-Answer Ploys
Keep a mental list of the wrong-answer types or ploys you learned about in this chapter. When you have trouble narrowing down the answer choices, review this list in your mind, and the remaining wrong answers should reveal themselves.

PART V

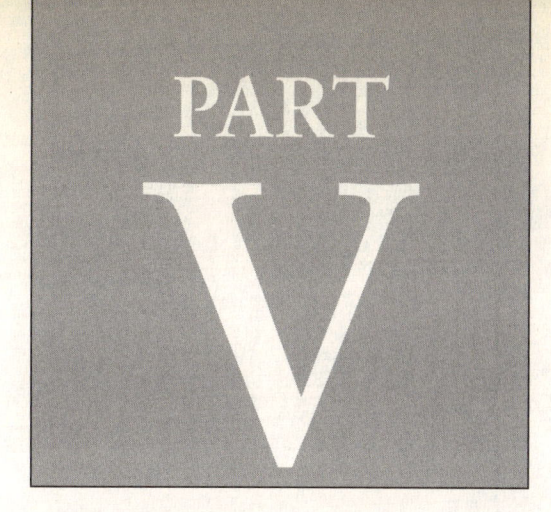

Three Practice Tests

Practice Test 1   *470*

Answers and Explanations   *497*

Practice Test 2   *512*

Answers and Explanations   *537*

Practice Test 3   *553*

Answers and Explanations   *577*

Practice Test 1

Analysis of an Issue

1 Question—30 Minutes

Directions: Using a word processor, compose a response to the following statement and directive. Do not use any spell-checking or grammar-checking functions.

> "As adults we prefer to define ourselves more by our occupation than by our affiliation with social groups."

In your view, how accurate is the foregoing statement? Use reasons and/or examples from your experience, observation, and/or reading to explain your viewpoint.

Analysis of an Argument

1 Question—30 Minutes

Directions: Using a word processor, compose an essay for the following argument and directive. Do not use any spell-checking or grammar-checking functions.

The following appeared as part of an article in a national business publication:

> "Workforce Systems, a consulting firm specializing in workplace productivity and efficiency, reports that nearly seventy percent of Maxtech's employees who enrolled in Workforce Systems' one-week seminar last year claim to be more content with their current jobs than prior to enrolling in the seminar. By requiring managers at all large corporations to enroll in the kinds of seminars that Workforce System offers, productivity in our economy's private sector is certain to improve."

Discuss how well reasoned you find this argument. In your discussion, be sure to analyze the line of reasoning and the use of evidence in the argument. For example, you may need to consider what questionable assumptions underlie the thinking and what alternative explanations or counterexamples might weaken the conclusion. You can also discuss what sort of evidence would strengthen or refute the argument, what changes in the argument would make it more logically sound, and what, if anything, would help you better evaluate its conclusion.

Quantitatiave Ability

37 Questions—75 Minutes

Directions for Problem Solving Questions: *(These directions will appear on your screen before your first Problem Solving question.)*

Solve this problem and indicate the best of the answer choices given.

<u>Numbers</u>: All numbers used are real numbers.

<u>Figures</u>: A figure accompanying a Problem Solving question is intended to provide information useful in solving the problem. Figures are drawn as accurately as possible EXCEPT when it is stated in a specific problem that its figure is not drawn to scale. Straight lines may sometimes appear jagged. All figures lie on a plane unless otherwise indicated.

To review these directions for subsequent questions of this type, click on HELP.

Directions for Data Sufficiency Questions: *(These directions will appear on your screen before your first Data Sufficiency question.)*

This Data Sufficiency problem consists of a question and two statement, labeled (1) and (2), in which certain data are given. You have to decide whether the data given in the statements are *sufficient* for answering the question. Using the data given in the statements *plus* your knowledge of mathematics and everyday facts (such as the number of days in July or the meaning of *counterclockwise*), you must indicate whether:

Statement (1) ALONE is sufficient, but statement (2) alone is not sufficient to answer the question asked;

Statement (2) ALONE is sufficient, but statement (1) alone is not sufficient to answer the question asked;

BOTH statements (1) and (2) TOGETHER are sufficient to answer the question asked; but NEITHER statement ALONE is sufficient;

EACH statement ALONE is sufficient to answer the question asked;

Statements (1) and (2) TOGETHER are NOT sufficient to answer the question asked, and additional data specific to the problem are needed.

Numbers: All numbers used are real numbers.

Figures: A figure accompanying a Data Sufficiency problem will conform to the information given in the question, but will not necessarily conform to the additional information in statements (1) and (2).

Lines shown as straight can be assumed to be straight and lines that appear jagged can also be assumed to be straight.

You may assume that positions of points, angles, regions, etc., exist in the order shown and that angle measures are greater than zero.

All figures lie in a plane unless otherwise indicated.

Note: In Data Sufficiency problems that ask you for the value of a quantity, the data given in the statements are sufficient only when it is possible to determine exactly one numerical value for the quantity.

To review these directions for subsequent questions of this type, click on HELP.

> **Note**
>
> Although the questions in this section cover all difficulty levels, you'll find fewer easy questions than challenging ones. Keep in mind that the GMAT CAT will determine the difficulty level of each question based on your responses to prior questions.

1. $4\frac{1}{2} + 3\frac{3}{4} - 2\frac{2}{5} =$

   A. $\frac{29}{5}$

   B. $\frac{23}{4}$

   C. $\frac{117}{20}$

   D. $\frac{231}{40}$

   E. $\frac{57}{10}$

2. Lyle's current age is 23 years, and Melanie's current age is 15 years. How many years ago was Lyle's age twice Melanie's age?

   A. 5
   B. 7
   C. 8
   D. 9
   E. 16

3. If x and y are integers, is $x + y - 1$ divisible by 3?

   (1) When x is divided by 3, the remainder is 2.

   (2) When y is divided by 6, the remainder is 5.

4. Four knots—A, B, C, and D—appear in that order along a straight length of rope. Is the distance between B and D the same as the distance between A and B?

   (1) The distance between A and C is less than the distance between B and D

   (2) Half the distance between A and D is the same as the distance between C and D.

5. Is $x > y$?

   (1) x is the arithmetic mean of all two-digit prime numbers less than 23.

   (2) y is the sum of all factors of 60 that are greater than -1 but less than 6.

6. In a boat race between David and Jeff, when Jeff had covered half the 30-mile race distance, David was two miles ahead of Jeff. How long did it take David to travel the entire 30-mile distance?

   (1) David traveled the last 15 miles of the race's distance in 40 minutes.

   (2) Jeff traveled the first 15 miles of the race's distance in 45 minutes.

7. IMPORTS AND EXPORTS FOR COUNTRY X AND COUNTRY Y, 1985-1990

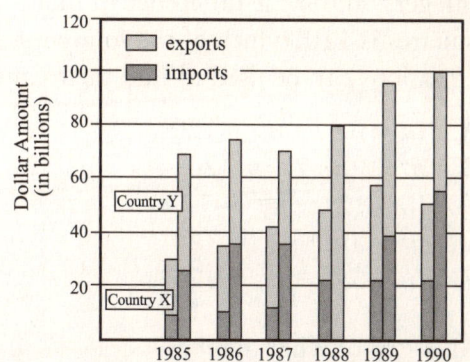

According to the chart shown above, during the year that Country X's exports exceeded its own imports by the greatest dollar amount, Country Y's imports exceeded Country X's imports by approximately

A. $23 billion.
B. $75 billion.
C. $90 billion.
D. $110 billion.
E. $160 billion.

8. A certain zoo charges exactly twice as much for an adult admission ticket as for a child's admission ticket. If the total admission price for the family of two adults and two children is $12.60, what is the price of a child's ticket?

A. $1.60
B. $2.10
C. $3.20
D. $3.30
E. $4.20

9. If *n* is the first of two consecutive odd integers, and if the difference of their squares is 120, which of the following equations can be used to find their values?

   A. $(n + 1)^2 - n^2 = 120$
   B. $n^2 - (n+2)^2 = 120$
   C. $[(n + 2) - n]^2 = 120$
   D. $n^2 - (n + 1)^2 = 120$
   E. $(n + 2)^2 - n^2 = 120$

10. *M* is *P*% of what number?

    A. $\dfrac{MP}{100}$
    B. $\dfrac{100P}{M}$
    C. $\dfrac{M}{100P}$
    D. $\dfrac{P}{100M}$
    E. $\dfrac{100M}{P}$

11.

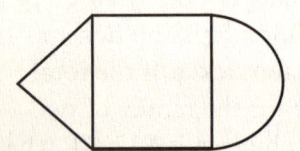

    Three carpet pieces—in the shapes of a square, a triangle, and a semicircle—are attached to one another, as shown in the figure above, to cover the floor of a room. If the area of the square is 144 feet and the perimeter of the triangle is 28 feet, what is the perimeter of the room's floor, in feet?

    A. $32 + 12\pi$
    B. $40 + 6\pi$
    C. $34 + 12\pi$
    D. $52 + 6\pi$
    E. $52 + 12\pi$

12. If $(b\square a\square c) = ab - c$, then $(4\square 3\square 5) + (6\square 5\square 7) =$

    A. 6
    B. 11
    C. 15
    D. 30
    E. 40

13. Two competitors battle each other in each match of a tournament with nine participants. What is the minimum number of matches that must occur for every competitor to battle every other competitor?

    A. 27
    B. 36
    C. 45
    D. 64
    E. 81

14. What is the value of *x*?

    (1) $4x^2 - 4x = -1$
    (2) $2x^2 + 9x = 5$

15. If, $\dfrac{2y}{9} = \dfrac{y-1}{3}$ then $y =$

    A. $\dfrac{1}{3}$
    B. $\dfrac{3}{5}$
    C. $\dfrac{4}{9}$
    D. $2\dfrac{1}{4}$
    E. 3

16. A 30-ounce pitcher is currently filled to exactly half its capacity with a lemonade mixture consisting of equal amounts of two lemonade brands—A and B. If the pitcher is then filled to capacity to conform to a certain recipe, how many ounces of each lemonade brand must be added to fill the pitcher?

    (1) The recipe calls for a mixture that includes 60 percent brand A.

    (2) When filled to capacity, the pitcher contains 12 ounces of brand B.

17. Lisa has 45 coins, which are worth a total of $3.50. If the coins are all nickels and dimes, what is the difference between the number of nickels and the number of dimes?

    A. 5
    B. 10
    C. 15
    D. 20
    E. 25

18. In an election between two candidates—Lange and Sobel—70% of the voters voted for Sobel. Of the election's voters, 60% were male. If 35% of the female voters voted for Lange, what percentage of the male voters voted for Sobel?

    A. 14
    B. 16
    C. 26
    D. 44
    E. 65

19. Barbara invests $2,400 in the National Bank at 5%. How much additional money must she invest at 8% so that the total annual income will be equal to 6% of her entire investment?

    A. $1,200
    B. $3,000
    C. $1,000
    D. $3,600
    E. $2,400

20. ABC Company pays an average of $140 per vehicle each month in outdoor parking fees for three of its eight vehicles. The company pays garage parking fees for the remaining five vehicles. If ABC pays an average of $240 per vehicle overall each month for parking, how much does ABC pay per month in garage parking fees for its vehicles?

    A. $300
    B. $420
    C. $912
    D. $1,420
    E. $1,500

21. If $m = n$ and $p < q$, which of the following must be true?

    A. $m - p > n - q$
    B. $p - m > q - n$
    C. $m - p < n - q$
    D. $mp > nq$
    E. $m + q < n + p$

22. If $ab \neq 0$, is $\dfrac{c}{a} > \dfrac{c}{b}$?

    (1) $c \neq 0$

    (2) $a > b$

23. If the price of a candy bar is doubled, by what percent will sales of the candy bar decrease?

    (1) For every ten cent increase in price, the sales will decease by 5 percent.

    (2) Each candy bar now costs sixty cents.

24. What is the numerical value of the second term in the following sequence: $x, x + 1, x + 3, x + 6, x + 10, x + 15, \ldots$?

    (1) The sum of the first and second terms is one-half the sum of the third and fourth terms.

    (2) The sum of the sixth and seventh terms is 43.

25. On the xy-plane, what is the area of a right triangle, one side of which is defined by the two points having the (x,y) coordinates $(2,3)$ and $(-4,0)$?

    (1) The triangle's perimeter crosses the y-axis at exactly two points altogether.

    (2) The y-coordinate of two of the triangle's three vertices is 0 (zero).

26.

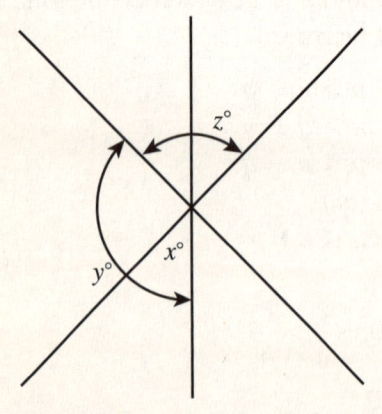

In the figure above, what is the value of x?

    (1) $y = 130$

    (2) $z = 100$

27. If $xy < 0$, and if x and y are both integers, what is the difference in value between x and y?

    (1) $x + y = 2$

    (2) $-3 < x < y$

28. A photographic negative measures $1\frac{7}{8}$ inches by $2\frac{1}{2}$ inches. If the longer side of the printed picture is to be 4 inches, what will be the length of the shorter side of the printed picture?

    A. $2\frac{3}{8}$ inches

    B. $2\frac{1}{2}$ inches

    C. $2\frac{3}{4}$ inches

    D. 3 inches

    E. $3\frac{1}{8}$ inches

29.

If the circumference of the circle pictured above is 16π, what is the length of $\overline{AC}$?

A. $4\sqrt{2}$
B. 16
C. $16\sqrt{2}$
D. 32
E. 16π

Questions 30 and 31 refer to the following figure:

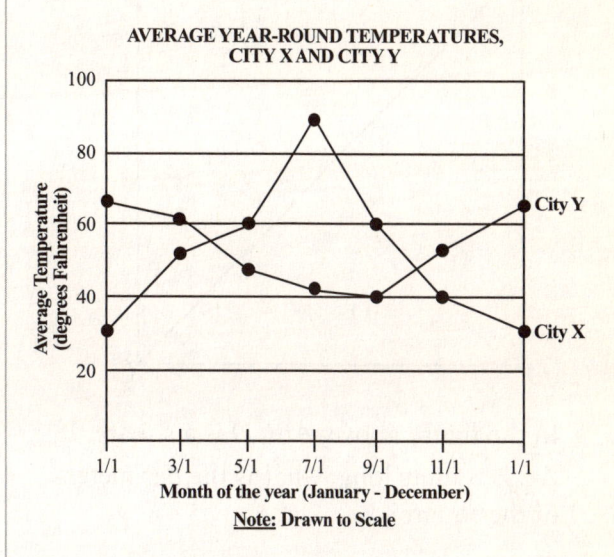

AVERAGE YEAR-ROUND TEMPERATURES, CITY X AND CITY Y

Note: Drawn to Scale

30. With respect to the two-month period over which the average daily temperature in City X increased by the greatest percentage, City Y's average daily temperature was approximately

   A. 38 degrees.
   B. 42 degrees.
   C. 52 degrees.
   D. 64 degrees.
   E. 68 degrees.

31. During the time periods in which City Y's average daily temperature was increasing while City X's was decreasing, the average daily temperature in City Y exceeded that in City X by approximately

   A. 0 degrees.
   B. 4 degrees.
   C. 10 degrees.
   D. 15 degrees.
   E. 19 degrees.

32.

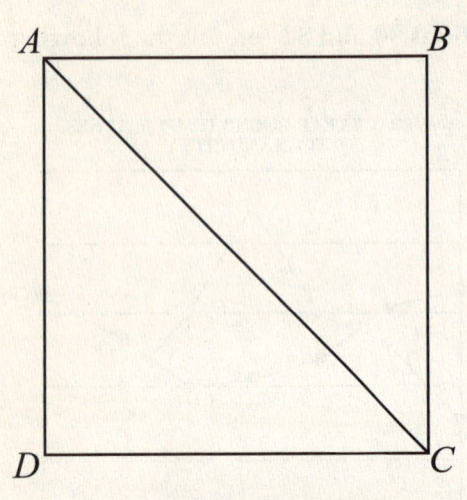

In the figure above, ABCD is a square. If $\overline{AC}$ is 8 units long, what is the perimeter of the square?

A. 16
B. $12\sqrt{2}$
C. 24
D. $16\sqrt{2}$
E. 30

33. Dan drove home from college at an average rate of 60 miles per hour. On his trip back to college, his rate was 10 miles per hour slower and the trip took him one hour longer than the drive home. How far is Dan's home from the college?

A. 65 miles
B. 100 miles
C. 200 miles
D. 280 miles
E. 300 miles

34. $\sqrt{\dfrac{y^2}{2} - \dfrac{y^2}{18}} =$

A. 0
B. $\dfrac{2y}{3}$
C. $\dfrac{19y}{3}$
D. $\dfrac{y\sqrt{3}}{6}$
E. $\dfrac{y\sqrt{5}}{3}$

35. A certain cylindrical tank set on its circular base is 7.5 feet in height. If the tank is filled with water, and if the water is then poured out of the tank into smaller cube-shaped tanks, how many cube-shaped tanks are required to hold all the water?

(1) The length of a cube-shaped tank's side is equal to the radius of the cylindrical tank's circular base.

(2) If 3 cube-shaped tanks are stacked on top of one another, the top of the third cube stacked is the same distance above the ground as the top of the cylindrical tank.

36. The average of seven numbers is 84. Six of the numbers are: 86, 82, 90, 92, 80, and 81. What is the seventh number?

A. 76
B. 77
C. 79
D. 81
E. 85

37. A solution of 60 ounces of sugar and water is 20% sugar. How much water must be added to make a solution that is 5% sugar?

   A. 20 ounces
   B. 80 ounces
   C. 100 ounces
   D. 120 ounces
   E. 180 ounces

Verbal Ability
41 Questions—75 Minutes

Directions for Sentence Correction Questions: *(These directions will appear on your screen before your first Sentence Correction question.)*

This question presents a sentence, all or part of which is underlined. Beneath the sentence you will find five ways of phrasing the underlined part. The first of these repeats the original; the other four are different. If you think the original is best, choose the first answer; otherwise choose one of the others.

This question tests correctness and effectiveness of expression. In choosing your answer, follow the requirements of Standard Written English; that is, pay attention to grammar, choice of words, and sentence construction. Choose the answer that produces the most effective sentence; this answer should be clear and exact, without awkwardness, ambiguity, redundancy, or grammatical error.

Directions for Critical Reasoning Questions: *(These directions will appear on your screen before your first Critical Reasoning question.)*

For this question, select the best of the answer choices given.

Directions for Reading Comprehension Questions: *(These directions will appear on your screen before your first group of Reading Comprehension questions.)*

The questions in this group are based on the content of a passage. After reading the passage, choose the best answer to each question. Answer all the questions following the passage on the basis of what is *stated* or *implied* in the passage.

1. Health professionals widely concur that, beyond a certain amount of exercise each day, the benefits that an individual can expect to derive <u>by further exercise is</u> negligible.

   A. by further exercise is
   B. from further exercise are
   C. in furthering exercise are
   D. by exercising further would be
   E. by exercising even more would be

2. <u>After bounty hunters turn over their captives to the authorities, they often are denied due process of law.</u>

   A. After bounty hunters turn over their captives to the authorities, they often are denied due process of law.
   B. After turning over bounty hunters' captives to the authorities, the authorities often deny them due process of law.
   C. The authorities often deny captives due process of law after bounty hunters turn the captives over to the authorities.
   D. Bounty hunters turn over their captives to the authorities, often being denied due process of law.
   E. A captive, when turned over by bounty hunters to the authorities, is often denied due process of law.

3. The media often hastens to chastise celebrities who have come into sudden and unexpected prominence, whether <u>they be actors, musicians, or some other high-profile vocation</u>.

   A. they be actors, musicians, or some other high-profile vocation
   B. their vocation be acting, music performance, or some other high-profile vocation
   C. they be actors, music, or some other high profile vocation
   D. their vocation is that of actor, musician, or otherwise a high-profile one
   E. they are actors, are musicians, or in some other high-profile vocation

4. In a recent survey, nine out of ten people using Slim-Ease for two weeks as directed reported that they lost weight during this period. This fact surely proves that Slim-Ease is effective for anyone wanting to shed some unwanted pounds.

   The claim made above depends on which of the following assumptions?

   A. The survey participants were not using Slim-Ease immediately prior to the two-week period.
   B. The survey participants did not exercise during the two-week period.
   C. The survey participants were overweight prior to the two-week period.
   D. The survey participants' dietary habits were otherwise similar during the two-week period as prior to that period.
   E. No other product is more effective than Slim-Ease to help lose weight.

5. Compared to older houses, new houses are sure to have newer, more efficient heating and cooling units, more modern kitchen appliances, and more contemporary-style bathroom fixtures. They also generally conform to current building-code regulations, whereas many older houses do not. Accordingly, it is always advantageous to purchase a new home rather than an old home.

Which of the following, if true, is the best criticism of the advice given in the argument above?

- **A.** Some people prefer more traditional styles of bathroom fixtures over contemporary styles.
- **B.** Whether a house has new equipment and fixtures and conforms to current code requirements are not the only factors home buyers consider important when choosing a house.
- **C.** New houses are generally more expensive than older houses of comparable size.
- **D.** When an older house is sold, correcting any code violations is the responsibility of the seller.
- **E.** In general, older houses have more of the kinds of details that lend charm to a home than do new houses.

Questions 6–8 are based on the following passage:

Line In the 1970s, the idea of building so-called "New Towns" to absorb growth was considered a potential cure-all for urban problems in the United
(5) States. It was erroneously assumed that by diverting residents from existing centers, current urban problems would at least get no worse. It was also wrongly assumed that, since European New
(10) Towns had been financially and socially successful, the same could be expected in the United States.

However, the ill-considered projects not only failed to relieve pressures on
(15) existing cities, but also weakened those cities further by drawing away high-income citizens. This increased the concentration of low-income groups—who were unable to provide the neces-
(20) sary tax base to support the cities. Taxpayers who remained were left to carry a greater burden, while industry and commerce sought to escape.

As it turned out, the promoters of
(25) New Towns were the developers, builders, and financial institutions, all whose main interest was financial gain. Not surprisingly, development occurred in areas where land was cheap and
(30) construction profitable rather than where New Towns were genuinely needed. Moreover, poor planning and legislation produced not the sort of successful New Towns seen in Britain but rather nothing
(35) more than sprawling suburbs. Federal regulations designed to promote the New Town concept failed to consider social needs as the European plans did. In fact, the regulations specified virtually all of
(40) the ingredients of the typical suburban community.

6. The author's primary concern in the passage is to
   A. describe the characteristics of American New Towns that made them unsuccessful.
   B. trace the development of the New Town concept in the United States.
   C. list the differences between New Towns in the United States with those in Europe.
   D. explain why New Towns in the United Stated failed to meet general expectations.
   E. analyze the impact of New Towns on urban centers in the United States.

7. Based only on the information in the passage, with which of the following statements about New Towns in the United States would the author most likely agree?
   A. They helped dissuade businesses in urban centers from relocating to other areas.
   B. They provided a thriving social center away from the problems of the older city.
   C. They helped reduce air pollution by relocating workplaces to suburbs, where most workers lived.
   D. They thwarted economic redevelopment plans for decaying urban centers.
   E. They provided affluent urban residents an escape from the city.

8. Which of the following phenomena is most closely analogous to the New Towns established in the United States?
   A. A business that fails as a result of insufficient demand for its products or services
   B. A new game that fails to attain widespread popularity because its rules are unfair
   C. New utility software that solves one computer problem but creates another
   D. A new drug whose side effects are severe enough to discourage people from using it
   E. A scientific theory that lacks supporting empirical evidence

9. The rules of etiquette for formal dinner parties with foreign diplomats require <u>citizens from both the host and from the diplomat's countries to be seated across from each other.</u>
   A. citizens from both the host and from the diplomat's countries to be seated across from each other
   B. citizens of the host country and of the diplomat's party to sit opposite each other
   C. that the host country and diplomat's country seat their citizens opposite one another
   D. that citizens of the host country be seated opposite those of the diplomat's country
   E. the host county's citizens to be seated opposite to the diplomat's country's citizens

10. *Company X spokesperson:* Although several of our key managerial employees have left our company since we merged with our leading competitor two months ago, we have no reason to believe that a significant number of our other employees will follow suit. Virtually all of Company X's current employees are the same people who we employed prior to the merger, and our employee-relations department is making every effort to ensure that these employees are content here.

    Which of the following, if true, would tend to support most effectively the spokesperson's prediction in the argument above?

    A. The employees who left Company X since the merger did so because they received more attractive employment offers from other firms.
    B. Worsening economic conditions may force Company X to reduce the size of its workforce in the near future.
    C. Company X has just hired a highly respected consultant who specializes in employee relations.
    D. None of the employees who worked for the company that has merged with Company X have left voluntarily.
    E. Most companies lose some workers to other firms as a result of a merger, but the number of workers lost is usually insignificant.

11. *Gwen:* As we both know, the most popular restaurants among college students here in Collegetown are the ones that provide delivery service. So, local economic conditions, which rely on the student population, would improve if expensive Collegetown restaurants were replaced by less expensive ones that also provide delivery service.

    Jose: I disagree. After all, many expensive Collegetown restaurants also provide delivery service.

    Which of the following best expresses the point of disagreement between Gwen and Jose?

    A. whether inexpensive restaurants are more popular among Collegetown students than expensive restaurants
    B. whether Collegetown should reduce the number of restaurants providing delivery service
    C. whether inexpensive restaurants in Collegetown should provide delivery service
    D. whether Collegetown students prefer delivery meal service over sit-down meal service
    E. whether inexpensive restaurants are popular among Collegetown students

12. Whether the universe is bound is frequently asked but impossible to answer.

A. Whether the universe is bound is frequently asked but impossible to answer.
B. A question asked frequently is whether the universe is bound, and it is impossible to answer.
C. As to whether the universe is bound is frequently asked but impossibly answered question.
D. Whether the universe is bound is frequently asked but impossible answered.
E. Whether or not the universe is bound is a question asked frequently but a question impossible to answer.

13. Of the 1,000 chemicals in coffee, less than thirty have been tested, most of which produce cancer in laboratory rats.

A. less than thirty have been tested, most of which produce cancer in laboratory rats
B. most of which produce cancer in laboratory rats, fewer than thirty have been tested
C. most of the less than thirty tested produced cancer in laboratory rats
D. less than thirty of which have been tested, most of them produce cancer in laboratory rats
E. fewer than thirty have been tested, and most of these produce cancer in laboratory rats

14. If the corporate bureaucracy persists in its discriminatory hiring and job advancement practices, its chief executives will expose themselves to class-action litigation by the groups prejudiced thereby.

A. its chief executives will expose themselves
B. its chief executives would expose themselves
C. their chief executives will expose themselves
D. its chief executives themselves would become exposed
E. the chief executives will, by themselves, be exposed

Questions 15–17 are based on the following passage:

Line   When Ralph Waldo Emerson pronounced America's declaration of cultural independence from Europe in his "American Scholar" address, he was
(5) actually articulating the transcendental assumptions of Jefferson's political independence. In the ideal new world envisioned by Emerson, America's becoming a perfect democracy of free
(10) and self-reliant individuals was within reach. Bringing Emerson's metaphysics down to earth, Henry David Thoreau's *Walden* (1854) asserted that one can live without encumbrances. Emerson wanted
(15) to visualize Thoreau as the ideal scholar in action that he had called for in the "American Scholar." In the end, however, Emerson regretted Thoreau's too-private individualism, which failed to signal the
(20) vibrant revolution in national consciousness that Emerson had prophesied. For Emerson, what Thoreau lacked, Walt Whitman embodied in full. On reading *Leaves of Grass* (1855), Emerson saw in

(25) Whitman the "prophet of democracy" whom he had sought. Other American Renaissance writers were less optimistic than Emerson and Whitman about the fulfillment of the democratic ideal. In
(30) *The Scarlet Letter* (1850), Nathaniel Hawthorne concluded that antinomianism such as the "heroics" displayed by Hester Prynne leads to moral anarchy; and Herman Melville, who saw in his
(35) story of *Pierre* (1852) a metaphor for the misguided assumptions of democratic idealism, declared the transcendentalist dream unrealizable. Ironically, the literary vigor with which both Hawthorne
(40) and Melville explored the ideal showed their deep sympathy with it even as they dramatized its delusions.

15. The author of the passage seeks primarily to

    A. explore the impact of the American Renaissance writers on the literature of the late 18th Century.
    B. illustrate how American literature of the mid-18th century differed in form from European literature of the same time period.
    C. identify two schools of thought among American Renaissance writers regarding the democratic ideal.
    D. point out how Emerson's democratic idealism was mirrored by the works of the American Renaissance writers.
    E. explain why the writers of the American Renaissance believed that an ideal world was forming in America.

16. Based on the passage's information, it can be inferred that Emerson might be characterized as any of the following EXCEPT

    A. a transcendentalist.
    B. an American Renaissance writer.
    C. a public speaker.
    D. a would-be prophet.
    E. a political pragmatist.

17. With which of the following statements about Melville and Hawthorne would the author most likely agree?

    A. Both men were disillusioned transcendentalists.
    B. Hawthorne sympathized with the transcendental dream more so than Melville.
    C. They agreed as to what the transcendentalist dream would ultimately lead to.
    D. Both men believed the idealists to be misguided.
    E. Hawthorne politicized the transcendental ideal, whereas Melville personalized it.

18. Last year, two drownings occurred at Lake Serene, so this year the lake's owner added one more lifeguard to the lakefront staff. No drownings have occurred at the lake this year. However, the new lifeguard has been home with the flu for nearly half the summer, so it appears that the new lifeguard was not needed after all.

    Which of the following, if true, would be most damaging to the argument above?

    A. This year, the lake's owner posted a warning about swimming without a lifeguard present.
    B. Drowning is not the lake owner's only safety concern.
    C. The lake has been equally crowded with swimmers this year as last year.
    D. Lake activities are safer in the presence of lifeguards.
    E. The new lifeguard has never saved a person from drowning.

19. Analyst Q predicts that the share price of MetaCorp stock will remain at its current level or higher as long as most stock analysts continue to recommend that investors buy the company's stock, and that stock analysts will continue to recommend MetaCorp stock to investors as long as the company continues to show a profit. Analyst T predicts that the share price of MetaCorp stock will at least remain at its current level, even if economic conditions worsen for MetaCorp's industry as a whole, as long as MetaCorp continues to show a profit.

    If the predictions of Analyst Q and Analyst T are all accurate, which of the following is logically inferable from them?

    A. Stock analysts would be more likely to recommend MetaCorp stock to investors if economic conditions for MetaCorp's industry are good than if they are poor.
    B. If MetaCorp discontinues to show a profit, stock analysts will be less inclined to recommend the company's stock to investors.
    C. If stock analysts stop recommending MetaCorp stock to investors, then the price of MetaCorp stock is less likely to at least remain at its current level than if stock analysts continue to recommend it.
    D. If economic conditions worsen for MetaCorp's industry as a whole, stock analysts will be less inclined to recommend MetaCorp stock.
    E. If MetaCorp continues to show a profit, then the price of MetaCorp stock will either remain at its current level or increase.

20. A national performing arts association conducted a survey that appears to confirm the public's interest in high culture. More than ninety percent of those surveyed said that they were either "somewhat interested" or "very interested" in attending performances of opera, ballet, or classical music.

Which of the following, if true, would most seriously weaken the argument above?

- A. Not all performances of opera, ballet, and classical music should be considered "high culture."
- B. Not all those who are interested in attending performances of opera, ballet, or classical music are willing to support an arts association.
- C. Most of those surveyed reported being "somewhat interested" rather than "highly interested."
- D. Other statistics show that more people attend sporting events than performances of opera, ballet, or classical music.
- E. The association conducting the survey receives most of its funding from sources other than the general public.

21. The high level of violence in television programming today has often been cited as an explanation for the increasing level of violence in our society. And, in fact, some recent studies show that the level of violence in television programming has increased considerably over the past twenty years. However, other recent studies indicate that the level, while high, is only slightly greater than it was twenty years ago.

Which of the following, if true, would provide the best explanation for the discrepancy among the recent studies cited in the argument above?

- A. Numerous studies of television violence have been conducted since the advent of television, and their results have not always been in agreement.
- B. All of those involved in conducting the cited studies shared the same perception of what constitutes "violence" in television programming.
- C. Television programming designed specifically for children accounts for a greater portion of television programming today than it did twenty years ago.
- D. Many factors other than violence in television programming carry a significant impact on the level of violence in society.
- E. Over the last twenty years, the level of violence in television programming has increased more than in society as a whole.

22. All modern computer languages derive from a more basic "assembly" language that originated many decades ago.

A. All modern computer languages derive from
B. Derived from all modern computer languages is
C. Resulting in all modern computer languages was
D. Modern computer languages, which all resulted from
E. All modern computer languages are derived from

23. Despite his admiration of the great jazz musicians that preceded him, Blakey opposed them trivializing the popular genre.

A. them trivializing the popular genre
B. their trivializing of the popular genre
C. them when trivializing the popular genre
D. the popular genre being trivialized by them
E. their trivializing the popular genre

24. Inventors have yet to learn that something that does two things does one of them better.

A. Inventors have yet to learn
B. Having not yet learned, inventors need to learn
C. Inventors have not as of yet learned
D. Inventors as yet have to learn
E. Not having yet learned, inventors have to learn

25. In general, obesity is caused not by the ingestion of foods that are high in fat content but rather by eating foods that contain too much sugar. For proof, consider that over the past ten years, even as sales of low-fat meals, snacks, and desserts have increased sharply throughout the world's developed countries, the incidence of obesity in those countries, as a percentage of overall population, has reached a new high.

Which of the following, if true, would most support the claim made in the argument above?

A. Ninety percent of the low-fat foods sold in developed countries are purchased by just ten percent of the population.
B. Sales of foods with a high sugar content have increased significantly over the past ten years.
C. Government-approved standards of obesity have changed several times during the past ten years.
D. Some foods labeled "low-fat" actually contain relatively high levels of fat.
E. Most physicians consider regular exercise to be an important component of any effective program to prevent or reverse obesity.

26. The increasing scarcity of available rental housing, particularly apartments with two or more bedrooms, is attributable to two recent trends: the increasing number of new office buildings as compared to new apartment buildings and the increasing number of rental apartments being sold as condominiums rather than rented.

    The passage above best supports which of the following conclusions?

    A. The rate at which new apartment buildings are being built is decreasing.
    B. The current demand for reasonably priced rental housing is greater than the current supply.
    C. Most rental apartments being sold as condominiums have at least two bedrooms.
    D. More new office buildings than rental apartment buildings are currently being built.
    E. The current demand for offices is greater than the current demand for rental apartments.

27. Scientist and artist Leonardo Da Vinci <u>was, and always will be considered by many,</u> as a singular figure among those whose scientific, artistic, and other cultural contributions defined the Renaissance period of European history.

    A. was, and always will be considered by many, as
    B. was and always will be considered by many as being
    C. was, and always will be by many, considered
    D. was, and always will be considered by many as,
    E. was considered by many and always will be by many

Questions 28–30 are based on the following passage:

Line   During the process of embryonic development, cells become progressively restricted in their developmental potential and finally acquire the biochemical
(5)   and morphological specialization necessary for their respective functions in an adult. Since enzymatic and structural proteins are required for the appearance and maintenance of this specialization,
(10)   the differentiated state results from the synthesis and activity of cell-specific proteins during development.

       Since all cells of an organism contain the same genotype as the fertilized egg,
(15)   cellular differentiation is the result of variable gene activity rather than selective gene loss. Thus, cellular specialization and cell-specific protein synthesis result from the expression of
(20)   appropriately selected groups of genes in each cell type. As development proceeds, the progressive differentiation of cells is correlated with changes in the population of protein species within the embryo,
(25)   which in turn reflect the accurate programming of the time and sequence of the biosynthesis of different proteins by the genome. In the absence of opportunities for genetic analysis, determining the
(30)   mechanisms involved in the regulation of protein synthesis is key to understanding genome control during development.

       The majority of studies on gene activity in embryogenesis have been done
(35)   on the sea urchin system, where large numbers of embryos undergoing relatively synchronous development can be easily obtained. Also, sea urchins' permeability to radioactive isotopes and
(40)   to inhibitors of RNA and protein

synthesis provides a distinct advantage for study over amphibian material. Especially well documented are the maternal programming of early develop-
(45) ment and the genomic control of later differentiation in the urchin. Maternal products, stored in the egg cytoplasm from oogenesis, can support development from fertilization through the hatching
(50) blastula stage; however, development from the mesenchyme blastula stage is dependent upon gene products synthesized under the direction of the embryonic genome.

28. With which of the following statements would the author of the passage most likely disagree?

   A. Morphological specialization requires the synthesis of cell-specific proteins.
   B. Embryonic development involves differentiation in cell genotype.
   C. The population of protein species with the embryo is dependent upon the timing of protein biosynthesis.
   D. Enzymatic proteins are required for an organism's full development.
   E. Selective gene loss is not a factor in cellular differentiation during embryonic development.

29. Which of the following statements about embryonic development in sea urchins is best supported by the passage?

   A. Genomic control over early embryonic development is especially well documented.
   B. Permeability to RNA inhibitors is comparable to that in amphibian embryos.
   C. Development during the hatching blastula stage requires gene products synthesized under the direction of the embryonic genome.
   D. Maternal products can support embryonic development following the mesenchyme blastula stage.
   E. Genomic control of later cell differentiation has been studied extensively.

30. The last paragraph of the passage (lines 33–54)

   A. illustrates a biological process by way of an example.
   B. describes a methodology for studying a biological phenomenon.
   C. compares two stages of biological development.
   D. defines and explains an important term mentioned earlier.
   E. provides an example which disproves a scientific theory.

31. Equipment used by private biotechnology-research firms becomes obsolete more quickly than any other business equipment, simply because biotechnology advances so rapidly. A proposed tax law would provide significant tax incentives for businesses in every industry to replace their old equipment with new equipment. Obviously, political lobbyists for the biotechnology industry were the instigators of this tax proposal.

Which of the following most supports the claim that biotechnology industry lobbyists are responsible for the tax proposal?

A. Equipment used in the biotechnology industry loses its value more quickly than equipment used in any other industry.
B. Biotechnology firms expect biotechnology advances to outpace those in other industries for the foreseeable future.
C. The legislator introducing the proposed law used to work in the biotechnology industry.
D. Other industries have not lobbied for the proposed law.
E. Unless a biotechnology firm replaces its obsolete equipment, it will be driven out of business by competing firms.

32. Due to sharply escalating tuition at four-year colleges, debt on student loans has increased to the point that many new graduates are forced either to pursue graduate-level degrees, thereby postponing repayment of their student loans, or to pursue only the highest-paying jobs. An unfortunate result of this trend is that fewer and fewer new graduates are entering important, but lower-paying, professions that require only a four-year degree.

Which of the following strategies would be most effective in reversing the decline in the number of college graduates entering lower-paying professions that require only a four-year degree?

A. Encourage college students to enroll in classes year-round in order to graduate early.
B. Expand opportunities for graduate-level students to obtain paying jobs while still in school.
C. Expand course offerings that prepare college students for these lower-paying professions.
D. Establish higher admission standards for graduate-level programs.
E. Increase the number of academic units required to obtain a four-year college degree.

33. International environmental regulations do not protect hybrid species, but they are protected by way of domestic laws.

   A. but they are protected by way of domestic laws
   B. although domestic laws do
   C. and so domestic laws only protect hybrid species
   D. yet the laws of domestic protection will so protect
   E. which require legal protection domestically

34. Even for high school freshmen and sophomores, theories concerning the psychology of death and dying among the elderly can hold considerable significance and interest for many students.

   A. Even for high school freshmen and sophomores, theories concerning the psychology of death and dying among the elderly can hold considerable significance and interest for many students.
   B. Even for high school freshmen and sophomore students with considerable interest in theories concerning the psychology of death and dying among the elderly, these theories can hold considerable significance.
   C. Theories concerning the psychology of death and dying among the elderly, for many students, even high school freshmen and sophomores, can hold considerable significance and interest.
   D. Theories concerning the psychology of death and dying among the elderly can hold considerable significance and interest even for high school freshmen and sophomore students.
   E. Considerable significance and interest for even high school freshmen and sophomores is held in theories concerning the psychology of death and dying among the elderly.

35. In order for a new third-world democratic country to achieve and maintain political stability, its government must afford its citizens the power to elect and remove the country's leaders. After all, Country X is among the most stable countries in the world, and its government affords its citizens this power.

The argument above is flawed in that it ignores the possibility that

   A. many third-world countries already grant their citizens the power to elect and remove their leaders.
   B. a large percentage of third-world countries have already achieved, and are maintaining, political stability.
   C. Country X's leaders are more popular among Country X's citizens than are the leaders of most third-world countries among their citizens.
   D. specific procedures for electing a country's leaders vary significantly from one country to another.
   E. Country X was already politically stable when its citizens were first afforded the power to elect and remove their leaders.

Questions 36–39 are based on the following passage:

Line The origin of the attempt to distinguish early from modern music and to establish the canons of performance practice for each lies in the eighteenth century. In the
(5) first half of that century, when Telemann and Bach ran the collegium musicum in Leipzig, Germany, they performed their own and other modern music. In the German universities of the early twenti-
(10) eth century, however, the reconstituted collegium musicum devoted itself to performing music from the centuries before the beginning of the "standard repertory," by which was understood
(15) music from before the time of Bach and Handel.

Alongside this modern collegium musicum, German musicologists developed the historical subdiscipline known
(20) as "performance practice," which included the deciphering of obsolete musical notation and its transcription into modern notation, the study of obsolete instruments, and—most
(25) importantly because all musical notation is incomplete—the re-establishment of lost oral traditions associated with those forgotten repertories. The cutoff date for this study was understood to be around
(30) 1750, the year of Bach's death. The reason for this demarcation was that the music of Bach, Handel, Telemann, and their contemporaries did call for obsolete instruments and voices and unannotated
(35) performing traditions. Furthermore, with a few exceptions, late baroque music had ceased to be performed for nearly a century, with the result that orally transmitted performing traditions
(40) associated with it were forgotten. In contrast, the notation in the music of Haydn and Mozart from the second half of the eighteenth century was more complete than in the earlier styles, and
(45) the instruments seemed familiar, so no "special" knowledge appeared necessary. Also, the music of Haydn and Mozart, having never ceased to be performed, had maintained some kind of oral tradition of
(50) performance practice.

36. It can be inferred that the "standard repertory" mentioned in lines 13–14 might have included music

   A. that called for the use of obsolete instruments.
   B. of the early twentieth century.
   C. written by the performance-practice composers.
   D. written before the time of Handel.
   E. composed before 1700.

37. According to the passage, performance practice in the early twentieth century involved all of the following EXCEPT

   A. deciphering outdated music notation.
   B. studying instruments no longer in common use.
   C. reestablishing unannotated performing traditions.
   D. determining which musical instrument to use.
   E. transcribing older music into modern notation.

38. According to the passage, German musicologists of the early twentieth century limited performance practice to pre-1750 works because

   A. special knowledge was generally not required to decipher pre-1750 music.
   B. unannotated performing traditions had been maintained for later works.
   C. generally speaking, only music written before 1750 had ceased to be performed.
   D. the annotation for earlier works was generally less complete than for the works of Bach and Handel.
   E. music written prior to 1750 was considered obsolete.

39. The author refers to modern performance practice as a "subdiscipline" (line 19) probably because it

   A. was not sanctioned by the mainstream.
   B. required more discipline than performing the standard repertory.
   C. focused on particular aspects of the music being performed at the German universities.
   D. involved deciphering obsolete musical notation.
   E. involved performing the works that were being transcribed at the universities.

40. Veterinarians have developed a new cat food that contains medication to prevent hair balls from accumulating in a cat's stomach and digestive tract. Hair balls are generally not harmful to cats, but they do cause discomfort. Although the medicated food is effective, many cats develop an allergic reaction to it that, left untreated, can result in a harmful infection. Accordingly, those concerned about the health of their cats should not feed this food to them.

   The answer to which of the following questions would be most useful to cat owners considering whether to feed the medicated food to their cats?

   A. How much of the medicated food must a cat eat in order to develop an allergic reaction?
   B. How noticeable to humans are the allergic reactions associated with ingesting the medicated food?
   C. Are there effective methods of preventing hairballs other than feeding a cat the medicated food?
   D. Do cats typically develop similar allergic reactions to other types of food as well?
   E. What percentage of all cat owners feed the medicated food to their pet cats?

41. On this issue, this state's elected officials ignored the wishes of their electorate, which cannot reasonably be disputed in light of the legislative record.

   A. On this issue, this state's elected officials ignored the wishes of their electorate, which
   B. This state's elected officials, ignoring on this issue the wishes of their electorate,
   C. That this state's elected officials ignored the wishes of their electorate
   D. On this issue, the wishes of the electorate were ignored by this state's elected officials, and
   E. That the wishes of the electorate on this issue were ignored by this state's elected officials

Answers and Explanations

See Appendix for score conversion tables to determine your score. Be sure to keep a tally of correct and incorrect answers for each test section.

Analysis of an Issue—Evaluation and Scoring

Evaluate your Issue-Analysis essay on a scale of 1 to 6 (6 being the highest score) according to the following five criteria:

1. Does your essay develop a position on the issue through the use of incisive reasons and persuasive examples?

2. Are your essay's ideas conveyed clearly and articulately?

3. Does your essay maintain proper focus on the issue, and is it well organized?

4. Does your essay demonstrate proficiency, fluency, and maturity in its use of sentence structure, vocabulary, and idiom?

5. Does your essay demonstrate command of the elements of Standard Written English, including grammar, word usage, spelling, and punctuation?

Analysis of an Argument—Evaluation and Scoring

Evaluate your Argument-Analysis essay on a scale of 1 to 6 (6 being the highest score) according to the following five criteria:

1. Does your essay identify the key features of the argument and analyze each one in a thoughtful manner?

2. Does your essay support each point of its critique with insightful reasons and examples?

3. Does your essay develop its ideas in a clear, organized manner, with appropriate transitions to help connect ideas?

4. Does your essay demonstrate proficiency, fluency, and maturity in its use of sentence structure, vocabulary, and idiom?

5. Does your essay demonstrate command of the elements of Standard Written English, including grammar, word usage, spelling, and punctuation?

The following series of questions, which serve to identify the Argument's five distinct problems, will help you evaluate your essay in terms of criteria 1 and 2. To earn a score of 4 or higher, your essay should identify at least three of these problems and, for each one, provide at least one example or counterexample that supports your critique. (Your examples need not be the same as the ones below.) Identifying and discussing at least four of the problems would help earn you an even higher score.

- Do Maxtech employees, at least those who claim Workforce cites, constitute a sufficiently *representative statistical sample* of the entire private-sector workforce? (Perhaps these Maxtech employees were more receptive or responsive to Workforce's particular methods than the average private-sector worker.)

- Is the report from Workforce Systems *credible*? (Perhaps the company overstates the benefits of its seminars in order to attract clients.)

- Was the seminar the *actual cause* of the improved level of contentment among the participants from Maxtech? (The answer might depend on how much time has passed since the seminar, whether Maxtech's participants have the same jobs as before, and whether the seminar is designed to help workers become more content to begin with.)

- Are the claims by Maxtech's employees *credible*? (Perhaps they felt pressure to exaggerate the benefits of the seminar, or falsely report improvement in order to take time off from work to enroll again in the seminar.)

- Might the argument assume that *all other conditions remain unchanged*? (Overall productivity of the economy's private sector depends also on many extrinsic factors having nothing to do with the benefits of these types of seminars.)

Quantitative Ability

1. **C** Your first step is to rewrite mixed numbers as fractions:

    $$\frac{9}{2} + \frac{15}{4} - \frac{12}{5}.$$

    The least common denominator is 20. You can eliminate answer choice (D). Rewrite each fraction, then combine:

    $$\frac{9}{2} + \frac{15}{4} - \frac{12}{5} = \frac{90 + 75 - 48}{20} = \frac{117}{20}$$

2. **B** You can solve the problem algebraically as follows:

    $$23 - x = 2(15 - x)$$
    $$23 - x = 30 - 2x$$
    $$x = 7$$

    An alternative method is to subtract the number given in each answer choice, in turn, from both Lyle's age and Melanie's age.

ANSWERS

3. C Neither statement (1) nor (2) alone provides any information about the second variable or, in turn, about the value of $x + y - 1$. Thus (A), (B), and (D) can easily be eliminated. Next, consider statements (1) and (2) together. Given a remainder of 2 when x is divided by 3, the value of x must be greater than a multiple of 3 by exactly 2: $x = \{5, 8, 11, 14, \ldots\}$. Given a remainder of 5 when y is divided by 6, the value of y must be greater than a multiple of 6 by exactly 5: $y = \{11, 17, 23, 29, \ldots\}$. Adding together any x-value and any y-value will always result in a sum that exceeds a multiple of 3 by exactly 7 (or by exactly 1). Accordingly, subtracting 1 from that sum will always result in a multiple of 3. Thus, given statements (1) and (2), $x = y - 1$ is divisible by 3.

4. D Statement (1) alone suffices to answer the question. Given $AC < BD$, AB (which is less than AC) must be less than BD. $BD > AB$, and the answer to the question is *no*.

Statement (2) also suffices alone to answer the question. Given $= \dfrac{AD}{2} = CD$, C bisects AD, and $AC = CD$. Thus, AB (which is smaller than AC) must be smaller than CD. Because CD is less than BD, $AB < BD$, and the answer to the question is *no*.

5. C Neither statement (1) nor (2) alone suffices to determine the values of both x and y. Thus, you can easily eliminate choices (A), (B), and (D). Next, consider both statements together. The two-digit prime numbers less than 23 include 11, 13, 17, and 19. Their sum is 60, and the average of the four numbers is 15. ($x = 15$.) Considering statement (2), the positive factors of 60 that are less than 6 include 1, 2, 3, 4, and 5. Their sum is 15 ($y = 15$). $x = y$, and the answer to the question, based on statements (1) and (2) together, is *no*.

6. E Statement (1) alone provides no information about how long it took David to travel the first 15 miles, and is therefore insufficient by itself to answer the question. Statement (2) alone provides even less information about how long it took David to travel the entire distance. Although you can determine from statement (2) that David traveled the first 17 miles in 45 minutes, you cannot determine how long it took David to travel the remaining 13 miles. Statements (1) and (2) together establish that David traveled 32 miles (17 + 15) in 85 minutes (45 + 40). However, 2 of the 32 miles are accounted for twice. Without knowing either the time that it took David to travel the 16th and 17th miles of the race, or his average speed over those two miles, you cannot determine David's total time for the 30-mile race. Thus, statements (1) and (2) together are insufficient to answer the question.

7. A This question involves two steps. First, visually compare the difference in height between Country X's solid bar and shaded bar for each year. (Be careful to look at County X's bar, *not* Country Y's.) You don't need too determine amounts at this point. A quick inspection reveals that 1987 was the year that Country X's exports exceeded its own imports by the greatest amount. Now go to the second step. During 1987, Country Y's imports were approximately $35 and Country X's imports were approximately $13. The difference is $22. Choice (A) is the only one that approximates this dollar figure.

8. **B** The price of two children's tickets together equals the price of one adult ticket. The total admission price is therefore equivalent to the price of three adult tickets.

$$3a = \$12.60$$
$$a = \$4.20$$

Child's ticket price $= \frac{1}{2}(\$4.20) = \$2.10$

9. **E** The other integer is $n + 2$. The difference between n and $(n + 2)$ must be positive, so the term $(n + 2)$ must appear first in the equation.

10. **E** Convert the question into an algebraic equation, and solve for x:

$$M = \frac{P}{100}(x)$$
$$100 = Px$$
$$\frac{100M}{P} = x$$

11. **B** The length of each side of the square is 12 feet. The length of the remaining two sides of the triangle totals 16 feet. The perimeter of the semicircle $= \frac{1}{2}\pi d = \frac{1}{2}\pi(12) = 6\pi$. The length of the two sides of the square included in the overall perimeter totals 24. The total perimeter of the floor $= 16 + 6\pi + 24 = 40 + 6\pi$.

12. **D** Apply the defined operation to each of the two expressions as follows:

$$(4\square 3\square 5) = 12 - 5 = 7$$
$$(6\square 5\square 7) = 30 - 7 = 23$$

Then add the two results: $7 + 23 = 30$

13. **B** Competitor 1 must engage in eight matches. Competitor 2 must engage in seven matches not already accounted for. (The match between competitors 1 and 2 has already been tabulated.) Similarly, competitor 3 must engage in six matches other than those accounted for, and so on. The minimum number of total matches $= 8 + 7 + 6 + 5 + 4 + 3 + 2 + 1 = 36$.

14. **A** Both equations are quadratic. For each one, you can determine the number of possible values of x by setting the quadratic expression equal to 0 (zero) and factoring that expression. Perform these tasks for equation in statement (1):

$$4x^2 - 4x = -1$$
$$4x^2 - 4x + 1 = 0$$
$$(2x - 1)(2x - 1) = 0$$

As you can see, the equation's two roots are the same—that is, there's only one possible value for *x*. Thus, statement (1) alone suffices to answer the question. Now perform the same tasks for the equation in statement (2):

$$2x^2 + 9x = 5$$
$$2x^2 + 9x - 5 = 0$$
$$(x + 5)(2x - 1) = 0$$

As you can see, based on the equation given in statement (2), there are two different roots—that is, two possible values of *x*. Thus, statement (2) alone is insufficient to answer the question.

15. **E** Cross-multiply to solve for *y*:

$$(9)(y - 1) = (2y)(3)$$
$$9y - 9 = 6y$$
$$3y = 9$$
$$y = 3$$

16. **D** The question itself provides that the pitcher currently contains $7\frac{1}{2}$ ounces of each brand. Given statement (1), 60% of the 30-quart mixture, or 18 ounces, must be brand A. Subtract $7\frac{1}{2}$ from 18 to find the remaining amount of B brand A needed ($10\frac{1}{2}$ ounces). Then subtract 18 from 30 to find the amount of brand B (12). Finally, subtract $7\frac{1}{2}$ from 12 to find the remaining amount of brand B needed $\left(4\frac{1}{2} \text{ ounces}\right)$. We've answered the question with statement (1) alone. Similarly, statement 2 would lead to the same answer.

17. **A** Let *x* equal the number of nickels:

$$45 - x = \text{the number of dimes}$$
$$5x = \text{the value of all nickels (in cents)}$$
$$450 - 10x = \text{the value of all dimes (in cents)}$$

Given a total value of 350 cents:

$$5x + 450 - 10x = 350$$
$$-5x = -100$$
$$x = 20$$

Lisa has 20 nickels and 25 dimes; thus, she has five more dimes than nickels.

18. **D** You can organize this problem's information in a table, as shown in this next figure:

	male	female	
Lange		14%	30%
Sobel	?		70%
	60%	40%	

Because 35% of 40% of the voters (female) voted for Lange, 14% (.40 × .35) of all voters were females who voted for Lange. You can now fill in the entire table (the four percentages must total 100%), as shown in this next figure:

	male	female	
Lange	16%	14%	30%
Sobel	44%	26%	70%
	60%	40%	

19. **A** If Barbara invests x additional dollars at 8%, her total investment will amount to $(2,400 + x)$ dollars.

$$.05(2,400) + .08x = .06(2,400) + x$$
$$5(2,400) + 8x = 6(2,400 + x)$$
$$12,000 + 8x = 14,400 + 6x$$
$$2x = 2,400$$
$$x = 1,200$$

20. **E** The total parking fee that ABC pays each month is $1,920 ($240 × 8). Of that amount, $420 is paid for outdoor parking for three cars. The difference ($1,920 − $420 = $1,500) is the total garage parking fee that the company pays for the other five cars.

21. **A** In choice (A), unequal quantities are subtracted from equal quantities. The differences are unequal, but the inequality is reversed because unequal numbers are being subtracted from, rather than added to, the equal numbers.

22. E Statement (1) alone is insufficient to answer the question, since it provides no information about a or b. Many test-takers would conclude incorrectly that Statement (2) alone is sufficient to answer the question. (About half of these test-takers would assert that the answer to the question is *no*, while the other half would claim that the answer to the question is *yes*.) Both groups would be wrong, of course. If $c < 0$, then dividing c by unequal quantities does not change the inequality. But if $c > 0$, dividing c by unequal quantity reverses the inequality. If you're the least bit unsure about this, it's a good idea to plug in a few simple numbers. For example, let $a = 2$ and $b = 1$. If $c = 1$ (a positive value), then $\frac{c}{a} < \frac{c}{b}$ because $\frac{1}{2} < \frac{1}{1}$. But if $c = -1$ (a negative number), then $\frac{c}{a} > \frac{c}{b}$ because $-\frac{1}{2} > -\frac{1}{1}$.

23. C Statement (1) alone is insufficient to answer the question because it fails to indicate what percent a 10 cent increase amounts to. Statement (2) alone is insufficient because it fails to provide any information as to the change in sales resulting from an increased price. Together, however, statements (1) and (2) provide the information needed. You do not need to calculate the percent decrease in sales; you know that the correct answer is (C). Here's how you would perform the calculation, however: A 60-cent increase is 6 increases of 10 cents, so the decrease in sales is 30% (6 × 5).

24. D Statement (1) establishes a linear equation in one variable:

$$x + (x + 1) = \frac{1}{2}[(x + 3) + (x + 6)].$$

You can determine the second term by solving for x, and statement (1) suffices to answer the question. [The second term is 4.5 ($x = 3.5$); however, you need not determine these values.] Statement (2) also establishes a linear equation in one variable: $(x + 15) + (x + 21) = 43$. The seventh term must be $(x + 21)$ because each successive term in the sequence adds to x a number that is one greater than the number that the previous term added to x. Statement (2) alone suffices to answer the question. (Again, $x = 3.5$ and the second term is 4.5, although you need not determine either value.)

25. B Statement (1) alone allows for more than one possible area, as illustrated below:

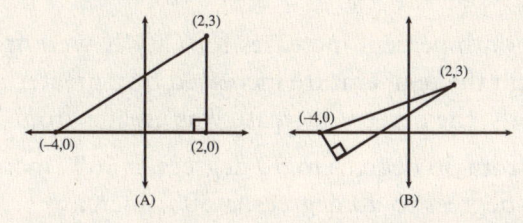

Statement (2) alone, however, allows for only one possible area (and shape and position) of the triangle—the one illustrated in diagram (A) above. Thus, statement (2) alone is sufficient to answer the question.

26. C It's obvious that neither statement (1) nor (2) alone provides sufficient information to determine the degree measure of ∠x. Thus, you can easily eliminate choices (A), (B), and (D). Next, consider statements (1) and (2) together. Notice that ∠y and ∠z together form an angle whose degree measure exceeds 180 (a straight line) by x. Thus, $y + z - x = 180$. Statements (1) and (2) provide the values of y and z and thus suffice to answer the question ($x = 50$).

27. E Given $xy < 0$, either x or y (but not both) must be negative. Despite this restriction, statement (1) alone is insufficient to answer the question because it specifies one equation in two variables. Statement (2) alone is also insufficient. Although x must equal either -2 or -1 (x must be a negative integer), y could be any positive integer. Now, consider statements (1) and (2) together. Since there are two possible values of x (-2 and -1) in the equation $x + y = 2$, the difference between x and y could be either 4 or 6. Thus, statements (1) and (2) together are insufficient to answer the question.

28. D Equate the proportions of the negative with those of the printed picture:

$$\frac{2\frac{1}{2}}{4} = \frac{1\frac{7}{8}}{x}$$

$$\frac{\frac{5}{2}}{4} = \frac{\frac{15}{8}}{x}$$

$$\frac{5}{2} = \frac{15}{2}$$

$$5x = 15$$

$$x = 3$$

29. C $\overline{AC}$ is a diagonal of the square ABCD. To find the length of any square's diagonal, multiply the length of any side by $\sqrt{2}$. So first you need to find the length of a side. Half the length of a side equals the circle's radius, and the perimeter of any circle equals $2\pi r$, where r is the radius. Thus, the radius here is 8, and the length of each of the square's sides is 16. Therefore, the length of diagonal $\overline{AC} = 16\sqrt{2}$

30. D The two greatest two-month percent increases for City X were from 1/1 to 3/1 and from 5/1 to 7/1. Although the temperature increased by a greater amount during the latter of these two periods, the percent increase was greater from 1/1 to 3/1.

January–February: from 30 degrees to 50 degrees, a 66% increase
May–June: from 60 degrees to 90 degrees, a 50% increase

During the period from 1/1 to 3/1, City Y's average daily temperature was midway between its highest and lowest temperatures (between 66 degrees and 62 degrees), or about 64 degrees.

ANSWERS

31. C The only two-month periods in which City Y's temperature was increasing while City X's was decreasing were September–October and November–December. Compare the two midpoints of the line segments for each period:

September–October: City X's average was 50 and City Y's was 46.
November–December: City X's average was 36 and City Y's average was 60.

For each city, find the average of the two midpoints:

City X's average: $\dfrac{50 + 36}{2} = 43$

City Y's average: $\dfrac{46 + 60}{2} = 53$

City Y's average overall temperature was about 10 degrees greater than City X's during these four months.

32. D The diagonal of a square is the hypotenuse of a $1:1:\sqrt{2}$ right triangle where the two legs are sides of the square. Given a hypotenuse of 8, the length of each side of the square is $\dfrac{8}{\sqrt{2}}$, or $4\sqrt{2}$. Accordingly, the square's perimeter $= 4 \times 4\sqrt{2} = 16\sqrt{2}$.

33. E You can express the distance both in terms of Dan's driving time going home and going back to college. Letting x equal the time (in hours) it took Dan to drive home, you can express the distance between his home and his workplace both as $60x$ and as $50(x + 1)$. Equate the two distances (because distance is constant) and solve for x as follows:

$$60x = 50(x + 1)$$
$$60x = 50x + 50$$
$$x = 5$$

It took Dan five hours at 60 miles per hour to drive from college to home, so the distance is 300 miles.

34. B Combine the terms under the radical into one fraction:

$$\sqrt{\dfrac{y^2}{2} - \dfrac{y^2}{18}} = \sqrt{\dfrac{9y^2 - y^2}{18}} = \sqrt{\dfrac{8y^2}{18}} = \sqrt{\dfrac{4y^2}{9}}$$

Then factor out "perfect squares" from both numerator and denominator:

$$\sqrt{\dfrac{4y^2}{9}} = \dfrac{2y}{3}$$

35. C To answer the question, you need to compare the volume of the cylindrical tank with the volume of a cube-shaped tank. Statement (1) fails to provide sufficient information to determine these volumes. The volume of the cylindrical tank is $7.5\pi r^2$ and, given statement (1), you can express the cube's volume as r^3. The ratio of the two volumes, then, is $7.5\pi r^2 : r^3$, or $7.5\pi : r$. Accordingly, the comparative volumes of the containers vary, depending on the value of r. Statement (2) is also insufficient to answer the question. Given statement (2), the length of a cube's side is 2.5 feet, and you can determine its volume (s^3). However, you cannot determine the cylindrical tank's volume because the size of its circular base remains unknown. Statement (1) provides this missing information. Thus, statements (1) and (2) together suffice to answer the question. Given statements (1) and (2), the ratio of V [cylinder] to V [cube] is $3\pi : 1$, so 10 cube-shaped tanks are required.

36. B You could solve the problem algebraically by using the arithmetic-mean formula (x is the seventh number):

$$84 = \frac{86 + 82 + 90 + 92 + 80 + 81 + x}{7}$$

There's a quicker way, however. 86 is 2 above the 84 average, and 82 is two below. These two numbers "cancel" each other. 90 is 6 above and 92 is 8 above the average (a total of 14 above), while 80 is 4 below and 81 is 3 below the average (a total of 7 below). Thus, the six terms average out to 7 above the average of 84. Accordingly, the seventh number is 7 below the average of 84, or 77.

37. E You can solve this problem by working backward from the answer choices—trying out each one in turn. Or, you can solve the problem algebraically. You can express the amount of sugar after you add water as $.05(60 + x)$, where $60 + x$ represents the total amount of solution after you add the additional water. This amount of sugar is the same as (equal to) the original amount of sugar (20% of 60). Set up an equation, multiply both sides by 100 to remove the decimal point, and solve for x:

$$5(60 + x) = 1{,}200$$
$$300 + 5x = 1{,}200$$
$$5x = 900$$
$$x = 180$$

Verbal Ability

1. B The original version (A) is faulty in two respects. First, the plural subject *benefits* is followed by the singular verb *is*. Second, the preposition *by* is not idiomatic in this context. (B) remedies both problems with the original sentence—by using the plural *are*, which agrees with *benefits*, and by replacing *by* with *from* (which is idiomatic here).

ANSWERS

2. C The original statement (A) includes an ambiguous pronoun reference. It is unclear whether *they* refers to the bounty hunters, their captives, or the authorities. (C) remedies the original sentence's ambiguous pronoun reference by reconstructing the sentence.

3. B The original sentence (A) suffers from faulty parallelism. Each of the three items in the underlined clause should be similar in grammatical construction. While *actors* and *musicians* both describe the celebrities themselves, *some other high-profile vocation* does not. (B) establishes a consistent (parallel) grammatical construction among the three items in the series; each of the three items refers clearly to a vocation.

4. D The claim (in the second sentence) relies on the assumption that all other factors in weight loss—such as exercise and dietary habits—remained unchanged from prior to the two-week period through the two-week period.

5. B The passage draws the general conclusion that home buyers should "always" buy a new house based on a few specific advantages that new houses offer. (B) is the best criticism of the argument because it suggests that these factors are not necessarily the only factors, or the most important ones, in the home-buying decision.

6. D In the first paragraph, the author cites certain erroneous assumptions upon which the U.S. New Town concept was based. Then, in the next two paragraphs, the author describes how and why New Towns in the United States failed to solve urban problems and to provide the sort of social environment hoped for. (D) provides a good recapitulation of this entire discussion.

7. E In the second paragraph, the author states that one of the effects of New Towns was to draw high-income citizens away from the cities—essentially what (E) indicates.

8. C According to the first sentence of the passage, New Towns were originally conceptualized as a way to absorb growth. Based on other information in the passage, it appears that U.S. New Towns achieved this objective—at least to some extent—since city residents who could afford to move away from urban centers did so. At the same time, however, the cities were left with new problems, such as an insufficient tax base to support themselves and to retain businesses. Thus, like the phenomenon that (C) describes, New Towns were a new innovation that served to solve one problem but created another along the way.

9. D The original sentence (A) suffers from faulty parallelism. The second occurrence of *from* should be deleted to restore the proper parallelism between the phrases *the host* and *the diplomat's*. At the same time, the word *both* is redundant in light of the words *the other* at the end of the sentence, thereby confusing the meaning of the sentence. (D) remedies the original sentence's faulty parallelism by reconstructing the phrase, using the subjunctive form (*that . . . be*).

10. **E** If the statement in (E) is true, it suggests that Company X's experience is comparable to that of other merging companies, and therefore it is unlikely that many more Company X workers will leave as a result of the merger.

11. **A** Gwen's argument relies on the assumption that expensive restaurants are not as popular among the college students as inexpensive restaurants. Jose provides one reason why expensive restaurants are *not necessarily* less popular among the college students, suggesting that the disagreement is about whether expensive restaurants are in fact less popular among the college students than inexpensive ones.

12. **A** The original version is the best one. The noun clause *whether the universe is bound* is properly considered the subject of the sentence.

13. **E** The original sentence (A) improperly uses *less* instead of *fewer* in reference to a numerical quantity (the number of chemicals tested). Also, the modifier *most of which* is separated from its antecedent (*thirty*), resulting in confusion as to whether *most of which* refers to the thirty chemicals tested or the tests themselves. (E) remedies both problems in the original sentence.

14. **A** The original sentence (A) correctly uses the singular pronoun *its* in referring to the singular *bureaucracy*. Also, (A) is consistent in its use of the future tense.

15. **C** The passage describes an imaginary debate over the American democratic ideal among the writers of the American Renaissance, in which Emerson, Thoreau, and Whitman are grouped together in one school of thought while Hawthorne and Melville are paired in another. Choice (C) nicely matches this recap.

16. **E** The passage is clear throughout that Emerson is an idealist, which is just the opposite of a pragmatist.

17. **D** According to the passage, Melville, through his story of *Pierre*, conveyed the notion that democratic idealism was based on "misguided assumptions." Although the author is not as explicit that Hawthorne also believed idealists to be misguided, Hawthorne's conclusion that transcendental freedom leads to moral anarchy can reasonably be interpreted this way.

18. **C** The argument's conclusion is that the new lifeguard was *not* a factor in the declining number of deaths from last year to this year. (C) rules out one other possible explanation for the decline in the number of drownings, in turn rendering it more likely that the additional lifeguard *did* contribute to the decline.

19. **E** The conclusion in (E) is logically inferable from two premises given in the passage: (1) If MetaCorp continues to show a profit, then analysts will continue to recommend it (in symbolic form: *If A, then B*), and (2) if analysts recommend MetaCorp stock, then the stock's price will at least remain at its current level—in other words, either remain the same or increase (in symbolic form: *If B, then C*). From these two premises, (E) is logically inferable (in symbolic form: *If A, then C*).

ANSWERS

20. A The argument that the public is interested in high culture relies on the assumption that opera, ballet, or classical music are considered "high culture." (A) provides some evidence that this necessary assumption is a questionable one.

21. A The discrepancy among the cited studies involves the increase in the level of violence in television programming over the last twenty years. One possible explanation for the discrepancy is that the recent studies relied on different previous studies, which disagreed as to what the level was twenty years ago.

22. E The original version improperly uses *derive* instead of the proper idiom *are derived from*. (E) corrects this diction error.

23. E The original sentence (A) is faulty in its use of the pronoun *them* instead of the possessive *their* where the object of a verb (*opposed*) is a gerund (*trivializing*) that it is not the musicians themselves but, instead, their actions or traits. (E) corrects the improper use of *them*, replacing it with the possessive *their*, which properly precedes the gerund *trivializing*.

24. A The original sentence (A) is correct in its use of the idiomatic phrase *have yet to*.

25. B The factual information cited in the passage suggests that eating high-fat foods does not cause obesity. However, that information is no help in determining the real cause. By showing that the rise in obesity has coincided with an increase in the sales of high-sugar foods, (B) suggests that excessive sugar consumption might be the cause. Although this correlation in itself does not irrefutably prove that sugar is the culprit, it nevertheless helps strengthen the case.

26. C The argument's first sentence suggests that the supply-demand ratio for rental apartments with two or more bedrooms is decreasing at a faster rate than the supply-demand ratio of rental apartments with one or fewer bedrooms. One possible explanation for the difference is the one that (C) provides.

27. D The original version (A) is faulty in two respects. First, the placement of the commas sets up a flawed parallel structure between the progressive verbs *was considered* and *will be considered*. Second, the phrase *considered as* is idiomatically questionable here. A person is *considered* or *considered to be*, not *considered as*, at least in the broader context of this sentence. (D) remedies both problems with the original sentence.

28. B According to the passage, all cells of an organism contain the same genotype as the fertilized egg (lines 13–14). Thus, (B) contradicts the information in the passage.

29. E According to the passage, the maternal programming of early development and the genomic control of later differentiation are "especially well documented" (line 43).

30. A In the first two paragraphs, the author discusses the process of cell differentiation in embryonic development. While the author is particularly concerned with examining the mechanisms involved, no specific type of organism (animal) is discussed as an illustration until the final paragraph (which focuses on the sea urchin). Accordingly, (A) properly reflects the flow of the author's discussion.

31. B It allows you to confidently conclude that biotechnology firms will in fact continue to replace equipment more frequently than other businesses, and therefore will stand to benefit from the proposed law more than other businesses. It would make sense, then, that the biotechnology lobbyists might be behind the proposal.

32. D It would reduce the number of options available to new college graduates, thereby increasing the likelihood that a new college graduate would enter one of the lower-paying professions that requires only a four-year degree.

33. B The original sentence awkwardly mixes the active voice (first clause) and the passive voice (second clause). It also includes the unnecessarily wordy *by way of*. (B) corrects both problems with a concise second clause in the active voice.

34. D The original sentence (A) misplaces the phrase *Even for high school freshmen and sophomores*. This phrase is intended to modify *many students*; therefore, the author should reconstruct the sentence so that the two phrases appear nearer to each other. (D) moves the initial phrase to the end of the sentence, clarifying the sentence's meaning.

35. E The argument suggests that the key to a third-world country's political stability is to afford its citizens certain powers. However, the argument relies entirely on one observed case (Country X) in which both characteristics are present. To be convincing, the argument must at least show that these powers actually contributed to Country X's political stability. (E) provides one plausible scenario in which these powers could have nothing to do with the country's political stability.

36. A It is reasonably inferable from the first paragraph as a whole that the "standard repertory" mentioned in lines 13–14 refers to the music of Bach and Telemann as well as to other ("modern") music from their time (first half of the eighteenth century). In the second paragraph, the author mentions that the music of Bach, Telemann, and their contemporaries called for obsolete instruments (lines 32–34). Thus, the standard repertory might have included music that called for the use of obsolete instruments, as response (E) indicates.

37. D Although the passage does indicate that early music often called for the use of obsolete instruments, the passage does not state explicitly that performance practice involved determining which musical instrument to use.

ANSWERS

38. B According to the passage, the German musicologists did not study the music of Mozart and Haydn (post-1750 music) because, among other reasons, their music, "having never ceased to be performed, had maintained some kind of oral tradition of performance practice" (lines 48–50). Unannotated music is music that is not written, but strictly oral. (B) restates the author's point in these lines.

39. C According to the passage, performance practice was developed alongside the modern (early twentieth-century) collegium musicum, which was part of the German university. While the modern collegium musicum performed music from before the time of Bach and Handel, scholars in the field of performance practice studied certain aspects (e.g., choice of instruments, deciphering notation) of music from the same time period.

40. C If there are other ways to prevent one's cat from accumulating hairballs, then there is no reason to risk the cat's developing an allergic reaction (and, in turn, a harmful infection) by feeding it the medicated food.

41. C The original sentence (A) contains a misplaced modifying phrase (following the comma). The sentence's construction suggests that it is the electorate that cannot reasonably be disputed, although this makes little sense in the context of the sentence as a whole. (C) remedies the underlined phrase's faulty construction by rephrasing it as a noun clause.

Practice Test 2

Analysis of an Issue
1 Question—30 Minutes

Directions: Using a word processor, compose a response to the following statement and directive. Do not use any spell-checking or grammar-checking functions.

"No business should sacrifice the quality of its products or services for the sake of maximizing profits."

Discuss the extent to which you agree or disagree with the foregoing statement. Support your perspective using reasons and/or examples from your experience, observation, reading, or academic studies.

Analysis of an Argument
1 Question—30 Minutes

Directions: Using a word processor, compose an essay for the following argument and directive. Do not use any spell-checking or grammar-checking functions.

The following is excerpted from an editorial appearing in a local newspaper:

"In order to prevent a decline of Oak City's property values and in rents that Oak City property owners can command, the residents of Oak City must speak out against the approval of a new four-year private college in their town. After all, in the nearby town of Mapleton the average rent for apartments has decreased by ten percent since its new community college opened last year, while the average value of Mapleton's single-family homes has declined by an even greater percentage over the same time period."

Discuss how well reasoned you find this argument. In your discussion be sure to analyze the line of reasoning and the use of evidence in the argument. For example, you may need to consider what questionable assumptions underlie the thinking and what alternative explanations or counterexamples might weaken the conclusion. You can also discuss what sort of evidence would strengthen or refute the argument, what changes in the argument would make it more logically sound, and what, if anything, would help you better evaluate its conclusion.

Quantitative Ability

37 Questions—75 Minutes

Directions for Problem Solving Questions: *(These directions will appear on your screen before your first Problem Solving question.)*

Solve this problem and indicate the best of the answer choices given.

Numbers: All numbers used are real numbers.

Figures: A figure accompanying a Problem Solving question is intended to provide information useful in solving the problem. Figures are drawn as accurately as possible EXCEPT when it is stated in a specific problem that its figure is not drawn to scale. Straight lines may sometimes appear jagged. All figures lie on a plane unless otherwise indicated.

To review these directions for subsequent questions of this type, click on HELP.

Directions for Data Sufficiency Questions: *(These directions will appear on your screen before your first Data Sufficiency question.)*

This Data Sufficiency problem consists of a question and two statements, labeled (1) and (2), in which certain data are given. You have to decide whether the data given in the statements are *sufficient* for answering the question. Using the data given in the statements *plus* your knowledge of mathematics and everyday facts (such as the number of days in July or the meaning of *counterclockwise*), you must indicate whether:

Statement (1) ALONE is sufficient, but statement (2) alone is not sufficient to answer the question asked;

Statement (2) ALONE is sufficient, but statement (1) alone is not sufficient to answer the question asked;

BOTH statements (1) and (2) TOGETHER are sufficient to answer the question asked; but NEITHER statement ALONE is sufficient;

EACH statement ALONE is sufficient to answer the question asked;

Statements (1) and (2) TOGETHER are NOT sufficient to answer the question asked, and additional data specific to the problem are needed.

Numbers: All numbers used are real numbers.

Figures: A figure accompanying a Data Sufficiency problem will conform to the information given in the question, but will not necessarily conform to the additional information in statements (1) and (2).

Lines shown as straight can be assumed to be straight and lines that appear jagged can also be assumed to be straight.

You may assume that positions of points, angles, regions, etc., exist in the order shown and that angle measures are greater than zero.

All figures lie in a plane unless otherwise indicated.

Note: In Data Sufficiency problems that ask you for the value of a quantity, the data given in the statements are sufficient only when it is possible to determine exactly one numerical value for the quantity.

To review these directions for subsequent questions of this type, click on HELP.

Note: Although the questions in this section cover all difficulty levels, you'll find fewer easy questions than challenging ones. Keep in mind that the GMAT CAT will determine the difficulty level of each question based on your responses to prior questions.

1. What is the sum of $\sqrt{.49}$, $\frac{3}{4}$, and 80%?

   A. .425
   B. 1.59
   C. 1.62
   D. 2.04
   E. 2.25

2. If the value of XYZ Company stock drops from $25 per share to $21 per share, what is the percent of decrease?

   A. 4
   B. 8
   C. 12
   D. 16
   E. 20

3. How many buses are required to transport 175 students to the museum?

   (1) No two buses have the same carrying capacity.
   (2) The average capacity of a bus is 55 students.

4. The storage capacity of disk drive A is 85% that of disk drive B. What percentage of drive B's storage capacity is currently used?

   (1) Disk drive B holds 3 more gigabytes than disk drive A.
   (2) 8.5 gigabytes of disk drive B's storage capacity is currently used.

5. Eight square window panes of equal size are to be pieced together to form a rectangular French door. What is the perimeter of the door, excluding framing between and around the panes?

   (1) The area of each pane is 1 square foot.
   (2) The area of the door, excluding framing between and around the panes, is 8 square feet.

6. The denominator of a certain fraction is twice as great as the numerator. If 4 were added to both the numerator and denominator, the new fraction would be $\frac{5}{8}$. What is the denominator of the fraction?

   A. 3
   B. 6
   C. 9
   D. 12
   E. 13

7. If $.2t = 2.2 - .6s$ and $.5s = .2t + 1.1$, then $s =$

   A. 1
   B. 3
   C. 10
   D. 11
   E. 30

Questions 8 and 9 refer to the following graph:

AREA OF WAREHOUSE UNITS A, B, C AND D (AS PORTIONS OF TOTAL WAREHOUSE AREA)

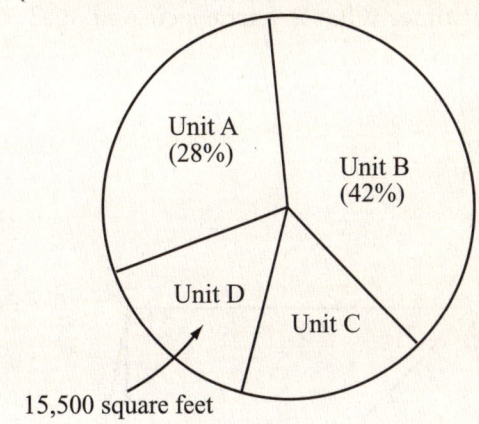

Unit A (28%)
Unit B (42%)
Unit C
Unit D
15,500 square feet

Total: 140,000 square feet
Note: Figure not drawn to scale.

8. By approximately how many square feet does the size of Unit A exceed that of Unit C?

   A. 9,000
   B. 11,000
   C. 12,500
   D. 15,500
   E. 19,000

9. The combined area of Unit B and Unit D is approximately

   A. 51,000 square feet.
   B. 57,500 square feet.
   C. 70,000 square feet.
   D. 74,500 square feet.
   E. 108,000 square feet.

10. Carrie's current age is 24 years greater than her son Benjamin's age. In 8 years, Carrie's age will be twice Benjamin's age at that time. What is Carrie's current age?

   A. 32
   B. 40
   C. 48
   D. 52
   E. 66

11.

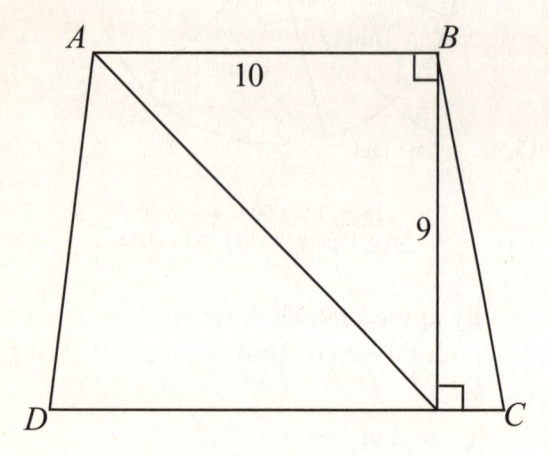

In the figure above, if the length of $\overline{DC}$ is 12, what is the area of *ABCD*?

   A. 99
   B. 108
   C. 112
   D. 120
   E. $50\sqrt{3}$

12. $\dfrac{\sqrt[3]{81x^7}}{\sqrt{9x^4}} - \dfrac{\sqrt{162x^5}}{\sqrt[3]{27x^6}} =$

   A. $3x^3 - \dfrac{1}{3}$
   B. $\sqrt[3]{2x} - 3$
   C. $\sqrt[3]{3x} - 3\sqrt{2x}$
   D. $3x^2 - \sqrt{2}$
   E. $9x - \sqrt{3}$

13. If the average (arithmetic mean) of the first sixteen positive integers is subtracted from the average (arithmetic mean) of the next sixteen positive integers, what is the result?

   A. 0
   B. 16
   C. 32
   D. 64
   E. 128

14. If $a > b$, and if $c > d$, then

   A. $a - b > c - d$
   B. $a - c > b - d$
   C. $c + d < a - b$
   D. $a - c < b + d$
   E. $b + d < a + c$

15.

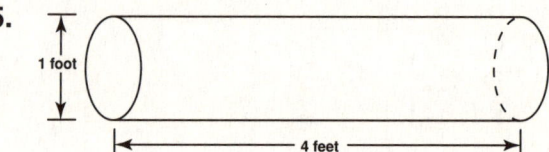

A closed cardboard box is to be designed for packing the cylindrical tube shown above. Will the entire tube fit inside the box?

   (1) The empty box contains 3 cubic feet.
   (2) The total surface area of the box is 14 square feet.

16. If *x* and *y* are negative integers, and if $x - y = 1$, what is the least possible value of *xy*?

   A. 0
   B. 1
   C. 2
   D. 3
   E. 4

17. A certain jar contains 20 jellybeans; each jellybean is either black, pink, or yellow. Does the jar contain more pink jellybeans than yellow jellybeans?

(1) The jar contains more black jellybeans than pink jellybeans.

(2) The jar contains 6 pink jellybeans.

18. Is the value of $a^2 - b^2$ greater than the value of $(3a + 3b)(2a - 2b)$?

(1) $b < a$

(2) $a < -1$

19. If $\blacktriangleleft x \blacktriangleright = (x + 2) - (x + 1) - (x - 1) - (x - 2)$, what is the value of $\blacktriangleleft -100 \blacktriangleright - \blacktriangleleft 100 \blacktriangleright$?

A. -196
B. -1
C. 0
D. 6
E. 400

20.

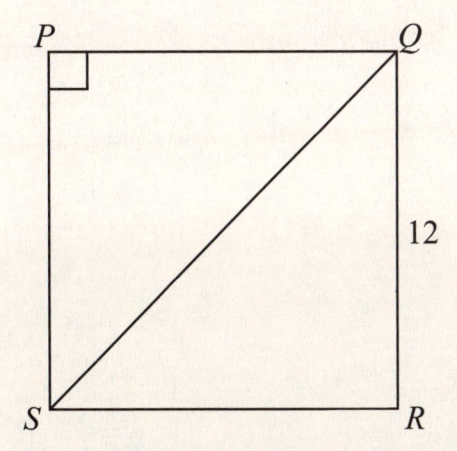

In the figure above, if PQRS is a rectangle, and if the length of $\overline{QR}$ is 12, is PQRS a square?

(1) The length of $\overline{SQ}$ is $12\sqrt{2}$.

(2) The length of $\overline{PS}$ is 12.

21. If a computer dealer bought a particular computer system for $10,000 and sold the computer system to a customer, how much did the customer pay for the computer system?

(1) The dealer's profit from the sale was 50%.

(2) The amount that the dealer paid for the computer system was two-thirds the amount that the customer paid for the computer system.

22. Which of the following distributions of numbers has the greatest standard deviation?

A. $\{-3, 1, 2\}$
B. $\{-2, -1, 1, 2\}$
C. $\{3, 5, 7\}$
D. $\{-1, 2, 3, 4\}$
E. $\{0, 2, 4\}$

23. Patrons at a certain restaurant can select two of three appetizers—fruit, soup, and salad—along with two of three vegetables—carrots, squash, and peas. What is the statistical probability that any patron will select fruit, salad, squash, and peas?

A. $\dfrac{1}{12}$
B. $\dfrac{1}{9}$
C. $\dfrac{1}{6}$
D. $\dfrac{1}{3}$
E. $\dfrac{1}{2}$

24. If bin *A* contains exactly twice as many potatoes as bin *B*, and if bin *A* contains exactly 11 more potatoes than bin *C*, does bin *B* contain more potatoes than bin *C*?

(1) The difference between the number of potatoes in bin *C* and the number in bin *A* is greater than the number of potatoes in bin *B*.

(2) If one potato were added to bin *A* and to bin *C*, bin *A* would contain exactly twice as many potatoes as bin *C*.

25. One of two ropes equal in length is cut into three segments to form the largest possible triangular area. The other rope is cut into four segments to form the largest possible rectangular area. Which of the following most closely approximates the ratio of the triangle's area to the rectangle's area?

A. 1:2
B. 2:3
C. 3:4
D. 1:1
E. 4:3

26. Code letters *X*, *Y*, and *Z* each represent one digit in the three-digit prime number *XYZ*. If neither *X* nor *Y* is an odd integer, what is the number represented by *XYZ*?

(1) The sum of the three digits is 7.
(2) $X - Y > 2$

27. If $abcd \neq 0$, and if $0 < c < b < a < 1$, is it true that $\dfrac{a^4bc}{d^2} < 1$?

(1) $a = \sqrt{d}$
(2) $d > 0$

28. If $x > 0$, and if $x + 3$ is a multiple of 3, which of the following is not a multiple of 3?

A. x
B. $x + 6$
C. $3x + 5$
D. $2x + 6$
E. $6x + 18$

29. If one dollar can buy *m* pieces of paper, how many dollars are needed to buy *p* reams of paper? (*Note:* 1 ream = 500 pieces of paper.)

A. $\dfrac{p}{500m}$

B. $\dfrac{m}{500p}$

C. $\dfrac{500}{p + m}$

D. $\dfrac{500p}{m}$

E. $500m(p - m)$

Questions 30 and 31 refer to the following chart:

SHARE PRICES OF COMMON STOCK
(ARDENT, BIOFIRM AND COMPUWIN CORPORATIONS)

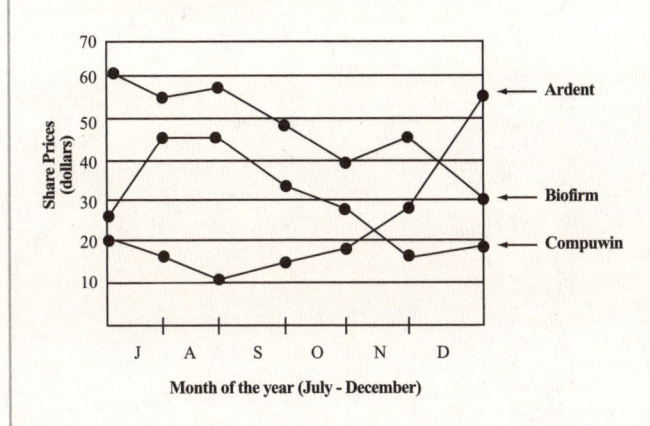

Month of the year (July - December)

30. At the end of September, the combined share price of Ardent stock and BioFirm stock exceeded the share price of Compu-Win stock by approximately

   A. 20%
   B. 35%
   C. 50%
   D. 100%
   E. 150%

31. During which of the following months did the aggregate share price of stock in all three companies change the LEAST?

   A. July
   B. August
   C. October
   D. November
   E. December

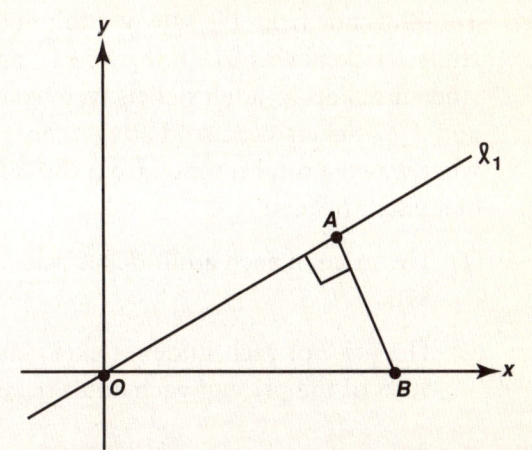

32. On the xy-plane above, if the equation of l_1 is $y = \frac{1}{2}x$ and if point B is defined by the xy-coordinate pair $(5,0)$, what is the area of $\triangle OAB$?

   A. 4
   B. $3\sqrt{2}$
   C. $2\sqrt{5}$
   D. 5
   E. 7

33. Twelve of 28 students are enrolled in English Literature, while 9 are enrolled in World History. How many of the 28 students are enrolled in Algebra I?

   (1) Three of the 28 students are enrolled in English Literature and World History but not Algebra I.

   (2) The total enrollment of all three classes is 35.

34. Total revenue from the sale of adult and student tickets was $180. If twice as many student tickets as adult tickets were sold, and if 27 tickets were sold altogether, what was the total revenue from the sale of student tickets?

(1) The price of each adult ticket was $10.

(2) The price of each student ticket was 50% of the price of each adult ticket.

35. If a, b, c and d are integers, is the sum of ab and cd an odd integer?

(1) a and c are both even integers.

(2) b is an even integer and d is an odd integer.

36.

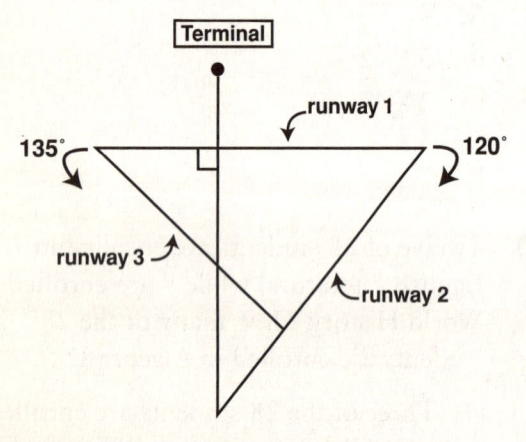

As shown in the figure above, from runway 1, airplanes must turn either 120° to the right onto runway 2 and 135° to the left onto runway 3. Which of the following does NOT indicate a complete turn from one runway to another?

A. 30°
B. 55°
C. 60°
D. 75°
E. 105°

37. A legislature passed a bill into law by a 5:3 margin. No legislator abstained. What part of the votes cast were cast in favor of the motion?

A. $\dfrac{3}{8}$

B. $\dfrac{2}{5}$

C. $\dfrac{8}{15}$

D. $\dfrac{3}{5}$

E. $\dfrac{5}{8}$

TEST 2

Verbal Ability
41 Questions—75 Minutes

Directions for Sentence Correction Questions: *(These directions will appear on your screen before your first Sentence Correction question.)*

This question presents a sentence, all or part of which is underlined. Beneath the sentence you will find five ways of phrasing the underlined part. The first of these repeats the original; the other four are different. If you think the original is best, choose the first answer; otherwise choose one of the others.

This question tests correctness and effectiveness of expression. In choosing your answer, follow the requirements of Standard Written English; that is, pay attention to grammar, choice of words, and sentence construction. Choose the answer that produces the most effective sentence; this answer should be clear and exact, without awkwardness, ambiguity, redundancy, or grammatical error.

Directions for Critical Reasoning Questions: *(These directions will appear on your screen before your first Critical Reasoning question.)*

For this question, select the best of the answer choices given.

Directions for Reading Comprehension Questions: *(These directions will appear on your screen before your first group of Reading Comprehension questions.)*

The questions in this group are based on the content of a passage. After reading the passage, choose the best answer to each question. Answer all the questions following the passage on the basis of what is *stated* or *implied* in the passage.

1. Either interest rates or the supply of money can, along with the level of government spending, be factors contributing to the amount of monetary inflation.

    A. can, along with the level of government spending, be factors contributing to
    B. along with the level of government spending, can one or the other be contributing factors in
    C. can, along with the level of government spending, contribute as factors to
    D. can be a contributing factor to, along with the level of government spending
    E. can contribute, along with the level of government spending, to

2. During his prolific career, Beethoven composed dozens of symphonies, out of which he never completed some of them.

    A. out of which he never completed some of them
    B. of which some of them were never completed by him
    C. which some he never completed
    D. some of which he never completed
    E. but some were not completed by him

3. The space program's missions to Mars have confirmed that the soil composition on that planet is similar to that on our planet.

    A. to that on our planet
    B. to our planet
    C. with the soil on our planet
    D. to this composition on our planet
    E. to our planet's soil's composition

4. According to life-insurance company statistics, nine out of ten alcoholics die before the age of seventy-five, as opposed to seven out of ten non-alcoholics. A recent report issued by the State Medical Board recounts these statistics and concludes that alcohol addiction increases a person's susceptibility to life-threatening diseases, thereby reducing life expectancy.

    The conclusion drawn by the State Medical Board depends on which of the following assumptions?

    A. People who are predisposed to life-threatening diseases are more likely than other people to become alcoholic.
    B. The statistics cited exclude deaths due to other alcohol-related events such as automobile accidents.
    C. Alcoholism does not also increase a person's susceptibility to diseases that are not life-threatening.
    D. The life expectancy of that portion of the general population not characterized by alcoholism increases over time.
    E. The author of the report is not biased in his or her personal opinion about the morality of alcohol consumption.

5. For the purpose of stimulating innovation at TechCorp, one of the company's long-standing goals has been to obtain at least 50 percent of its annual revenues from sales of products that are no more than three years old. Last year, TechCorp achieved this goal, despite the fact that the company introduced no new products during the year.

Which of the following, if true, best explains the results described above?

A. None of the company's competitors introduced any new products during the last year.
B. Scientists at the company report that they are close to breakthroughs that should result in several new products during the coming year.
C. Sales of some of the company's older products were discontinued during that last year.
D. The company has introduced very few new products during the last three years.
E. Company spending on research and development has increased sharply over the past five years.

Questions 6–8 are based on the following passage:

Line   The Pan-American land bridge, or isthmus, connecting North and South America was formed volcanically long after dinosaurs became extinct. The
(5)   isthmus cleaved populations of marine organisms, creating sister species. These twin species, called "geminates," then evolved independently. Scientists observe, for example, that Pacific pistol shrimp no
(10)   longer mate with those from the Atlantic Ocean. Yet the two oceans had already begun to form their distinctive personalities long before the isthmus was fully formed. As the seabed rose, Pacific
(15)   waters grew cooler, their upswelling currents carrying rich nutrients, while the Atlantic side grew shallower, warmer, and nutrient poor. In fact, it was these new conditions, and not so much the
(20)   fully-formed isthmus, that spawned changes in the shrimp population.
        For terrestrial life, the impact of the isthmus was more immediate. Animals traversed the newly formed bridge in
(25)   both directions, although North American creatures proved better colonizers— more than half of South America's mammals trace direct lineage to this so-called Great American Biotic Ex-
(30)   change. Only three animals—the armadillo, opossum, and hedgehog— survive as transplants in the north today.

6. Which of the following statements finds the LEAST support in the passage?

   A. Population divergences resulting from the formation of the Pan-American isthmus were more a process than an event.
   B. The divergence in ocean temperature during the formation of the Pan-American isthmus resulted in a divergence in the ocean's nutrient value.
   C. Genetic differences among pistol shrimp have grown to the point that there are now at least two distinct species of these shrimp.
   D. The part of ocean which is now the Pacific grew deeper due to the geologic forces that created the Pan-American isthmus.
   E. Not until the Pan-American isthmus was fully formed did geminate marine organisms begin to develop in that area of the ocean.

7. The author mentions the mating habits of pistol shrimp in order to show that

   A. some species of marine organisms inhabiting the Pacific Ocean are now entirely distinct from those in the Atlantic Ocean.
   B. twin species of marine organisms can each survive even though one species can no longer mate with the other.
   C. since the formation of the Pan-American isthmus, some marine geminates no longer mate with their sister species.
   D. geminate species that do not mate with one another are considered separate species.
   E. the evolutionary impact of the Pan-American isthmus was greater for marine organisms than for land animals.

8. Which of the following statements is most readily inferable from the information in the passage?

   A. Species of marine organisms in the Atlantic Ocean number fewer today than before the formation of the Pan-American isthmus.
   B. The number of terrestrial animal species in South America today exceeds the number prior to the formation of the Pan-American isthmus.
   C. Of the indigenous South American species that migrated north across the Pan-American isthmus, more than three survive to this day.
   D. Since the formation of the Pan-American isthmus, fewer terrestrial animals have traveled north across the isthmus than south.
   E. As the Pan-American isthmus began to form, most pistol shrimp migrated west to what is now the Pacific Ocean.

9. <u>That which is self-evident cannot be disputed, and that in itself is self-evident.</u>

   A. That which is self-evident cannot be disputed, and that in
   B. That that is self-evident cannot be disputed, of which
   C. It is self-evident that which cannot be disputed, and this fact
   D. The self-evident cannot be disputed, and this fact
   E. That which is self-evident cannot be disputed, a fact which

10. People who discontinue regular exercise typically claim that exercising amounted to wasted time for them. But this claim is born of laziness, in light of the overwhelming evidence that regular exercise improves one's health.

Which of the following statements, if true, would most seriously weaken the argument above?

A. Exercise has been shown to not only improve one's health, but also to increase longevity, or life span.
B. People who have discontinued regular exercise now make productive use of the time they formerly devoted to exercise.
C. People who are in good health are more likely to exercise regularly than people who are in poor health.
D. A person need not exercise every day to experience improved health from the exercise.
E. People who are in poor health are less likely to exercise than other people.

11. Very few software engineers have left MicroFirm Corporation to seek employment elsewhere. Thus, unless CompTech Corporation increases the salaries of its software engineers to the same level as those of MicroFirm's, these CompTech employees are likely to leave CompTech for another employer.

The flawed reasoning in the argument above is most similar to the reasoning in which of the following arguments?

A. Robert does not gamble, and he has never been penniless. Therefore, if Gina refrains from gambling she will also avoid being penniless.
B. If Dan throws a baseball directly at the window, the window pane will surely break. The window pane is not broken, so Dan has not thrown a baseball directly at it.
C. If a piano sits in a humid room the piano will need tuning within a week. This piano needs tuning; therefore, it must have sat in a humid room for at least a week.
D. Diligent practice results in perfection. Thus, one must practice diligently in order to achieve perfection.
E. More expensive cars are stolen than inexpensive cars. Accordingly, owners of expensive cars should carry auto theft insurance, whereas owners of inexpensive cars should not.

12. The technique of "ping-ponging," which permits overdubbing of audio sound tracks, has not been used as much from the time of the advent of computer-based recording.

    A. as much from the time of
    B. as much since
    C. as much as
    D. much as after
    E. much because of

13. The volatility of a balanced portfolio of stocks and bonds, less than eighty percent of the overall stock market.

    A. The volatility of a balanced portfolio of stocks and bonds, less than eighty percent of the overall stock market.
    B. A balanced portfolio of stocks and bonds is less than eighty percent as volatile as the overall stock market.
    C. A balanced portfolio of stocks and bonds is less than eighty percent as volatile as that of the overall stock market.
    D. Volatility is less than eighty percent for a balanced portfolio of stocks and bonds compared to the overall stock market.
    E. The volatility of a balanced portfolio of stocks and bonds is less than eighty percent of the overall stock market.

14. In 19th-century Europe, a renewed interest in Middle Eastern architecture was kindled not only by increased trade but also by increased tourism and improved diplomatic relations.

    A. not only by increased trade but also by
    B. by not only increased trade but also by
    C. not only by increased trade but also
    D. not only by increased trade but
    E. by increased trade and also by

Questions 15–17 are based on the following passage:

Line Historians sometimes forget that no matter how well they might come to know a particular historical figure, they are not free to claim a godlike knowledge
(5)   of the figure or of the events surrounding the figure's life. Richard III, one of England's monarchs, is an apt case because we all think we "know" what he was like. In his play *Richard III*, Shakes-
(10) peare provided a portrait of a monster of a man, twisted in both body and soul. Shakespeare's great artistry and vivid depiction of Richard has made us accept this creature for the man. We are
(15) prepared, therefore, to interpret all the events around him in such a way as to justify our opinion of him.

   We accept that Richard executed his brother Clarence, even though the
(20) records of the time show that Richard pleaded for his brother's life. We assume that Richard supervised the death of King Henry VI, overlooking that there is no proof that Henry was actually murdered.
(25) And we recoil at Richard's murdering his two nephews, children of his brother's wife Elizabeth; yet we forget that

Elizabeth had spent her time on the throne plotting to replace her husband's
(30) family in power with her own family. Once we appreciate the historical context, especially the actions of Richard's opponents, we no longer see his actions as monstrous. Richard becomes,
(35) if not lovable, at least understandable. What's more, when we account for the tone of the times during which Richard lived, as illuminated in literary works of that era such as Machiavelli's *The Prince*,
(40) Richard's actions seem to us all the more reasonable.

15. With which of the following statements would the author of the passage most likely agree?

    A. In *Richard III*, Shakespeare portrays the king as more noble than he actually was.
    B. The deeds of Elizabeth were even more evil than those of Richard III.
    C. Richard III may have been innocent of some of the crimes that Shakespeare leads us to believe he committed.
    D. Richard III may have had a justifiable reason for killing Henry VI.
    E. Shakespeare was unaware of many of the historical facts about the life of Richard III.

16. The author of the passage refers to Shakespeare's "great artistry and vivid depiction of Richard" (lines 10-11) most probably in order to

    A. make the point that studying *Richard III* is the best way to understand Richard as an historical figure.
    B. explain why *Richard III* is widely acclaimed as one of Shakespeare's greatest works.
    C. contrast Shakespeare's depiction of Richard with how Richard might have described himself.
    D. illustrate how historians might become prejudiced in their view of historical figures.
    E. point out that historians should never rely on fictional works to understand and interpret historical events.

17. It can be inferred from the passage information that Machiavelli's *The Prince* helps show

    A. that, in his play *Richard III*, Shakespeare's depictions of the king was historically accurate.
    B. that Richard's actions were an accurate reflection of the times in which he lived.
    C. that different authors often depict the same historical figures in very different ways.
    D. that Machiavelli was a more astute than Shakespeare as an observer of human nature.
    E. that Richard's actions as a king are not surprising in light of his earlier actions as a prince.

18. PharmaCorp, which manufactures the drug Aidistan, claims that Aidistan is more effective than the drug Betatol in treating Puma Syndrome. To support its claim, PharmaCorp cites the fact that one of every two victims of Puma Syndrome is treated successfully with Aidistan alone, as opposed to one out of every three treated with Betatol alone. However, PharmaCorp's claim cannot be taken seriously in light of the fact that the presence of Gregg's Syndrome has been known to render Puma Syndrome more resistant to any treatment.

    Which of the following, if true, would most support the allegation that PharmaCorp's claim cannot be taken seriously?

    A. Among people who suffer from both Puma Syndrome and Gregg's Syndrome, fewer are treated with Aidistan than with Betatol.
    B. Among people who suffer from both Puma Syndrome and Gregg's Syndrome, fewer are treated with Betatol than with Aidistan.
    C. Gregg's Syndrome reduces Aidistan's effectiveness in treating Puma Syndrome more than Betatol's effectiveness in treating the same syndrome.
    D. Betatol is less effective than Aidistan in treating Gregg's Syndrome.
    E. Neither Aidistan nor Betatol is effective in treating Gregg's Syndrome.

19. *City official:* In order to revitalize our city's downtown business district, we should increase the number of police officers that patrol the district during business hours. Three years ago, the city reduced the total size of its police force by nearly 20 percent. Since then, retail businesses in the district have experienced a steady decline in revenue.

    Any of the following, if true, would be an effective criticism of the city official's recommendation EXCEPT:

    A. Two years ago, the city established more rigorous standards for the retention and hiring of its police officers.
    B. New businesses offering products or services similar to those in the district have emerged outside the district recently.
    C. The number of people who reside in the district has not changed significantly over the last three years.
    D. Businesses operating in the city but outside the district have experienced declining revenues during the last three years.
    E. Some of the city's police officers patrol areas outside as well as inside the district.

20. Which of the following provides the most logical completion of the passage below?

    More and more consumers are being attracted to sport utility vehicles because they are safer to drive than regular cars, and because of the feeling of power a person experiences when driving a sport utility vehicle. In its current advertising campaign, Jupiter Auto Company emphasizes the low price of its new sport utility vehicle compared to the price of other such vehicles. However, this marketing strategy is unwise because _____.

    A. Jupiter's sport utility vehicle is not as safe as those produced by competing automobile manufacturers.
    B. If Jupiter reduces the price of its sport utility vehicle even further, Jupiter would sell even more of these vehicles.
    C. the retail price of Jupiter's most expensive luxury car is less than that of its new sport utility vehicle.
    D. most consumers who purchase sport utility vehicles are also concerned about the reliability of their vehicle.
    E. consumers who purchase sport utility vehicles associate affordability with lack of safety.

21. Since City X reduced the frequency with which its service vehicles pick up recyclable materials from residences for transport to its recycling center, the volume of material that its service vehicles transport to landfills for permanent disposal has increased to unmanageable levels. However, the city cannot increase the frequency of either its trash pickup or its recycling pickup at city residences.

    Based only the information above, which of the following strategies seems most appropriate for City X in the interest of reducing the volume of material that the city's service vehicles transport to landfills?

    A. Provide larger recycling containers to the residents of the city
    B. Establish a community program to increase awareness of the benefits of recycling
    C. Establish additional recycling centers as near as possible to the city's residential areas
    D. Provide incentives to the city's residents to reuse, rather than discard for pickup by the city's service vehicles, whatever they can
    E. Ease restrictions on the types of materials the city's service vehicles will pick up for transport to its recycling center

22. The pesticide Azocide, introduced to central valley farms three summers ago, has proven ineffective <u>because other pesticides' chemical compositions already in wide use</u> neutralizing its desired effect.

    A. because other pesticides' chemical compositions already in wide use
    B. because of the chemical compositions of the pesticides already in wide use
    C. due to other pesticides already in wide use, whose chemical compositions have been
    D. since, due to the chemical compositions of other pesticides already in use, those pesticides have been
    E. because of other pesticides and their chemical compositions already in use, which have been

23. To relieve anxiety, moderate exercise can be equally <u>effective as, and</u> less addictive than, most sedatives.

    A. effective as, and
    B. as effective as, while being
    C. effectively equal to, but
    D. as effective as, and
    E. effective, and

24. The government's means <u>of disposal of</u> war surplus following World War II met with vociferous objections by industrialists, prominent advisors, and many others.

    A. of disposal of
    B. in disposing
    C. for the disposition of
    D. used in disposing
    E. of disposing

25. No nation in the world has experienced as significant a decline in its Yucaipa tree population as our nation. Yet only our nation imposes a law prohibiting the use of Yucaipa tree-bark oil in cosmetics. The purpose of this law in the first place was to help maintain the Yucaipa tree population, at least in this nation. But the law is clearly unnecessary and therefore should be repealed.

    Which of the following, if true, would most seriously weaken the conclusion drawn in the passage?

    A. This nation contains more Yucaipa trees than any other nation.
    B. Yucaipa tree-bark oil is not used for any consumer goods other than cosmetics.
    C. The demand for cosmetics containing Yucaipa tree-bark oil is expected to decline in the future in other nations while continuing unabated in this nation.
    D. In other countries, labor used to harvest Yucaipa trees for cosmetics is less expensive than comparable labor in this nation.
    E. In this nation, some wild animals eat Yucaipa tree bark, thereby contributing to their destruction.

26. Some official Web sites of regionally accredited colleges have received the highest possible rating from the Federal Department of Education. However, all official Web sites of nationally accredited colleges have received the highest possible rating from the same department.

   Which of the following, if added to the statements above, would provide most support for the conclusion that all Web sites administered by individuals holding advanced degrees in educational technology have received the highest possible rating from the Federal Department of Education?

   A. Only official Web sites of nationally accredited colleges are administered by individuals holding advanced degrees in educational technology.
   B. All official Web sites of nationally accredited colleges are administered by individuals holding advanced degrees in educational technology.
   C. Only Web sites that have not received the highest possible rating from the Federal Department of Education are administered by individuals not holding advanced degrees in educational technology.
   D. All official Web sites of nationally accredited colleges are administered by individuals holding advanced degrees in educational technology.
   E. No Web site administered by individuals holding advanced degrees in educational technology is an official Web site of a regionally accredited college.

27. The time it takes for a star to change its brightness is directly related to <u>the luminosity of it</u>.

   A. the luminosity of it
   B. the luminosity of its brightness
   C. the luminosity of a star
   D. luminosity of it
   E. its luminosity

Questions 28–30 are based on the following passage:

Line   Diseases associated with aging in women are difficult to correlate explicitly with estrogen deficiency because aging and genetics are important influences in the
(5)   development of such diseases. A number of studies, however, indicate a profound effect of estrogen deficiency in syndromes such as cardiovascular disease (including atherosclerosis and stroke) and os-
(10)   teoporosis—the loss and increasing fragility of bone in aging individuals.
        The amount of bone in the elderly skeleton—a key determinant in its susceptibility to fractures—is believed to
(15)   be a function of two major factors. The first is the peak amount of bone mass attained, determined to a large extent by genetic inheritance. The marked effect of gender is obvious—elderly men experi-
(20)   ence only one-half as many hip fractures per capita as elderly women. However, African-American women have a lower incidence of osteoporotic fractures than Caucasian women. Other important
(25)   variables include diet, exposure to sunlight, and physical activity. The second major factor is the rate of bone loss after peak bone mass has been attained. While many of the variables
(30)   that affect peak bone mass also affect rates of bone loss, additional factors

influencing bone loss include physiological stresses such as pregnancy and lactation. It is hormonal status, however, (35) reflected primarily by estrogen and progesterone levels, that may exert the greatest effect on rates of decline in skeletal mass.

28. Based upon the passage, which of the following is LEAST clearly a factor affecting the rate of decline in bone mass?

    A. Gender
    B. Exposure to sunlight
    C. Progesterone levels
    D. Age
    E. Estrogen levels

29. In discussing the "marked effect of gender" (lines 18–19), the author assumes all of the following EXCEPT

    A. the difference in incidence of hip fractures is not due instead to different rates of bone loss.
    B. the incidence of hip fractures among elderly men as compared to elderly women is representative of the total number of bone fractures among elderly men as compared to elderly women.
    C. elderly women are not more accident-prone than elderly men.
    D. the population upon which the cited statistic is based includes both African-Americans and Caucasians.
    E. men achieve peak bone mass at the same age as women.

30. It can be inferred from the passage that the peak amount of bone mass in women

    A. is not affected by either pregnancy or lactation.
    B. is determined primarily by diet.
    C. depends partly upon hormonal status.
    D. may play a role in determining the rate of decrease in estrogen and progesterone levels.
    E. is not dependent upon genetic makeup.

31. Vining University's teacher credential program should be credited for the high grade-point averages of high school students who enroll in classes taught by Vining graduates. More new graduates of Vining's credential program accept entry-level positions at Franklin High School than at any other high school. And during the most recent academic year, just prior to which many of Franklin's teachers transferred to Valley View High School, the median grade point average of the students at Franklin has declined while at Franklin it has increased.

    The argument above depends on which of the following assumptions?

    A. The two high schools employ differing methods of computing student grade point averages.
    B. Neither high school has a peer tutoring program that would afford the school an advantage over the other in terms of student academic performance.
    C. Just prior to last year, more teachers transferred from Franklin to Valley View than from Valley View to Franklin.
    D. The teachers who transferred from Franklin to Valley View were replaced with teachers who are also graduates of Vining University's teacher credential program.
    E. The teachers who transferred from Franklin to Valley View last year were graduates of Vining's teacher credential program.

32. More airplane accidents are caused by pilot error than any other single factor. The military recently stopped requiring its pilots to obtain immunization shots against chemical warfare agents. These shots are known to cause unpredictable dizzy spells which can result in pilot error. Since many military pilots also pilot commercial passenger airliners, the reason for the military's decision must have been to reduce the number of commercial airline accidents.

Which of the following, if true, provides most support for the conclusion drawn above?

A. Recently, more pilots have been volunteering for the immunization shots.
B. All commercial airline flights are piloted by two co-pilots, whereas military flights are usually piloted by only one.
C. Chemical warfare is likely to escalate in the future.
D. Military pilots are choosing to resign rather than obtain the immunization shots.
E. Recently, the number of military pilots also piloting commercial airliners has declined.

33. While few truly great artists consider themselves visionary, many lesser talents boast about their own destiny to lead the way to higher artistic ground.

A. While few truly great artists consider themselves visionary, many lesser talents boast about their own destiny to lead the way to higher artistic ground.
B. While many lesser talents boast about their own destinies to lead the way to higher ground, few truly great artists consider themselves as visionary.
C. Many lesser talents boast about their own destiny to lead the way to higher artistic ground while few truly great artists consider themselves as being visionary.
D. Few truly great artists consider himself or herself a visionary while many lesser talents boast about their own destinies to lead the way to higher artistic ground.
E. While many lesser talents boast about their own destiny, few truly great artists consider themselves visionary, to lead the way to higher artistic ground.

34. History shows that while simultaneously attaining global or even regional dominance, a country generally succumbs to erosion of its social infrastructure.

A. History shows that while simultaneously attaining
B. History would show that, while attaining
C. History bears out that, in the course of attaining
D. During the course of history, the attainment of
E. Throughout history, during any country's attaining

35. *Connie:* This season, new episodes of my favorite television program are even more entertaining than previous episodes; so the program should be even more popular this season than last season.

Karl: I disagree. After all, we both know that the chief aim of television networks is to maximize advertising revenue by increasing the popularity of their programs. But this season the television networks that compete with the one that shows your favorite program are showing reruns of old programs during the same time slot as your favorite program.

Which of the following, if true, would provide the most support for Karl's response to Connie's argument?

A. What Connie considers entertaining does not necessarily coincide with what most television viewers consider entertaining.
B. Entertaining television shows are not necessarily popular as well.
C. Television networks generally schedule their most popular shows during the same time slots as their competitors' most popular shows.
D. Certain educational programs which are not generally considered entertaining are nevertheless among the most popular programs.
E. The most common reason for a network to rerun a television program is that a great number of television viewers request the rerun.

Questions 36–39 are based on the following passage:

(The following passage was written in 1991.)

Line One of the cornerstones of economic reform in the formerly Communist states is privatization, which can be approached either gradually or rapidly. Under the
(5) gradual approach, a state bureau would decide if and when an enterprise is prepared for privatization and which form is most suitable for it. However, gradual privatization would only prolong
(10) the core problems of inefficiency and misallocation of both labor and capital. Under one of two approaches to rapid privatization, shares of an enterprise would be distributed among the enter-
(15) prise's employees so that the employees would become the owners of the enterprise. This socialist-reform approach discriminates in favor of workers who happen to be employed by a modern and
(20) efficient enterprise as well as by placing workers' property at great risk by requiring them to invest their property in the same enterprise in which they are employed rather than permitting them to
(25) diversify their investments.

A better approach involves distribution of shares in enterprises, free of charge, among all the people by means of vouchers—a kind of investment money.
(30) Some critics charge that voucher holders would not be interested in how their enterprises are managed, as may be true of small corporate shareholders in capitalist countries who pay little
(35) attention to their investments until the corporation's profits fail to meet expectations, at which time these shareholders rush to sell their securities. While the resulting fall in stock prices can cause
(40) serious problems for a corporation, it is this very pressure that drives private firms toward efficiency and profitability. Other detractors predict that most people will sell their vouchers to foreign
(45) capitalists. These skeptics ignore the capacity of individuals to consider their

own future—that is, to compare the future flow of income secured by a voucher to the benefits of immediate consumption. Even if an individual should decide to sell, the aim of voucher privatization is not to secure equality of property but rather equality of opportunity.
(50)

38. In responding to those "skeptics" who claim that people will sell their vouchers to foreign capitalists (lines 43–45), the author implies that

    A. foreign capitalists will not be willing to pay a fair price for the vouchers.
    B. the future flow of income is likely in many cases to exceed the present exchange value of a voucher.
    C. foreign investment in a nation's enterprises may adversely affect currency exchange rates.
    D. although the skeptics are correct, their point is irrelevant in evaluating the merits of voucher privatization.
    E. foreign capitalists are less interested in the success of voucher privatization than in making a profit.

37. Which of the following would the author probably agree is the LEAST desirable outcome of economic reform in formerly Communist countries?

    A. Effective allocation of labor
    B. Equitable distribution of property among citizens
    C. Financial security of citizens
    D. Equal opportunity for financial success among citizens
    E. Financial security of private enterprises

36. Which of the following is NOT mentioned in the passage as a possible adverse consequence of rapid privatization?

    A. Undue prolongation of inefficiency and misallocation
    B. Loss of ownership in domestic private enterprises to foreign concerns
    C. Financial devastation for employees of private enterprises
    D. Inequitable distribution of wealth among employees of various enterprises
    E. Instability in stock prices

39. Which of the following is LEAST accurate in characterizing the author's method of argumentation in discussing the significance of falling stock prices (lines 38–42)?

    A. Describing a paradox that supports the author's position
    B. Asserting that one drawback of an approach is outweighed by countervailing considerations
    C. Rebutting an opposing position by suggesting an alternative explanation
    D. Discrediting an opposing argument by questioning its relevance
    E. Characterizing an argument against a course of action instead as an argument in its favor

40. Currently, the supply of office buildings in this state far exceeds demand, while demand for single-family housing far exceeds supply. As a result, real estate developers have curtailed office building construction until demand meets supply, and have stepped up construction of single-family housing. The state legislature recently enacted a law eliminating a state income tax on corporations whose primary place of business is this state. In response, many large private employers from other states have already begun to relocate to this state, and according to a reliable study, this trend will continue during the next five years.

Which of the following predictions is best supported by the information above?

- **A.** During the next five years, fewer new office buildings than single-family houses will be constructed in the state.
- **B.** Five years from now, the available supply of single-family housing in the state will exceed demand.
- **C.** Five years from now, the per capita income of the state's residents will exceed current levels.
- **D.** During the next five years, the cost of purchasing new single-family residential housing will decrease.
- **E.** During the next five years, the number of state residents working at home as opposed to working in office buildings will decrease.

41. Humans naturally crave to do good, act reasonably, and to think decently, these urges must have a global purpose in order to have meaning.

- **A.** to think decently, these
- **B.** think decently, yet these
- **C.** to decently think, and these
- **D.** thinking decently, but these
- **E.** think decent, these

Answers and Explanations

See Appendix for score conversion tables to determine your score. Be sure to keep a tally of correct and incorrect answers for each test section.

Analysis of an Issue—Evaluation and Scoring

Evaluate your Issue-Analysis essay on a scale of 1 to 6 (6 being the highest score) according to the following five criteria:

1. Does your essay develop a position on the issue through the use of incisive reasons and persuasive examples?
2. Are your essay's ideas conveyed clearly and articulately?
3. Does your essay maintain proper focus on the issue, and is it well organized?
4. Does your essay demonstrate proficiency, fluency, and maturity in its use of sentence structure, vocabulary, and idiom?
5. Does your essay demonstrate command of the elements of Standard Written English, including grammar, word usage, spelling, and punctuation?

Analysis of an Argument—Evaluation and Scoring

Evaluate your Argument-Analysis essay on a scale of 1 to 6 (6 being the highest score) according to the following five criteria:

1. Does your essay identify the key features of the argument and analyze each one in a thoughtful manner?
2. Does your essay support each point of its critique with insightful reasons and examples?
3. Does your essay develop its ideas in a clear, organized manner, with appropriate transitions to help connect ideas together?
4. Does your essay demonstrate proficiency, fluency, and maturity in its use of sentence structure, vocabulary, and idiom?
5. Does your essay demonstrate command of the elements of Standard Written English, including grammar, word usage, spelling, and punctuation?

The following series of questions, which serve to identify the Argument's four distinct problems, will help you evaluate your essay in terms of criteria 1 and 2. To earn a score of 4 or higher, your essay should identify at least three of these problems and, for each one, provide at least one example or counterexample that supports your critique. (Your examples need not be the same as the ones below.) Identifying and discussing all four problems would help earn you an even higher score.

- Does the Argument draw a *questionable analogy* between Oak City's circumstances and Mapleton's? (Perhaps the percentage of students needing off-campus housing, which might affect property values, is significantly greater in one town than the other.)

- Does the Argument draw a *questionable analogy* between four-year colleges and community colleges? (Perhaps a four-year college would bring greater prestige or higher culture to the town.)

- Is the presence of Mapleton's new community college necessarily the *actual cause* of the decline in Mapleton's property values and rents? (Perhaps some other recent development is responsible instead.)

- Is it *necessary* to refuse the new college in order to prevent a decline in property values and rents? (Perhaps Oak City can counteract downward pressure on property values and rents through some means.)

Quantitative Ability

1. **E** Since the answer choices are expressed in decimal terms, rewrite all three terms in the question to decimals, then add:

$$\sqrt{.49} = .7$$
$$\frac{3}{4} = .75$$
$$80\% = .8$$
$$.7 + .75 + .8 = 2.25$$

2. **D** The amount of the decrease is $4. The percent of the decrease is $\frac{4}{25}$, or $\frac{16}{100}$, or 16%.

3. **E** Statement (1) alone provides no information about how many students a bus can carry, so it is insufficient to answer the question. Statement (2) provides only an average. Some buses might have a greater capacity, while others might have a lesser capacity.

4. **C** To answer the question, you need to know drive B's total capacity as well as the amount (number of gigabytes) of drive B's capacity currently used. Statement (1), together with the information given in the question stem, provides the former, while Statement (2) provides the latter. [The storage capacities of drives A and B are 17 and 20, respectively. Of drive B's 20 gigabyte capacity, 42.5% (8.5 gigabytes) is currently used.]

5. **E** You could piece together the panes into either a single column (or row) of 8 panes or into 2 adjacent columns (or rows) of 4 panes each. In the first case, the door's perimeter would be 18. In the second case, the door's perimeter would be 12. Thus, statement (1) alone is insufficient to answer the question. Statement (2) alone is insufficient for the same reason. Both statements together still fail to provide sufficient information to determine the shape (or perimeter) of the door.

6. **D** One way to solve this problem is to substitute each answer choice in turn into the given fraction. You can also solve the problem algebraically. Let $\frac{x}{2x}$ represent the original fraction. Add 4 to both the numerator and denominator, then cross-multiply to solve for x:

$$\frac{x+4}{2x+4} = \frac{5}{8}$$
$$8x + 32 = 10x + 20$$
$$12 = 2x$$
$$6 = x$$

The original denominator is $2x$, or 12.

7. **B** Because the t-terms are the same ($.2t$), the quickest way to solve for s is with the addition-subtraction method. Manipulate both equations so that corresponding terms "line up," then add the two equations:

$$.2t + .6s = 2.2$$
$$-.2t + .5s = 1.1$$
$$\overline{1.1s = 3.3}$$
$$s = 3$$

8. **C** To determine the size of Unit C, first determine the size of Unit D as a percentage of the total warehouse size. Unit D occupies 15,500 square feet, or approximately 11%, of the total 140,000 square feet in the warehouse. Thus, Unit C occupies 19% of that total (100% − 28% − 42% − 11% = 19%). The question asks for the difference in size between Unit A (28%) and Unit D (19%). That difference is 9% of the 140,000 total square feet, or 12,600 square feet.

9. **D** The size of Unit B is 42% of 140,000 square feet, or about 59,000 square feet. Thus, the combined size of Unit B and Unit D is approximately 74,500 square feet.

10. B One way to solve this problem is to substitute each answer choice, in turn, for Carrie's current age. You can also solve the problem by setting up an algebraic equation. Letting x equal Benjamin's present age, you can express Benjamin's age eight years from now as $x + 8$. Similarly, you can express Carrie's present age as $(x + 24)$, and her age eight years from now as $(x + 32)$. Set up the following equation relating Carrie's age and Benjamin's age eight years from now:

$$x + 32 = 2(x + 8)$$
$$x + 32 = 2x + 16$$
$$16 = x$$

Benjamin's current age is 16 and Carrie's current age is 40.

11. A Because of the two right angles indicated in the figure, $AB \parallel DC$, and $ABCD$ is a trapezoid. The area of a trapezoid $= \frac{1}{2}h(b_1 + b_2)$, where h is the height and each b is a parallel base (side):

$$A = \frac{1}{2}(9)(10 + 12) = 99$$

12. C Simplify all four terms by removing perfect squares or cubes. Then, for each fraction, divide common factors:

$$\frac{\sqrt[3]{81x^7}}{\sqrt{9x^4}} - \frac{\sqrt{162x^5}}{\sqrt[3]{27x^6}} = \frac{(3x^2)\sqrt[3]{3x}}{3x^2} - \frac{(9x^2)\sqrt{2x}}{3x^2} = \sqrt[3]{3x} - 3\sqrt{2x}$$

13. B Since each of the two series is strictly arithmetic (all terms are evenly spaced), for each series the mean is the same as the median: exactly midway between the least and greatest numbers.

Mean of first series: $\dfrac{1 + 16}{2} = \dfrac{17}{2}$

Mean of second series: $\dfrac{17 + 32}{2} = \dfrac{49}{2}$

Now, do the subtraction: $\dfrac{49}{2} - \dfrac{17}{2} = \dfrac{32}{2}$, or 16.

14. E If unequal quantities (c and d) are added to unequal quantities of the same order (a and b), the result is an inequality of the same order. (E) essentially states this rule.

ANSWERS

15. **D** First, you need to determine the volume of the cylindrical tube. The tube's radius (r) is $\frac{1}{2}$ and its length is 4. Apply the formula for the volume of a right cylinder ($V = \pi r^2 h$):

    $$V = \pi \left(\frac{1}{2}\right)^2 (4) = \pi \left(\frac{1}{4}\right)(4) = \pi$$

    The tube's volume is π (approximately 3.1) cubic feet. Regardless of its shape, the tube will not fit into a box containing only 3 cubic feet. Thus, given statement (1) alone, you can answer the question. (The answer is *no*.) Statement (2) alone allows for an infinite variety of box shapes. However, no shape with a surface area of 14 will accommodate the tube. How do you know this? Assume that the box's dimensions are $3 \times 1 \times 1$. It's total surface area is exactly 14, yet it's too short (only 3 feet long) to accommodate the tube, which is 4 feet long. Visualize altering the box's shape (making it either "fatter" or "skinnier") while maintaining a surface area of 14. To increase its length, you must sacrifice surface area of the base (and vice versa). In any case, a box with surface area of 14 cannot accommodate the tube. Thus, statement (2) alone suffices to answer the question. (Again, the answer is *no*.)

16. **C** Using negative integers with the least absolute value yields the least product. Start with -1, then decrease the values of x and y if necessary. The first two values that satisfy the equation are: $y = -2$, $x = -1$ $[-1 - (-2) = 1]$. Accordingly, $xy = 2$.

17. **E** Neither statement (1) nor (2) alone provides any information about the number of yellow jellybeans. Considering both statements together, however, we know that the jar must contain 7 or more black jellybeans (along with exactly 6 pink jellybeans). Accordingly, the jar can contain a maximum of 7 yellow jellybeans. If the jar contains either 6 or 7 yellow jellybeans, the answer to the question is *no*. However, if the jar contains 5 or fewer jellybeans, the answer to the question is *yes*.

18. **C** The expression $a^2 - b^2$ can also be expressed in its factored form: $(a + b)(a - b)$. Notice the similarity between this form and the binomial expression given in the question. Factor out the constants (numbers) in the binomial so that it more closely resembles the factored form of $a^2 - b^2$:

    $$(3a + 3b)(2a - 2b) = 6(a + b)(a - b) = 6(a^2 - b^2)$$

    So the question is asking: Is $a^2 - b^2$ greater than $6(a^2 - b^2)$? Considering statement (1) alone, $(a^2 - b^2)$ might be either positive or negative, depending on whether the absolute value of b is less than a or greater than a. Accordingly, $(6)(a^2 - b^2)$ might be either greater or less than $(a^2 - b^2)$, and statement (1) alone does not suffice to answer the question. Considering statement (2) alone, whether $(a^2 - b^2)$ is positive or negative depends on the value of b, and therefore $(6)(a^2 - b^2)$ might be either greater or less than $(a^2 - b^2)$. Thus, statement (2) alone does not suffice to answer the question. However, both statements together do suffice to answer the question. Given that $b < a < -1$, $(a^2 - b^2)$ must be a negative number. Multiplying this negative number by 6 yields an even lesser number (to the left on the real number line). Therefore, $6(a^2 - b^2) < a^2 - b^2$. (The answer to the question is *yes*.)

19. E Apply the defined operation to -100 and to 100 in turn, by substituting each value for x in the operation:

$$◂-100▸ = -98 - (99) - (-101) - (-102) = -98 + 99 + 101 + 102 = 204$$

$$◂100▸ = 102 - 101 - 99 - 98 = -196$$

Then combine the two results:

$$◂-100▸ - ◂100▸ = 204 - (-196) = 204 + 196 = 400$$

20. A Given statement (1) alone, $\triangle QRS$ must be a $1:1:\sqrt{2}$ triangle. Accordingly, $\overline{QR} \cong \overline{SR}$. Since $PQRS$ is a rectangle, $\overline{QR}$ and $\overline{SR}$ are congruent to their respective opposite sides. Thus, all four sides are congruent, and $PQRS$ must be a square. Statement (2) alone provides no new information. We already know that $PQRS$ is a rectangle and, accordingly, that the length of $\overline{PS}$ is 12. $\overline{PQ}$ and $\overline{SR}$ could be any length, so the rectangle might, but need not, be a square.

21. D Consider statement (1) alone. If the dealer earned a 50% profit from the sale to the customer, determining the amount the customer paid is a simple matter of adding 50% of $10,000 to $10,000. Thus, statement (1) alone suffices to answer the question. Consider statement (2) alone. If the dealer's cost was two thirds the amount the customer paid, then the customer paid $\frac{3}{2}$ of dealer's cost. Determining how much the customer paid is a simple matter of multiplying $10,000 by $\frac{3}{2}$. Thus, statement (2) alone suffices to answer the question.

22. A Computing standard deviation involves these steps:

(1) Compute the arithmetic mean (simple average) of all terms in the set

(2) Compute the difference between the mean and each term

(3) Square each difference you computed in step (2)

(4) Compute the mean of the squares you computed in step (3)

(5) Compute the non-negative square root of the mean you computed in step (4)

Applying steps 1–4 to each of the five answer choices yields the following results:

(A) $\frac{14}{3}$ (B) $\frac{5}{2}$ (C) $\frac{8}{3}$ (D) $\frac{7}{2}$ (E) $\frac{8}{3}$

Choice (A) is the only fraction that exceeds 4. [There's no need to compute the square roots of any of these fractions (step 5), since their relative values would remain the same.]

23. B In each set are three distinct member pairs. Thus the probability of selecting any pair is one in three, or $\frac{1}{3}$. Accordingly, the probability of selecting fruit and salad from the appetizer menu along with squash and peas from the vegetable menu is $\frac{1}{3} \times \frac{1}{3} = \frac{1}{9}$.

24. D Statement (1) says essentially: $A - C > B$. Given that bin A contains exactly twice as many potatoes as bin B, you can substitute $2B$ for A in the inequality, then determine the relationship between the number of potatoes in bins B and C:

$$A - C > B$$
$$2B - C > B$$
$$B - C > 0$$
$$B > C$$

Thus, statement (1) alone suffices to answer the question. (The answer is *yes*.) Given statement (2) alone, C must be less than $\frac{1}{2}A$. (If you're not certain of this, use a few simple numbers to confirm it.) Given that $B = \frac{1}{2}A$, you can conclude from statement (2) alone that $B > C$. Statement (2) alone also suffices to answer the question. (Notice that you can answer the question with either statement alone without the additional fact that bin A contains *exactly* 11 more potatoes than bin C. This additional information appears to make the problem more complicated than it really is.)

25. C The largest possible rectangular area is formed by a square, the area of which is the square of any side. (The length of each side is one-fourth the rope's length.) The largest possible triangular area is formed by an equilateral triangle, the area of which is defined as follows (s = the length of any side):

$$\text{Area} = \frac{s^2 \sqrt{3}}{4}$$

One way to compare the two areas is to substitute a hypothetical value for the length of the ropes. Assume the length of each rope before it was cut was 12. The length of each of the triangle's sides is 4, while the length of the square's sides is 3:

The triangle's area $= \frac{4^2 \sqrt{3}}{4} = 4\sqrt{3} \approx 4(1.7) \approx 6.8$

The square's area $= 3^2 = 9$

The ratio of 6.8 to 9 is approximately 3 to 4.

26. E Any multiple-digit prime number must end in an odd digit other than 5 (1, 3, 7, or 9). Considering statement (1) alone, Z must be either 1 or 3, and five possibilities emerge:

601
421
241
403
223

Statement (2) alone allows for many possibilities, since Z can be either 1, 3, 7 or 9. Statements (1) and (2) together eliminate only three of the possibilities, leaving more than one answer.

27. A Given statement (1), $a^2 = d$. Substituting a^2 for d in the fraction: $\frac{a^4 bc}{a^4}$, or simply bc. Given that b and c are both positive but less than 1, $bc < 1$, and statement (1) alone suffices to answer the question. (The answer to the question is *yes*.) However, statement (2) alone is insufficient to answer the question. Even if d is greater than zero, statement (2) fails to provide sufficient information to determine the relative values of the numerator and denominator. A sufficiently small d-value relative to the values of a, b, and c results in a quotient greater than 1, whereas a sufficiently greate relative d-value results in a quotient less than 1.

28. C $3x$ is a multiple of 3; thus, adding 5 to that number yields a number that is not a multiple of 3. None of the other choices fit the bill. (A) is incorrect because $x > 0$ and therefore must equal 3 or some multiple of 3. (B), (D) and (E) are incorrect because any integer multiplied by 3 is a multiple of 3, and any multiple of 3 (such as 6 or 18) added to a multiple of 3 is also a multiple of 3.

29. D The number of dollars increases proportionately with the number of pieces of paper. The question is essentially asking: "1 is to m as what is to p?" First, set up a proportion (equate two ratios, or fractions). Then convert pieces of paper to reams (divide m by 500) or reams to pieces (multiply p by 500). (The second conversion method is used below.) Cross-multiply to solve for x:

$$\frac{1}{m} = \frac{x}{500p}$$

$$mx = 500p$$

$$x = \frac{500p}{m}$$

30. **D** At the end of September the approximate share prices of the three companies' stocks were as follows:

    Ardent stock: $16
    BioFirm stock: $50
    CompuWin stock: $34

The aggregate price of Ardent stock and BioFirm stock was $66, which exceeds the price of CompuWin stock ($34) by approximately 100%.

31. **B** During August, the price of BioFirm stock and CompuWin stock increased by a combined amount of about $5. During the same month the price of Ardent stock decreased by about $6. The net aggregate change is nearly zero.

32. **D** The key to this problem involves perpendicular lines and the concept of slope. The slope of l_1 is $\frac{1}{2}$, which means that every 2 units from left to right (the line's "run") corresponds to 1 unit upward (vertically) on the plane (the line's "rise"). Since the angle at point A is a right angle, the slope of $\overline{AB}$ must be -2 (a "drop" or "negative rise" of 2 units for every 1 unit from left to right). Drawing a plumb line down from point A reveals that, in order to attain these slopes, the height (altitude) of $\triangle OAB$ must be 2:

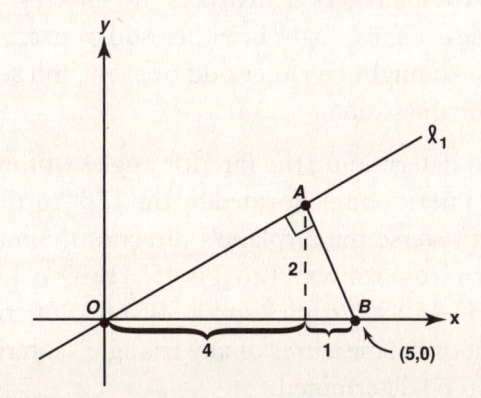

The area of any triangle is defined as one-half the product of its base and height (altitude). Given a base ($\overline{OB}$) of 5 and an altitude of 2, the area of $\triangle OAB$ must equal 5.

33. **B** Considering statement (1) alone, it is possible that any number of the remaining students, from 0 to 25, are enrolled in Algebra I. Statement (2) alone suffices to answer the question. Given that 12 students are enrolled in English Literature while 9 are enrolled in World History, if the total enrollment for all three classes is 35, then 14 students must be enrolled in Algebra I.

34. D Given that twice as many student tickets as adult tickets were sold, two-thirds (18) of the 27 tickets sold were student tickets, while one-third (9) were adult tickets. You can express the ticket sales revenue by way of the following equation (A = adult ticket price, S = student ticket price):

$$9A + 18S = \$180$$

Statement (1) provides the value of A, which allows you to determine the value of S (the answer to the question):

$$9(10) + 18S = 180$$
$$18S = 90$$
$$S = 5$$

Statement (2) allows you to substitute $2S$ for A in the equation above, thereby allowing you to determine the value of S (the answer to the question):

$$9(2S) + 18S = \$180$$
$$36S = \$180$$
$$S = \$5$$

35. A The product of an even integer and any other integer is always even. Therefore, statement (1) alone establishes that ab and cd are both even and, accordingly, that $ab + cd$ is even (the sum of two even integers is always even). Given statement (2) alone, however, although ab must be even, cd might be either odd or even, depending on the value of c. Accordingly, $ab + cd$ might be either odd or even, and statement (2) alone does not suffice to answer the question.

36. B The key to this problem is in determining the interior angles of the various triangles formed by the runways. The interior angle formed by the 120° turn from runway 1 to 2 is 60° (a 180° turn would reverse the airplane's direction). Similarly, the interior angle formed by the 135° turn from runway 1 to 3 is 45° (180° − 135°). Two triangle "angle triplets" emerge: a 45°-45°-90° triplet and a 30°-60°-90° triplet, as shown in the next figure. Since the sum of the measures of any triangle's interior angles is 180°, the remaining angles can also be determined:

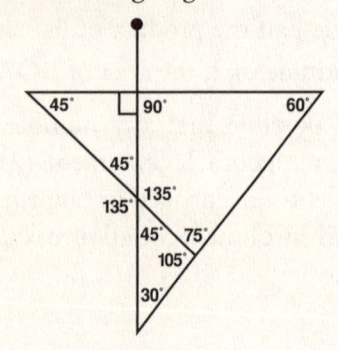

The only angle measure listed among the answer choices that does not appear in the figure above is 55°.

37. E You can answer this question without knowing the total number of legislators who voted, because the question involves ratios only. Think of the legislature as containing 8 voters divided into two parts: $\frac{5}{8} + \frac{3}{8} = \frac{8}{8}$. For every 5 votes in favor, 3 were cast against the motion. Thus, 5 out of every 8 votes, or $\frac{5}{8}$, were cast in favor of the motion.

Verbal Ability

1. E The original sentence (A) is faulty in two respects. First, the sentence treats the compound subject (*interest rates* and *the supply of money*) as singular by using *either . . . or*; the predicate should agree by also referring to the subject in the singular form, using *a factor* rather than *factors*. Second, the verb phrase *can . . . be* is improperly split. Third, the phrase *can . . . be factors contributing to* is redundant and wordy. (E) remedies all the original sentence problems by uniting the verb parts, rewording the predicate to agree in form with the subject, and removing the redundant language.

2. D The original version is wordy and very awkward. (D) is clear and concise.

3. A The original version is perfectly fine. The phrase *similar to* sets up a comparison between soil composition on Mars and soil composition on Earth. The relative pronoun *that* is proper here to refer to the latter.

4. B The argument relies on the assumption that alcoholics die relatively young only because alcoholism increases a person's susceptibility to life-threatening diseases, and not for other reasons as well. (B) provides explicitly that those other possible reasons were ruled out in compiling the insurance statistics cited in the report.

5. C Statement (C) helps explain last year's sales results by suggesting that sales of products three years old and older could have fallen sharply during the year. Thus, the proportion of sales produced by newer products could have grown, even without popular new products.

6. E It can reasonably be inferred that the "new conditions" which sparked the divergence in pistol shrimp are an aspect of the two oceans' "distinctive personalities," which the author states began to emerge "long before the isthmus was fully formed." Statement (E) contradicts the inference.

7. A The author discusses pistol shrimp as an example of twin species, or geminates. Thus, (A) expresses the author's immediate purpose in mentioning the mating habits of pistol shrimp.

8. C The second paragraph provides ample support for this inference. The author states that the terrestrial species migrating south were "better colonizers" than the ones migrating north, that *more than half* of those in the south today came from the north, and that *only three* animal species migrating north across the isthmus survive today. It is readily inferable, then, that more than three species that migrated south across the isthmus survive today.

9. **D** The original sentence (A) contains a vague pronoun reference. It is unclear as to what the second *that* refers. (D) restates the idea of the first clause of the original sentence more succinctly and clearly, as well as making it clear by the use of the phrase, *and this fact*, that the latter part of the sentence refers to the earlier part.

10. **B** The conclusion of the argument is that the claim made by those who have discontinued regular exercise is born of laziness; in other words, these people are making this claim because they are lazy. One effective way to refute the argument is to provide convincing evidence that directly contradicts the conclusion. (B) provides just such evidence, by showing that these people are not in fact lazy.

11. **D** The original argument's line of reasoning is essentially as follows:

    Premise: The well-paid engineers at CompTech do not quit their jobs.

    Conclusion: If MicroFirm engineers are not well-paid, they will quit their jobs.

    You can express this argument symbolically as follows:

    Premise: All A's are B's.

    Conclusion: If not A, then not B.

    The reasoning is fallacious (flawed), because it fails to account for other possible reasons why MicroFirm engineers have not left their jobs. (Some B's might not be A's.) (D) is the only answer choice that demonstrates the same essential pattern of flawed reasoning. To recognize the similarity, rephrase the argument's sentence structure to match the essence of the original argument:

    Premise: All people who practice diligently (A) achieve perfection (B).

    Conclusion: If one does not practice diligently (not A) one cannot achieve perfection (not B).

12. **B** In the original version, *the advent* and *from the time of* are redundant. Also, *since* is more appropriate than *from* to express the sentence's intended meaning. (B) corrects both problems.

13. **B** The original sentence (A) is not a complete sentence. (B) completes the sentence without committing any errors in grammar or diction.

14. **A** The original sentence (A) properly uses the correlative *not only . . . but also*. The two modifying phrases (*not only by increased* and *but also by increased*) are grammatically parallel.

15. **C** Shakespeare depicts Richard III as a monster with a twisted soul—a depiction that leads us to believe that Richard could well have been responsible for the deaths of both his brother Clarence and Henry VI. However, the author of the passage tells us that there is historical evidence that Richard did not kill his brother, and that there is no proof that Henry VI was actually murdered.

ANSWERS

16. D In the passage, the author first tells us that historians sometimes think they know an historical figure better than they really do. Then the passage's author explains how this can happen by providing an illustrative example—a biographical work (*Richard III*) that is so compelling in its development of the main character that even an historian can be unduly influenced by it.

17. B According to passage, Machiavelli's *The Prince* provides information about the tone of the times in which Richard lived. The passage's final sentence tells us that Richard's actions seem "reasonable" in light of the tone of the times—in other words, that his actions reflected the times.

18. A This argument relies on the assumption that Gregg's Syndrome is more prevalent among Puma Syndrome victims who take Betatol than among those who take Aidistan. (A) essentially affirms this assumption, although it expresses it in a somewhat different way. Given that Gregg's Syndrome renders any Puma Syndrome treatment less effective, if victims who have both syndromes are treated with Betatol while victims who have only Puma Syndrome are treated with Aidistan, then Aidistan will appear to be more effective, although the absence of Gregg's Syndrome might in fact be the key factor that explains the differing results.

19. C In all likelihood, the district's residents contribute to the revenues of businesses there by purchasing goods and services from them. A net loss in the number of district residents would provide an alternative explanation for the loss of revenue. (C) rules out this possibility, thereby *strengthening* the claim that the loss in revenue was due to the city's reduction in its police force and, accordingly, that increasing the size of the force will reverse the decline in revenues.

20. E The passage boils down to the following:

> *Premise:* People buy sport utility vehicles because they believe these vehicles are safe.
>
> *Conclusion:* To sell a vehicle, a manufacturer should not emphasize affordability.

Choice (E) provides the assumption needed to render the argument logically convincing:

> *Premise:* People buy sport utility vehicles because they believe these vehicles are safe.
>
> *Premise (E):* People do not believe that affordable vehicles are safe.
>
> *Conclusion:* To sell a sport utility vehicle, a manufacturer should not emphasize its affordability.

21. D Regardless of the reason for the increase in the volume of material transported to landfills, reducing the volume of material available for transport to landfills would serve the stated objective. (D) suggests a plan of action that, if successful, would help.

22. C The original sentence (A) is faulty in two respects. First, it improperly uses *because* instead of *because of*. Second, the construction leaves it unclear as to whether the modifying phrase *already in wide use* refers to *other pesticides* or to *chemical compositions*. (C) corrects the misuse of *because* by replacing it with *due to* (an alternative to *because of*).

23. D Instead of using the proper idiom *equal . . . to* or the proper correlative pair *as . . . as*, the original version attempts to make a comparison by using the improper *equal . . . as*. (D) corrects this error with the correlative pair *as . . . as*.

24. E The original sentence (A) uses *of* twice; the result is wordy and awkward. (E) is idiomatically proper and more concise than the original version.

25. D Choice (D) weakens the argument by providing some evidence that in this nation it would be comparatively expensive to produce cosmetics with Yucaipa tree-bark oil and, accordingly, that the tree population in this nation might not be significantly depleted even if the law were repealed.

26. A You can rephrase (A) as follows: *All* Web sites administered by individuals holding advanced degrees in educational technology are official Web sites of nationally accredited colleges. In other words, the following two symbolic statements are logically equivalent:

Only A are B.

All B are A.

Given that all Web sites of nationally accredited colleges have received the highest possible rating from the Department, and given that all Web sites administered by individuals holding advanced degrees in educational technology are official Web sites of nationally accredited colleges, it follows logically that all Web sites administered by individuals holding advanced degrees in educational technology have received the highest possible rating from the Department. To follow the logical steps, it helps to express the premises and conclusion symbolically:

Premise: All A are C.

Premise: All B are A.

Conclusion: All B are C.

27. E The original version is grammatically correct, but the pronoun reference is vague. (To what does *it* refer?) (E) clarifies the pronoun reference by using the possessive *its luminosity*.

28. B Exposure to sunlight was mentioned as one factor determining peak bone mass. Although the passage states that "many of the factors that affect the attainment of peak bone mass also affect rates of bone loss," it is unwarranted to infer that exposure to sunlight is one such factor.

ANSWERS

29. E As long as the population upon which the cited statistic was based excluded those who had not yet achieved peak bone mass, it does not make a difference whether the men in the group achieved their peak bone mass at a different age than the women.

30. A In lines 12–25, the author lists various factors affecting peak bone mass, then asserts that many of these factors also affect the rate of bone loss. In mentioning pregnancy and lactation as "additional factors" affecting bone loss, the author implies that these two factors do not also affect peak bone mass.

31. E The argument relies on two important assumptions. One is that the teachers who transferred from Franklin to Valley View were Vining graduates; the other is that teachers who transferred from Valley View to Franklin were not Vining graduates. If neither or only one were the case, then it would be unreasonable to conclude that Vining graduates are responsible for high academic performance. Admittedly, these assumptions involve a matter of degree; for example, the greater the percentage of Vining alumni among the teachers transferring from Franklin to Valley View, the stronger the argument's conclusion. And, admittedly, (E) does not acknowledge this fact. Nevertheless, (E) provides the essence of one of these two crucial assumptions.

32. C The argument concludes that the reason for the military's decision was to reduce pilot error during commercial flights. (C) is the only answer choice that supports this conclusion. Given that chemical warfare is likely to escalate in the future, it would seem that the military would *continue* to require immunization shots. But the military stopped requiring the shots. So the military's decision must have been based on some factor outweighing the potential danger of chemical warfare to pilots. One such possible factor is the increased danger of commercial airline accidents resulting from the immunization shots.

33. A The original sentence contains no grammatical errors, ambiguous references, or idiomatically improper words or phrases. The word *visionary*, used as an adjective here, is proper, although you could use the word *visionaries* (a noun) instead.

34. C The original sentence (A) is unclear in meaning; the use of the word *simultaneously* suggests that two or more items are attained. If the sentence had continued with the phrase *global and regional dominance*, the use of the word *simultaneously* would have made more sense. (C) excludes the confusing word *simultaneously* and properly sets off the prepositional phrase beginning with *in the course* with commas to clarify the sentence's meaning.

35. E Karl's response relies on two alternative but interrelated assumptions: (1) the reruns are likely to be popular enough to compete with Connie's favorite program, and (2) Connie's favorite program will not in fact be popular. (E) provides evidence that helps affirm both of these assumptions by suggesting that the reruns might very well be popular enough to draw the viewing audience away from Connie's favorite program, thus rendering it less popular. Admittedly, (E) would provide even greater support if it explicitly indicated that one popular program can draw viewers away from another. Nevertheless, (E) is the best among the five answer choices.

36. A The author foresees prolonged inefficiency and misallocation as a consequence of gradual, not rapid, privatization (lines 8–11).

37. E In the third paragraph the author suggests a willingness to place a private enterprise at risk for the broader purpose of achieving a free-market system. While advocating voucher privatization, the author admits that this approach may very well result in the instability of stock prices; yet, the author seems to view the insecurity caused by market pressures as "good" for private enterprises in that it will drive them to efficiency—a sort of sink-or-swim approach.

38. B The author responds to the skeptics' claim by pointing out that people are likely to weigh the future flow of income from a voucher against the benefits of selling their vouchers now and using the proceeds for consumption. If people were not likely, at least in many cases, to hold their vouchers after weighing these two alternatives, the author would not have made this argument. Thus, the author is implying that, in many cases, the future flow of income from a voucher will exceed the present value of the voucher.

39. C Although the author does respond to what might be one undesired result of voucher privatization—falling stock prices, as well as explain the cause of falling stock prices—the author does not offer an "alternative" explanation for this phenomenon, as suggested by (C). Moreover, the author's purpose in discussing falling stock prices is not to explain their cause, but rather to acknowledge that what appears to be an undesirable consequence of voucher privatization may actually help bring about a desirable result.

40. A The passage indicates that developers have curtailed construction of new office buildings until demand grows to meet supply, while stepping up construction of single-family houses. This evidence in itself strongly supports (A). Admittedly, it is possible that an influx of businesses from other states will deplete the current oversupply of office buildings and create sufficient demand for new ones. Nevertheless, (A) is the best of the five choices.

41. B The original sentence (A) lacks proper parallelism; *to* should be omitted. Also, the original sentence is comprised of two main clauses (each of which could stand on its own as a complete sentences) separated only by a comma. This comma splice should be corrected by inserting an appropriate connecting word, such as *but*, *yet*, or *although*. (B) corrects both problems with the original version.

Practice Test 3

Analysis of an Issue
1 Question—30 Minutes

Directions: Using a word processor, compose a response to the following statement and directive. Do not use any spell-checking or grammar-checking functions.

"Most great achievements are the result of careful planning and a long, sustained effort rather than to sudden bursts of creativity or insight."

In your view, how accurate is the foregoing statement? Use reasons and/or examples from your experience, observation, and/or reading to explain your viewpoint.

Analysis of an Argument
1 Question—30 Minutes

Directions: Using a word processor, compose an essay for the following argument and directive. Do not use any spell-checking or grammar-checking functions.

The following appeared in a speech by a prominent state politician:

"At Giant Industries, our state's largest private business, the average production worker is now forty-two years old. Recently, Giant's revenue from the sale of textiles and paper, which together account for the majority of Giant's manufacturing business, has declined significantly. Since an increasing percentage of new graduates from our state's colleges and universities are finding jobs in other states, our state will soon face a crisis in which the size of our workforce will be insufficient to replace our current workers as they retire, in turn resulting in widespread business failure and a reduced quality of life in our state."

Discuss how well reasoned you find this argument. In your discussion be sure to analyze the line of reasoning and the use of evidence in the argument. For example, you may need to consider what questionable assumptions underlie the thinking and what alternative explanations or counterexamples might weaken the conclusion. You can also discuss what sort of evidence would strengthen or refute the argument, what changes in the argument would make it more logically sound, and what, if anything, would help you better evaluate its conclusion.

Quantitative Ability

37 Questions—75 Minutes

Directions for Problem Solving Questions: *(These directions will appear on your screen before your first Problem Solving question.)*

Solve this problem and indicate the best of the answer choices given.

<u>Numbers</u>: All numbers used are real numbers.

<u>Figures</u>: A figure accompanying a Problem Solving question is intended to provide information useful in solving the problem. Figures are drawn as accurately as possible EXCEPT when it is stated in a specific problem that its figure is not drawn to scale. Straight lines may sometimes appear jagged. All figures lie on a plane unless otherwise indicated.

To review these directions for subsequent questions of this type, click on HELP.

Directions for Data Sufficiency Questions: *(These directions will appear on your screen before your first Data Sufficiency question.)*

This Data Sufficiency problem consists of a question and two statements, labeled (1) and (2), in which certain data are given. You have to decide whether the data given in the statements are *sufficient* for answering the question. Using the data given in the statements *plus* your knowledge of mathematics and everyday facts (such as the number of days in July or the meaning of *counterclockwise*), you must indicate whether:

Statement (1) ALONE is sufficient, but statement (2) alone is not sufficient to answer the question asked;

Statement (2) ALONE is sufficient, but statement (1) alone is not sufficient to answer the question asked;

BOTH statements (1) and (2) TOGETHER are sufficient to answer the question asked; but NEITHER statement ALONE is sufficient;

EACH statement ALONE is sufficient to answer the question asked;

Statements (1) and (2) TOGETHER are NOT sufficient to answer the question asked, and additional data specific to the problem are needed.

Numbers: All numbers used are real numbers.

Figures: A figure accompanying a Data Sufficiency problem will conform to the information given in the question, but will not necessarily conform to the additional information in statements (1) and (2).

Lines shown as straight can be assumed to be straight and lines that appear jagged can also be assumed to be straight.

You may assume that positions of points, angles, regions, etc., exist in the order shown and that angle measures are greater than zero.

All figures lie in a plane unless otherwise indicated.

Note: In Data Sufficiency problems that ask you for the value of a quantity, the data given in the statements are sufficient only when it is possible to determine exactly one numerical value for the quantity.

To review these directions for subsequent questions of this type, click on HELP.

Note

Although the questions in this section cover all difficulty levels, you'll find fewer easy questions than challenging ones. Keep in mind that the GMAT CAT will determine the difficulty level of each question based on your responses to prior questions.

1. If $\dfrac{a}{b} \cdot \dfrac{b}{c} \cdot \dfrac{c}{d} \cdot \dfrac{d}{e} \cdot x = 1$, then $x =$

    A. $\dfrac{a}{e}$

    B. $\dfrac{e}{a}$

    C. e

    D. $\dfrac{1}{a}$

    E. $\dfrac{be}{a}$

2. Three of four women—A, B, C, and D—are to be selected randomly to serve on a certain committee. Two of three men—X, Y, and Z—are to be selected randomly to serve on the same committee. What is the probability that the committee will consist of B, C, D, Y, and Z?

    A. $\dfrac{1}{12}$

    B. $\dfrac{1}{9}$

    C. $\dfrac{1}{6}$

    D. $\dfrac{3}{16}$

    E. $\dfrac{2}{9}$

3. Who takes less time to drive to work, Maria or Lupe?

   (1) Maria drives to work in 20 minutes.
   (2) Lupe and Maria drive the same distance to work.

4. The arithmetic mean (average) of two numbers is $P \times Q$. If the first number is Q, what is the other number?

   A. $2PQ - Q$
   B. $PQ - 2Q$
   C. $2PQ - P$
   D. P
   E. $PQ - Q$

5. What is the minimum value of $|a + b|$?

   (1) $|a| = 3$
   (2) $|a - b| = 1$

6.

   In the simple light show pictured above, a light starts at the center (white) at time zero and moves once every second in the following pattern: from white (W) to blue (B), back to white, then to green (G), back to white, then to red (R), and back to white—in a *counterclockwise* direction. If the light continues to move in this way, what will be the color sequence from the 208th second to the 209th second?

   A. White to green
   B. White to blue
   C. White to red
   D. Red to white
   E. Green to white

7. What is the value of x?

   (1) $x > 0$
   (2) $x^2 - 6x + 9 = 0$

8. If $\blacktriangleleft u \blacktriangleright = u^2 - u$, what is the value of $\blacktriangleleft \dfrac{2}{3} \blacktriangleright + \blacktriangleleft -\dfrac{2}{3} \blacktriangleright$?

   A. $-\dfrac{2}{3}$
   B. 0
   C. $\dfrac{2}{3}$
   D. $\dfrac{4}{9}$
   E. $\dfrac{8}{9}$

9.

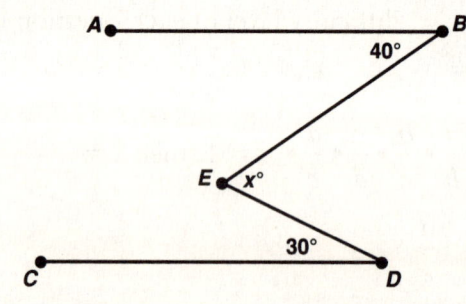

   In the figure above, if $\overline{AB} \parallel \overline{CD}$, then $x =$

   A. 40
   B. 50
   C. 60
   D. 70
   E. 80

10. Kirk sent $54 to the newspaper dealer for whom he delivers papers after deducting a 10% commission for himself. If newspapers sell for 40 cents each, how many papers did Kirk deliver?

    A. 135
    B. 150
    C. 160
    D. 540
    E. 600

11. If $x + y = a$, and if $x - y = b$, then $x =$

    A. $\frac{1}{2}(a + b)$
    B. $a + b$
    C. $a - b$
    D. $\frac{1}{2}ab$
    E. $\frac{1}{2}(a - b)$

12. Four of the five interior angles of a pentagon measure 110°, 60°, 120°, and 100°. What is the measure of the fifth interior angle?

    A. 100°
    B. 110°
    C. 125°
    D. 135°
    E. 150°

13. A certain animal shelter houses two different types of animals—dogs and cats. If d represents the number of dogs, and c the number of cats, which of the following expresses the portion of animals at the shelter that are dogs?

    A. $\dfrac{d}{c + d}$
    B. $\dfrac{c}{c + d}$
    C. $\dfrac{c}{d}$
    D. $\dfrac{c}{d}$
    E. $d + \dfrac{c}{d}$

14. HARVESTED CROP REVENUES (YEAR X)
    (Percent of total revenue among four counties)

	non-subsidized farms	subsidized farms
Willot County	7%	
Tilson County		12%
Stanton County		
Osher County	8%	
(Total Percentages)	30%	

    Based on the table above, if the total harvested crop revenues for Willot and Tilson counties combined equaled those for Stanton and Osher counties combined, then Stanton County's subsidized farm revenues accounted for what percentage of the total harvested crop revenues for all four counties?

    (1) During year X, Osher County's total harvested crop revenues totaled twice those of Tilson County.

    (2) During year X, Tilson County's farms contributed 18% of all harvested crop revenues for the four counties.

15.

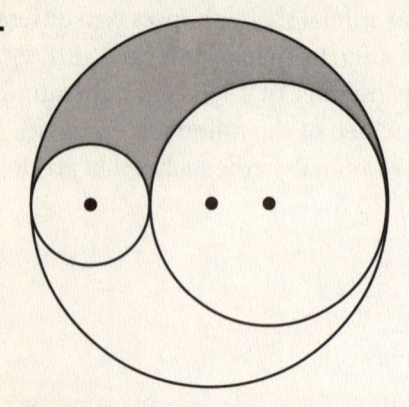

In the figure above, the centers of all three circles lie on the same line. The radius of the middle-sized circle is twice that of the smallest circle. If the radius of the smallest circle is 1, what is the length of the boundary of the shaded region?

A. 9
B. 3π
C. 12
D. 6π
E. 12π

16. If $a^m = b^n$, and if $a \neq b \neq m \neq n$, what is the value of $a + b + m + n$?

(1) $a, b, m,$ and n are all non-negative integers less than 10.

(2) $b^n = 81$.

17. M college students agree to rent an apartment for D dollars per month, sharing the rent equally. If the rent is increased by $100, what amount must each student contribute?

A. $\dfrac{D + 100}{M}$

B. $\dfrac{D}{M} + 100$

C. $\dfrac{D}{M}$

D. $\dfrac{M}{D + 100}$

E. $\dfrac{M + 100}{D}$

18. If n is a positive even integer, and if $n \div 3$ results in a quotient with a remainder of 1, which of the following expressions is NOT divisible by 3?

A. $n + 2$
B. $n + 5$
C. $n - 1$
D. $n \times 2$
E. $n \times 3$

19. $\sqrt{\dfrac{a^2}{b^2} + \dfrac{a^2}{b^2}} =$

A. $\dfrac{a^2}{b^2}$

B. $\dfrac{a}{b}$

C. $\dfrac{a^4}{b^4}$

D. $\dfrac{a}{b}\sqrt{\dfrac{a}{b}}$

E. $\dfrac{a\sqrt{2}}{b}$

20. Is it true that $\sqrt[3]{a} < a$?

(1) $a < 0$

(2) $a > -1$

21. A certain purse contains 30 coins. Each coin is either a nickel or a quarter. If the total value of all coins in the purse is $4.70, how many nickels does the purse contain?

A. 12
B. 14
C. 16
D. 20
E. 22

22.

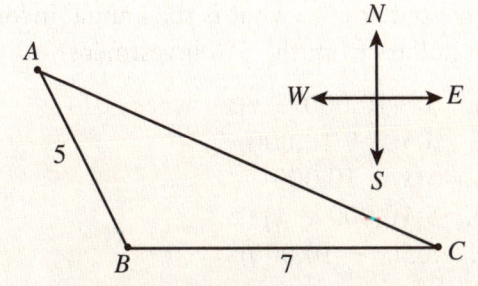

Once a month, a crop duster sprays a triangular area defined by three farm houses—A, B, and C—as indicated in the figure above. Farmhouse B lies due west of Farmhouse C. Given the compass directions and distances (in miles) indicated in the figure, what is the total area that the crop duster sprays?

(1) Farmhouse C is located 4 miles further south than farmhouse A.

(2) Farmhouse C is located 10 miles further east than farmhouse A.

23. Each computer system in a graphic-arts classroom is equipped with either a scanner, a printer, or both. What percentage of the computer systems are equipped with scanners but not printers?

(1) 20 percent of the computer systems are equipped with both scanners and printers.

(2) 25 percent of the computer systems are equipped with printers but not with scanners.

24. Daniel, Carl, and Todd working together can load a moving van in 8 hours. How long would it take Daniel working alone to load the van?

(1) Working alone, Carl can load the van in 15 hours.

(2) Carl and Todd working together can load the van in 12 hours.

25. What is the unit area of circle O on the standard xy-coordinate plane?

(1) Point $R(7,-3)$ and point $S(7,7)$ both lie along the circumference of circle O.

(2) R and S are the endpoints of the longest possible chord of circle O.

26. If A and B denote the digits of a three-digit number BAB, is BAB divisible by 4?

(1) The product of A and B is divisible by 4.

(2) The sum of B, A, and B is divisible by 4.

27. If a total of 55 books were sold at a community book fair, and if each book was either hardback or paperback, how many hardback books were sold at the book fair?

    (1) The total proceeds from the sale of paperback books, each of which was sold for 75 cents, was $19.50.

    (2) The proceeds from the book fair totaled $48.50.

Questions 28 and 29 refer to the following figure:

AVERAGE NUMBER OF HOURS PER WEEK SPENT WATCHING TELEVISION

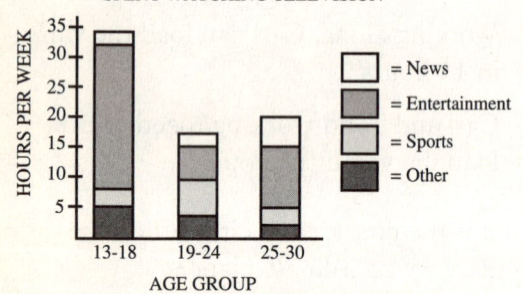

☐ = News
▨ = Entertainment
▢ = Sports
■ = Other

28. According to the graph, the two age groups, other than the group that spent the greatest number of hours per week watching sports on television, accounted for approximately what percent of the total hours spent watching television among all three age groups?

    A. 27
    B. 36
    C. 60
    D. 76
    E. 85

29. Which of the following is the approximate ratio of the average number of hours per week that the youngest age group spent watching entertainment on television to the average number of hours that the other two groups combined spent watching the same type of programming?

    A. 3:4
    B. 1:1
    C. 4:3
    D. 5:3
    E. 3:2

30. If a portion of $10,000 is invested at 6% and the remaining portion is invested at 5%, and if x represents the amount invested at 6%, what is the annual income in dollars from the 5% investment?

    A. $.05(10,000 - x)$
    B. $.05(x + 10,000)$
    C. $5(x - 10,000)$
    D. $5(10,000 - x)$
    E. $.05(x - 10,000)$

31. In a geometric series, each term is a constant multiple of the preceding one. If the first three terms in a geometric series are -2, x, and -8, which of the following could be the sixth term in the series?

    A. -128
    B. -17
    C. 64
    D. 256
    E. 512

32. What is the maximum number of rectangular boxes, each measuring 2 inches by 3 inches by 5 inches, that can be packed into a rectangular packing box measuring 18 inches by 19 inches by 35 inches, if all of the smaller boxes are aligned in the same direction?

- A. 296
- B. 356
- C. 378
- D. 412
- E. 424

33. If J is a set of six integers, what is the median value of those integers?

(1) The difference between the least and greatest integers in set J is 40.

(2) The arithmetic mean (average) of the six integers in set J is 15.

34.

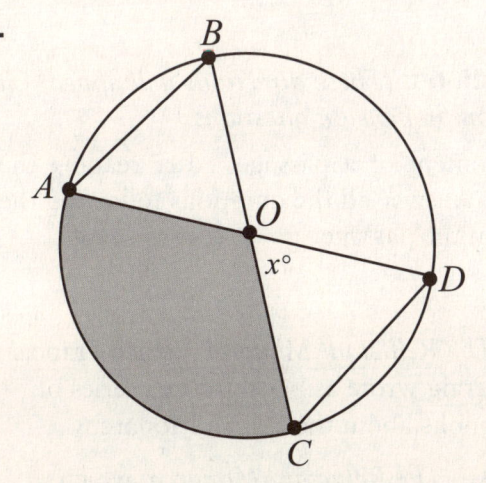

In the figure above, is the area of the shaded region less than the combined area of the two triangles?

(1) $x = 60$.

(2) The length of chord AB equals the circle's radius.

35. Two buses are 515 miles apart. At 9:30 a.m., they start traveling toward each other at rates of 48 and 55 miles per hour. At what time will they pass each other?

- A. 1:30 p.m.
- B. 2:00 p.m.
- C. 2:30 p.m.
- D. 3:00 p.m.
- E. 3:30 p.m.

36. $\dfrac{7^{77} - 7^{76}}{6} =$

- A. 7
- B. $7^{\frac{77}{76}}$
- C. 49
- D. 7^{75}
- E. 7^{76}

37. An investor can sell her MicroTron stock for $36 per share and her Dynaco stock for $52 per share. If she sells 300 shares altogether, some of each stock, at an average price per share of $40, how many shares of Dynaco stock has she sold?

- A. 52
- B. 75
- C. 92
- D. 136
- E. 184

Verbal Ability
41 Questions—75 Minutes

> **Directions for Sentence Correction Questions:** *(These directions will appear on your screen before your first Sentence Correction question.)*
>
> This question presents a sentence, all or part of which is underlined. Beneath the sentence you will find five ways of phrasing the underlined part. The first of these repeats the original; the other four are different. If you think the original is best, choose the first answer; otherwise choose one of the others.
>
> This question tests correctness and effectiveness of expression. In choosing your answer, follow the requirements of Standard Written English; that is, pay attention to grammar, choice of words, and sentence construction. Choose the answer that produces the most effective sentence; this answer should be clear and exact, without awkwardness, ambiguity, redundancy, or grammatical error.

> **Directions for Critical Reasoning Questions:** *(These directions will appear on your screen before your first Critical Reasoning question.)*
>
> For this question, select the best of the answer choices given.

> **Directions for Reading Comprehension Questions:** *(These directions will appear on your screen before your first group of Reading Comprehension questions.)*
>
> The questions in this group are based on the content of a passage. After reading the passage, choose the best answer to each question. Answer all the questions following the passage on the basis of what is *stated* or *implied* in the passage.

1. Not only smoking cigarettes but also cigar smoking has been banned now from many public places.
   - A. Not only smoking cigarettes but also cigar smoking has been banned now
   - B. Cigarette smoking and cigar smoking are both banned now
   - C. Not only has smoking cigarettes been banned but so has cigar smoking
   - D. Both smoking cigarettes and cigar smoking is now banned
   - E. Smoking cigarettes as well as cigars is now banned

2. *The Reluctant Monarch*, which Francis Craig wrote as her third in a series of books about the British Monarchy.
   - A. *The Reluctant Monarch*, which Francis Craig wrote as her third
   - B. *The Reluctant Monarch* is the third book written by Francis Craig
   - C. Written by Francis Craig, *The Reluctant Monarch*, which is her third book
   - D. Francis Craig wrote *The Reluctant Monarch*, which book is her third
   - E. *The Reluctant Monarch*, written by Francis Craig, is her third

3. Some varieties of parrots live as long as the age of one hundred years.

   A. as long as the age of one hundred years
   B. as long as one hundred
   C. as long as one hundred years old
   D. as long as one hundred years
   E. to be one hundred years old in age

4. Two years ago, a court found a certain cigarette manufacturer legally liable for the deaths of several thousand people who smoked the company's cigarettes, and ordered the company to pay a large sum to the families of those victims. The next year, the company's profits increased to record levels. The lesson for other large corporations is clear: Produce products that are unsafe or unhealthy for consumers, and your company will become more profitable.

   Which of the following, if true, would provide the best reason for rejecting the conclusion drawn in the last sentence above?

   A. Publicity resulting from court judgments against large businesses often affects their profitability.
   B. Manufacturers of potentially unsafe or unhealthy products are required by law to provide appropriate warnings to consumers.
   C. Manufacturers of dangerous products are often held liable for injuries to consumers resulting from the use of those products.
   D. The risks involved in using any product are just one of many types of factors consumers consider when buying a product.
   E. Compared to cigarettes, most consumer products pose insignificant risks to the health or safety of those who use them.

5. *John:* If a person believes in the inevitability of success, then that person will surely succeed.

   Jolanda: I disagree. According to a recent magazine article entitled "The 100 Most Successful Women in History," most of these 100 women did not believe they would ever become successful.

   Which of the following would be John's most logically convincing response to Jolanda's counter-argument above?

   A. Success does not depend on whether a person believes in its inevitability.
   B. Successful people are often viewed by others as unsuccessful.
   C. Success is inevitable for some people but not for others.
   D. Society's definition of success might have changed throughout history.
   E. None of the successful people listed in the magazine article were men.

Questions 6–8 are based on the following passage:

Line   The decline of the Iroquois Indian nations began during the American Revolution of 1776, when disagreement among them as to whether they should
(5) become involved in the war began to divide the Iroquois. Because of the success of the revolutionaries and the encroachment upon Iroquois lands that followed, many Iroquois resettled in
(10) Canada, while those who remained behind lost the respect they had enjoyed among other Indian nations. The introduction of distilled spirits resulted in widespread alcoholism, leading in turn to
(15) the rapid decline of both the culture and population. The influence of the Quakers impeded, yet in another sense contrib-

uted, to this decline. By establishing schools for the Iroquois and by introduc-
(20) ing them to modern technology for agriculture and husbandry, the Quakers instilled in the Iroquois some hope for the future yet undermined the Iroquois' sense of national identity.
(25)   Ironically, it was Handsome Lake who can be credited with reviving the Iroquois culture. Lake, the alcoholic half-brother of Seneca Cornplanter, perhaps the most outspoken proponent
(30) among the Iroquois for assimilation of white customs and institutions, was a former member of the Great Council of Iroquois nations. Inspired by a near-death vision in 1799, Lake established a
(35) new religion among the Iroquois which tied the more useful aspects of Christianity to traditional Indian beliefs and customs.

6. The passage mentions all the following events as contributing to the decline of the Iroquois culture EXCEPT:

   A. new educational opportunities for the Iroquois people.
   B. divisive power struggles among the leaders of the Iroquois nations.
   C. introduction of new farming technologies.
   D. territorial threats against the Iroquois nations.
   E. discord among the nations regarding their role in the American Revolution.

7. Among the following reasons, it is most likely that the author considers Handsome Lake's leading a rival of the Iroquois culture to be "ironic" because

   A. he was a former member of the Great Council.
   B. he was not a full-blooded relative of Seneca Cornplanter.
   C. he was related by blood to an important proponent of assimilation.
   D. Seneca Cornplanter was Lake's alcoholic half-brother.
   E. his religious beliefs conflicted with traditional Iroquois beliefs.

8. Assuming that the reasons asserted by the author for the decline of the Iroquois culture are historically representative of the decline of cultural minorities, which of the following developments would most likely contribute to the demise of a modern-day ethnic minority?

   A. A bilingual education program in which children who are members of the minority group learn to read and write in both their traditional language and the language prevalent in the present culture.
   B. A tax credit for residential-property owners who lease their property to members of the minority group.
   C. Increased efforts by local government to eradicate the availability of illegal drugs.
   D. The declaration of a national holiday commemorating a past war in which the minority group played an active role.
   E. A government-sponsored program to assist minority-owned businesses in using computer technology to improve efficiency.

9. Over thirty million illegal immigrants live in the United States, including greater than two million alone in California.

   A. greater than two million alone in California.
   B. in California greater than two million.
   C. more in California than two million.
   D. more than two million in California alone.
   E. greater than two million such illegal immigrants in California.

10. Babies who are breast fed instead of bottle fed until at least their first birthday are seventy percent less likely to become obese children than babies who are bottle fed but not breast fed. A child is obese if the ratio of the child's weight to height is among the highest three percent of all children. But breast feeding instead of bottle feeding during the first three months of a baby's life also reduces the likelihood that the baby will become an obese child.

    Which of the following can be most properly inferred from the information in the passage?

    A. Genetic propensity for obesity is not significant in determining whether a baby will become an obese child.
    B. Bottle feeding is more likely than breast feeding to result in obesity in children.
    C. Unless a baby is breast fed instead of bottle fed until at least its first birthday, the baby is likely to become an obese child.
    D. If a child is obese, there is a seventy-percent likelihood that, as a baby, the child was bottle fed but not breast fed.
    E. Breast feeding is ineffective to prevent obesity unless it is continued until at least the baby's first birthday.

11. When people are worried about general economic conditions, they tend to spend less on consumer goods. Official government figures show that retail inventory levels throughout the economy have been increasing in recent months. However, consumer-confidence levels are currently the highest they've been in several years.

    Any of the following, if true, would help to explain the apparent discrepancy described above EXCEPT:

    A. High interest rates tend to discourage consumers from buying products on credit that they otherwise could not afford.
    B. Businesses often increase production of consumer goods in anticipation of improving economic conditions.
    C. Consumer-spending levels tend to follow seasonal patterns.
    D. When the domestic currency's value increases compared to that of foreign currencies, foreign products become less expensive for domestic consumers.
    E. Increased business spending generally precedes a decline in consumer confidence levels.

12. Ignorance of the law does not preclude one being arrested for violating it.

    A. one being arrested for violating it
    B. arrest for one's violation of it
    C. one's violation and arrest for it
    D. one from being arrested for violating that law
    E. one from an arrest for having violated the law

13. <u>Rationalizing the protracted and bloody war</u> with the Philippines, President McKinley described the process of subjugating the Filipinos as "benign assimilation."

    A. Rationalizing the protracted and bloody war
    B. To rationalize the protracted war and bloody war
    C. The protracted and bloody war was rationalized
    D. Rationalizing the war, which was protracted as well as bloody
    E. To rationalize the war, a protracted and bloody one

14. Cambodia <u>remains being</u> a largely underdeveloped country because virtually all educated citizens were slaughtered during the regime of Pon Pen.

    A. remains being
    B. is still remaining
    C. is being
    D. remains
    E. remains still

Questions 15–17 are based on the following passage:

Line   For absolute dating of archeological artifacts, the radiocarbon method emerged during the latter half of the twentieth century as the most reliable
(5)   and precise method. The results of obsidian (volcanic glass) dating, a method based on the belief that newly exposed obsidian surfaces absorb moisture from the surrounding atmo-
(10)   sphere at a constant rate, proved uneven. It was initially thought that the thickness of the hydration layer would provide a means of calculating the time elapsed since the fresh surface was made. But this
(15)   method failed to account for the chemical variability in the physical and chemical mechanism of obsidian hydration. Moreover, each geographic source presented unique chemical characteris-
(20)   tics, necessitating a trace element analysis for each such source.
        Yet despite its limitations, obsidian dating helped archeologists identify the sources of many obsidian artifacts, and
(25)   to identify in turn ancient exchange networks for the flow of goods. Nor were ceramic studies and fluoride analysis supplanted entirely by the radiocarbon method, which in use allows
(30)   for field labeling and laboratory errors, as well as sample contamination. In addition, in the 1970s dendrochronological (tree-ring) studies on the bristlecone pine showed that deviation from radio-
(35)   carbon values increases as one moves back in time. Eventually calibration curves were developed to account for this phenomenon; but in the archeological literature we still find dual references to
(40)   radiocarbon and sidereal, or calendar, time.

15. Based on the information in the passage, which of the following is LEAST likely to have been a means of dating archeological artifacts?

    A. Ceramics studies
    B. Radiocarbon dating
    C. Dendrochronological studies
    D. Fluoride analysis
    E. Obsidian hydration-layer analysis

16. In the passage, the author mentions all of the following as problems with radiocarbon dating EXCEPT:

    A. disparities with the calendar dating system.
    B. deterioration of samples.
    C. identification errors by archeological field workers.
    D. contamination of artifacts.
    E. mistakes by laboratory workers.

17. With which of the following statements would the passage's author most likely agree?

    A. The greater the time that has elapsed since exposure of obsidian surface to moisture the less reliable the results of obsidian dating.
    B. The hydration layer accumulating through obsidian moisture absorption varies in thickness depending on the amount of surface area exposed to moisture.
    C. The unpredictability of the obsidian hydration process renders the obsidian dating method problematic as a means of determining historical trade routes.
    D. The results of obsidian dating are as reliable and precise as those of fluoride analysis only if trace element analysis is performed for the geographic source of the obsidian.
    E. An obsidian artifact can be reliably dated using the obsidian method only if certain environmental conditions where the artifact was found are considered.

18. When inhaled, asbestos fibers are known to significantly increase the likelihood of lung cancer and other respiratory ailments. Thousands of buildings in this state, especially apartment houses, are insulated with asbestos. Some local governments in the state have initiated massive and costly efforts to remove this asbestos.

    Which of the following, if true, taken together with the information above, best supports the conclusion that the health of those who occupy the buildings would be better preserved by leaving the asbestos in place than by removing it?

    A. In removing the asbestos, millions of fibers are likely to be dislodged and sent into circulation in the air.
    B. Asbestos removal is a hazardous procedure, posing significant health dangers to those who perform it.
    C. Fewer than one person in a hundred who breathes asbestos-contaminated air is likely to contract a respiratory ailment as a result.
    D. Apartment dwellers typically move from one residence to another more frequently than people who live in single family homes.
    E. Most people who live in apartment buildings insulated with asbestos are aware of that fact.

19. Over the last year, the price that toy manufacturer FunTime charges for each toy it produces and sells directly to consumers has, on average, nearly doubled, prompting complaints to the company by many consumers. To combat this problem, FunTime's management must make every effort to improve relations with its union workers in order to help prevent them from striking, as these workers did for several weeks during the past year.

    Which of the following, if true, would cast the most doubt on the effectiveness of the proposal suggested above?

    A. Despite the complaints from consumers, sales of FunTime toys directly to consumers have increased steadily over the last year.
    B. FunTime's union workers are likely to be skeptical of any attempt by management to improve its relations with them.
    C. Some consumers who buy FunTime toys don't mind paying more for them because they are the highest quality toys available.
    D. FunTime's union workers are likely to strike again in the near future, regardless of management's efforts to improve relations with them.
    E. Most of the increase in the prices of FunTime toys is attributable to an increase in the cost of the raw materials the company uses to manufacture its toys.

20. The emission of fluorocarbons into the earth's atmosphere has been shown to deplete the ozone layer in the atmosphere. Therefore, if we were to eliminate all sources of fluorocarbon emission, we could successfully halt ozone layer depletion.

    Which of the following demonstrates a pattern of reasoning that is most similar to the flawed reasoning in the argument above?

    A. When challenged to prove their psychic abilities, several of the world's most celebrated so-called psychics were unable to do so, clearly proving that the psychic phenomenon is fiction rather than fact.
    B. The theory that the earth's temperature would be shown to be cyclical if measured over millions of years is convincing, in light of the fact that the extinction of the dinosaurs occurred due to changes in the earth's temperature.
    C. Flag burning is ultimately in the state's interest as well as the individual's interest, because the First Amendment right to free expression was created for the purpose of preserving our democratic way of life.
    D. Any person suffering from phlebitis must take the drug Anatol in order to prevent the condition from worsening, as evidenced by the fact that doctors have used Anatol successfully for many years to treat and control phlebitis.
    E. Autopsies of the residents of Huiki Island killed by a recent volcanic eruption have shown excessive bone deterioration, which leads to my conclusion that the Huikan culture encourages a diet that promotes bone marrow disease.

21. *Advertising executive:* Those who oppose the use of humor in advertising, whether print and television, either lack a sense of humor or fail to understand the advantage of using humor to advertise a product or service. After all, numerous surveys show that ordinary consumers are almost twice as likely to recall a humorous commercial as they are to recall a serious commercial.

    Which of the following, if true, would cast the most serious doubt on the accuracy of the advertising executive's contention?

    A. Although most consumers surveyed were able to recall viewing humorous commercials, many said they enjoyed the serious commercials more.
    B. For certain types of products, humorous advertising would be inappropriate and potentially offensive.
    C. Although most consumers surveyed were able to recall viewing humorous commercials, most failed to recall the name of the product advertised.
    D. The consumers surveyed about humorous commercials included people considered unlikely to buy the particular product advertised.
    E. The use of humorous television commercials by advertisers has been declining over the last few years.

22. Upon man-made toxins' invading the human body, special enzymes are deployed, rebuilding any damaged DNA strands that result.

    A. Upon man-made toxins invading the human body, special enzymes are deployed, rebuilding any damaged DNA strands that result.
    B. Upon man-made toxins, invasion of the human body, special enzymes are deployed that rebuild any damaged DNA strands resulting from the invasion.
    C. When man-made toxins invade the human body, special enzymes are deployed to rebuild any DNA strands damaged as a result.
    D. Special enzymes are deployed whenever man-made toxins invade the human body; they rebuild any damage that results to DNA strands.
    E. Damage to DNA strands that results when man-made toxins invade the human body are repaired by deployed special enzymes.

23. The fact that the tie between the Manchus and the Chinese was cultural rather than racial helps to account for the homogeneity of the Chinese people.

    A. cultural rather than racial helps to account for
    B. not racial but cultural in nature helps explain
    C. a cultural tie but not racial helps explain
    D. cultural rather than a racial one helps to explain
    E. cultural rather than a racial tie helps to account for

24. The atmospheric study reported last month in the Journal of the Environment would not have been taken seriously by the scientific community if they were cognizant of the questionable methodology employed.

A. have been taken seriously by the scientific community if they were
B. be taken seriously by the scientific community in the event that it had become
C. have been taken seriously by the scientific community were they
D. have been taken seriously by the scientific community when the scientific community became
E. have been taken seriously by the scientific community had scientists been

25. Although the use of fertilizers tends to diminish the flavor of fruits, the use of pesticides makes virtually no difference in flavor, assuming the fruit is washed thoroughly. Moreover, the use of pesticides repels insects that would otherwise leave unsightly blemishes on the fruit. Therefore, in the interest of appealing to consumer tastes, fruit growers would be well advised to use pesticides but not artificial fertilizers.

Which of the following, if true, could proponents of the argument most appropriately cite as evidence for the soundness of the advice to fruit growers given in the last sentence?

A. The use of natural fertilizer results in larger, more colorful fruit than the use of artificial fertilizer.
B. The use of pesticides and fertilizers increase fruit growers' costs, which the growers generally pass on to consumers in the form of higher fruit prices.
C. Consumers generally consider a fruit's flavor to be important but consider a fruit's appearance to be less important.
D. Chemicals in artificial fertilizers pose a health threat to consumers who eat fruits produced using artificial fertilizers.
E. The use of artificial fertilizers in growing fruit has no effect on the appearance of the fruit.

26. A recent research study of a particular state's prison systems indicates that prisoners participating in the weekend furlough program are less likely to become repeat offenders after they are released than prisoners who do not participate in the program. The study confirms the researchers' hypothesis that weekend furlough programs at the state's prisons are an effective means of reducing crime.

Which of the following, if true, would cast the most serious doubt on the hypothesis to which the last sentence above refers?

- A. The furlough program was available only to prisoners who had demonstrated good behavior while in prison.
- B. The crime rate in other states with similar furlough programs is lower overall than the crime rate in states without furlough programs.
- C. Whether the weekend furlough program is effective depends on how greatly one values the reform of any one prisoner.
- D. Less than half of the prisoners not involved in the furlough program become repeat offenders after they are released.
- E. Less than half of all the prisoners studied participated in the furlough program.

27. Too many naive consumers <u>hasty and happily provide</u> credit information to unscrupulous merchants, who provide nothing in exchange but a credit fraud nightmare.

- A. hasty and happily provide
- B. hastily and happily provide
- C. hasty and happy providing
- D. hastily and happily providing
- E. providing hastily and happily

Questions 28–30 are based on the following passage:

Line The 35-millimeter (mm) format for movie production became a de facto standard around 1913. The mid-1920s through the mid-1930s, however, saw a
(5) resurgence of wide-film formats. During this time period, formats used by studios ranged in gauge from 55mm to 70mm. Research and development then slackened until the 1950s, when wide-screen
(10) film-making came back in direct response to the erosion of box-office receipts because of the rising popularity of television. This Cinerama (1952) is generally considered to mark the
(15) beginning of the modern era of wide-screen film-making, which saw another flurry of specialized formats, such as Cinemascope. In 1956, Panavision developed Camera 65 for MGM Studios;
(20) it was first used during the filming of *Raintree Country*. Panavision soon contributed another key technical advance by developing spherical 65mm lenses, which eliminated the "fat faces"
(25) syndrome that had plagued earlier CinemaScope films.

Some forty "roadshow" films were filmed in wide-screen formats during this period. But wide-screen formats floun-
(30) dered due to expense, unwieldy cameras, and slow film stocks and lenses. After the invention of a set of 35mm anamorphic lenses, which could be used in conjunction with much more mobile cameras to
(35) squeeze a wide-screen image onto theatrical screens, film technology improved to the point where quality 70mm prints could be blown up from 35mm negatives.

28. It can be inferred from the information in the passage that wide-film formats were

  A. in use before 1913.
  B. not used during the 1940s.
  C. more widely used during the 1920s than during the 1930s.
  D. not used after 1956.
  E. more widely used for some types of movies than for others.

29. The passage mentions all the following as factors contributing to the increased use of wide-film formats for moviemaking EXCEPT:

  A. spherical camera lenses.
  B. Panavision's Camera 65.
  C. television.
  D. anamorphic camera lenses.
  E. movie theater revenues.

30. Which of the following statements is most strongly supported by the passage's information?

  A. If a movie does not suffer from the "fat faces" syndrome, then it was not produced in a wide-film format.
  B. Prior to the invention of the 35mm anamorphic lens, quality larger prints could not be made from smaller negatives.
  C. The same factors that contributed to the resurgence of wide-film formats in the 1950s also led to the subsequent decline in their use.
  D. The most significant developments in 35mm technology occurred after the release of *Raintree Country*.
  E. Movie-theater revenues are not significantly affected by whether the movies shown are in wide-screen format.

31. Many individuals take antihistamine medications to alleviate the symptoms of allergies. Although all antihistamines are essentially similar, there is sufficient variation among the available formulas to make some more effective than others for any particular individual. Therefore, by trying different antihistamine formulations, any allergy sufferer can eventually find one that is effective.

Which of the following, if true, would most strengthen the conclusion drawn in the argument above?

  A. Antihistamines are the only types of medications proven effective in treating allergy symptoms.
  B. At least one antihistamine will relieve any individual's allergy symptoms.
  C. The effectiveness of an antihistamine is partially determined by the drug's specific formulation.
  D. The specific formulation used most often by allergy sufferers is not the one that would be most effective for the greatest number of allergy sufferers.
  E. Most allergy sufferers experience allergy symptoms that are typical of many different types of allergies.

32. All college students read either literary classics or current best-selling books as a habit, but some avid readers of current best-selling books do not read literary classics as a habit because they do not appreciate these books. People who enjoy classical music do not find current best-selling books interesting, and therefore do not read them as a habit. Since Javier is a college student who enjoys classical music, he must appreciate literary classics.

    Which of the following must be true for the conclusion drawn above to be logically correct?

    A. Literary classics are more interesting than current best-selling books.
    B. All college students who appreciate literary classics read them as a habit.
    C. Literary classics are more interesting than classical music.
    D. All avid readers of literary classics appreciate this type of book.
    E. All college students who find classical music enjoyable also read current best-selling books as a habit.

33. Due to racial discrimination, some of the most gifted and influential jazz musicians were prohibited from dining at the venues they have performed in.

    A. at the venues they have performed in
    B. at the very same venues they have performed in
    C. where they have performed
    D. at the same venues at which they performed
    E. in venues, which were where they performed

34. In asserting that a thing is honorable, a favorable distinction is bestowed upon it.

    A. a favorable distinction is bestowed upon it
    B. we bestow a distinction upon it favorably
    C. we bestow upon it a favorable distinction
    D. a favorable distinction upon it is bestowed
    E. bestowing a favorable distinction upon it

35. A proposed law would prohibit any individual who has been employed as a lobbyist on behalf of a particular industry from serving as the director of a government agency charged with regulating that same industry. The purpose of the proposed law is to prevent conflicts of interest. However, if passed, the law would prove counterproductive because it would prevent individuals who are knowledgeable about industries from serving as government regulators.

The argument above depends most directly on which the following assumptions?

- **A.** The individuals in government that hold the power to enact the proposed law are susceptible to influence on the part of industry lobbyists.
- **B.** Government has a legitimate role to play in the regulation of most industries.
- **C.** Only individuals who have served as lobbyists on behalf of an industry are knowledgeable about that industry.
- **D.** Those who have served as lobbyists on behalf of an industry are capable of objective, unbiased decisions as regulators.
- **E.** The primary objective of government regulation of industry should be to strengthen and support that industry.

Questions 36–39 are based on the following passage:

Line In 1930, a century after the birth of Victorian poetess Christina Rossetti, writer and scholar Virginia Woolf identified her as "one of Shakespeare's
(5) more recent sisters" whose life had been reclusively Victorian but whose artistic achievement was enduring. Woolf remembered Rossetti for the explosive originality, vivid imagery, and emotional
(10) energy of her poems. "A Birthday," for instance, is no typical Victorian poem and is certainly unlike predictable works of the era's best-known women poets. Rossetti's most famous poem, "Goblin
(15) Market," is at once Christian, psychological, and pro-feminist. Like many of Rossetti's works, it is extraordinarily original, risky in subject matter, and unorthodox in form. Its Christian
(20) allusions are obvious but grounded in opulent images whose lushness borders on the erotic.

From Rossetti's work emerge not only emotional force, frequently-ironic
(25) playfulness, and intellectual vigor, but also an intriguing, enigmatic quality. "Winter: My Secret," for example, combines these traits along with a very high (and un-Victorian) level of poetic
(30) self-consciousness. "How does one reconcile the aesthetic sensuality of Rossetti's poetry with her repressed, ascetic lifestyle?" Woolf wondered. That Rossetti did indeed withhold a "secret"
(35) both from those intimate with her and from posterity is Lorna Packer's thesis in her 1963 biography of Rossetti. Packer's claim that Rossetti's was a secret of the heart has since been disproved through
(40) the discovery of hundreds of letters by

Rossetti, which reinforce the conventional image of her as pious, scrupulously abstinent, and semi-reclusive.

(45) Yet the passions expressed in Rossetti's love poems do expose the "secret" at the heart of both her life and art: a willingness to forego worldly pleasures in favor of an aestheticized Christian version of transcendent
(50) fulfillment in heaven. The world, for Rossetti, is a fallen place, and her work is pervasively designed to convey this inescapable truth. The beauty of her poetry must be seen, therefore, as an
(55) artistic strategy, a means toward a moral end.

36. All of the following are mentioned in the passage as qualities that emerge from Rossetti's work EXCEPT:

    A. lush imagery.
    B. ironic playfulness.
    C. stark realism.
    D. unorthodox form.
    E. intellectual vigor.

37. Which of the following statements is most reasonably inferable from the passage?

    A. "Winter: My Secret" is Rossetti's best-known poem.
    B. Rossetti was not among the best-known poets during her era.
    C. The accounts of Rossetti's life contained in Packer's biography of Rossetti differ from those included in Woolf's biography of Rossetti.
    D. Rossetti's display of poetic self-consciousness drew criticism from her contemporaries.
    E. "Goblin Market" was published later than "A Birthday."

38. The author discusses Packer's thesis and its flaws in order to

    A. contrast the sensuality of Rossetti's poetry with the relative starkness of her devotional commentary.
    B. reveal the secret to which Rossetti alludes in "Winter: My Secret."
    C. call into question the authenticity of recently discovered letters written by Rossetti.
    D. compare Woolf's understanding of Rossetti with a recent, more enlightened view.
    E. provide a foundation for the author's own theory about Rossetti's life and work.

39. Which of the following best expresses the main idea of the passage?

    A. Newly-discovered evidence suggests that Rossetti's works were misinterpreted by earlier critics and scholars.
    B. Rossetti can be compared to Shakespeare both in her private life and in the enduring quality of her work.
    C. Victorian poetry can be properly interpreted only by considering the personal life of the particular poet.
    D. The apparent inconsistency between Rossetti's personal life and literary work are explained by Rossetti's poems themselves.
    E. Rossetti's artistic integrity served as a model for later women poets.

40. Everyone agrees that current licensing requirements for child care facilities are reasonably necessary to ensure public safety. Current licensing requirements for handgun ownership are far less stringent than those for operating child care facilities. Yet the recent flurry of school shootings by young children using their parents' handguns shows that handgun ownership poses a significant potential threat to public safety.

    The author is arguing that

    A. the recent school shootings would not have occurred were it not for lenient handgun ownership laws.
    B. parents of young children should not be allowed to own handguns.
    C. the legal requirements for obtaining a license for operating a child care facility are more stringent than those for handgun ownership.
    D. unlicensed child care and unlicensed handgun ownership both pose a potential threat to public safety.
    E. it would be reasonable to impose more stringent requirements for handgun ownership.

41. The ancient Greek states boasted that <u>within their domains word and speech were free</u>.

    A. within their domains word and speech were free
    B. within its domain word and speech were free
    C. word and speech were within their domains free
    D. within their domains both word as well as speech were free
    E. free word and speech were within their domains

Answers and Explanations

See Appendix for score conversion tables to determine your score. Be sure to keep a tally of correct and incorrect answers for each test section.

Analysis of an Issue—Evaluation and Scoring

Evaluate your Issue-Analysis essay on a scale of 1 to 6 (6 being the highest score) according to the following five criteria:

1. Does your essay develop a position on the issue through the use of incisive reasons and persuasive examples?
2. Are your essay's ideas conveyed clearly and articulately?
3. Does your essay maintain proper focus on the issue, and is it well organized?
4. Does your essay demonstrate proficiency, fluency, and maturity in its use of sentence structure, vocabulary, and idiom?
5. Does your essay demonstrate command of the elements of Standard Written English, including grammar, word usage, spelling, and punctuation?

Analysis of an Argument—Evaluation and Scoring

Evaluate your Argument-Analysis essay on a scale of 1 to 6 (6 being the highest score) according to the following five criteria:

1. Does your essay identify the key features of the argument and analyze each one in a thoughtful manner?
2. Does your essay support each point of its critique with insightful reasons and examples?
3. Does your essay develop its ideas in a clear, organized manner, with appropriate transitions to help connect ideas?
4. Does your essay demonstrate proficiency, fluency, and maturity in its use of sentence structure, vocabulary, and idiom?
5. Does your essay demonstrate command of the elements of Standard Written English, including grammar, word usage, spelling, and punctuation?

The following series of questions, which serve to identify the Argument's *five* distinct problems, will help you evaluate your essay in terms of criteria 1 and 2. To earn a score of 4 or higher, your essay should identify at least three of these problems and, for each one, provide at least one example or counterexample that supports your critique. (Your examples need not be the same as the ones below.) Identifying and discussing at least four of the problems would help earn you an even higher score.

- Are key characteristics of one group member (Giant Industries) also characteristics of the group as a whole (all employers in a certain state)? (Perhaps Giant is not typical of the state's employers, as a group, with respect to either its financial strength or its the average age of its workforce.)

- Does the term "largest private business" necessarily mean that Giant employs more workers than any other business in the state? (The smaller the workforce at Giant, the less likely that Giant is representative of the state's employers as a group.)

- Doesn't the prediction's accuracy require that other *future conditions* remain unchanged? (For example, the argument ignores a possible influx of workers from other states.)

- Would a reduced workforce necessarily result in business failure? (Perhaps businesses will be more profitable by trimming their workforce.)

- What is the *definition* of "quality of life"? (The argument's ultimate prediction depends on this missing definition.)

Quantitative Ability

1. **B** In combining fractions, you can divide across fractions all variables except a (in the numerator) and e (in the denominator), leaving $\frac{a}{e} \cdot x = 1$. Then, to isolate x on one side of the equation, multiply both sides by $\frac{e}{a}$:

$$\frac{e}{a} \cdot \frac{a}{e} \cdot x = 1 \cdot \frac{e}{a}$$

$$x = \frac{e}{a}$$

2. **A** Any one of four distinct groups of three women might be selected: *ABC*, *ABD*, *ACD*, or *BCD*. The probability that the selections will result in any particular one of these groupings is 1 in 4, or $\frac{1}{4}$. Similarly, any one of three distinct pairs of two men might be selected: *XY*, *XZ*, and *YZ*. The probability that the selections will result in any particular one of these pairs is 1 in 3, or $\frac{1}{3}$. To determine the combined probability, multiply one individual probability by the other: $\frac{1}{4} \times \frac{1}{3} = \frac{1}{12}$.

3. **E** The question asks you to compare rates of motion, or speeds. To determine a speed, you need to know time and distance. Statement (1) provides only Maria's time, not Lupe's, so it is insufficient alone to answer the question. Statement (2) compares their driving distances, but it provides no information about Lupe's driving time. Since Lupe's driving time is a critical fact but is missing from both statements, the correct answer is (E).

4. **A** Apply the formula for determining arithmetic mean (*AM* below), or simple average. Letting x equal the other number, solve for x:

$$AM = \frac{Q + x}{2}$$

$$PQ = \frac{Q + x}{2}$$

$$2PQ = Q + x$$

$$2PQ - Q = x$$

5. **C** Statement (1) alone provides no information about b and is therefore insufficient to answer the question. Statement (2) alone is also insufficient because is provides two distinct equations in two variables: $a - b = 1$ and $a - b = -1$. Now consider both statements together. Given statement (1), $a = 3, -3$. Substituting 3 and -3 for a into each of the two equations that statement (2) suggests yields four possible values for b: 2, -4, 4, and -2. Since you now know all possible values for a and b, you can determine the minimum value of $|a + b|$. (The answer to the question is *1*.)

6. **C** Here's the sequence up to the 12th second:

   0 W   1 B   2 W   3 G   4 W   5 R   6 W

   7 B   8 W   9 G   10 W   11 R   12 W

   Every time you reach a time divisible by 6, the sequence starts over with *W* and proceeds: *W-B-W-G-W-R*. 204 is divisible by 6; hence, starting at the 204th second, here are the light's movements through the 209th second:

   204 W   205 B   206 W

   207 G   208 W   209 R

   As you can see, the movement from the 208th to the 209th second is from white (*W*) to red (*R*).

7. **D** Statement (1) alone is obviously insufficient to answer the question. Considering statement (2) alone, the factored form of the quadratic expression $x^2 - 6x + 9$ is $(x - 3)(x - 3)$. As you can see, the two roots of the equation in statement (2) are the same. The only possible value of x is 3. Thus, statement (2) alone suffices to answer the question.

8. **E** Substitute $\frac{2}{3}$ and $-\frac{2}{3}$ individually for u in the defined operation $\blacktriangleleft u \blacktriangleright = u^2 - u$:

$$\blacktriangleleft \frac{2}{3} \blacktriangleright = \frac{4}{9} - \frac{2}{3} = \frac{4}{9} - \frac{6}{9} = -\frac{2}{9}$$

$$\blacktriangleleft -\frac{2}{3} \blacktriangleright = \frac{4}{9} + \frac{2}{3} = \frac{4}{9} + \frac{6}{9} = \frac{10}{9}$$

Then add the two results together:.

$$-\frac{2}{9} + \frac{10}{9} = \frac{8}{9}.$$

9. **D** Extend $\overline{BE}$ to F (as in the diagram below). m∠EFD = m∠ABE = 40°. m∠FED must be 110° because a triangles amgle measures sum to 180°. Since ∠BED and ∠FED are supplementary, m∠BED = 70°.

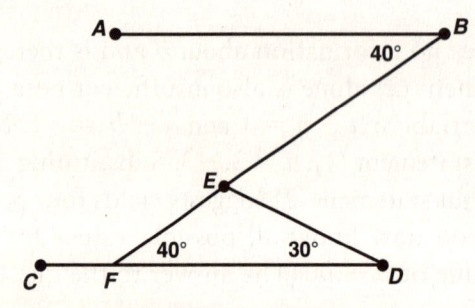

10. **B** $54 is 90% of what Kirk collected. Express this as an equation:

$$54 = .90x$$
$$540 = 9x$$
$$x = 60$$

Kirk collected $60. If each paper sells for 40 cents, the number of paper Kirk sold is.

$$\frac{60}{.40} = \frac{600}{4} = 150.$$

11. **A** Add the two equations:

$$x + y = a$$
$$\underline{x - y = b}$$
$$2x = a + b$$
$$x = \frac{1}{2}(a + b)$$

12. **E** Since the figure has 5 sides, the sum of the measures of the angles is 540°:

    $$180(5 - 2) = 540$$

    The sum of the mesures of the five angles is 540°. Set up an equation, and then solve for x:

    $$540 = x + 110 + 60 + 120 + 100$$
    $$540 = x + 390$$
    $$150 = x$$

13. **A** The shelter houses $d + c$ animals altogether. Of these animals, d are dogs. That portion can be expressed as the fraction $\dfrac{d}{c + d}$.

14. **C** Statement (1) establishes the total contributions of Willot and Tilson counties relative to those of Stanton and Osher counties, but the statement provides no additional information about Stanton County's specific percentage contribution. Statement (1) alone is therefore insufficient to answer the question. Based on statement (2) alone, Tilson County's non-subsidized farms must have accounted for 6% of all revenues (18% − 12%). Accordingly, Stanton County's non-subsidized farms must have accounted for 9% of all revenues. (The percentages in the leftmost column must total 30.) However, this information is insufficient to determine Stanton County's subsidized farm contribution. With statements (1) and (2) together, Osher County's revenues must total 36% (because statement (2) stipulates that Osher County contributed twice the revenues of Tilson County, which you now know contributed 18% of all revenues). At this point, you've partially completed the table:

	non-subsidized farms	subsidized farms		
Willot County	7%			
Tilson County	(6%)	12%	(18%)	} 50%
Stanton County	(9%)			
Osher County	8%	(28%)	(36%)	} 50%
(Total Percentages)	30%	(70%)		

    Now you can see that Stanton County's subsidized farms contributed 6% of the total revenues. (Stanton and Osher revenues must account for 50% of the total.) Thus, statements (1) and (2) together suffice to answer the question.

15. **D** Since the smallest circle has a radius of 1, the medium circle has a radius of 2, and, therefore, the diameter of the large circle must be 6, which makes its radius 3. The arc of a semicircle is half the circle's circumference—that is, πr. So the length of the boundary of the shaded region is the sum of the arcs of the three semicircles:

    $$\pi + 2\pi + 3\pi = 6\pi.$$

16. C Statement (1) alone is insufficient because you can make several possible equations using the integers 0 through 9. Statement (2) alone is insufficient for the same reason. Considering statements (1) and (2) together leaves you with only two possibilities for b^n: 3^4 or 9^2. Given that $a^m = b^n$, you can now answer the question. The sum of the four integers is $3 + 4 + 9 + 2$, or 18.

17. A The total rent is $D + 100$, which must be divided by the number of students (M).

18. D Start with 2, then 4, then 6, and so forth (positive even integers), as the value of n. Test each value in turn. You'll find that only the numbers in the following sequence leave a remainder of 1 when divided by 3: $\{4, 10, 16, \ldots\}$. Notice that the numbers increase by 6 in sequence. Next, try a few of these numbers as the value of n in each of the five expressions. You'll find that all but ($n \times 2$) are divisible by 3.

19. E First combine the two terms inside the radical using the common denominator b^2. Then remove perfect squares from the radical:

$$\sqrt{\frac{a^2}{b^2} + \frac{a^2}{b^2}} = \sqrt{\frac{a^2 + a^2}{b^2}} = \sqrt{\frac{2a^2}{b^2}} = \frac{a}{b}\sqrt{2}$$

20. C First consider statement (1) alone. If $a = -1$, then the two quantities are equal, while if a has any other value less than 0, the two quantities are unequal. Thus, you can easily dismiss statement (1) as insufficient to answer the question. Consider statement (2) alone. If $-1 < a < 0$, then $\sqrt[3]{a} < a$ (and the answer to the question is *yes*). For example, $\sqrt[3]{-\frac{1}{8}} = -\frac{1}{2}$, which is less than $-\frac{1}{8}$. But, if $0 < a < 1$, then $\sqrt[3]{a} > a$ (and the answer to the question is *no*). For example $\sqrt[3]{\frac{1}{8}} = \frac{1}{2}$, which is greater than $\frac{1}{8}$. Thus, statement (2) does not suffice. Considering both statements together, $-1 < a < 0$. As already noted, under this constraint the answer to the question is always *yes*. If $a < -1$, then $\sqrt[3]{a} > a$ (and the answer to the question is *no*). For example, $\sqrt[3]{-8} = -2$, which is greater than -8.

21. B You can solve the problem by trying each answer choice in turn. Or, you can solve the problem algebraically. Let x = the number of nickels. $30 - x$ = the number of quarters. Convert both expressions to cents:

$5x$ = the value of nickels in cents

$750 - 25x$ = the value of quarters in cents

The total of these two expressions is 470. Set up the equation, then solve for x:

$$5x + 750 - 25x = 470$$
$$-20x = -280$$
$$x = 14$$

22. D The area of any triangle equals $\frac{1}{2} \times base \times height$. Using 7 miles as the base of the triangle in this problem, the triangle's height is the north-south (vertical) distance from A to an imaginary line extending west from B. Statement (1) explicitly provides the triangle's height. Statement (2) also provides sufficient information to determine this height.

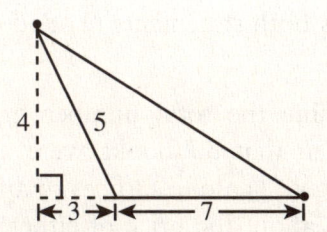

As indicated in the figure above, the triangle's height is 4 miles ($3^2 + 4^2 = 5^2$, per the Pythagorean theorem). Accordingly, either statement alone suffices to determine the triangle's area. (The area $= \frac{1}{2} \times 7 \times 4 = 14$.)

23. C Neither statement (1) nor (2) alone suffices to answer the question. You still do not know what portion of the remaining computer systems are equipped only with scanners. However, both statements together establish that 55% (100% − 20% − 25%) are equipped only with scanners.

24. B To answer the question, you need to compare Daniel's rate of work with that of Carl and Todd working together. Statement (1) provides Carl's rate, but not Todd's; therefore, statement (1) alone is insufficient to answer the question. Statement (2) provides Carl's and Todd's combined rate. By comparing this combined rate with the rate of all three working together, you can determine Daniel's rate. Statement (2) alone suffices to answer the question. Although you don't have to do the math, here's how you would answer the question. All three workers can load $\frac{1}{8}$ of the van in one hour. Similarly, Carl and Todd can load $\frac{1}{12}$ of the van in one hour. Subtract $\frac{1}{12}$ from $\frac{1}{8}$ to obtain Daniel's rate: $\frac{1}{8} - \frac{1}{12} = \frac{3}{24} - \frac{2}{24} = \frac{1}{24}$. Daniel can do $\frac{1}{24}$ of the job (loading the van) in one hour, so it would take Daniel 24 hours to load the van.

25. C By definition, the longest possible chord of a circle is equal in length to the circle's diameter. Thus, the coordinates of R and S allow you to calculate the circle's diameter and, in turn, its area. Statements (1) and (2) together suffice to answer the question.

26. E This problem requires a bit of trial and error. Given statement (1), a bit of experimenting with a few numbers—e.g., AB = 43 and AB = 24—quickly reveals that statement (1) alone is insufficient to answer the question: 4 × 3 = 12 (divisible by 4), but BAB (343) is not divisible by 4. 2 × 4 = 8 (divisible by 4), and BAB (424) is also divisible by 4. Similarly, given statement (2), substituting a few different value pairs for A and B that satisfy statement (2) quickly reveals that statement (2) alone is insufficient to answer the question. 3 + 6 + 3 = 12 (divisible by 4), but 363 (BAB) is not divisible by 4. 2 + 4 + 2 = 8 (divisible by 4), and 242 is divisible by 4. Even considered together, statements (1) and (2) are insufficient to answer the question. For example, the number 242 satisfies both statements (1) and (2) but is not divisible by 4, whereas the number 484 satisfies both statements (1) and (2) and is divisible by 4.

27. A Given statement (1), you can determine the total number of paperbacks sold: ($.75)(P) = $19.50, or P = 26. Given that 55 books were sold altogether, 29 hardback books were sold, and statement (1) alone suffices to answer the question. Statement (2) provides no information about the price of either type of book, and therefore alone is insufficient to answer the question.

28. D The age group that spent the most time per week watching sports on television was the 19–24 year-old group (who spent an average of approximately 6 hours per week watching sports programming). The average hours for all three groups totals approximately 76 (33 + 17 + 22). Of that total, the two groups other than the 19 − 24 age group accounted for 55 hours, or about 76% $\left(\frac{55}{72}\right)$ of the total hours for all three age groups.

29. D You're task here is to compare the size of the entertainment portion of the left-hand bar to the combined sizes of the same portion of the other two bars. Size up the ratio visually. The portion on the first chart is a just a bit larger than the other two combined, isn't it? So you're looking for a ratio that's greater than 1:1. You can rule out answer choices (A) and (B). Approximate the height of each three portions:

13–18 age group: 25 hours

19–24 age group: 5 hours

25–30 age group: 10 hours

The ratio in question is 25:15, or 5:3.

30. A The amount invested at 5% is (10,000 − x) dollars. Thus, the income from that amount is .05(10,000 − x) dollars.

31. C Based on the definition of a geometric series in the question, all pairs of successive terms must have the same ratio. Thus, $\frac{x}{-2} = \frac{-8}{x}$. Cross-multiplying, $x^2 = 16$; hence $x = \pm 4$. The constant multiple is either 2 or −2. If the second term is +4, the sixth term would be $(-2)(2)^{(6-1)} = (-2)(2)^5 = -64$. If the second term is −4, the sixth term would be $(-2)(-2)^5 = 64$.

32. C This question requires a bit of intuition. The objective is to minimize the unused space in the packing box by turning the smaller boxes on their appropriate sides. Align the 2-inch edge of each box along the 18-inch edge of the packing box (9 boxes make up a row). Align the 5-inch side of each box along the 35-inch edge of the packing box (7 boxes make up a row). Arranged in this manner with the 18-inch by 35-inch face of the packing box as the base, one layer of small boxes 3 inches high includes 63 boxes (9 × 7). Given that the packing box's third dimension is 19 inches, 6 layers of boxes, each 3 inches high, will fit into the packing box, for a total of 378 boxes. An unused 1-inch layer remains at the top of the box. (You could reverse the alignment of the 2- and 3-inch sides and arrive at the same result.)

33. E A median is the number that ranks exactly in the middle of the set. To know the median here, you would need to know what the six specific values are, not just their range and/or average.

34. D Statement (1) alone suffices to answer the question. Given that $x = 60$, the area of each of the two triangles must be less than $\frac{60}{360}$ (or $\frac{1}{6}$) of the area of the circle (the difference is the region between each triangle and the circle's circumference). So, the combined area of the two triangles is less than $\frac{1}{3}$ the area of the circle. Given that $x = 60$, m∠AOC = 120, and the area of the shaded region is exactly $\frac{120}{360}$ (or $\frac{1}{3}$) that of the circle. Statement (2) alone also suffices to answer the question. Given that the length of *AB* equals the radius, each of the two triangles must be equilateral, and all angles measure 60°. You can now apply the same reasoning as with statement (1) to answer the question.

35. C The total distance is equal to the distance that one bus traveled plus the distance that the other bus traveled (to the point where they pass each other). Letting *x* equal the number of hours traveled, you can express the distances that the two buses travel in that time as $48x$ and $55x$. Equate the sum of these distances with the total distance and solve for *x*:

$$48x + 55x = 515$$
$$103x = 515$$
$$x = 5$$

The buses will pass each other five hours after 9:30 a.m.—at 2:30 p.m.

36. **E** The expression involves subtraction, so neither the base numbers nor the exponents can be combined. Only (E) is equivalent to the original expression. To confirm this without using a calculator, factor 7^{76} from both terms:

$$\frac{7^{77} - 7^{76}}{6} = \frac{7^{76}(7^1 - 1)}{6} = \frac{7^{76}(6)}{6} = 7^{76}$$

37. **B** The value of Dynaco shares sold plus the value of MicroTron shares sold must be equal to the value of all shares sold. Letting x represent the number of Dynaco shares sold, you can represent the number of MicroTron shares sold by $300 - x$. Set up an equation in which the value of Dynaco shares sold plus the value of MicroTron shares sold equals the total value of all shares sold. Then solve for x:

$$52x + 36(300 - x) = 40(300)$$
$$52x + 10{,}800 - 36x = 12{,}000$$
$$16x = 1{,}200$$
$$x = 75$$

The investor has sold 75 shares of Dynaco stock.

Verbal Ability

1. **B** In the original version, the terms following each part of the correlative *not only . . . but also* are not parallel. The sentence is also awkward. (B) reconstructs the sentence in a clear and concise manner.

2. **E** The original sentence (A) is a long sentence fragment with no predicate. (E) completes the sentence by reconstructing it.

3. **D** The original version contains superfluous words; either *the age of* or *years* should be omitted. (D) corrects the original version by omitting *the age of*. (E) is redundant; either *old* or *in age* should be omitted.

4. **D** The argument suggests that the company's improved profitability the year after the court judgement was attributable to that judgment. However, the mere fact that one event follows the other does not necessarily mean that it was *caused* by the other event. (D) points out this critical flaw in the argument by recognizing that consumer buying decisions and, in turn, the profitability of product manufacturers, can depend on a variety of possible factors.

5. **A** John's statement does *not* logically infer, as Jolanda seems to think, that a person must believe in the inevitability of success in order to be successful. (B) is an effective rebuttal for John because it points out Jolanda's apparent reasoning error.

6. **B** Nowhere in the passage does the author mention any power struggles among the leaders of the Iroquois nations. Although the first paragraph does refer to a dispute among the Iroquois leaders, the dispute involved the role that the Iroquois should

play in the American Revolution. Thus, (B) confuses the information in the passage by referring to unrelated details.

7. **C** The passage states that Cornplanter was an outspkoken proponent of assimilation and that Handsome Lake was related to Cornplanter as a half-brother. The fact that Lake was responsible for the Iroquois reasserting their national identity is ironic, then, in light of Lake's blood relationship to Cornplanter.

8. **E** According to the author, the Quakers' introduction of new technology to the Iroquois was partly responsible for the decline of the Iroquois culture in that it contributed to the tribe's loss of national identity. (E) presents a similar situation.

9. **D** In the original version, the position of *alone* suggests improperly that the immigrants are alone. (D) corrects this problem (*more* and *greater* are both acceptable here).

10. **B** The first and third sentences, considered together, strongly infer the conclusion expressed by (B). Admittedly, the passage does not rule out the possibility that babies who are breast fed during some portion of the first year other than the first three months are more likely than other babies to become obese. However, this possible scenario runs completely contrary to the passage information. Thus, despite this remote possibility, (B) is the best answer choice.

11. **E** The passage's first sentence implies that a high level of consumer confidence leads to increased consumer spending, which in turn leads to depletion of retail inventories. However, the passage indicates that, at a time when consumer confidence is great, retail inventories are *increasing* instead. Each answer choice except (E) provides a logical explanation for this apparent discrepancy. However, (E) suggests that an increase in consumer confidence levels should be preceded by decreased business spending, which would tend to *decrease*, rather than increase, retail inventory levels. Thus, (E) actually renders the discrepancy more inexplicable.

12. **D** In the original version, *one being arrested* should be replaced either with *one from being arrested*, with *one's arrest*, or with the noun clause *one's being arrested*. (Noun clauses take the possessive verb form.) Also, *it* would more clearly refer to its antecedent *the law* if it were positioned closer to the antecedent or replaced with the antecedent. (D) corrects both problems with the original version. An even better version would include *one's arrest* instead of *one from being arrested*; nevertheless, (D) is the best of the five choices.

13. **A** The original version is correct; the first clause modifies *President McKinley*, and the two elements are appropriately juxtaposed to form a clear expression of the intended idea.

14. **D** The original version uses the awkward (and improper) *remains being*. Either *is still* or simply *remains* should be used instead. (D) corrects the problem.

15. **C** As the passage indicates, dendrochronological studies involve analyzing tree rings. Although the wood from trees might have been used for creating items which are now

considered archeological artifacts, the author does not indicate explicitly that tree rings are studied for the purpose of dating such artifacts.

16. B In the second paragraph, the author mentions (A), (C), (D), and (E) as problems with radiocarbon dating. Nowhere in the passage, however, does the author mention any problem involving sample deterioration.

17. E In mentioning that a trace element analysis is needed for the geographic source of an obsidian artifact, the author strongly infers that an accounting for specific conditions of the geographic area is needed in order to determine the age of the obsidian artifact by measuring its hydration layer.

18. A Statement (A), if true, suggests that the removal of the asbestos could endanger the health of the building's occupants by sending dangerous fibers into the atmosphere. Since it is possible that this health risk outweighs the health risk of leaving the asbestos in place, the statement provides strong support for the conclusion that the asbestos should be left in place in the interest of the occupants' health.

19. E The argument assumes that union-relations problems are the major cause of the price increase. (E) undermines the logic of the proposed solution by suggesting that another factor—the cost of raw materials—may be more important.

20. D The original argument essentially demonstrates the following reasoning:

Premise: If fluorocarbons are emitted, then ozone depletion will occur.

Conclusion: If fluorocarbons are not emitted, then ozone depletion will not occur.

You can express this reasoning symbolically as follows:

Premise: If A, then B.

Conclusion: If not A, then not B.

The reasoning is fallacious (flawed), because it fails to account for other possible causes of ozone depletion. (B might occur whether or not A occurs.)

Choice (D) is the only answer choice that demonstrates the same essential pattern of flawed reasoning.

Premise: If a person with phlebitis takes Anatol, the phlebitis will be controlled.

Conclusion: If a person does not take Anatol, the phlebitis will not be controlled.

Note that (D) begins with the conclusion, whereas the original argument begins with the premise. This fact makes no difference, however, in assessing the reasoning itself.

21. C The argument relies on the assumption that consumers are more likely to buy a particular product (or service) if they remember a particular advertisement for it than if they don't remember. (C) undermines this crucial assumption. Even if consumers remember an advertisement, unless they also remember the particular product advertised, they're no more likely to buy that product than had they not remembered the advertisement at all.

22. C In the original sentence, the antecedent of *that result* is unclear. Is it DNA strands or damage to those strands that result from the deployment of enzymes? Also, the use of the noun clause *man-made toxins' invading* in a prepositional phrase here is somewhat awkward, albeit grammatically correct. (B) improperly uses *that* instead of *which*. Also, it is unclear what "resulting" refers to here—DNA strands or damage to the DNA strands. (C) improves on the awkward use of a noun clause in the first part of the original sentence. The infinitive *to rebuild* and the phrase *as a result* clarify the meaning of the second part of the sentence. In spite of its use of the passive voice (*enzymes are deployed*), (C) is the best version.

23. A The original version is correct. By omitting *rather*, (B) obscures the meaning of the sentence; the original version is clearer. (C) sets up a faulty parallel between *cultural tie* and *racial*. (D) also sets up a faulty parallel—between *cultural* and *a racial one*. (E) also sets up a faulty parallel—between *cultural* and *a racial tie*.

24. E The original sentence (A) confuses the subjunctive verb form (which deals with possibilities rather than facts) and past-perfect tense. (A) also contains a pronoun-antecedent agreement problem; *scientific community* is singular, calling for the singular pronoun *it* rather than *they*. (E) remedies both problems. It uses the subjunctive form consistently—at both the beginning and end of the phrase. It also replaces the incorrect plural pronoun *they* with *scientists*.

25. C The argument recommends that fruit growers not use artificial fertilizers if they wish to appeal to consumer tastes because these fertilizers diminish flavor. This recommendation depends on the assumption that flavor enhances a fruit's appeal to consumers. Statement (C) helps substantiate this assumption. (Presumably, flavorful fruit is more appealing than flavorless fruit.)

26. A The argument relies on the assumption that the furlough program is responsible for, or at least contributes to, a prisoner's refraining from committing crimes after release. One effective way of weakening the argument is to refute this assumption by providing evidence that the program does *not* contribute to the reform of prisoners. (A) provides strong evidence to this effect—specifically, that program participants are less likely than non-participants to commit crimes upon their release, regardless of their participation in the program.

27. B The original sentence (A) improperly uses the adjective *hasty* instead of the adverb *hastily* to modify the verb *provide*. (B) remedies the problem.

28. A The passage refers to the establishment of a de facto 35mm standard around 1913, followed by a "resurgence" of wide-film formats (in the mid-1920s to the mid-1930s). This resurgence suggests that wide-film formats were not new because they had been used before the 35mm standard was established—that is, before 1913.

29. D According to the passage's last sentence, anamorphic lenses, used with more mobile cameras, made it possible to create quality 70mm prints from 35mm negatives. In this respect, the invention of the anamorphic camera lens contributed to the demise (not the increased use) of wide-film moviemaking.

30. B The passage's final sentence states that after the invention of the 35mm anamorphic lens, quality 70mm (larger) prints could be made from 35mm (smaller) negatives. It is reasonable to assume that larger prints could not be made from smaller negatives prior to that invention.

31. B The argument relies on the assumption that every allergy sufferer can be helped by one or another antihistamine. (B) substantiates this necessary assumption.

32. D Based on the passage's premise, we can conclude that Javier reads literary classics. In order to also conclude that Javier appreciates literary classics, we must assume that all readers of literary classics appreciate these types of books. (D) provides the additional premise needed to draw that conclusion.

33. D The original version incorrectly mixes the past tense (*were prohibited*) with the present perfect tense (*have performed*), resulting in confusion as to the proper time frame. Also, ending the sentence with a preposition (*in*), although not grammatically incorrect, is somewhat awkward and should be avoided if possible. (D) corrects both problems, as well as clarifying the meaning of the sentence by adding the word *same*. (E) is awkward and distorts the meaning of the original sentence by suggesting that these musicians were prohibited from dining at any "venue" and that "venues" were the only places they performed.

34. C The original version includes a dangling modifier. The sentence fails to refer to whomever is doing the asserting. The original version also uses the awkward passive voice. (C) corrects both problems. The first clause now refers clearly to *we*, and the underlined clause has been reconstructed using the active voice.

35. C The argument's conclusion, stated in the passage's final sentence, is true only if it is also true that the government has no other choice but to turn to former industry lobbyists if it wants to find knowledgeable regulators. (This is the assumption that (C) provides.) If such people are available elsewhere—for example, among university professors—then the conclusion is faulty.

36. C In describing Rossetti's work, the author never uses the words "stark" or "realism," nor does the author describe her work in any way that might be expressed by either of these terms. (The term "vivid imagery," appearing in line 9, does not carry the same meaning as "stark realism.")

37. **B** In lines 10–13, the author states that "'A Birthday' is no typical Victorian poem and is certainly unlike predictable works of the era's best-known women poets." It is reasonably inferable that Rossetti was not among the era's best-known women poets, at least during her time.

38. **E** The author's threshold purpose in discussing Packer's biography is to affirm that Rossetti's style of writing was not a reflection of her personal lifestyle. Having dismissed the theory that Rossetti was keeping secrets about her life, the author goes on (in the final paragraph) to offer a better explanation for the apparent contradiction between Rossetti's lifestyle and the emotional, sensual style of her poetry.

39. **D** In the passage, the author's first concern is to point out that Rossetti's work conflicts with her apparently conservative personal life. The author's own impressions of Rossetti's work are corroborated by those of Woolf. Then, in the second paragraph, the author asks how to reconcile this apparent conflict. (The newly discovered letters discussed in that paragraph only reinforce the inconsistency between her personal life and literary work.) In the last paragraph, the author attempts to explain the inconsistency by way of Rossetti's love poems. (D) nicely embraces all these ideas.

40. **E** The argument boils down to the following:

Premise: Child care license requirements are reasonable because they ensure public safety.

Premise: Handgun ownership laws are not as stringent as child care license laws.

Intermediate Conclusion: Current handgun ownership laws do not ensure public safety.

Final conclusion: More stringent handgun ownership laws would be reasonable.

(E) expresses the argument's final conclusion.

41. **A** The original version is clear and grammatically correct. (B) incorrectly uses the singular form *its*; the verb should agree in number with its plural subject *states*. (C) awkwardly splits the grammatical element *were free*. (D) uses the redundant and improper correlative *both . . . as well as . . .* (E) confuses the meaning of the sentence; the construction unfairly suggests that free word and speech could be found *only* in the Greek states.

PART VI

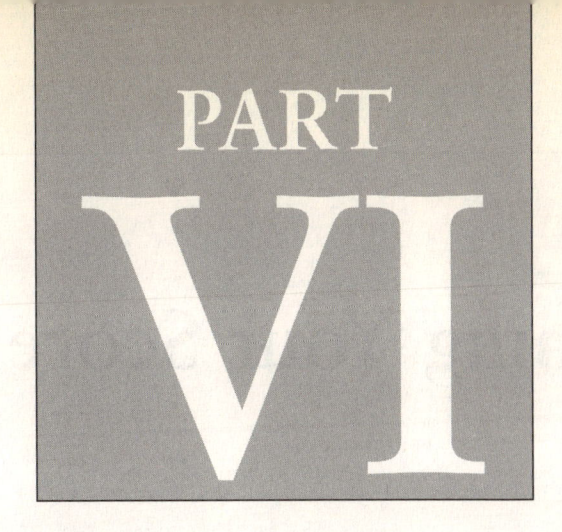

Appendix

Determining Your Score 594

Determining Your Score

Determining Your Verbal, Quantitative, and Total Scaled Scores

To determine your scaled score for either the Quantitative or Verbal section of the practice tests, follow these steps:

Step 1: Determine your total number of correct responses for the section, based on the answer explanations. This is your raw score.

Corrected Raw Score

Corrected Raw Score	Verbal	Quantitative	Corrected Raw Score	Verbal	Quantitative
41	52	—	19	27	31
40	51	—	18	25	30
39	50	—	17	24	28
38	48	—	16	23	27
37	47	53	15	22	25
36	46	52	14	21	24
35	45	51	13	20	23
34	44	50	12	19	22
33	43	49	11	18	21
32	42	48	10	17	20
31	41	47	9	16	18
30	39	45	8	15	17
29	38	44	7	14	16
28	37	43	6	13	14
27	36	41	5	12	13
26	35	40	4	11	12
25	33	38	3	10	11
24	32	37	2	9	10
23	31	36	1	8	9
22	30	34	0	7	8
21	29	33			
20	28	32			

Determining Your Score

Step 2: Subtract one-quarter point from that total for each *incorrect* response; round off this number to the nearest integer. The result is your *corrected raw score*. (This is how the pencil-and-paper GMAT penalizes test-takers for incorrect responses.) See "Corrected Raw Score" table on the previous page.

Total Scaled Score (200–800)

Corrected Raw Score	Total Scaled Score	Corrected Raw Score	Total Scaled Score	Corrected Raw Score	Total Scaled Score
63 and up	800	41	580	19	370
62	790	40	570	18	360
61	780	39	560	17	350
60	770	38	550	16	340
59	760	37	540	15	330
58	750	36	530	14	330
57	740	35	530	13	320
56	730	34	520	12	310
55	720	33	510	11	300
54	710	32	500	10	290
53	700	31	490	9	280
52	690	30	480	8	270
51	680	29	470	7	260
50	670	28	460	6	250
49	660	27	450	5	240
48	650	26	440	4	230
47	640	25	430	3	220
46	630	24	420	2	310
45	620	23	410	0–1	200
44	610	22	400		
43	600	21	390		
42	590	20	380		

Step 3: To determine your total scaled score, add your two corrected raw scores together and convert the total corrected raw score to a scaled score (200–800) using the "Total Scaled Score" table.

NOTES

NOTES

NOTES

NOTES

NOTES

Give Your Admissions Essay An Edge At...

EssayEdge.com

Put Harvard-Educated Editors To Work For You

As the largest and most critically acclaimed admissions essay service, EssayEdge.com has assisted countless college, graduate, business, law, and medical program applicants gain acceptance to their first choice schools. With more than 250 Harvard-educated editors on staff, EssayEdge.com provides superior editing and admissions consulting, giving you an edge over hundreds of applicants with comparable academic credentials.

Use this coupon code when ordering an EssayEdge.com service and **SAVE $7.50** — 12164

Visit

www.essayedge.com today, and take your admissions essay to a new level.

"One of the Best Essay Services on the Internet"
—*The Washington Post*

"The World's Premier Application Essay Editing Service"
—*The New York Times Learning Network*

THOMSON
PETERSON'S

THOMSON
★
PETERSON'S

Want to pursue your education?

Get there with the graduate resources at **Petersons.com!**

Explore
more than 30,000 graduate programs

Prep for success
with Peterson's online practice tests

Wow admissions officials
with a well-written, eye-catching personal statement

Get recruited
by grad programs interested in applicants like you

> Visit www.petersons.com today.

PETERSON'S
getting you there

GRADPUB04